Pride and Prejudice
Webster's Italian
Thesaurus Edition

for ESL, EFL, ELP, TOEFL®, TOEIC®, and AP® Test Preparation

Jane Austen

ICON CLASSICS

Published by ICON Group International, Inc.
7404 Trade Street
San Diego, CA 92121 USA

www.icongrouponline.com

Pride and Prejudice: Webster's Italian Thesaurus Edition for ESL, EFL, ELP, TOEFL®, TOEIC®, and AP® Test Preparation

This edition published by ICON Classics in 2005
Printed in the United States of America.

ISBN 0-497-89970-1

Contents

iv

PREFACE FROM THE EDITOR

Webster's paperbacks take advantage of the fact that classics are frequently assigned readings in English courses. By using a running English-to-Italian thesaurus at the bottom of each page, this edition of *Pride and Prejudice* by Jane Austen was edited for three audiences. The first includes Italian-speaking students enrolled in an English Language Program (ELP), an English as a Foreign Language (EFL) program, an English as a Second Language Program (ESL), or in a TOEFL® or TOEIC® preparation program. The second audience includes English-speaking students enrolled in bilingual education programs or Italian speakers enrolled in English speaking schools. The third audience consists of students who are actively building their vocabularies in Italian in order to take foreign service, translation certification, Advanced Placement® (AP®)[1] or similar examinations. By using the Webster's Italian Thesaurus Edition when assigned for an English course, the reader can enrich their vocabulary in anticipation of an examination in Italian or English.

Webster's edition of this classic is organized to expose the reader to a maximum number of difficult and potentially ambiguous English words. Rare or idiosyncratic words and expressions are given lower priority compared to "difficult, yet commonly used" words. Rather than supply a single translation, many words are translated for a variety of meanings in Italian, allowing readers to better grasp the ambiguity of English, and avoid them using the notes as a pure translation crutch. Having the reader decipher a word's meaning within context serves to improve vocabulary retention and understanding. Each page covers words not already highlighted on previous pages. If a difficult word is not translated on a page, chances are that it has been translated on a previous page. A more complete glossary of translations is supplied at the end of the book; translations are extracted from Webster's Online Dictionary.

Definitions of remaining terms as well as translations can be found at www.websters-online-dictionary.org. Please send suggestions to websters@icongroupbooks.com

The Editor
Webster's Online Dictionary
www.websters-online-dictionary.org

---

[1] TOEFL®, TOEIC®, AP® and Advanced Placement® are trademarks of the Educational Testing Service which has neither reviewed nor endorsed this book. All rights reserved.

CHAPTER 1

It is a **truth universally acknowledged**, that a **single** man in **possession** of a good **fortune**, must be in want of a **wife**.

However little known the feelings or **views** of such a man may be on his first **entering** a **neighbourhood**, this truth is so well **fixed** in the minds of the **surrounding** families, that he is **considered** the **rightful property** of some one or other of their **daughters**.

"My **dear** Mr. **Bennet**," said his **lady** to him one day, "have you **heard** that Netherfield Park is let at last?"

Mr. Bennet replied that he had not.

"But it is," **returned** she; "for Mrs. Long has just been here, and she told me all about it."

Mr. Bennet made no **answer**.

"Do you not want to know who has taken it?" cried his wife **impatiently**.

"*You* want to tell me, and I have no **objection** to **hearing** it."

This was **invitation** enough.

"Why, my dear, you must know, Mrs. Long says that Netherfield is taken by a young man of large fortune from the north of England; that he came down on Monday in a **chaise** and four to see the place, and was so much **delighted** with it,

Italian

acknowledged: riconosciuto.
answer: risposta, rispondere, replicare, rispondere a.
bennet: cariofillata, erba benedetta.
chaise: calesse.
considered: considerato.
daughters: figlie.
dear: caro, costoso, egregio.
delighted: lietissimo.
entering: entrando, entrare.
fixed: fissato, riparato, fisso, fermo.
fortune: fortuna, sorte, patrimonio.

heard: udito, sentito.
hearing: udendo, sentendo, udito, udienza, ascolto.
impatiently: impazientemente.
invitation: invito.
lady: signora, dama.
neighbourhood: circondario, distretto, vicinato, quartiere.
objection: obiezione, opposizione.
possession: possesso.
property: proprietà, patrimonio, possesso, fattoria, caratteristica.

returned: ritornato.
rightful: legittimo.
single: singolo, celibe, nubile, solo, single.
surrounding: circondando, circostante.
truth: verità.
universally: universalmente.
views: viste.
wife: moglie, la moglie.

that he **agreed** with Mr. Morris immediately; that he is to take possession before Michaelmas, and some of his servants are to be in the house by the end of next week."

"What is his name?"

"Bingley."

"Is he **married** or single?"

"Oh! Single, my dear, to be sure! A single man of large fortune; four or five thousand a year. What a fine thing for our girls!"

"How so? How can it **affect** them?"

"My dear Mr. Bennet," replied his wife, "how can you be so **tiresome**! You must know that I am thinking of his **marrying** one of them."

"Is that his design in **settling** here?"

"Design! Nonsense, how can you talk so! But it is very likely that he *may* fall in love with one of them, and therefore you must visit him as soon as he comes."

"I see no **occasion** for that. You and the girls may go, or you may send them by themselves, which perhaps will be still better, for as you are as **handsome** as any of them, Mr. Bingley may like you the best of the party."

"My dear, you **flatter** me. I certainly *have* had my share of **beauty**, but I do not **pretend** to be anything **extraordinary** now. When a woman has five grown-up daughters, she **ought** to give over thinking of her own beauty."

"In such cases, a woman has not often much beauty to think of."

"But, my dear, you must indeed go and see Mr. Bingley when he comes into the neighbourhood."

"It is more than I **engage** for, I **assure** you."

"But consider your daughters. Only think what an **establishment** it would be for one of them. Sir William and Lady Lucas are **determined** to go, **merely** on that account, for in general, you know, they visit no newcomers. Indeed you must go, for it will be **impossible** for *us* to visit him if you do not."

Italian

affect: riguardare, riguarda, riguardo, riguardano, riguardate, riguardi, riguardiamo, affettare.
agreed: concordato, pattuito.
assure: assicurare, assicura, assicuriamo, assicurate, assicuri, assicurano, assicuro, garantire.
beauty: bellezza.
determined: definito, fissato, determinato.
engage: innestare, innestiamo, innesta, innestano, innestate, innesti,

ingaggiare, ingranare, impegnare, assumere, innesto.
establishment: stabilimento, fondazione, azienda.
extraordinary: straordinario, eccezionale.
flatter: lusingare, lusingate, lusingo, lusinghi, lusingano, lusinghiamo, lusinga, adulare.
handsome: bello, carino.
impossible: impossibile.
married: sposato, si sposato.

marrying: sposandosi.
merely: soltanto.
occasion: occasione.
ought: dovere.
pretend: fingere, fingete, fingi, fingiamo, fingo, fingono, pretendere, simulare.
settling: regolando, saldando, sistemando, assestamento, regolare, sedimentazione.
tiresome: seccante, fastidioso, noioso, faticoso.

"You are over-scrupulous, surely. I **dare** say Mr. Bingley will be very **glad** to see you; and I will send a few lines by you to assure him of my **hearty** consent to his marrying **whichever** he **chooses** of the girls; though I must throw in a good word for my little Lizzy."

"I desire you will do no such thing. Lizzy is not a bit better than the others; and I am sure she is not half so handsome as Jane, nor half so good-humoured as Lydia. But you are always giving *her* the preference."

"They have none of them much to **recommend** them," replied he; "they are all **silly** and **ignorant** like other girls; but Lizzy has something more of **quickness** than her sisters."

"Mr. Bennet, how *can* you abuse your own children in such a way? You take **delight** in **vexing** me. You have no **compassion** for my poor **nerves**."

"You mistake me, my dear. I have a high respect for your nerves. They are my old friends. I have heard you mention them with consideration these last twenty years at least."

Mr. Bennet was so odd a mixture of quick parts, **sarcastic humour, reserve,** and **caprice,** that the experience of three-and-twenty years had been **insufficient** to make his wife understand his character. *her* mind was less difficult to develop. She was a woman of mean understanding, little information, and **uncertain temper.** When she was **discontented,** she **fancied** herself **nervous.** The business of her life was to get her daughters married; its **solace** was **visiting** and news.

Italian

caprice: capriccio.
chooses: sceglie, elegge.
compassion: compassione.
dare: osare, oso, osiamo, osi, osate, osano, osa, sfida.
delight: delizia, deliziare, dilettare, diletto, godimento, rallegrare, gioia.
discontented: scontento.
fancied: fantastico.
glad: contento, felice, lieto.
hearty: cordiale, caloroso.
humour: umore, umorismo.

ignorant: ignorante.
insufficient: insufficiente.
nerves: nervi, nervo.
nervous: nervoso.
quickness: prontezza, rapidità, lestezza.
recommend: raccomandare, raccomanda, raccomandano, raccomandate, raccomandi, raccomandiamo, raccomando, consigliare, vantare.
reserve: riservare, riserva, prenotare,

ordinare.
sarcastic: sarcastico.
silly: sciocco, stupido.
solace: conforto, consolare.
temper: umore, temperamento, tempra.
uncertain: incerto, malsicuro.
vexing: irritando, vessando, contrariando, indispettendo.
visiting: visitando.
whichever: qualunque, chiunque, qualsiasi.

CHAPTER 2

Mr. Bennet was among the earliest of those who **waited** on Mr. Bingley. He had always **intended** to visit him, though to the last always **assuring** his wife **that** he should not go; and **till** the evening after the visit was paid she had no knowledge of it. It was then **disclosed** in the following **manner**. **Observing** his second daughter **employed** in **trimming** a hat, he suddenly **addressed** her with:

"I hope Mr. Bingley will like it, Lizzy."

"We are not in a way to know *what* Mr. Bingley likes," said her mother resentfully, "since we are not to visit."

"But you forget, mamma," said Elizabeth, "that we shall meet him at the **assemblies**, and that Mrs. Long **promised** to **introduce** him."

"I do not believe Mrs. Long will do any such thing. She has two nieces of her own. She is a **selfish**, **hypocritical** woman, and I have no **opinion** of her."

"No more have I," said Mr. Bennet; "and I am glad to find that you do not **depend** on her serving you."

Mrs. Bennet **deigned** not to make any **reply**, but, **unable** to **contain** herself, began **scolding** one of her daughters.

"Don't keep **coughing** so, Kitty, for Heaven's **sake**! Have a little compassion on my nerves. You **tear** them to pieces."

Italian

addressed: rivolto.
assemblies: complessivi.
assuring: assicurando.
contain: contenere, contenete, contengo, conteniamo, contengono, contieni.
cough: tossire, tosse.
coughing: tosse, tossire.
deigned: degnato.
depend: dipendere, dipendete, dipendiamo, dipendo, dipendono, dipendi.

disclosed: dischiuso, svelato.
employed: impiegato.
hat: cappello.
hypocritical: ipocrita.
intended: inteso.
introduce: presentare, presenta, presenti, presentiamo, presentate, presentano, presento, introdurre, introduci, introduciamo, introduco.
manner: maniera, modo.
opinion: parere, opinione, avviso.
promised: promesso.

reply: risposta, rispondere, replicare, replica.
sake: causa.
scolding: rimprovero, sgridata.
selfish: egoistico, egoista.
serving: servendo.
tear: strappo, lagrima, strappare, lacerare, lacrima.
till: finchè, coltivare, cassa, fino, arare.
trimming: guarnizione.
unable: incapace.
waited: aspettato.

"Kitty has no **discretion** in her coughs," said her father; "she times them ill."

"I do not cough for my own amusement," replied Kitty fretfully. "When is your next **ball** to be, Lizzy?"

"To-morrow **fortnight**."

"Aye, so it is," cried her mother, "and Mrs. Long does not come back till the day before; so it will be impossible for her to introduce him, for she will not know him herself."

"Then, my dear, you may have the **advantage** of your friend, and introduce Mr. Bingley to *her*."

"Impossible, Mr. Bennet, impossible, when I am not **acquainted** with him myself; how can you be so teasing?"

"I **honour** your **circumspection**. A fortnight's **acquaintance** is certainly very little. One **cannot** know what a man really is by the end of a fortnight. But if *we* do not **venture somebody** else will; and after all, Mrs. Long and her daughters must **stand** their chance; and, therefore, as she will think it an act of **kindness**, if you **decline** the office, I will take it on myself."

The **girls** stared at their father. Mrs. Bennet said only, "Nonsense, **nonsense!**"

"What can be the **meaning** of that **emphatic** exclamation?" cried he. "Do you consider the forms of **introduction**, and the **stress** that is **laid** on them, as nonsense? I cannot quite agree with you *there*. What say you, Mary? For you are a young lady of **deep reflection**, I know, and read great books and make extracts."

Mary **wished** to say something **sensible**, but knew not how.

"While Mary is **adjusting** her ideas," he **continued**, "let us return to Mr. Bingley."

"I am **sick** of Mr. Bingley," cried his wife.

"I am sorry to hear *that*; but why did not you tell me that before? If I had known as much this morning I certainly would not have called on him. It is very

Italian

acquaintance: conoscenza, conoscente.
acquainted: informato.
adjusting: aggiustando, regolando.
advantage: vantaggio, beneficio, guadagno, profitto.
ball: palla, ballo, sfera, globo, pallone, la palla, gomitolo.
cannot: non potere.
circumspection: circospezione.
continued: continuato, durato.
decline: declinare, declino, deperire, peggiorare, ribasso, regressione.

deep: profondo, fondo, intenso, cupo.
discretion: discrezione.
emphatic: enfatico.
fortnight: due settimane.
girls: ragazze.
honour: onore.
introduction: introduzione, presentazione.
kindness: gentilezza, bontà, cortesia.
laid: posato.
meaning: significato, intenzione, accezione, senso.

nonsense: nonsenso.
reflection: riflesso, riflessione.
sensible: sensato, ragionevole, sensibile.
sick: malato, ammalato.
somebody: qualcuno, qualcheduno.
stand: stare in piedi, granaio, alzarsi, bancarella.
stress: accento, tensione, stress, accentare, sollecitazione, sforzo.
venture: arrischiare, impresa.
wished: desiderato.

unlucky; but as I have actually paid the visit, we cannot **escape** the acquaintance now."

The **astonishment** of the **ladies** was just what he wished; that of Mrs. Bennet perhaps **surpassing** the rest; though, when the first **tumult** of **joy** was over, she began to **declare** that it was what she had expected all the while.

"How good it was in you, my dear Mr. Bennet! But I knew I should **persuade** you at last. I was sure you **loved** your girls too well to **neglect** such an acquaintance. Well, how **pleased** I am! and it is such a good **joke**, too, that you should have gone this morning and never said a word about it till now."

"Now, Kitty, you may cough as much as you choose," said Mr. Bennet; and, as he spoke, he left the room, **fatigued** with the raptures of his wife.

"What an **excellent** father you have, girls!" said she, when the door was **shut**. "I do not know how you will ever make him **amends** for his kindness; or me, either, for that matter. At our time of life it is not so **pleasant**, I can tell you, to be making new **acquaintances** every day; but for your sakes, we would do anything. Lydia, my love, though you *are* the youngest, I dare say Mr. Bingley will **dance** with you at the next ball."

"Oh!" said Lydia stoutly, "I am not **afraid**; for though I *am* the youngest, I'm the tallest."

The rest of the evening was spent in conjecturing how soon he would return Mr. Bennet's visit, and **determining** when they should ask him to dinner.

Italian

acquaintances: conoscenze.
afraid: pauroso, inquieto, spaventato, angoscioso, impaurito.
amends: emenda, ammenda.
astonishment: stupore, meraviglia, sorpresa.
dance: ballare, ballo, danza.
declare: dichiarare, dichiara, dichiaro, dichiariamo, dichiari, dichiarano, dichiarate.
determining: definendo, fissando, definito, fissato, determinato,
determinando.
escape: scarico, evasione, scappare, sfuggire, evadere, fuoriuscire, fuga.
excellent: eccellente, esimio, ottimo.
fatigued: affaticato.
joke: scherzo, scherzare, barzelletta, celia, lazzo.
joy: gioia.
ladies: signore.
loved: benvoluto.
neglect: trascurare, negligere, negligenza, trascuratezza.
persuade: convincere, convincono, convincete, convinci, convinciamo, convinco, persuadere, persuadono, persuado, persuadiamo, persuadi.
pleasant: piacevole, gradevole, ameno.
pleased: contento, soddisfatto.
shut: chiudere, chiuso.
surpassing: senza pari, superare, sorpassando, sovrastando, superando.
tumult: tumulto.
unlucky: sfortunato, disgraziato.

CHAPTER 3

Not all that Mrs. Bennet, however, with the **assistance** of her five daughters, could ask on the subject, was **sufficient** to draw from her husband any **satisfactory description** of Mr. Bingley. They attacked him in various ways--with **barefaced** questions, **ingenious** suppositions, and **distant** surmises; but he **eluded** the **skill** of them all, and they were at last **obliged** to accept the second-hand **intelligence** of their **neighbour**, Lady Lucas. Her report was highly **favourable**. Sir William had been delighted with him. He was quite young, **wonderfully** handsome, extremely **agreeable**, and, to **crown** the whole, he meant to be at the next assembly with a large party. Nothing could be more **delightful!** To be **fond** of **dancing** was a certain step towards **falling** in love; and very **lively hopes** of Mr. Bingley's heart were **entertained**.

"If I can but see one of my daughters **happily settled** at Netherfield," said Mrs. Bennet to her husband, "and all the others **equally** well married, I shall have nothing to wish for."

In a few days Mr. Bingley returned Mr. Bennet's visit, and sat about ten minutes with him in his library. He had entertained hopes of being **admitted** to a sight of the young ladies, of whose beauty he had heard much; but he saw only the father. The ladies were **somewhat** more **fortunate**, for they had the advantage of **ascertaining** from an **upper** window that he wore a blue **coat**, and rode a black horse.

Italian

admitted: confessato, ammesso.
agreeable: gradevole, piacevole, amabile.
ascertaining: constatando, accertando.
assistance: assistenza, aiuto.
barefaced: impudente.
coat: cappotto, rivestire.
crown: corona.
dancing: ballando.
delightful: delizioso, piacevole.
description: descrizione.
distant: distante, lontano.

eluded: eluso, schivato.
entertained: intrattenuto.
equally: ugualmente.
falling: cadendo.
favourable: favorevole.
fond: tenero, affettuoso, affezionato.
fortunate: fortunato, felice.
happily: felicemente.
hopes: spera.
ingenious: ingegnoso.
intelligence: intelligenza.
lively: vivace, spiritoso, vivo, animato,

vispo.
neighbour: vicino.
obliged: obbligato.
satisfactory: soddisfacente.
settled: regolato, stabilito, stabile, fermo, fisso, popolato, saldato, sistemato, deciso.
skill: abilità, destrezza, maestria.
somewhat: piuttosto, alquanto.
sufficient: sufficiente.
upper: tomaia, superiore.
wonderfully: meravigliosamente.

An invitation to dinner was soon afterwards **dispatched**; and already had Mrs. Bennet planned the courses that were to do credit to her **housekeeping**, when an answer arrived which **deferred** it all. Mr. Bingley was obliged to be in town the following day, and, **consequently**, unable to accept the honour of their invitation, etc. Mrs. Bennet was quite **disconcerted**. She could not imagine what business he could have in town so soon after his arrival in Hertfordshire; and she began to fear that he might be always **flying** about from one place to another, and never settled at Netherfield as he ought to be. Lady Lucas quieted her fears a little by starting the idea of his being gone to London only to get a large party for the ball; and a report soon followed that Mr. Bingley was to bring twelve ladies and seven gentlemen with him to the assembly. The girls **grieved** over such a number of ladies, but were **comforted** the day before the ball by hearing, that instead of twelve he brought only six with him from London--his five sisters and a **cousin**. And when the party entered the assembly room it **consisted** of only five altogether--Mr. Bingley, his two sisters, the husband of the **eldest**, and another young man.

Mr. Bingley was good-looking and gentlemanlike; he had a pleasant **countenance**, and easy, **unaffected manners**. His sisters were fine women, with an air of decided fashion. His brother-in-law, Mr. Hurst, merely looked the gentleman; but his friend Mr. Darcy soon drew the attention of the room by his fine, tall person, handsome features, **noble mien**, and the report which was in general **circulation** within five minutes after his **entrance**, of his having ten thousand a year. The gentlemen **pronounced** him to be a fine figure of a man, the ladies **declared** he was much handsomer than Mr. Bingley, and he was looked at with great **admiration** for about half the evening, till his manners gave a **disgust** which turned the **tide** of his **popularity**; for he was discovered to be **proud**; to be above his company, and above being pleased; and not all his large estate in Derbyshire could then save him from having a most **forbidding**, **disagreeable** countenance, and being **unworthy** to be compared with his friend.

Mr. Bingley had soon made himself acquainted with all the **principal** people in the room; he was lively and unreserved, **danced** every dance, was angry that

Italian

admiration: ammirazione.
circulation: circolazione, diffusione.
comforted: confortato.
consequently: conseguentemente.
consisted: consistito, constato.
countenance: approvare, viso.
cousin: cugino, cugina.
danced: ballato, ballavo ballava.
declared: dichiarato.
deferred: differito.
disagreeable: sgradevole.
disconcerted: sconcertato, turbato.

disgust: ripugnanza, avversione, disgustare, disgusto, nauseare.
dispatched: spedito.
eldest: maggiore, il più vecchio.
entrance: entrata, ingresso, accesso, l'entrata, adito.
flying: volando, volare, volante.
forbidding: vietando, proibendo, ostile, spaventevole.
grieved: accorato, addolorato.
housekeeping: economia domestica, operazioni di gestione interna.

manners: educazione.
mien: aspetto.
noble: nobile, gentilizio, nobiliare.
popularity: popolarità.
principal: principale, committente, capitale, mandante.
pronounced: pronunciato.
proud: orgoglioso, fiero.
tide: marea.
unaffected: spontaneo, non affettato, semplice.
unworthy: indegno.

the ball closed so early, and **talked** of giving one himself at Netherfield. Such **amiable** qualities must speak for themselves. What a contrast between him and his friend! Mr. Darcy danced only once with Mrs. Hurst and once with Miss Bingley, declined being introduced to any other lady, and spent the rest of the evening in **walking** about the room, **speaking occasionally** to one of his own party. His character was decided. He was the proudest, most disagreeable man in the world, and everybody **hoped** that he would never come there again. Amongst the most **violent** against him was Mrs. Bennet, whose **dislike** of his general behaviour was **sharpened** into particular **resentment** by his having slighted one of her daughters.

Elizabeth Bennet had been obliged, by the **scarcity** of gentlemen, to sit down for two dances; and during part of that time, Mr. Darcy had been standing near enough for her to hear a **conversation** between him and Mr. Bingley, who came from the dance for a few minutes, to press his friend to join it.

"Come, Darcy," said he, "I must have you dance. I **hate** to see you standing about by yourself in this **stupid** manner. You had much better dance."

"I certainly shall not. You know how I **detest** it, unless I am particularly acquainted with my **partner**. At such an **assembly** as this it would be insupportable. Your sisters are **engaged**, and there is not another woman in the room whom it would not be a **punishment** to me to stand up with."

"I would not be so **fastidious** as you are," cried Mr. Bingley, "for a kingdom! Upon my honour, I never met with so many pleasant girls in my life as I have this evening; and there are several of them you see **uncommonly pretty**."

"*You* are dancing with the only handsome girl in the room," said Mr. Darcy, looking at the eldest Miss Bennet.

"Oh! She is the most beautiful **creature** I ever **beheld**! But there is one of her sisters sitting down just behind you, who is very pretty, and I dare say very agreeable. Do let me ask my partner to introduce you."

"Which do you mean?" and **turning** round he looked for a moment at Elizabeth, till **catching** her eye, he withdrew his own and **coldly** said: "She is

Italian

amiable: amabile.
assembly: montaggio, accumulazione, assemblea, complesso, adunanza, riunione, assemblaggio.
beheld: guardato.
catching: contagioso, prendendo, infettivo, colpendo, prendere.
coldly: freddamente.
conversation: conversazione, discorso.
creature: creatura.
detest: detestare, detestate, detesto, detesti, detestano, detesta,

detestiamo.
dislike: avversione, ripugnanza, antipatia.
engaged: occupato, innestato, impegnato.
fastidious: fastidioso.
hate: odiare, odio, detestare.
hoped: sperato.
occasionally: occasionalmente.
partner: socio, partner.
pretty: grazioso, bellino, carino, bello.
punishment: punizione, castigo, pena.

resentment: risentimento, astio.
scarcity: scarsità.
sharpened: affilato, acuito.
speaking: parlando, parlare.
stupid: stupido, sciocco, ignorante, balordo.
talked: parlato.
turning: girando, svoltando, svolta, cambiando.
uncommonly: insolitamente.
violent: violento.
walking: camminando, camminare.

tolerable, but not handsome enough to **tempt** *me*; I am in no humour at present to give **consequence** to young ladies who are slighted by other men. You had better return to your partner and enjoy her smiles, for you are **wasting** your time with me."

Mr. Bingley followed his advice. Mr. Darcy walked off; and Elizabeth remained with no very **cordial** feelings **toward** him. She told the story, however, with great spirit among her friends; for she had a lively, **playful disposition,** which delighted in anything ridiculous.

The evening **altogether** passed off **pleasantly** to the whole family. Mrs. Bennet had seen her eldest daughter much **admired** by the Netherfield party. Mr. Bingley had danced with her twice, and she had been **distinguished** by his sisters. Jane was as much **gratified** by this as her mother could be, though in a quieter way. Elizabeth felt Jane's **pleasure.** Mary had heard herself **mentioned** to Miss Bingley as the most **accomplished** girl in the neighbourhood; and Catherine and Lydia had been fortunate enough never to be without partners, which was all that they had yet learnt to care for at a ball. They returned, therefore, in good spirits to Longbourn, the village where they **lived,** and of which they were the principal **inhabitants.** They found Mr. Bennet still up. With a book he was **regardless** of time; and on the present occasion he had a good deal of **curiosity** as to the events of an evening which had raised such **splendid expectations.** He had rather hoped that his wife's views on the **stranger** would be **disappointed;** but he soon found out that he had a different story to hear.

"Oh! my dear Mr. Bennet," as she **entered** the room, "we have had a most delightful evening, a most excellent ball. I wish you had been there. Jane was so admired, nothing could be like it. **Everybody** said how well she looked; and Mr. Bingley thought her quite beautiful, and danced with her twice! Only think of *that,* my dear; he actually danced with her twice! and she was the only creature in the room that he asked a second time. First of all, he asked Miss Lucas. I was so **vexed** to see him stand up with her! But, however, he did not admire her at all; indeed, **nobody** can, you know; and he seemed quite **struck** with Jane as she

Italian

accomplished: compiuto.
admire: ammirare, ammiriamo, ammira, ammirano, ammiro, ammiri, ammirate.
admired: ammirato.
altogether: tutto, complessivamente.
consequence: conseguenza, risultato.
cordial: cordiale.
curiosity: curiosità.
disappointed: deluso.
disposition: disposizione, predisposizione, ingegno, talento.

distinguished: distinto.
entered: entrato.
everybody: ognuno, tutti, ogni, tutto.
expectations: aspettativa, aspettative.
gratified: gratificato.
inhabitants: fruitori della casa.
lived: vissuto, abitato.
mentioned: menzionato.
nobody: nessuno.
playful: giocoso.
pleasantly: piacevolmente.
pleasure: piacere, gradimento.

regardless: incurante.
splendid: splendido, magnifico.
stranger: sconosciuto, estraneo, forestiero.
struck: colpito.
tempt: tentare, tento, tentiamo, tenti, tentate, tenta, tentano.
tolerable: tollerabile.
toward: verso, a.
vexed: irritato, indispettito, vessato, contrariato.
wasting: sprecare, sprecando.

was going down the dance. So he **inquired** who she was, and got **introduced**, and asked her for the two next. Then the two third he danced with Miss King, and the two **fourth** with Maria Lucas, and the two **fifth** with Jane again, and the two **sixth** with Lizzy, and the Boulanger--"

"If he had had any compassion for *me*," cried her **husband** impatiently, "he would not have danced half so much! For God's sake, say no more of his partners. O that he had sprained his **ankle** in the first **place**!"

"Oh! my dear, I am quite delighted with him. He is so **excessively** handsome! And his sisters are **charming** women. I never in my life saw anything more **elegant** than their dresses. I dare say the lace upon Mrs. Hurst's gown--"

Here she was **interrupted** again. Mr. Bennet protested against any description of finery. She was therefore obliged to **seek** another **branch** of the subject, and **related**, with much **bitterness** of **spirit** and some **exaggeration**, the **shocking rudeness** of Mr. Darcy.

"But I can assure you," she added, "that Lizzy does not **lose** much by not suiting *his* **fancy**; for he is a most disagreeable, **horrid** man, not at all worth **pleasing**. So high and so **conceited** that there was no **enduring** him! He **walked** here, and he walked there, fancying himself so very great! Not handsome enough to dance with! I wish you had been there, my dear, to have given him one of your set-downs. I quite detest the man."

Italian

ankle: caviglia.
bitterness: amarezza.
branch: ramo, filiale, succursale, diramazione, agenzia, diramarsi, branca.
charming: affascinante, grazioso, amabile, incantevole.
conceited: vanitoso, presuntuoso.
elegant: elegante.
enduring: sopportando, durando, durevole.
exaggeration: esagerazione.

excessively: eccessivamente.
fancy: figurarsi, capriccio, immaginazione.
fifth: quinto, quinta.
fourth: quarto, quarta.
horrid: orrendo.
husband: marito, sposo.
inquired: domandato.
interrupted: interrotto, sospeso.
introduced: presentato, introdotto.
lace: pizzo, laccio, merletto, allacciare, stringa.

lose: perdere, perdiamo, perdete, perdi, perdo, perdono.
pleasing: piacevole.
related: raccontato, imparentato, congiunto.
rudeness: villania, maleducazione.
seek: cercare, cercano, cerchiamo, cercate, cerchi, cerco, cerca.
shocking: irritante, scandaloso.
sixth: sesto, sesta.
spirit: spirito, anima.
walked: camminato.

CHAPTER 4

When Jane and Elizabeth were **alone**, the **former**, who had been **cautious** in her **praise** of Mr. Bingley before, **expressed** to her **sister** just how very much she **admired** him.

"He is just what a young man ought to be," said she, "sensible, good-humoured, **lively**; and I never saw such **happy** manners!--so much **ease**, with such **perfect** good breeding!"

"He is also handsome," replied Elizabeth, "which a young man ought **likewise** to be, if he **possibly** can. His **character** is **thereby** complete."

"I was very much **flattered** by his **asking** me to dance a second time. I did not **expect** such a compliment."

"Did not you? I did for you. But that is one great **difference** between us. Compliments always take *you* by **surprise**, and *me* never. What could be more **natural** than his asking you again? He could not help **seeing** that you were about five times as pretty as every other woman in the room. No **thanks** to his **gallantry** for that. Well, he **certainly** is very **agreeable**, and I give you **leave** to like him. You have liked many a stupider person."

"Dear Lizzy!"

Italian

admired: ammirato.
agreeable: gradevole, piacevole, amabile.
alone: solo, da solo, solamente.
asking: chiedendo, domandando.
cautious: cauto, prudente.
certainly: certamente.
character: carattere, natura, indole, segno.
difference: differenza.
ease: agio, facilità.
expect: aspettare, aspettate, aspetti,
aspetta, aspettiamo, aspettano, aspetto, aspettarsi.
expressed: espresso.
flattered: lusingato.
former: precedente, passato.
gallantry: galanteria, valore, prodezza.
happy: felice, contento, lieto, beato.
leave: lasciare, abbandonare, partire, lasciano, partono, partite, partiamo, parti, lasciate, lasciamo, lascia.
likewise: anche, altrettanto.
lively: vivace, spiritoso, vivo, animato,
vispo.
natural: naturale.
perfect: perfetto, perfezionare.
possibly: forse, possibilmente.
praise: lodare, lode, elogiare, encomio, elogio.
seeing: vedendo, segando.
sister: sorella, la sorella.
surprise: sorprendere, sorpresa, meraviglia, stupore.
thanks: grazie, ringrazia.
thereby: con ciò.

"Oh! you are a great deal too **apt**, you know, to like people in general. You never see a fault in anybody. All the world are good and agreeable in your eyes. I never heard you speak **ill** of a human being in your life."

"I would not wish to be **hasty** in censuring anyone; but I always speak what I think."

"I know you do; and it is *that* which makes the wonder. With *your* good sense, to be so **honestly blind** to the follies and nonsense of others! Affectation of **candour** is common enough--one **meets** with it everywhere. But to be **candid** without **ostentation** or design--to take the good of everybody's character and make it still better, and say nothing of the bad--belongs to you alone. And so you like this man's sisters, too, do you? Their manners are not equal to his."

"Certainly not--at first. But they are very pleasing women when you **converse** with them. Miss Bingley is to live with her brother, and keep his house; and I am much **mistaken** if we shall not find a very charming neighbour in her."

Elizabeth **listened** in silence, but was not **convinced**; their behaviour at the assembly had not been **calculated** to please in general; and with more quickness of **observation** and less pliancy of temper than her sister, and with a **judgement** too unassailed by any attention to herself, she was very little **disposed** to **approve** them. They were in fact very fine ladies; not **deficient** in good humour when they were pleased, nor in the power of making themselves agreeable when they chose it, but proud and conceited. They were rather handsome, had been **educated** in one of the first private seminaries in town, had a fortune of twenty thousand pounds, were in the **habit** of spending more than they ought, and of **associating** with people of **rank**, and were therefore in every respect **entitled** to think well of themselves, and **meanly** of others. They were of a **respectable** family in the north of England; a **circumstance** more deeply **impressed** on their memories than that their brother's fortune and their own had been acquired by trade.

Mr. Bingley **inherited** property to the amount of nearly a hundred thousand pounds from his father, who had intended to purchase an estate, but did not live to do it. Mr. Bingley intended it likewise, and sometimes made choice of his

Italian

approve: approvare, approvate, approvano, approvi, approvo, approva, approviamo.
apt: adatto.
associating: associare.
blind: cieco, accecare, acceca, accechi, accechiamo, accecate, accecano, acceco.
calculated: calcolato.
candid: franco.
candour: franchezza.
circumstance: circostanza.

converse: contrario.
convinced: convinto.
deficient: deficiente, carente, difettoso, insufficiente.
disposed: disposto.
educated: istruito, educato.
entitled: intitolato.
habit: abitudine, costume, vizio, consuetudine.
hasty: affrettato, frettoloso.
honestly: onestamente.
ill: malato, ammalato.

impressed: impressionato.
inherited: ereditato.
judgement: giudizio, decreto, deliberazione, sentenza.
listened: ascoltato.
meanly: meschinamente.
meets: incontra.
mistaken: sbagliato.
observation: osservazione.
ostentation: ostentazione.
rank: rango, ordine, classificare.
respectable: rispettabile, onorevole.

county; but as he was now provided with a good house and the **liberty** of a **manor**, it was **doubtful** to many of those who best knew the **easiness** of his temper, whether he might not spend the **remainder** of his days at Netherfield, and leave the next generation to purchase.

His sisters were anxious for his having an estate of his own; but, though he was now only established as a tenant, Miss Bingley was by no means **unwilling** to **preside** at his table--nor was Mrs. Hurst, who had married a man of more fashion than fortune, less disposed to consider his house as her home when it suited her. Mr. Bingley had not been of age two years, when he was **tempted** by an **accidental recommendation** to look at Netherfield House. He did look at it, and into it for half-an-hour--was pleased with the situation and the principal rooms, **satisfied** with what the owner said in its praise, and took it immediately.

Between him and Darcy there was a very steady **friendship**, in **spite** of great opposition of character. Bingley was endeared to Darcy by the easiness, **openness**, and **ductility** of his temper, though no disposition could offer a greater contrast to his own, and though with his own he never appeared **dissatisfied**. On the strength of Darcy's regard, Bingley had the firmest **reliance**, and of his judgement the highest opinion. In understanding, Darcy was the **superior**. Bingley was by no means deficient, but Darcy was clever. He was at the same time **haughty, reserved**, and fastidious, and his manners, though well-bred, were not **inviting**. In that respect his friend had greatly the advantage. Bingley was sure of being liked wherever he appeared, Darcy was **continually** giving **offense**.

The manner in which they spoke of the Meryton assembly was sufficiently **characteristic**. Bingley had never met with more pleasant people or prettier girls in his life; everybody had been most kind and **attentive** to him; there had been no **formality**, no **stiffness**; he had soon felt acquainted with all the room; and, as to Miss Bennet, he could not **conceive** an **angel** more beautiful. Darcy, on the **contrary**, had seen a collection of people in whom there was little beauty and no fashion, for none of whom he had felt the smallest interest, and from none

Italian

accidental: accidentale, fortuito.
angel: angelo.
attentive: attento, premuroso.
characteristic: caratteristico, caratteristica.
conceive: concepire, concepiamo, concepisci, concepisco, concepiscono, concepite.
continually: continuamente.
contrary: contrario.
dissatisfied: insoddisfatto.
doubtful: dubbioso.

ductility: duttilità.
easiness: facilità, agevolezza, comodità, con facilità.
formality: formalità.
friendship: amicizia.
haughty: altezzoso.
inviting: invitando, invitare, invitante.
liberty: libertà.
manor: feudo.
offense: offesa.
openness: apertura, franchezza.
preside: presiedere.

recommendation: raccomandazione, consiglio.
reliance: fiducia.
remainder: resto, rimanenza.
reserved: riservato.
satisfied: soddisfatto, contento, accontentato.
spite: dispetto.
stiffness: rigidezza, rigidità.
superior: superiore.
tempted: tentato.
unwilling: riluttante, restio.

received either **attention** or **pleasure**. Miss Bennet he **acknowledged** to be **pretty**, but she **smiled** too much.

Mrs. Hurst and her **sister allowed** it to be so--but still they **admired** her and liked her, and **pronounced** her to be a **sweet girl**, and one **whom** they would not **object** to know more of. Miss Bennet was therefore **established** as a sweet girl, and their **brother** felt **authorized** by such **commendation** to think of her as he chose.

Italian

acknowledged: riconosciuto.
admired: ammirato.
allowed: permesso.
attention: attenzione.
authorized: autorizzato.
brother: fratello, il fratello.
commendation: raccomandazione.
established: stabilito, fuso, constatato.
girl: ragazza, piccola, la ragazza.
mrs: signora.
object: oggetto, cosa, scopo.
pleasure: piacere, gradimento.

pretty: grazioso, bellino, carino, bello.
pronounced: pronunciato.
received: ricevuto, accolto.
sister: sorella, la sorella.
smiled: sorriso.
sweet: dolce, soave, caramella.
whom: chi, cui.

CHAPTER 5

Within a short walk of Longbourn lived a family with whom the Bennets were particularly **intimate**. Sir William Lucas had been **formerly** in trade in Meryton, where he had made a tolerable fortune, and **risen** to the honour of **knighthood** by an address to the king during his mayoralty. The **distinction** had perhaps been felt too **strongly**. It had given him a disgust to his business, and to his **residence** in a small market town; and, in **quitting** them both, he had **removed** with his family to a house about a **mile** from Meryton, **denominated** from that period Lucas Lodge, where he could think with pleasure of his own importance, and, unshackled by business, **occupy** himself **solely** in being civil to all the world. For, though **elated** by his rank, it did not **render** him **supercilious**; on the contrary, he was all attention to everybody. By nature **inoffensive**, **friendly**, and **obliging**, his **presentation** at St. James's had made him **courteous**.

Lady Lucas was a very good kind of woman, not too **clever** to be a **valuable** neighbour to Mrs. Bennet. They had several children. The eldest of them, a sensible, **intelligent** young woman, about twenty-seven, was Elizabeth's intimate friend.

That the Miss Lucases and the Miss Bennets should meet to talk over a ball was absolutely necessary; and the morning after the assembly brought the former to Longbourn to hear and to **communicate**.

Italian

clever: intelligente, destro, abile, lesto, sveglio.
communicate: comunicare, comunicano, comunico, comunichi, comunica, communicate, comunichiamo, annunciare, infettare.
courteous: cortese.
denominated: denominato.
distinction: distinzione.
elated: esaltato, esultante.
formerly: precedentemente, davanti, in passato, un tempo.

friendly: amichevole, cortese, amicale, gradevole, benevole, carino, grazioso.
inoffensive: inoffensivo.
intelligent: intelligente.
intimate: intimo.
knighthood: cavalierato.
mile: miglio.
obliging: obbligando, accomodante.
occupy: occupare, occupano, occupo, occupiamo, occupate, occupa, occupi.
presentation: presentazione, rappresentazione.

quitting: abbandonando.
removed: tolto, asportato, rimosso.
render: rendere, rendono, rendete, rendi, rendiamo, rendo.
residence: residenza, alloggio, appartamento.
risen: sorto.
solely: solamente, soltanto, unicamente.
strongly: fortemente.
supercilious: altezzoso.
valuable: costoso, caro, prezioso.

"*You* **began** the evening well, Charlotte," said Mrs. Bennet with **civil** self-command to Miss Lucas. "*You* were Mr. Bingley's first choice."

"Yes; but he seemed to like his second better."

"Oh! you mean Jane, I **suppose**, because he danced with her **twice**. To be sure that *did* seem as if he admired her--indeed I rather believe he *did*--I heard something about it--but I **hardly** know what--something about Mr. Robinson."

"Perhaps you mean what I **overheard** between him and Mr. Robinson; did not I **mention** it to you? Mr. Robinson's asking him how he liked our Meryton assemblies, and whether he did not think there were a great many pretty women in the room, and *which* he thought the prettiest? and his **answering immediately** to the last question: 'Oh! the eldest Miss Bennet, **beyond** a **doubt**; there cannot be two opinions on that point.'"

"Upon my word! Well, that is very **decided** indeed--that does seem as if--but, however, it may all come to nothing, you know."

"*My* overhearings were more to the **purpose** than *yours*, Eliza," said Charlotte. "Mr. Darcy is not so well worth **listening** to as his friend, is he?--poor Eliza!--to be only just *tolerable*."

"I beg you would not put it into Lizzy's head to be vexed by his ill-treatment, for he is such a disagreeable man, that it would be quite a **misfortune** to be liked by him. Mrs. Long told me last night that he **sat** close to her for half-an-hour without once **opening** his lips."

"Are you quite sure, ma'am?--is not there a little mistake?" said Jane. "I certainly saw Mr. Darcy speaking to her."

"Aye--because she asked him at last how he liked Netherfield, and he could not help answering her; but she said he seemed quite **angry** at being **spoke** to."

"Miss Bingley told me," said Jane, "that he never **speaks** much, **unless** among his intimate acquaintances. With *them* he is **remarkably** agreeable."

"I do not believe a word of it, my dear. If he had been so very agreeable, he would have talked to Mrs. Long. But I can **guess** how it was; everybody says

Italian

angry: arrabbiato, irato, stizzito.
answering: risposta, rispondere.
beg: mendicare, mendicano, mendica, mendicate, mendico, mendichiamo, mendichi, chiedere, elemosinare, supplicare.
beyond: oltre, dopo, attraverso, in seguito, poi.
civil: civile.
decided: deciso.
doubt: dubitare, dubbio.
guess: supporre, indovinare,

supposizione, congettura.
hardly: appena, a malapena, a stento.
immediately: immediatamente, subito, direttamente, fra poco.
listening: ascoltando, ascolto.
mention: menzionare, menzione, cenno.
misfortune: sfortuna, traversia, disgrazia.
opening: apertura, aprendo, pertugio, inaugurazione, bocca, orificio, luce.
overheard: origliato.

purpose: scopo, proposito, fine, intenzione.
remarkably: notevolmente.
sat: seduto, covato.
speaks: parla.
spoke: raggio.
suppose: supporre, supponiamo, supponete, suppongo, suppongono, supponi.
twice: due volte.
unless: a meno che, eccetto che.
yours: il vostro, vostro.

that he is eat up with **pride**, and I dare say he had heard **somehow** that Mrs. Long does not keep a **carriage**, and had come to the ball in a **hack** chaise."

"I do not mind his not talking to Mrs. Long," said Miss Lucas, "but I wish he had danced with Eliza."

"Another time, Lizzy," said her mother, "I would not dance with *him*, if I were you."

"I believe, ma'am, I may **safely promise** you *never* to dance with him."

"His pride," said Miss Lucas, "does not **offend** *me* so much as pride often does, because there is an **excuse** for it. One cannot wonder that so very fine a young man, with family, fortune, everything in his **favour**, should think highly of himself. If I may so express it, he has a *right* to be proud."

"That is very true," replied Elizabeth, "and I could easily **forgive** *his* pride, if he had not **mortified** *mine*."

"Pride," **observed** Mary, who piqued herself upon the **solidity** of her reflections, "is a very common **failing**, I believe. By all that I have ever read, I am convinced that it is very common indeed; that human nature is particularly **prone** to it, and that there are very few of us who do not **cherish** a feeling of self-complacency on the **score** of some quality or other, real or **imaginary**. Vanity and pride are different things, though the words are often used **synonymously**. A person may be proud without being **vain**. Pride **relates** more to our opinion of ourselves, **vanity** to what we would have others think of us."

"If I were as rich as Mr. Darcy," cried a young Lucas, who came with his sisters, "I should not care how proud I was. I would keep a **pack** of foxhounds, and drink a bottle of wine a day."

"Then you would drink a great deal more than you ought," said Mrs. Bennet; "and if I were to see you at it, I should take away your bottle directly."

The boy protested that she should not; she continued to declare that she would, and the argument ended only with the visit.

Italian

carriage: vettura, carrello, vagone, carro, carrozza.
cherish: adoriamo, adori, adorate, adorano, adora, adoro, adorare, curare teneramente.
excuse: scusa, scusare, giustificazione, pretesto.
failing: in mancanza di.
favour: favorire, favore.
forgive: perdonare, perdonano, perdoniamo, perdona, perdonate, perdoni, perdono.

hack: fare a pezzi.
imaginary: immaginario.
mortified: mortificato.
observed: osservato.
offend: offendere, offendiamo, offendo, offendi, offendete, offendono, insultare, insulto, insulti, insultate, insultano.
pack: pacco, avvolgere, imballare, impaccare, muta.
pride: orgoglio, fierezza.
promise: promessa, promettere,

promettono, promettete, prometti, promettiamo, prometto.
prone: prono, incline.
relates: racconta.
safely: al sicuro, sicuramente.
score: punteggio, segnare, partitura, punto, segno, marcare.
solidity: solidità.
somehow: in qualche modo.
synonymously: sinonimo.
vain: vanitoso, vano.
vanity: vanità.

CHAPTER 6

The ladies of Longbourn **soon** waited on those of Netherfield. The visit was soon returned in **due** form.   Miss Bennet's pleasing manners grew on the **goodwill** of Mrs. Hurst and Miss Bingley; and though the mother was found to be **intolerable**, and the **younger** sisters not **worth** speaking to, a wish of being better acquainted with *them* was expressed towards the two eldest.   By Jane, this attention was received with the greatest pleasure, but Elizabeth still saw superciliousness in their **treatment** of everybody, hardly **excepting** even her sister, and could not like them; though their kindness to Jane, such as it was, had a value as **arising** in all **probability** from the influence of their brother's admiration.   It was **generally evident whenever** they **met**, that he *did* admire her and to *her* it was equally evident that Jane was **yielding** to the **preference** which she had **begun** to **entertain** for him from the first, and was in a way to be very much in love; but she considered with pleasure that it was not likely to be **discovered** by the world in general, since Jane united, with great strength of **feeling**, a **composure** of temper and a **uniform cheerfulness** of manner which would guard her from the suspicions of the **impertinent**.   She mentioned this to her **friend** Miss Lucas.

"It may perhaps be pleasant," replied Charlotte, "to be able to **impose** on the public in such a case; but it is sometimes a **disadvantage** to be so very **guarded**. If a woman **conceals** her **affection** with the same skill from the object of it, she

Italian

affection: affetto, affezione, amore.
arising: nascendo, sorgendo.
begun: cominciato, iniziato.
cheerfulness: contentezza, allegria.
composure: calma, compostezza.
conceals: nasconde.
disadvantage: svantaggio.
discovered: scoperto.
due: dovuto.
entertain: intrattenere, intrattenete, intrattieni, intratteniamo, intrattengo, intrattengono, ricevere.

evident: evidente, chiaro, palese, lampante.
excepting: salvo.
feeling: sentimento, sensazione.
friend: amico, amica.
generally: generalmente.
goodwill: avviamento, buona volontà, avviamento commerciale.
guarded: guardingo, custodito.
impertinent: impertinente, insolente.
impose: imporre, imponete, imponiamo, imponi, impongo,

impongono.
intolerable: intollerabile.
met: incontrato.
preference: preferenza.
probability: probabilità.
soon: fra poco, presto.
treatment: trattamento.
uniform: uniforme, divisa.
whenever: ogni volta che, quando.
worth: valore.
yielding: cedendo.
younger: più giovane.

may lose the opportunity of **fixing** him; and it will then be but poor **consolation** to believe the world equally in the dark. There is so much of **gratitude** or vanity in almost every **attachment**, that it is not safe to leave any to itself. We can all *begin* freely--a **slight** preference is natural enough; but there are very few of us who have heart enough to be really in love without **encouragement**. In nine cases out of ten a women had better show *more* affection than she **feels**. Bingley likes your sister **undoubtedly**; but he may never do more than like her, if she does not help him on."

"But she does help him on, as much as her nature will allow. If I can **perceive** her regard for him, he must be a **simpleton**, indeed, not to **discover** it too."

"Remember, Eliza, that he does not know Jane's disposition as you do."

"But if a woman is **partial** to a man, and does not **endeavour** to **conceal** it, he must find it out."

"Perhaps he must, if he **sees** enough of her. But, though Bingley and Jane meet **tolerably** often, it is never for many hours together; and, as they always see each other in large **mixed** parties, it is impossible that every moment should be employed in conversing together. Jane should therefore make the most of every half-hour in which she can **command** his attention. When she is secure of him, there will be more **leisure** for falling in love as much as she chooses."

"Your plan is a good one," replied Elizabeth, "where nothing is in question but the desire of being well married, and if I were determined to get a rich husband, or any husband, I dare say I should **adopt** it. But these are not Jane's feelings; she is not acting by design. As yet, she cannot even be certain of the degree of her own regard nor of its **reasonableness**. She has known him only a fortnight. She danced four dances with him at Meryton; she saw him one morning at his own house, and has since **dined** with him in company four times. This is not quite enough to make her understand his character."

"Not as you represent it. Had she merely *dined* with him, she might only have discovered whether he had a good **appetite**; but you must remember that

---

Italian

adopt: adottare, adotta, adotto, adottiamo, adotti, adottano, adottate.
appetite: appetito.
attachment: accessorio, allegato, attaccamento.
command: comando, ordine, comandare, padronanza.
conceal: nascondere, nascondono, nascondete, nascondi, nascondiamo, nascondo, occultare.
consolation: consolazione.
dined: pranzato, cenato.

discover: scoprire, scopri, scoprono, scopro, scoprite, scopriamo.
encouragement: incoraggiamento.
endeavour: tentare, tentativo, sforzarsi.
feels: sente, tasta, tocca, trova, prova.
fixing: fissando, riparando, fissazione, fissaggio, quotazione.
gratitude: gratitudine, riconoscenza, grazie.
leisure: tempo libero, ozio, svago.
mixed: misto, mescolato.

partial: parziale.
perceive: percepire, accorgersi, scorgere, percepiamo, scorgo, scorgiamo, scorgi, scorgete, percepite, scorgono, percepiscono.
reasonableness: ragionevolezza.
sees: vede, sega.
simpleton: sempliciotto.
slight: leggero, lieve.
tolerably: tollerabilmente.
undoubtedly: indubbiamente, si capisce.

four evenings have also been spent together--and four evenings may do a great deal."

"Yes; these four evenings have **enabled** them to **ascertain** that they both like Vingt-un better than Commerce; but with respect to any other leading characteristic, I do not imagine that much has been unfolded."

"Well," said Charlotte, "I wish Jane success with all my heart; and if she were married to him to-morrow, I should think she had as good a chance of **happiness** as if she were to be **studying** his character for a twelvemonth. Happiness in marriage is entirely a matter of chance. If the dispositions of the parties are ever so well known to each other or ever so similar **beforehand**, it does not advance their **felicity** in the least. They always continue to grow **sufficiently** unlike **afterwards** to have their share of **vexation**; and it is better to know as little as possible of the defects of the person with whom you are to pass your life."

"You make me **laugh**, Charlotte; but it is not sound. You know it is not sound, and that you would never act in this way yourself."

Occupied in **observing** Mr. Bingley's attentions to her sister, Elizabeth was far from suspecting that she was herself becoming an object of some interest in the eyes of his friend. Mr. Darcy had at first **scarcely** allowed her to be pretty; he had looked at her without admiration at the ball; and when they next met, he looked at her only to **criticise**. But no **sooner** had he made it clear to himself and his friends that she hardly had a good feature in her face, than he began to find it was **rendered** uncommonly intelligent by the beautiful expression of her dark eyes. To this **discovery succeeded** some others equally **mortifying**. Though he had **detected** with a critical eye more than one failure of perfect **symmetry** in her form, he was forced to **acknowledge** her figure to be light and pleasing; and in spite of his **asserting** that her manners were not those of the **fashionable** world, he was caught by their easy playfulness. Of this she was **perfectly unaware**; to her he was only the man who made himself agreeable **nowhere**, and who had not thought her handsome enough to dance with.

Italian

acknowledge: riconoscere, riconoscono, riconosco, riconosciamo, riconosci, riconoscete, confessare, confermare, prendere atto.
afterwards: dopo, dietro, in seguito, successivamente.
ascertain: constatare, constatiamo, constati, constatate, constato, constatano, constata, accertare, accerto, accertiamo, accerti.
asserting: asserendo.
beforehand: in anticipo.

criticise: criticare.
detected: scoperto.
discovery: scoperta.
enabled: abilitato.
fashionable: alla moda.
felicity: felicità.
happiness: felicità.
laugh: ridere, riso, risata.
mortifying: mortificando, umiliante.
nowhere: in nessun luogo, da nessuna parte.
observing: osservando.

perfectly: perfettamente.
rendered: reso.
scarcely: appena, a stento.
sooner: prima.
studying: studio.
succeeded: riuscito.
sufficiently: abbastanza, sufficientemente.
symmetry: simmetria.
unaware: inconsapevole, ignaro, inconscio.
vexation: irritazione.

He began to wish to know more of her, and as a **step** towards **conversing** with her himself, **attended** to her conversation with others. His doing so drew her notice. It was at Sir William Lucas's, where a large party were assembled.

"What does Mr. Darcy mean," said she to Charlotte, "by listening to my conversation with Colonel Forster?"

"That is a question which Mr. Darcy only can answer."

"But if he does it any more I shall certainly let him know that I see what he is about. He has a very **satirical** eye, and if I do not **begin** by being impertinent myself, I shall soon **grow** afraid of him."

On his **approaching** them soon afterwards, though without **seeming** to have any **intention** of speaking, Miss Lucas **defied** her friend to mention such a subject to him; which immediately **provoking** Elizabeth to do it, she turned to him and said:

"Did you not think, Mr. Darcy, that I expressed myself uncommonly well just now, when I was teasing Colonel Forster to give us a ball at Meryton?"

"With great energy; but it is always a subject which makes a lady energetic."

"You are **severe** on us."

"It will be *her* turn soon to be teased," said Miss Lucas. "I am going to open the **instrument**, Eliza, and you know what follows."

"You are a very **strange** creature by way of a friend!--always **wanting** me to play and sing before **anybody** and everybody! If my vanity had taken a **musical** turn, you would have been **invaluable**; but as it is, I would really rather not sit down before those who must be in the habit of hearing the very best performers." On Miss Lucas's **persevering**, however, she added, "Very well, if it must be so, it must." And **gravely** glancing at Mr. Darcy, "There is a fine old saying, which everybody here is of course **familiar** with: 'Keep your **breath** to **cool** your porridge'; and I shall keep **mine** to **swell** my **song**."

Her performance was pleasing, though by no means capital. After a song or two, and before she could reply to the entreaties of several that she would sing

---

Italian

anybody: qualcuno, nessuno.
approaching: avvicinamento.
attended: visitato, curato, assistito.
begin: cominciare, cominci, cominciate, cominciano, comincia, cominciamo, comincio, iniziare, inizi, iniziate, iniziano.
breath: alito, respiro, fiato, soffio.
cool: fresco, raffreddare, freddo.
defied: sfidato.
familiar: familiare.
gravely: tomba, seriamente.

grow: crescere, crescete, crescono, cresco, cresci, cresciamo, coltivare, coltiviamo, coltivo, coltivi, coltivate.
instrument: strumento, apparecchio.
intention: intenzione, proposito.
invaluable: inestimabile.
mine: miniera, mina, minare, estrarre.
musical: musicale, musical.
persevering: perseverando.
provoking: incitando, provocando, spronando.
satirical: satirico.

seeming: parendo, sembrando, sembrare.
severe: severo.
sing: cantare, canta, cantano, cantate, canti, cantiamo, canto.
song: canzone, canto.
step: passo, gradino, scalino.
strange: strano.
swell: gonfiare, dilatare, rigonfiamento, mare lungo, crescendo.
wanting: volendo.

again, she was **eagerly** succeeded at the instrument by her sister Mary, who having, in consequence of being the only **plain** one in the family, worked hard for knowledge and **accomplishments**, was always **impatient** for display.

Mary had neither **genius** nor **taste**; and though vanity had given her application, it had given her likewise a **pedantic** air and conceited manner, which would have **injured** a higher degree of **excellence** than she had reached. Elizabeth, easy and unaffected, had been listened to with much more pleasure, though not playing half so well; and Mary, at the end of a long concerto, was glad to **purchase** praise and gratitude by Scotch and Irish airs, at the **request** of her younger sisters, who, with some of the Lucases, and two or three officers, **joined** eagerly in dancing at one end of the room.

Mr. Darcy stood near them in **silent indignation** at such a **mode** of **passing** the evening, to the **exclusion** of all conversation, and was too much **engrossed** by his thoughts to perceive that Sir William Lucas was his neighbour, till Sir William thus began:

"What a charming **amusement** for young people this is, Mr. Darcy! There is nothing like dancing after all. I consider it as one of the first refinements of **polished** society."

"Certainly, sir; and it has the advantage also of being in **vogue amongst** the less polished societies of the world. Every **savage** can dance."

Sir William only smiled. "Your friend **performs** delightfully," he continued after a **pause**, on seeing Bingley join the group; "and I doubt not that you are an **adept** in the science yourself, Mr. Darcy."

"You saw me dance at Meryton, I believe, sir."

"Yes, indeed, and received no inconsiderable pleasure from the sight. Do you often dance at St. James's?"

"Never, sir."

"Do you not think it would be a **proper compliment** to the place?"

"It is a compliment which I never pay to any place if I can avoid it."

Italian

accomplishments: compimenti.
adept: esperto, abile.
amongst: fra, tra.
amusement: divertimento, spasso, svago.
compliment: complimento.
eagerly: ardentemente.
engrossed: assorbito.
excellence: eccellenza.
exclusion: esclusione.
genius: genio.
impatient: impaziente.

indignation: indignazione, sdegno.
injured: danneggiato, ferito.
joined: congiunto, legato, unito, collegato.
mode: modo, moda, maniera.
passing: passeggero, passare, passaggio.
pause: pausa, sosta.
pedantic: pedante.
performs: esegue.
plain: piano, pianura, evidente, distinto, chiaro.

polished: lucidato.
proper: decente, proprio.
purchase: acquisto, comperare, comprare, compra, acquistare, compera.
request: richiesta, richiedere, chiedere, domanda.
savage: selvaggio, crudele.
silent: silenzioso, zitto.
taste: gustare, gusto, assaggiare, sapore.
vogue: moda.

"You have a house in town, I conclude?"

Mr. Darcy bowed.

"I had once had some thought of fixing in town myself--for I am fond of superior society; but I did not feel quite certain that the air of London would agree with Lady Lucas."

He paused in hopes of an answer; but his **companion** was not disposed to make any; and Elizabeth at that **instant** moving towards them, he was struck with the action of doing a very **gallant** thing, and called out to her:

"My dear Miss Eliza, why are you not dancing? Mr. Darcy, you must allow me to present this young lady to you as a very **desirable** partner. You cannot **refuse** to dance, I am sure when so much beauty is before you." And, taking her hand, he would have given it to Mr. Darcy who, though extremely **surprised**, was not unwilling to receive it, when she **instantly** drew back, and said with some discomposure to Sir William:

"Indeed, sir, I have not the **least** intention of dancing. I **entreat** you not to suppose that I moved this way in order to beg for a partner."

Mr. Darcy, with **grave propriety**, requested to be allowed the honour of her hand, but in vain. Elizabeth was determined; nor did Sir William at all **shake** her purpose by his attempt at **persuasion**.

"You **excel** so much in the dance, Miss Eliza, that it is **cruel** to **deny** me the happiness of seeing you; and though this **gentleman** dislikes the amusement in general, he can have no objection, I am sure, to **oblige** us for one half-hour."

"Mr. Darcy is all politeness," said Elizabeth, **smiling**.

"He is, indeed; but, **considering** the **inducement**, my dear Miss Eliza, we cannot **wonder** at his complaisance--for who would object to such a partner?"

Elizabeth looked **archly**, and turned away. Her **resistance** had not injured her with the gentleman, and he was thinking of her with some **complacency**, when thus **accosted** by Miss Bingley:

"I can guess the subject of your reverie."

Italian

accosted: abbordato, accostato, avvicinato.
archly: arco.
companion: compagno, accompagnatore.
complacency: compiacimento.
considering: considerando.
cruel: crudele.
deny: negare, negate, negano, neghi, neghiamo, nego, nega.
desirable: desiderabile.
entreat: supplicare.
excel: eccellere, eccelli, eccellono, eccello, eccellete, eccelliamo.
gallant: galante, coraggioso, valoroso.
gentleman: signore, galantuomo, gentiluomo.
grave: tomba, grave.
inducement: incitamento.
instant: istante, momento, immediato.
instantly: direttamente, istantaneamente, immediatamente.
least: minimo, meno.
oblige: obbligare, obblighiamo, obbliga, obbligano, obbligate, obblighi, obbligo.
persuasion: persuasione.
propriety: convenienza.
refuse: rifiutare, rifiutarsi, rifiuti.
resistance: resistenza.
shake: scuotere, scuotono, scuoto, scuotiamo, scuoti, scuotete, scossa.
smiling: sorridere.
surprised: sorpreso, sorpresa.
wonder: stupirsi, stupore, meraviglia, domandarsi, meravigliarsi.

"I should **imagine** not."

"You are considering how insupportable it would be to **pass** many evenings in this manner--in such society; and indeed I am quite of your opinion. I was never more **annoyed**! The **insipidity**, and yet the noise--the **nothingness**, and yet the self-importance of all those people! What would I give to hear your strictures on them!"

"You **conjecture** is **totally** wrong, I assure you. My mind was more **agreeably** engaged. I have been **meditating** on the very great pleasure which a **pair** of fine eyes in the face of a pretty woman can bestow."

Miss Bingley immediately fixed her eyes on his face, and **desired** he would tell her what lady had the **credit** of **inspiring** such reflections. Mr. Darcy replied **with** great intrepidity:

"Miss Elizabeth Bennet."

"Miss Elizabeth Bennet!" **repeated** Miss Bingley. "I am all astonishment. How long has she been such a favourite?--and **pray**, when am I to **wish** you joy?"

"That is **exactly** the question which I **expected** you to ask. A lady's **imagination** is very **rapid**; it jumps from admiration to love, from love to **matrimony**, in a moment. I knew you would be wishing me joy."

"Nay, if you are **serious** about it, I shall consider the matter is **absolutely** settled. You will be having a charming **mother**-in-law, indeed; and, of course, she will always be at Pemberley with you."

He listened to her with perfect **indifference** while she chose to entertain herself in this manner; and as his composure convinced her that all was **safe**, her wit flowed long.

Italian

absolutely: assolutamente, infatti, davvero, completamente.
agreeably: piacevolmente.
annoyed: infastidito, irritato, seccato.
conjecture: congettura.
credit: credito, accreditare, avere.
desired: desiderato.
exactly: esattamente, giusto, giustamente, precisamente.
expected: aspettato, atteso.
imagination: immagine, immaginazione, fantasia.

imagine: immaginare, figurarsi, immagino, immaginiamo, immagini, immaginano, immaginate, immagina.
indifference: indifferenza.
insipidity: insipidezza.
inspiring: ispirando.
matrimony: matrimonio.
meditating: meditando.
mother-in-law: suocera.
nothingness: inutilità, nullità.
pair: paio, coppia, accoppiarsi, accoppiare.

pass: passare, passaggio, lasciapassare, passata, trascorrere, passo.
pray: pregare, pregate, prego, preghi, prega, preghiamo, pregano.
rapid: rapido.
repeated: ripetuto.
safe: sicuro, cassaforte.
serious: serio, grave, importante.
totally: totalmente.
wish: desiderio, volere, desiderare, volontà, voglia.
wit: arguzia.

CHAPTER 7

Mr. Bennet's property consisted almost **entirely** in an **estate** of two thousand a year, which, **unfortunately** for his daughters, was entailed, in **default** of heirs **male**, on a distant **relation**; and their mother's fortune, though **ample** for her situation in life, could but ill supply the **deficiency** of his. Her father had been an **attorney** in Meryton, and had left her four thousand pounds.

She had a sister married to a Mr. Phillips, who had been a **clerk** to their father and succeeded him in the business, and a brother settled in London in a respectable line of trade.

The village of Longbourn was only one mile from Meryton; a most **convenient distance** for the young ladies, who were usually tempted **thither** three or four times a week, to pay their **duty** to their **aunt** and to a milliner's shop just over the way. The two youngest of the family, Catherine and Lydia, were particularly **frequent** in these attentions; their minds were more **vacant** than their sisters', and when nothing better **offered**, a walk to Meryton was necessary to **amuse** their morning hours and **furnish** conversation for the evening; and however **bare** of news the country in general might be, they always **contrived** to learn some from their aunt. At present, indeed, they were well **supplied** both with news and happiness by the recent **arrival** of a **militia regiment** in the neighbourhood; it was to remain the whole **winter**, and Meryton was the **headquarters**.

Italian

ample: ampio.
amuse: divertire, divertiamo, divertono, diverto, diverti, divertite.
arrival: arrivo, venuta.
attorney: procuratore, avvocato.
aunt: zia, la zia.
bare: nudo, denudare.
clerk: commesso, cancelliere, impiegato.
contrived: escogitato.
convenient: conveniente.
default: predefinito, inadempienza,

contumacia, difetto, mancanza.
deficiency: deficienza, mancanza, carenza, difetto, disavanzo.
distance: distanza.
duty: dovere, dazio, imposta, mansione.
entirely: completamente, interamente.
estate: fattoria, patrimonio, tenuta.
frequent: frequente, bazzicare.
furnish: fornire, fornite, forniscono, fornisco, fornisci, forniamo, arredare.
headquarters: sede centrale.

male: maschio, maschile.
militia: milizia.
offered: offerto, offerta.
regiment: reggimento.
relation: relazione, rapporto.
supplied: fornito.
thither: là.
unfortunately: purtroppo, per sfortuna, per fortuna, sfortunatamente.
vacant: vacante, libero.
winter: inverno, l'inverno.

Their **visits** to Mrs. Phillips were now **productive** of the most **interesting** intelligence. Every day added something to their knowledge of the **officers'** **names** and **connections**. Their lodgings were not long a **secret**, and at **length** they began to know the officers themselves. Mr. Phillips **visited** them all, and this **opened** to his nieces a **store** of felicity **unknown** before. They could talk of nothing but officers; and Mr. Bingley's large fortune, the mention of which gave **animation** to their mother, was **worthless** in their eyes when **opposed** to the regimentals of an ensign.

After listening one morning to their effusions on this subject, Mr. Bennet **coolly** observed:

"From all that I can **collect** by your manner of talking, you must be two of the silliest girls in the country. I have suspected it some time, but I am now convinced."

Catherine was disconcerted, and made no answer; but Lydia, with perfect **indifference**, continued to **express** her admiration of Captain Carter, and her hope of seeing him in the course of the day, as he was going the next morning to London.

"I am **astonished**, my dear," said Mrs. Bennet, "that you should be so **ready** to think your own children silly. If I wished to think slightingly of anybody's children, it should not be of my own, however."

"If my children are silly, I must hope to be always sensible of it."

"Yes--but as it **happens**, they are all of them very clever."

"This is the only point, I flatter myself, on which we do not **agree**. I had hoped that our sentiments **coincided** in every particular, but I must so far differ from you as to think our two youngest daughters uncommonly foolish."

"My dear Mr. Bennet, you must not expect such girls to have the sense of their father and mother. When they get to our age, I dare say they will not think about officers any more than we do. I remember the time when I liked a red coat myself very well--and, indeed, so I do still at my heart; and if a **smart** young **colonel**, with five or six **thousand** a year, should want one of my girls I shall not

Italian

agree: concordare, concordi, concorda, concordate, concordiamo, concordo, concordano, convenire, essere d'accordo, pattuire, pattuisco.
animation: animazione, vivacità.
astonished: stupito, si stupito.
coincided: coinciso.
collect: raccogliere, raccolgono, raccolgo, raccogliete, raccogliamo, raccogli.
colonel: colonnello.
connections: accesso.

coolly: frescamente.
differ: differire.
express: espresso, esprimere, esprimete, esprimi, esprimiamo, esprimo, esprimono, direttissimo.
happens: succede, avviene.
interesting: interessante.
length: lunghezza, durata.
names: nomi.
officers: ufficiali.
opened: aperto.
opposed: opposto, contrapposto.

productive: produttivo.
ready: pronto, disposto.
secret: segreto.
smart: intelligente.
store: negozio, magazzino, deposito, immagazzinare, memorizzare.
thousand: mille.
unknown: sconosciuto, ignoto.
visited: visitato.
visits: visita.
worthless: immeritevole, dappoco, indegno.

say **nay** to him; and I thought Colonel Forster looked very **becoming** the other night at Sir William's in his regimentals."

"Mamma," cried Lydia, "my aunt says that Colonel Forster and Captain Carter do not go so often to Miss Watson's as they did when they first came; she sees them now very often **standing** in Clarke's library."

Mrs. **Bennet** was **prevented** replying by the entrance of the **footman** with a **note** for Miss Bennet; it came from Netherfield, and the **servant** waited for an answer. Mrs. Bennet's eyes sparkled with **pleasure**, and she was **eagerly calling** out, while her **daughter** read,

"Well, Jane, who is it from? What is it about? What does he say? Well, Jane, make **haste** and tell us; make haste, my love."

"It is from Miss Bingley," said Jane, and then read it aloud.

"My Dear Friend,

"If you are not so **compassionate** as to **dine** to-day with Louisa and me, we shall be in **danger** of **hating** each other for the **rest** of our **lives**, for a whole day's tete-a-tete between two women can never end without a **quarrel**. Come as soon as you can on **receipt** of this. My brother and the gentlemen are to dine with the officers. Yours ever.

"Caroline Bingley"

"With the officers!" cried Lydia. "I wonder my aunt did not tell us of *that*."

"Dining out," said Mrs. Bennet, "that is very unlucky."

"Can I have the carriage?" said Jane.

"No, my dear, you had better go on **horseback**, because it seems likely to **rain**; and then you must **stay** all night."

"That would be a good scheme," said Elizabeth, "if you were sure that they would not **offer** to **send** her home."

Italian

becoming: conveniente, divenendo.
bennet: cariofillata, erba benedetta.
calling: chiamando, chiamata.
compassionate: compassionevole.
danger: pericolo.
daughter: figlia, figliola, figliuola, la figlia.
dine: cenare.
eagerly: ardentemente.
footman: lacchè.
haste: fretta, furia.
hating: odiare.

horseback: groppa, dorso del cavallo.
lives: vive, abita.
nay: anzi.
note: nota, biglietto, appunto, annotazione, notare, annotare.
offer: offerta, offrire, proporre, presentare, proposta.
prevented: impedito, prevenuto.
quarrel: lite, litigare, bisticciare, bisticcio, litigio.
rain: pioggia, piovere, la pioggia.
receipt: ricevuta, quietanza,

quietanzare, ricezione, scontrino.
rest: riposo, riposarsi, riposare, resto, pausa.
send: mandare, mandano, mandiamo, mandi, mandate, manda, mando, spedire, spediamo, spedisco, spedite.
servant: servire, servo, servitore.
standing: in piedi.
stay: stare, sta', stanno, sto, state, stiamo, stai, restare, rimanere, soggiorno, resta.
sure: certo, sicuro.

"Oh! but the gentlemen will have Mr. Bingley's chaise to go to Meryton, and the Hursts have no horses to theirs."

"I had much rather go in the coach."

"But, my dear, your father cannot **spare** the horses, I am sure. They are wanted in the **farm**, Mr. Bennet, are they not?"

"They are wanted in the farm much oftener than I can get them."

"But if you have got them to-day," said Elizabeth, "my mother's purpose will be answered."

She did at last **extort** from her father an **acknowledgment** that the horses were engaged. Jane was therefore obliged to go on horseback, and her mother attended her to the door with many **cheerful** prognostics of a **bad** day. Her hopes were answered; Jane had not been gone long before it rained hard. Her sisters were **uneasy** for her, but her mother was delighted. The rain continued the whole **evening** without **intermission**; Jane certainly could not come back.

"This was a **lucky** idea of mine, indeed!" said Mrs. Bennet more than once, as if the credit of making it rain were all her own. Till the next morning, however, she was not **aware** of all the felicity of her **contrivance**. Breakfast was scarcely over when a servant from Netherfield **brought** the following note for Elizabeth:

"My Dearest Lizzy,

"I find **myself** very **unwell** this morning, which, I suppose, is to be **imputed** to my getting **wet** through yesterday. My kind friends will not **hear** of my returning till I am better. They **insist** also on my seeing Mr. Jones--therefore do not be **alarmed** if you should hear of his having been to me--and, excepting a **sore throat** and **headache**, there is not much the matter with me. Yours, etc."

"Well, my dear," said Mr. Bennet, when Elizabeth had read the note **aloud**, "if your daughter should have a **dangerous fit** of illness--if she should **die**, it

Italian

acknowledgment: riconoscimento.
alarmed: allarmato.
aloud: ad alta voce.
aware: cosciente, consapevole.
bad: cattivo, male.
brought: portato.
cheerful: allegro.
contrivance: congegno.
dangerous: pericoloso.
die: morire, muoio, muori, muoiono, morite, moriamo, dado, cubo, matrice, stampo.

evening: sera, la sera, serata.
extort: estorcere, estorci, estorcono, estorcete, estorco, estorciamo.
farm: fattoria, podere, la fattoria, coltivare.
fit: adattare, aggiustare, apoplessia, in forma, adatto.
headache: mal di testa, cefalea.
hear: udire, odono, odi, odo, udite, udiamo, sentire, sentono, sento, sentite, senti.
imputed: attribuito, imputato.

insist: insistere, insistiamo, insisto, insistete, insistono, insisti.
intermission: interruzione, intervallo.
lucky: fortunato.
myself: mi, me stesso, io stesso.
sore: piaga, dolente.
spare: risparmiare, scorta.
throat: gola, la gola.
uneasy: inquieto.
unwell: indisposto.
wet: bagnato, bagnare, umido, inumidire.

would be a **comfort** to know that it was all in **pursuit** of Mr. Bingley, and under your orders."

"Oh! I am not afraid of her **dying**. People do not die of little **trifling** colds. She will be taken good care of. As long as she **stays** there, it is all very well. I would go an see her if I could have the carriage."

Elizabeth, feeling really **anxious**, was determined to go to her, though the carriage was not to be had; and as she was no **horsewoman**, walking was her only **alternative**. She declared her resolution.

"How can you be so silly," cried her mother, "as to think of such a thing, in all this **dirt**! You will not be fit to be seen when you get there."

"I shall be very fit to see Jane--which is all I want."

"Is this a **hint** to me, Lizzy," said her father, "to send for the horses?"

"No, indeed, I do not wish to avoid the walk. The distance is nothing when one has a **motive**; only three miles. I shall be back by dinner."

"I admire the activity of your benevolence," observed Mary, "but every **impulse** of feeling should be **guided** by reason; and, in my opinion, **exertion** should always be in **proportion** to what is required."

"We will go as far as Meryton with you," said Catherine and Lydia. Elizabeth **accepted** their company, and the three young ladies set off together.

"If we make haste," said Lydia, as they walked along, "perhaps we may see something of Captain Carter before he goes."

In Meryton they parted; the two youngest **repaired** to the lodgings of one of the officers' wives, and Elizabeth continued her walk alone, **crossing** field after field at a **quick pace, jumping** over stiles and **springing** over puddles with impatient activity, and **finding** herself at last within view of the house, with **weary** ankles, **dirty** stockings, and a face **glowing** with the **warmth** of exercise.

She was shown into the breakfast-parlour, where all but Jane were **assembled**, and where her **appearance created** a great deal of surprise. That she should have walked three miles so early in the day, in such dirty **weather**, and

Italian

accepted: accettato.
alternative: alternativa, alternativo.
anxious: ansioso.
appearance: apparenza, aspetto, aria, comparizione, comparsa.
assembled: montato, assemblato.
comfort: consolare, comodità, confortare, comfort, benessere.
created: creato.
crossing: attraversamento, incrocio, traversata, passaggio.
dirt: sporcizia, fango, sudiciume.

dirty: sporco, sporcare, imbrattare, insudiciare.
dying: morendo, morente.
exertion: sforzo.
finding: fondendo, fondando.
glowing: raggiante, ardente.
guided: guidato.
hint: alludere, suggerimento, allusione, cenno.
horsewoman: amazzone, cavallerizza.
impulse: impulso.
jumping: saltare.

motive: motivo, movente, ragione.
pace: passo, andatura, velocità.
proportion: proporzione.
pursuit: inseguimento, ricerca.
quick: rapido, svelto, veloce.
repaired: riparato.
springing: saltare, correzione.
stays: sta, resta.
trifling: insignificante.
warmth: calore, cordialità, tepore.
weary: stanco, stancare, fiacco.
weather: tempo.

by herself, was almost **incredible** to Mrs. Hurst and Miss Bingley; and Elizabeth was convinced that they held her in **contempt** for it. She was received, however, very **politely** by them; and in their brother's manners there was something better than **politeness**; there was good humour and kindness. Mr. Darcy said very little, and Mr. Hurst nothing at all. The former was divided between admiration of the **brilliancy** which exercise had given to her **complexion**, and doubt as to the occasion's **justifying** her coming so far alone. The latter was thinking only of his breakfast.

Her inquiries after her sister were not very **favourably** answered. Miss Bennet had **slept** ill, and though up, was very **feverish**, and not well enough to leave her room. Elizabeth was glad to be taken to her immediately; and Jane, who had only been **withheld** by the fear of giving **alarm** or **inconvenience** from **expressing** in her note how much she longed for such a visit, was delighted at her entrance. She was not equal, however, to much conversation, and when Miss Bingley left them together, could attempt little **besides expressions** of gratitude for the extraordinary kindness she was treated with. Elizabeth **silently** attended her.

When breakfast was over they were joined by the sisters; and Elizabeth began to like them herself, when she saw how much affection and **solicitude** they showed for Jane. The **apothecary** came, and having examined his patient, said, as might be supposed, that she had caught a violent cold, and that they must endeavour to get the better of it; **advised** her to return to bed, and promised her some **draughts**. The advice was followed **readily**, for the feverish symptoms increased, and her head ached **acutely**. Elizabeth did not **quit** her room for a moment; nor were the other ladies often **absent**; the gentlemen being out, they had, in fact, nothing to do elsewhere.

When the clock struck three, Elizabeth felt that she must go, and very **unwillingly** said so. Miss Bingley offered her the carriage, and she only wanted a little pressing to accept it, when Jane **testified** such concern in **parting** with her, that Miss Bingley was obliged to **convert** the offer of the chaise to an invitation to remain at Netherfield for the present. Elizabeth most **thankfully consented**, and

Italian

absent: assente.
acutely: acutamente.
advised: consigliato.
alarm: allarme, sveglia, allarmare.
apothecary: farmacista.
besides: inoltre, d'altronde.
brilliancy: splendore.
complexion: carnagione.
consented: acconsentito.
contempt: sprezzo, disprezzo.
convert: convertito, convertire.
draughts: dama.

expressing: esprimendo.
expressions: espressioni.
favourably: favorevolmente.
feverish: febbrile, febbricitante.
inconvenience: inconvenienza, disagio, disturbo.
incredible: incredibile.
justifying: giustificando.
parting: separazione, divisione.
politely: cortesemente.
politeness: cortesia, garbo.
pressing: pressatura, urgente.

quit: abbandonare, abbandonato, abbandono, abbandoni, abbandonate, abbandonano, abbandona, abbandoniamo, smettere.
readily: prontamente.
silently: silenziosamente.
slept: dormito.
solicitude: sollecitudine.
testified: testimoniato.
thankfully: riconoscentemente.
unwillingly: malvolentieri.
withheld: trattenuto.

a **servant** was **dispatched** to Longbourn to **acquaint** the family with her **stay** and **bring** back a **supply** of clothes.

Italian

acquaint: informare, informi, informa, informate, informiamo, informo, informano, insegnare.
bring: portare, portiamo, porti, portano, portate, porto, porta.
dispatched: spedito.
servant: servire, servo, servitore.
stay: stare, sta', stanno, sto, state, stiamo, stai, restare, rimanere, soggiorno, resta.
supply: fornitura, rifornimento, fornire, approvvigionamento, erogare, alimentazione, offerta, provvedere, scorta.

CHAPTER 8

At five o'clock the two ladies **retired** to **dress**, and at half-past six Elizabeth was **summoned** to dinner. To the civil inquiries which then **poured** in, and amongst which she had the pleasure of **distinguishing** the much superior **solicitude** of Mr. Bingley's, she could not make a very favourable answer. Jane was by no means better. The sisters, on hearing this, repeated three or four times how much they were **grieved**, how **shocking** it was to have a bad **cold**, and how **excessively** they disliked being ill themselves; and then thought no more of the matter: and their indifference towards Jane when not immediately before them **restored** Elizabeth to the **enjoyment** of all her former dislike.

Their brother, **indeed**, was the only one of the party whom she could **regard** with any **complacency**. His **anxiety** for Jane was evident, and his attentions to **herself** most **pleasing**, and they prevented her feeling herself so much an **intruder** as she **believed** she was considered by the others. She had very little notice from any but him. Miss Bingley was **engrossed** by Mr. Darcy, her sister scarcely less so; and as for Mr. Hurst, by whom Elizabeth sat, he was an **indolent** man, who lived only to eat, **drink**, and play at **cards**; who, when he found her to **prefer** a plain **dish** to a **ragout**, had nothing to say to her.

When dinner was over, she returned **directly** to Jane, and Miss Bingley began **abusing** her as soon as she was out of the room. Her manners were pronounced

Italian

abusing: abusando.
anxiety: ansia, ansietà, angoscia, inquietudine.
believed: creduto.
cards: carte.
cold: freddo, raffreddore.
complacency: compiacimento.
directly: direttamente.
dish: piatto, pietanza.
distinguishing: distinguendo.
dress: vestire, vestito, vestirsi, abito, abbigliare.

drink: bere, bevanda, bibita.
engrossed: assorbito.
enjoyment: godimento.
excessively: eccessivamente.
grieved: accorato, addolorato.
herself: stesso, sè.
indeed: davvero, infatti, di fatto, veramente.
indolent: indolente.
intruder: intruso.
pleasing: piacevole.
poured: versato.

prefer: preferire, preferisci, preferite, preferiscono, preferisco, preferiamo.
ragout: cibreo.
regard: riguardo, considerazione, considerare, rispetto, considerano, consideriamo, considero, considera, consideri, considerate, stima.
restored: ripristinato, restaurato.
retired: pensionato, ritirato, a riposo.
shocking: irritante, scandaloso.
solicitude: sollecitudine.
summoned: convocato.

to be very bad indeed, a **mixture** of pride and **impertinence**; she had no conversation, no **style**, no beauty. Mrs. Hurst thought the same, and added:

"She has nothing, in short, to recommend her, but being an excellent **walker**. I shall never **forget** her appearance this morning. She really looked almost wild."

"She did, indeed, Louisa. I could hardly keep my countenance. Very **nonsensical** to come at all! Why must *she* be **scampering** about the country, because her sister had a cold? Her hair, so **untidy**, so blowsy!"

"Yes, and her **petticoat**; I hope you saw her petticoat, six inches deep in **mud**, I am absolutely certain; and the **gown** which had been let down to **hide** it not doing its office."

"Your **picture** may be very **exact**, Louisa," said Bingley; "but this was all lost upon me. I thought Miss Elizabeth Bennet looked remarkably well when she came into the room this morning. Her dirty petticoat quite escaped my notice."

"*You* observed it, Mr. Darcy, I am sure," said Miss Bingley; "and I am **inclined** to think that you would not wish to see *your* sister make such an exhibition."

"Certainly not."

"To walk three miles, or four miles, or five miles, or whatever it is, above her ankles in dirt, and alone, quite alone! What could she mean by it? It seems to me to show an **abominable** sort of conceited **independence**, a most country-town indifference to decorum."

"It **shows** an affection for her sister that is very pleasing," said Bingley.

"I am afraid, Mr. Darcy," observed Miss Bingley in a half **whisper**, "that this **adventure** has rather **affected** your admiration of her fine eyes."

"Not at all," he replied; "they were brightened by the exercise." A short pause followed this **speech**, and Mrs. Hurst began again:

Italian

abominable: abominevole, orribile, orrendo.
adventure: avventura.
affected: riguardato.
exact: esatto, preciso.
forget: dimenticare, dimentichi, dimentichiamo, dimenticate, dimenticano, dimentica, dimentico, scordare.
gown: abito, vestito, toga.
hide: nascondere, nascondo, nascondiamo, nascondono,

nascondete, nascondi, pelle, nascondersi, pellame, celare, occultare.
impertinence: impertinenza.
inclined: disposto, inclinato, propenso.
independence: indipendenza.
mixture: mistura, miscela, commistione, impasto, mescolanza, miscuglio.
mud: fango, melma.
nonsensical: assurdo, privo di senso.

petticoat: sottana, sottogonna, sottoveste.
picture: immagine, illustrazione, pittura, figura, quadro.
scampering: sgambettando.
shows: mostra.
speech: discorso, orazione, parola.
style: stile, stilo, modello, moda.
untidy: trasandato.
walker: deambulatore, camminatore.
whisper: sussurrare, bisbigliare, bisbiglio.

"I have a **excessive** regard for Miss Jane Bennet, she is really a very sweet girl, and I wish with all my heart she were well settled. But with such a father and mother, and such low connections, I am afraid there is no chance of it."

"I think I have heard you say that their **uncle** is an attorney on Meryton."

"Yes; and they have another, who lives **somewhere** near Cheapside."

"That is capital," added her sister, and they both laughed heartily.

"If they had uncles enough to **fill** *all* Cheapside," cried Bingley, "it would not make them one **jot** less agreeable."

"But it must very **materially lessen** their chance of marrying men of any **consideration** in the world," replied Darcy.

To this speech Bingley made no answer; but his sisters gave it their hearty **assent**, and **indulged** their **mirth** for some time at the **expense** of their dear friend's **vulgar** relations.

With a **renewal** of **tenderness**, however, they returned to her room on leaving the dining-parlour, and sat with her till summoned to **coffee**. She was still very **poorly**, and Elizabeth would not quit her at all, till late in the evening, when she had the comfort of seeing her **sleep**, and when it seemed to her rather right than pleasant that she should go **downstairs** herself. On entering the drawing-room she found the whole party at **loo**, and was immediately **invited** to join them; but suspecting them to be playing high she declined it, and making her sister the excuse, said she would amuse herself for the short time she could stay below, with a book. Mr. Hurst looked at her with astonishment.

"Do you prefer **reading** to cards?" said he; "that is rather singular."

"Miss Eliza Bennet," said Miss Bingley, "despises cards. She is a great **reader**, and has no pleasure in anything else."

"I **deserve neither** such praise nor such censure," cried Elizabeth; "I am *not* a great reader, and I have pleasure in many things."

"In **nursing** your sister I am sure you have pleasure," said Bingley; "and I hope it will be soon **increased** by seeing her quite well."

Italian

assent: affermare, assentire, approvazione, assenso, acconsentire.
coffee: caffè.
consideration: corrispettivo, considerazione.
deserve: meritare, meritano, merita, meritate, meritiamo, meriti, merito.
downstairs: giù dalle scale.
excessive: eccessivo.
expense: spese, spesa.
fill: riempire, riempimento.
increased: aumentato.
indulged: compiaciuto, indulto.
invited: invitato.
jot: annotare in fretta.
lessen: diminuire, diminuiamo, diminuisci, diminuisco, diminuiscono, diminuite.
loo: gabinetto.
materially: materialmente.
mirth: gaiezza, allegria, ilarità, gioia.
neither: ne, neanche, nemmeno, neppure.
nursing: allattamento.
poorly: male, poveramente.
reader: lettore, lettrice.
reading: leggendo, lettura.
renewal: rinnovo, rinnovamento.
sleep: sonno, dormire, dormi, dormiamo, dormite, dormo, dormono.
somewhere: in qualche luogo, da qualche parte.
tenderness: tenerezza, affettuosità.
uncle: zio, lo zio.
vulgar: volgare, triviale.

Elizabeth **thanked** him from her heart, and then walked towards the table where a few books were **lying**. He immediately offered to **fetch** her others--all that his **library afforded**.

"And I wish my **collection** were **larger** for your benefit and my own credit; but I am an **idle fellow**, and though I have not many, I have more than I ever looked into."

Elizabeth **assured** him that she could **suit** herself perfectly with those in the room.

"I am astonished," said Miss Bingley, "that my father should have left so small a collection of books. What a delightful library you have at Pemberley, Mr. Darcy!"

"It ought to be good," he replied, "it has been the work of many generations."

"And then you have added so much to it yourself, you are always **buying** books."

"I cannot **comprehend** the neglect of a family library in such days as these."

"Neglect! I am sure you neglect nothing that can add to the beauties of that noble place. Charles, when you **build** *your* house, I wish it may be half as delightful as Pemberley."

"I wish it may."

"But I would really **advise** you to make your purchase in that neighbourhood, and take Pemberley for a kind of model. There is not a finer **county** in England than Derbyshire."

"With all my heart; I will buy Pemberley itself if Darcy will **sell** it."

"I am talking of **possibilities**, Charles."

"Upon my word, Caroline, I should think it more possible to get Pemberley by purchase than by imitation."

Elizabeth was so much **caught** with what **passed**, as to leave her very little attention for her book; and soon **laying** it **wholly aside**, she drew near the **card-**

Italian

advise: consigliare, consigliano, consigli, consiglia, consigliamo, consigliate, consiglio, raccomandare.
afforded: permesso.
aside: da parte, a parte.
assured: assicurato, certo.
build: costruire, fabbricare, edificare, build.
buying: acquisto.
card: carta, scheda.
caught: preso, colpito.
collection: collezione, raccolta,

incasso, gruppo.
comprehend: comprendere, comprendo, comprendono, comprendiamo, comprendi, comprendete.
county: contea.
fellow: uomo.
fetch: portare, portiamo, porto, porti, portate, portano, porta, ottenere, andare a prendere.
idle: ozioso, pigro, folle, inattivo.
larger: più grande.

laying: posando, posa.
library: biblioteca, libreria, la biblioteca.
lying: mentire, bugiardo, giacente.
passed: passato.
possibilities: possibilità.
sell: vendere, vendo, vendono, vendiamo, vendi, vendete.
suit: abito, costume, vestito, tailleur, completo.
thanked: ringraziato.
wholly: interamente, completamente.

table, and stationed herself between Mr. Bingley and his eldest sister, to **observe** the game.

"Is Miss Darcy much **grown** since the spring?" said Miss Bingley; "will she be as **tall** as I am?"

"I think she will. She is now about Miss Elizabeth **Bennet's height,** or rather taller."

"How I long to see her again! I never met with anybody who delighted me so much. Such a countenance, such manners! And so extremely accomplished for her age! Her performance on the pianoforte is exquisite."

"It is **amazing** to me," said Bingley, "how young ladies can have **patience** to be so very accomplished as they all are."

"All young ladies accomplished! My dear Charles, what do you mean?"

"Yes, all of them, I think. They all **paint tables,** cover screens, and net **purses.** I scarcely know anyone who cannot do all this, and I am sure I never heard a young lady **spoken** of for the first time, without being **informed** that she was very accomplished."

"Your list of the common extent of accomplishments," said Darcy, "has too much truth. The word is **applied** to many a woman who **deserves** it no otherwise than by **netting** a purse or **covering** a screen. But I am very far from **agreeing** with you in your **estimation** of ladies in general. I cannot **boast** of **knowing** more than half-a-dozen, in the whole range of my acquaintance, that are really accomplished."

"Nor I, I am sure," said Miss Bingley.

"Then," observed Elizabeth, "you must comprehend a great deal in your idea of an accomplished woman."

"Yes, I do comprehend a great deal in it."

"Oh! certainly," cried his **faithful assistant,** "no one can be really **esteemed** accomplished who does not **greatly surpass** what is usually met with. A woman must have a **thorough** knowledge of music, **singing, drawing,** dancing, and the

Italian

agreeing: concordando, pattuendo.
amazing: sbalordendo, stupefacente, stupendosi, sorprendente, strabiliante.
applied: applicato.
assistant: assistente, aggiunto, aiutante, aiuto, coadiutore.
boast: vanteria, vantarsi.
covering: copertura, rivestimento, coprire, monta.
deserves: merita.
drawing: disegno, disegnando,

prelievo.
esteemed: stimato.
estimation: stima, valutazione.
faithful: fedele, leale.
greatly: molto, grandemente.
grown: cresciuto, coltivato.
height: altezza, altitudine, altura.
informed: informato.
knowing: conoscendo, sapendo.
net: rete, netto.
netting: reticolato.
observe: osservare, osservano,

osservo, osserviamo, osservate, osserva, osservi, eseguire, compiere.
paint: dipingere, pittura, vernice, verniciare, tinta, tingere, pitturare.
patience: pazienza.
purse: borsa, borsellino, portamonete.
singing: cantando, canto.
spoken: parlato.
surpass: sorpassare, superare.
tables: tavoli.
tall: alto, grande, elevato.
thorough: completo, accurato.

modern languages, to deserve the word; and besides all this, she must **possess** a certain something in her air and manner of walking, the tone of her voice, her address and expressions, or the word will be but half-deserved."

"All this she must possess," added Darcy, "and to all this she must yet add something more substantial, in the improvement of her mind by **extensive** reading."

"I am no longer surprised at your knowing *only* six accomplished women. I rather wonder now at your knowing *any*."

"Are you so severe upon your own sex as to doubt the possibility of all this?"

"I never saw such a woman. I never saw such capacity, and taste, and application, and **elegance**, as you describe united."

Mrs. Hurst and Miss Bingley both cried out against the **injustice** of her **implied** doubt, and were both **protesting** that they knew many women who answered this description, when Mr. Hurst called them to order, with **bitter complaints** of their **inattention** to what was going forward. As all conversation was thereby at an end, **Elizabeth** soon afterwards left the room.

"Elizabeth Bennet," said Miss Bingley, when the door was closed on her, "is one of those young ladies who seek to recommend themselves to the other sex by **undervaluing** their own; and with many men, I dare say, it **succeeds**. But, in my opinion, it is a **paltry device**, a very mean art."

"Undoubtedly," replied Darcy, to whom this **remark** was **chiefly** addressed, "there is a meanness in *all* the arts which ladies sometimes **condescend** to **employ** for **captivation**. Whatever bears **affinity** to **cunning** is despicable."

Miss Bingley was not so entirely satisfied with this reply as to continue the subject.

Elizabeth joined them again only to say that her sister was worse, and that she could not leave her. Bingley urged Mr. Jones being sent for immediately; while his sisters, convinced that no country advice could be of any service, **recommended** an express to town for one of the most **eminent** physicians. This she would not hear of; but she was not so unwilling to **comply** with their

Italian

affinity: affinità, parentela, parentado.
bitter: amaro.
captivation: attrazione.
chiefly: principalmente, soprattutto.
complaints: reclami.
comply: ottemperi, accondiscendiamo, ottemperiamo, ottempero, ottemperate, ottemperano, ottempera, accondiscendo, accondiscendi, accondiscendete, accondiscendono.
condescend: degna, degnano, degnate, degni, degniamo, degno, degnare.
cunning: astuzia, astuto, furbo.
device: dispositivo, apparecchio, congegno.
elegance: eleganza.
elizabeth: Elisabetta.
eminent: eminente.
employ: usare, impiegare, assumere, occupare.
extensive: vasto, esteso.
implied: significato, implicito, implicato.
inattention: disattenzione.
injustice: ingiustizia.
paltry: meschino.
possess: possedere, possedete, possediamo, possiedi, possiedo, possiedono.
protesting: protestare.
recommended: raccomandato.
remark: commento, osservazione, nota.
succeeds: riesce.
undervaluing: sottovalutando.

brother's **proposal**; and it was **settled** that Mr. Jones should be **sent** for early in the morning, if Miss Bennet were not **decidedly** better. Bingley was quite **uncomfortable**; his sisters **declared** that they were **miserable**. They solaced their wretchedness, however, by duets after **supper**, while he could find no better **relief** to his feelings than by **giving** his **housekeeper directions** that every **attention** might be **paid** to the **sick lady** and her sister.

Italian

attention: attenzione.
decidedly: decisamente.
declared: dichiarato.
directions: avvertenze.
giving: dando, regalando.
housekeeper: governante.
lady: signora, dama.
miserable: miserabile, misero, afflitto, cattivo, triste, povero, miserevole, miserando.
paid: pagato.
proposal: proposta.

relief: rilievo, sollievo.
sent: mandato, spedito.
settled: regolato, stabilito, stabile, fermo, fisso, popolato, saldato, sistemato, deciso.
sick: malato, ammalato.
supper: cena.
uncomfortable: scomodo, disagiato.

CHAPTER 9

Elizabeth passed the **chief** of the night in her sister's room, and in the morning had the pleasure of being able to send a **tolerable** answer to the inquiries which she very early **received** from Mr. Bingley by a **housemaid**, and some time afterwards from the two elegant ladies who waited on his sisters. In **spite** of this **amendment**, however, she requested to have a note sent to Longbourn, desiring her mother to visit Jane, and form her own judgement of her **situation**. The note was immediately dispatched, and its **contents** as quickly **complied** with. Mrs. **Bennet**, **accompanied** by her two youngest girls, reached Netherfield soon after the family **breakfast**.

Had she found Jane in any **apparent** danger, Mrs. Bennet would have been very miserable; but being satisfied on seeing her that her **illness** was not **alarming**, she had no wish of her **recovering** immediately, as her **restoration** to health would probably **remove** her from Netherfield. She would not **listen**, therefore, to her daughter's proposal of being **carried** home; neither did the **apothecary**, who **arrived** about the same time, think it at all **advisable**. After **sitting** a little while with Jane, on Miss Bingley's appearance and invitation, the mother and three daughter all attended her into the breakfast **parlour**. Bingley met them with hopes that Mrs. Bennet had not found Miss Bennet **worse** than she expected.

Italian

accompanied: accompagnato.
advisable: consigliabile.
alarming: allarmante.
amendment: emendamento, modifica, correzione.
apothecary: farmacista.
apparent: apparente, evidente.
arrived: arrivato.
bennet: cariofillata, erba benedetta.
breakfast: colazione, prima colazione.
carried: portato, trasportato.
chief: capo, principale.

complied: accondisceso, ottemperato.
contents: contenuto.
housemaid: domestica.
illness: malattia.
listen: ascoltare, ascolti, ascoltiamo, ascoltate, ascoltano, ascolta, ascolto.
parlour: salotto.
receive: ricevere, ricevono, ricevo, riceviamo, ricevi, ricevete, accogliere, accogliete, accolgo, accogliamo, accogli.
recovering: ricuperando.

remove: togliere, togliamo, togli, tolgo, tolgono, togliete, asportare, rimuovere, asporti, rimuovete, rimuovi.
restoration: restauro, ripristino, ristabilimento, restituzione, restaurazione.
sitting: sedendo, covando, seduta.
situation: situazione.
spite: dispetto.
tolerable: tollerabile.
worse: peggiore, peggio.

"Indeed I have, sir," was her answer. "She is a great **deal** too ill to be **moved**. Mr. Jones says we must not think of **moving** her. We must **trespass** a little **longer** on your kindness."

"Removed!" cried Bingley. "It must not be thought of. My sister, I am sure, will not hear of her removal."

"You may depend upon it, Madam," said Miss Bingley, with cold **civility**, "that Miss Bennet will receive every possible attention while she **remains** with us."

Mrs. Bennet was **profuse** in her acknowledgments.

"I am sure," she **added**, "if it was not for such good friends I do not know what would become of her, for she is very ill indeed, and **suffers** a **vast** deal, though with the greatest patience in the world, which is always the way with her, for she has, without **exception**, the sweetest temper I have ever met with. I often tell my other girls they are nothing to *her*. You have a sweet room here, Mr. Bingley, and a charming **prospect** over the **gravel walk**. I do not know a place in the country that is **equal** to Netherfield. You will not think of quitting it in a **hurry**, I hope, though you have but a **short** lease."

"Whatever I do is done in a hurry," replied he; "and therefore if I should **resolve** to quit Netherfield, I should probably be off in five minutes. At present, however, I **consider** myself as quite fixed here."

"That is exactly what I should have **supposed** of you," said Elizabeth.

"You begin to comprehend me, do you?" cried he, turning towards her.

"Oh! yes--I understand you perfectly."

"I wish I might take this for a compliment; but to be so **easily** seen through I am afraid is pitiful."

"That is as it happens. It does not **follow** that a deep, **intricate** character is more or less **estimable** than such a one as yours."

"Lizzy," cried her mother, "remember where you are, and do not run on in the **wild** manner that you are **suffered** to do at home."

Italian

added: aggiunto, addizionato.
civility: civiltà, cortesia.
consider: considerare, consideri, considerano, consideriamo, considera, considerate, considero, guardare.
deal: affare, trattare, accordo.
easily: facilmente.
equal: eguale, uguale, pari.
estimable: stimabile.
exception: eccezione.
follow: seguire, seguiamo, seguite,
seguo, seguono, segui.
gravel: ghiaia.
hurry: affrettarsi, fretta.
intricate: complicato, intricato.
longer: oltre, più lungo.
moved: commosso.
moving: toccante, commovente, spostamento.
profuse: abbondante, profuso.
prospect: prospettiva, esplorare.
remains: rimane, resta, resti.
resolve: risolvere.
short: corto, breve, basso.
suffered: sofferto, patito.
suffers: soffre, patisce.
supposed: supposto.
trespass: trasgredire, trasgressione, infrazione, sconfinare.
vast: vasto.
walk: camminare, cammino, cammina, camminano, camminate, cammini, camminiamo, camminata, passeggiare, passeggiata.
wild: selvaggio, feroce, selvatico.

"I did not know before," continued Bingley immediately, "that your were a studier of character. It must be an **amusing** study."

"Yes, but **intricate** characters are the *most* amusing. They have at least that advantage."

"The country," said Darcy, "can in general supply but a few subjects for such a study. In a country neighbourhood you move in a very **confined** and unvarying society."

"But people themselves **alter** so much, that there is something new to be observed in them for ever."

"Yes, indeed," cried Mrs. **Bennet, offended** by his manner of mentioning a country neighbourhood. "I **assure** you there is quite as much of *that* going on in the country as in **town**."

Everybody was surprised, and Darcy, after looking at her for a moment, **turned silently** away. Mrs. Bennet, who **fancied** she had **gained** a **complete victory** over him, continued her triumph.

"I **cannot** see that London has any great advantage over the country, for my part, **except the shops** and public places. The country is a vast deal pleasanter, is it not, Mr. Bingley?"

"When I am in the country," he replied, "I never wish to leave it; and when I am in town it is pretty much the same. They have each their **advantages**, and I can be equally happy in either."

"Aye--that is because you have the right **disposition**. But that gentleman," looking at Darcy, "seemed to think the country was nothing at all."

"Indeed, Mamma, you are mistaken," said Elizabeth, **blushing** for her mother. "You quite mistook Mr. Darcy. He only **meant** that there was not such a **variety** of people to be met with in the country as in the town, which you must **acknowledge** to be true."

Italian

acknowledge: riconoscere, riconoscono, riconosco, riconosciamo, riconosci, riconoscete, confessare, confermare, prendere atto.
advantages: vantaggi.
alter: cambiarsi, alterare, altera, alteriamo, alterano, alteri, alterate, altero, modificare, mutare, cambiare.
amusing: divertente, divertendo, spassoso.
assure: assicurare, assicura, assicuriamo, assicurate, assicuri,

assicurano, assicuro, garantire.
bennet: cariofillata, erba benedetta.
blushing: rosso, arrossire, rossore.
cannot: non potere.
complete: completo, completare, pieno, ultimare, finire.
confined: limitato.
disposition: disposizione, predisposizione, ingegno, talento.
except: eccetto, salvo, tranne, eccettuare.
fancied: fantastico.

gained: guadagnato.
intricate: complicato, intricato.
meant: significato.
offended: offeso, insultato, oltraggiato.
shops: negozi.
silently: silenziosamente.
town: città.
turned: girato, svoltato, cambiato.
variety: varietà, variazione.
victory: vittoria.

"Certainly, my dear, nobody said there were; but as to not **meeting** with many people in this neighbourhood, I believe there are **few** neighbourhoods larger. I know we dine with four-and-twenty families."

Nothing but **concern** for Elizabeth could **enable** Bingley to keep his countenance. His sister was less **delicate**, and **directed** her eyes towards Mr. Darcy with a very **expressive smile**. Elizabeth, for the sake of **saying** something that might **turn** her mother's thoughts, now asked her if Charlotte Lucas had been at Longbourn since *her* **coming** away.

"Yes, she called **yesterday** with her father. What an agreeable man Sir William is, Mr. Bingley, is not he? So much the man of **fashion**! So **genteel** and **easy**! He had always something to say to everybody. *That* is my idea of good **breeding**; and those persons who fancy themselves very important, and never open their mouths, quite **mistake** the matter."

"Did Charlotte dine with you?"

"No, she would go home. I fancy she was wanted about the mince-pies. For my part, Mr. Bingley, I always keep servants that can do their own work; *my* daughters are brought up very **differently**. But everybody is to **judge** for themselves, and the Lucases are a very good sort of girls, I assure you. It is a **pity** they are not handsome! Not that I think Charlotte so *very* plain--but then she is our particular friend."

"She seems a very pleasant young woman."

"Oh! dear, yes; but you must own she is very plain. Lady Lucas herself has often said so, and **envied** me Jane's beauty. I do not like to boast of my own child, but to be sure, Jane--one does not often see anybody better looking. It is what everybody says. I do not **trust** my own **partiality**. When she was only **fifteen**, there was a man at my brother Gardiner's in town so much in love with her that my **sister-in-law** was sure he would make her an offer before we came away. But, however, he did not. Perhaps he thought her too young. However, he wrote some verses on her, and very pretty they were."

Italian

breeding: allevamento, riproduzione.
coming: venendo.
concern: riguardare, concernere, cura, azienda, importanza, preoccupazione.
delicate: delicato.
differently: diversamente, in modo diverso.
directed: diretto.
easy: facile, semplice.
enable: abilitare, abilita, abilitano, abilitate, abiliti, abilitiamo, abilito,

attivare, permettere.
envied: invidiato.
expressive: espressivo.
fashion: moda, modo.
few: pochi, poco.
fifteen: quindici.
genteel: distinto.
judge: giudice, giudicare, critico.
meeting: incontrando, convegno, riunione, incontro, adunanza, comizio, assemblea.
mistake: errore, sbaglio, sbagliare,

confondere, fallo.
partiality: parzialità, predilezione.
pity: compassione, pietà.
saying: dicendo, detto, proverbio.
sister-in-law: cognata.
smile: sorriso, sorridere.
trust: fiducia, trust, confidenza, affidamento.
turn: girare, giro, svoltare, gira, giriamo, giri, girate, girano, svolta, rovesciare, svoltiamo.
yesterday: ieri.

"And so ended his affection," said Elizabeth impatiently. "There has been many a one, I fancy, **overcome** in the same way. I wonder who first discovered the **efficacy** of **poetry** in **driving** away love!"

"I have been used to consider poetry as the *food* of love," said Darcy.

"Of a fine, **stout, healthy** love it may. **Everything nourishes** what is strong already. But if it be only a **slight**, thin sort of **inclination**, I am convinced that one good **sonnet** will **starve** it entirely away."

Darcy only smiled; and the general pause which **ensued** made Elizabeth **tremble lest** her mother should be **exposing** herself again. She longed to speak, but could think of nothing to say; and after a short **silence** Mrs. Bennet began **repeating** her thanks to Mr. Bingley for his kindness to Jane, with an **apology** for troubling him also with Lizzy. Mr. Bingley was unaffectedly civil in his answer, and **forced** his younger sister to be civil also, and say what the occasion required. She **performed** her part indeed without much graciousness, but Mrs. Bennet was satisfied, and soon afterwards **ordered** her carriage. Upon this **signal**, the youngest of her daughters put herself forward. The two girls had been **whispering** to each other during the whole visit, and the result of it was, that the youngest should tax Mr. Bingley with having promised on his first coming into the country to give a ball at Netherfield.

Lydia was a stout, well-grown girl of fifteen, with a fine complexion and good-humoured countenance; a **favourite** with her mother, whose affection had brought her into public at an **early** age. She had high animal spirits, and a sort of natural self-consequence, which the attention of the officers, to whom her uncle's good dinners, and her own easy manners recommended her, had increased into **assurance**. She was very equal, therefore, to address Mr. Bingley on the subject of the ball, and **abruptly reminded** him of his promise; **adding,** that it would be the most **shameful** thing in the world if he did not keep it. His answer to this **sudden** attack was delightful to their mother's ear:

"I am perfectly ready, I assure you, to keep my **engagement**; and when your sister is **recovered**, you shall, if you please, name the very day of the ball. But you would not wish to be dancing when she is ill."

Italian

abruptly: improvvisamente.
adding: aggiungendo, addizionando.
apology: scusa, apologia.
assurance: assicurazione, promessa.
driving: guida.
ear: orecchio, spiga, l'orecchio, pannocchia.
efficacy: efficacia.
engagement: fidanzamento, assunzione.
ensued: seguito.
exposing: esponendo.

favourite: preferito.
forced: forzato.
healthy: sano.
inclination: inclinazione, pendenza.
lest: affinchè non, per paura che.
nourishes: alimenta, nutrisce.
ordered: ordinato, disposto.
overcome: superare.
performed: eseguito.
poetry: poesia.
recovered: ricuperato.
reminded: ricordato.

repeating: ripetendo.
shameful: vergognoso.
signal: segnale, segno.
silence: silenzio.
sonnet: sonetto.
starve: affamare.
stout: forte, corpulento, robusto, birra scura.
sudden: subitaneo, improvviso.
thin: magro, sottile.
tremble: tremare.
whispering: sussurrio.

Lydia **declared** herself **satisfied**. "Oh! yes--it would be much better to **wait** till Jane was well, and by that time most likely Captain Carter would be at Meryton again. And when you have given *your* ball," she **added**, "I shall **insist** on their **giving** one also. I shall tell Colonel Forster it will be quite a **shame** if he does not."

Mrs. **Bennet** and her **daughters** then **departed**, and Elizabeth **returned** **instantly** to Jane, **leaving** her own and her **relations' behaviour** to the **remarks** of the two **ladies** and Mr. Darcy; the **latter** of whom, however, could not be **prevailed** on to **join** in their **censure** of *her*, in spite of all Miss Bingley's witticisms on *fine eyes*.

Italian

added: aggiunto, addizionato.
behaviour: comportamento, condotta.
bennet: cariofillata, erba benedetta.
censure: disapprovazione, criticare, censura.
daughters: figlie.
declared: dichiarato.
departed: partito.
fine: multa, contravvenzione, multare, bello, delicato, carino, eccellente, penale, ammenda.
giving: dando, regalando.

insist: insistere, insistiamo, insisto, insistete, insistono, insisti.
instantly: direttamente, istantaneamente, immediatamente.
join: congiungere, congiungi, congiungiamo, congiungo, congiungono, congiungete, legare, unirsi, lego, lega, legano.
ladies: signore.
latter: ultimo.
leaving: abbandonando, lasciando, partendo.

prevailed: prevalso.
relations: parentado.
remarks: osservazioni.
returned: ritornato.
satisfied: soddisfatto, contento, accontentato.
shame: vergogna, pudore.
spite: dispetto.
till: finchè, coltivare, cassa, fino, arare.
wait: aspettare, aspetto, aspetta, aspettano, aspettate, aspetti, aspettiamo, attesa.

CHAPTER 10

The day passed much as the day before had done. Mrs. Hurst and Miss Bingley had **spent** some **hours** of the morning with the **invalid**, who continued, though **slowly**, to **mend**; and in the evening Elizabeth joined their party in the drawing-room. The loo-table, however, did not appear. Mr. Darcy was **writing**, and Miss Bingley, **seated near** him, was **watching** the **progress** of his **letter** and **repeatedly** calling off his attention by **messages** to his sister. Mr. Hurst and Mr. Bingley were at piquet, and Mrs. Hurst was observing their game.

Elizabeth took up some **needlework**, and was sufficiently **amused** in **attending** to what passed between Darcy and his companion. The **perpetual** commendations of the lady, either on his **handwriting**, or on the **evenness** of his **lines**, or on the length of his letter, with the perfect **unconcern** with which her praises were received, **formed a curious dialogue**, and was exactly in **union** with her opinion of each.

"How delighted Miss Darcy will be to receive such a letter!"

He made no answer.

"You **write** uncommonly fast."

"You are mistaken. I write rather slowly."

"How many **letters** you must have occasion to write in the course of a year! Letters of business, too! How **odious** I should think them!"

Italian

amused: divertito.
attending: visitando, curando, assistendo.
curious: curioso.
dialogue: dialogo.
evenness: uniformità.
formed: formato.
handwriting: calligrafia.
hours: ore.
invalid: non valido, invalido.
letter: lettera, la lettera.
letters: lettere.

lines: linee.
mend: riparare, rammendare, accomodare.
messages: messaggio.
near: vicino, prossimo, presso.
needlework: cucito, lavoro ad ago, ricamo.
odious: odioso.
pen: penna.
perpetual: perpetuo.
progress: progresso, avanzamento, miglioramento, fare progressi,

avanzare, procedere, progredire.
repeatedly: ripetutamente.
seated: seduto.
slowly: lentamente.
spent: speso, passato.
unconcern: noncuranza.
union: unione, sindacato.
watching: guardare.
write: scrivere, scrivi, scrivono, scriviamo, scrivete, scrivo.
writing: scrivendo, scrittura.

"It is fortunate, then, that they **fall** to my **lot instead** of yours."

"Pray tell your sister that I long to see her."

"I have already told her so once, by your desire."

"I am afraid you do not like your pen. Let me mend it for you. I mend pens remarkably well."

"Thank you--but I always mend my own."

"How can you **contrive** to write so even?"

He was silent.

"Tell your sister I am delighted to hear of her **improvement** on the **harp**; and pray let her know that I am quite in raptures with her **beautiful** little design for a table, and I think it **infinitely** superior to Miss Grantley's."

"Will you give me leave to **defer** your raptures till I write again? At present I have not room to do them justice."

"Oh! it is of no consequence. I shall see her in January. But do you always write such charming long letters to her, Mr. Darcy?"

"They are generally long; but whether always charming it is not for me to determine."

"It is a **rule** with me, that a person who can write a long letter with ease, cannot write ill."

"That will not do for a compliment to Darcy, Caroline," cried her brother, "because he does *not* write with ease. He **studies** too much for words of four syllables. Do not you, Darcy?"

"My style of writing is very different from yours."

"Oh!" cried Miss Bingley, "Charles **writes** in the most **careless** way **imaginable**. He **leaves** out half his words, and blots the rest."

"My ideas **flow** so **rapidly** that I have not time to express them--by which means my letters sometimes **convey** no ideas at all to my correspondents."

"Your **humility**, Mr. Bingley," said Elizabeth, "must **disarm** reproof."

Italian

beautiful: bello, carino, bella, bellissimo.
careless: sbadato, noncurante, negligente, trascurato.
contrive: escogitano, escogito, escogitiamo, escogitate, escogita, escogiti, escogitare.
convey: trasportare.
defer: rinviate, rinvio, dilaziono, differiamo, differisci, differisco, differiscono, differite, dilaziona, dilazionano, dilazionate.

disarm: disarmare, disarmiamo, disarma, disarmano, disarmi, disarmate, disarmo.
fall: cadere, caduta, autunno, cadono, cado, cadiamo, cadi, cadete, diminuire, calo, piombare.
flow: scorrere, flusso, fluire, corrente, scorrimento, affluire, portata, defluire.
harp: arpa.
humility: umiltà.
imaginable: immaginabile.

improvement: miglioramento, perfezionamento.
infinitely: infinitamente.
instead: invece.
leaves: parte, lascia, abbandona.
lot: lotto, sorte, destino, partita.
rapidly: rapidamente.
rule: regola, governare, dominare, norma, canone, rigare, governo, regolamento.
studies: studi.
writes: scrive.

"Nothing is more deceitful," said Darcy, "than the appearance of humility. It is often only **carelessness** of opinion, and sometimes an **indirect** boast."

"And which of the two do you call *my* little recent **piece** of modesty?"

"The indirect boast; for you are really proud of your defects in writing, because you consider them as **proceeding** from a **rapidity** of thought and carelessness of **execution**, which, if not estimable, you think at least **highly** interesting. The power of doing anything with quickness is always prized much by the **possessor**, and often without any attention to the **imperfection** of the performance. When you told Mrs. Bennet this morning that if you ever **resolved** upon quitting Netherfield you should be gone in five minutes, you meant it to be a sort of **panegyric**, of compliment to **yourself**--and yet what is there so very **laudable** in a precipitance which must leave very necessary business **undone**, and can be of no real advantage to yourself or **anyone** else?"

"Nay," cried Bingley, "this is too much, to remember at night all the **foolish** things that were said in the morning. And yet, upon my honour, I believe what I said of myself to be true, and I believe it at this moment. At least, therefore, I did not **assume** the character of **needless** precipitance merely to show off before the ladies."

"I dare say you believed it; but I am by no means convinced that you would be gone with such **celerity**. Your **conduct** would be quite as **dependent** on **chance** as that of any man I know; and if, as you were **mounting** your **horse**, a friend were to say, 'Bingley, you had better stay till next week,' you would probably do it, you would probably not go--and at another word, might stay a month."

"You have only **proved** by this," cried Elizabeth, "that Mr. Bingley did not do **justice** to his own disposition. You have shown him off now much more than he did himself."

"I am **exceedingly** gratified," said Bingley, "by your converting what my friend says into a compliment on the **sweetness** of my temper. But I am afraid you are giving it a turn which that gentleman did by no means **intend**; for he

Italian

anyone: chiunque, nessuno.
assume: presumere, presumo, presumono, presumiamo, presumi, presumete, assumere, supporre.
carelessness: negligenza.
celerity: celerità.
chance: caso.
conduct: condotta, condurre, guidare, comportamento.
dependent: dipendente, persona a carico.
exceedingly: estremamente.

execution: esecuzione.
foolish: sciocco, stupido, stolto, ignorante, fesso.
highly: altamente, estremamente.
horse: cavallo, il cavallo.
imperfection: imperfezione.
indirect: indiretto.
intend: intendere, intendono, intendo, intendete, intendiamo, intendi.
justice: giustizia.
laudable: lodevole.
mounting: montaggio, salita.

needless: inutile.
panegyric: panegirico.
piece: pezzo, parte, porzione.
possessor: possessore.
proceeding: procedendo, procedimento.
proved: provato.
rapidity: rapidità, velocità.
resolved: risolto.
sweetness: dolcezza.
undone: disfatto.
yourself: ti.

would certainly think better of me, if under such a circumstance I were to give a flat **denial**, and **ride** off as fast as I could."

"Would Mr. Darcy then consider the **rashness** of your original intentions as **atoned** for by your **obstinacy** in **adhering** to it?"

"Upon my word, I cannot exactly explain the matter; Darcy must speak for himself."

"You expect me to account for opinions which you choose to call mine, but which I have never acknowledged. Allowing the case, however, to stand **according** to your representation, you must remember, Miss Bennet, that the friend who is supposed to desire his return to the house, and the **delay** of his plan, has merely desired it, asked it without offering one argument in favour of its propriety."

"To **yield** readily--easily--to the *persuasion* of a friend is no **merit** with you."

"To yield without **conviction** is no compliment to the understanding of either."

"You appear to me, Mr. Darcy, to allow nothing for the influence of friendship and affection. A regard for the requester would often make one readily yield to a request, without waiting for arguments to reason one into it. I am not particularly speaking of such a case as you have supposed about Mr. Bingley. We may as well wait, perhaps, till the circumstance occurs before we discuss the discretion of his behaviour **thereupon**. But in general and ordinary cases between friend and friend, where one of them is desired by the other to change a resolution of no very great moment, should you think ill of that person for **complying** with the desire, without waiting to be argued into it?"

"Will it not be advisable, before we **proceed** on this subject, to **arrange** with rather more **precision** the degree of importance which is to **appertain** to this request, as well as the degree of **intimacy subsisting** between the parties?"

"By all means," cried Bingley; "let us hear all the **particulars**, not **forgetting** their **comparative** height and size; for that will have more weight in the argument, Miss Bennet, than you may be aware of. I assure you, that if Darcy

Italian

according: secondo.
adhering: aderendo.
appertain: appartieni, apparteniamo, appartengono, appartenete, appartengo, appartenere.
arrange: sistemare, sistemiamo, sistemate, sistemano, sistemo, sistemi, sistema, predisporre, predisponete, predispongo, predisponi.
atoned: espiato.
comparative: comparativo.

complying: accondiscendendo, ottemperando.
conviction: convinzione, condanna.
delay: ritardo, tardare, ritardare, indugio, indugiare.
denial: negazione, rifiuto, smentita.
forgetting: dimenticando.
intimacy: intimità.
merit: meritare, merito, benemerenza, pregio.
obstinacy: ostinazione.
particulars: particolari.

precision: precisione, accuratezza.
proceed: procedere, procedete, procedono, procedo, procediamo, procedi.
rashness: avventatezza.
ride: camminare, giro, corsa, cavalcare, cavalcata.
subsisting: sussistendo, esistendo.
thereupon: in merito.
yield: cedere, cedete, cedi, cediamo, cedo, cedono, resa, rendimento, prodotto, fruttare.

were not such a great tall fellow, in **comparison** with myself, I should not pay him half so much **deference**. I declare I do not know a more **awful** object than Darcy, on particular **occasions**, and in particular places; at his own house especially, and of a Sunday evening, when he has nothing to do."

Mr. Darcy smiled; but Elizabeth thought she could perceive that he was rather offended, and therefore **checked** her laugh. Miss Bingley **warmly** resented the **indignity** he had received, in an expostulation with her brother for **talking** such nonsense.

"I see your design, Bingley," said his friend. "You dislike an **argument**, and want to silence this."

"Perhaps I do. Arguments are too much like disputes. If you and Miss Bennet will defer yours till I am out of the room, I shall be very **thankful**; and then you may say whatever you like of me."

"What you ask," said Elizabeth, "is no **sacrifice** on my side; and Mr. Darcy had much better **finish** his letter."

Mr. Darcy took her **advice**, and did finish his letter.

When that business was over, he applied to Miss Bingley and Elizabeth for an **indulgence** of some music. Miss Bingley moved with some **alacrity** to the pianoforte; and, after a **polite** request that Elizabeth would lead the way which the other as politely and more **earnestly** negatived, she seated herself.

Mrs. Hurst sang with her sister, and while they were thus employed, Elizabeth could not help observing, as she turned over some music-books that **lay** on the instrument, how **frequently** Mr. Darcy's eyes were fixed on her. She hardly knew how to suppose that she could be an object of admiration to so great a man; and yet that he should look at her because he disliked her, was still more strange. She could only imagine, however, at last that she drew his **notice** because there was something more wrong and **reprehensible**, according to his ideas of right, than in any other person present. The **supposition** did not **pain** her. She liked him too little to care for his **approbation**.

Italian

advice: consiglio, avviso, comunicato, annunzio.
alacrity: entusiasmo, alacrità.
approbation: approvazione.
argument: argomento.
awful: orribile, orrendo, tremendo, terribile.
checked: quadrettato.
comparison: confronto, riscontro, comparazione, paragone.
deference: deferenza.
earnestly: seriamente.

finish: finire, finisci, finite, finisco, finiamo, finiscono, terminare, fine, finitura, preparare, ultimare.
frequently: frequentemente, spesso, sovente.
indignity: trattamento indegno.
indulgence: indulgenza.
lay: posare, posiamo, poso, posi, posate, posano, posa, laico.
notice: avviso, osservare, preavviso, notare, affisso, cartellone, comunicato, osservazione, annunzio,

notifica.
occasions: occasioni.
pain: dolore, male, addolorare, pena, affliggere.
polite: cortese, educato.
reprehensible: riprovevole, biasimevole.
sacrifice: sacrificio, sacrificare, offrire.
supposition: supposizione.
talking: parlando, parlare.
thankful: riconoscente, grato.
warmly: caldamente, calorosamente.

After playing some Italian songs, Miss Bingley **varied** the **charm** by a lively Scotch air; and soon afterwards Mr. Darcy, drawing near Elizabeth, said to her:

"Do not you feel a great inclination, Miss Bennet, to **seize** such an opportunity of dancing a **reel**?"

She smiled, but made no answer. He repeated the question, with some surprise at her silence.

"Oh!" said she, "I heard you before, but I could not immediately determine what to say in reply. You wanted me, I know, to say 'Yes,' that you might have the pleasure of **despising** my taste; but I always delight in **overthrowing** those kind of schemes, and **cheating** a person of their **premeditated** contempt. I have, therefore, made up my mind to tell you, that I do not want to dance a reel at all-- and now **despise** me if you dare."

"Indeed I do not dare."

Elizabeth, having rather expected to **affront** him, was **amazed** at his gallantry; but there was a mixture of sweetness and **archness** in her manner which made it difficult for her to affront anybody; and Darcy had never been so **bewitched** by any woman as he was by her. He really believed, that were it not for the **inferiority** of her connections, he should be in some danger.

Miss Bingley saw, or suspected enough to be **jealous**; and her great anxiety for the recovery of her dear friend Jane received some assistance from her desire of getting rid of Elizabeth.

She often tried to **provoke** Darcy into disliking her **guest**, by talking of their supposed marriage, and planning his happiness in such an alliance.

"I hope," said she, as they were walking together in the **shrubbery** the next day, "you will give your mother-in-law a few hints, when this desirable event takes place, as to the advantage of holding her **tongue**; and if you can **compass** it, do sure the younger girls of running after officers. And, if I may mention so delicate a subject, endeavour to check that little something, **bordering** on **conceit** and impertinence, which your lady possesses."

"Have you anything else to **propose** for my domestic felicity?"

Italian

affront: affronto, insulto, insultare.
amazed: sbalordito, stupito, si stupito.
archness: malizia.
bewitched: incantato.
bordering: orlare, confinante, cingente.
charm: fascino, incanto.
cheating: ingannare, frode, imbrogliare.
compass: bussola, la bussola, compasso.
conceit: presunzione.

despise: disprezzare, disprezza, disprezzano, disprezzate, disprezzi, disprezziamo, disprezzo.
despising: disprezzando.
guest: ospite, invitato.
inferiority: inferiorità.
jealous: geloso.
overthrowing: rovesciando.
premeditated: premeditato.
propose: proporre, proponiamo, proponi, propongono, proponete, propongo.

provoke: spronare, provocare, incitare, provochi, sproniamo, sprono, sproni, spronate, spronano, sprona, provoco.
reel: bobina, aspo, mulinello, rocchetto.
seize: afferrare, afferro, afferra, afferrano, afferrate, afferri, afferriamo, acciuffare, acchiappare, confiscare, prendere.
shrubbery: boschetto.
tongue: lingua, linguetta, la lingua.
varied: variato, vario.

"Oh! yes. Do let the portraits of your uncle and aunt Phillips be placed in the **gallery** at Pemberley. Put them next to your great-uncle the judge. They are in the same **profession**, you know, only in different lines. As for your Elizabeth's picture, you must not have it taken, for what **painter** could do justice to those beautiful eyes?"

"It would not be easy, indeed, to **catch** their **expression**, but their **colour** and **shape**, and the **eyelashes**, so remarkably fine, might be copied."

At that moment they were met from another walk by Mrs. Hurst and Elizabeth herself.

"I did not know that you intended to walk," said Miss Bingley, in some **confusion**, lest they had been overheard.

"You used us **abominably** ill," answered Mrs. Hurst, "running away without **telling** us that you were coming out."

Then taking the **disengaged** arm of Mr. Darcy, she left Elizabeth to walk by herself. The **path** just admitted three. Mr. Darcy felt their rudeness, and immediately said:

"This walk is not **wide** enough for our party. We had better go into the avenue."

But Elizabeth, who had not the least inclination to **remain** with them, **laughingly** answered:

"No, no; stay where you are. You are **charmingly grouped**, and appear to **uncommon** advantage. The **picturesque** would be spoilt by **admitting** a fourth. Good-bye."

She then ran **gaily** off, **rejoicing** as she rambled about, in the hope of being at home again in a day or two. Jane was already so much recovered as to intend leaving her room for a couple of hours that evening.

Italian

abominably: abominevolmente.
admitting: confessando, ammettendo.
arm: armare, braccio, arma, il braccio, armi.
catch: prendere, prendi, prendono, prendete, prendiamo, prendo, fermo, colpire, colpiscono, colpisco, colpiamo.
charmingly: affascinantemente.
colour: colore.
confusion: confusione.
disengaged: disimpegnato,
disinnestato.
expression: espressione, aria, locuzione.
eyelashes: ciglio.
gaily: gaiamente.
gallery: galleria, ballatoio.
grouped: raggruppato.
laughingly: ridere.
painter: pittore.
path: sentiero, percorso, viottolo, traiettoria, cammino, viale, via.
picturesque: pittoresco.
profession: professione, mestiere.
rejoicing: gioia.
remain: rimanere, rimangono, rimani, rimango, rimanete, rimaniamo, restare, restiamo, resti, restate, restano.
shape: forma, formare, figura, foggia, modellare, sagoma.
telling: dicendo, raccontando, narrando.
uncommon: insolito, raro.
wide: largo, vasto, ampio.

CHAPTER 11

When the ladies removed after **dinner,** Elizabeth ran up to her sister, and seeing her well guarded from cold, attended her into the drawing-room, where she was **welcomed** by her two friends with many professions of pleasure; and Elizabeth had never seen them so agreeable as they were during the **hour** which passed before the gentlemen **appeared.** Their **powers** of conversation were considerable. They could describe an **entertainment** with **accuracy, relate** an **anecdote** with humour, and laugh at their acquaintance with spirit.

But when the gentlemen entered, Jane was no longer the first object; Miss Bingley's eyes were instantly turned toward Darcy, and she had something to say to him before he had **advanced** many **steps.** He addressed himself to Miss Bennet, with a polite **congratulation;** Mr. Hurst also made her a slight **bow,** and said he was "very glad;" but diffuseness and warmth **remained** for Bingley's **salutation.** He was full of joy and attention. The first half-hour was spent in **piling** up the fire, lest she should **suffer** from the change of room; and she removed at his **desire** to the other side of the **fireplace,** that she might be further from the door. He then sat down by her, and talked scarcely to anyone else. Elizabeth, at work in the **opposite corner,** saw it all with great delight.

When **tea** was over, Mr. Hurst reminded his sister-in-law of the card-table-- but in vain. She had **obtained** private intelligence that Mr. Darcy did not wish for cards; and Mr. Hurst soon found even his open **petition rejected.** She

Italian

accuracy: accuratezza, esattezza, precisione.
advanced: avanzato, progredito.
anecdote: aneddoto.
appeared: apparso.
bow: arco, prua, fiocco, inchino, inchinarsi, curva, archetto.
congratulation: felicitazione, rallegramento, congratulazione.
corner: angolo.
desire: desiderio, desiderare, bramare.
dinner: pranzo, colazione, cena, desinare.

entertainment: divertimento, spettacolo.
fireplace: camino, caminetto.
hour: ora, l'ora.
obtained: ottenuto.
opposite: dirimpetto, opposto, contrario, contro, di fronte a, di fronte.
petition: petizione, istanza, supplica.
piling: accatastamento.
powers: poteri.

rejected: respinto.
relate: raccontare, raccontiamo, racconta, raccontano, raccontate, racconti, racconto, narrare.
remained: rimasto, restato.
salutation: saluto.
steps: passi, gradinata, gradini.
suffer: soffrire, soffri, soffro, soffrono, soffrite, soffriamo, patire, subire, patiamo, patite, patiscono.
tea: tè.
welcomed: accolto.

assured him that no one intended to play, and the silence of the whole party on the subject seemed to **justify** her. Mr. Hurst had therefore nothing to do, but to **stretch** himself on one of the sofas and go to sleep. Darcy took up a book; Miss Bingley did the same; and Mrs. Hurst, **principally occupied** in playing with her bracelets and **rings**, joined now and then in her brother's conversation with Miss Bennet.

Miss Bingley's attention was quite as much engaged in watching Mr. Darcy's progress through *his* book, as in reading her own; and she was **perpetually** either making some **inquiry**, or looking at his page. She could not **win** him, however, to any conversation; he merely answered her **question**, and read on. At length, quite **exhausted** by the attempt to be amused with her own book, which she had only **chosen** because it was the second **volume** of his, she gave a great **yawn** and said, "How pleasant it is to **spend** an evening in this way! I declare after all there is no enjoyment like reading! How much sooner one tires of anything than of a book! When I have a house of my own, I shall be miserable if I have not an excellent library."

No one made any reply. She then yawned again, threw aside her book, and **cast** her eyes round the room in quest for some amusement; when hearing her brother mentioning a ball to Miss Bennet, she turned suddenly towards him and said:

"By the **bye**, Charles, are you really serious in meditating a dance at Netherfield? I would advise you, before you **determine** on it, to **consult** the wishes of the present party; I am much mistaken if there are not some among us to whom a ball would be rather a punishment than a pleasure."

"If you mean Darcy," cried her brother, "he may go to bed, if he chooses, before it begins--but as for the ball, it is quite a settled thing; and as soon as Nicholls has made white **soup** enough, I shall send round my cards."

"I should like **balls** infinitely better," she replied, "if they were carried on in a different manner; but there is something insufferably **tedious** in the **usual** process of such a meeting. It would **surely** be much more **rational** if conversation instead of dancing were made the order of the day."

Italian

balls: sfere, palla, balli.
bye: arrivederci, addio, ciao.
cast: calco, fuso, getto.
chosen: scelto, eletto.
consult: consultare.
determine: definire, fissare, fissi, definiscono, fissano, fissate, fissa, definiamo, definite, fisso, definisci.
exhausted: esausto, sfinito, esaurito.
inquiry: inchiesta.
justify: giustificare, giustificate, giustifico, giustifichiamo, giustificano, giustifici, giustifica.
occupied: occupato.
perpetually: perennemente, perpetuamente.
principally: principalmente, soprattutto.
quest: ricerca.
rational: razionale, ragionevole.
rings: anelli.
soup: minestra, brodo, zuppa, la minestra.
spend: spendere, spendiamo, spendo, spendi, spendete, spendono, passare, passo, passiamo, passi, passate.
stretch: stendere, tendere, allungamento.
surely: certamente, sicuramente.
tedious: noioso, tedioso.
usual: usuale, consueto, solito, generale, abituale.
volume: volume, tomo.
win: vincere, vincete, vinco, vincono, vinci, vinciamo, guadagnare, vittoria.
yawn: sbadigliare, sbadiglio.

"Much more rational, my dear Caroline, I dare say, but it would not be near so much like a ball."

Miss Bingley made no answer, and soon afterwards she got up and walked about the room. Her figure was elegant, and she walked well; but Darcy, at whom it was all **aimed**, was still **inflexibly studious**. In the **desperation** of her feelings, she resolved on one **effort** more, and, turning to Elizabeth, said:

"Miss Eliza Bennet, let me persuade you to follow my **example**, and take a turn about the room. I assure you it is very **refreshing** after sitting so long in one attitude."

Elizabeth was surprised, but agreed to it immediately. Miss Bingley succeeded no less in the real object of her civility; Mr. Darcy looked up. He was as much **awake** to the **novelty** of attention in that **quarter** as Elizabeth herself could be, and **unconsciously closed** his book. He was directly invited to join their party, but he declined it, observing that he could imagine but two motives for their **choosing** to walk up and down the room together, with either of which motives his **joining** them would **interfere**. "What could he mean? She was dying to know what could be his meaning?"--and asked Elizabeth whether she could at all understand him?

"Not at all," was her answer; "but depend upon it, he means to be severe on us, and our surest way of **disappointing** him will be to ask nothing about it."

Miss Bingley, however, was **incapable** of disappointing Mr. Darcy in anything, and **persevered** therefore in **requiring** an **explanation** of his two motives.

"I have not the smallest objection to **explaining** them," said he, as soon as she allowed him to speak. "You either **choose** this **method** of passing the evening because you are in each other's **confidence**, and have secret **affairs** to **discuss**, or because you are conscious that your figures appear to the greatest advantage in walking; if the first, I would be **completely** in your way, and if the second, I can admire you much better as I sit by the fire."

Italian

affairs: affari.
aimed: puntato, intenzionato, mirato.
awake: sveglio, svegliarsi.
choose: scegliere, scegli, scegliamo, scegliete, scelgo, scelgono, eleggere, eleggete, eleggi, eleggiamo, eleggo.
choosing: scegliendo, eleggendo.
closed: chiuso.
completely: completamente.
confidence: fiducia, confidenza, affidamento.
conscious: cosciente.

desperation: disperazione.
disappointing: deludendo.
discuss: discutere, discutono, discuto, discutiamo, discutete, discuti.
effort: sforzo, fatica.
example: esempio, modello.
explaining: spiegando.
explanation: spiegazione.
incapable: incapace.
inflexibly: inflessibilmente.
interfere: interferire, interferiamo, interferite, interferiscono, interferisco,

interferisci.
joining: congiungendo, legando, unendo, collegando.
method: metodo, modo.
novelty: novità.
persevered: perseverato.
quarter: quarto, quartiere, circondario, distretto, trimestre.
refreshing: rinfrescante.
requiring: richiedendo.
studious: studioso.
unconsciously: inconsciamente.

"Oh! shocking!" cried Miss Bingley. "I never heard anything so abominable. How shall we **punish** him for such a speech?"

"Nothing so easy, if you have but the inclination," said Elizabeth. "We can all **plague** and punish one another. Tease him--laugh at him. Intimate as you are, you must know how it is to be done."

"But upon my honour, I do *not*. I do assure you that my intimacy has not yet **taught** me *that*. Tease **calmness** of manner and **presence** of mind! No, no--feel he may **defy** us there. And as to **laughter**, we will not **expose ourselves**, if you please, by **attempting** to laugh without a subject. Mr. Darcy may **hug** himself."

"Mr. Darcy is not to be laughed at!" cried Elizabeth. "That is an uncommon advantage, and uncommon I hope it will **continue**, for it would be a great **loss** to *me* to have many such acquaintances. I **dearly** love a laugh."

"Miss Bingley," said he, "has given me more credit than can be. The **wisest** and the best of men--nay, the wisest and best of their actions--may be rendered **ridiculous** by a person whose first object in life is a joke."

"Certainly," replied Elizabeth--"there are such people, but I hope I am not one of *them*. I hope I never **ridicule** what is wise and good. Follies and nonsense, whims and inconsistencies, *do* **divert** me, I own, and I laugh at them whenever I can. But these, I suppose, are **precisely** what you are without."

"Perhaps that is not possible for anyone. But it has been the study of my life to **avoid** those **weaknesses** which often expose a **strong understanding** to ridicule."

"Such as vanity and pride."

"Yes, vanity is a weakness indeed. But pride--where there is a real **superiority** of mind, pride will be always under good regulation."

Elizabeth turned away to hide a smile.

"Your **examination** of Mr. Darcy is over, I presume," said Miss Bingley; "and pray what is the result?"

Italian

attempting: provando.
avoid: evitare, evitano, evito, evitiamo, evitate, evita, eviti.
calmness: calma.
continue: continuare, continui, continuate, continua, continuiamo, continuano, continuo, durare, duro, duriamo, duri.
dearly: caramente.
defy: sfidare, sfidano, sfidiamo, sfidate, sfidi, sfido, sfida.
divert: deviare.

examination: esame, verifica.
expose: esporre, esponete, espongo, espongono, esponi, esponiamo.
hug: abbracciare, abbraccio.
laughter: risa, risata, riso.
loss: perdita, danno, smarrimento, deficit.
ourselves: ci.
plague: peste.
precisely: precisamente.
presence: presenza.
punish: punire, puniamo, punisci,

punisco, puniscono, punite, castigare, castiga, castigano, castigate, castighi.
ridicule: ridicolo, ridicolizzare.
ridiculous: ridicolo, assurdo.
strong: forte, robusto.
superiority: superiorità.
taught: insegnato.
understanding: capendo, comprendendo, comprensione, intesa.
weakness: debolezza.
wise: saggio, assennato.

"I am perfectly convinced by it that Mr. Darcy has no **defect**. He owns it himself without disguise."

"No," said Darcy, "I have made no such **pretension**. I have **faults** enough, but they are not, I **hope**, of understanding. My temper I dare not **vouch** for. It is, I believe, too little yielding--certainly too little for the **convenience** of the world. I cannot forget the follies and vices of other so soon as I ought, **nor** their **offenses** against myself. My feelings are not puffed about with every **attempt** to **move** them. My temper would perhaps be called **resentful**. My good opinion once **lost**, is lost forever."

"*That* is a failing indeed!" cried Elizabeth. "Implacable resentment *is* a **shade** in a character. But you have chosen your fault well. I really cannot *laugh* at it. You are safe from me."

"There is, I believe, in every disposition a **tendency** to some particular evil--a natural defect, which not even the best education can overcome."

"And *your* defect is to hate everybody."

"And yours," he replied with a smile, "is willfully to **misunderstand** them."

"Do let us have a little music," cried Miss Bingley, **tired** of a conversation in which she had no **share**. "Louisa, you will not mind my **waking** Mr. Hurst?"

Her sister had not the smallest objection, and the pianoforte was opened; and Darcy, after a few moments' **recollection**, was not **sorry** for it. He began to feel the danger of **paying** Elizabeth too much attention.

CHAPTER 12

In consequence of an agreement between the sisters, Elizabeth wrote the next morning to their mother, to **beg** that the **carriage** might be sent for them in the course of the day. But Mrs. **Bennet**, who had **calculated** on her **daughters remaining** at Netherfield till the following Tuesday, which would exactly finish Jane's week, could not bring herself to receive them with pleasure before. Her answer, therefore, was not **propitious**, at least not to Elizabeth's wishes, for she was **impatient** to get home. Mrs. Bennet sent them word that they could not possibly have the carriage before Tuesday; and in her **postscript** it was added, that if Mr. Bingley and his sister **pressed** them to stay longer, she could spare them very well. Against **staying** longer, however, Elizabeth was **positively** resolved--nor did she much expect it would be asked; and **fearful**, on the **contrary**, as being considered as **intruding** themselves **needlessly** long, she urged Jane to **borrow** Mr. Bingley's carriage immediately, and at length it was **settled** that their original design of leaving Netherfield that morning should be mentioned, and the request made.

The communication **excited** many professions of concern; and enough was said of wishing them to stay at least till the following day to work on Jane; and till the **morrow** their going was **deferred**. Miss Bingley was then sorry that she had proposed the **delay**, for her **jealousy** and **dislike** of one sister much **exceeded** her **affection** for the other.

Italian

affection: affetto, affezione, amore.
beg: mendicare, mendicano, mendica, mendicate, mendico, mendichiamo, mendichi, chiedere, elemosinare, supplicare.
bennet: cariofillata, erba benedetta.
borrow: prendere in prestito.
calculated: calcolato.
carriage: vettura, carrello, vagone, carro, carrozza.
contrary: contrario.
daughters: figlie.

deferred: differito.
delay: ritardo, tardare, ritardare, indugio, indugiare.
dislike: avversione, ripugnanza, antipatia.
exceeded: ecceduto.
excited: eccitato, concitato, emozionato.
fearful: spaventoso, pauroso.
impatient: impaziente.
intruding: imponendo.
jealousy: gelosia.

morrow: domani.
needlessly: inutilmente.
positively: positivamente.
postscript: poscritto.
pressed: premuto.
propitious: propizio.
remaining: rimanendo, restando, rimanente, restante.
settled: regolato, stabilito, stabile, fermo, fisso, popolato, saldato, sistemato, deciso.
staying: stando, restando.

The **master** of the house heard with real **sorrow** that they were to go so soon, and repeatedly **tried** to persuade Miss Bennet that it would not be safe for her-- that she was not enough recovered; but Jane was **firm** where she felt herself to be right.

To Mr. Darcy it was **welcome** intelligence--Elizabeth had been at Netherfield long enough. She **attracted** him more than he liked--and Miss Bingley was **uncivil** to *her*, and more teasing than usual to himself. He **wisely** resolved to be particularly **careful** that no **sign** of admiration should *now* escape him, nothing that could **elevate** her with the hope of influencing his felicity; sensible that if such an idea had been **suggested**, his behaviour during the last day must have **material weight** in **confirming** or **crushing** it. Steady to his purpose, he scarcely spoke ten words to her through the whole of Saturday, and though they were at one time left by themselves for half-an-hour, he **adhered** most **conscientiously** to his book, and would not even look at her.

On Sunday, after morning service, the **separation**, so agreeable to almost all, took place. Miss Bingley's civility to Elizabeth increased at last very rapidly, as well as her affection for Jane; and when they parted, after assuring the latter of the pleasure it would always give her to see her either at Longbourn or Netherfield, and embracing her most **tenderly**, she even shook hands with the former. Elizabeth took leave of the whole party in the liveliest of spirits.

They were not welcomed home very **cordially** by their mother. Mrs. Bennet **wondered** at their coming, and thought them very wrong to give so much **trouble**, and was sure Jane would have caught cold again. But their father, though very **laconic** in his expressions of pleasure, was really glad to see them; he had felt their **importance** in the family **circle**. The evening conversation, when they were all assembled, had lost much of its animation, and almost all its sense by the **absence** of Jane and Elizabeth.

They found Mary, as usual, deep in the study of thorough-bass and human nature; and had some extracts to admire, and some new **observations** of **threadbare morality** to listen to. Catherine and Lydia had information for them of a different sort. Much had been done and much had been said in the regiment

Italian

absence: assenza, mancanza.
adhered: aderito.
attracted: attirato, attratto.
careful: accurato, attento, cauto.
circle: circolo, cerchio, compagnia.
confirming: confermando.
conscientiously: coscienziosamente.
cordially: cordialmente.
crushing: schiacciamento.
elevate: elevare, elevate, elevo, elevi, eleva, eleviamo, elevano.
firm: ditta, azienda, impresa, stabile,

saldo, sodo, fermo.
importance: importanza.
laconic: laconico.
master: maestro, padrone, principale, master, dominare, anagrafica.
material: materiale, materia.
morality: virtù, moralità, morale.
observations: osservazioni.
separation: separazione, distacco.
sign: firmare, segno, segnale, prova, augurio.
sorrow: tristezza, cordoglio.

suggested: proposto, suggerito.
tenderly: teneramente.
threadbare: liso.
tried: sperimentato, tentativo.
trouble: problema, disturbare, disturbo, guasto, fastidio.
uncivil: incivile.
weight: peso, carico.
welcome: benvenuto, bene arrivate, accoglienza, gradito, accogliere.
wisely: saggiamente.
wondered: domandato.

since the **preceding** Wednesday; several of the **officers** had **dined lately** with their **uncle**, a **private** had been **flogged**, and it had actually been **hinted** that Colonel Forster was going to be married.

Italian

dined: pranzato, cenato.
flogged: frustato, fustigato.
hinted: suggerito.
lately: ultimamente, recentemente.
officers: ufficiali.
preceding: precedendo, precedente.
private: privato, senza impiego,
 riservato.
uncle: zio, lo zio.

CHAPTER 13

"I hope, my dear," said Mr. **Bennet** to his wife, as they were at **breakfast** the next morning, "that you have **ordered** a good dinner to-day, because I have reason to expect an **addition** to our family party."

"Who do you mean, my dear? I know of nobody that is coming, I am sure, unless Charlotte Lucas should **happen** to call in--and I hope *my* dinners are good enough for her. I do not believe she often **sees** such at home."

"The person of whom I **speak** is a **gentleman**, and a **stranger**."

Mrs. Bennet's eyes sparkled. "A gentleman and a stranger! It is Mr. Bingley, I am sure! Well, I am sure I shall be **extremely glad** to see Mr. Bingley. But-- good Lord! how **unlucky**! There is not a bit of **fish** to be got to-day. Lydia, my love, **ring** the bell--I must speak to Hill this moment."

"It is *not* Mr. Bingley," said her husband; "it is a person whom I never saw in the whole course of my life."

This **roused** a general **astonishment**; and he had the pleasure of being **eagerly** questioned by his wife and his five **daughters** at once.

After **amusing** himself some time with their **curiosity**, he thus **explained**:

"About a month ago I received this letter; and about a **fortnight** ago I answered it, for I thought it a case of some **delicacy**, and **requiring** early

Italian

addition: aggiunta, addizione.
amusing: divertente, divertendo, spassoso.
astonishment: stupore, meraviglia, sorpresa.
bennet: cariofillata, erba benedetta.
breakfast: colazione, prima colazione.
curiosity: curiosità.
daughters: figlie.
delicacy: delicatezza.
eagerly: ardentemente.
explain: spiegare, spieghi, spiego,

spieghiamo, spiegano, spiega, spiegate.
explained: spiegato.
extremely: estremamente, assai, molto.
fish: pesce, pescare, il pesce.
fortnight: due settimane.
gentleman: signore, galantuomo, gentiluomo.
glad: contento, felice, lieto.
happen: succedere, succedete, succedono, succedo, succedi, succediamo, accadere, avvenire,

arrivare, avvenite, avveniamo.
ordered: ordinato, disposto.
requiring: richiedendo.
ring: anello, circolo.
roused: incitato, spronato, stimolato.
sees: vede, sega.
speak: parlare, parla, parlo, parliamo, parli, parlate, parlano, favellare.
stranger: sconosciuto, estraneo, forestiero.
unlucky: sfortunato, disgraziato.

attention. It is from my cousin, Mr. Collins, who, when I am **dead**, may turn you all out of this house as soon as he pleases."

"Oh! my dear," cried his wife, "I cannot **bear** to hear that mentioned. Pray do not **talk** of that odious man. I do think it is the hardest thing in the world, that your estate should be **entailed** away from your own children; and I am sure, if I had been you, I should have tried long ago to do something or other about it."

Jane and Elizabeth tried to explain to her the nature of an entail. They had often **attempted** to do it before, but it was a **subject** on which Mrs. Bennet was beyond the **reach** of reason, and she continued to **rail bitterly** against the **cruelty** of settling an estate away from a family of five daughters, in favour of a man whom nobody cared anything about.

"It certainly is a most **iniquitous** affair," said Mr. Bennet, "and nothing can clear Mr. Collins from the **guilt** of **inheriting** Longbourn. But if you will listen to his letter, you may perhaps be a little **softened** by his manner of expressing himself."

"No, that I am sure I shall not; and I think it is very impertinent of him to write to you at all, and very hypocritical. I hate such **false friends**. Why could he not keep on quarreling with you, as his father did before him?"

"Why, indeed; he does seem to have had some **filial** scruples on that head, as you will hear."

Hunsford, near Westerham, Kent, 15th October.

Dear Sir,

The **disagreement** subsisting between yourself and my **late** honoured father always gave me much **uneasiness**, and since I have had the misfortune to lose him, I have frequently wished to **heal** the **breach**; but for some time I was **kept** back by my own **doubts**, fearing lest it might seem **disrespectful** to his **memory** for me to be on good **terms** with anyone with whom it had always pleased him to be at variance.--'There, Mrs. Bennet.'--My mind, however, is now made up on the subject, for

Italian

attempted: provato.
bear: orso, produrre, ribassista, partorire, l'orso, portare.
bitterly: amaramente.
breach: violazione, breccia, rottura, infrazione, inadempimento.
cruelty: crudeltà.
dead: morto.
disagreement: disaccordo.
disrespectful: irriverente.
doubts: dubbio.
entail: comportare.

false: falso, finto.
filial: filiale.
friends: amici.
guilt: colpa.
heal: guarire, guarisco, guariscono, guariamo, guarite, guarisci, sanare.
inheriting: ereditando.
iniquitous: iniquo.
kept: conservato, osservato, trattenuto.
late: tardi, tardo, in ritardo, tardivo.
memory: memoria, ricordo.
rail: rotaia, parapetto, guida.

reach: arrivare, portata, raggiungere, pervenire, estendersi.
softened: ammorbidito.
subject: soggetto, argomento, oggetto, sottoporre, tema, suddito, assoggettato.
talk: parlare, parlo, parliamo, parli, parlate, parlano, parla, discorso, discorrere, conversazione, conversare.
terms: condizioni.
uneasiness: disagio.

having received **ordination** at Easter, I have been so fortunate as to be distinguished by the **patronage** of the Right Honourable Lady Catherine de Bourgh, **widow** of Sir Lewis de Bourgh, whose **bounty** and **beneficence** has **preferred** me to the valuable **rectory** of this **parish**, where it shall be my **earnest** endeavour to demean myself with **grateful respect** towards her **ladyship**, and be ever ready to perform those rites and ceremonies which are **instituted** by the Church of England. As a **clergyman**, **moreover**, I feel it my duty to **promote** and establish the **blessing** of peace in all families within in the reach of my influence; and on these grounds I flatter myself that my present overtures are highly **commendable**, and that the circumstance of my being next in the entail of Longbourn estate will be **kindly** overlooked on your side, and not lead you to **reject** the offered olive-branch. I cannot be otherwise than concerned at being the means of **injuring** your amiable daughters, and beg leave to **apologise** for it, as well as to assure you of my **readiness** to make them every possible amends--but of this **hereafter**. If you should have no objection to receive me into your house, I propose myself the **satisfaction** of waiting on you and your family, Monday, November 18th, by four o'clock, and shall probably trespass on your **hospitality** till the Saturday se'ennight following, which I can do without any inconvenience, as Lady Catherine is far from objecting to my **occasional** absence on a Sunday, provided that some other clergyman is engaged to do the duty of the day.--I remain, dear sir, with **respectful compliments** to your lady and daughters, your well-wisher and friend,

"William Collins"

"At four o'clock, therefore, we may expect this peace-making gentleman," said Mr. Bennet, as he **folded** up the letter. "He seems to be a most **conscientious** and polite young man, upon my word, and I doubt not will prove a valuable acquaintance, especially if Lady Catherine should be so **indulgent** as to let him come to us again."

Italian

apologise: scusarsi.
beneficence: beneficenza.
blessing: benedicendo, benedizione.
bounty: generosità.
clergyman: ecclesiastico, prete, curato, sacerdote.
commendable: lodevole.
compliments: complimenti.
conscientious: coscienzioso.
earnest: serio, caparra.
folded: piegato.
grateful: riconoscente, grato.

hereafter: in futuro.
hospitality: ospitalità.
indulgent: indulgente.
injuring: danneggiando, ferendo.
instituted: istituito.
kindly: gentilmente, gentile.
ladyship: signoria.
moreover: inoltre, d'altronde.
occasional: occasionale.
ordination: ordinazione.
parish: parrocchia.
patronage: patrocinio, patronato.

preferred: preferito.
promote: promuovere, promuovi, promuovono, promuoviamo, promuovete, promuovo, favorire.
readiness: prontezza.
rectory: canonica.
reject: rifiutare, respingere, scarto, rigettare, rifiutarsi, bocciare, scartare.
respect: rispettare, rispetto, stima.
respectful: rispettoso.
satisfaction: soddisfazione.
widow: vedova.

"There is some sense in what he says about the girls, however, and if he is **disposed** to make them any **amends**, I shall not be the person to **discourage** him."

"Though it is difficult," said Jane, "to guess in what way he can mean to make us the **atonement** he **thinks** our due, the wish is certainly to his credit."

Elizabeth was chiefly struck by his extraordinary **deference** for Lady Catherine, and his kind intention of **christening, marrying,** and **burying** his parishioners whenever it were required.

"He must be an **oddity,** I think," said she. "I **cannot** make him out.--There is something very **pompous** in his style.--And what can he mean by apologising for being next in the entail?--We cannot suppose he would help it if he could.--Could he be a sensible man, sir?"

"No, my dear, I think not. I have great hopes of finding him quite the **reverse.** There is a mixture of **servility** and self-importance in his letter, which **promises** well. I am impatient to see him."

"In point of composition," said Mary, "the letter does not **seem defective.** The idea of the olive-branch perhaps is not wholly new, yet I think it is well expressed."

To Catherine and Lydia, neither the letter nor its **writer** were in any **degree** interesting. It was next to impossible that their cousin should come in a **scarlet** coat, and it was now some **weeks** since they had received pleasure from the society of a man in any other colour. As for their mother, Mr. Collins's letter had done away much of her ill-will, and she was **preparing** to see him with a degree of **composure** which astonished her husband and daughters.

Mr. Collins was **punctual** to his time, and was received with great **politeness** by the whole family. Mr. **Bennet** indeed said little; but the ladies were ready enough to talk, and Mr. Collins seemed neither in need of encouragement, nor inclined to be silent himself. He was a tall, heavy-looking young man of five-and-twenty. His **air** was grave and **stately,** and his manners were very **formal.** He had not been long seated before he complimented Mrs. Bennet on having so

Italian

air: aria.
amends: emenda, ammenda.
atonement: espiazione, riparazione.
bennet: cariofillata, erba benedetta.
burying: seppellendo.
cannot: non potere.
christening: battesimo, battezzando.
composure: calma, compostezza.
defective: difettoso, difettivo.
deference: deferenza.
degree: grado, laurea.
discourage: impaurire, scoraggiare,

spaventare, impaurite, spavento, spaventiamo, spaventi, spaventate, spaventano, spaventa, scoraggio.
disposed: disposto.
formal: formale, convenzionale.
marrying: sposandosi.
oddity: stranezza.
politeness: cortesia, garbo.
pompous: ampolloso, pomposo.
preparing: preparando, allestendo, apprestando.
promises: promette.

punctual: esatto, puntuale, preciso.
reverse: retromarcia, inverso, contrario, invertire, rovescio.
scarlet: scarlatto.
seem: parere, paiono, paiamo, pari, paio, parete, sembrare, sembra, sembrano, sembrate, sembri.
servility: servilismo.
stately: imponente.
thinks: pensa.
weeks: settimane.
writer: autore.

fine a family of daughters; said he had heard much of their beauty, but that in this **instance fame** had **fallen** short of the truth; and added, that he did not doubt her seeing them all in due time disposed of in marriage. This gallantry was not much to the taste of some of his hearers; but Mrs. Bennet, who quarreled with no compliments, answered most readily.

"You are very kind, I am sure; and I wish with all my heart it may **prove** so, for else they will be **destitute** enough. Things are settled so oddly."

"You **allude**, perhaps, to the entail of this estate."

"Ah! sir, I do indeed. It is a **grievous affair** to my poor girls, you must **confess**. Not that I mean to find fault with *you*, for such things I know are all chance in this world. There is no **knowing** how estates will go when once they come to be entailed."

"I am very sensible, madam, of the **hardship** to my fair cousins, and could say much on the subject, but that I am cautious of **appearing** forward and **precipitate**. But I can assure the young ladies that I come prepared to admire them. At present I will not say more; but, perhaps, when we are better acquainted--"

He was interrupted by a **summons** to dinner; and the girls smiled on each other. They were not the only **objects** of Mr. Collins's admiration. The hall, the dining-room, and all its **furniture**, were **examined** and praised; and his commendation of everything would have **touched** Mrs. Bennet's heart, but for the mortifying supposition of his **viewing** it all as his own future property. The dinner too in its turn was highly admired; and he **begged** to know to which of his fair cousins the **excellency** of its **cooking** was owing. But he was set right there by Mrs. Bennet, who assured him with some **asperity** that they were very well able to keep a good cook, and that her daughters had nothing to do in the kitchen. He begged **pardon** for having **displeased** her. In a softened **tone** she declared herself not at all offended; but he continued to apologise for about a quarter of an hour.

Italian

affair: affare, faccenda, caso.
allude: alludere, alludi, alludiamo, alludo, alludono, alludete.
appearing: apparendo.
asperity: asperità.
begged: mendicato.
confess: confessare, confessa, confessano, confessate, confessi, confessiamo, confesso.
cook: cuoco, cuoca, cucinare, cuocere.
cooking: cucina.
destitute: indigente.

displeased: scontentato, scontento.
examined: esaminato.
excellency: eccellenza.
fair: biondo, fiera, giusto, bazar, correttamente, bello, equo.
fallen: caduto.
fame: fama.
furniture: mobili, mobilia.
grievous: doloroso.
hardship: avversità.
instance: istanza, esempio.
objects: oggetti.

owing: dovere.
pardon: grazia, perdono, perdonare, scusare, scusa.
precipitate: precipitare, precipitato.
prove: provare, proviamo, provi, provate, provano, provo, prova, comprovare, dimostrare.
summons: citazione, ingiunzione.
tone: tono.
touched: toccato.
viewing: veduta, osservare, osservazione.

CHAPTER 14

During dinner, Mr. **Bennet** scarcely spoke at all; but when the servants were **withdrawn**, he thought it time to have some conversation with his guest, and therefore started a subject in which he expected him to **shine**, by **observing** that he seemed very fortunate in his **patroness**. Lady Catherine de Bourgh's attention to his wishes, and consideration for his comfort, appeared very **remarkable**. Mr. Bennet could not have chosen better. Mr. Collins was **eloquent** in her praise. The subject **elevated** him to more than usual **solemnity** of manner, and with a most important **aspect** he protested that "he had never in his life **witnessed** such behaviour in a person of rank--such **affability** and **condescension**, as he had himself **experienced** from Lady Catherine. She had been **graciously** pleased to **approve** of both of the discourses which he had already had the honour of **preaching** before her. She had also asked him twice to **dine** at Rosings, and had sent for him only the Saturday before, to make up her **pool** of **quadrille** in the evening. Lady Catherine was **reckoned** proud by many people he knew, but *he* had never seen anything but affability in her. She had always spoken to him as she would to any other gentleman; she made not the smallest objection to his joining in the society of the neighbourhood nor to his leaving the parish occasionally for a week or two, to **visit** his relations.   She had even **condescended** to advise him to **marry** as soon as he could, provided he chose with discretion; and had once paid him a visit in his **humble parsonage**, where

Italian

affability: affabilità.
approve: approvare, approvate, approvano, approvi, approvo, approva, approviamo.
aspect: aspetto, apparenza, aria.
bennet: cariofillata, erba benedetta.
condescended: degnato.
condescension: condiscendenza.
dine: cenare.
elevated: elevato.
eloquent: eloquente.
experienced: esperto.

graciously: graziosamente.
humble: umile, modesto.
marry: sposare, sposati, sposatevi, si sposi, si sposate, si sposano, ci sposiamo, mi sposo, maritarsi, ammogliarsi, maritare.
observing: osservando.
parsonage: canonica.
patroness: patrona, patronessa.
pool: piscina, unirsi, consorzio.
preaching: predicando.
quadrille: quadriglia.

reckoned: contato, calcolato, computato.
remarkable: notevole, eccezionale.
shine: risplendere, brillare, lustro, splendere.
solemnity: solennità.
visit: visita, visitare, visitano, visitate, visiti, visitiamo, visito, andare a trovare.
withdrawn: ritirato, prelevato.
witnessed: testimoniato.

she had perfectly **approved** all the alterations he had been making, and had even vouchsafed to **suggest** some herself--some **shelves** in the **closet** upstairs."

"That is all very proper and civil, I am sure," said Mrs. Bennet, "and I dare say she is a very agreeable woman. It is a pity that great ladies in general are not more like her. Does she live near you, sir?"

"The **garden** in which stands my humble **abode** is **separated** only by a **lane** from Rosings Park, her ladyship's residence."

"I think you said she was a widow, sir? Has she any family?"

"She has only one daughter, the **heiress** of Rosings, and of very extensive property."

"Ah!" said Mrs. Bennet, **shaking** her head, "then she is better off than many girls. And what sort of young lady is she? Is she handsome?"

"She is a most charming young lady indeed. Lady Catherine herself says that, in point of true beauty, Miss de Bourgh is far superior to the handsomest of her **sex**, because there is that in her **features** which marks the young lady of distinguished **birth**. She is unfortunately of a **sickly constitution**, which has prevented her from making that progress in many accomplishments which she could not have **otherwise failed** of, as I am informed by the lady who **superintended** her education, and who still **resides** with them. But she is perfectly amiable, and often **condescends** to **drive** by my humble abode in her little phaeton and ponies."

"Has she been **presented**? I do not remember her name among the ladies at court."

"Her **indifferent** state of health **unhappily prevents** her being in town; and by that means, as I told Lady Catherine one day, has **deprived** the British court of its brightest ornaments. Her ladyship seemed pleased with the idea; and you may imagine that I am happy on every occasion to offer those little delicate compliments which are always **acceptable** to ladies. I have more than once observed to Lady Catherine, that her charming daughter seemed **born** to be a **duchess**, and that the most elevated rank, instead of giving her consequence,

Italian

abode: residenza, appartamento, alloggio, dimora.
acceptable: accettabile.
approved: approvato, omologato.
birth: nascita, parto.
born: nato.
closet: armadio.
condescends: degna.
constitution: costituzione.
deprived: privato, deprivato.
drive: azionamento, comando, guidare, impulso, trasmissione,

spingere.
duchess: duchessa.
failed: fallito, non riuscito.
features: caratteristiche, fattezze.
garden: giardino.
heiress: erede.
indifferent: indifferente.
lane: vicolo, corsia.
otherwise: altrimenti.
presented: presentato.
prevents: impedisce, previene.
resides: risiede.

separated: separato.
sex: sesso.
shaking: scuotendo.
shelves: ripiani, scaffali.
sickly: cagionevole, malaticcio, malatamente.
suggest: proporre, indicare, proponi, proponiamo, propongo, proponete, propongono, mostrare, suggerire, suggerisci, suggeriamo.
superintended: soprinteso.
unhappily: infelicemente.

would be **adorned** by her. These are the kind of little things which please her ladyship, and it is a sort of attention which I conceive myself **peculiarly bound** to pay."

"You judge very properly," said Mr. Bennet, "and it is happy for you that you possess the **talent** of **flattering** with delicacy. May I ask whether these pleasing attentions proceed from the impulse of the moment, or are the result of previous study?"

"They **arise** chiefly from what is passing at the time, and though I sometimes amuse myself with **suggesting** and **arranging** such little elegant compliments as may be **adapted** to ordinary occasions, I always wish to give them as **unstudied** an air as possible."

Mr. Bennet's expectations were fully answered. His cousin was as **absurd** as he had hoped, and he listened to him with the keenest enjoyment, **maintaining** at the same time the most **resolute** composure of countenance, and, except in an occasional **glance** at Elizabeth, requiring no partner in his pleasure.

By tea-time, however, the **dose** had been enough, and Mr. Bennet was glad to take his guest into the drawing-room again, and, when tea was over, glad to **invite** him to read aloud to the ladies. Mr. Collins readily assented, and a book was produced; but, on **beholding** it (for everything **announced** it to be from a **circulating** library), he started back, and **begging** pardon, protested that he never read novels. Kitty stared at him, and Lydia **exclaimed**. Other books were produced, and after some **deliberation** he chose Fordyce's Sermons. Lydia gaped as he opened the volume, and before he had, with very **monotonous** solemnity, read three **pages**, she interrupted him with:

"Do you know, **mamma**, that my uncle Phillips **talks** of turning away Richard; and if he does, Colonel Forster will **hire** him. My aunt told me so herself on Saturday. I shall walk to Meryton to-morrow to hear more about it, and to ask when Mr. Denny comes back from town."

Lydia was **bid** by her two eldest sisters to hold her tongue; but Mr. Collins, much offended, laid aside his book, and said:

Italian

absurd: assurdo.
adapted: adattato.
adorned: decorato.
announced: annunciato, annunziato.
arise: nascere, nasciamo, nasco, nasci, nascete, nascono, salire, sorgere, sorgete, sorgono, sorgi.
arranging: sistemando, predisponendo, ordinando.
begging: mendicando.
beholding: guardando.
bid: offerta, offrire, chiedere.

bound: limite, confine.
circulating: circolante, circolare.
deliberation: deliberazione.
dose: dose.
exclaimed: esclamato.
flattering: lusingando, adulatorio.
glance: occhiata, sguardo.
hire: prendere in affitto, noleggio, noleggiare, noleggiate, noleggiano, noleggiamo, noleggia, noleggi, affitto, assumere.
invite: invitare, invita, invitano,

invitate, inviti, invitiamo, invito.
maintaining: mantenendo, conservando.
mamma: mamma.
monotonous: monotono, uniforme.
pages: pagine.
peculiarly: particolarmente.
resolute: risoluto, deciso.
suggesting: proponendo, suggerendo.
talent: talento, ingegno.
talks: parla.
unstudied: spontaneo.

"I have often observed how little young ladies are **interested** by books of a serious **stamp**, though written solely for their benefit. It **amazes** me, I **confess**; for, certainly, there can be nothing so **advantageous** to them as **instruction**. But I will no longer **importune** my young cousin."

Then turning to Mr. **Bennet**, he offered himself as his **antagonist** at **backgammon**. Mr. Bennet accepted the **challenge**, observing that he acted very **wisely** in leaving the girls to their own **trifling** amusements. Mrs. Bennet and her daughters apologised most **civilly** for Lydia's **interruption**, and promised that it should not **occur** again, if he would **resume** his book; but Mr. Collins, after **assuring** them that he **bore** his young cousin no ill-will, and should never resent her behaviour as any **affront**, seated himself at another table with Mr. Bennet, and **prepared** for backgammon.

Italian

advantageous: vantaggioso, utile.
affront: affronto, insulto, insultare.
amazes: sbalordisce, si stupisce.
antagonist: antagonista.
assuring: assicurando.
backgammon: backgammon.
bennet: cariofillata, erba benedetta.
bore: annoiare, alesaggio, foro, forare, succiello, seccare, alesare, perforare, trivellare.
challenge: contestare, sfida, sfidare, disputare.

civilly: civile, civilmente.
confess: confessare, confessa, confessano, confessate, confessi, confessiamo, confesso.
importune: importunare.
instruction: istruzione.
interested: interessato.
interruption: interruzione.
occur: succedere, accadere, succedete, succedono, succedo, succediamo, succedi, accado, accadiamo, accadete, accadi.

prepared: preparato, allestito, apprestato.
resume: riprendere, riprendete, riprendiamo, riprendo, riprendono, riprendi.
stamp: francobollo, bollo, bollare, timbro, affrancare, timbrare.
trifling: insignificante.
wisely: saggiamente.

CHAPTER 15

Mr. Collins was not a sensible man, and the deficiency of **nature** had been but little **assisted** by education or society; the greatest part of his life having been spent under the **guidance** of an **illiterate** and **miserly** father; and though he **belonged** to one of the universities, he had merely kept the **necessary** terms, without **forming** at it any **useful** acquaintance. The **subjection** in which his father had brought him up had given him **originally** great humility of manner; but it was now a good deal **counteracted** by the self-conceit of a **weak** head, **living** in **retirement**, and the **consequential** feelings of early and **unexpected** **prosperity**. A fortunate chance had recommended him to Lady Catherine de Bourgh when the living of Hunsford was vacant; and the respect which he felt for her high rank, and his **veneration** for her as his **patroness**, **mingling** with a very good opinion of himself, of his **authority** as a clergyman, and his right as a **rector**, made him altogether a mixture of pride and **obsequiousness**, self-importance and humility.

Having now a good house and a very sufficient **income**, he intended to marry; and in **seeking** a **reconciliation** with the Longbourn family he had a wife in view, as he meant to choose one of the daughters, if he found them as handsome and amiable as they were **represented** by **common** report. This was his **plan** of amends--of atonement--for inheriting their father's estate; and he

Italian

assisted: assistito, aiutato.
authority: autorità.
belonged: appartenuto.
common: comune, volgare, ordinario.
consequential: conseguente.
counteracted: neutralizzato.
forming: formazione.
guidance: guida.
illiterate: analfabeta, illetterato.
income: reddito, rendita, entrate, introito.
living: vivendo, abitando, vivo, vivente.
mingling: mescolando, mischiando.
miserly: avaro.
nature: natura, indole, carattere.
necessary: necessario, occorrente.
obsequiousness: ossequiosità.
originally: originalmente.
patroness: patrona, patronessa.
plan: progetto, progettare, piano, intenzione, pianificare, programma, pianta, disegno.
prosperity: prosperità.
reconciliation: riconciliazione, conciliazione.
rector: rettore, parroco.
represented: rappresentato, figurato.
retirement: pensionamento, ritiro.
seeking: cercando.
subjection: sottomissione, soggezione.
unexpected: inatteso, imprevisto, inaspettato.
useful: utile.
veneration: venerazione.
weak: debole, fiacco.

thought it an excellent one, full of **eligibility** and suitableness, and excessively **generous** and **disinterested** on his own part.

His plan did not **vary** on seeing them. Miss Bennet's **lovely** face **confirmed** his views, and established all his strictest notions of what was due to **seniority**; and for the first evening *she* was his settled choice. The next morning, however, made an **alteration**; for in a quarter of an hour's tete-a-tete with Mrs. Bennet before breakfast, a conversation beginning with his parsonage-house, and leading **naturally** to the **avowal** of his hopes, that a **mistress** might be found for it at Longbourn, **produced** from her, **amid** very **complaisant** smiles and general encouragement, a **caution** against the very Jane he had fixed on. "As to her *younger* daughters, she could not take upon her to say--she could not positively answer--but she did not *know* of any prepossession; her *eldest* daughter, she must just mention--she felt it **incumbent** on her to hint, was likely to be very soon engaged."

Mr. Collins had only to change from Jane to Elizabeth--and it was soon done--done while Mrs. Bennet was **stirring** the fire. Elizabeth, equally next to Jane in birth and beauty, succeeded her of course.

Mrs. Bennet treasured up the hint, and **trusted** that she might soon have two daughters married; and the man whom she could not bear to speak of the day before was now high in her good graces.

Lydia's intention of walking to Meryton was not **forgotten**; every sister except Mary agreed to go with her; and Mr. Collins was to **attend** them, at the request of Mr. Bennet, who was most anxious to get **rid** of him, and have his library to himself; for thither Mr. Collins had followed him after breakfast; and there he would continue, **nominally** engaged with one of the largest folios in the collection, but really talking to Mr. Bennet, with little **cessation**, of his house and garden at Hunsford. Such doings discomposed Mr. Bennet exceedingly. In his library he had been always sure of leisure and **tranquillity**; and though prepared, as he told Elizabeth, to meet with **folly** and conceit in every other room of the house, he was used to be free from them there; his civility, therefore, was most **prompt** in inviting Mr. Collins to join his daughters in their walk; and

Italian

alteration: alterazione, modifica, cambiamento, variazione.
amid: tra, fra.
attend: visitare, curare, assistere, curiamo, curi, curo, curano, visitate, visitiamo, cura, visiti.
avowal: ammissione.
caution: avvertire, prudenza, avvertenza, cautela.
cessation: cessazione.
complaisant: compiacente.
confirmed: confermato.

disinterested: disinteressato, imparziale.
eligibility: eleggibilità.
folly: follia.
forgotten: dimenticato.
generous: generoso, liberale, munifico.
incumbent: incombente.
lovely: bello, piacevole, amabile, grazioso, gradevole, affascinante, caro, carino.
mistress: padrona.
naturally: naturalmente.

nominally: nominalmente.
produced: prodotto.
prompt: preciso, esatto, sollecito, pronto.
rid: sbarazzare.
seniority: anzianità.
stirring: mescolare, eccitante, agitazione.
tranquillity: tranquillità.
trusted: fidato.
vary: variare, vario, variate, vari, varia, variamo, variano.

Mr. Collins, being in fact much better **fitted** for a walker than a reader, was extremely pleased to close his large book, and go.

In pompous nothings on his side, and civil assents on that of his cousins, their time passed till they entered Meryton. The attention of the younger ones was then no longer to be gained by him. Their eyes were immediately **wandering** up in the street in quest of the **officers**, and nothing less than a very smart **bonnet** indeed, or a really new **muslin** in a shop window, could **recall** them.

But the attention of every lady was soon caught by a young man, whom they had never seen before, of most gentlemanlike appearance, walking with another officer on the other side of the way. The officer was the very Mr. Denny **concerning** whose return from London Lydia came to **inquire**, and he **bowed** as they passed. All were struck with the stranger's air, all wondered who he could be; and Kitty and Lydia, determined if possible to find out, led the way across the street, under **pretense** of wanting something in an opposite shop, and **fortunately** had just gained the **pavement** when the two gentlemen, turning back, had reached the same **spot**. Mr. Denny **addressed** them directly, and **entreated permission** to introduce his friend, Mr. Wickham, who had returned with him the day before from town, and he was happy to say had accepted a commission in their **corps**. This was exactly as it should be; for the young man wanted only regimentals to make him completely charming. His appearance was greatly in his favour; he had all the best part of beauty, a fine countenance, a good figure, and very pleasing address. The introduction was followed up on his side by a happy readiness of conversation--a readiness at the same time perfectly **correct** and **unassuming**; and the whole party were still standing and talking together very agreeably, when the sound of horses drew their notice, and Darcy and Bingley were seen **riding** down the street. On distinguishing the ladies of the group, the two gentlemen came directly towards them, and began the usual civilities. Bingley was the principal **spokesman**, and Miss Bennet the principal object. He was then, he said, on his way to Longbourn on purpose to inquire after her. Mr. Darcy **corroborated** it with a bow, and was beginning to determine not to **fix** his eyes on Elizabeth, when they were suddenly **arrested** by

Italian

address: indirizzo, indirizzare, recapito, discorso, l'indirizzo.
arrested: arrestato.
bonnet: cofano, cappotta, cuffia.
bowed: chino.
concerning: concernere.
corps: corpo.
correct: correggere, corretto, giusto, esatto, rettificare.
corroborated: confermato, corroborato.
entreated: supplicato.

fitted: aderente, adatto, attrezzato.
fix: fissare, fissa, fissano, fissate, fissi, fissiamo, fisso, riparare, aggiustare, ripara, ripariamo.
fortunately: fortunatamente, per fortuna.
inquire: domandare, informarsi, domandano, domandate, domandi, domandiamo, domando, indagare, domanda.
muslin: mussolina, mussola.
officer: funzionario, ufficiale,

impiegato.
pavement: marciapiede, selciato.
permission: permesso, accordo, autorizzazione, nullaosta, licenza.
pretense: pretesa, finta, finzione.
recall: richiamo, ricordare, richiamare.
riding: equitazione, cavalcata.
spokesman: portavoce.
spot: luogo, macchia, punto, posto, spot, macchiare.
unassuming: senza pretese.
wandering: vagando, peregrinazione.

the **sight** of the stranger, and Elizabeth **happening** to see the countenance of both as they looked at each other, was all astonishment at the effect of the meeting. Both changed colour, one looked white, the other **red**. Mr. Wickham, after a few moments, touched his hat--a **salutation** which Mr. Darcy just **deigned** to **return**. What could be the meaning of it? It was impossible to imagine; it was impossible not to long to know.

In another **minute**, Mr. Bingley, but without seeming to have noticed what passed, took leave and rode on with his friend.

Mr. Denny and Mr. Wickham walked with the young ladies to the door of Mr. Phillip's house, and then made their **bows**, in spite of Miss Lydia's pressing entreaties that they should come in, and even in spite of Mrs. Phillips's **throwing** up the parlour **window** and **loudly** seconding the invitation.

Mrs. Phillips was always glad to see her nieces; and the two eldest, from their **recent** absence, were particularly welcome, and she was eagerly expressing her surprise at their sudden return home, which, as their own carriage had not **fetched** them, she should have known nothing about, if she had not **happened** to see Mr. Jones's shop-boy in the **street**, who had told her that they were not to send any more draughts to Netherfield because the Miss Bennets were come away, when her **civility** was **claimed** towards Mr. Collins by Jane's introduction of him. She received him with her very best politeness, which he returned with as much more, apologising for his **intrusion**, without any **previous** acquaintance with her, which he could not help flattering himself, however, might be **justified** by his **relationship** to the young ladies who introduced him to her notice. Mrs. Phillips was quite awed by such an **excess** of good breeding; but her **contemplation** of one stranger was soon put to an end by exclamations and inquiries about the other; of whom, however, she could only tell her nieces what they already knew, that Mr. Denny had brought him from London, and that he was to have a lieutenant's **commission** in the ----shire. She had been watching him the last hour, she said, as he walked up and down the street, and had Mr. Wickham appeared, Kitty and Lydia would certainly have continued the **occupation**, but **unluckily** no one passed **windows** now except a few of the

Italian

bows: archetti.
civility: civiltà, cortesia.
claimed: reclamato.
commission: commissione, provvigione.
contemplation: contemplazione.
deigned: degnato.
excess: eccesso, eccedenza, franchigia.
fetched: portato.
happened: successo, avvenuto.
happening: succedendo, avvenendo, avvenimento.

intrusion: intrusione.
justified: giustificato.
loudly: forte, ad alta voce.
minute: minuto, il minuto, minuscolo, momento.
occupation: occupazione, mestiere, professione, impiego, lavoro.
previous: precedente.
recent: recente, fresco.
red: rosso.
relationship: parentela, relazione, rapporto, parentado.

return: ritorno, ritornare, restituire, rientro, contraccambiare, resa, rendere, rivenire, restituzione.
salutation: saluto.
sight: vista, aspetto, avvistare, aria, apparenza.
street: via, strada.
throwing: lancio.
unluckily: sfortunatamente.
window: finestra, sportello, finestrino, la finestra.
windows: finestre.

officers, who, in comparison with the stranger, were become "stupid, **disagreeable** fellows." Some of them were to dine with the Phillipses the next day, and their aunt promised to make her husband **call** on Mr. Wickham, and give him an invitation also, if the family from Longbourn would come in the evening. This was agreed to, and Mrs. Phillips protested that they would have a **nice comfortable noisy game** of **lottery tickets**, and a little **bit** of **hot** supper afterwards. The prospect of such delights was very **cheering**, and they parted in **mutual** good spirits. Mr. Collins repeated his **apologies** in **quitting** the room, and was assured with unwearying **civility** that they were perfectly needless.

As they walked home, Elizabeth related to Jane what she had seen pass between the two gentlemen; but though Jane would have **defended** either or both, had they appeared to be in the **wrong**, she could no more explain such behaviour than her sister.

Mr. Collins on his return highly **gratified** Mrs. **Bennet** by **admiring** Mrs. Phillips's manners and **politeness**. He protested that, except Lady Catherine and her daughter, he had never seen a more elegant woman; for she had not only received him with the **utmost** civility, but even pointedly **included** him in her invitation for the next evening, although **utterly** unknown to her before. Something, he supposed, might be **attributed** to his **connection** with them, but yet he had never met with so much attention in the whole **course** of his life.

Italian

admiring: ammirando, ammirativo.
apologies: scuse.
attributed: attribuito.
bennet: cariofillata, erba benedetta.
bit: pezzo, morso, punta, pezzetto, bit.
call: chiamare, chiami, chiamiamo, chiamo, chiamano, chiama, chiamate, chiamata, appello.
cheering: applauso.
civility: civiltà, cortesia.
comfortable: comodo, confortevole.
connection: coincidenza, accoppiamento, connessione, collegamento, relazione, banda.
course: corso, percorso, piatto, andamento, decorso, direzione, rotta, portata.
defended: difeso.
disagreeable: sgradevole.
game: gioco, giuoco, cacciagione, selvaggina, partita.
gratified: gratificato.
hot: caldo, piccante.
included: incluso, contenuto.
lottery: lotteria.
mutual: reciproco.
nice: piacevole, buono, gradevole, gentile, simpatico, Nizza.
noisy: rumoroso, chiassoso.
politeness: cortesia, garbo.
quitting: abbandonando.
tickets: biglietti.
utmost: massimo.
utterly: totalmente.
wrong: sbagliato, torto, errato, scorretto.

CHAPTER 16

As no **objection** was made to the young people's **engagement** with their aunt, and all Mr. Collins's scruples of leaving Mr. and Mrs. **Bennet** for a single evening during his visit were most **steadily resisted**, the **coach conveyed** him and his five **cousins** at a suitable hour to Meryton; and the girls had the pleasure of hearing, as they entered the drawing-room, that Mr. Wickham had accepted their uncle's **invitation**, and was then in the house.

When this information was given, and they had all taken their seats, Mr. Collins was at leisure to look around him and **admire**, and he was so much struck with the size and furniture of the **apartment**, that he declared he might almost have supposed himself in the small summer breakfast **parlour** at Rosings; a comparison that did not at first convey much **gratification**; but when Mrs. Phillips **understood** from him what Rosings was, and who was its proprietor-- when she had **listened** to the description of only one of Lady Catherine's drawing-rooms, and found that the chimney-piece alone had cost eight hundred pounds, she felt all the force of the **compliment**, and would hardly have resented a comparison with the housekeeper's room.

In **describing** to her all the **grandeur** of Lady Catherine and her **mansion**, with **occasional** digressions in **praise** of his own **humble abode**, and the improvements it was **receiving**, he was **happily** employed until the gentlemen joined them; and he found in Mrs. Phillips a very **attentive listener**, whose

Italian

abode: residenza, appartamento, alloggio, dimora.
admire: ammirare, ammiriamo, ammira, ammirano, ammiro, ammiri, ammirate.
apartment: appartamento.
attentive: attento, premuroso.
bennet: cariofillata, erba benedetta.
coach: vettura, vagone, carrozza, allenatore, allenare.
compliment: complimento.
convey: trasportare.

conveyed: trasportato.
cousin: cugino, cugina.
describing: descrivendo.
engagement: fidanzamento, assunzione.
grandeur: grandiosità.
gratification: gratificazione, soddisfazione.
happily: felicemente.
humble: umile, modesto.
invitation: invito.
listened: ascoltato.

listener: ascoltatore.
mansion: palazzo.
objection: obiezione, opposizione.
occasional: occasionale.
parlour: salotto.
praise: lodare, lode, elogiare, encomio, elogio.
receiving: ricevendo, accogliendo, ricezione, ricevere, ricevente.
resisted: resistito.
steadily: costantemente, fermamente.
understood: capito, compreso.

opinion of his consequence increased with what she heard, and who was resolving to **retail** it all among her neighbours as soon as she could. To the girls, who could not listen to their cousin, and who had nothing to do but to wish for an instrument, and **examine** their own indifferent imitations of china on the mantelpiece, the **interval** of **waiting** appeared very long. It was over at last, however. The gentlemen did approach, and when Mr. Wickham walked into the room, Elizabeth felt that she had neither been seeing him before, nor **thinking** of him since, with the smallest degree of **unreasonable** admiration. The officers of the ----shire were in general a very **creditable**, gentlemanlike set, and the best of them were of the present party; but Mr. Wickham was as far beyond them all in person, countenance, air, and walk, as *they* were superior to the broad-faced, stuffy uncle Phillips, **breathing port wine**, who **followed** them into the room.

Mr. Wickham was the happy man towards whom almost every **female eye** was turned, and Elizabeth was the happy woman by whom he **finally** seated himself; and the agreeable manner in which he immediately **fell** into conversation, though it was only on its being a wet night, made her feel that the commonest, dullest, most threadbare **topic** might be rendered interesting by the skill of the **speaker**.

With such rivals for the notice of the fair as Mr. Wickham and the officers, Mr. Collins seemed to **sink** into **insignificance**; to the young ladies he certainly was nothing; but he had still at intervals a kind listener in Mrs. Phillips, and was by her **watchfulness**, most **abundantly** supplied with coffee and **muffin**. When the card-tables were placed, he had the **opportunity** of obliging her in turn, by sitting down to whist.

"I know little of the game at present," said he, "but I shall be glad to **improve** myself, for in my situation in life--" Mrs. Phillips was very glad for his **compliance**, but could not wait for his reason.

Mr. Wickham did not play at whist, and with ready delight was he received at the other table between Elizabeth and Lydia. At first there seemed danger of Lydia's **engrossing** him entirely, for she was a most determined talker; but being likewise extremely fond of lottery tickets, she soon grew too much interested in

Italian

abundantly: abbondantemente.
breathing: respirando, respirazione, respiro.
compliance: conformità, compliance, cedevolezza.
creditable: lodevole.
engrossing: assorbendo, assorbire.
examine: esaminare, esaminate, esamino, esamini, esaminano, esamina, esaminiamo.
eye: occhio, cruna.
fell: abbattere.

female: femmina, femminile.
finally: finalmente, alla fine, infine.
followed: seguito.
improve: migliorare, miglioro, miglioriamo, migliori, migliorate, migliora, migliorano, perfezionare, perfezioni, perfeziono, perfezioniamo.
insignificance: banalità, futilità.
interval: intervallo.
muffin: focaccina.
opportunity: opportunità, occasione.

port: porto, porta, portello.
retail: al dettaglio.
sink: lavandino, lavello, affondare, acquaio.
speaker: oratore, vivavoce, altoparlante, conferenziere.
thinking: pensando.
topic: argomento, tema.
unreasonable: irragionevole.
waiting: aspettando, attesa, servizio.
watchfulness: vigilanza.
wine: vino.

the game, too **eager** in making bets and **exclaiming** after prizes to have attention for anyone in particular. Allowing for the common demands of the game, Mr. Wickham was therefore at leisure to talk to Elizabeth, and she was very **willing** to hear him, though what she **chiefly** wished to hear she could not hope to be told--the **history** of his **acquaintance** with Mr. Darcy. She **dared** not even mention that gentleman. Her **curiosity**, however, was **unexpectedly relieved**. Mr. Wickham began the subject himself. He **inquired** how far Netherfield was from Meryton; and, after **receiving** her answer, asked in a **hesitating** manner how long Mr. Darcy had been staying there.

"About a month," said Elizabeth; and then, **unwilling** to let the subject **drop**, added, "He is a man of very large **property** in Derbyshire, I understand."

"Yes," replied Mr. Wickham; "his estate there is a **noble** one. A clear ten thousand per annum. You could not have met with a person more **capable** of giving you certain information on that head than myself, for I have been **connected** with his family in a particular manner from my infancy."

Elizabeth could not but look surprised.

"You may well be surprised, Miss Bennet, at such an **assertion**, after seeing, as you probably might, the very cold **manner** of our meeting yesterday. Are you much **acquainted** with Mr. Darcy?"

"As much as I ever wish to be," cried Elizabeth very **warmly**. "I have spent four days in the same house with him, and I think him very **disagreeable**."

"I have no right to give *my* opinion," said Wickham, "as to his being agreeable or otherwise. I am not **qualified** to form one. I have known him too long and too well to be a fair judge. It is impossible for *me* to be **impartial**. But I believe your opinion of him would in general astonish--and perhaps you would not express it quite so strongly **anywhere** else. Here you are in your own family."

"Upon my **word**, I say no more *here* than I might say in any house in the **neighbourhood**, except Netherfield. He is not at all liked in Hertfordshire.

Italian

acquaintance: conoscenza, conoscente.
acquainted: informato.
agreeable: gradevole, piacevole, amabile.
anywhere: dovunque, in qualche luogo, da qualche parte.
assertion: asserzione, affermazione.
capable: capace, abile, idoneo, adatto.
chiefly: principalmente, soprattutto.
connected: collegato, legato, connesso.
curiosity: curiosità.
dared: osato.

drop: goccia, diminuire, abbassamento, abbassare, caduta.
eager: avido, desideroso, bramoso, impaziente.
exclaiming: esclamando.
hesitating: esitando, titubando, esitare.
history: storia, la storia.
impartial: imparziale.
inquired: domandato.
neighbourhood: circondario, distretto, vicinato, quartiere.

noble: nobile, gentilizio, nobiliare.
per: a.
qualified: qualificato, abilitato.
receiving: ricevendo, accogliendo, ricezione, ricevere, ricevente.
relieved: alleviato.
unexpectedly: inaspettatamente.
unwilling: riluttante, restio.
warmly: caldamente, calorosamente.
willing: disposto, volenteroso.
word: parola, vocabolo, termine, verbo, formulare.

Everybody is disgusted with his pride. You will not find him more **favourably** spoken of by anyone."

"I **cannot** pretend to be sorry," said Wickham, after a short **interruption**, "that he or that any man should not be **estimated** beyond their deserts; but with *him* I believe it does not often happen. The world is **blinded** by his fortune and consequence, or **frightened** by his high and **imposing** manners, and sees him only as he chooses to be seen."

"I should take him, even on *my* slight acquaintance, to be an ill-tempered man." Wickham only shook his head.

"I wonder," said he, at the next opportunity of speaking, "whether he is likely to be in this country much longer."

"I do not at all know; but I *heard* nothing of his going away when I was at Netherfield. I hope your plans in favour of the ----shire will not be affected by his being in the neighbourhood."

"Oh! no--it is not for *me* to be **driven** away by Mr. Darcy. If *he* wishes to avoid seeing *me*, he must go. We are not on friendly terms, and it always **gives** me pain to **meet** him, but I have no **reason** for **avoiding** *him* but what I might **proclaim** before all the world, a sense of very great ill-usage, and most **painful** regrets at his being what he is. His father, Miss Bennet, the late Mr. Darcy, was one of the best men that ever **breathed**, and the truest friend I ever had; and I can never be in company with this Mr. Darcy without being **grieved** to the **soul** by a thousand **tender** recollections. His behaviour to myself has been **scandalous**; but I **verily** believe I could forgive him anything and **everything**, rather than his disappointing the hopes and **disgracing** the memory of his father."

Elizabeth found the interest of the subject **increase**, and listened with all her **heart**; but the **delicacy** of it prevented further inquiry.

Mr. Wickham began to speak on more general topics, Meryton, the neighbourhood, the society, appearing highly pleased with all that he had yet seen, and speaking of the latter with **gentle** but very **intelligible gallantry**.

Italian

avoiding: evitando.
blinded: accecato.
breathed: respirato.
cannot: non potere.
delicacy: delicatezza.
disgracing: disonorare.
driven: guidato.
estimated: stimato.
everything: tutto.
favourably: favorevolmente.
frightened: spaventato.
gallantry: galanteria, valore, prodezza.

gentle: mite, gentile, dolce, delicato.
gives: dà, regala.
grieved: accorato, addolorato.
heart: cuore, il cuore.
imposing: imponente, imponendo.
increase: aumento, aumentare, ingrandire, incremento, incrementare, accrescere.
intelligible: intelligibile.
interruption: interruzione.
meet: incontrare, incontra, incontriamo, incontri, incontrano,

incontrate, incontro, confluire.
painful: doloroso, penoso.
proclaim: proclamare, proclami, proclamiamo, proclamate, proclamano, proclamo, proclama, pubblicare.
reason: ragione, causa, intelletto, ragionare, argomentare, motivo.
scandalous: scandaloso.
soul: anima.
tender: tenero, dolce, offerta, tender.
verily: molto.

"It was the prospect of **constant** society, and good society," he added, "which was my chief inducement to **enter** the ----shire. I knew it to be a most respectable, agreeable corps, and my friend Denny tempted me further by his account of their present quarters, and the very great attentions and excellent acquaintances Meryton had **procured** them. Society, I own, is necessary to me. I have been a disappointed man, and my spirits will not bear **solitude**. I *must* have **employment** and society. A **military** life is not what I was intended for, but **circumstances** have now made it **eligible**. The church *ought* to have been my profession--I was brought up for the church, and I should at this time have been in possession of a most valuable living, had it pleased the gentleman we were speaking of just now."

"Indeed!"

"Yes--the late Mr. Darcy bequeathed me the next presentation of the best living in his **gift**. He was my **godfather**, and excessively **attached** to me. I cannot do justice to his kindness. He meant to provide for me **amply**, and thought he had done it; but when the living fell, it was given elsewhere."

"Good heavens!" cried Elizabeth; "but how could *that* be? How could his will be **disregarded**? Why did you not seek legal redress?"

"There was just such an **informality** in the terms of the **bequest** as to give me no hope from law. A man of honour could not have doubted the intention, but Mr. Darcy chose to doubt it--or to **treat** it as a merely **conditional** recommendation, and to **assert** that I had forfeited all **claim** to it by **extravagance**, imprudence--in short anything or nothing. Certain it is, that the living became vacant two years ago, exactly as I was of an age to hold it, and that it was given to another man; and no less certain is it, that I cannot **accuse** myself of having really done anything to deserve to lose it. I have a **warm**, **unguarded** temper, and I may have spoken my opinion *of* him, and *to* him, too **freely**. I can recall nothing worse. But the fact is, that we are very different sort of men, and that he hates me."

"This is quite shocking! He deserves to be **publicly** disgraced."

Italian

accuse: accusare, accusate, accusi, accusiamo, accuso, accusano, accusa, caricare, caricano, carico, carichiamo.
amply: ampiamente.
assert: asserire, asserite, asseriscono, asserisci, asserisco, asseriamo, sostenere, affermare.
attached: fissato, attaccato, allegato.
bequest: lascito.
circumstances: circostanze.
claim: reclamo, rivendicazione, richiesta, pretendere, credito,

affermazione, pretesa.
conditional: condizionale.
constant: costante, fedele.
disregarded: ignorato.
eligible: eleggibile.
employment: occupazione, impiego, lavoro.
enter: entrare, entra, entrano, entrate, entri, entriamo, entro, invio.
extravagance: stravaganza, prodigalità.
freely: liberamente.

gift: regalo, dono, presente, donazione, omaggio.
godfather: padrino, compare.
informality: tono familiare, familiarità, irregolarità.
military: militare.
procured: procurato.
publicly: pubblicamente.
solitude: solitudine.
treat: trattare, guarire.
unguarded: incustodito.
warm: caldo, caloroso, scaldare.

"Some time or other he *will* be--but it shall not be by *me*. Till I can forget his father, I can never **defy** or expose *him*."

Elizabeth honoured him for such feelings, and thought him handsomer than ever as he expressed them.

"But what," said she, after a pause, "can have been his motive? What can have **induced** him to **behave** so cruelly?"

"A thorough, determined dislike of me--a dislike which I **cannot** but **attribute** in some **measure** to jealousy. Had the late Mr. Darcy liked me less, his **son** might have borne with me better; but his father's uncommon attachment to me **irritated** him, I believe, very early in life. He had not a temper to bear the sort of **competition** in which we stood--the sort of preference which was often given me."

"I had not thought Mr. Darcy so bad as this--though I have never liked him. I had not thought so very ill of him. I had supposed him to be **despising** his fellow-creatures in general, but did not **suspect** him of **descending** to such **malicious revenge**, such injustice, such **inhumanity** as this."

After a few **minutes'** reflection, however, she continued, "I *do* remember his **boasting** one day, at Netherfield, of the **implacability** of his resentments, of his having an unforgiving temper. His disposition must be dreadful."

"I will not trust myself on the subject," replied Wickham; "I can hardly be just to him."

Elizabeth was again deep in thought, and after a time exclaimed, "To treat in such a manner the **godson**, the friend, the favourite of his father!" She could have added, "A young man, too, like *you*, whose very **countenance** may **vouch** for your being amiable"--but she **contented** herself with, "and one, too, who had probably been his companion from **childhood**, connected together, as I think you said, in the closest manner!"

"We were born in the same parish, within the same **park**; the greatest part of our **youth** was passed together; inmates of the same house, **sharing** the same amusements, objects of the same **parental** care. *my* father began life in the

Italian

attribute: attributo, attribuire.
behave: comportarsi, condursi.
boasting: vanteria.
cannot: non potere.
childhood: infanzia, fanciullezza.
competition: concorrenza, concorso, competizione, gara.
contented: contento.
countenance: approvare, viso.
defy: sfidare, sfidano, sfidiamo, sfidate, sfidi, sfido, sfida.
descending: scendendo, discendendo.

despising: disprezzando.
godson: figlioccio.
implacability: implacabilità.
induced: indotto, concluso, dedotto.
inhumanity: inumanità.
irritated: irritato.
malicious: maligno, doloso, malizioso.
measure: misura, misurare, provvedimento.
minutes: verbale, contravvenzione, minuti.
parental: parentale.

park: parco, parcheggiare.
revenge: vendetta.
sharing: condivisione.
son: figlio, figliolo, il figlio.
suspect: sospettare, sospetto.
vouch: attestare, attestano, attestate, attesti, attestiamo, attesto, attesta.
youth: gioventù, giovinezza, adolescenza, giovane.

profession which your uncle, Mr. Phillips, **appears** to do so much credit to--but he gave up everything to be of use to the late Mr. Darcy and **devoted** all his time to the care of the Pemberley property. He was most highly esteemed by Mr. Darcy, a most intimate, **confidential** friend. Mr. Darcy often **acknowledged** himself to be under the greatest obligations to my father's **active** **superintendence**, and when, immediately before my father's death, Mr. Darcy gave him a **voluntary** promise of **providing** for me, I am convinced that he felt it to be as much a **debt** of gratitude to *him*, as of his affection to myself."

"How strange!" cried Elizabeth. "How abominable! I wonder that the very pride of this Mr. Darcy has not made him just to you! If from no better motive, that he should not have been too proud to be dishonest--for **dishonesty** I must call it."

"It *is* wonderful," replied Wickham, "for almost all his actions may be traced to pride; and pride had often been his best friend. It has connected him nearer with **virtue** than with any other feeling. But we are **none** of us **consistent**, and in his behaviour to me there were stronger **impulses** even than pride."

"Can such abominable pride as his have ever done him good?"

"Yes. It has often led him to be **liberal** and generous, to give his money freely, to **display** hospitality, to **assist** his tenants, and **relieve** the poor. Family pride, and *filial* pride--for he is very proud of what his father was--have done this. Not to appear to **disgrace** his family, to **degenerate** from the **popular** qualities, or lose the **influence** of the Pemberley House, is a **powerful** motive. He has also *brotherly* pride, which, with *some* brotherly affection, makes him a very kind and careful **guardian** of his sister, and you will hear him generally cried up as the most attentive and best of brothers."

"What sort of girl is Miss Darcy?"

He shook his head. "I wish I could call her amiable. It gives me pain to speak ill of a Darcy. But she is too much like her brother--very, very proud. As a child, she was **affectionate** and pleasing, and extremely fond of me; and I have devoted hours and hours to her amusement. But she is nothing to me now. She

Italian

active: attivo, operoso, laborioso.
affectionate: affettuoso.
appear: apparire, apparite, appariamo, appari, appaiono, appaio, parere, comparire.
appears: appare.
assist: assistere, assistono, assistiamo, assistete, assisti, assisto, aiutare, aiuti, aiuta, aiutano, aiutate.
brotherly: fraterno.
confidential: confidenziale.
consistent: costante.

debt: debito.
degenerate: degenerare, degenerato.
devoted: devoto.
disgrace: vergogna, disgrazia, disonorare, disonore.
dishonesty: disonestà.
display: visualizzazione, esposizione, esporre.
guardian: guardiano, tutore.
impulses: impulsi.
influence: influenza, influsso, influenzare, influire.

led: condotto, guidato.
liberal: liberale.
none: nessuno.
popular: popolare.
powerful: potente.
providing: provvedendo, fornendo.
relieve: alleviare, allevio, allevi, allevia, alleviamo, alleviano, alleviate, rilevare.
superintendence: soprintendenza.
virtue: virtù.
voluntary: volontario.

is a handsome girl, about fifteen or **sixteen**, and, I **understand**, highly accomplished. Since her father's death, her home has been London, where a lady lives with her, and **superintends** her education."

After many pauses and many trials of other subjects, Elizabeth could not help **reverting** once more to the first, and saying:

"I am **astonished** at his **intimacy** with Mr. Bingley! How can Mr. Bingley, who seems good humour itself, and is, I really believe, **truly amiable**, be in friendship with such a man? How can they suit each other? Do you know Mr. Bingley?"

"Not at all."

"He is a sweet-tempered, amiable, charming man. He **cannot** know what Mr. Darcy is."

"Probably not; but Mr. Darcy can **please** where he **chooses**. He does not want **abilities**. He can be a conversible companion if he thinks it worth his while. Among those who are at all his equals in consequence, he is a very different man from what he is to the less **prosperous**. His pride never deserts him; but with the **rich** he is liberal-minded, just, **sincere**, rational, **honourable**, and perhaps agreeable--allowing something for fortune and figure."

The whist party soon afterwards **breaking** up, the players **gathered** round the other table and Mr. Collins took his **station** between his cousin Elizabeth and Mrs. Phillips. The usual inquiries as to his **success** was made by the latter. It had not been very great; he had lost every point; but when Mrs. Phillips began to express her concern **thereupon**, he assured her with much **earnest gravity** that it was not of the least importance, that he considered the money as a **mere trifle**, and **begged** that she would not make herself uneasy.

"I know very well, madam," said he, "that when persons **sit** down to a card-table, they must take their chances of these things, and happily I am not in such circumstances as to make five shillings any object. There are undoubtedly many who could not say the same, but thanks to Lady Catherine de Bourgh, I am removed far beyond the **necessity** of **regarding** little matters."

Italian

abilities: abilità.
amiable: amabile.
astonished: stupito, si stupito.
begged: mendicato.
breaking: rottura.
cannot: non potere.
chooses: sceglie, elegge.
earnest: serio, caparra.
gathered: raccolto.
gravity: gravità.
honourable: onorevole.
intimacy: intimità.

mere: mero, laghetto, semplice.
necessity: necessità, bisogno.
please: piacere, per favore, per piacere, prego.
prosperous: prospero, fiorente.
regarding: considerando.
reverting: ritornando.
rich: ricco.
sincere: sincero.
sit: sedere, sediamo, siedono, siedi, sedete, siedo, covare, covo, covi, cova, covate.

sixteen: sedici.
station: stazione, posto, posta.
success: successo, riuscita.
superintends: soprintende.
thereupon: in merito.
trifle: inezia, sciocchezza.
truly: davvero, infatti, veramente.
understand: capire, capite, capiamo, capisci, capisco, capiscono, comprendere, comprendono, comprendo, comprendiamo, comprendete.

Mr. Wickham's attention was caught; and after **observing** Mr. Collins for a few moments, he asked Elizabeth in a **low** voice whether her relation was very **intimately acquainted** with the family of de Bourgh.

"Lady Catherine de Bourgh," she replied, "has very lately given him a living. I hardly know how Mr. Collins was first introduced to her notice, but he certainly has not known her long."

"You know of course that Lady Catherine de Bourgh and Lady Anne Darcy were sisters; consequently that she is aunt to the **present** Mr. Darcy."

"No, indeed, I did not. I knew nothing at all of Lady Catherine's connections. I never heard of her **existence** till the day before yesterday."

"Her daughter, Miss de Bourgh, will have a very large fortune, and it is believed that she and her cousin will **unite** the two estates."

This information made Elizabeth smile, as she thought of **poor** Miss Bingley. Vain indeed must be all her attentions, **vain** and **useless** her affection for his sister and her praise of himself, if he were already self-destined for another.

"Mr. Collins," said she, "speaks highly both of Lady Catherine and her daughter; but from some **particulars** that he has related of her **ladyship**, I suspect his gratitude **misleads** him, and that in **spite** of her being his **patroness**, she is an **arrogant, conceited** woman."

"I believe her to be both in a great degree," replied Wickham; "I have not seen her for many years, but I very well **remember** that I never liked her, and that her manners were **dictatorial** and **insolent**. She has the **reputation** of being remarkably sensible and clever; but I rather believe she **derives** part of her abilities from her rank and fortune, part from her **authoritative** manner, and the rest from the pride for her **nephew**, who **chooses** that **everyone** connected with him should have an understanding of the first class."

Elizabeth allowed that he had given a very rational **account** of it, and they continued talking together, with mutual satisfaction till supper put an end to cards, and gave the rest of the ladies their share of Mr. Wickham's attentions. There could be no conversation in the **noise** of Mrs. Phillips's supper party, but

Italian

account: conto, considerare, rendiconto, spiegazione, pareggiamento dei conti, credere, account.
acquainted: informato.
arrogant: arrogante, altezzoso.
authoritative: autoritario, autorevole.
chooses: sceglie, elegge.
conceited: vanitoso, presuntoso.
derives: deriva.
dictatorial: dittatoriale.
everyone: ognuno, tutti.

existence: esistenza.
insolent: insolente.
intimately: intimamente.
ladyship: signoria.
low: basso.
misleads: travia, fuorvia.
nephew: nipote.
noise: rumore, schiamazzo.
observing: osservando.
particulars: particolari.
patroness: patrona, patronessa.
poor: povero, cattivo.

present: presente, regalo, dono, presentare, attuale.
remember: ricordare, ricordiamo, ricorda, ricordano, ricordate, ricordi, ricordo.
reputation: reputazione, fama.
spite: dispetto.
unite: unire, congiungere, unirsi, unite, uniscono, unisco, uniamo, unisci.
useless: inutile, inservibile.
vain: vanitoso, vano.

his **manners recommended** him to everybody. Whatever he said, was said well; and whatever he did, done **gracefully**. Elizabeth went away with her head full of him. She could think of nothing but of Mr. Wickham, and of what he had told her, all the way home; but there was not time for her even to **mention** his name as they went, for **neither** Lydia nor Mr. Collins were once **silent**. Lydia **talked incessantly** of **lottery tickets,** of the fish she had lost and the fish she had **won;** and Mr. Collins in **describing** the **civility** of Mr. and Mrs. Phillips, **protesting** that he did not in the **least regard** his **losses** at whist, **enumerating** all the **dishes** at **supper,** and **repeatedly** fearing that he **crowded** his cousins, had more to say than he could well **manage** before the **carriage stopped** at Longbourn House.

Italian

carriage: vettura, carrello, vagone, carro, carrozza.
civility: civiltà, cortesia.
crowded: affollato.
describing: descrivendo.
dishes: stoviglie.
enumerating: enumerando.
everybody: ognuno, tutti, ogni, tutto.
gracefully: con garbo.
incessantly: incessantemente.
least: minimo, meno.
losses: perdite.

lottery: lotteria.
manage: dirigere, dirigiamo, dirigo, dirigi, dirigete, dirigono, amministrare, gestire.
manners: educazione.
mention: menzionare, menzione, cenno.
neither: ne, neanche, nemmeno, neppure.
protesting: protestare.
recommended: raccomandato.
regard: riguardo, considerazione,

considerare, rispetto, considerano, consideriamo, considero, considera, consideri, considerate, stima.
repeatedly: ripetutamente.
silent: silenzioso, zitto.
stopped: fermato, cessato, interrotto, smesso, arrestato.
supper: cena.
talked: parlato.
tickets: biglietti.
won: vinto.

CHAPTER 17

Elizabeth related to Jane the next day what had passed between Mr. Wickham and herself. Jane **listened** with **astonishment** and concern; she knew not how to believe that Mr. Darcy could be so **unworthy** of Mr. Bingley's regard; and yet, it was not in her nature to question the **veracity** of a young man of such **amiable** appearance as Wickham. The possibility of his having **endured** such **unkindness**, was enough to interest all her **tender** feelings; and nothing remained therefore to be done, but to think well of them both, to **defend** the **conduct** of each, and **throw** into the account of accident or **mistake** whatever could not be otherwise **explained**.

"They have both," said she, "been **deceived**, I **dare** say, in some way or other, of which we can form no idea. Interested people have perhaps **misrepresented** each to the other. It is, in short, impossible for us to **conjecture** the causes or circumstances which may have **alienated** them, without actual **blame** on either side."

"Very true, indeed; and now, my dear Jane, what have you got to say on behalf of the interested people who have probably been concerned in the business? Do clear *them* too, or we shall be **obliged** to think **ill** of somebody."

"Laugh as much as you choose, but you will not **laugh** me out of my opinion. My dearest Lizzy, do but consider in what a **disgraceful** light it places Mr. Darcy, to be **treating** his father's **favourite** in such a **manner**, one whom his father had

Italian

alienated: alienato.
amiable: amabile.
astonishment: stupore, meraviglia, sorpresa.
blame: colpa, biasimare, riprendere, incolpare, biasimo.
conduct: condotta, condurre, guidare, comportamento.
conjecture: congettura.
dare: osare, oso, osiamo, osi, osate, osano, osa, sfida.
deceived: ingannato, truffato.

defend: difendere, difendi, difendiamo, difendo, difendono, difendete.
disgraceful: disgraziata, vergognoso, disonorevole.
endured: sopportato, durato.
explained: spiegato.
favourite: preferito.
ill: malato, ammalato.
laugh: ridere, riso, risata.
listened: ascoltato.
manner: maniera, modo.

misrepresented: falsato, travisato.
mistake: errore, sbaglio, sbagliare, confondere, fallo.
obliged: obbligato.
tender: tenero, dolce, offerta, tender.
throw: gettare, lanciare, lancio, tiro, alzata.
treating: trattare.
unkindness: cattiveria, scortesia.
unworthy: indegno.
veracity: veracità.

promised to provide for. It is impossible. No man of common **humanity**, no man who had any value for his character, could be capable of it. Can his most intimate friends be so **excessively deceived** in him? Oh! no."

"I can much more easily believe Mr. Bingley's being **imposed** on, than that Mr. Wickham should **invent** such a history of himself as he gave me last night; names, **facts**, everything mentioned without **ceremony**. If it be not so, let Mr. Darcy **contradict** it. Besides, there was truth in his looks."

"It is difficult indeed--it is **distressing**. One does not know what to think."

"I **beg** your pardon; one **knows** exactly what to think."

But Jane could think with **certainty** on only one point--that Mr. Bingley, if he *had* been imposed on, would have much to suffer when the affair became public.

The two young ladies were summoned from the **shrubbery**, where this conversation passed, by the arrival of the very persons of whom they had been speaking; Mr. Bingley and his sisters came to give their **personal** invitation for the long-expected ball at Netherfield, which was fixed for the following Tuesday. The two ladies were delighted to see their dear friend again, called it an age since they had met, and repeatedly asked what she had been doing with herself since their separation. To the rest of the family they paid little attention; avoiding Mrs. **Bennet** as much as possible, saying not much to Elizabeth, and nothing at all to the others. They were soon gone again, **rising** from their seats with an **activity** which took their brother by surprise, and hurrying off as if eager to escape from Mrs. Bennet's civilities.

The prospect of the Netherfield ball was extremely **agreeable** to every female of the family. Mrs. Bennet chose to consider it as given in **compliment** to her eldest daughter, and was particularly **flattered** by receiving the invitation from Mr. Bingley himself, instead of a **ceremonious** card. Jane pictured to herself a happy evening in the society of her two friends, and the attentions of her brother; and Elizabeth thought with pleasure of dancing a great deal with Mr. Wickham, and of seeing a **confirmation** of everything in Mr. Darcy's look and **behavior**.

Italian

activity: attività, occupazione.
agreeable: gradevole, piacevole, amabile.
beg: mendicare, mendicano, mendica, mendicate, mendico, mendichiamo, mendichi, chiedere, elemosinare, supplicare.
behavior: condotta, comportamento.
bennet: cariofillata, erba benedetta.
ceremonious: cerimonioso.
ceremony: cerimonia.
certainty: certezza.

compliment: complimento.
confirmation: conferma.
contradict: contraddire, contraddiciamo, contraddite, contraddico, contraddici, contraddi', contraddicono.
deceived: ingannato, truffato.
distressing: doloroso, penoso, angoscioso.
excessively: eccessivamente.
facts: fatti.
flattered: lusingato.

humanity: umanità.
imposed: imposto.
invent: inventare, inventano, inventate, inventi, inventiamo, invento, inventa.
knows: conosce, sa.
personal: personale, proprio.
rising: aumento, salita, sorgere, sorgente, levata, ascendente, ascesa, nascente, sommossa, levante, crescita.
shrubbery: boschetto.

The happiness **anticipated** by Catherine and Lydia **depended** less on any single **event**, or any particular person, for though they each, like Elizabeth, meant to dance half the evening with Mr. Wickham, he was by no means the only partner who could **satisfy** them, and a ball was, at any rate, a ball. And even Mary could assure her family that she had no **disinclination** for it.

"While I can have my mornings to myself," said she, "it is enough--I think it is no sacrifice to join occasionally in evening engagements. Society has **claims** on us all; and I **profess** myself one of those who consider intervals of **recreation** and amusement as desirable for everybody."

Elizabeth's spirits were so high on this occasion, that though she did not often speak **unnecessarily** to Mr. Collins, she could not help asking him whether he intended to **accept** Mr. Bingley's invitation, and if he did, whether he would think it proper to join in the evening's amusement; and she was rather surprised to find that he entertained no **scruple whatever** on that head, and was very far from dreading a **rebuke** either from the Archbishop, or Lady Catherine de Bourgh, by venturing to dance.

"I am by no means of the opinion, I assure you," said he, "that a ball of this kind, given by a young man of character, to respectable people, can have any **evil** tendency; and I am so far from objecting to dancing myself, that I shall hope to be honoured with the **hands** of all my fair cousins in the course of the evening; and I take this opportunity of **soliciting** yours, Miss Elizabeth, for the two first dances **especially**, a preference which I trust my cousin Jane will attribute to the right **cause**, and not to any **disrespect** for her."

Elizabeth felt herself completely taken in. She had **fully proposed** being engaged by Mr. Wickham for those very dances; and to have Mr. Collins instead! her **liveliness** had never been worse timed. There was no help for it, however. Mr. Wickham's happiness and her own were **perforce delayed** a little longer, and Mr. Collins's proposal accepted with as good a **grace** as she could. She was not the better pleased with his gallantry from the idea it suggested of something more. It now first struck her, that *she* was **selected** from among her sisters as **worthy** of being mistress of Hunsford Parsonage, and of **assisting** to form a

Italian

accept: accettare, accettano, accetto, accettiamo, accetti, accettate, accetta, accogliere.
anticipated: anticipato.
assisting: assistendo, aiutando.
cause: causa, causare, provocare.
claims: rivendicazioni.
delayed: ritardato.
depended: dipeso.
disinclination: avversione.
disrespect: mancanza di rispetto.
especially: soprattutto, specialmente, principalmente.
event: evento, avvenimento.
evil: male, cattivo, malvagio.
fully: completamente, pienamente.
grace: grazia.
hands: mani.
liveliness: vivacità.
perforce: necessariamente.
profess: dichiarare, professare.
proposed: proposto.
rebuke: biasimare, disapprovare, riprendere, sgridare, rimproverare.
recreation: ricreazione.
satisfy: soddisfare, accontentare, soddisfano, soddisfiamo, soddisfa, soddisfate, soddisfo, accontentate, accontento, soddisfi, accontentano.
scruple: scrupolo.
selected: selezionato, scelto.
soliciting: adescamento, sollecitando.
unnecessarily: inutilmente.
whatever: qualunque, qualsiasi cosa, qualunque cosa.
worthy: degno, meritevole.

quadrille table at Rosings, in the absence of more **eligible** visitors. The idea soon reached to conviction, as she observed his **increasing** civilities **toward** herself, and heard his frequent attempt at a **compliment** on her **wit** and **vivacity;** and though more **astonished** than **gratified** herself by this effect of her charms, it was not long before her mother gave her to understand that the **probability** of their **marriage** was extremely **agreeable** to *her.* Elizabeth, however, did not choose to take the **hint,** being well aware that a serious **dispute** must be the consequence of any reply. Mr. Collins might never make the offer, and till he did, it was **useless** to **quarrel** about him.

If there had not been a Netherfield ball to **prepare** for and talk of, the younger Miss Bennets would have been in a very **pitiable** state at this time, for from the day of the **invitation,** to the day of the ball, there was such a **succession** of rain as **prevented** their walking to Meryton once. No aunt, no officers, no **news** could be **sought** after--the very shoe-roses for Netherfield were got by **proxy.** Even Elizabeth might have found some **trial** of her **patience** in weather which totally **suspended** the improvement of her **acquaintance** with Mr. Wickham; and nothing less than a dance on Tuesday, could have made such a Friday, Saturday, Sunday, and Monday **endurable** to Kitty and Lydia.

Italian

acquaintance: conoscenza, conoscente.
agreeable: gradevole, piacevole, amabile.
astonished: stupito, si stupito.
compliment: complimento.
dispute: controversia.
eligible: eleggibile.
endurable: sopportabile, tollerabile.
gratified: gratificato.
hint: alludere, suggerimento, allusione, cenno.
increasing: crescente, in aumento.

invitation: invito.
marriage: matrimonio.
news: notizie, novità, notizia.
patience: pazienza.
pitiable: pietoso.
prepare: preparare, prepari, prepariamo, preparate, preparano, prepara, preparo, allestire, allestiamo, allestisci, allestisco.
prevented: impedito, prevenuto.
probability: probabilità.
proxy: procura, procuratore,

mandatario.
quadrille: quadriglia.
quarrel: lite, litigare, bisticciare, bisticcio, litigio.
sought: cercato.
succession: successione.
suspended: sospeso.
toward: verso, a.
trial: prova, esperimento.
useless: inutile, inservibile.
vivacity: vivacità.
wit: arguzia.

CHAPTER 18

Till Elizabeth **entered** the drawing-room at Netherfield, and looked in **vain** for Mr. Wickham among the **cluster** of red coats there **assembled**, a doubt of his being present had never **occurred** to her. The **certainty** of meeting him had not been **checked** by any of those recollections that might not unreasonably have **alarmed** her. She had **dressed** with more than usual care, and prepared in the highest spirits for the **conquest** of all that remained unsubdued of his heart, **trusting** that it was not more than might be won in the course of the evening. But in an **instant** arose the **dreadful suspicion** of his being **purposely omitted** for Mr. Darcy's pleasure in the Bingleys' **invitation** to the officers; and though this was not exactly the case, the **absolute** fact of his absence was **pronounced** by his friend Denny, to whom Lydia **eagerly** applied, and who told them that Wickham had been **obliged** to go to town on business the day before, and was not yet returned; **adding**, with a significant smile, "I do not imagine his business would have called him away just now, if he had not wanted to avoid a certain gentleman here."

This part of his **intelligence**, though **unheard** by Lydia, was caught by Elizabeth, and, as it **assured** her that Darcy was not less **answerable** for Wickham's absence than if her first **surmise** had been just, every feeling of **displeasure** against the former was so **sharpened** by immediate **disappointment**, that she could hardly **reply** with **tolerable civility** to the polite

Italian

absolute: assoluto, completo.	disappunto.	**pronounced**: pronunciato.
adding: aggiungendo, addizionando.	**displeasure**: scontento, dispiacere.	**purposely**: intenzionalmente.
alarmed: allarmato.	**dreadful**: terribile.	**reply**: risposta, rispondere, replicare,
answerable: responsabile.	**dressed**: vestito.	replica.
assembled: montato, assemblato.	**eagerly**: ardentemente.	**sharpened**: affilato, acuito.
assured: assicurato, certo.	**entered**: entrato.	**surmise**: supporre, congetturare.
certainty: certezza.	**instant**: istante, momento, immediato.	**suspicion**: sospetto.
checked: quadrettato.	**intelligence**: intelligenza.	**tolerable**: tollerabile.
civility: civiltà, cortesia.	**invitation**: invito.	**trusting**: fiducioso.
cluster: gruppo, grappolo, cluster.	**obliged**: obbligato.	**unheard**: non sentito.
conquest: conquista.	**occurred**: successo, accaduto.	**vain**: vanitoso, vano.
disappointment: delusione,	**omitted**: omesso.	

inquiries which he directly afterwards approached to make. Attendance, **forbearance**, patience with Darcy, was **injury** to Wickham. She was resolved against any sort of conversation with him, and turned away with a degree of ill-humour which she could not wholly **surmount** even in speaking to Mr. Bingley, **whose** blind partiality **provoked** her.

But Elizabeth was not formed for ill-humour; and though every prospect of her own was **destroyed** for the evening, it could not **dwell** long on her spirits; and having told all her griefs to Charlotte Lucas, whom she had not seen for a week, she was soon able to make a voluntary **transition** to the **oddities** of her cousin, and to point him out to her particular notice. The first two dances, however, brought a return of **distress**; they were dances of **mortification**. Mr. Collins, **awkward** and **solemn**, apologising instead of attending, and often moving wrong without being aware of it, gave her all the shame and **misery** which a disagreeable partner for a couple of dances can give. The moment of her **release** from him was **ecstasy**.

She danced next with an officer, and had the **refreshment** of talking of Wickham, and of hearing that he was universally liked. When those dances were over, she returned to Charlotte Lucas, and was in conversation with her, when she found herself suddenly addressed by Mr. Darcy who took her so much by surprise in his **application** for her hand, that, without knowing what she did, she accepted him. He walked away again immediately, and she was left to **fret** over her own want of presence of mind; Charlotte tried to **console** her:

"I dare say you will find him very agreeable."

"Heaven **forbid**! *that* would be the greatest misfortune of all! To find a man agreeable whom one is determined to hate! Do not wish me such an evil."

When the dancing recommenced, however, and Darcy approached to claim her hand, Charlotte could not help cautioning her in a whisper, not to be a simpleton, and **allow** her fancy for Wickham to make her appear **unpleasant** in the eyes of a man ten times his consequence. Elizabeth made no answer, and took her place in the set, amazed at the **dignity** to which she was arrived in being allowed to stand opposite to Mr. Darcy, and reading in her neighbours' **looks**,

Italian

allow: permettere, permettete, permettono, permetto, permettiamo, permetti, lasciare, consentire.
application: applicazione, domanda, richiesta, programma.
awkward: goffo, sgraziato.
console: consolare, consolle, console.
destroyed: distrutto.
dignity: dignità, decoro.
distress: pericolo.
dwell: abitare, dimorare, dimorate, dimoro, dimori, dimorano, dimora,

abitiamo, abiti, abitate, abitano.
ecstasy: estasi.
forbearance: pazienza.
forbid: vietare, vieti, vietate, vietano, vietiamo, vieta, vieto, proibire, proibite, proibiamo, proibisci.
fret: agitazione, consumare, greca.
injury: ferita, lesione, danno, torto.
looks: guarda.
misery: miseria.
mortification: mortificazione.
oddities: stranezze.

provoked: spronato, incitato, provocato.
refreshment: rinfresco, ristoro.
release: liberare, rilasciare, rilascio, disinnesto, liberazione, svincolo, versione.
solemn: solenne.
surmount: sormontare.
transition: transizione, passaggio.
unpleasant: rude, spiacevole, brusco, sgradevole, scostante.
whose: di chi, il cui.

their equal **amazement** in **beholding** it. They stood for some time without speaking a word; and she began to imagine that their silence was to last through the two dances, and at first was resolved not to **break** it; till **suddenly** fancying that it would be the greater punishment to her partner to **oblige** him to talk, she made some slight observation on the dance. He replied, and was again silent. After a pause of some minutes, she addressed him a second time with:--"It is *your* turn to say something now, Mr. Darcy. I talked about the dance, and *you* ought to make some sort of remark on the size of the room, or the number of couples."

He smiled, and assured her that whatever she wished him to say should be said.

"Very well. That reply will do for the present. Perhaps by and by I may observe that private balls are much pleasanter than public ones. But *now* we may be silent."

"Do you talk by rule, then, while you are dancing?"

"Sometimes. One must speak a little, you know. It would look **odd** to be entirely silent for half an hour together; and yet for the advantage of *some*, conversation ought to be so **arranged**, as that they may have the trouble of saying as little as possible."

"Are you **consulting** your own feelings in the present case, or do you imagine that you are **gratifying** mine?"

"Both," replied Elizabeth **archly**; "for I have always seen a great **similarity** in the turn of our minds. We are each of an unsocial, **taciturn disposition**, unwilling to speak, unless we expect to say something that will amaze the whole room, and be handed down to **posterity** with all the eclat of a proverb."

"This is no very **striking resemblance** of your own character, I am sure," said he. "How near it may be to *mine*, I **cannot** pretend to say. *you* think it a faithful **portrait** undoubtedly."

"I must not **decide** on my own performance."

Italian

amaze: sbalordire, sbalordiamo, sbalordisci, sbalordisco, sbalordiscono, sbalordite, stupire, si stupiscono, ci stupiamo, si stupisci, si stupite.
amazement: stupore, meraviglia.
archly: arco.
arranged: sistemato, predisposto, ordinato.
beholding: guardando.
break: rompere, rottura, spezzare, rompersi, frattura, pausa, schiantare,

infrangere, sosta, spaccare.
cannot: non potere.
consulting: consultando, interpellando, consultare.
decide: decidere, decidono, decidete, decidi, decidiamo, decido.
disposition: disposizione, predisposizione, ingegno, talento.
gratifying: gratificando, gratificante.
oblige: obbligare, obblighiamo, obbliga, obbligano, obbligate, obblighi, obbligo.

odd: strano, dispari.
portrait: ritratto, verticale.
posterity: posterità.
resemblance: somiglianza, rassomiglianza.
similarity: somiglianza, similarità.
striking: impressionante.
suddenly: improvvisamente, ad un tratto.
taciturn: taciturno.

He made no answer, and they were again silent till they had gone down the dance, when he asked her if she and her sisters did not very often walk to Meryton. She answered in the **affirmative**, and, unable to **resist** the **temptation**, added, "When you met us there the other day, we had just been forming a new acquaintance."

The effect was **immediate**. A deeper shade of hauteur **overspread** his features, but he said not a word, and Elizabeth, though **blaming** herself for her own weakness, could not go on. At length Darcy spoke, and in a **constrained** manner said, "Mr. Wickham is **blessed** with such happy manners as may **ensure** his *making* friends--whether he may be equally capable of *retaining* them, is less certain."

"He has been so unlucky as to lose *your* friendship," replied Elizabeth with **emphasis**, "and in a manner which he is likely to suffer from all his life."

Darcy made no answer, and seemed **desirous** of **changing** the subject. At that moment, Sir William Lucas appeared close to them, meaning to pass through the set to the other side of the room; but on **perceiving** Mr. Darcy, he stopped with a bow of superior **courtesy** to compliment him on his dancing and his partner.

"I have been most highly gratified indeed, my dear sir. Such very superior dancing is not often seen. It is evident that you **belong** to the first circles. Allow me to say, however, that your fair partner does not disgrace you, and that I must hope to have this pleasure often repeated, especially when a certain desirable event, my dear Eliza (glancing at her sister and Bingley) shall take place. What **congratulations** will then flow in! I **appeal** to Mr. Darcy:--but let me not **interrupt** you, sir. You will not thank me for **detaining** you from the **bewitching** converse of that young lady, whose **bright** eyes are also **upbraiding** me."

The latter part of this address was scarcely heard by Darcy; but Sir William's **allusion** to his friend seemed to **strike** him forcibly, and his eyes were directed with a very serious expression towards Bingley and Jane, who were dancing together. Recovering himself, however, **shortly**, he turned to his partner, and said, "Sir William's interruption has made me forget what we were talking of."

Italian

affirmative: affermativo.
allusion: allusione.
appeal: appello, impugnazione, preghiera, ricorso, domanda, attrazione.
belong: appartenere, appartieni, apparteniamo, appartengono, appartenete, appartengo.
bewitching: incantando, affascinante.
blaming: biasimare.
blessed: benedetto, beato.
bright: brillante, luminoso,

splendente, chiaro.
changing: cambiare.
congratulations: congratulazioni.
constrained: costretto.
courtesy: cortesia.
desirous: desideroso.
detaining: ritenendo.
emphasis: enfasi.
ensure: assicurare, assicura, assicurano, assicurate, assicuri, assicuriamo, assicuro, garantire.
immediate: immediato.

interrupt: interrompere, interruzione.
overspread: coprire, cospargere.
perceiving: percependo, scorgendo, intravedendo.
resist: resistere, resistete, resistono, resisto, resistiamo, resisti.
retaining: ritenendo, trattenendo.
shortly: prossimamente.
strike: picchiare, colpire, battere, sciopero, scioperare, fare sciopero.
temptation: tentazione.
upbraiding: rimproverando.

"I do not think we were **speaking** at all. Sir William could not have **interrupted** two people in the room who had less to say for themselves. We have tried two or three subjects already without success, and what we are to talk of next I **cannot** imagine."

"What think you of books?" said he, smiling.

"Books--oh! no. I am sure we never read the same, or not with the same feelings."

"I am sorry you think so; but if that be the case, there can at least be no want of subject. We may **compare** our different opinions."

"No--I cannot talk of books in a ball-room; my head is always full of something else."

"The *present* always **occupies** you in such scenes--does it?" said he, with a look of doubt.

"Yes, always," she replied, without **knowing** what she said, for her thoughts had **wandered** far from the subject, as soon **afterwards** appeared by her suddenly **exclaiming**, "I remember **hearing** you once say, Mr. Darcy, that you hardly ever forgave, that you **resentment** once created was unappeasable. You are very **cautious**, I suppose, as to its *being created*."

"I am," said he, with a firm voice.

"And never allow yourself to be **blinded** by prejudice?"

"I hope not."

"It is particularly **incumbent** on those who never change their opinion, to be **secure** of **judging properly** at first."

"May I **ask** to what these questions tend?"

"Merely to the **illustration** of *your* character," said she, endeavouring to **shake** off her **gravity**. "I am **trying** to make it out."

"And what is your success?"

She shook her head. "I do not get on at all. I hear such different **accounts** of you as **puzzle** me exceedingly."

Italian

accounts: clienti, situazione contabile.
afterwards: dopo, dietro, in seguito, successivamente.
ask: chiedere, chiedi, chiediamo, chiedo, chiedete, chiedono, domandare, domando, domandate, domandi, domandiamo.
blinded: accecato.
cannot: non potere.
cautious: cauto, prudente.
compare: confrontare, confronta, confrontiamo, confronti, confrontano,

confrontate, confronto, paragonare, paragono, paragona, paragonate.
exclaiming: esclamando.
gravity: gravità.
hearing: udendo, sentendo, udito, udienza, ascolto.
illustration: illustrazione.
incumbent: incombente.
interrupted: interrotto, sospeso.
judging: giudicare.
knowing: conoscendo, sapendo.
occupies: occupa.

properly: propriamente.
puzzle: puzzle, enigma, confondere, rendere perplesso, rompicapo.
resentment: risentimento, astio.
secure: fissare, fissa, fissano, fissate, fissi, fissiamo, fisso, sicuro, assicurare.
shake: scuotere, scuotono, scuoto, scuotiamo, scuoti, scuotete, scossa.
speaking: parlando, parlare.
trying: duro, difficile, tentare.
wandered: vagato.

"I can readily believe," answered he gravely, "that **reports** may vary greatly with respect to me; and I could wish, Miss Bennet, that you were not to **sketch** my character at the present moment, as there is reason to **fear** that the **performance** would **reflect** no credit on either."

"But if I do not take your **likeness** now, I may never have another opportunity."

"I would by no means **suspend** any pleasure of yours," he coldly replied. She said no more, and they went down the other dance and parted in silence; and on each side dissatisfied, though not to an equal degree, for in Darcy's **breast** there was a tolerable powerful feeling towards her, which soon **procured** her pardon, and directed all his **anger** against another.

They had not long separated, when Miss Bingley came towards her, and with an expression of civil **disdain accosted** her:

"So, Miss Eliza, I hear you are quite delighted with George Wickham! Your sister has been talking to me about him, and asking me a thousand questions; and I find that the young man quite **forgot** to tell you, among his other **communication**, that he was the son of old Wickham, the late Mr. Darcy's **steward**. Let me recommend you, however, as a friend, not to give **implicit** confidence to all his assertions; for as to Mr. Darcy's using him ill, it is perfectly false; for, on the contrary, he has always been remarkably kind to him, though George Wickham has **treated** Mr. Darcy in a most **infamous** manner. I do not know the particulars, but I know very well that Mr. Darcy is not in the least to blame, that he **cannot** bear to hear George Wickham mentioned, and that though my brother thought that he could not well avoid including him in his invitation to the officers, he was excessively glad to find that he had taken himself out of the way. His coming into the country at all is a most **insolent** thing, indeed, and I wonder how he could **presume** to do it. I pity you, Miss Eliza, for this discovery of your favourite's guilt; but really, considering his **descent**, one could not expect much better."

"His guilt and his descent appear by your account to be the same," said Elizabeth **angrily**; "for I have heard you accuse him of nothing worse than of

Italian

accosted: abbordato, accostato, avvicinato.
anger: collera, rabbia, ira.
angrily: irosamente.
breast: petto, seno, mammella.
cannot: non potere.
communication: comunicazione, annunzio, comunicato.
descent: discesa, discendenza.
disdain: sdegno, sdegnare.
fear: paura, temere, angoscia, timore, aver timore.

forgot: dimenticato.
implicit: implicito.
infamous: infame.
insolent: insolente.
likeness: somiglianza, rassomiglianza.
performance: prestazione, adempimento, prestazioni, esecuzione, rappresentazione.
presume: supporre, supponiamo, supponi, suppongono, suppongo, supponete, presumere, presumiamo, presumo, presumi, presumete.

procured: procurato.
reflect: riflettere, rifletti, riflettiamo, rifletto, riflettono, riflettete.
reports: relazioni.
sketch: schizzo, abbozzare, bozzetto, disegno, abbozzo, progetto, progettare, schema.
steward: maggiordomo, dispensiere.
suspend: sospendere, sospendi, sospendono, sospendiamo, sospendete, sospendo.
treated: trattato.

being the son of Mr. Darcy's **steward**, and of *that*, I can **assure** you, he informed me himself."

"I **beg** your pardon," replied Miss Bingley, turning away with a **sneer**. "Excuse my interference--it was kindly meant."

"Insolent girl!" said Elizabeth to herself. "You are much mistaken if you expect to influence me by such a **paltry attack** as this. I see nothing in it but your own **wilful ignorance** and the **malice** of Mr. Darcy." She then sought her eldest sister, who has **undertaken** to make inquiries on the same subject of Bingley. Jane met her with a smile of such sweet **complacency**, a **glow** of such happy expression, as sufficiently **marked** how well she was satisfied with the occurrences of the evening. Elizabeth instantly read her feelings, and at that moment **solicitude** for Wickham, **resentment** against his enemies, and everything else, gave way before the hope of Jane's being in the fairest way for happiness.

"I want to know," said she, with a **countenance** no less smiling than her sister's, "what you have learnt about Mr. Wickham. But perhaps you have been too **pleasantly** engaged to think of any third person; in which case you may be sure of my pardon."

"No," replied Jane, "I have not forgotten him; but I have nothing satisfactory to tell you. Mr. Bingley does not know the whole of his history, and is quite **ignorant** of the circumstances which have **principally offended** Mr. Darcy; but he will **vouch** for the good conduct, the **probity**, and honour of his friend, and is perfectly convinced that Mr. Wickham has **deserved** much less attention from Mr. Darcy than he has received; and I am sorry to say by his account as well as his sister's, Mr. Wickham is by no means a respectable young man. I am afraid he has been very **imprudent**, and has deserved to lose Mr. Darcy's regard."

"Mr. Bingley does not know Mr. Wickham himself?"

"No; he never saw him till the other morning at Meryton."

"This account then is what he has received from Mr. Darcy. I am satisfied. But what does he say of the living?"

Italian

assure: assicurare, assicura, assicuriamo, assicurate, assicuri, assicurano, assicuro, garantire.
attack: attacco, attaccare, assalto, aggredire, assalire, aggressione, accesso.
beg: mendicare, mendicano, mendica, mendicate, mendico, mendichiamo, mendichi, chiedere, elemosinare, supplicare.
complacency: compiacimento.
countenance: approvare, viso.

deserved: meritato.
glow: ardore.
ignorance: ignoranza.
ignorant: ignorante.
imprudent: imprudente.
malice: malevolenza, livore, dolo, malizia, malignità.
marked: marcato, contrassegnato.
offended: offeso, insultato, oltraggiato.
paltry: meschino.
pleasantly: piacevolmente.

principally: principalmente, soprattutto.
probity: probità.
resentment: risentimento, astio.
sneer: sogghigno, sogghignare, scherno.
solicitude: sollecitudine.
steward: maggiordomo, dispensiere.
undertaken: intrapreso.
vouch: attestare, attestano, attestate, attesti, attestiamo, attesto, attesta.
wilful: intenzionale, testardo.

"He does not exactly **recollect** the circumstances, though he has heard them from Mr. Darcy more than once, but he **believes** that it was left to him *conditionally* only."

"I have not a doubt of Mr. Bingley's sincerity," said Elizabeth **warmly**; "but you must excuse my not being convinced by assurances only. Mr. Bingley's **defense** of his friend was a very able one, I dare say; but since he is **unacquainted** with several **parts** of the **story**, and has learnt the rest from that friend himself, I shall venture to still think of both gentlemen as I did before."

She then changed the **discourse** to one more **gratifying** to each, and on which there could be no difference of **sentiment**. Elizabeth listened with delight to the happy, though **modest** hopes which Jane **entertained** of Mr. Bingley's regard, and said all in her power to **heighten** her confidence in it. On their being joined by Mr. Bingley himself, Elizabeth withdrew to Miss Lucas; to whose inquiry after the **pleasantness** of her last partner she had scarcely replied, before Mr. Collins came up to them, and told her with great **exultation** that he had just been so fortunate as to make a most important discovery.

"I have found out," said he, "by a **singular accident**, that there is now in the room a near relation of my **patroness**. I happened to **overhear** the gentleman himself mentioning to the young lady who does the honours of the house the names of his cousin Miss de Bourgh, and of her mother Lady Catherine. How **wonderfully** these sort of things occur! Who would have thought of my meeting with, perhaps, a nephew of Lady Catherine de Bourgh in this assembly! I am most **thankful** that the discovery is made in time for me to pay my respects to him, which I am now going to do, and trust he will excuse my not having done it before. My **total** ignorance of the connection must **plead** my apology."

"You are not going to introduce yourself to Mr. Darcy!"

"Indeed I am. I shall **entreat** his pardon for not having done it **earlier**. I believe him to be Lady Catherine's *nephew*. It will be in my power to assure him that her **ladyship** was quite well yesterday se'nnight."

Italian

accident: incidente, accidente, disgrazia, sinistro, infortunio.
believes: crede.
conditionally: condizionalmente.
defense: difesa.
discourse: discorso.
earlier: prima.
entertained: intrattenuto.
entreat: supplicare.
exultation: esultanza.
gratifying: gratificando, gratificante.
heighten: innalzare.

ladyship: signoria.
modest: modesto, pudico.
overhear: origlia, origliate, origlio, origli, origliano, origliamo, origliare, udire per caso.
parts: ricambi, parte.
patroness: patrona, patronessa.
plead: peroro, supplico, supplichiamo, supplichi, supplicate, supplica, peroriamo, perori, perorano, perora, imploro.
pleasantness: piacevolezza.

recollect: rammenta, rammentano, rammentate, rammenti, rammentiamo, rammento, rammentare, ricordarsi.
sentiment: sentimento.
singular: singolare, strano.
story: storia, piano, racconto.
thankful: riconoscente, grato.
total: totale, completo.
unacquainted: non abituato.
warmly: caldamente, calorosamente.
wonderfully: meravigliosamente.

Elizabeth tried hard to **dissuade** him from such a scheme, assuring him that Mr. Darcy would consider his **addressing** him without introduction as an impertinent freedom, rather than a compliment to his aunt; that it was not in the least necessary there should be any notice on either side; and that if it were, it must belong to Mr. Darcy, the superior in consequence, to begin the acquaintance. Mr. Collins listened to her with the determined air of following his own inclination, and, when she **ceased** speaking, replied thus:

"My dear Miss Elizabeth, I have the **highest** opinion in the world in your excellent judgement in all matters within the **scope** of your understanding; but **permit** me to say, that there must be a wide difference between the established forms of ceremony amongst the **laity**, and those which **regulate** the **clergy**; for, give me leave to observe that I consider the **clerical** office as equal in point of dignity with the highest rank in the kingdom--provided that a proper humility of behaviour is at the same time **maintained**. You must therefore allow me to follow the **dictates** of my **conscience** on this occasion, which **leads** me to **perform** what I look on as a point of duty. Pardon me for neglecting to **profit** by your advice, which on every other subject shall be my constant **guide**, though in the case before us I consider myself more fitted by education and **habitual** study to decide on what is right than a young lady like yourself." And with a low bow he left her to attack Mr. Darcy, whose **reception** of his **advances** she eagerly **watched**, and whose astonishment at being so addressed was very evident. Her cousin prefaced his speech with a solemn bow and though she could not hear a word of it, she felt as if hearing it all, and saw in the **motion** of his lips the words "apology," "Hunsford," and "Lady Catherine de Bourgh." It vexed her to see him expose himself to such a man. Mr. Darcy was eyeing him with **unrestrained** wonder, and when at last Mr. Collins allowed him time to speak, replied with an air of distant civility. Mr. Collins, however, was not **discouraged** from speaking again, and Mr. Darcy's contempt seemed abundantly increasing with the length of his second speech, and at the end of it he only made him a slight bow, and moved another way. Mr. Collins then returned to Elizabeth.

Italian

addressing: indirizzamento.
advances: avanzamenti.
ceased: cessato.
clergy: clero.
clerical: clericale.
conscience: coscienza.
dictates: detta.
discouraged: impaurito, spaventato, scoraggiato.
dissuade: dissuadere, dissuadi, dissuadono, dissuadiamo, dissuadete, dissuado.

guide: guidare, guida, condurre, cicerone.
habitual: abituale.
highest: sommo.
laity: laicato.
leads: conduce, guida.
maintained: mantenuto, conservato.
motion: movimento, mozione, moto.
perform: eseguire, eseguono, eseguo, eseguite, eseguiamo, esegui, compiere, fare, apparire, entrare, commettere.

permit: permettere, permesso, autorizzazione.
profit: profitto, guadagno, beneficio, vantaggio, utile, approfittare, profittare, tornaconto.
reception: ricezione, ricevimento, accettazione, reception, portineria.
regulate: regolare, regolano, regolate, regoli, regoliamo, regolo, regola.
scope: portata, scopo, ambito, campo.
unrestrained: non represso.
watched: guardato.

"I have no reason, I assure you," said he, "to be **dissatisfied** with my reception. Mr. Darcy seemed much pleased with the attention. He answered me with the **utmost civility,** and even paid me the compliment of saying that he was so well convinced of Lady Catherine's **discernment** as to be certain she could never **bestow** a favour **unworthily.** It was really a very handsome thought. Upon the whole, I am much pleased with him."

As Elizabeth had no longer any interest of her own to **pursue,** she turned her attention almost entirely on her sister and Mr. Bingley; and the **train** of **agreeable** reflections which her observations gave birth to, made her perhaps almost as happy as Jane. She saw her in idea settled in that very house, in all the **felicity** which a marriage of **true** affection could bestow; and she felt capable, under such circumstances, of endeavouring even to like Bingley's two sisters. Her mother's thoughts she plainly saw were **bent** the same way, and she determined not to venture near her, **lest** she might hear too much. When they sat down to supper, therefore, she considered it a most unlucky perverseness which placed them within one of each other; and **deeply** was she **vexed** to find that her mother was talking to that one person (Lady Lucas) freely, **openly**, and of nothing else but her **expectation** that Jane would soon be married to Mr. Bingley. It was an animating subject, and Mrs. **Bennet** seemed incapable of **fatigue** while **enumerating** the advantages of the **match.** His being such a charming young man, and so rich, and living but three miles from them, were the first **points** of self-gratulation; and then it was such a comfort to think how fond the two sisters were of Jane, and to be certain that they must desire the connection as much as she could do. It was, moreover, such a **promising** thing for her younger daughters, as Jane's marrying so greatly must throw them in the way of other rich men; and **lastly**, it was so pleasant at her time of life to be able to **consign** her single daughters to the care of their sister, that she might not be obliged to go into company more than she liked. It was necessary to make this circumstance a **matter** of pleasure, because on such occasions it is the **etiquette**; but no one was less likely than Mrs. Bennet to find comfort in staying home at any period of her life. She **concluded** with many good wishes that Lady Lucas might soon be

Italian

agreeable: gradevole, piacevole, amabile.
bennet: cariofillata, erba benedetta.
bent: curvo, piegato.
bestow: tributare, concedere.
civility: civiltà, cortesia.
concluded: concluso.
consign: consegnare.
deeply: profondamente.
discernment: discernimento.
dissatisfied: insoddisfatto.
enumerating: enumerando.

etiquette: etichetta, galateo.
expectation: attesa, aspettativa.
fatigue: fatica, affaticare, stancare, stanchezza, affaticamento.
felicity: felicità.
lastly: infine, ultimamente, per finire.
lest: affinchè non, per paura che.
match: fiammifero, accoppiare, corrispondenza, partita, cerino.
matter: materia, faccenda, affare, questione, importare, caso, sostanza.
openly: apertamente.

points: punti, scambio.
promising: promettendo, promettente.
pursue: perseguire, persegui, perseguite, perseguo, perseguiamo, perseguono, perseguitare, inseguire.
train: treno, addestrare, il treno, ammaestrare, educare.
true: vero.
unworthily: indegnamente.
utmost: massimo.
vexed: irritato, indispettito, vessato, contrariato.

equally fortunate, though **evidently** and **triumphantly believing** there was no chance of it.

In vain did Elizabeth endeavour to **check** the rapidity of her mother's words, or persuade her to **describe** her felicity in a less **audible** whisper; for, to her **inexpressible** vexation, she could perceive that the chief of it was overheard by Mr. Darcy, who sat opposite to them. Her mother only scolded her for being nonsensical.

"What is Mr. Darcy to me, pray, that I should be afraid of him? I am sure we **owe** him no such particular civility as to be obliged to say nothing *he* may not like to hear."

"For heaven's sake, madam, speak lower. What advantage can it be for you to offend Mr. Darcy? You will never recommend yourself to his friend by so doing!"

Nothing that she could say, however, had any influence. Her mother would talk of her views in the same intelligible tone. Elizabeth **blushed** and blushed again with **shame** and vexation. She could not help frequently glancing her eye at Mr. Darcy, though every glance convinced her of what she dreaded; for though he was not always looking at her mother, she was convinced that his attention was **invariably** fixed by her. The expression of his face changed **gradually** from **indignant** contempt to a **composed** and **steady** gravity.

At length, however, Mrs. Bennet had no more to say; and Lady Lucas, who had been long **yawning** at the **repetition** of delights which she saw no **likelihood** of sharing, was left to the comforts of cold ham and **chicken**. Elizabeth now began to **revive**. But not long was the interval of tranquillity; for, when supper was over, singing was talked of, and she had the mortification of seeing Mary, after very little **entreaty**, preparing to oblige the company. By many **significant** looks and silent entreaties, did she endeavour to prevent such a **proof** of **complaisance**, but in vain; Mary would not understand them; such an opportunity of exhibiting was delightful to her, and she began her song. Elizabeth's eyes were fixed on her with most painful sensations, and she watched her progress through the several stanzas with an **impatience** which was very ill

Italian

audible: udibile.
believing: credendo, credere.
blushed: arrossito.
check: verificare, assegno, controllare, assegno bancario, controllo, verifica.
chicken: pollo, gallina, il pollo, pollastro.
complaisance: compiacenza.
composed: composto.
describe: descrivere, descrivete, descrivi, descrivo, descriviamo, descrivono.

entreaty: preghiera, domanda, supplica.
evidently: evidentemente.
gradually: gradualmente, poco a poco.
ham: prosciutto, il prosciutto.
impatience: impazienza.
indignant: indignato.
inexpressible: inesprimibile.
invariably: invariabilmente.
likelihood: verosimiglianza, probabilità.
owe: dovere.

proof: prova, bozza, dimostrazione, provino, impermeabilizzare, resistente.
repetition: ripetizione, replica.
revive: rianimare, rianima, rianimano, rianimate, rianimi, rianimiamo, rianimo, rinascere.
significant: significativo, importante.
steady: fisso.
triumphantly: trionfalmente.
yawning: sbadiglio, sbadigliando.

rewarded at their close; for Mary, on receiving, amongst the thanks of the table, the hint of a hope that she might be prevailed on to favour them again, after the pause of half a minute began another. Mary's powers were by no means fitted for such a display; her voice was weak, and her manner affected. Elizabeth was in agonies. She looked at Jane, to see how she bore it; but Jane was very composedly talking to Bingley. She looked at his two sisters, and saw them making **signs** of **derision** at each other, and at Darcy, who continued, however, imperturbably grave. She looked at her father to entreat his **interference**, lest Mary should be singing all night. He took the hint, and when Mary had **finished** her second song, said **aloud**, "That will do extremely well, child. You have **delighted** us long enough. Let the other young ladies have time to exhibit."

Mary, though **pretending** not to hear, was somewhat disconcerted; and Elizabeth, sorry for her, and sorry for her father's speech, was afraid her anxiety had done no good. Others of the party were now applied to.

"If I," said Mr. Collins, "were so fortunate as to be able to sing, I should have great pleasure, I am sure, in obliging the company with an air; for I consider **music** as a very **innocent diversion**, and perfectly **compatible** with the profession of a clergyman. I do not mean, however, to assert that we can be justified in **devoting** too much of our time to music, for there are certainly other things to be attended to. The rector of a parish has much to do. In the first place, he must make such an **agreement** for tithes as a may be **beneficial** to himself and not **offensive** to his **patron**. He must write his own sermons; and the time that remains will not be too much for his parish duties, and the care and improvement of his **dwelling**, which he cannot be excused from making as a comfortable as possible. And I do not think it of light importance that he should have attentive and **conciliatory** manner towards everybody, especially towards those to whom he owes his preferment. I cannot **acquit** him of that duty; nor could I think well of the man who should **omit** an occasion of **testifying** his respect towards anybody connected with the family." And with a bow to Mr. Darcy, he concluded his speech, which had been spoken so loud as a to be heard by half the room. Many stared--many smiled; but no one looked more amused

Italian

acquit: assolvere, assolvete, assolviamo, assolvo, assolvono, assolvi.
agreement: accordo, patto, accomodamento, contratto, convenzione, consenso, concordanza.
beneficial: giovevole, che reca giovamento, che fa bene, benefico, vantaggioso.
compatible: compatibile.
conciliatory: conciliativo.
derision: derisione.

devoting: dedicando, consacrando.
diversion: diversione, deviazione, dirottamento.
dwelling: dimorando, abitando, dimora, abitazione.
finished: finito, pronto, ultimato, terminato, rifinito.
innocent: innocente.
interference: interferenza.
light: luce, leggero, accendere, chiaro, illuminare, fanale, lampada, luminoso, debole.

loud: forte, alto, rumoroso.
music: musica, la musica.
offensive: offensivo, offensiva.
omit: omettere, omettete, ometti, omettiamo, omettono, trascurare, ometto.
patron: patrono, mecenate.
pretending: fingendo.
signs: segnaletica.
testifying: testimoniando.

than Mr. **Bennet** himself, while his wife **seriously commended** Mr. Collins for having spoken so **sensibly**, and observed in a half-whisper to Lady Lucas, that he was a remarkably clever, good kind of young man.

To Elizabeth it appeared that, had her family made an agreement to expose themselves as a much as a they could during the evening, it would have been impossible for them to play their parts with more spirit or finer success; and happy did she think it for Bingley and her sister that some of the **exhibition** had escaped his notice, and that his feelings were not of a sort to be much **distressed** by the folly which he must have witnessed. That his two sisters and Mr. Darcy, however, should have such an opportunity of **ridiculing** her relations, was bad enough, and she could not determine whether the silent contempt of the gentleman, or the **insolent** smiles of the ladies, were more **intolerable**.

The rest of the evening brought her little amusement. She was teased by Mr. Collins, who continued most perseveringly by her side, and though he could not **prevail** on her to dance with him again, put it out of her power to dance with others. In **vain** did she **entreat** him to stand up with somebody else, and offer to introduce him to any young lady in the room. He assured her, that as to dancing, he was perfectly indifferent to it; that his chief object was by delicate attentions to recommend himself to her and that he should therefore make a point of remaining **close** to her the whole evening. There was no **arguing** upon such a **project**. She owed her greatest relief to her friend Miss Lucas, who often joined them, and good-naturedly engaged Mr. Collins's conversation to herself.

She was at least free from the **offense** of Mr. Darcy's further notice; though often standing within a very short distance of her, quite **disengaged**, he never came near enough to speak. She felt it to be the **probable** consequence of her allusions to Mr. Wickham, and **rejoiced** in it.

The Longbourn party were the last of all the company to **depart**, and, by a **manoeuvre** of Mrs. Bennet, had to wait for their carriage a quarter of an hour after everybody else was **gone**, which gave them time to see how **heartily** they were wished away by some of the family. Mrs. Hurst and her sister scarcely opened their mouths, except to **complain** of **fatigue**, and were evidently

Italian

arguing: argomentando, discutendo, disputando.
bennet: cariofillata, erba benedetta.
close: chiudere, vicino, chiudo, chiudono, chiudiamo, chiudete, chiudi, prossimo, chiuso.
commended: lodato.
complain: lagnarsi, lamentarsi, lamentare.
depart: partire, partite, partiamo, parti, partono, parto, andarsene.
disengaged: disimpegnato,

disinnestato.
distressed: afflitto.
entreat: supplicare.
exhibition: esposizione, mostra, fiera.
fatigue: fatica, affaticare, stancare, stanchezza, affaticamento.
gone: andato.
heartily: cordialmente.
insolent: insolente.
intolerable: intollerabile.
manoeuvre: manovra, manovrare.
offense: offesa.

prevail: prevalere, prevalete, prevalgo, prevalgono, prevali, prevaliamo.
probable: probabile.
project: progetto, proiettare, piano, progettare.
rejoiced: allietato, gioito, rallegrato.
ridiculing: ridicolizzare.
sensibly: assennatamente.
seriously: seriamente, gravemente.
vain: vanitoso, vano.

impatient to have the house to themselves. They repulsed every attempt of Mrs. **Bennet** at conversation, and by so doing threw a **languor** over the whole party, which was very little **relieved** by the long speeches of Mr. Collins, who was complimenting Mr. Bingley and his sisters on the **elegance** of their **entertainment**, and the **hospitality** and **politeness** which had marked their behaviour to their guests. Darcy said nothing at all. Mr. Bennet, in equal silence, was **enjoying the scene**. Mr. Bingley and Jane were standing together, a little **detached** from the rest, and talked only to each other. Elizabeth **preserved** as steady a silence as either Mrs. Hurst or Miss Bingley; and even Lydia was too much **fatigued** to **utter** more than the occasional **exclamation** of "Lord, how tired I am!" accompanied by a violent yawn.

When at length they arose to take leave, Mrs. Bennet was most pressingly civil in her hope of seeing the whole family soon at Longbourn, and addressed herself especially to Mr. Bingley, to **assure** him how happy he would make them by **eating** a family dinner with them at any time, without the **ceremony** of a formal invitation. Bingley was all grateful pleasure, and he readily **engaged** for taking the earliest opportunity of waiting on her, after his return from London, **whither** he was **obliged** to go the next day for a short time.

Mrs. Bennet was perfectly satisfied, and quitted the house under the **delightful persuasion** that, **allowing** for the necessary **preparations** of settlements, new carriages, and **wedding clothes**, she should undoubtedly see her daughter settled at Netherfield in the course of three or four months. Of having another daughter married to Mr. Collins, she thought with equal **certainty**, and with considerable, though not equal, pleasure. Elizabeth was the least dear to her of all her children; and though the man and the match were quite good enough for *her*, the worth of each was eclipsed by Mr. Bingley and Netherfield.

Italian

allowing: permettendo.
assure: assicurare, assicura, assicuriamo, assicurate, assicuri, assicurano, assicuro, garantire.
bennet: cariofillata, erba benedetta.
ceremony: cerimonia.
certainty: certezza.
clothes: veste, vestiti.
delightful: delizioso, piacevole.
detached: isolato, staccato, distaccato.
eating: mangiando.
elegance: eleganza.

engaged: occupato, innestato, impegnato.
enjoying: piacendo, fruendo, godendo.
entertainment: divertimento, spettacolo.
exclamation: esclamazione.
fatigued: affaticato.
hospitality: ospitalità.
impatient: impaziente.
languor: languore.
obliged: obbligato.

persuasion: persuasione.
politeness: cortesia, garbo.
preparations: preparativi.
preserved: conservato.
relieved: alleviato.
scene: scena.
utter: totale, completo, proferire, emettere.
wedding: nozze, matrimonio, sposalizio.
whither: dove.

CHAPTER 19

The next day **opened** a new **scene** at Longbourn. Mr. Collins made his **declaration** in form. Having **resolved** to do it without loss of time, as his leave of **absence** extended only to the following Saturday, and having no feelings of **diffidence** to make it **distressing** to himself even at the moment, he set about it in a very **orderly manner**, with all the **observances**, which he **supposed** a regular part of the business. On **finding** Mrs. **Bennet**, Elizabeth, and one of the **younger** girls together, soon after **breakfast**, he **addressed** the mother in these words:

"May I hope, madam, for your interest with your fair daughter Elizabeth, when I **solicit** for the **honour** of a private audience with her in the course of this morning?"

Before Elizabeth had time for anything but a **blush** of surprise, Mrs. Bennet answered **instantly**, "Oh dear!--yes--certainly. I am sure Lizzy will be very happy--I am sure she can have no **objection**. Come, Kitty, I want you upstairs." And, **gathering** her work together, she was **hastening** away, when Elizabeth called out:

"Dear madam, do not go. I **beg** you will not go. Mr. Collins must **excuse** me. He can have nothing to say to me that **anybody** need not hear. I am going away myself."

Italian

absence: assenza, mancanza.
addressed: rivolto.
anybody: qualcuno, nessuno.
beg: mendicare, mendicano, mendica, mendicate, mendico, mendichiamo, mendichi, chiedere, elemosinare, supplicare.
bennet: cariofillata, erba benedetta.
blush: rossore, arrossire.
breakfast: colazione, prima colazione.
declaration: dichiarazione.
diffidence: timidezza.

distress: pericolo.
distressing: doloroso, penoso, angoscioso.
excuse: scusa, scusare, giustificazione, pretesto.
finding: fondendo, fondando.
gathering: convegno, raccolta.
hastening: affrettando, sollecitando.
honour: onore.
instantly: direttamente, istantaneamente, immediatamente.
manner: maniera, modo.

objection: obiezione, opposizione.
observances: osservanze.
opened: aperto.
orderly: attendente.
resolved: risolto.
scene: scena.
solicit: sollecito, sollecitare, sollecitate, solleciti, sollecitano, sollecita, sollecitiamo.
supposed: supposto.
younger: più giovane.

"No, no, nonsense, Lizzy. I desire you to stay where you are." And upon Elizabeth's seeming really, with vexed and **embarrassed** looks, about to escape, she **added**: "Lizzy, I *insist* upon your staying and hearing Mr. Collins."

Elizabeth would not **oppose** such an injunction--and a moment's consideration making her also sensible that it would be wisest to get it over as soon and as **quietly** as possible, she sat down again and tried to conceal, by **incessant** employment the feelings which were **divided** between distress and diversion. Mrs. Bennet and Kitty walked off, and as soon as they were gone, Mr. Collins began.

"Believe me, my dear Miss Elizabeth, that your **modesty**, so far from doing you any **disservice**, rather **adds** to your other perfections. You would have been less amiable in my eyes had there *not* been this little **unwillingness**; but allow me to assure you, that I have your **respected** mother's permission for this address. You can hardly doubt the **purport** of my discourse, however your natural delicacy may **lead** you to **dissemble**; my attentions have been too marked to be mistaken. Almost as soon as I entered the house, I singled you out as the companion of my **future** life. But before I am run away with by my feelings on this subject, perhaps it would be advisable for me to state my reasons for marrying--and, moreover, for coming into Hertfordshire with the **design** of **selecting** a wife, as I certainly did."

The idea of Mr. Collins, with all his solemn composure, being run away with by his feelings, made Elizabeth so near **laughing**, that she could not use the short pause he allowed in any attempt to stop him further, and he continued:

"My reasons for marrying are, first, that I think it a right thing for every clergyman in easy circumstances (like myself) to set the example of matrimony in his parish; **secondly**, that I am convinced that it will add very greatly to my happiness; and thirdly--which perhaps I ought to have mentioned earlier, that it is the particular advice and recommendation of the very noble lady whom I have the honour of calling patroness. Twice has she condescended to give me her opinion (unasked too!) on this subject; and it was but the very Saturday night before I left Hunsford--between our **pools** at **quadrille**, while Mrs. Jenkinson was

Italian

add: aggiungere, aggiungiamo, aggiungete, aggiungi, aggiungo, aggiungono, addizionare, addizioniamo, addizioni, addizionate, addizionano.
adds: aggiunge, addiziona.
design: disegno, progetto, disegnare, progettazione, design, progettare, piano, costruttive.
dissemble: dissimuli, dissimulo, dissimuliamo, dissimulano, dissimula, dissimulate, dissimulare.

disservice: danno, disservizio.
divided: diviso, separato.
embarrassed: imbarazzato.
future: futuro, avvenire.
incessant: incessante.
laughing: ridere, risata.
lead: piombo, condurre, conduciamo, conducono, conduco, conducete, conduci, guidare, guidiamo, guidano, guidate.
modesty: modestia, verecondia.
oppose: contrapporre, contrapponete,

contrapponi, contrapponiamo, contrappongono, contrappongo, opporre.
pools: piscina, totocalcio.
purport: senso, significare, significato.
quadrille: quadriglia.
quietly: tranquillamente.
respected: rispettato.
secondly: in secondo luogo, secondariamente.
selecting: selezionando.
unwillingness: renitenza, malavoglia.

arranging Miss de Bourgh's **footstool**, that she said, 'Mr. Collins, you must marry. A **clergyman** like you must marry. Choose properly, choose a **gentlewoman** for *my* sake; and for your *own*, let her be an active, useful sort of person, not brought up high, but able to make a small income go a good way. This is my advice. Find such a woman as soon as you can, bring her to Hunsford, and I will visit her.' Allow me, by the way, to observe, my fair cousin, that I do not **reckon** the notice and kindness of Lady Catherine de Bourgh as among the least of the advantages in my power to offer. You will find her manners beyond anything I can describe; and your wit and **vivacity**, I think, must be acceptable to her, especially when **tempered** with the silence and respect which her rank will **inevitably excite**. Thus much for my general intention in favour of **matrimony**; it remains to be told why my views were directed towards Longbourn instead of my own neighbourhood, where I can assure you there are many **amiable** young women. But the fact is, that being, as I am, to **inherit** this estate after the death of your honoured father (who, however, may **live** many years longer), I could not satisfy myself without resolving to choose a wife from among his daughters, that the loss to them might be as little as possible, when the **melancholy** event **takes** place--which, however, as I have already said, may not be for several years. This has been my motive, my fair cousin, and I **flatter** myself it will not sink me in your **esteem**. And now nothing remains but for me but to assure you in the most **animated language** of the **violence** of my affection. To fortune I am perfectly indifferent, and shall make no **demand** of that nature on your father, since I am well aware that it could not be complied with; and that one thousand pounds in the four per cents, which will not be yours till after your mother's **decease**, is all that you may ever be entitled to. On that head, therefore, I shall be **uniformly** silent; and you may assure yourself that no ungenerous **reproach** shall ever pass my lips when we are married."

It was absolutely necessary to interrupt him now.

"You are too hasty, sir," she cried. "You forget that I have made no answer. Let me do it without further loss of time. Accept my thanks for the compliment

Italian

amiable: amabile.
animated: animato.
clergyman: ecclesiastico, prete, curato, sacerdote.
decease: decedere, decesso.
demand: richiesta, esigere, domanda, vendita, smercio, rivendicazione, pretesa.
esteem: stima, rispetto, stimare, considerazione, considerare, rispettare, riguardo.
excite: eccitare, ecciti, eccitiamo,

eccitano, eccita, eccito, eccitate, spronare, incitare.
flatter: lusingare, lusingate, lusingo, lusinghi, lusingano, lusinghiamo, lusinga, adulare.
footstool: sgabello.
gentlewoman: signora, gentildonna.
inevitably: inevitabilmente.
inherit: ereditare, erediti, ereditiamo, ereditano, ereditate, eredito, eredita.
language: lingua, linguaggio, idioma.
live: vivere, vivete, vivono, viviamo,

vivi, vivo, abitare, abiti, abita, abitano, abitare.
matrimony: matrimonio.
melancholy: malinconia, malinconico.
reckon: contare, computare, calcolare.
reproach: rimprovero, rimproverare, riprendere.
takes: prende.
tempered: temperato.
uniformly: uniformemente.
violence: violenza.
vivacity: vivacità.

you are paying me. I am very sensible of the honour of your proposals, but it is impossible for me to do otherwise than to decline them."

"I am not now to learn," replied Mr. Collins, with a formal **wave** of the hand, "that it is usual with young ladies to reject the **addresses** of the man whom they **secretly** mean to accept, when he first **applies** for their favour; and that sometimes the **refusal** is repeated a second, or even a third time. I am therefore by no means **discouraged** by what you have just said, and shall hope to lead you to the **altar** ere long."

"Upon my word, sir," cried Elizabeth, "your hope is a rather extraordinary one after my declaration. I do **assure** you that I am not one of those young ladies (if such young ladies there are) who are so **daring** as to **risk** their happiness on the chance of being asked a second time. I am perfectly serious in my refusal. You could not make *me* happy, and I am convinced that I am the last woman in the world who could make you so. Nay, were your friend Lady Catherine to know me, I am **persuaded** she would find me in every respect ill qualified for the situation."

"Were it certain that Lady Catherine would think so," said Mr. Collins very gravely--"but I **cannot** imagine that her **ladyship** would at all **disapprove** of you. And you may be certain when I have the honour of seeing her again, I shall speak in the very highest terms of your **modesty, economy**, and other **amiable** qualification."

"Indeed, Mr. Collins, all praise of me will be **unnecessary**. You must give me leave to judge for myself, and pay me the **compliment** of **believing** what I say. I wish you very happy and very rich, and by refusing you hand, do all in my power to **prevent** your being otherwise. In making me the offer, you must have satisfied the **delicacy** of your feelings with regard to my family, and may take possession of Longbourn estate whenever it **falls**, without any self-reproach. This matter may be considered, therefore, as finally settled." And rising as she thus spoke, she would have quitted the room, had Mr. Collins not thus addressed her:

Italian

addresses: indirizzi.
altar: altare.
amiable: amabile.
applies: applica.
assure: assicurare, assicura, assicuriamo, assicurate, assicuri, assicurano, assicuro, garantire.
believing: credendo, credere.
cannot: non potere.
compliment: complimento.
daring: osando, audace.
delicacy: delicatezza.

disapprove: disapprovare, disapprova, disapprovo, disapproviamo, disapprovi, disapprovate, disapprovano, biasimare, biasima, biasimano, biasimate.
discouraged: impaurito, spaventato, scoraggiato.
economy: economia.
falls: cade.
ladyship: signoria.
modesty: modestia, verecondia.

persuaded: convinto, persuaso.
prevent: impedire, impediamo, impedisci, impedisco, impediscono, impedite, prevenire, prevenite, previeni, preveniamo, prevengono.
refusal: rifiuto.
risk: rischio, arrischiare, rischiare, cimento.
secretly: segretamente.
unnecessary: inutile, non necessario.
wave: onda, ondata, sventolare, l'onda, ondeggiare.

"When I do myself the honour of speaking to you next on the subject, I shall hope to receive a more favourable answer than you have now given me; though I am far from **accusing** you of cruelty at present, because I know it to be the established **custom** of your sex to reject a man on the first application, and perhaps you have even now said as much to **encourage** my suit as would be consistent with the true delicacy of the female character."

"Really, Mr. Collins," cried Elizabeth with some warmth, "you puzzle me exceedingly. If what I have **hitherto** said can appear to you in the form of encouragement, I know not how to express my refusal in such a way as to **convince** you of its being one."

"You must give me leave to flatter myself, my dear cousin, that your refusal of my addresses is merely words of course. My reasons for believing it are **briefly** these: It does not appear to me that my hand is **unworthy** your **acceptance**, or that the establishment I can offer would be any other than highly **desirable**. My situation in life, my connections with the family of de Bourgh, and my relationship to your own, are circumstances highly in my favour; and you should take it into further consideration, that in **spite** of your **manifold** attractions, it is by no means certain that another offer of marriage may ever be made you. Your **portion** is unhappily so small that it will in all likelihood **undo** the effects of your **loveliness** and amiable qualifications. As I must therefore **conclude** that you are not serious in your **rejection** of me, I shall choose to attribute it to your wish of increasing my love by **suspense**, **according** to the usual **practice** of elegant females."

"I do assure you, sir, that I have no pretensions whatever to that kind of elegance which **consists** in **tormenting** a respectable man. I would rather be paid the compliment of being believed sincere. I **thank** you again and again for the honour you have done me in your proposals, but to accept them is absolutely impossible. My feelings in every respect forbid it. Can I speak plainer? Do not consider me now as an elegant female, **intending** to plague you, but as a rational creature, speaking the truth from her heart."

Italian

acceptance: accettazione, accoglienza, accoglimento.
according: secondo.
accusing: accusando, caricando.
briefly: brevemente.
conclude: concludere, concludo, concludono, concludiamo, concludi, concludete.
consists: consiste, consta.
convince: convincere, convincete, convinci, convinciamo, convinco, convincono, persuadere.

custom: costume, usanza, uso, abitudine, consuetudine.
encourage: incoraggiare, incoraggio, incoraggi, incoraggia, incoraggiamo, incoraggiano, incoraggiate.
hitherto: finora.
intending: intendendo.
loveliness: bellezza.
manifold: collettore, molteplice.
portion: parte, porzione.
practice: pratica, esercizio, praticare, applicare, esercitare.

rejection: rifiuto, rigetto.
sir: signore.
spite: dispetto.
suspense: apprensione.
thank: ringraziare, ringraziano, ringraziate, ringraziamo, ringrazia, ringrazi, ringrazio.
tormenting: tormentoso, tormento.
undo: disfare, disfate, disfa', disfacciamo, disfaccio, disfai, disfanno.
unworthy: indegno.

"You are **uniformly** charming!" cried he, with an air of **awkward gallantry**; "and I am **persuaded** that when sanctioned by the **express** authority of both your **excellent** parents, my proposals will not **fail** of being acceptable."

To such **perseverance** in **wilful** self-deception Elizabeth would make no **reply**, and **immediately** and in **silence** withdrew; **determined**, if he **persisted** in **considering** her **repeated** refusals as **flattering encouragement**, to **apply** to her father, whose **negative** might be uttered in such a **manner** as to be **decisive**, and whose **behavior** at **least** could not be **mistaken** for the **affectation** and **coquetry** of an **elegant** female.

Italian

affectation: affettazione, posa.
apply: applicare, applico, applichi, applicano, applicate, applichiamo, applica.
awkward: goffo, sgraziato.
behavior: condotta, comportamento.
considering: considerando.
coquetry: civetteria.
decisive: decisivo.
determined: definito, fissato, determinato.
elegant: elegante.

encouragement: incoraggiamento.
excellent: eccellente, esimio, ottimo.
express: espresso, esprimere, esprimete, esprimi, esprimiamo, esprimo, esprimono, direttissimo.
fail: fallire, morire, mancare.
flattering: lusingando, adulatorio.
gallantry: galanteria, valore, prodezza.
immediately: immediatamente, subito, direttamente, fra poco.
least: minimo, meno.
manner: maniera, modo.

mistaken: sbagliato.
negative: negativo.
perseverance: perseveranza.
persisted: persistito.
persuaded: convinto, persuaso.
repeated: ripetuto.
reply: risposta, rispondere, replicare, replica.
silence: silenzio.
uniformly: uniformemente.
wilful: intenzionale, testardo.

CHAPTER 20

Mr. Collins was not left long to the **silent contemplation** of his successful love; for Mrs. **Bennet**, having **dawdled** about in the **vestibule** to watch for the end of the conference, no **sooner** saw Elizabeth open the door and with quick step pass her towards the **staircase**, than she **entered** the breakfast-room, and **congratulated** both him and herself in warm terms on the happy **prospect** or their nearer **connection**. Mr. Collins received and returned these felicitations with equal pleasure, and then **proceeded** to **relate** the **particulars** of their interview, with the result of which he **trusted** he had every reason to be **satisfied**, since the **refusal** which his **cousin** had steadfastly given him would **naturally** flow from her **bashful modesty** and the genuine **delicacy** of her character.

This information, however, **startled** Mrs. Bennet; she would have been **glad** to be equally satisfied that her daughter had meant to encourage him by **protesting** against his proposals, but she **dared** not believe it, and could not help saying so.

"But, depend upon it, Mr. Collins," she added, "that Lizzy shall be brought to reason. I will speak to her about it directly. She is a very **headstrong, foolish** girl, and does not know her own interest but I will *make* her know it."

"Pardon me for interrupting you, madam," cried Mr. Collins; "but if she is really headstrong and foolish, I know not whether she would **altogether** be a

Italian

altogether: tutto, complessivamente.
bashful: timido.
bennet: cariofillata, erba benedetta.
congratulated: felicitato.
connection: coincidenza, accoppiamento, connessione, collegamento, relazione, banda.
contemplation: contemplazione.
cousin: cugino, cugina.
dared: osato.
dawdled: bighellonato, gingillato.
delicacy: delicatezza.

entered: entrato.
foolish: sciocco, stupido, stolto, ignorante, fesso.
glad: contento, felice, lieto.
headstrong: testardo.
modesty: modestia, verecondia.
naturally: naturalmente.
particulars: particolari.
proceeded: proceduto.
prospect: prospettiva, esplorare.
protesting: protestare.
refusal: rifiuto.

relate: raccontare, raccontiamo, racconta, raccontano, raccontate, racconti, racconto, narrare.
satisfied: soddisfatto, contento, accontentato.
silent: silenzioso, zitto.
sooner: prima.
staircase: scala.
startled: spaventato.
trusted: fidato.
vestibule: vestibolo.

very desirable wife to a man in my situation, who naturally looks for **happiness** in the marriage state. If therefore she actually **persists** in rejecting my suit, perhaps it were better not to force her into **accepting** me, because if **liable** to such defects of **temper**, she could not **contribute** much to my felicity."

"Sir, you quite **misunderstand** me," said Mrs. **Bennet**, **alarmed**. "Lizzy is only **headstrong** in such matters as these. In everything else she is as **good-natured** a girl as ever lived. I will go directly to Mr. Bennet, and we shall very soon **settle** it with her, I am sure."

She would not give him time to reply, but hurrying **instantly** to her husband, called out as she entered the library, "Oh! Mr. Bennet, you are wanted immediately; we are all in an **uproar**. You must come and make Lizzy marry Mr. Collins, for she vows she will not have him, and if you do not make **haste** he will change his mind and not have *her*."

Mr. Bennet **raised** his eyes from his book as she entered, and fixed them on her face with a **calm unconcern** which was not in the least **altered** by her communication.

"I have not the pleasure of understanding you," said he, when she had finished her speech. "Of what are you talking?"

"Of Mr. Collins and Lizzy. Lizzy **declares** she will not have Mr. Collins, and Mr. Collins **begins** to say that he will not have Lizzy."

"And what am I to do on the occasion? It seems an **hopeless** business."

"Speak to Lizzy about it yourself. Tell her that you **insist** upon her **marrying** him."

"Let her be called down. She shall hear my opinion."

Mrs. Bennet rang the **bell**, and Miss Elizabeth was **summoned** to the library.

"Come here, child," cried her father as she appeared. "I have sent for you on an affair of importance. I understand that Mr. Collins has made you an offer of marriage. Is it true?" Elizabeth replied that it was. "Very well--and this offer of marriage you have refused?"

Italian

accepting: accettando.
alarmed: allarmato.
altered: alterato.
begins: comincia, inizia.
bell: campana, campanello.
bennet: cariofillata, erba benedetta.
calm: calmo, calmare, tranquillo, calma, placare.
contribute: contribuire, contribuiamo, contribuisci, contribuisco, contribuiscono, contribuite.
declares: dichiara.

good-natured: gradevole, cortese.
happiness: felicità.
haste: fretta, furia.
headstrong: testardo.
hopeless: disperato, senza speranza.
insist: insistere, insistiamo, insisto, insistete, insistono, insisti.
instantly: direttamente, istantaneamente, immediatamente.
liable: responsabile.
marrying: sposandosi.
misunderstand: fraintendere,

fraintendi, fraintendono, fraintendiamo, fraintendete, fraintendo.
persists: persiste.
raised: a rilievo, garzato.
settle: sistemare, regolare, saldare.
summoned: convocato.
temper: umore, temperamento, tempra.
unconcern: noncuranza.
uproar: baccano.

"I have, sir."

"Very well. We now come to the point. Your mother **insists** upon your accepting it. Is it not so, Mrs. **Bennet**?"

"Yes, or I will never see her again."

"An **unhappy** alternative is before you, Elizabeth. From this day you must be a stranger to one of your parents. Your mother will never see you again if you do *not* marry Mr. Collins, and I will never see you again if you *do*."

Elizabeth could not but smile at such a **conclusion** of such a **beginning**, but Mrs. Bennet, who had persuaded herself that her husband **regarded** the affair as she wished, was excessively disappointed.

"What do you mean, Mr. Bennet, in talking this way? You promised me to *insist* upon her marrying him."

"My dear," replied her husband, "I have two small favours to request. First, that you will allow me the free use of my understanding on the present occasion; and secondly, of my room. I shall be glad to have the library to myself as soon as may be."

Not yet, however, in **spite** of her disappointment in her husband, did Mrs. Bennet give up the point. She talked to Elizabeth again and again; **coaxed** and **threatened** her by **turns**. She endeavoured to secure Jane in her interest; but Jane, with all possible **mildness**, declined **interfering**; and Elizabeth, sometimes with real **earnestness**, and sometimes with **playful gaiety**, replied to her attacks. Though her manner varied, however, her **determination** never did.

Mr. Collins, **meanwhile**, was **meditating** in **solitude** on what had passed. He thought too well of himself to **comprehend** on what motives his cousin could refuse him; and though his pride was **hurt**, he suffered in no other way. His regard for her was quite imaginary; and the **possibility** of her **deserving** her mother's **reproach** prevented his feeling any **regret**.

While the family were in this confusion, Charlotte Lucas came to spend the day with them. She was met in the **vestibule** by Lydia, who, flying to her, cried in a half whisper, "I am glad you are come, for there is such **fun** here! What do

Italian

beginning: inizio, cominciando, principio, iniziando.
bennet: cariofillata, erba benedetta.
coaxed: persuaso, blandito.
comprehend: comprendere, comprendo, comprendono, comprendiamo, comprendi, comprendete.
conclusion: conclusione, risultato.
determination: determinazione.
earnestness: serietà.

fun: divertimento, spasso, piacere.
gaiety: gaiezza.
hurt: ferire, far male, ferita, dolere.
insists: insiste.
interfering: interferendo, interferire.
meanwhile: intanto, nel frattempo, frattanto, mentre.
meditating: meditando.
mildness: mitezza.
playful: giocoso.
possibility: possibilità, eventualità.
regarded: considerato.

regret: rincrescere, rammarico, rimpiangere, rimpianto, rincrescimento.
reproach: rimprovero, rimproverare, riprendere.
solitude: solitudine.
spite: dispetto.
threatened: minacciato.
turns: gira, svolta, cambia.
unhappy: infelice, triste.
vestibule: vestibolo.

you think has happened this morning? Mr. Collins has made an offer to Lizzy, and she will not have him."

Charlotte hardly had time to answer, before they were joined by Kitty, who came to tell the same news; and no sooner had they entered the breakfast-room, where Mrs. **Bennet** was alone, than she **likewise** began on the subject, calling on Miss Lucas for her **compassion**, and **entreating** her to persuade her friend Lizzy to **comply** with the wishes of all her family. "Pray do, my dear Miss Lucas," she added in a **melancholy** tone, "for nobody is on my side, nobody takes part with me. I am **cruelly** used, nobody feels for my poor nerves."

Charlotte's reply was **spared** by the entrance of Jane and Elizabeth.

"Aye, there she comes," continued Mrs. Bennet, "looking as **unconcerned** as may be, and **caring** no more for us than if we were at York, provided she can have her own way. But I tell you, Miss Lizzy--if you take it into your head to go on refusing every offer of marriage in this way, you will never get a husband at all--and I am sure I do not know who is to **maintain** you when your father is dead. I shall not be able to keep you--and so I **warn** you. I have done with you from this very day. I told you in the library, you know, that I should never speak to you again, and you will find me as good as my word. I have no pleasure in talking to undutiful children. Not that I have much pleasure, indeed, in talking to anybody. People who suffer as I do from nervous **complaints** can have no great **inclination** for talking. Nobody can tell what I suffer! But it is always so. Those who do not complain are never pitied."

Her daughters listened in silence to this **effusion**, sensible that any attempt to reason with her or **soothe** her would only increase the **irritation**. She talked on, therefore, without **interruption** from any of them, till they were joined by Mr. Collins, who entered the room with an air more **stately** than usual, and on **perceiving** whom, she said to the girls, "Now, I do insist upon it, that you, all of you, hold your tongues, and let me and Mr. Collins have a little conversation together."

Elizabeth passed quietly out of the room, Jane and Kitty followed, but Lydia stood her ground, determined to hear all she could; and Charlotte, **detained** first

Italian

bennet: cariofillata, erba benedetta.
caring: premuroso.
compassion: compassione.
complain: lagnarsi, lamentarsi, lamentare.
comply: ottemperi, accondiscendiamo, ottemperiamo, ottempero, ottemperate, ottemperano, ottempera, accondiscendo, accondiscendi, accondiscendete, accondiscendono.
cruelly: crudelmente.

detained: ritenuto.
effusion: versamento, effusione.
entreating: supplicando, supplicare.
inclination: inclinazione, pendenza.
interruption: interruzione.
irritation: irritazione.
likewise: anche, altrettanto.
maintain: mantenere, mantengono, manteniamo, mantengo, mantenete, mantieni, conservare, conservo, conserviamo, conservi, conservate.
melancholy: malinconia, malinconico.

perceiving: percependo, scorgendo, intravedendo.
soothe: calmare, calmano, calmiamo, calmi, calmate, calmo, calma, placare, lenire.
spared: risparmiato.
stately: imponente.
unconcerned: indifferente.
warn: avvertire, avvertiamo, avvertono, avverti, avverto, avvertite, ammonire, avvisare.

by the **civility** of Mr. Collins, whose inquiries after herself and all her family were very minute, and then by a little **curiosity**, satisfied herself with walking to the window and **pretending** not to hear. In a doleful voice Mrs. **Bennet began** the **projected** conversation: "Oh! Mr. Collins!"

"My dear madam," replied he, "let us be for ever silent on this point. Far be it from me," he **presently** continued, in a voice that marked his **displeasure**, "to resent the behaviour of your daughter. **Resignation** to **inevitable evils** is the evil duty of us all; the **peculiar** duty of a young man who has been so **fortunate** as I have been in early preferment; and I trust I am **resigned**. Perhaps not the less so from feeling a doubt of my **positive happiness** had my fair cousin honoured me with her hand; for I have often observed that resignation is never so perfect as when the **blessing denied** begins to lose somewhat of its **value** in our **estimation**. You will not, I hope, consider me as **showing** any **disrespect** to your family, my dear madam, by thus **withdrawing** my pretensions to your daughter's favour, without having paid yourself and Mr. Bennet the **compliment** of requesting you to **interpose** your authority in my behalf. My conduct may, I fear, be **objectionable** in having accepted my dismission from your daughter's lips instead of your own. But we are all liable to **error**. I have certainly meant well through the whole affair. My object has been to secure an **amiable** companion for myself, with due consideration for the advantage of all your family, and if my *manner* has been at all **reprehensible**, I here beg leave to apologise."

CHAPTER 21

The discussion of Mr. Collins's offer was now nearly at an end, and Elizabeth had only to suffer from the **uncomfortable** feelings **necessarily attending** it, and occasionally from some **peevish** allusions of her mother. As for the gentleman himself, *his* feelings were **chiefly** expressed, not by **embarrassment** or **dejection**, or by trying to avoid her, but by **stiffness** of manner and **resentful** silence. He **scarcely** ever spoke to her, and the **assiduous** attentions which he had been so sensible of himself were **transferred** for the rest of the day to Miss Lucas, whose **civility** in listening to him was a **seasonable** relief to them all, and especially to her friend.

The **morrow** produced no **abatement** of Mrs. Bennet's ill-humour or ill health. Mr. Collins was also in the same state of angry pride. Elizabeth had hoped that his **resentment** might **shorten** his visit, but his plan did not appear in the least affected by it. He was always to have gone on Saturday, and to Saturday he meant to stay.

After breakfast, the girls walked to Meryton to **inquire** if Mr. Wickham were returned, and to **lament** over his absence from the Netherfield ball. He joined them on their entering the town, and attended them to their aunt's where his **regret** and **vexation**, and the concern of everybody, was well talked over. To Elizabeth, however, he **voluntarily acknowledged** that the necessity of his absence *had* been self-imposed.

Italian

abatement: riduzione, detrazione, diminuzione, abbattimento, abolizione.
acknowledged: riconosciuto.
assiduous: assiduo, diligente.
attending: visitando, curando, assistendo.
chiefly: principalmente, soprattutto.
civility: civiltà, cortesia.
dejection: deiezione, abbattimento, scoraggiamento, depressione.
embarrassment: imbarazzo.

inquire: domandare, informarsi, domandano, domandate, domandi, domandiamo, domando, indagare, domanda.
lament: lamento, lamentare.
morrow: domani.
necessarily: necessariamente.
peevish: permaloso, stizzoso.
regret: rincrescere, rammarico, rimpiangere, rimpianto, rincrescimento.
resentful: risentito, astioso.

resentment: risentimento, astio.
scarcely: appena, a stento.
seasonable: stagionale, di stagione.
shorten: abbreviare, accorciare, accorciate, accorciano, accorciamo, accorcia, accorci, abbreviate, abbreviano, abbreviamo, abbrevia.
stiffness: rigidezza, rigidità.
transferred: trasferito, attraversato.
uncomfortable: scomodo, disagiato.
vexation: irritazione.
voluntarily: volontariamente.

"I found," said he, "as the time drew near that I had better not meet Mr. Darcy; that to be in the same room, the same party with him for so many hours together, might be more than I could bear, and that scenes might arise unpleasant to more than myself."

She highly approved his **forbearance**, and they had leisure for a full **discussion** of it, and for all the **commendation** which they **civilly bestowed** on each other, as Wickham and another officer walked back with them to Longbourn, and during the walk he particularly attended to her. His **accompanying** them was a **double** advantage; she felt all the **compliment** it offered to herself, and it was most acceptable as an occasion of **introducing** him to her father and mother.

Soon after their return, a letter was **delivered** to Miss Bennet; it came from Netherfield. The **envelope contained** a **sheet** of elegant, little, hot-pressed **paper**, well **covered** with a lady's fair, **flowing** hand; and Elizabeth saw her sister's **countenance** change as she read it, and saw her **dwelling intently** on some particular passages. Jane **recollected** herself soon, and **putting** the letter away, tried to join with her usual **cheerfulness** in the general conversation; but Elizabeth felt an anxiety on the subject which drew off her attention even from Wickham; and no sooner had he and he companion taken leave, than a glance from Jane invited her to follow her **upstairs**. When they had gained their own room, Jane, taking out the letter, said:

"This is from Caroline Bingley; what it **contains** has surprised me a good deal. The whole party have left Netherfield by this time, and are on their way to town--and without any intention of coming back again. You shall hear what she says."

She then read the first **sentence aloud**, which **comprised** the information of their having just resolved to follow their brother to town directly, and of their meaning to **dine** in Grosvenor Street, where Mr. Hurst had a house. The next was in these words: "I do not pretend to regret anything I shall leave in Hertfordshire, except your society, my dearest friend; but we will hope, at some future period, to **enjoy** many returns of that delightful **intercourse** we have

Italian

accompanying: accompagnando.
aloud: ad alta voce.
bestowed: concesso, tributato.
cheerfulness: contentezza, allegria.
civilly: civile, civilmente.
commendation: raccomandazione.
compliment: complimento.
comprised: compreso, contenuto.
contained: contenuto.
contains: contiene.
countenance: approvare, viso.
covered: coperto.

delivered: consegnato.
dine: cenare.
discussion: discussione.
double: doppio, sosia, raddoppiare, duplice.
dwelling: dimorando, abitando, dimora, abitazione.
enjoy: fruire, godere.
envelope: busta, la busta, involucro.
flowing: fluente.
forbearance: pazienza.
intently: intensamente.

intercourse: rapporti.
introducing: presentando, introducendo.
paper: carta, documento, tappezzare, relazione, giornale, la carta.
putting: mettendo, ponendo.
recollected: rammentato.
sentence: frase, condannare, giudizio, sentenza.
sheet: foglio, lenzuolo, foglia, scotta, lastra.
upstairs: di sopra.

known, and in the meanwhile may **lessen** the pain of separation by a very frequent and most unreserved **correspondence**. I depend on you for that." To these highflown expressions Elizabeth listened with all the **insensibility** of **distrust**; and though the **suddenness** of their **removal** surprised her, she saw nothing in it really to **lament**; it was not to be supposed that their absence from Netherfield would prevent Mr. Bingley's being there; and as to the loss of their society, she was persuaded that Jane must **cease** to regard it, in the enjoyment of his.

"It is unlucky," said she, after a short pause, "that you should not be able to see your friends before they leave the country. But may we not hope that the period of future happiness to which Miss Bingley looks **forward** may **arrive** earlier than she is aware, and that the delightful intercourse you have known as friends will be **renewed** with yet **greater** satisfaction as sisters? Mr. Bingley will not be detained in London by them."

"Caroline decidedly says that none of the party will return into Hertfordshire this winter. I will read it to you:"

"When my brother left us yesterday, he **imagined** that the business which took him to London might be concluded in three or four days; but as we are certain it **cannot** be so, and at the same time convinced that when Charles **gets** to town he will be in no hurry to leave it again, we have determined on following him **thither**, that he may not be obliged to spend his vacant hours in a comfortless **hotel**. Many of my acquaintances are already there for the winter; I wish that I could hear that you, my dearest friend, had any intention of making one of the crowd--but of that I **despair**. I **sincerely** hope your Christmas in Hertfordshire may **abound** in the gaieties which that **season** generally **brings**, and that your **beaux** will be so **numerous** as to prevent your feeling the loss of the three of whom we shall **deprive** you."

"It is evident by this," added Jane, "that he **comes** back no more this winter."

"It is only evident that Miss Bingley does not mean that he *should*."

Italian

abound: abbondare, abbondano, abbondate, abbondi, abbondiamo, abbondo, abbonda.
arrive: arrivare, arrivano, arriva, arrivi, arriviamo, arrivate, arrivo, giungere.
beaux: fidanzati.
brings: porta.
cannot: non potere.
cease: cessare.
comes: viene.
correspondence: corrispondenza,

carteggio.
deprive: privare.
despair: disperazione, disperare.
distrust: diffidenza.
forward: avanti, spedire, attaccante, in avanti, inoltrare.
gets: ottiene.
greater: maggiore.
hotel: albergo.
imagined: immaginato.
insensibility: insensibilità, indifferenza.

lament: lamento, lamentare.
lessen: diminuire, diminuiamo, diminuisci, diminuisco, diminuiscono, diminuite.
numerous: numeroso.
removal: rimozione, asportazione, eliminazione.
renewed: rinnovato.
season: stagione, condire.
sincerely: sinceramente, francamente.
suddenness: subitaneità.
thither: là.

"Why will you think so? It must be his own doing. He is his own master.
But you do not know *all*. I *will* read you the **passage** which particularly hurts
me. I will have no **reserves** from *you*."

"Mr. Darcy is **impatient** to see his sister; and, to **confess** the truth, *we* are
scarcely less eager to meet her again. I really do not think Georgiana Darcy has
her equal for beauty, **elegance**, and **accomplishments**; and the affection she
inspires in Louisa and myself is **heightened** into something still more
interesting, from the hope we dare **entertain** of her being **hereafter** our sister. I
do not know whether I ever before mentioned to you my feelings on this subject;
but I will not leave the country without **confiding** them, and I trust you will not
esteem them unreasonable. My brother **admires** her greatly already; he will
have frequent opportunity now of seeing her on the most intimate **footing**; her
relations all wish the connection as much as his own; and a sister's **partiality** is
not **misleading** me, I think, when I call Charles most capable of **engaging** any
woman's heart. With all these circumstances to favour an **attachment**, and
nothing to prevent it, am I wrong, my dearest Jane, in **indulging** the hope of an
event which will secure the happiness of so many?"

"What do you think of *this* sentence, my dear Lizzy?" said Jane as she
finished it. "Is it not clear enough? Does it not **expressly** declare that Caroline
neither **expects** nor wishes me to be her sister; that she is perfectly convinced of
her brother's **indifference**; and that if she suspects the nature of my feelings for
him, she means (most kindly!) to put me on my **guard**? Can there be any other
opinion on the subject?"

"Yes, there can; for mine is totally different. Will you hear it?"

"Most willingly."

"You shall have it in a few words. Miss Bingley sees that her brother is in
love with you, and wants him to marry Miss Darcy. She follows him to town in
hope of **keeping** him there, and tries to persuade you that he does not care about
you."

Jane shook her head.

Italian

accomplishments: compimenti.
admires: ammira.
attachment: accessorio, allegato,
  attaccamento.
confess: confessare, confessa,
  confessano, confessate, confessi,
  confessiamo, confesso.
confiding: confidando, confidare.
elegance: eleganza.
engaging: innestando, attraente.
entertain: intrattenere, intrattenete,
  intrattieni, intratteniamo, intrattengo,

intrattengono, ricevere.
esteem: stima, rispetto, stimare,
  considerazione, considerare,
  rispettare, riguardo.
expects: aspetta.
expressly: espressamente.
footing: punto d'appoggio.
guard: capotreno, protezione,
  proteggere, guardia, carter, riparo,
  custodire, sorvegliare.
heightened: innalzato.
hereafter: in futuro.

impatient: impaziente.
indifference: indifferenza.
indulging: indulgendo, compiacendo.
inspires: ispira.
keeping: conservando, osservando,
  trattenendo.
misleading: fuorviante.
partiality: parzialità, predilezione.
passage: passaggio, corridoio, brano,
  varco, corsia.
reserves: riserve.

"Indeed, Jane, you ought to believe me. No one who has ever seen you together can doubt his affection. Miss Bingley, I am sure, **cannot**. She is not such a **simpleton**. Could she have seen half as much love in Mr. Darcy for herself, she would have ordered her wedding clothes. But the case is this: We are not rich enough or grand enough for them; and she is the more anxious to get Miss Darcy for her brother, from the **notion** that when there has been *one* **intermarriage**, she may have less trouble in **achieving** a second; in which there is certainly some **ingenuity**, and I dare say it would **succeed**, if Miss de Bourgh were out of the way. But, my dearest Jane, you cannot seriously imagine that because Miss Bingley **tells** you her brother greatly **admires** Miss Darcy, he is in the smallest degree less sensible of *your* **merit** than when he took leave of you on Tuesday, or that it will be in her power to persuade him that, instead of being in love with you, he is very much in love with her friend."

"If we thought **alike** of Miss Bingley," replied Jane, "your **representation** of all this might make me quite easy. But I know the **foundation** is **unjust**. Caroline is **incapable** of wilfully **deceiving** anyone; and all that I can hope in this case is that she is deceiving herself."

"That is right. You could not have started a more happy idea, since you will not take comfort in mine. Believe her to be **deceived**, by all means. You have now done your duty by her, and must **fret** no longer."

"But, my dear sister, can I be happy, even **supposing** the best, in accepting a man whose sisters and friends are all wishing him to marry elsewhere?"

"You must decide for yourself," said Elizabeth; "and if, upon **mature deliberation**, you find that the misery of **disobliging** his two sisters is more than **equivalent** to the happiness of being his wife, I advise you by all means to refuse him."

"How can you talk so?" said Jane, **faintly** smiling. "You must know that though I should be **exceedingly grieved** at their **disapprobation**, I could not hesitate."

Italian

achieving: compiendo, conseguendo.
admires: ammira.
alike: simile, similmente.
cannot: non potere.
deceived: ingannato, truffato.
deceiving: ingannando, truffando, ingannare.
deliberation: deliberazione.
disapprobation: disapprovazione.
disobliging: scortese.
equivalent: equivalente.
exceedingly: estremamente.

faintly: debolmente.
foundation: fondazione, fondamento, fondo, base, fondamenta.
fret: agitazione, consumare, greca.
grieved: accorato, addolorato.
incapable: incapace.
ingenuity: ingegnosità.
intermarriage: matrimonio tra consanguinei.
mature: maturo, maturare, maturano, maturate, maturi, maturiamo, matura.

merit: meritare, merito, benemerenza, pregio.
notion: nozione, idea.
representation: rappresentanza, rappresentazione, figura.
simpleton: sempliciotto.
succeed: riuscire, riusciamo, riuscite, riescono, riesco, riesci, succedere.
supposing: supponendo.
tells: dice, racconta, narra.
unjust: ingiusto.

"I did not think you would; and that being the case, I **cannot** consider your situation with much compassion."

"But if he returns no more this winter, my **choice** will never be **required**. A thousand things may **arise** in six months!"

The idea of his returning no more Elizabeth treated with the **utmost contempt**. It appeared to her merely the **suggestion** of Caroline's interested wishes, and she could not for a moment suppose that those wishes, however **openly** or **artfully spoken**, could influence a young man so totally **independent** of everyone.

She **represented** to her sister as forcibly as possible what she felt on the subject, and had soon the pleasure of seeing its happy effect. Jane's **temper** was not desponding, and she was **gradually** led to hope, though the **diffidence** of **affection** sometimes overcame the hope, that Bingley would return to Netherfield and answer every wish of her heart.

They agreed that Mrs. **Bennet** should only hear of the **departure** of the family, without being **alarmed** on the **score** of the gentleman's conduct; but even this **partial** communication gave her a great deal of concern, and she **bewailed** it as **exceedingly unlucky** that the **ladies** should happen to go away just as they were all getting so **intimate** together. After lamenting it, however, at some length, she had the **consolation** that Mr. Bingley would be soon down again and soon **dining** at Longbourn, and the conclusion of all was the comfortable **declaration**, that though he had been **invited** only to a family dinner, she would take care to have two full **courses**.

Italian

affection: affetto, affezione, amore.
alarmed: allarmato.
arise: nascere, nasciamo, nasco, nasci, nascete, nascono, salire, sorgere, sorgete, sorgono, sorgi.
artfully: astutamente.
bennet: cariofillata, erba benedetta.
bewailed: si lamentato.
cannot: non potere.
choice: scelta.
consolation: consolazione.
contempt: sprezzo, disprezzo.

courses: mestruazioni.
declaration: dichiarazione.
departure: partenza.
diffidence: timidezza.
dining: pranzando, cenando.
exceedingly: estremamente.
gradually: gradualmente, poco a poco.
independent: indipendente.
intimate: intimo.
invited: invitato.
ladies: signore.
openly: apertamente.

partial: parziale.
represented: rappresentato, figurato.
required: richiesto.
score: punteggio, segnare, partitura, punto, segno, marcare.
spoken: parlato.
suggestion: suggerimento, proposta, suggestione.
temper: umore, temperamento, tempra.
unlucky: sfortunato, disgraziato.
utmost: massimo.

CHAPTER 22

The Bennets were engaged to **dine** with the Lucases and again during the chief of the day was Miss Lucas so kind as to listen to Mr. Collins. Elizabeth took an opportunity of **thanking** her. "It **keeps** him in good humour," said she, "and I am more **obliged** to you than I can express." Charlotte assured her friend of her satisfaction in being useful, and that it **amply repaid** her for the little **sacrifice** of her time. This was very **amiable**, but Charlotte's **kindness extended farther** than Elizabeth had any **conception** of; its object was nothing else than to secure her from any return of Mr. Collins's **addresses**, by **engaging** them towards herself. Such was Miss Lucas's **scheme**; and appearances were so **favourable**, that when they parted at night, she would have felt almost secure of success if he had not been to leave Hertfordshire so very soon. But here she did **injustice** to the **fire** and independence of his character, for it led him to escape out of Longbourn House the next morning with **admirable slyness**, and **hasten** to Lucas Lodge to throw himself at her **feet**. He was anxious to avoid the notice of his cousins, from a conviction that if they saw him **depart**, they could not fail to **conjecture** his design, and he was not willing to have the attempt known till its success might be known **likewise**; for though feeling almost secure, and with reason, for Charlotte had been **tolerably encouraging**, he was **comparatively diffident** since the adventure of Wednesday. His reception, however, was of the most **flattering** kind. Miss Lucas **perceived** him from an upper window as he walked towards

Italian

addresses: indirizzi.
admirable: ammirabile, ammirevole, mirabile.
amiable: amabile.
amply: ampiamente.
comparatively: comparativamente.
conception: concepimento, concezione.
conjecture: congettura.
depart: partire, partite, partiamo, parti, partono, parto, andarsene.
diffident: timido.

dine: cenare.
encouraging: incoraggiando, incoraggiante.
engaging: innestando, attraente.
extended: esteso.
farther: più lontano.
favourable: favorevole.
feet: piedi.
fire: fuoco, incendio, sparare, rogo.
flattering: lusingando, adulatorio.
hasten: affrettarsi, affrettare.
injustice: ingiustizia.

keeps: osserva, conserva, trattiene.
kindness: gentilezza, bontà, cortesia.
likewise: anche, altrettanto.
obliged: obbligato.
perceived: scorto, percepito, intravisto.
repaid: rimborsato, ripagato.
sacrifice: sacrificio, sacrificare, offrire.
scheme: progetto, schema, piano.
slyness: astuzia.
thanking: ringraziando.
tolerably: tollerabilmente.

the house, and instantly set out to meet him **accidentally** in the lane. But little had she dared to hope that so much love and **eloquence awaited** her there.

In as short a time as Mr. Collins's long speeches would allow, everything was settled between them to the satisfaction of both; and as they entered the house he earnestly **entreated** her to name the day that was to make him the happiest of men; and though such a **solicitation** must be **waived** for the present, the lady felt no inclination to trifle with his happiness. The **stupidity** with which he was **favoured** by nature must guard his **courtship** from any charm that could make a woman wish for its continuance; and Miss Lucas, who accepted him solely from the **pure** and **disinterested** desire of an establishment, cared not how soon that establishment were gained.

Sir William and Lady Lucas were **speedily** applied to for their **consent**; and it was **bestowed** with a most **joyful alacrity**. Mr. Collins's present circumstances made it a most eligible match for their daughter, to whom they could give little fortune; and his prospects of future **wealth** were exceedingly fair. Lady Lucas began directly to **calculate**, with more interest than the matter had ever excited before, how many years longer Mr. **Bennet** was likely to live; and Sir William gave it as his decided opinion, that whenever Mr. Collins should be in possession of the Longbourn estate, it would be highly **expedient** that both he and his wife should make their appearance at St. James's. The whole family, in short, were properly **overjoyed** on the occasion. The younger girls formed hopes of *coming out* a year or two sooner than they might otherwise have done; and the boys were relieved from their **apprehension** of Charlotte's dying an old **maid**. Charlotte herself was **tolerably** composed. She had gained her point, and had time to consider of it. Her reflections were in general satisfactory. Mr. Collins, to be sure, was neither sensible nor agreeable; his society was **irksome**, and his attachment to her must be imaginary. But still he would be her husband. Without thinking highly either of men or **matrimony**, marriage had always been her object; it was the only provision for well-educated young women of small fortune, and however uncertain of giving happiness, must be their pleasantest **preservative** from want. This preservative she had now obtained; and at the age

Italian

accidentally: accidentalmente.
alacrity: entusiasmo, alacrità.
apprehension: apprensione, arresto.
awaited: aspettato, atteso.
bennet: cariofillata, erba benedetta.
bestowed: concesso, tributato.
calculate: calcolare, calcoliamo, calcola, calcolano, calcolate, calcoli, calcolo.
consent: consenso, concordare, essere d'accordo, accordo, benestare, assenso, acconsentire.

courtship: corteggiamento.
disinterested: disinteressato, imparziale.
eloquence: eloquenza.
entreated: supplicato.
expedient: espediente, conveniente.
favoured: favorito.
irksome: seccante.
joyful: gioioso.
maid: cameriera, ragazza.
matrimony: matrimonio.
overjoyed: felicissimo.

preservative: conservante, preservativo, conservativo.
pure: puro.
solicitation: sollecitazione.
speedily: rapidamente.
stupidity: stupidità.
tolerably: tollerabilmente.
waived: rinunciato.
wealth: ricchezza, abbondanza, opulenza.

of twenty-seven, without having ever been handsome, she felt all the good **luck** of it. The least agreeable circumstance in the business was the surprise it must occasion to Elizabeth **Bennet**, whose friendship she **valued** beyond that of any other person. Elizabeth would wonder, and probably would blame her; and though her **resolution** was not to be **shaken**, her feelings must be hurt by such a **disapprobation**. She resolved to give her the information herself, and therefore **charged** Mr. Collins, when he returned to Longbourn to dinner, to drop no hint of what had passed before any of the family. A promise of **secrecy** was of course very dutifully given, but it could not be kept without **difficulty**; for the curiosity excited by his long absence **burst forth** in such very **direct** questions on his return as required some ingenuity to **evade**, and he was at the same time exercising great self-denial, for he was **longing** to **publish** his prosperous love.

As he was to begin his **journey** too early on the **morrow** to see any of the family, the ceremony of leave-taking was performed when the ladies moved for the night; and Mrs. Bennet, with great **politeness** and **cordiality**, said how happy they should be to see him at Longbourn again, whenever his engagements might allow him to visit them.

"My dear madam," he replied, "this invitation is particularly **gratifying**, because it is what I have been **hoping** to receive; and you may be very certain that I shall **avail** myself of it as soon as possible."

They were all astonished; and Mr. Bennet, who could by no means wish for so **speedy** a return, immediately said:

"But is there not danger of Lady Catherine's disapprobation here, my good sir? You had better neglect your relations than run the risk of **offending** your patroness."

"My dear sir," replied Mr. Collins," I am particularly obliged to you for this friendly caution, and you may depend upon my not taking so material a step without her ladyship's concurrence."

"You **cannot** be too much upon your guard. Risk anything rather than her **displeasure**; and if you find it likely to be raised by your coming to us again,

---

Italian

avail: giovare, essere utile, servire, utilizzare.
bennet: cariofillata, erba benedetta.
burst: scoppiare, scoppio, crepa, screpolatura, fessura, esplosione, crepare, irrompere, burst.
cannot: non potere.
charged: caricato.
cordiality: cordialità.
difficulty: difficoltà.
direct: diretto, guidare, destro, condurre, dirigere.

disapprobation: disapprovazione.
displeasure: scontento, dispiacere.
evade: evitare, evitano, evita, evitate, eviti, evito, evitiamo, eludere, eludiamo, eludo, eludi.
forth: avanti.
gratifying: gratificando, gratificante.
hoping: sperando.
journey: viaggio, viaggiare.
longing: bramoso.
luck: fortuna.
morrow: domani.

offending: offendendo, insultando, oltraggiando.
politeness: cortesia, garbo.
publish: pubblicare, pubblicate, pubblichi, pubblichiamo, pubblica, pubblicano, pubblico.
resolution: risoluzione, definizione, deliberazione.
secrecy: segretezza.
shaken: scosso.
speedy: rapido.
valued: valutato, stimato.

which I should think **exceedingly** probable, stay quietly at home, and be satisfied that *we* shall take no offence."

"Believe me, my dear sir, my **gratitude** is **warmly** excited by such **affectionate** attention; and depend upon it, you will **speedily** receive from me a letter of thanks for this, and for every other **mark** of your regard during my stay in Hertfordshire. As for my fair cousins, though my absence may not be long enough to **render** it necessary, I shall now take the liberty of wishing them health and happiness, not **excepting** my cousin Elizabeth."

With proper civilities the ladies then withdrew; all of them equally surprised that he **meditated** a quick return. Mrs. **Bennet** wished to understand by it that he thought of paying his addresses to one of her younger girls, and Mary might have been **prevailed** on to accept him. She **rated** his abilities much **higher** than any of the **others**; there was a **solidity** in his reflections which often struck her, and though by no means so clever as herself, she thought that if **encouraged** to read and improve himself by such an example as hers, he might become a very **agreeable** companion. But on the following morning, every hope of this kind was done away. Miss Lucas called soon after breakfast, and in a private **conference** with Elizabeth related the event of the day before.

The possibility of Mr. Collins's fancying herself in love with her friend had once occurred to Elizabeth within the last day or two; but that Charlotte could encourage him seemed almost as far from possibility as she could encourage him herself, and her **astonishment** was consequently so great as to overcome at first the bounds of **decorum**, and she could not help **crying** out:

"Engaged to Mr. Collins! My dear Charlotte--impossible!"

The steady **countenance** which Miss Lucas had **commanded** in telling her story, gave way to a **momentary** confusion here on receiving so direct a **reproach**; though, as it was no more than she expected, she soon **regained** her **composure**, and **calmly** replied:

Italian

affectionate: affettuoso.
agreeable: gradevole, piacevole, amabile.
astonishment: stupore, meraviglia, sorpresa.
bennet: cariofillata, erba benedetta.
calmly: con calma.
commanded: comandato.
composure: calma, compostezza.
conference: conferenza, congresso.
countenance: approvare, viso.
crying: pianto, piangente, piangere.

decorum: decoro.
encouraged: incoraggiato.
exceedingly: estremamente.
excepting: salvo.
gratitude: gratitudine, riconoscenza, grazie.
hers: suo.
higher: più alto.
mark: segno, marcare, marco, marchio, contrassegnare, marca, segnare, contrassegno, voto.
meditated: meditato.

momentary: momentaneo.
prevailed: prevalso.
rated: nominale.
regained: riacquistato, riconquistato, ricuperato, riguadagnato, ripreso.
render: rendere, rendono, rendete, rendi, rendiamo, rendo.
reproach: rimprovero, rimproverare, riprendere.
solidity: solidità.
speedily: rapidamente.
warmly: caldamente, calorosamente.

"Why should you be surprised, my dear Eliza? Do you think it **incredible** that Mr. Collins should be able to **procure** any woman's good opinion, because he was not so happy as to succeed with you?"

But Elizabeth had now **recollected** herself, and making a strong effort for it, was able to **assure** with **tolerable firmness** that the prospect of their relationship was highly grateful to her, and that she wished her all **imaginable happiness**.

"I see what you are feeling," replied Charlotte. "You must be surprised, very much surprised--so **lately** as Mr. Collins was wishing to marry you. But when you have had time to think it over, I hope you will be **satisfied** with what I have done. I am not **romantic**, you know; I never was. I ask only a comfortable home; and considering Mr. Collins's character, connection, and situation in life, I am convinced that my chance of happiness with him is as fair as most people can **boast** on **entering** the marriage state."

Elizabeth quietly answered "Undoubtedly;" and after an **awkward pause**, they returned to the rest of the family. Charlotte did not stay much longer, and Elizabeth was then left to reflect on what she had heard. It was a long time before she became at all **reconciled** to the idea of so **unsuitable** a match. The **strangeness** of Mr. Collins's making two offers of marriage within three days was nothing in comparison of his being now accepted. She had always felt that Charlotte's opinion of **matrimony** was not exactly like her own, but she had not supposed it to be possible that, when called into action, she would have **sacrificed** every better feeling to **worldly** advantage. Charlotte the wife of Mr. Collins was a most **humiliating** picture! And to the **pang** of a friend **disgracing** herself and sunk in her **esteem**, was added the **distressing conviction** that it was impossible for that friend to be **tolerably** happy in the lot she had chosen.

Italian

assure: assicurare, assicura, assicuriamo, assicurate, assicuri, assicurano, assicuro, garantire.
awkward: goffo, sgraziato.
boast: vanteria, vantarsi.
conviction: convinzione, condanna.
disgracing: disonorare.
distressing: doloroso, penoso, angoscioso.
entering: entrando, entrare.
esteem: stima, rispetto, stimare, considerazione, considerare,

rispettare, riguardo.
firmness: fermezza.
happiness: felicità.
humiliating: umiliando, umiliante.
imaginable: immaginabile.
incredible: incredibile.
lately: ultimamente, recentemente.
matrimony: matrimonio.
pang: dolore acuto, spasimo.
pause: pausa, sosta.
procure: procurare, procurate, procuro, procuri, procurano,

procuriamo, procacciare, procura.
recollected: rammentato.
reconciled: conciliato, riconciliato.
romantic: romantico.
sacrificed: sacrificato.
satisfied: soddisfatto, contento, accontentato.
strangeness: stravaganza, stranezza.
tolerable: tollerabile.
tolerably: tollerabilmente.
unsuitable: disadatto.
worldly: mondano.

CHAPTER 23

Elizabeth was sitting with her mother and sisters, **reflecting** on what she had heard, and **doubting** whether she was authorised to mention it, when Sir William Lucas himself appeared, sent by his daughter, to **announce** her engagement to the family. With many **compliments** to them, and much self-gratulation on the prospect of a connection between the **houses**, he **unfolded** the matter--to an **audience** not merely wondering, but **incredulous**; for Mrs. **Bennet**, with more **perseverance** than **politeness**, protested he must be entirely mistaken; and Lydia, always **unguarded** and often **uncivil**, boisterously exclaimed:

"Good Lord! Sir William, how can you tell such a story? Do not you know that Mr. Collins **wants** to marry Lizzy?"

Nothing less than the **complaisance** of a **courtier** could have borne without anger such treatment; but Sir William's good breeding carried him through it all; and though he **begged** leave to be positive as to the truth of his information, he listened to all their **impertinence** with the most **forbearing** courtesy.

Elizabeth, feeling it **incumbent** on her to **relieve** him from so unpleasant a situation, now put herself forward to **confirm** his account, by mentioning her **prior knowledge** of it from Charlotte herself; and endeavoured to put a **stop** to the exclamations of her mother and sisters by the **earnestness** of her **congratulations** to Sir William, in which she was readily joined by Jane, and by making a variety of remarks on the happiness that might be expected from the

Italian

announce: annunciare, annunciate, annunci, annuncia, annunciamo, annunciano, annunziare, annuncio, annunziate, annunzi, annunzia.
audience: udienza, uditorio, pubblico.
begged: mendicato.
bennet: cariofillata, erba benedetta.
complaisance: compiacenza.
compliments: complimenti.
confirm: confermare, confermiamo, confermo, confermano, confermate, confermi, conferma.

congratulations: congratulazioni.
courtier: cortigiano.
doubting: dubitare.
earnestness: serietà.
forbearing: indulgente, paziente.
houses: case.
impertinence: impertinenza.
incredulous: incredulo.
incumbent: incombente.
knowledge: conoscenza, cognizione.
perseverance: perseveranza.
politeness: cortesia, garbo.

prior: anteriore, precedente.
reflecting: riflettendo.
relieve: alleviare, allevio, allevi, allevia, alleviamo, alleviano, alleviate, rilevare.
stop: fermare, ferma, fermarsi, fermo, fermi, fermate, fermano, fermiamo, fermata, cessare, cesso.
uncivil: incivile.
unfolded: spiegato.
unguarded: incustodito.
wants: vuole.

match, the excellent character of Mr. Collins, and the convenient distance of Hunsford from London.

Mrs. **Bennet** was in fact too much **overpowered** to say a great deal while Sir William remained; but no sooner had he left them than her feelings found a rapid **vent**. In the first place, she persisted in disbelieving the whole of the matter; secondly, she was very sure that Mr. Collins had been taken in; **thirdly**, she trusted that they would never be happy together; and **fourthly**, that the match might be **broken** off. Two inferences, however, were plainly **deduced** from the whole: one, that Elizabeth was the real cause of the **mischief**; and the other that she herself had been **barbarously** misused by them all; and on these two points she principally dwelt during the rest of the day. Nothing could **console** and nothing could **appease** her. Nor did that day **wear** out her resentment. A week **elapsed** before she could see Elizabeth without **scolding** her, a **month** passed away before she could speak to Sir William or Lady Lucas without being **rude**, and many months were gone before she could at all forgive their daughter.

Mr. Bennet's emotions were much more **tranquil** on the occasion, and such as he did experience he pronounced to be of a most agreeable sort; for it **gratified** him, he said, to discover that Charlotte Lucas, whom he had been used to think **tolerably** sensible, was as foolish as his wife, and more foolish than his daughter!

Jane **confessed** herself a little surprised at the match; but she said less of her astonishment than of her **earnest** desire for their happiness; nor could Elizabeth persuade her to consider it as **improbable**. Kitty and Lydia were far from **envying** Miss Lucas, for Mr. Collins was only a **clergyman**; and it affected them in no other way than as a piece of news to **spread** at Meryton.

Lady Lucas could not be **insensible** of **triumph** on being able to **retort** on Mrs. Bennet the comfort of having a daughter well married; and she called at Longbourn rather oftener than usual to say how happy she was, though Mrs. Bennet's **sour** looks and ill-natured remarks might have been enough to drive happiness away.

Italian

appease: placare, placo, plachiamo, plachi, placate, placano, placa, calmare.
barbarously: barbaramente.
bennet: cariofillata, erba benedetta.
broken: rotto, spezzato.
clergyman: ecclesiastico, prete, curato, sacerdote.
confessed: confessato.
console: consolare, consolle, console.
deduced: dedotto.
earnest: serio, caparra.

elapsed: trascorso.
envying: invidiando.
fourthly: in quarto luogo.
gratified: gratificato.
improbable: improbabile.
insensible: insensibile.
mischief: birichinata.
month: mese, il mese.
overpowered: sopraffatto.
retort: replica, storta.
rude: scortese, rozzo, maleducato.
scolding: rimprovero, sgridata.

sour: acido, agro, brusco, rude, acerbo, aspro.
spread: diffondere, spargere, diffusione, spalmare, propagare, scarto.
thirdly: in terzo luogo.
tolerably: tollerabilmente.
tranquil: tranquillo, calmo.
triumph: vittoria, trionfo.
vent: sfogo, apertura.
wear: portare, usura, logoramento, indossare.

Between Elizabeth and Charlotte there was a **restraint** which kept them **mutually** silent on the subject; and Elizabeth felt persuaded that no real confidence could ever **subsist** between them again. Her disappointment in Charlotte made her turn with **fonder** regard to her sister, of whose **rectitude** and **delicacy** she was sure her opinion could never be shaken, and for whose happiness she grew **daily** more anxious, as Bingley had now been gone a week and nothing more was heard of his return.

Jane had sent Caroline an early answer to her letter, and was **counting** the days till she might **reasonably** hope to hear again. The promised letter of thanks from Mr. Collins arrived on Tuesday, addressed to their father, and **written** with all the **solemnity** of gratitude which a twelvemonth's **abode** in the family might have prompted. After discharging his conscience on that head, he proceeded to **inform** them, with many **rapturous** expressions, of his happiness in having obtained the affection of their **amiable** neighbour, Miss Lucas, and then explained that it was merely with the view of enjoying her society that he had been so ready to close with their kind wish of seeing him again at Longbourn, **whither** he hoped to be able to return on Monday fortnight; for Lady Catherine, he added, so **heartily** approved his marriage, that she wished it to take place as soon as possible, which he trusted would be an **unanswerable** argument with his amiable Charlotte to name an early day for making him the happiest of men.

Mr. Collins's return into Hertfordshire was no longer a matter of pleasure to Mrs. **Bennet**. On the contrary, she was as much disposed to complain of it as her husband. It was very strange that he should come to Longbourn instead of to Lucas Lodge; it was also very **inconvenient** and **exceedingly troublesome**. She **hated** having visitors in the house while her health was so indifferent, and lovers were of all people the most **disagreeable**. Such were the gentle murmurs of Mrs. Bennet, and they gave way only to the greater distress of Mr. Bingley's continued absence.

Neither Jane nor Elizabeth were comfortable on this subject. Day after day passed away without **bringing** any other tidings of him than the report which shortly **prevailed** in Meryton of his coming no more to Netherfield the whole

Italian

abode: residenza, appartamento, alloggio, dimora.
amiable: amabile.
bennet: cariofillata, erba benedetta.
bringing: portando.
counting: contare, conteggio.
daily: quotidiano, giornaliero, quotidianamente, ogni giorno, giornalmente.
delicacy: delicatezza.
disagreeable: sgradevole.
exceedingly: estremamente.

fonder: più affettuoso.
hated: odiato.
heartily: cordialmente.
inconvenient: difficile, pesante, inconveniente, incomodo.
inform: informare, informano, informate, informi, informiamo, informo, informa, insegnare.
mutually: reciprocamente.
prevailed: prevalso.
rapturous: estatico.
reasonably: ragionevolmente.

rectitude: rettitudine.
restraint: restrizione.
solemnity: solennità.
subsist: esistere, sussistere, sussisti, sussistono, sussistiamo, sussistete, esisto, esistiamo, esisti, esistete, sussisto.
troublesome: fastidioso, noioso.
unanswerable: incontestabile, irrefutabile.
whither: dove.
written: scritto.

winter; a report which highly **incensed** Mrs. Bennet, and which she never failed to contradict as a most scandalous falsehood.

Even Elizabeth began to fear--not that Bingley was indifferent--but that his sisters would be **successful** in keeping him away. Unwilling as she was to **admit** an idea so **destructive** of Jane's happiness, and so **dishonorable** to the **stability** of her **lover**, she could not prevent its frequently **occurring**. The **united** efforts of his two **unfeeling** sisters and of his **overpowering** friend, assisted by the attractions of Miss Darcy and the amusements of London might be too much, she **feared**, for the **strength** of his attachment.

As for Jane, *her* anxiety under this suspense was, of course, more painful than Elizabeth's, but whatever she felt she was desirous of **concealing**, and between herself and Elizabeth, therefore, the subject was never **alluded** to. But as no such delicacy **restrained** her mother, an hour **seldom** passed in which she did not talk of Bingley, express her impatience for his arrival, or even **require** Jane to confess that if he did not come back she would think herself very ill used. It needed all Jane's steady mildness to bear these attacks with tolerable tranquillity.

Mr. Collins returned most **punctually** on Monday fortnight, but his reception at Longbourn was not quite so **gracious** as it had been on his first introduction. He was too happy, however, to need much attention; and **luckily** for the others, the business of love-making relieved them from a great deal of his company. The chief of every day was spent by him at Lucas Lodge, and he sometimes returned to Longbourn only in time to make an apology for his absence before the family went to **bed**.

Mrs. Bennet was really in a most **pitiable** state. The very mention of anything concerning the match threw her into an **agony** of ill-humour, and **wherever** she went she was sure of hearing it talked of. The sight of Miss Lucas was odious to her. As her **successor** in that house, she regarded her with jealous **abhorrence**. Whenever Charlotte came to see them, she concluded her to be **anticipating** the hour of possession; and whenever she spoke in a low voice to Mr. Collins, was convinced that they were talking of the Longbourn estate, and

Italian

abhorrence: orrore, avversione, ribrezzo, ripugnanza.
admit: confessare, confessa, confessiamo, confessi, confessate, confessano, confesso, ammettere, permettere, ammetto, ammettiamo.
agony: agonia, angoscia.
alluded: alluso.
anticipating: anticipando.
bed: letto, il letto.
concealing: nascondendo.
destructive: distruttivo.

dishonorable: disonorevole.
feared: temuto.
gracious: grazioso.
incensed: incenso.
lover: amante.
luckily: fortunatamente.
occurring: accadendo, succedendo.
overpowering: sopraffacendo, opprimente, prepotente, schiacciante.
pitiable: pietoso.
punctually: puntualmente.
require: aver bisogno di, richiedere,

richiedete, richiedono, richiedo, richiedi, richiediamo, necessitare.
restrained: dominato.
seldom: raramente.
stability: stabilità.
strength: forza, resistenza, robustezza, potenza.
successful: riuscito.
successor: successore, discendente.
unfeeling: insensibile.
united: unito.
wherever: dovunque, laddove.

resolving to turn herself and her **daughters** out of the house, as soon as Mr. **Bennet** were **dead**. She **complained bitterly** of all this to her husband.

"Indeed, Mr. Bennet," said she, "it is very **hard** to think that Charlotte Lucas should ever be **mistress** of this house, that I should be **forced** to make way for *her*, and live to see her take her place in it!"

"My **dear**, do not give way to such **gloomy** thoughts. Let us hope for better things. Let us **flatter ourselves** that I may be the survivor."

This was not very **consoling** to Mrs. Bennet, and therefore, **instead** of making any **answer**, she went on as before.

"I **cannot bear** to think that they should have all this **estate**. If it was not for the **entail**, I should not mind it."

"What should not you mind?"

"I should not mind anything at all."

"Let us be **thankful** that you are **preserved** from a state of such insensibility."

"I never can be thankful, Mr. Bennet, for anything about the entail. How **anyone** could have the **conscience** to entail away an estate from one's own daughters, I cannot **understand**; and all for the **sake** of Mr. Collins too! Why should *he* have it more than **anybody** else?"

"I leave it to **yourself** to determine," said Mr. Bennet.

Italian

answer: risposta, rispondere, replicare, rispondere a.
anybody: qualcuno, nessuno.
anyone: chiunque, nessuno.
bear: orso, produrre, ribassista, partorire, l'orso, portare.
bennet: cariofillata, erba benedetta.
bitterly: amaramente.
cannot: non potere.
complained: reclamato, si lamentato.
conscience: coscienza.
consoling: consolare.

daughters: figlie.
dead: morto.
dear: caro, costoso, egregio.
entail: comportare.
estate: fattoria, patrimonio, tenuta.
flatter: lusingare, lusingate, lusingo, lusinghi, lusingano, lusinghiamo, lusinga, adulare.
forced: forzato.
gloomy: tetro, tenebroso, oscuro.
hard: duro, pesante, difficile, dura, solido.

instead: invece.
mistress: padrona.
ourselves: ci.
preserved: conservato.
sake: causa.
thankful: riconoscente, grato.
understand: capire, capite, capiamo, capisci, capisco, capiscono, comprendere, comprendono, comprendo, comprendiamo, comprendete.
yourself: ti.

CHAPTER 24

Miss Bingley's letter arrived, and put an end to doubt. The very first sentence **conveyed** the **assurance** of their being all settled in London for the winter, and concluded with her brother's **regret** at not having had time to pay his respects to his friends in Hertfordshire before he left the country.

Hope was over, entirely over; and when Jane could attend to the rest of the letter, she found little, except the **professed affection** of the writer, that could give her any comfort. Miss Darcy's **praise occupied** the chief of it. Her many attractions were again dwelt on, and Caroline **boasted joyfully** of their increasing **intimacy**, and **ventured** to **predict** the **accomplishment** of the wishes which had been **unfolded** in her former letter. She wrote also with great pleasure of her brother's being an inmate of Mr. Darcy's house, and mentioned with raptures some plans of the latter with regard to new furniture.

Elizabeth, to whom Jane very soon **communicated** the chief of all this, heard it in silent **indignation**. Her heart was divided between concern for her sister, and **resentment** against all others. To Caroline's **assertion** of her brother's being **partial** to Miss Darcy she paid no credit. That he was really **fond** of Jane, she doubted no more than she had ever done; and much as she had always been **disposed** to like him, she could not think without anger, hardly without **contempt**, on that **easiness** of **temper**, that want of proper resolution, which now made him the **slave** of his **designing** friends, and led him to **sacrifice** of his own

Italian

accomplishment: compimento, adempimento.
affection: affetto, affezione, amore.
assertion: asserzione, affermazione.
assurance: assicurazione, promessa.
boasted: vantato.
communicated: comunicato.
contempt: sprezzo, disprezzo.
conveyed: trasportato.
designing: progettazione, disegnare.
disposed: disposto.
easiness: facilità, agevolezza,

comodità, con facilita.
fond: tenero, affettuoso, affezionato.
indignation: indignazione, sdegno.
intimacy: intimità.
joyfully: gioiosamente.
occupied: occupato.
partial: parziale.
praise: lodare, lode, elogiare, encomio, elogio.
predict: predire, predici, prediciamo, predico, predicono, predite, predi'.
professed: professato, dichiarare,

dichiarato.
regret: rincrescere, rammarico, rimpiangere, rimpianto, rincrescimento.
resentment: risentimento, astio.
sacrifice: sacrificio, sacrificare, offrire.
slave: schiavo, sgobbare.
temper: umore, temperamento, tempra.
unfolded: spiegato.
ventured: avventurato.

happiness to the **caprice** of their **inclination**. Had his own happiness, however, been the only **sacrifice**, he might have been allowed to **sport** with it in whatever manner he thought best, but her **sister's** was **involved** in it, as she thought he must be sensible himself. It was a subject, in short, on which **reflection** would be long **indulged**, and must be **unavailing**. She could think of nothing else; and yet whether Bingley's regard had really **died** away, or were **suppressed** by his friends' **interference**; whether he had been aware of Jane's **attachment**, or whether it had escaped his observation; whatever were the case, though her opinion of him must be **materially** affected by the difference, her sister's situation remained the same, her **peace** equally wounded.

A day or two passed before Jane had **courage** to speak of her feelings to Elizabeth; but at last, on Mrs. Bennet's leaving them together, after a longer **irritation** than usual about Netherfield and its master, she could not help saying:

"Oh, that my dear mother had more command over herself! She can have no idea of the pain she gives me by her **continual** reflections on him. But I will not repine. It **cannot** last long. He will be **forgot**, and we shall all be as we were before."

Elizabeth looked at her sister with **incredulous solicitude**, but said nothing.

"You doubt me," cried Jane, **slightly colouring**; "indeed, you have no reason. He may live in my memory as the most **amiable** man of my **acquaintance**, but that is all. I have nothing either to hope or fear, and nothing to **reproach** him with. Thank God! I have not *that* pain. A little time, therefore--I shall certainly try to get the better."

With a stronger voice she soon added, "I have this comfort immediately, that it has not been more than an error of **fancy** on my side, and that it has done no **harm** to anyone but myself."

"My dear Jane!" **exclaimed** Elizabeth, "you are too good. Your **sweetness** and **disinterestedness** are really **angelic**; I do not know what to say to you. I feel as if I had never done you justice, or loved you as you deserve."

Italian

acquaintance: conoscenza, conoscente.
amiable: amabile.
angelic: angelico.
attachment: accessorio, allegato, attaccamento.
cannot: non potere.
caprice: capriccio.
colouring: coloritura.
continual: continuo, costante.
courage: coraggio.
died: morto.
disinterestedness: disinteresse.

exclaimed: esclamato.
fancy: figurarsi, capriccio, immaginazione.
forgot: dimenticato.
happiness: felicità.
harm: danno, nuocere, danneggiare.
inclination: inclinazione, pendenza.
incredulous: incredulo.
indulged: compiaciuto, indulto.
interference: interferenza.
involved: coinvolto.
irritation: irritazione.

materially: materialmente.
peace: pace.
reflection: riflesso, riflessione.
reproach: rimprovero, rimproverare, riprendere.
sacrifice: sacrificio, sacrificare, offrire.
slightly: leggermente, lievemente.
solicitude: sollecitudine.
sport: sport.
suppressed: soffocato, soppresso.
sweetness: dolcezza.
unavailing: inutile.

Miss Bennet eagerly **disclaimed** all extraordinary merit, and threw back the praise on her sister's warm affection.

"Nay," said Elizabeth, "this is not fair. *you* wish to think all the world respectable, and are hurt if I speak ill of anybody. I only want to think *you* perfect, and you set yourself against it. Do not be afraid of my **running** into any excess, of my encroaching on your **privilege** of **universal** good-will. You need not. There are few people whom I really love, and still **fewer** of whom I think well. The more I see of the world, the more am I dissatisfied with it; and every day **confirms** my **belief** of the **inconsistency** of all **human** characters, and of the little **dependence** that can be placed on the appearance of merit or sense. I have met with two instances lately, one I will not mention; the other is Charlotte's marriage. It is **unaccountable**! In every view it is unaccountable!"

"My dear Lizzy, do not give way to such feelings as these. They will **ruin** your happiness. You do not make **allowance** enough for difference of situation and temper. Consider Mr. Collins's **respectability**, and Charlotte's steady, **prudent** character. Remember that she is one of a large family; that as to fortune, it is a most eligible match; and be ready to believe, for everybody's sake, that she may feel something like regard and esteem for our cousin."

"To **oblige** you, I would try to believe almost anything, but no one else could be benefited by such a belief as this; for were I persuaded that Charlotte had any regard for him, I should only think worse of her understanding than I now do of her heart. My dear Jane, Mr. Collins is a **conceited**, **pompous**, narrow-minded, silly man; you know he is, as well as I do; and you must feel, as well as I do, that the woman who married him **cannot** have a proper way of thinking. You shall not defend her, though it is Charlotte Lucas. You shall not, for the sake of one **individual**, change the meaning of **principle** and **integrity**, nor endeavour to persuade yourself or me, that **selfishness** is **prudence**, and **insensibility** of danger **security** for happiness."

"I must think your language too strong in speaking of both," replied Jane; "and I hope you will be convinced of it by seeing them happy together. But enough of this. You **alluded** to something else. You mentioned *two* instances. I

Italian

allowance: indennità, assegno, tolleranza, abbuono, detrazione, sconto, permesso.
alluded: alluso.
belief: credenza, fede, opinione.
cannot: non potere.
conceited: vanitoso, presuntuoso.
confirms: conferma.
dependence: dipendenza.
disclaimed: negato.
fewer: meno.
human: umano.

inconsistency: inconsistenza, incoerenza.
individual: individuale, individuo, singolo.
insensibility: insensibilità, indifferenza.
integrity: integrità.
oblige: obbligare, obblighiamo, obbliga, obbligano, obbligate, obblighi, obbligo.
pompous: ampolloso, pomposo.
principle: principio.

privilege: privilegio, privilegiare.
prudence: prudenza.
prudent: prudente, sensato.
respectability: rispettabilità.
ruin: rovinare, rovina.
running: correndo, funzionamento, scorrendo, corsa, marcia, corrente.
security: sicurezza, garanzia, titolo.
selfishness: egoismo.
unaccountable: inesplicabile, irresponsabile.
universal: universale.

cannot misunderstand you, but I entreat you, dear Lizzy, not to pain me by thinking *that person* to blame, and saying your opinion of him is sunk. We must not be so ready to fancy ourselves intentionally injured. We must not expect a lively young man to be always so guarded and circumspect. It is very often nothing but our own vanity that deceives us. Women fancy admiration means more than it does."

"And men take care that they should."

"If it is designedly done, they cannot be justified; but I have no idea of there being so much design in the world as some persons imagine."

"I am far from attributing any part of Mr. Bingley's conduct to design," said Elizabeth; "but without scheming to do wrong, or to make others unhappy, there may be error, and there may be misery. Thoughtlessness, want of attention to other people's feelings, and want of resolution, will do the business."

"And do you impute it to either of those?"

"Yes; to the last. But if I go on, I shall displease you by saying what I think of persons you esteem. Stop me whilst you can."

"You persist, then, in supposing his sisters influence him?"

"Yes, in conjunction with his friend."

"I cannot believe it. Why should they try to influence him? They can only wish his happiness; and if he is attached to me, no other woman can secure it."

"Your first position is false. They may wish many things besides his happiness; they may wish his increase of wealth and consequence; they may wish him to marry a girl who has all the importance of money, great connections, and pride."

"Beyond a doubt, they *do* wish him to choose Miss Darcy," replied Jane; "but this may be from better feelings than you are supposing. They have known her much longer than they have known me; no wonder if they love her better. But, whatever may be their own wishes, it is very unlikely they should have opposed their brother's. What sister would think herself at liberty to do it, unless there

Italian

admiration: ammirazione.
attached: fissato, attaccato, allegato.
attributing: attribuire.
cannot: non potere.
circumspect: circospetto.
conjunction: congiunzione.
deceives: inganna, truffa.
displease: dispiacere.
entreat: supplicare.
esteem: stima, rispetto, stimare, considerazione, considerare, rispettare, riguardo.

fancy: figurarsi, capriccio, immaginazione.
guarded: guardingo, custodito.
happiness: felicità.
impute: attribuire.
intentionally: intenzionalmente.
justified: giustificato.
liberty: libertà.
lively: vivace, spiritoso, vivo, animato, vispo.
misery: miseria.
misunderstand: fraintendere,

fraintendi, fraintendono, fraintendiamo, fraintendete, fraintendo.
opposed: opposto, contrapposto.
persist: persistere, persistono, persisto, persistiamo, persisti, persistete.
scheming: intrigante.
supposing: supponendo.
unhappy: infelice, triste.
unlikely: improbabile.
vanity: vanità.
whilst: durante.

were something very **objectionable**? If they believed him attached to me, they would not try to part us; if he were so, they could not succeed. By **supposing** such an affection, you make everybody **acting unnaturally** and wrong, and me most unhappy. Do not distress me by the idea. I am not **ashamed** of having been mistaken--or, at least, it is light, it is nothing in comparison of what I should feel in thinking ill of him or his sisters. Let me take it in the best light, in the light in which it may be understood."

Elizabeth could not **oppose** such a wish; and from this time Mr. Bingley's name was scarcely ever mentioned between them.

Mrs. **Bennet** still continued to wonder and repine at his returning no more, and though a day seldom passed in which Elizabeth did not account for it clearly, there was little chance of her ever considering it with less **perplexity**. Her daughter endeavoured to **convince** her of what she did not believe herself, that his attentions to Jane had been merely the effect of a common and **transient liking**, which ceased when he saw her no more; but though the probability of the statement was admitted at the time, she had the same story to **repeat** every day. Mrs. Bennet's best comfort was that Mr. Bingley must be down again in the summer.

Mr. Bennet treated the matter differently. "So, Lizzy," said he one day, "your sister is **crossed** in love, I find. I **congratulate** her. Next to being married, a girl likes to be crossed a little in love now and then. It is something to think of, and it gives her a sort of distinction among her companions. When is your turn to come? You will hardly bear to be long **outdone** by Jane. Now is your time. Here are officers enough in Meryton to **disappoint** all the young ladies in the country. Let Wickham be *your* man. He is a pleasant fellow, and would **jilt** you creditably."

"Thank you, sir, but a less **agreeable** man would satisfy me. We must not all expect Jane's good fortune."

"True," said Mr. Bennet, "but it is a comfort to think that whatever of that kind may **befall** you, you have an **affectionate** mother who will make the most of it."

Italian

acting: recitazione, rappresentazione.
affectionate: affettuoso.
agreeable: gradevole, piacevole, amabile.
ashamed: vergognoso.
befall: succedete, succedi, succediamo, succedo, succedono, succedere.
bennet: cariofillata, erba benedetta.
congratulate: felicitare, felicitate, felicito, feliciti, felicitano, felicita, felicitiamo.
convince: convincere, convincete, convinci, convinciamo, convinco, convincono, persuadere.
crossed: attraversato.
disappoint: deludere, deludo, deludete, deludi, deludiamo, deludono.
jilt: pianta, piantano, piantate, pianti, piantiamo, pianto, piantare, civetta.
liking: predilezione, simpatia.
objectionable: biasimevole.
oppose: contrapporre, contrapponete, contrapponi, contrapponiamo, contrappongono, contrappongo, opporre.
outdone: superato, sorpassato.
perplexity: perplessità.
repeat: ripetere, ripetono, ripetete, ripetiamo, ripeto, ripeti, ripetizione.
supposing: supponendo.
transient: transitorio.
unnaturally: innaturalmente.

Mr. Wickham's society was of **material** service in **dispelling** the **gloom** which the **late perverse** occurrences had **thrown** on many of the Longbourn family. They saw him often, and to his other **recommendations** was now **added** that of general unreserve. The whole of what Elizabeth had already **heard**, his **claims** on Mr. Darcy, and all that he had **suffered** from him, was now **openly acknowledged** and **publicly** canvassed; and **everybody** was **pleased** to know how much they had always disliked Mr. Darcy before they had known anything of the matter.

Miss Bennet was the only **creature** who could **suppose** there might be any **extenuating circumstances** in the case, **unknown** to the society of Hertfordshire; her **mild** and **steady candour** always pleaded for allowances, and urged the **possibility** of mistakes--but by everybody else Mr. Darcy was **condemned** as the **worst** of men.

Italian

acknowledged: riconosciuto.
added: aggiunto, addizionato.
candour: franchezza.
circumstances: circostanze.
claims: rivendicazioni.
condemned: condannato, biasimato.
creature: creatura.
dispelling: dissipando, scacciando.
everybody: ognuno, tutti, ogni, tutto.
extenuating: attenuante.
gloom: malinconia, tristezza.
heard: udito, sentito.

late: tardi, tardo, in ritardo, tardivo.
material: materiale, materia.
mild: mite, dolce.
openly: apertamente.
perverse: perverso.
pleased: contento, soddisfatto.
possibility: possibilità, eventualità.
publicly: pubblicamente.
recommendations: raccomandazioni.
steady: fisso.
suffered: sofferto, patito.
suppose: supporre, supponiamo,

supponete, suppongo, suppongono, supponi.
thrown: gettato.
unknown: sconosciuto, ignoto.
worst: peggiore.

CHAPTER 25

After a week spent in professions of love and schemes of **felicity**, Mr. Collins was called from his **amiable** Charlotte by the **arrival** of Saturday. The pain of **separation**, however, might be **alleviated** on his side, by **preparations** for the **reception** of his **bride**; as he had reason to hope, that shortly after his return into Hertfordshire, the day would be fixed that was to make him the happiest of men. He took leave of his relations at Longbourn with as much **solemnity** as before; **wished** his fair cousins health and **happiness** again, and promised their father another letter of thanks.

On the following Monday, Mrs. **Bennet** had the pleasure of **receiving** her brother and his wife, who came as usual to spend the Christmas at Longbourn. Mr. Gardiner was a **sensible**, gentlemanlike man, **greatly superior** to his sister, as well by nature as education. The Netherfield **ladies** would have had difficulty in **believing** that a man who lived by trade, and within view of his own warehouses, could have been so well-bred and **agreeable**. Mrs. Gardiner, who was several years younger than Mrs. Bennet and Mrs. Phillips, was an amiable, **intelligent**, **elegant** woman, and a great **favourite** with all her Longbourn nieces. Between the two **eldest** and herself especially, there **subsisted** a particular regard. They had frequently been **staying** with her in town.

The first part of Mrs. Gardiner's business on her arrival was to **distribute** her **presents** and describe the newest fashions. When this was done she had a less

Italian

agreeable: gradevole, piacevole, amabile.
alleviated: alleviato.
amiable: amabile.
arrival: arrivo, venuta.
believing: credendo, credere.
bennet: cariofillata, erba benedetta.
bride: sposa, fidanzata, novella sposa.
distribute: distribuire, distribuite, distribuiscono, distribuiamo, distribuisco, distribuisci.
eldest: maggiore, il più vecchio.

elegant: elegante.
favourite: preferito.
felicity: felicità.
greatly: molto, grandemente.
happiness: felicità.
intelligent: intelligente.
ladies: signore.
preparations: preparativi.
presents: presenta.
receiving: ricevendo, accogliendo, ricezione, ricevere, ricevente.
reception: ricezione, ricevimento,

accettazione, reception, portineria.
sensible: sensato, ragionevole, sensibile.
separation: separazione, distacco.
solemnity: solennità.
staying: stando, restando.
subsisted: esistito, sussistito.
superior: superiore.
wished: desiderato.

active part to **play**. It became her turn to listen. Mrs. **Bennet** had many grievances to **relate**, and much to **complain** of. They had all been very ill-used since she last saw her sister. Two of her girls had been upon the point of marriage, and after all there was nothing in it.

"I do not **blame** Jane," she continued, "for Jane would have got Mr. Bingley if she could. But Lizzy! Oh, sister! It is very hard to think that she might have been Mr. Collins's wife by this time, had it not been for her own perverseness. He made her an offer in this very room, and she **refused** him. The consequence of it is, that Lady Lucas will have a daughter married before I have, and that the Longbourn estate is just as much entailed as ever. The Lucases are very **artful** people indeed, sister. They are all for what they can get. I am sorry to say it of them, but so it is. It **makes** me very **nervous** and **poorly**, to be **thwarted** so in my own family, and to have neighbours who think of themselves before anybody else. However, your coming just at this time is the greatest of comforts, and I am very glad to hear what you tell us, of long sleeves."

Mrs. Gardiner, to whom the chief of this news had been given before, in the course of Jane and Elizabeth's **correspondence** with her, made her sister a **slight** answer, and, in **compassion** to her nieces, turned the conversation.

When alone with Elizabeth afterwards, she spoke more on the subject. "It seems likely to have been a **desirable** match for Jane," said she. "I am sorry it went off. But these things happen so often! A young man, such as you describe Mr. Bingley, so easily **falls** in love with a pretty girl for a few weeks, and when accident **separates** them, so easily **forgets** her, that these sort of inconsistencies are very frequent."

"An excellent **consolation** in its way," said Elizabeth, "but it will not do for *us*. We do not **suffer** by *accident*. It does not often happen that the **interference** of friends will **persuade** a young man of independent **fortune** to think no more of a girl whom he was **violently** in love with only a few days before."

"But that expression of 'violently in love' is so **hackneyed**, so **doubtful**, so **indefinite**, that it gives me very little idea. It is as often applied to feelings which

Italian

artful: astuto.
bennet: cariofillata, erba benedetta.
blame: colpa, biasimare, riprendere, incolpare, biasimo.
compassion: compassione.
complain: lagnarsi, lamentarsi, lamentare.
consolation: consolazione.
correspondence: corrispondenza, carteggio.
desirable: desiderabile.
doubtful: dubbioso.

falls: cade.
forgets: dimentica.
fortune: fortuna, sorte, patrimonio.
hackneyed: trito, trito e ritrito.
indefinite: indefinito.
interference: interferenza.
makes: fa, commette.
nervous: nervoso.
persuade: convincere, convincono, convincete, convinci, conviniciamo, convinco, persuadere, persuadono, persuado, persuadiamo, persuadi.

play: giocare, giocano, giocate, giochiamo, gioca, giochi, gioco, suonare, suona, suoni, suoniamo.
poorly: male, poveramente.
refused: rifiutato.
relate: raccontare, raccontiamo, racconta, raccontano, raccontate, racconti, racconto, narrare.
separates: separa.
slight: leggero, lieve.
thwarted: contrastato, ostacolato.
violently: violentemente.

arise from a half-hour's **acquaintance**, as to a real, strong **attachment**. Pray, how *violent was* Mr. Bingley's love?"

"I never saw a more **promising inclination**; he was **growing** quite **inattentive** to other people, and **wholly engrossed** by her. Every time they met, it was more decided and remarkable. At his own ball he **offended** two or three young ladies, by not asking them to dance; and I spoke to him twice myself, without **receiving** an answer. Could there be finer **symptoms**? Is not general incivility the very **essence** of love?"

"Oh, yes!--of that kind of love which I suppose him to have felt. Poor Jane! I am sorry for her, because, with her **disposition**, she may not get over it immediately. It had better have happened to *you*, Lizzy; you would have laughed yourself out of it **sooner**. But do you think she would be **prevailed** upon to go back with us? Change of scene might be of service--and perhaps a little relief from home may be as useful as anything."

Elizabeth was **exceedingly** pleased with this proposal, and felt **persuaded** of her sister's ready acquiescence.

"I hope," added Mrs. Gardiner, "that no consideration with regard to this young man will influence her. We live in so different a part of town, all our **connections** are so different, and, as you well know, we go out so little, that it is very **improbable** that they should meet at all, unless he really comes to see her."

"And *that* is quite impossible; for he is now in the **custody** of his friend, and Mr. Darcy would no more suffer him to call on Jane in such a part of London! My dear aunt, how could you think of it? Mr. Darcy may perhaps have *heard* of such a place as Gracechurch Street, but he would hardly think a month's **ablution** enough to **cleanse** him from its **impurities**, were he once to enter it; and depend upon it, Mr. Bingley never stirs without him."

"So much the better. I hope they will not meet at all. But does not Jane **correspond** with his sister? *she* will not be able to help calling."

"She will drop the acquaintance entirely."

Italian

ablution: abluzione.
acquaintance: conoscenza, conoscente.
arise: nascere, nasciamo, nasco, nasci, nascete, nascono, salire, sorgere, sorgete, sorgono, sorgi.
attachment: accessorio, allegato, attaccamento.
cleanse: pulire, puliamo, pulisci, puliscono, pulite.
connections: accesso.
correspond: corrispondere, corrispondete, corrispondi,

corrispondiamo, corrispondo,
corrispondono, avere la coincidenza.
custody: custodia.
disposition: disposizione,
predisposizione, ingegno, talento.
engrossed: assorbito.
essence: essenza.
exceedingly: estremamente.
growing: crescendo, coltivando.
improbable: improbabile.
impurities: impurità.
inattentive: disattento.

inclination: inclinazione, pendenza.
offended: offeso, insultato, oltraggiato.
persuaded: convinto, persuaso.
prevailed: prevalso.
promising: promettendo, promettente.
receiving: ricevendo, accogliendo, ricezione, ricevere, ricevente.
sooner: prima.
symptoms: sintomi.
violent: violento.
wholly: interamente, completamente.

But in **spite** of the certainty in which Elizabeth affected to place this point, as well as the still more interesting one of Bingley's being **withheld** from seeing Jane, she felt a **solicitude** on the subject which convinced her, on examination, that she did not consider it entirely **hopeless**. It was possible, and sometimes she thought it **probable**, that his affection might be **reanimated**, and the influence of his friends **successfully** combated by the more natural influence of Jane's attractions.

Miss **Bennet** accepted her aunt's invitation with pleasure; and the Bingleys were no otherwise in her thoughts at the same time, than as she hoped by Caroline's not living in the same house with her brother, she might occasionally spend a morning with her, without any danger of seeing him.

The Gardiners **stayed** a week at Longbourn; and what with the Phillipses, the Lucases, and the officers, there was not a day without its **engagement**. Mrs. Bennet had so **carefully provided** for the entertainment of her brother and sister, that they did not once sit down to a family dinner. When the engagement was for home, some of the officers always made part of it--of which officers Mr. Wickham was sure to be one; and on these occasion, Mrs. Gardiner, **rendered suspicious** by Elizabeth's warm **commendation**, narrowly observed them both. Without **supposing** them, from what she saw, to be very seriously in love, their preference of each other was plain enough to make her a little **uneasy**; and she resolved to speak to Elizabeth on the subject before she left Hertfordshire, and **represent** to her the **imprudence** of encouraging such an **attachment**.

To Mrs. Gardiner, Wickham had one means of **affording** pleasure, unconnected with his general powers. About ten or a **dozen** years **ago**, before her marriage, she had spent a **considerable** time in that very part of Derbyshire to which he **belonged**. They had, therefore, many **acquaintances** in common; and though Wickham had been little there since the death of Darcy's father, it was yet in his power to give her **fresher** intelligence of her former friends than she had been in the way of **procuring**.

Mrs. Gardiner had seen Pemberley, and known the late Mr. Darcy by character perfectly well. Here consequently was an **inexhaustible** subject of

Italian

acquaintances: conoscenze.
affording: permettendo.
ago: fa.
attachment: accessorio, allegato, attaccamento.
belonged: appartenuto.
bennet: cariofillata, erba benedetta.
carefully: attentamente.
commendation: raccomandazione.
considerable: considerevole, notevole, ragguardevole, rilevante.
dozen: dozzina.

engagement: fidanzamento, assunzione.
fresher: matricola.
hopeless: disperato, senza speranza.
imprudence: imprudenza.
inexhaustible: inesauribile.
probable: probabile.
procuring: procurando.
provided: provvisto, fornito.
reanimated: rianimato.
rendered: reso.
represent: rappresentare, rappresenta,

rappresento, rappresentate, rappresenti, rappresentano, rappresentiamo, figurare, figuri, figurate, figuriamo.
solicitude: sollecitudine.
spite: dispetto.
stayed: stato, restato.
successfully: con successo.
supposing: supponendo.
suspicious: sospettoso, sospetto.
uneasy: inquieto.
withheld: trattenuto.

discourse.   In **comparing** her **recollection** of Pemberley with the **minute description** which Wickham could give, and in **bestowing** her **tribute** of **praise** on the **character** of its **late possessor**, she was delighting both him and **herself**. On being made **acquainted** with the **present** Mr. Darcy's **treatment** of him, she **tried** to remember some of that gentleman's **reputed disposition** when quite a **lad** which might **agree** with it, and was **confident** at last that she **recollected** having **heard** Mr. Fitzwilliam Darcy **formerly spoken** of as a very **proud**, ill-natured boy.

Italian

acquainted: informato.
agree: concordare, concordi, concorda, concordate, concordiamo, concordo, concordano, convenire, essere d'accordo, pattuire, pattuisco.
bestowing: concedendo, tributando.
character: carattere, natura, indole, segno.
comparing: confrontando, paragonando.
confident: fiducioso.
description: descrizione.

discourse: discorso.
disposition: disposizione, predisposizione, ingegno, talento.
formerly: precedentemente, davanti, in passato, un tempo.
heard: udito, sentito.
herself: stesso, sè.
lad: ragazzo.
late: tardi, tardo, in ritardo, tardivo.
minute: minuto, il minuto, minuscolo, momento.
possessor: possessore.

praise: lodare, lode, elogiare, encomio, elogio.
present: presente, regalo, dono, presentare, attuale.
proud: orgoglioso, fiero.
recollected: rammentato.
recollection: memoria, ricordo.
reputed: reputato, stimato, supposto.
spoken: parlato.
treatment: trattamento.
tribute: tributo.
tried: sperimentato, tentativo.

CHAPTER 26

Mrs. Gardiner's **caution** to Elizabeth was **punctually** and **kindly** given on the first **favourable** opportunity of **speaking** to her alone; after **honestly** telling her what she thought, she thus went on:

"You are too sensible a girl, Lizzy, to fall in love merely because you are warned against it; and, therefore, I am not afraid of speaking **openly**. Seriously, I would have you be on your guard. Do not involve yourself or **endeavour** to involve him in an **affection** which the want of **fortune** would make so very **imprudent**. I have nothing to say against *him*; he is a most interesting young man; and if he had the fortune he ought to have, I should think you could not do better. But as it is, you must not let your **fancy** run away with you. You have sense, and we all expect you to use it. Your father would depend on *your* **resolution** and good **conduct**, I am sure. You must not **disappoint** your father."

"My dear **aunt**, this is being serious indeed."

"Yes, and I hope to **engage** you to be serious likewise."

"Well, then, you need not be under any **alarm**. I will take care of myself, and of Mr. Wickham too. He shall not be in love with me, if I can prevent it."

"Elizabeth, you are not serious now."

"I **beg** your **pardon**, I will try again. At present I am not in love with Mr. Wickham; no, I certainly am not. But he is, beyond all **comparison**, the most

Italian

affection: affetto, affezione, amore.
alarm: allarme, sveglia, allarmare.
aunt: zia, la zia.
beg: mendicare, mendicano, mendica, mendicate, mendico, mendichiamo, mendichi, chiedere, elemosinare, supplicare.
caution: avvertire, prudenza, avvertenza, cautela.
comparison: confronto, riscontro, comparazione, paragone.
conduct: condotta, condurre, guidare,
comportamento.
disappoint: deludere, deludo, deludete, deludi, deludiamo, deludono.
endeavour: tentare, tentativo, sforzarsi.
engage: innestare, innestiamo, innesta, innestano, innestate, innesti, ingaggiare, ingranare, impegnare, assumere, innesto.
fancy: figurarsi, capriccio, immaginazione.
favourable: favorevole.
fortune: fortuna, sorte, patrimonio.
honestly: onestamente.
imprudent: imprudente.
kindly: gentilmente, gentile.
openly: apertamente.
pardon: grazia, perdono, perdonare, scusare, scusa.
punctually: puntualmente.
resolution: risoluzione, definizione, deliberazione.
speaking: parlando, parlare.

agreeable man I ever saw--and if he **becomes** really attached to me--I believe it will be better that he should not. I see the **imprudence** of it. Oh! *that* **abominable** Mr. Darcy! My father's opinion of me does me the greatest honour, and I should be **miserable** to **forfeit** it. My father, however, is partial to Mr. Wickham. In short, my dear aunt, I should be very sorry to be the means of making any of you unhappy; but since we see every day that where there is affection, young people are seldom **withheld** by immediate want of fortune from entering into engagements with each other, how can I promise to be wiser than so many of my fellow-creatures if I am **tempted**, or how am I even to know that it would be **wisdom** to resist? All that I can promise you, therefore, is not to be in a hurry. I will not be in a hurry to believe myself his first object. When I am in company with him, I will not be wishing. In short, I will do my best."

"Perhaps it will be as well if you **discourage** his coming here so very often. At least, you should not *remind* you mother of **inviting** him."

"As I did the other day," said Elizabeth with a conscious smile: "very true, it will be wise in me to **refrain** from *that*. But do not imagine that he is always here so often. It is on your account that he has been so frequently invited this week. You know my mother's ideas as to the necessity of constant company for her friends. But really, and upon my honour, I will try to do what I think to be the wisest; and now I hope you are satisfied."

Her aunt assured her that she was, and Elizabeth having **thanked** her for the **kindness** of her hints, they parted; a **wonderful** instance of advice being given on such a point, without being resented.

Mr. Collins returned into Hertfordshire soon after it had been quitted by the Gardiners and Jane; but as he took up his **abode** with the Lucases, his arrival was no great **inconvenience** to Mrs. **Bennet**. His marriage was now **fast** approaching, and she was at length so far resigned as to think it inevitable, and even repeatedly to say, in an ill-natured tone, that she *"wished* they might be happy." Thursday was to be the wedding day, and on Wednesday Miss Lucas paid her **farewell** visit; and when she **rose** to take leave, Elizabeth, **ashamed** of her mother's ungracious and **reluctant** good wishes, and **sincerely** affected

Italian

abode: residenza, appartamento, alloggio, dimora.
abominable: abominevole, orribile, orrendo.
ashamed: vergognoso.
becomes: diviene, diventa.
bennet: cariofillata, erba benedetta.
discourage: impaurire, scoraggiare, spaventare, impaurite, spavento, spaventiamo, spaventi, spaventate, spaventano, spaventa, scoraggio.
farewell: addio, congedo.

fast: veloce, digiuno, velocemente, presto, digiunare, rapido.
forfeit: penalità, penale.
imprudence: imprudenza.
inconvenience: inconvenienza, disagio, disturbo.
inviting: invitando, invitare, invitante.
kindness: gentilezza, bontà, cortesia.
miserable: miserabile, misero, afflitto, cattivo, triste, povero, miserevole, miserando.
refrain: ritornello, astenersi.

reluctant: riluttante, ritroso, restio.
remind: ricordare, ricorda, ricordo, ricordiamo, ricordi, ricordate, ricordano.
rose: rosa.
sincerely: sinceramente, francamente.
tempted: tentato.
thanked: ringraziato.
wisdom: saggezza, freccia, sapienza.
withheld: trattenuto.
wonderful: meraviglioso, stupendo, splendido.

herself, **accompanied** her out of the room. As they went **downstairs** together, Charlotte said:

"I shall depend on hearing from you very often, Eliza."

"*That* you certainly shall."

"And I have another **favour** to ask you. Will you come and see me?"

"We shall often meet, I hope, in Hertfordshire."

"I am not likely to leave Kent for some time. Promise me, therefore, to come to Hunsford."

Elizabeth could not **refuse**, though she foresaw little pleasure in the visit.

"My father and Maria are coming to me in March," added Charlotte, "and I hope you will consent to be of the party. Indeed, Eliza, you will be as welcome as either of them."

The wedding took place; the **bride** and **bridegroom** set off for Kent from the church door, and everybody had as much to say, or to hear, on the subject as usual. Elizabeth soon heard from her friend; and their **correspondence** was as **regular** and **frequent** as it had ever been; that it should be equally unreserved was impossible. Elizabeth could never address her without feeling that all the **comfort** of **intimacy** was over, and though determined not to **slacken** as a **correspondent**, it was for the **sake** of what had been, rather than what was. Charlotte's first letters were received with a good deal of **eagerness**; there could not but be **curiosity** to know how she would speak of her new home, how she would like Lady Catherine, and how happy she would **dare pronounce** herself to be; though, when the letters were read, Elizabeth felt that Charlotte expressed herself on every point exactly as she might have **foreseen**. She wrote **cheerfully**, seemed **surrounded** with comforts, and mentioned nothing which she could not **praise**. The house, furniture, **neighbourhood**, and **roads**, were all to her taste, and Lady Catherine's behaviour was most friendly and **obliging**. It was Mr. Collins's picture of Hunsford and Rosings **rationally softened**; and Elizabeth **perceived** that she must wait for her own visit there to know the rest.

Italian

accompanied: accompagnato.
bride: sposa, fidanzata, novella sposa.
bridegroom: sposo.
cheerfully: allegramente.
comfort: consolare, comodità, confortare, comfort, benessere.
correspondence: corrispondenza, carteggio.
correspondent: corrispondente.
curiosity: curiosità.
dare: osare, oso, osiamo, osi, osate, osano, osa, sfida.

downstairs: giù dalle scale.
eagerness: impazienza.
favour: favorire, favore.
foreseen: previsto.
frequent: frequente, bazzicare.
intimacy: intimità.
neighbourhood: circondario, distretto, vicinato, quartiere.
obliging: obbligando, accomodante.
perceived: scorto, percepito, intravisto.
praise: lodare, lode, elogiare, encomio,

elogio.
pronounce: pronunciare, pronunciano, pronunciate, pronunciamo, pronunci, pronuncio, pronuncia.
rationally: razionalmente.
refuse: rifiutare, rifiutarsi, rifiuti.
regular: regolare, normale.
roads: strade.
sake: causa.
slacken: allentare.
softened: ammorbidito.
surrounded: circondato.

Jane had already written a few lines to her sister to **announce** their safe arrival in London; and when she wrote again, Elizabeth hoped it would be in her power to say something of the Bingleys.

Her **impatience** for this second letter was as well rewarded as impatience generally is. Jane had been a week in town without either seeing or hearing from Caroline. She accounted for it, however, by **supposing** that her last letter to her friend from Longbourn had by some accident been lost.

"My aunt," she continued, "is going to-morrow into that part of the town, and I shall take the opportunity of calling in Grosvenor Street."

She wrote again when the visit was paid, and she had seen Miss Bingley. "I did not think Caroline in spirits," were her words, "but she was very glad to see me, and **reproached** me for giving her no notice of my coming to London. I was right, therefore, my last letter had never reached her. I **inquired** after their brother, of course. He was well, but so much **engaged** with Mr. Darcy that they **scarcely** ever saw him. I found that Miss Darcy was expected to dinner. I wish I could see her. My visit was not long, as Caroline and Mrs. Hurst were going out. I dare say I shall see them soon here."

Elizabeth shook her head over this letter. It convinced her that accident only could discover to Mr. Bingley her sister's being in town.

Four weeks passed away, and Jane saw nothing of him. She endeavoured to persuade herself that she did not **regret** it; but she could no longer be blind to Miss Bingley's **inattention**. After waiting at home every morning for a **fortnight**, and **inventing** every evening a fresh excuse for her, the **visitor** did at last appear; but the **shortness** of her stay, and yet more, the **alteration** of her manner would allow Jane to **deceive** herself no longer. The letter which she wrote on this occasion to her sister will prove what she felt.

"My dearest Lizzy will, I am sure, be **incapable** of triumphing in her better judgement, at my expense, when I **confess** myself to have been entirely **deceived** in Miss Bingley's regard for me. But, my dear sister, though the event has proved you right, do not think me **obstinate** if I still **assert** that, considering what her

Italian

alteration: alterazione, modifica, cambiamento, variazione.
announce: annunciare, annunciate, annunci, annuncia, annunciamo, annunciano, annunziare, annuncio, annunziate, annunzi, annunzia.
assert: asserire, asserite, asseriscono, asserisci, asserisco, asseriamo, sostenere, affermare.
confess: confessare, confessa, confessano, confessate, confessi, confessiamo, confesso.

deceive: ingannare, ingannano, inganniamo, ingannate, inganna, inganni, inganno, truffare, truffate, truffano, truffiamo.
deceived: ingannato, truffato.
engaged: occupato, innestato, impegnato.
fortnight: due settimane.
impatience: impazienza.
inattention: disattenzione.
incapable: incapace.
inquired: domandato.

inventing: inventando.
obstinate: ostinato.
regret: rincrescere, rammarico, rimpiangere, rimpianto, rincrescimento.
reproached: rimproverato.
scarcely: appena, a stento.
shortness: bassa statura, brevità.
supposing: supponendo.
visitor: visitatore, ospite.

behaviour was, my confidence was as natural as your **suspicion**. I do not at all **comprehend** her reason for wishing to be **intimate** with me; but if the same circumstances were to happen again, I am sure I should be **deceived** again. Caroline did not return my visit till yesterday; and not a note, not a line, did I receive in the **meantime**. When she did come, it was very evident that she had no pleasure in it; she made a slight, formal **apology**, for not calling before, said not a word of wishing to see me again, and was in every respect so **altered** a creature, that when she went away I was perfectly resolved to continue the **acquaintance** no longer. I pity, though I **cannot** help **blaming** her. She was very wrong in singling me out as she did; I can safely say that every **advance** to **intimacy** began on her side. But I pity her, because she must feel that she has been acting wrong, and because I am very sure that anxiety for her brother is the cause of it. I need not explain myself **farther**; and though *we* know this anxiety to be quite **needless**, yet if she feels it, it will easily account for her behaviour to me; and so deservedly dear as he is to his sister, whatever anxiety she must feel on his behalf is natural and **amiable**. I cannot but wonder, however, at her having any such fears now, because, if he had at all cared about me, we must have met, long ago. He knows of my being in town, I am certain, from something she said herself; and yet it would seem, by her manner of talking, as if she wanted to persuade herself that he is really partial to Miss Darcy. I cannot understand it. If I were not afraid of **judging harshly**, I should be almost **tempted** to say that there is a strong appearance of **duplicity** in all this. But I will **endeavour** to **banish** every painful thought, and think only of what will make me happy--your **affection**, and the **invariable kindness** of my dear uncle and aunt. Let me hear from you very soon. Miss Bingley said something of his never returning to Netherfield again, of giving up the house, but not with any **certainty**. We had better not mention it. I am extremely glad that you have such pleasant accounts from our friends at Hunsford. Pray go to see them, with Sir William and Maria. I am sure you will be very comfortable there.--Yours, etc."

   This letter gave Elizabeth some pain; but her spirits returned as she considered that Jane would no longer be duped, by the sister at least. All **expectation** from the brother was now absolutely over. She would not even wish

Italian

acquaintance: conoscenza, conoscente.
advance: avanzare, anticipo, proporre, avvicinarsi, anticipazione, avanzamento, avanzata, acconto, progredire, prestito, progresso.
affection: affetto, affezione, amore.
altered: alterato.
amiable: amabile.
apology: scusa, apologia.
banish: bandire, bandisci, bandisco, bandiscono, bandite, bandiamo, esiliare.

blaming: biasimare.
cannot: non potere.
certainty: certezza.
comprehend: comprendere, comprendo, comprendono, comprendiamo, comprendi, comprendete.
deceived: ingannato, truffato.
duplicity: duplicità.
endeavour: tentare, tentativo, sforzarsi.
expectation: attesa, aspettativa.

farther: più lontano.
harshly: duramente.
intimacy: intimità.
intimate: intimo.
invariable: invariabile.
judging: giudicare.
kindness: gentilezza, bontà, cortesia.
meantime: frattanto, nel frattempo, intanto.
needless: inutile.
suspicion: sospetto.
tempted: tentato.

for a renewal of his attentions. His character sunk on every **review** of it; and as a punishment for him, as well as a possible advantage to Jane, she seriously hoped he might really soon marry Mr. Darcy's sister, as by Wickham's account, she would make him **abundantly** regret what he had thrown away.

Mrs. Gardiner about this time reminded Elizabeth of her promise concerning that gentleman, and required information; and Elizabeth had such to send as might rather give **contentment** to her aunt than to herself. His apparent **partiality** had **subsided**, his attentions were over, he was the **admirer** of some one else. Elizabeth was **watchful** enough to see it all, but she could see it and write of it without material pain. Her heart had been but slightly touched, and her **vanity** was satisfied with believing that *she* would have been his only choice, had fortune **permitted** it. The sudden **acquisition** of ten thousand pounds was the most remarkable charm of the young lady to whom he was now **rendering** himself agreeable; but Elizabeth, less clear-sighted perhaps in this case than in Charlotte's, did not quarrel with him for his wish of independence. Nothing, on the contrary, could be more natural; and while able to suppose that it **cost** him a few **struggle** to **relinquish** her, she was ready to allow it a wise and desirable measure for both, and could very sincerely wish him happy.

All this was acknowledged to Mrs. Gardiner; and after **relating** the circumstances, she thus went on: "I am now convinced, my dear aunt, that I have never been much in love; for had I really experienced that pure and **elevating** **passion**, I should at present **detest** his very name, and wish him all manner of evil. But my feelings are not only **cordial** towards *him*; they are even **impartial** towards Miss King. I **cannot** find out that I hate her at all, or that I am in the least unwilling to think her a very good sort of girl. There can be no love in all this. My **watchfulness** has been **effectual**; and though I certainly should be a more interesting object to all my **acquaintances** were I distractedly in love with him, I cannot say that I regret my comparative **insignificance**. Importance may sometimes be **purchased** too **dearly**. Kitty and Lydia take his **defection** much more to heart than I do. They are young in the **ways** of the world, and not yet

open to the **mortifying conviction** that **handsome** young men must have
something to **live** on as well as the plain."

Italian

conviction: convinzione, condanna.
handsome: bello, carino.
live: vivere, vivete, vivono, viviamo,
  vivi, vivo, abitare, abiti, abita,
  abitano, abitate.
mortifying: mortificando, umiliante.

CHAPTER 27

With no greater events than these in the Longbourn family, and otherwise **diversified** by little beyond the walks to Meryton, sometimes dirty and sometimes cold, did January and February **pass** away. March was to take Elizabeth to Hunsford. She had not at first thought very **seriously** of going **thither**; but Charlotte, she soon found, was **depending** on the plan and she **gradually** learned to consider it herself with greater **pleasure** as well as greater **certainty**. Absence had increased her **desire** of **seeing** Charlotte again, and **weakened** her **disgust** of Mr. Collins. There was **novelty** in the scheme, and as, with such a mother and such uncompanionable sisters, home could not be **faultless**, a little change was not **unwelcome** for its own **sake**. The **journey** would **moreover** give her a **peep** at Jane; and, in short, as the time drew near, she would have been very sorry for any **delay**. Everything, however, went on **smoothly**, and was finally settled **according** to Charlotte's first **sketch**. She was to **accompany** Sir William and his second daughter. The improvement of spending a night in London was added in time, and the plan became **perfect** as plan could be.

The only pain was in leaving her father, who would certainly miss her, and who, when it came to the point, so little liked her going, that he told her to write to him, and almost **promised** to answer her letter.

Italian

accompany: accompagnare, accompagna, accompagniamo, accompagno, accompagni, accompagnate, accompagnano.
according: secondo.
certainty: certezza.
delay: ritardo, tardare, ritardare, indugio, indugiare.
depending: dipendendo.
desire: desiderio, desiderare, bramare.
disgust: ripugnanza, avversione, disgustare, disgusto, nauseare.

diversified: diversificato, differenziato.
faultless: irreprensibile, perfetto.
gradually: gradualmente, poco a poco.
journey: viaggio, viaggiare.
moreover: inoltre, d'altronde.
novelty: novità.
pass: passare, passaggio, lasciapassare, passata, trascorrere, passo.
peep: occhieggiare, pigolio, pigolare, sbirciare.
perfect: perfetto, perfezionare.

pleasure: piacere, gradimento.
promised: promesso.
sake: causa.
seeing: vedendo, segando.
seriously: seriamente, gravemente.
sketch: schizzo, abbozzare, bozzetto, disegno, abbozzo, progetto, progettare, schema.
smoothly: facilmente, agevolmente.
thither: là.
unwelcome: sgradito.
weakened: indebolito, debilitato.

The farewell between herself and Mr. Wickham was perfectly friendly; on his side even more. His present pursuit could not make him forget that Elizabeth had been the first to **excite** and to deserve his attention, the first to listen and to pity, the first to be admired; and in his manner of **bidding** her **adieu**, wishing her every enjoyment, **reminding** her of what she was to expect in Lady Catherine de Bourgh, and trusting their opinion of her--their opinion of everybody--would always **coincide**, there was a **solicitude**, an interest which she felt must ever **attach** her to him with a most sincere regard; and she parted from him convinced that, whether married or single, he must always be her **model** of the amiable and pleasing.

Her fellow-travellers the next day were not of a kind to make her think him less agreeable. Sir William Lucas, and his daughter Maria, a good-humoured girl, but as empty-headed as himself, had nothing to say that could be worth hearing, and were listened to with about as much delight as the **rattle** of the **chaise**. Elizabeth loved absurdities, but she had known Sir William's too long. He could tell her nothing new of the wonders of his presentation and **knighthood**; and his civilities were **worn** out, like his information.

It was a journey of only twenty-four miles, and they began it so early as to be in Gracechurch Street by **noon**. As they **drove** to Mr. Gardiner's door, Jane was at a drawing-room window watching their arrival; when they entered the passage she was there to welcome them, and Elizabeth, looking earnestly in her face, was pleased to see it **healthful** and lovely as ever. On the **stairs** were a **troop** of little boys and girls, whose eagerness for their cousin's appearance would not allow them to wait in the drawing-room, and whose **shyness**, as they had not seen her for a twelvemonth, prevented their coming **lower**. All was joy and kindness. The day passed most pleasantly away; the morning in **bustle** and **shopping**, and the evening at one of the theatres.

Elizabeth then contrived to sit by her aunt. Their first object was her sister; and she was more **grieved** than astonished to hear, in reply to her minute inquiries, that though Jane always **struggled** to support her spirits, there were periods of **dejection**. It was **reasonable**, however, to hope that they would not

Italian

adieu: addio.
attach: fissare, attaccare, fissi, attacca, fissate, fissano, fisso, attacchi, attacchiamo, attaccate, attaccano.
bidding: offerta, licitazione, comando.
bustle: trambusto.
chaise: calesse.
coincide: coincidere, coincidete, coincidi, coincidiamo, coincido, coincidono.
dejection: deiezione, abbattimento, scoraggiamento, depressione.

drove: gregge.
excite: eccitare, ecciti, eccitiamo, eccitano, eccita, eccito, eccitate, spronare, incitare.
grieved: accorato, addolorato.
healthful: sano, salubre.
knighthood: cavalierato.
lower: inferiore, abbassare, abbassate, abbassi, abbassiamo, abbassano, abbassa, abbasso, calare, abbattere.
model: modello, esempio, indossatrice.

noon: mezzogiorno, mezzodì.
rattle: sonaglio, rantolo.
reasonable: ragionevole, sensato.
reminding: ricordando.
shopping: shopping.
shyness: timidezza.
solicitude: sollecitudine.
stairs: scala, scale.
struggled: lottato.
troop: truppa.
worn: consumato, usato, esausto, portato, logoro.

continue long. Mrs. Gardiner gave her the **particulars** also of Miss Bingley's visit in Gracechurch Street, and **repeated** conversations **occurring** at different times between Jane and herself, which **proved** that the former had, from her heart, given up the acquaintance.

Mrs. Gardiner then rallied her **niece** on Wickham's **desertion**, and complimented her on **bearing** it so well.

"But my dear Elizabeth," she added, "what sort of girl is Miss King? I should be sorry to think our friend **mercenary**."

"Pray, my dear **aunt**, what is the difference in **matrimonial** affairs, between the mercenary and the **prudent motive**? Where does **discretion** end, and **avarice** begin? Last Christmas you were afraid of his **marrying** me, because it would be **imprudent**; and now, because he is trying to get a girl with only ten thousand pounds, you want to find out that he is mercenary."

"If you will only tell me what sort of girl Miss King is, I shall know what to think."

"She is a very good kind of girl, I believe. I know no **harm** of her."

"But he paid her not the smallest attention **till** her grandfather's death made her **mistress** of this fortune."

"No--what should he? If it were not **allowable** for him to **gain** *my* affections because I had no money, what **occasion** could there be for making love to a girl whom he did not care about, and who was equally poor?"

"But there seems an **indelicacy** in directing his attentions towards her so soon after this event."

"A man in **distressed** circumstances has not time for all those **elegant** decorums which other people may **observe**. If *she* does not **object** to it, why should *we*?"

"*Her* not objecting does not **justify** *him*. It only shows her being **deficient** in something herself--sense or feeling."

Italian

allowable: ammissibile.
aunt: zia, la zia.
avarice: avarizia.
bearing: cuscinetto, rapporto.
deficient: deficiente, carente, difettoso, insufficiente.
desertion: diserzione.
discretion: discrezione.
distressed: afflitto.
elegant: elegante.
gain: guadagno, profitto, guadagnare, vantaggio, beneficio.

harm: danno, nuocere, danneggiare.
imprudent: imprudente.
indelicacy: indelicatezza.
justify: giustificare, giustificate, giustifico, giustificiamo, giustificano, giustifici, giustifica.
marrying: sposandosi.
matrimonial: matrimoniale.
mercenary: mercenario.
mistress: padrona.
motive: motivo, movente, ragione.
niece: nipote.

object: oggetto, cosa, scopo.
observe: osservare, osservano, osservo, osserviamo, osservate, osserva, osservi, eseguire, compiere.
occasion: occasione.
occurring: accadendo, succedendo.
particulars: particolari.
proved: provato.
prudent: prudente, sensato.
repeated: ripetuto.
till: finchè, coltivare, cassa, fino, arare.

"Well," cried Elizabeth, "have it as you choose. *He* shall be **mercenary**, and *she* shall be foolish."

"No, Lizzy, that is what I do *not* choose. I should be sorry, you know, to think ill of a young man who has lived so long in Derbyshire."

"Oh! if that is all, I have a very poor opinion of young men who live in Derbyshire; and their **intimate** friends who live in Hertfordshire are not much better. I am sick of them all. Thank Heaven! I am going to-morrow where I shall find a man who has not one **agreeable quality**, who has neither manner nor sense to **recommend** him. Stupid men are the only ones worth knowing, after all."

"Take care, Lizzy; that speech savours strongly of **disappointment**."

Before they were **separated** by the conclusion of the play, she had the unexpected **happiness** of an **invitation** to **accompany** her uncle and aunt in a **tour** of pleasure which they proposed taking in the summer.

"We have not determined how far it shall **carry** us," said Mrs. Gardiner, "but, perhaps, to the Lakes."

No scheme could have been more agreeable to Elizabeth, and her acceptance of the invitation was most ready and grateful. "Oh, my dear, dear aunt," she rapturously cried, "what delight! what **felicity**! You give me **fresh** life and **vigour**. Adieu to disappointment and **spleen**. What are young men to rocks and **mountains**? Oh! what hours of **transport** we shall spend! And when we *do* return, it shall not be like other travellers, without being able to give one **accurate** idea of anything. We *will* know where we have gone--we *will* **recollect** what we have seen. Lakes, mountains, and rivers shall not be jumbled together in our imaginations; nor when we attempt to describe any particular scene, will we begin quarreling about its **relative** situation. Let *our* first effusions be less insupportable than those of the **generality** of travellers."

Italian

accompany: accompagnare, accompagna, accompagniamo, accompagno, accompagni, accompagnate, accompagnano.
accurate: esatto, preciso, accurato.
agreeable: gradevole, piacevole, amabile.
carry: portare, porti, portate, portiamo, portano, porto, porta, trasportare, trasporta, trasportano, trasportate.
disappointment: delusione, disappunto.

felicity: felicità.
fresh: fresco.
generality: generalità.
happiness: felicità.
intimate: intimo.
invitation: invito.
mercenary: mercenario.
mountains: montagne.
quality: qualità.
recollect: rammenta, rammentano, rammentate, rammenti, rammentiamo, rammento,

rammentare, ricordarsi.
recommend: raccomandare, raccomanda, raccomandano, raccomandate, raccomandi, raccomandiamo, raccomando, consigliare, vantare.
relative: parente, relativo, familiare.
separated: separato.
spleen: milza, malumore.
tour: giro.
transport: trasporto, trasportare.
vigour: forza, vigore.

CHAPTER 28

Every object in the next day's journey was new and interesting to Elizabeth; and her spirits were in a state of **enjoyment**; for she had seen her sister looking so well as to **banish** all fear for her health, and the prospect of her northern tour was a constant source of delight.

When they left the high road for the lane to Hunsford, every eye was in **search** of the Parsonage, and every turning expected to bring it in view. The **palings** of Rosings Park was their **boundary** on one side. Elizabeth smiled at the **recollection** of all that she had heard of its **inhabitants**.

At length the Parsonage was **discernible**. The garden **sloping** to the road, the house standing in it, the green pales, and the **laurel hedge**, everything declared they were **arriving**. Mr. Collins and Charlotte appeared at the door, and the carriage stopped at the small **gate** which led by a short **gravel** walk to the house, **amidst** the nods and smiles of the whole party. In a moment they were all out of the **chaise**, **rejoicing** at the sight of each other. Mrs. Collins welcomed her friend with the liveliest pleasure, and Elizabeth was more and more satisfied with coming when she found herself so **affectionately** received. She saw **instantly** that her cousin's **manners** were not **altered** by his marriage; his formal **civility** was just what it had been, and he **detained** her some minutes at the gate to hear and **satisfy** his inquiries after all her family. They were then, with no other delay than his **pointing** out the **neatness** of the entrance, taken into the

Italian

affectionately: affettuosamente.
altered: alterato.
amidst: tra, fra.
arriving: arrivando.
banish: bandire, bandisci, bandisco, bandiscono, bandite, bandiamo, esiliare.
boundary: confine, frontiera, limite, delimitazione, contorno.
chaise: calesse.
civility: civiltà, cortesia.
detained: ritenuto.

discernible: distinguibile, discernibile.
enjoyment: godimento.
gate: cancello, porta, saracinesca, paratoia, uscita.
gravel: ghiaia.
hedge: siepe, copertura, barriera.
inhabitants: fruitori della casa.
instantly: direttamente, istantaneamente, immediatamente.
laurel: alloro, lauro.
manners: educazione.
neatness: pulizia, accuratezza.

palings: steccato, palizzata.
pointing: indicare.
recollection: memoria, ricordo.
rejoicing: gioia.
satisfy: soddisfare, accontentare, soddisfano, soddisfiamo, soddisfa, soddisfate, soddisfo, accontentate, accontento, soddisfi, accontentano.
search: ricerca, cerca, ricercare, cercare, perquisizione.
sloping: inclinato.

house; and as soon as they were in the parlour, he welcomed them a second time, with **ostentatious** formality to his humble abode, and punctually repeated all his wife's offers of refreshment.

Elizabeth was prepared to see him in his **glory**; and she could not help in fancying that in displaying the good proportion of the room, its aspect and its furniture, he addressed himself particularly to her, as if wishing to make her feel what she had lost in refusing him. But though everything seemed **neat** and comfortable, she was not able to **gratify** him by any **sigh** of **repentance**, and rather looked with wonder at her friend that she could have so cheerful an air with such a companion. When Mr. Collins said anything of which his wife might reasonably be ashamed, which certainly was not unseldom, she **involuntarily** turned her eye on Charlotte. Once or twice she could **discern** a **faint** blush; but in general Charlotte wisely did not hear. After sitting long enough to admire every article of furniture in the room, from the **sideboard** to the **fender**, to give an account of their journey, and of all that had happened in London, Mr. Collins invited them to take a **stroll** in the garden, which was large and well laid out, and to the **cultivation** of which he attended himself. To work in this garden was one of his most respectable pleasures; and Elizabeth admired the command of countenance with which Charlotte talked of the healthfulness of the exercise, and **owned** she encouraged it as much as possible. Here, leading the way through every walk and **cross** walk, and scarcely allowing them an interval to utter the praises he asked for, every view was **pointed** out with a **minuteness** which left beauty entirely behind. He could number the **fields** in every direction, and could tell how many tress there were in the most distant **clump**. But of all the views which his garden, or which the country or kingdom could boast, none were to be compared with the prospect of Rosings, afforded by an opening in the trees that bordered the park nearly opposite the front of his house. It was a handsome modern building, well **situated** on rising ground.

From his garden, Mr. Collins would have led them round his two meadows; but the ladies, not having **shoes** to **encounter** the remains of a white **frost**, turned back; and while Sir William accompanied him, Charlotte took her sister and

Italian

clump: gruppo.

cross: croce, attraversare, irato, incrociare, incrocio, varcare, valicare, traversare, accavallare.

cultivation: coltivazione.

discern: distinguo, distingui, percepiamo, percepiscono, percepisco, percepisci, distinguiamo, percepite, distinguete, discernono, discerno.

encounter: incontro, incontrare, incontra, incontriamo, incontri, incontrano, incontrate.

faint: debole, svenire, svengo, svengono, sveniamo, svenite, svieni, svenimento, vago.

fender: parafango, parabordo.

fields: campi.

frost: gelo, brina, gelata.

glory: gloria.

gratify: gratificare, gratificano, gratifico, gratifichiamo, gratifichi, gratificate, gratifica.

involuntarily: involontariamente.

minuteness: minuziosità, minutezza.

neat: pulito, puro, ordinato.

ostentatious: ostentato.

owned: posseduto.

pointed: appuntato, appuntito, acuto, aguzzo.

repentance: pentimento, rimpianto.

shoes: scarpe.

sideboard: armadio, credenza.

sigh: sospirare, sospiro.

situated: situato.

stroll: passeggiata, passeggiare.

friend over the house, extremely well pleased, probably, to have the opportunity of showing it without her husband's help. It was rather small, but well **built** and convenient; and everything was fitted up and arranged with a **neatness** and **consistency** of which Elizabeth gave Charlotte all the credit. When Mr. Collins could be forgotten, there was really an air of great comfort **throughout**, and by Charlotte's evident enjoyment of it, Elizabeth supposed he must be often forgotten.

She had already learnt that Lady Catherine was still in the country. It was spoken of again while they were at dinner, when Mr. Collins joining in, observed:

"Yes, Miss Elizabeth, you will have the honour of seeing Lady Catherine de Bourgh on the **ensuing** Sunday at church, and I need not say you will be delighted with her. She is all **affability** and **condescension**, and I doubt not but you will be honoured with some portion of her notice when service is over. I have scarcely any **hesitation** in saying she will **include** you and my sister Maria in every invitation with which she honours us during your stay here. Her behaviour to my dear Charlotte is charming. We **dine** at Rosings twice every week, and are never allowed to walk home. Her ladyship's carriage is **regularly** ordered for us. I *should* say, one of her ladyship's carriages, for she has several."

"Lady Catherine is a very respectable, sensible woman indeed," added Charlotte, "and a most **attentive** neighbour."

"Very true, my dear, that is exactly what I say. She is the sort of woman whom one **cannot** regard with too much deference."

The evening was spent **chiefly** in talking over Hertfordshire news, and telling again what had already been written; and when it closed, Elizabeth, in the **solitude** of her **chamber**, had to **meditate** upon Charlotte's degree of **contentment**, to understand her address in **guiding**, and **composure** in bearing with, her husband, and to acknowledge that it was all done very well. She had also to **anticipate** how her visit would pass, the **quiet tenor** of their usual employments, the **vexatious** interruptions of Mr. Collins, and the gaieties of their intercourse with Rosings. A lively imagination soon settled it all.

Italian

affability: affabilità.
anticipate: anticipare, anticipiamo, anticipi, anticipate, anticipa, anticipano, anticipo, prevedere, prevenire.
attentive: attento, premuroso.
built: costruito.
cannot: non potere.
chamber: camera.
chiefly: principalmente, soprattutto.
composure: calma, compostezza.
condescension: condiscendenza.

consistency: consistenza, coerenza.
contentment: soddisfazione.
dine: cenare.
ensuing: seguendo.
guiding: guidare.
hesitation: esitazione, tentennamento.
include: contenere, contenete, conteniamo, contieni, contengo, contengono, includere, includo, includono, includiamo, includi.
meditate: meditare, mediti, meditiamo, meditate, meditano,

medita, medito.
neatness: pulizia, accuratezza.
quiet: calmare, tranquillo, placare, quieto, calmo, zitto, silenzioso, quiete.
regularly: regolarmente, spesso, frequentemente, sovente.
solitude: solitudine.
tenor: tenore.
throughout: dappertutto, in tutto, completamente, per tutto.
vexatious: irritante.

About the **middle** of the next day, as she was in her room getting ready for a walk, a sudden noise **below** seemed to speak the whole house in **confusion**; and, after listening a moment, she heard somebody running **upstairs** in a **violent hurry**, and calling **loudly** after her. She opened the door and met Maria in the **landing** place, who, **breathless** with **agitation**, cried out--

"Oh, my dear Eliza! **pray** make **haste** and come into the dining-room, for there is such a sight to be seen! I will not tell you what it is. Make haste, and come down this moment."

Elizabeth asked **questions** in **vain**; Maria would tell her nothing more, and down they ran into the dining-room, which fronted the lane, in quest of this wonder; It was two ladies **stopping** in a low phaeton at the garden gate.

"And is this all?" cried Elizabeth. "I expected at least that the pigs were got into the garden, and here is nothing but Lady Catherine and her daughter."

"La! my dear," said Maria, quite shocked at the mistake, "it is not Lady Catherine. The old lady is Mrs. Jenkinson, who lives with them; the other is Miss de Bourgh. Only look at her. She is quite a little **creature**. Who would have thought that she could be so thin and small?"

"She is **abominably rude** to keep Charlotte out of doors in all this **wind**. Why does she not come in?"

"Oh, Charlotte says she hardly ever does. It is the greatest of favours when Miss de Bourgh comes in."

"I like her appearance," said Elizabeth, **struck** with other ideas. "She looks **sickly** and cross. Yes, she will do for him very well. She will make him a very proper wife."

Mr. Collins and Charlotte were both standing at the gate in conversation with the ladies; and Sir William, to Elizabeth's high **diversion**, was stationed in the **doorway**, in **earnest contemplation** of the **greatness** before him, and **constantly bowing** whenever Miss de Bourgh looked that way.

At length there was nothing more to be said; the ladies drove on, and the others returned into the house. Mr. Collins no **sooner** saw the two girls than he

Italian

abominably: abominevolmente.
agitation: agitazione.
below: sotto, giù, dabbasso.
bowing: archeggio.
breathless: ansante, senza fiato.
confusion: confusione.
constantly: costantemente.
contemplation: contemplazione.
creature: creatura.
diversion: diversione, deviazione, dirottamento.
doorway: entrata, vano della porta.

earnest: serio, caparra.
greatness: grandezza.
haste: fretta, furia.
hurry: affrettarsi, fretta.
landing: pianerottolo, sbarco, approdo, atterraggio.
loudly: forte, ad alta voce.
middle: mezzo, medio, metà, di mezzo.
pray: pregare, pregate, prego, preghi, prega, preghiamo, pregano.
quest: ricerca.

rude: scortese, rozzo, maleducato.
sickly: cagionevole, malaticcio, malatamente.
sooner: prima.
stopping: fermando, cessando, interrompendo, smettendo, arrestando.
struck: colpito.
upstairs: di sopra.
vain: vanitoso, vano.
violent: violento.
wind: vento, flatulenza, avvolgere.

began to **congratulate** them on their good **fortune**, which Charlotte **explained** by **letting** them know that the whole party was asked to **dine** at Rosings the next day.

Italian

congratulate: felicitare, felicitate,
  felicito, feliciti, felicitano, felicita,
  felicitiamo.
dine: cenare.
explained: spiegato.
fortune: fortuna, sorte, patrimonio.
letting: affittando.

CHAPTER 29

Mr. Collins's **triumph**, in **consequence** of this **invitation**, was complete. The power of displaying the **grandeur** of his **patroness** to his wondering visitors, and of **letting** them see her **civility** towards himself and his wife, was exactly what he had **wished** for; and that an opportunity of doing it should be given so soon, was such an **instance** of Lady Catherine's **condescension**, as he knew not how to **admire** enough.

"I confess," said he, "that I should not have been at all **surprised** by her **ladyship's asking** us on Sunday to **drink** tea and spend the evening at Rosings. I rather expected, from my knowledge of her **affability**, that it would happen. But who could have **foreseen** such an attention as this? Who could have **imagined** that we should receive an invitation to **dine** there (an invitation, **moreover**, including the whole party) so immediately after your arrival!"

"I am the less surprised at what has happened," replied Sir William, "from that knowledge of what the **manners** of the great really are, which my situation in life has allowed me to acquire. About the court, such instances of **elegant breeding** are not uncommon."

Scarcely anything was **talked** of the whole day or next morning but their visit to Rosings. Mr. Collins was **carefully instructing** them in what they were to expect, that the **sight** of such rooms, so many servants, and so **splendid** a dinner, might not **wholly overpower** them.

Italian

admire: ammirare, ammiriamo, ammira, ammirano, ammiro, ammiri, ammirate.
affability: affabilità.
asking: chiedendo, domandando.
breeding: allevamento, riproduzione.
carefully: attentamente.
civility: civiltà, cortesia.
condescension: condiscendenza.
consequence: conseguenza, risultato.
dine: cenare.
drink: bere, bevanda, bibita.

elegant: elegante.
foreseen: previsto.
grandeur: grandiosità.
imagined: immaginato.
instance: istanza, esempio.
instructing: istruendo.
invitation: invito.
ladyship: signoria.
letting: affittando.
manners: educazione.
moreover: inoltre, d'altronde.
overpower: sopraffa', sopraffacciamo,

soppraffaccio, sopraffai, sopraffanno, sopraffate, sopraffare.
patroness: patrona, patronessa.
sight: vista, aspetto, avvistare, aria, apparenza.
splendid: splendido, magnifico.
surprised: sorpreso, sorpresa.
talked: parlato.
triumph: vittoria, trionfo.
wholly: interamente, completamente.
wished: desiderato.

When the ladies were **separating** for the toilette, he said to Elizabeth--

"Do not make yourself **uneasy**, my dear **cousin**, about your **apparel**. Lady Catherine is far from **requiring** that **elegance** of dress in us which becomes herself and her daughter. I would advise you merely to put on whatever of your clothes is superior to the rest--there is no occasion for anything more. Lady Catherine will not think the worse of you for being **simply** dressed. She likes to have the distinction of rank preserved."

While they were **dressing**, he came two or three times to their different doors, to **recommend** their being quick, as Lady Catherine very much objected to be kept waiting for her dinner. Such **formidable** accounts of her **ladyship**, and her manner of living, quite frightened Maria Lucas who had been little used to company, and she looked forward to her introduction at Rosings with as much **apprehension** as her father had done to his presentation at St. James's.

As the weather was fine, they had a pleasant walk of about half a mile across the park. Every park has its beauty and its prospects; and Elizabeth saw much to be pleased with, though she could not be in such raptures as Mr. Collins expected the scene to **inspire**, and was but slightly affected by his **enumeration** of the windows in **front** of the house, and his relation of what the **glazing** altogether had originally cost Sir Lewis de Bourgh.

When they **ascended** the steps to the **hall**, Maria's alarm was every moment increasing, and even Sir William did not look perfectly **calm**. Elizabeth's **courage** did not fail her. She had heard nothing of Lady Catherine that spoke her awful from any extraordinary talents or **miraculous virtue**, and the mere **stateliness** of money or rank she thought she could **witness** without **trepidation**.

From the entrance-hall, of which Mr. Collins pointed out, with a **rapturous** air, the fine proportion and the finished ornaments, they followed the servants through an ante-chamber, to the room where Lady Catherine, her daughter, and Mrs. Jenkinson were sitting. Her ladyship, with great **condescension**, arose to receive them; and as Mrs. Collins had settled it with her husband that the office of introduction should be hers, it was performed in a proper manner, without any of those **apologies** and thanks which he would have thought necessary.

Italian

apologies: scuse.
apparel: vestimento, abito.
apprehension: apprensione, arresto.
ascended: salito, asceso.
calm: calmo, calmare, tranquillo, calma, placare.
condescension: condiscendenza.
courage: coraggio.
cousin: cugino, cugina.
dressing: fasciatura, condimento.
elegance: eleganza.
enumeration: enumerazione.

formidable: formidabile, straordinario.
front: fronte, facciata, anteriore, davanti.
glazing: vetrata.
hall: sala, salone.
inspire: ispirare, ispira, ispirate, ispiri, ispiro, ispirano, ispiriamo.
ladyship: signoria.
miraculous: miracoloso.
rapturous: estatico.
recommend: raccomandare,

raccomanda, raccomandano, raccomandate, raccomandi, raccomandiamo, raccomando, consigliare, vantare.
requiring: richiedendo.
separating: separare.
simply: semplicemente.
stateliness: grandiosità.
trepidation: trepidazione.
uneasy: inquieto.
virtue: virtù.
witness: testimone, testimoniare.

In **spite** of having been at St. James's Sir William was so completely awed by the **grandeur** surrounding him, that he had but just courage enough to make a very low bow, and take his **seat** without saying a word; and his daughter, frightened almost out of her **senses**, sat on the **edge** of her **chair**, not knowing which way to look. Elizabeth found herself quite equal to the scene, and could observe the three ladies before her composedly. Lady Catherine was a tall, large woman, with strongly-marked features, which might once have been handsome. Her air was not **conciliating**, nor was her manner of receiving them such as to make her visitors forget their **inferior** rank. She was not rendered formidable by silence; but whatever she said was spoken in so authoritative a tone, as marked her self-importance, and brought Mr. Wickham immediately to Elizabeth's mind; and from the observation of the day altogether, she believed Lady Catherine to be exactly what he represented.

When, after **examining** the mother, in whose **countenance** and **deportment** she soon found some resemblance of Mr. Darcy, she turned her eyes on the daughter, she could almost have joined in Maria's astonishment at her being so thin and so small. There was neither in **figure** nor face any **likeness** between the ladies. Miss de Bourgh was **pale and sickly**; her features, though not plain, were **insignificant**; and she spoke very little, except in a low voice, to Mrs. Jenkinson, in whose appearance there was nothing remarkable, and who was entirely engaged in listening to what she said, and **placing** a **screen** in the proper **direction** before her eyes.

After sitting a few minutes, they were all sent to one of the windows to admire the view, Mr. Collins attending them to point out its beauties, and Lady Catherine kindly **informing** them that it was much better worth looking at in the **summer**.

The dinner was **exceedingly** handsome, and there were all the servants and all the articles of **plate** which Mr. Collins had promised; and, as he had likewise **foretold**, he took his seat at the **bottom** of the table, by her ladyship's desire, and looked as if he felt that life could **furnish** nothing greater. He **carved**, and ate, and praised with delighted **alacrity**; and every dish was **commended**, first by

Italian

alacrity: entusiasmo, alacrità.
bottom: fondo, basso, carena.
carved: intagliato, tagliato, scolpito.
chair: sedia, la sedia.
commended: lodato.
conciliating: conciliando, conciliare.
countenance: approvare, viso.
deportment: condotta, comportamento.
direction: direzione, senso.
edge: orlo, bordo, spigolo, margine, lembo.

examining: esaminando, esaminare.
exceedingly: estremamente.
figure: figura, calcolare, cifra, numero.
foretold: predetto.
furnish: fornire, fornite, forniscono, fornisco, fornisci, forniamo, arredare.
grandeur: grandiosità.
inferior: inferiore.
informing: informando.
insignificant: insignificante.
likeness: somiglianza, rassomiglianza.
pale: pallido, smorto, impallidire.

placing: collocamento.
plate: piatto, lastra, piastra, placca, lamiera, targa.
screen: schermo, vaglio, retino, riparo, schermare, schermata, riparare, paravento.
seat: posto, sede, sedile, seggio, sedia.
senses: sensi.
sickly: cagionevole, malaticcio, malatamente.
spite: dispetto.
summer: estate, l'estate.

him and then by Sir William, who was now enough recovered to **echo** whatever his son-in-law said, in a manner which Elizabeth wondered Lady Catherine could bear. But Lady Catherine seemed **gratified** by their excessive **admiration**, and gave most **gracious** smiles, especially when any **dish** on the table proved a **novelty** to them. The party did not supply much conversation. Elizabeth was ready to speak whenever there was an opening, but she was **seated** between Charlotte and Miss de Bourgh--the former of whom was **engaged** in listening to Lady Catherine, and the latter said not a word to her all dinner-time. Mrs. Jenkinson was **chiefly** employed in watching how little Miss de Bourgh ate, **pressing** her to try some other dish, and fearing she was **indisposed**. Maria thought speaking out of the question, and the gentlemen did nothing but eat and admire.

When the ladies returned to the drawing-room, there was little to be done but to hear Lady Catherine talk, which she did without any **intermission** till coffee came in, **delivering** her opinion on every subject in so **decisive** a manner, as proved that she was not used to have her judgement controverted. She **inquired** into Charlotte's **domestic** concerns **familiarly** and **minutely**, gave her a great deal of advice as to the management of them all; told her how everything ought to be **regulated** in so small a family as hers, and **instructed** her as to the care of her **cows** and her **poultry**. Elizabeth found that nothing was **beneath** this great lady's attention, which could **furnish** her with an occasion of **dictating** to others. In the intervals of her discourse with Mrs. Collins, she addressed a variety of questions to Maria and Elizabeth, but especially to the latter, of whose connections she knew the least, and who she observed to Mrs. Collins was a very **genteel**, pretty kind of girl. She asked her, at different times, how many sisters she had, whether they were **older** or younger than herself, whether any of them were likely to be married, whether they were **handsome**, where they had been **educated**, what carriage her father kept, and what had been her mother's **maiden** name? Elizabeth felt all the **impertinence** of her questions but answered them very composedly. Lady Catherine then observed,

Italian

admiration: ammirazione.
beneath: sotto.
chiefly: principalmente, soprattutto.
cows: vacche.
decisive: decisivo.
delivering: consegnando.
dictating: dettando.
dish: piatto, pietanza.
domestic: domestico, nazionale.
eat: mangiare, mangi, mangia, mangiamo, mangiano, mangiate, mangio.

echo: eco, echeggiare.
educated: istruito, educato.
engaged: occupato, innestato, impegnato.
familiarly: familiarmente.
furnish: fornire, fornite, forniscono, fornisco, fornisci, forniamo, arredare.
genteel: distinto.
gracious: grazioso.
gratified: gratificato.
handsome: bello, carino.
impertinence: impertinenza.

indisposed: indisposto.
inquired: domandato.
instructed: istruito.
intermission: interruzione, intervallo.
maiden: nubile, fanciulla.
minutely: minutamente.
novelty: novità.
older: più vecchio.
poultry: pollame.
pressing: pressatura, urgente.
regulated: regolato.
seated: seduto.

"Your father's **estate** is entailed on Mr. Collins, I think. For your sake," **turning** to Charlotte, "I am **glad** of it; but otherwise I see no **occasion** for **entailing** estates from the **female** line. It was not **thought** necessary in Sir Lewis de Bourgh's family. Do you play and **sing**, Miss Bennet?"

"A little."

"Oh! then--some time or other we shall be happy to hear you. Our **instrument** is a **capital** one, probably **superior** to----You shall try it some day. Do your sisters play and sing?"

"One of them does."

"Why did not you all **learn**? You ought all to have **learned**. The Miss Webbs all play, and their father has not so good an income as **yours**. Do you draw?"

"No, not at all."

"What, **none** of you?"

"Not one."

"That is very **strange**. But I suppose you had no opportunity. Your mother should have taken you to town every **spring** for the **benefit** of masters."

"My mother would have had no **objection**, but my father hates London."

"Has your **governess** left you?"

"We never had any governess."

"No governess! How was that possible? Five **daughters** brought up at home without a governess! I never heard of such a thing. Your mother must have been quite a **slave** to your education."

Elizabeth could hardly help **smiling** as she **assured** her that had not been the case.

"Then, who **taught** you? who **attended** to you? Without a governess, you must have been neglected."

"Compared with some families, I believe we were; but such of us as **wished** to learn never wanted the means. We were always **encouraged** to read, and had

Italian

assured: assicurato, certo.
attended: visitato, curato, **assistito**.
benefit: beneficio, profitto, vantaggio, guadagno, prestazione, beneficiare, avvantaggiare.
capital: capitale, capitello.
daughters: figlie.
encouraged: incoraggiato.
entailing: comportare.
estate: fattoria, patrimonio, tenuta.
female: femmina, femminile.
glad: contento, felice, lieto.

governess: istitutrice, governante.
instrument: strumento, apparecchio.
learn: imparare, impari, impariamo, imparate, imparano, impara, imparo, apprendere.
learned: imparato, erudito, colto, dotto, istruito.
none: nessuno.
objection: obiezione, opposizione.
occasion: occasione.
ought: dovere.
sing: cantare, canta, cantano, cantate,

canti, cantiamo, canto.
slave: schiavo, sgobbare.
smiling: sorridere.
spring: molla, sorgente, primavera, fonte, saltare, la primavera.
strange: strano.
superior: superiore.
taught: insegnato.
turning: girando, svoltando, svolta, cambiando.
wished: desiderato.
yours: il vostro, vostro.

all the masters that were necessary. Those who chose to be **idle**, certainly might."

"Aye, no doubt; but that is what a **governess** will prevent, and if I had known your mother, I should have **advised** her most **strenuously** to **engage** one. I always say that nothing is to be done in education without **steady** and regular **instruction**, and nobody but a governess can give it. It is wonderful how many families I have been the means of **supplying** in that way. I am always glad to get a young person well placed out. Four nieces of Mrs. Jenkinson are most delightfully **situated** through my means; and it was but the other day that I **recommended** another young person, who was merely **accidentally** mentioned to me, and the family are quite **delighted** with her. Mrs. Collins, did I tell you of Lady Metcalf's **calling** yesterday to thank me? She **finds** Miss Pope a **treasure**. 'Lady Catherine,' said she, 'you have given me a treasure.' Are any of your younger sisters out, Miss Bennet?"

"Yes, ma'am, all."

"All! What, all five out at once? Very odd! And you only the second. The younger ones out before the **elder** ones are married! Your younger sisters must be very young?"

"Yes, my youngest is not **sixteen**. Perhaps *she* is full young to be much in company. But really, ma'am, I think it would be very hard upon younger sisters, that they should not have their share of society and **amusement**, because the elder may not have the means or **inclination** to **marry** early. The last-born has as good a right to the pleasures of youth at the first. And to be kept back on *such* a **motive**! I think it would not be very likely to promote **sisterly affection** or **delicacy** of mind."

"Upon my word," said her **ladyship**, "you give your opinion very **decidedly** for so young a person. Pray, what is your age?"

"With three younger sisters grown up," replied Elizabeth, **smiling**, "your ladyship can hardly expect me to own it."

Italian

accidentally: accidentalmente.
advised: consigliato.
affection: affetto, affezione, amore.
amusement: divertimento, spasso, svago.
calling: chiamando, chiamata.
decidedly: decisamente.
delicacy: delicatezza.
delighted: lietissimo.
elder: maggiore, sambuco.
engage: innestare, innestiamo, innesta, innestano, innestate, innesti,

ingaggiare, ingranare, impegnare, assumere, innesto.
finds: fonde, fonda.
governess: istitutrice, governante.
idle: ozioso, pigro, folle, inattivo.
inclination: inclinazione, pendenza.
instruction: istruzione.
ladyship: signoria.
marry: sposare, sposati, sposatevi, si sposi, si sposate, si sposano, ci sposiamo, mi sposo, maritarsi, ammogliarsi, maritare.

motive: motivo, movente, ragione.
recommended: raccomandato.
sisterly: sorella.
situated: situato.
sixteen: sedici.
smiling: sorridere.
steady: fisso.
strenuously: strenuamente.
supplying: approvvigionamento, fornitura.
treasure: tesoro.

Lady Catherine seemed quite **astonished** at not receiving a direct answer; and Elizabeth suspected herself to be the first creature who had ever **dared** to **trifle** with so much **dignified** impertinence.

"You **cannot** be more than **twenty**, I am sure, therefore you need not **conceal** your age."

"I am not one-and-twenty."

When the gentlemen had joined them, and tea was over, the card-tables were placed. Lady Catherine, Sir William, and Mr. and Mrs. Collins sat down to **quadrille**; and as Miss de Bourgh chose to play at cassino, the two girls had the honour of **assisting** Mrs. Jenkinson to make up her party. Their table was superlatively stupid. Scarcely a **syllable** was uttered that did not relate to the game, except when Mrs. Jenkinson expressed her fears of Miss de Bourgh's being too hot or too cold, or having too much or too little light. A great deal more passed at the other table. Lady Catherine was generally speaking--stating the mistakes of the three others, or relating some **anecdote** of herself. Mr. Collins was employed in **agreeing** to everything her **ladyship** said, **thanking** her for every fish he won, and apologising if he thought he won too many. Sir William did not say much. He was **storing** his memory with anecdotes and **noble** names.

When Lady Catherine and her daughter had **played** as long as they chose, the tables were broken up, the carriage was offered to Mrs. Collins, **gratefully** accepted and immediately ordered. The party then gathered round the fire to hear Lady Catherine determine what weather they were to have on the **morrow**. From these **instructions** they were **summoned** by the arrival of the coach; and with many speeches of **thankfulness** on Mr. Collins's side and as many **bows** on Sir William's they **departed**. As soon as they had driven from the door, Elizabeth was called on by her cousin to give her opinion of all that she had seen at Rosings, which, for Charlotte's sake, she made more **favourable** than it really was. But her **commendation**, though **costing** her some trouble, could by no means satisfy Mr. Collins, and he was very soon **obliged** to take her ladyship's **praise** into his own hands.

Italian

agreeing: concordando, pattuendo.
anecdote: aneddoto.
assisting: assistendo, aiutando.
astonished: stupito, si stupito.
bows: archetti.
cannot: non potere.
commendation: raccomandazione.
conceal: nascondere, nascondono, nascondete, nascondi, nascondiamo, nascondo, occultare.
costing: valutazione dei costi, determinazione dei costi, costo,

costare.
dared: osato.
departed: partito.
dignified: dignitoso.
favourable: favorevole.
gratefully: con gratitudine.
instructions: istruzioni.
ladyship: signoria.
morrow: domani.
noble: nobile, gentilizio, nobiliare.
obliged: obbligato.
played: giocato, suonato.

praise: lodare, lode, elogiare, encomio, elogio.
quadrille: quadriglia.
storing: immagazzinamento, memorizzazione.
summoned: convocato.
syllable: sillaba.
thankfulness: gratitudine, riconoscenza.
thanking: ringraziando.
trifle: inezia, sciocchezza.
twenty: venti.

CHAPTER 30

Sir William **stayed** only a week at Hunsford, but his visit was long enough to **convince** him of his daughter's being most **comfortably settled**, and of her **possessing** such a husband and such a **neighbour** as were not often met with. While Sir William was with them, Mr. Collins **devoted** his morning to **driving** him out in his **gig**, and showing him the country; but when he went away, the whole family returned to their usual employments, and Elizabeth was **thankful** to find that they did not see more of her **cousin** by the **alteration**, for the chief of the time between breakfast and dinner was now passed by him either at work in the garden or in reading and writing, and looking out of the window in his own book-room, which fronted the road. The room in which the **ladies** sat was **backwards**. Elizabeth had at first rather wondered that Charlotte should not **prefer** the dining-parlour for common use; it was a better sized room, and had a more **pleasant** aspect; but she soon saw that her friend had an excellent reason for what she did, for Mr. Collins would **undoubtedly** have been much less in his own **apartment**, had they sat in one equally **lively**; and she gave Charlotte credit for the arrangement.

From the drawing-room they could **distinguish** nothing in the lane, and were **indebted** to Mr. Collins for the knowledge of what carriages went along, and how often especially Miss de Bourgh **drove** by in her phaeton, which he never failed coming to **inform** them of, though it happened almost every day. She not

Italian

alteration: alterazione, modifica, cambiamento, variazione.
apartment: appartamento.
backwards: indietro, a rovescio, all'indietro, supino.
comfortably: piacevolmente.
convince: convincere, convincete, convinci, convinciamo, convinco, convincono, persuadere.
cousin: cugino, cugina.
devoted: devoto.
distinguish: distinguere, distingui,

distinguono, distinguiamo, distinguete, distinguo.
driving: guida.
drove: gregge.
gig: calesse.
indebted: obbligato, indebitato.
inform: informare, informano, informate, informi, informiamo, informo, informa, insegnare.
ladies: signore.
lively: vivace, spiritoso, vivo, animato, vispo.

neighbour: vicino.
pleasant: piacevole, gradevole, ameno.
possessing: possedendo.
prefer: preferire, preferisci, preferite, preferiscono, preferisco, preferiamo.
settled: regolato, stabilito, stabile, fermo, fisso, popolato, saldato, sistemato, deciso.
stayed: stato, restato.
thankful: riconoscente, grato.
undoubtedly: indubbiamente, si capisce.

unfrequently stopped at the Parsonage, and had a few minutes' conversation with Charlotte, but was scarcely ever **prevailed** upon to get out.

Very few days passed in which Mr. Collins did not walk to Rosings, and not many in which his wife did not think it necessary to go **likewise**; and till Elizabeth **recollected** that there might be other family livings to be **disposed** of, she could not understand the **sacrifice** of so many hours. Now and then they were honoured with a call from her **ladyship**, and nothing escaped her observation that was passing in the room during these visits. She examined into their employments, looked at their work, and advised them to do it differently; found fault with the **arrangement** of the furniture; or **detected** the **housemaid** in **negligence**; and if she accepted any **refreshment**, seemed to do it only for the sake of finding out that Mrs. Collins's **joints** of **meat** were too large for her family.

Elizabeth soon perceived, that though this great lady was not in commission of the peace of the county, she was a most active **magistrate** in her own parish, the minutest concerns of which were carried to her by Mr. Collins; and whenever any of the cottagers were disposed to be **quarrelsome**, **discontented**, or too poor, she sallied forth into the **village** to settle their **differences**, silence their complaints, and **scold** them into **harmony** and **plenty**.

The entertainment of **dining** at Rosings was repeated about twice a week; and, allowing for the loss of Sir William, and there being only one card-table in the evening, every such entertainment was the **counterpart** of the first. Their other engagements were few, as the style of living in the **neighbourhood** in general was beyond Mr. Collins's reach. This, however, was no evil to Elizabeth, and upon the whole she spent her time **comfortably** enough; there were half-hours of pleasant conversation with Charlotte, and the weather was so fine for the time of year that she had often great **enjoyment** out of doors. Her favourite walk, and where she frequently went while the others were calling on Lady Catherine, was **along** the open **grove** which edged that side of the park, where there was a nice **sheltered** path, which no one seemed to value but herself, and where she felt beyond the reach of Lady Catherine's **curiosity**.

Italian

along: lungo.
arrangement: accomodamento, disposizione, sistemazione, ordinamento, arrangiamento, assestamento, adattamento.
comfortably: piacevolmente.
counterpart: controparte.
curiosity: curiosità.
detected: scoperto.
differences: differenze.
dining: pranzando, cenando.
discontented: scontento.

disposed: disposto.
enjoyment: godimento.
grove: boschetto.
harmony: armonia, accordo.
housemaid: domestica.
joints: giunti.
ladyship: signoria.
likewise: anche, altrettanto.
magistrate: magistrato.
meat: carne, la carne.
negligence: negligenza, trascuratezza, condotta negligente.

neighbourhood: circondario, distretto, vicinato, quartiere.
plenty: abbondanza, affluenza, molto.
prevailed: prevalso.
quarrelsome: litigioso.
recollected: rammentato.
refreshment: rinfresco, ristoro.
sacrifice: sacrificio, sacrificare, offrire.
scold: sgridare, rimproverare, riprendere.
sheltered: riparato.
village: villaggio, paese, borgo.

In this quiet way, the first **fortnight** of her visit soon passed away. Easter was **approaching**, and the week **preceding** it was to bring an **addition** to the family at Rosings, which in so small a circle must be important. Elizabeth had heard soon after her arrival that Mr. Darcy was expected there in the course of a few weeks, and though there were not many of her **acquaintances** whom she did not prefer, his coming would **furnish** one **comparatively** new to look at in their Rosings parties, and she might be **amused** in seeing how **hopeless** Miss Bingley's designs on him were, by his behaviour to his **cousin**, for whom he was **evidently destined** by Lady Catherine, who talked of his coming with the greatest satisfaction, spoke of him in terms of the highest **admiration**, and seemed almost angry to find that he had already been frequently seen by Miss Lucas and herself.

His arrival was soon known at the Parsonage; for Mr. Collins was walking the whole morning within view of the lodges opening into Hunsford Lane, in order to have the earliest **assurance** of it, and after making his **bow** as the **carriage** turned into the Park, **hurried** home with the great intelligence. On the following morning he **hastened** to Rosings to pay his respects. There were two nephews of Lady Catherine to require them, for Mr. Darcy had brought with him a Colonel Fitzwilliam, the younger son of his uncle Lord ----, and, to the great surprise of all the party, when Mr. Collins returned, the gentleman accompanied him. Charlotte had seen them from her husband's room, **crossing** the road, and immediately running into the other, told the girls what an honour they might expect, adding:

"I may thank you, Eliza, for this piece of **civility**. Mr. Darcy would never have come so soon to wait upon me."

Elizabeth had **scarcely** time to **disclaim** all right to the **compliment**, before their approach was announced by the door-bell, and shortly afterwards the three gentlemen entered the room. Colonel Fitzwilliam, who led the way, was about **thirty**, not **handsome**, but in person and address most truly the gentleman. Mr. Darcy looked just as he had been used to look in Hertfordshire--paid his **compliments**, with his usual **reserve**, to Mrs. Collins, and whatever might be his

Italian

acquaintances: conoscenze.
addition: aggiunta, addizione.
admiration: ammirazione.
amused: divertito.
approach: accesso, approccio, avvicinare, avvicinamento, avvicinarsi, accostare.
approaching: avvicinamento.
assurance: assicurazione, promessa.
bow: arco, prua, fiocco, inchino, inchinarsi, curva, archetto.
carriage: vettura, carrello, vagone, carro, carrozza.
civility: civiltà, cortesia.
comparatively: comparativamente.
compliment: complimento.
compliments: complimenti.
cousin: cugino, cugina.
crossing: attraversamento, incrocio, traversata, passaggio.
destined: destinato.
disclaim: negare, nego, neghiamo, neghi, negate, negano, nega.
evidently: evidentemente.
fortnight: due settimane.
furnish: fornire, fornite, forniscono, fornisco, fornisci, forniamo, arredare.
handsome: bello, carino.
hastened: affrettato, sollecitato.
hopeless: disperato, senza speranza.
hurried: affrettato, frettoloso.
preceding: precedendo, precedente.
reserve: riservare, riserva, prenotare, ordinare.
scarcely: appena, a stento.
thirty: trenta.

feelings **toward** her friend, met her with every appearance of **composure**. Elizabeth merely curtseyed to him without saying a word.

Colonel Fitzwilliam **entered** into conversation directly with the **readiness** and **ease** of a well-bred man, and **talked** very **pleasantly**; but his **cousin**, after having **addressed** a **slight observation** on the house and garden to Mrs. Collins, sat for some time without **speaking** to **anybody**. At length, however, his **civility** was so far **awakened** as to **inquire** of Elizabeth after the health of her family. She answered him in the usual way, and after a moment's **pause**, added:

"My **eldest** sister has been in town these three months. Have you never happened to see her there?"

She was **perfectly sensible** that he never had; but she **wished** to see whether he would **betray** any **consciousness** of what had passed between the Bingleys and Jane, and she thought he looked a little **confused** as he answered that he had never been so **fortunate** as to meet Miss Bennet. The subject was **pursued** no **farther**, and the gentlemen soon **afterwards** went away.

Italian

addressed: rivolto.
afterwards: dopo, dietro, in seguito, successivamente.
anybody: qualcuno, nessuno.
awakened: svegliato, risvegliato.
betray: tradire, tradisci, tradite, tradisco, tradiamo, tradiscono.
civility: civiltà, cortesia.
composure: calma, compostezza.
confused: confuso.
consciousness: consapevolezza, coscienza.

cousin: cugino, cugina.
ease: agio, facilità.
eldest: maggiore, il più vecchio.
entered: entrato.
farther: più lontano.
fortunate: fortunato, felice.
inquire: domandare, informarsi, domandano, domandate, domandi, domandiamo, domando, indagare, domanda.
observation: osservazione.
pause: pausa, sosta.

perfectly: perfettamente.
pleasantly: piacevolmente.
pursued: perseguito.
readiness: prontezza.
sensible: sensato, ragionevole, sensibile.
slight: leggero, lieve.
speaking: parlando, parlare.
talked: parlato.
toward: verso, a.
wished: desiderato.

CHAPTER 31

Colonel Fitzwilliam's **manners** were very much **admired** at the Parsonage, and the **ladies** all felt that he must add **considerably** to the pleasures of their engagements at Rosings. It was some days, however, before they received any **invitation** thither--for while there were visitors in the house, they could not be necessary; and it was not **till** Easter-day, almost a week after the gentlemen's **arrival**, that they were honoured by such an attention, and then they were **merely** asked on leaving church to come there in the evening. For the last week they had seen very little of Lady Catherine or her daughter. Colonel Fitzwilliam had called at the Parsonage more than once during the time, but Mr. Darcy they had seen only at church.

The invitation was **accepted** of course, and at a **proper** hour they **joined** the party in Lady Catherine's drawing-room. Her **ladyship** received them **civilly**, but it was **plain** that their company was by no means so **acceptable** as when she could get **nobody** else; and she was, in fact, almost **engrossed** by her nephews, **speaking** to them, especially to Darcy, much more than to any other person in the room.

Colonel Fitzwilliam seemed really **glad** to see them; anything was a welcome **relief** to him at Rosings; and Mrs. Collins's **pretty** friend had **moreover caught** his **fancy** very much. He now **seated** himself by her, and **talked** so **agreeably** of Kent and Hertfordshire, of **travelling** and **staying** at home, of new books and

Italian

acceptable: accettabile.
accepted: accettato.
admired: ammirato.
agreeably: piacevolmente.
arrival: arrivo, venuta.
caught: preso, colpito.
civilly: civile, civilmente.
colonel: colonnello.
considerably: considerevolmente.
engrossed: assorbito.
fancy: figurarsi, capriccio, immaginazione.

glad: contento, felice, lieto.
invitation: invito.
joined: congiunto, legato, unito, collegato.
ladies: signore.
ladyship: signoria.
manners: educazione.
merely: soltanto.
moreover: inoltre, d'altronde.
nobody: nessuno.
plain: piano, pianura, evidente, distinto, chiaro.

pretty: grazioso, bellino, carino, bello.
proper: decente, proprio.
relief: rilievo, sollievo.
seated: seduto.
speaking: parlando, parlare.
staying: stando, restando.
talked: parlato.
till: finchè, coltivare, cassa, fino, arare.
travelling: itinerante, viaggiante, viaggiare.

music, that Elizabeth had never been half so well **entertained** in that room before; and they **conversed** with so much spirit and flow, as to **draw** the attention of Lady Catherine herself, as well as of Mr. Darcy. *His* eyes had been soon and **repeatedly** turned towards them with a look of **curiosity**; and that her **ladyship**, after a while, **shared** the feeling, was more **openly acknowledged**, for she did not **scruple** to call out:

"What is that you are saying, Fitzwilliam? What is it you are talking of? What are you telling Miss Bennet? Let me hear what it is."

"We are speaking of music, madam," said he, when no longer able to avoid a reply.

"Of music! Then **pray** speak **aloud**. It is of all subjects my **delight**. I must have my share in the conversation if you are speaking of music. There are few people in England, I suppose, who have more true **enjoyment** of music than myself, or a better natural taste. If I had ever learnt, I should have been a great **proficient**. And so would Anne, if her health had allowed her to apply. I am confident that she would have performed delightfully. How does Georgiana get on, Darcy?"

Mr. Darcy spoke with **affectionate praise** of his sister's **proficiency**.

"I am very glad to hear such a good account of her," said Lady Catherine; "and pray tell her from me, that she **cannot** expect to **excel** if she does not practice a good deal."

"I **assure** you, madam," he replied, "that she does not need such advice. She practises very constantly."

"So much the better. It cannot be done too much; and when I next write to her, I shall charge her not to **neglect** it on any account. I often tell young ladies that no **excellence** in music is to be **acquired** without constant practice. I have told Miss Bennet several times, that she will never play really well unless she practises more; and though Mrs. Collins has no instrument, she is very welcome, as I have often told her, to come to Rosings every day, and play on the pianoforte

Italian

acknowledged: riconosciuto.
acquired: acquisito.
affectionate: affettuoso.
aloud: ad alta voce.
assure: assicurare, assicura, assicuriamo, assicurate, assicuri, assicurano, assicuro, garantire.
cannot: non potere.
conversed: conversato.
curiosity: curiosità.
delight: delizia, deliziare, dilettare, diletto, godimento, rallegrare, gioia.

draw: disegnare, disegna, disegniamo, disegni, disegnate, disegnano, disegno, tirare, attrarre, sorteggio, eguaglianza.
enjoyment: godimento.
entertained: intrattenuto.
excel: eccellere, eccelli, eccellono, eccello, eccellete, eccelliamo.
excellence: eccellenza.
ladyship: signoria.
neglect: trascurare, negligere, negligenza, trascuratezza.

openly: apertamente.
praise: lodare, lode, elogiare, encomio, elogio.
pray: pregare, pregate, prego, preghi, prega, preghiamo, pregano.
proficiency: competenza.
proficient: competente.
repeatedly: ripetutamente.
scruple: scrupolo.
shared: dividere, condiviso, diviso.

in Mrs. Jenkinson's room. She would be in nobody's way, you know, in that part of the house."

Mr. Darcy looked a little **ashamed** of his aunt's ill-breeding, and made no answer.

When coffee was over, Colonel Fitzwilliam reminded Elizabeth of having promised to play to him; and she sat down directly to the instrument. He drew a chair near her. Lady Catherine listened to half a song, and then talked, as before, to her other **nephew**; till the latter walked away from her, and making with his usual **deliberation** towards the pianoforte stationed himself so as to command a full view of the fair performer's **countenance**. Elizabeth saw what he was doing, and at the first convenient pause, turned to him with an **arch** smile, and said:

"You mean to **frighten** me, Mr. Darcy, by coming in all this state to hear me? I will not be **alarmed** though your sister *does* play so well. There is a **stubbornness** about me that never can bear to be frightened at the will of others. My courage always rises at every attempt to **intimidate** me."

"I shall not say you are mistaken," he replied, "because you could not really believe me to **entertain** any design of **alarming** you; and I have had the pleasure of your **acquaintance** long enough to know that you find great **enjoyment** in occasionally **professing** opinions which in fact are not your own."

Elizabeth laughed **heartily** at this picture of herself, and said to Colonel Fitzwilliam, "Your cousin will give you a very pretty notion of me, and **teach** you not to believe a word I say. I am particularly **unlucky** in meeting with a person so able to **expose** my real character, in a part of the world where I had hoped to pass myself off with some degree of credit. Indeed, Mr. Darcy, it is very ungenerous in you to mention all that you knew to my disadvantage in Hertfordshire--and, give me leave to say, very **impolitic** too--for it is **provoking** me to **retaliate,** and such things may come out as will **shock** your relations to hear."

"I am not afraid of you," said he, **smilingly**.

Italian

acquaintance: conoscenza, conoscente.
alarmed: allarmato.
alarming: allarmante.
arch: arco, volta.
ashamed: vergognoso.
countenance: approvare, viso.
deliberation: deliberazione.
enjoyment: godimento.
entertain: intrattenere, intrattenete, intrattieni, intratteniamo, intrattengo, intrattengono, ricevere.
expose: esporre, esponete, espongo, espongono, esponi, esponiamo.
frighten: spaventare, spaventiamo, spaventi, spaventate, spaventano, spaventa, spavento, impaurire, intimorire.
heartily: cordialmente.
impolitic: impolitico.
intimidate: intimidire, intimidiamo, intimidisci, intimidisco, intimidiscono, intimidite, intimorire.
nephew: nipote.
professing: dichiarando, professando.
provoking: incitando, provocando, spronando.
retaliate: rivalersi.
shock: shock, urto, scossa, colpo, choc, scandalizzare, scioccare.
smilingly: sorridere.
stubbornness: testardaggine, cocciutaggine.
teach: insegnare, insegna, insegnano, insegniamo, insegni, insegnate, insegno, istruire.
unlucky: sfortunato, disgraziato.

"Pray let me hear what you have to **accuse** him of," cried Colonel **Fitzwilliam**. "I should like to know how he **behaves** among strangers."

"You shall hear then--but prepare yourself for something very **dreadful**. The first time of my ever seeing him in Hertfordshire, you must know, was at a ball-- and at this ball, what do you think he did? He **danced** only four dances, though gentlemen were **scarce**; and, to my certain knowledge, more than one young lady was sitting down in want of a partner. Mr. Darcy, you **cannot deny** the fact."

"I had not at that time the **honour** of knowing any lady in the assembly beyond my own party."

"True; and nobody can ever be introduced in a ball-room. Well, Colonel Fitzwilliam, what do I play next? My **fingers** wait your orders."

"Perhaps," said Darcy, "I should have **judged** better, had I sought an introduction; but I am ill-qualified to **recommend** myself to strangers."

"Shall we ask your **cousin** the reason of this?" said Elizabeth, still **addressing** Colonel Fitzwilliam. "Shall we ask him why a man of sense and education, and who has lived in the world, is ill **qualified** to recommend himself to strangers?"

"I can answer your question," said Fitzwilliam, "without **applying** to him. It is because he will not give himself the trouble."

"I certainly have not the **talent** which some people possess," said Darcy, "of conversing easily with those I have never seen before. I cannot catch their tone of conversation, or appear interested in their concerns, as I often see done."

"My fingers," said Elizabeth, "do not move over this instrument in the **masterly** manner which I see so many women's do. They have not the same **force** or **rapidity**, and do not **produce** the same expression. But then I have always supposed it to be my own fault--because I will not take the trouble of **practising**. It is not that I do not believe *my* fingers as capable as any other woman's of **superior** execution."

Darcy smiled and said, "You are perfectly right. You have employed your time much better. No one admitted to the **privilege** of hearing you can think anything **wanting**. We neither of us perform to strangers."

Italian

accuse: accusare, accusate, accusi, accusiamo, accuso, accusano, accusa, caricare, caricano, carico, carichiamo.
addressing: indirizzamento.
applying: applicando.
behaves: agisce.
cannot: non potere.
cousin: cugino, cugina.
danced: ballato, ballavo ballava.
deny: negare, negate, negano, neghi, neghiamo, nego, nega.
dreadful: terribile.

fingers: dito.
force: forza, forzare, costringere, vigore.
honour: onore.
ill: malato, ammalato.
judged: giudicato.
masterly: magistrale.
practising: praticante.
privilege: privilegio, privilegiare.
produce: produrre, produciamo, produco, produci, producete, producono, produzione, prodotti,

fabbricare, prodotto.
qualified: qualificato, abilitato.
rapidity: rapidità, velocità.
recommend: raccomandare, raccomanda, raccomandano, raccomandate, raccomandi, raccomandiamo, raccomando, consigliare, vantare.
scarce: scarso, raro.
superior: superiore.
talent: talento, ingegno.
wanting: volendo.

Here they were **interrupted** by Lady Catherine, who called out to know what they were talking of.   **Elizabeth** immediately began playing again.   Lady Catherine approached, and, after **listening** for a few minutes, said to Darcy:

"Miss Bennet would not play at all **amiss** if she practised more, and could have the advantage of a London master.   She has a very good **notion** of **fingering**, though her taste is not equal to Anne's.   Anne would have been a **delightful performer**, had her health allowed her to learn."

Elizabeth looked at Darcy to see how **cordially** he assented to his cousin's **praise**; but neither at that moment nor at any other could she **discern** any **symptom** of love; and from the whole of his behaviour to Miss de Bourgh she **derived** this **comfort** for Miss Bingley, that he might have been just as likely to **marry** *her*, had she been his relation.

Lady Catherine continued her **remarks** on Elizabeth's performance, **mixing** with them many **instructions** on **execution** and taste. Elizabeth received them with all the **forbearance** of **civility**, and, at the request of the gentlemen, remained at the **instrument till** her ladyship's **carriage** was ready to take them all home.

Italian

amiss: male, inopportuno.
carriage: vettura, carrello, vagone, carro, carrozza.
civility: civiltà, cortesia.
comfort: consolare, comodità, confortare, comfort, benessere.
cordially: cordialmente.
delightful: delizioso, piacevole.
derived: derivato.
discern: distinguo, distingui, percepiamo, percepiscono, percepisco, percepisci, distinguiamo,

percepite, distinguete, discernono, discerno.
elizabeth: Elisabetta.
execution: esecuzione.
fingering: diteggiatura.
forbearance: pazienza.
instructions: istruzioni.
instrument: strumento, apparecchio.
interrupted: interrotto, sospeso.
listening: ascoltando, ascolto.
marry: sposare, sposati, sposatevi, si sposi, si sposate, si sposano, ci

sposiamo, mi sposo, maritarsi, ammogliarsi, maritare.
mixing: mescolamento, miscelazione.
notion: nozione, idea.
performer: esecutore.
praise: lodare, lode, elogiare, encomio, elogio.
remarks: osservazioni.
symptom: sintomo, segno.
till: finchè, coltivare, cassa, fino, arare.

CHAPTER 32

Elizabeth was sitting by herself the next morning, and writing to Jane while Mrs. Collins and Maria were gone on business into the village, when she was **startled** by a **ring** at the door, the certain **signal** of a **visitor**. As she had heard no **carriage**, she thought it not **unlikely** to be Lady Catherine, and under that **apprehension** was putting away her half-finished letter that she might **escape** all **impertinent** questions, when the door **opened**, and, to her very great surprise, Mr. Darcy, and Mr. Darcy only, **entered** the room.

He seemed **astonished** too on **finding** her **alone**, and apologised for his **intrusion** by **letting** her know that he had **understood** all the **ladies** were to be within.

They then sat down, and when her inquiries after Rosings were made, seemed in **danger** of **sinking** into total **silence**. It was absolutely necessary, therefore, to think of something, and in this **emergence recollecting** *when* she had seen him last in Hertfordshire, and feeling **curious** to know what he would say on the subject of their **hasty departure**, she **observed**:

"How very suddenly you all quitted Netherfield last November, Mr. Darcy! It must have been a most **agreeable** surprise to Mr. Bingley to see you all after him so soon; for, if I recollect right, he went but the day before. He and his sisters were well, I hope, when you left London?"

Italian

agreeable: gradevole, piacevole, amabile.
alone: solo, da solo, solamente.
apprehension: apprensione, arresto.
astonished: stupito, si stupito.
carriage: vettura, carrello, vagone, carro, carrozza.
curious: curioso.
danger: pericolo.
departure: partenza.
emergence: emersione.
entered: entrato.

escape: scarico, evasione, scappare, sfuggire, evadere, fuoriuscire, fuga.
finding: fondendo, fondando.
hasty: affrettato, frettoloso.
impertinent: impertinente, insolente.
intrusion: intrusione.
ladies: signore.
letting: affittando.
observed: osservato.
opened: aperto.
recollect: rammenta, rammentano, rammentate, rammenti,

rammentiamo, rammento, rammentare, ricordarsi.
recollecting: rammentando.
ring: anello, circolo.
signal: segnale, segno.
silence: silenzio.
sinking: affondamento, sprofondamento.
startled: spaventato.
understood: capito, compreso.
unlikely: improbabile.
visitor: visitatore, ospite.

"Perfectly so, I thank you."

She found that she was to receive no other answer, and, after a short **pause** added:

"I think I have **understood** that Mr. Bingley has not much idea of ever returning to Netherfield again?"

"I have never heard him say so; but it is **probable** that he may spend very little of his time there in the future. He has many friends, and is at a time of life when friends and engagements are **continually** increasing."

"If he means to be but little at Netherfield, it would be better for the **neighbourhood** that he should give up the place entirely, for then we might possibly get a **settled** family there. But, perhaps, Mr. Bingley did not take the house so much for the **convenience** of the neighbourhood as for his own, and we must expect him to keep it or **quit** it on the same principle."

"I should not be surprised," said Darcy, "if he were to give it up as soon as any **eligible purchase** offers."

Elizabeth made no answer. She was **afraid** of talking longer of his friend; and, having nothing else to say, was now **determined** to leave the trouble of **finding** a subject to him.

He took the **hint,** and soon began with, "This seems a very **comfortable** house. Lady Catherine, I believe, did a great deal to it when Mr. Collins first came to Hunsford."

"I believe she did--and I am sure she could not have **bestowed** her **kindness** on a more **grateful** object."

"Mr. Collins appears to be very **fortunate** in his choice of a wife."

"Yes, indeed, his friends may well **rejoice** in his having met with one of the very few **sensible** women who would have **accepted** him, or have made him happy if they had. My friend has an **excellent** understanding--though I am not certain that I consider her **marrying** Mr. Collins as the wisest thing she ever did.

Italian

accepted: accettato.
afraid: pauroso, inquieto, spaventato, angoscioso, impaurito.
bestowed: concesso, tributato.
comfortable: comodo, confortevole.
continually: continuamente.
convenience: convenienza.
determined: definito, fissato, determinato.
eligible: eleggibile.
excellent: eccellente, esimio, ottimo.
finding: fondendo, fondando.

fortunate: fortunato, felice.
grateful: riconoscente, grato.
hint: alludere, suggerimento, allusione, cenno.
kindness: gentilezza, bontà, cortesia.
marrying: sposandosi.
neighbourhood: circondario, distretto, vicinato, quartiere.
pause: pausa, sosta.
probable: probabile.
purchase: acquisto, comperare, comprare, compra, acquistare,

compera.
quit: abbandonare, abbandonato, abbandono, abbandoni, abbandonate, abbandonano, abbandona, abbandoniamo, smettere.
rejoice: allietare, rallegrare.
sensible: sensato, ragionevole, sensibile.
settled: regolato, stabilito, stabile, fermo, fisso, popolato, saldato, sistemato, deciso.
understood: capito, compreso.

She seems perfectly happy, however, and in a **prudential** light it is certainly a very good match for her."

"It must be very **agreeable** for her to be **settled** within so easy a distance of her own family and friends."

"An easy distance, do you call it? It is **nearly fifty** miles."

"And what is fifty miles of good road? Little more than half a day's journey. Yes, I call it a *very* easy distance."

"I should never have considered the distance as one of the *advantages* of the match," cried Elizabeth. "I should never have said Mrs. Collins was settled *near* her family."

"It is a **proof** of your own **attachment** to Hertfordshire. Anything beyond the very **neighbourhood** of Longbourn, I suppose, would appear far."

As he spoke there was a sort of smile which Elizabeth **fancied** she understood; he must be **supposing** her to be thinking of Jane and Netherfield, and she **blushed** as she answered:

"I do not mean to say that a woman may not be settled too near her family. The far and the near must be relative, and **depend** on many **varying** circumstances. Where there is **fortune** to make the **expenses** of **travelling unimportant**, distance becomes no **evil**. But that is not the case *here*. Mr. and Mrs. Collins have a **comfortable** income, but not such a one as will allow of **frequent** journeys--and I am **persuaded** my friend would not call herself *near* her family under less than *half* the present distance."

Mr. Darcy drew his chair a little towards her, and said, "*You* **cannot** have a right to such very strong local attachment. *You* cannot have been always at Longbourn."

Elizabeth looked **surprised**. The gentleman experienced some change of feeling; he drew back his chair, took a **newspaper** from the table, and glancing over it, said, in a colder voice:

"Are you **pleased** with Kent?"

Italian

advantages: vantaggi.
agreeable: gradevole, piacevole, amabile.
attachment: accessorio, allegato, attaccamento.
blushed: arrossito.
cannot: non potere.
comfortable: comodo, confortevole.
depend: dipendere, dipendete, dipendiamo, dipendo, dipendono, dipendi.
evil: male, cattivo, malvagio.

expenses: spese.
fancied: fantastico.
fifty: cinquanta.
fortune: fortuna, sorte, patrimonio.
frequent: frequente, bazzicare.
nearly: quasi.
neighbourhood: circondario, distretto, vicinato, quartiere.
newspaper: giornale.
persuaded: convinto, persuaso.
pleased: contento, soddisfatto.
proof: prova, bozza, dimostrazione,

provino, impermeabilizzare, resistente.
prudential: prudenziale.
settled: regolato, stabilito, stabile, fermo, fisso, popolato, saldato, sistemato, deciso.
supposing: supponendo.
surprised: sorpreso, sorpresa.
travelling: itinerante, viaggiante, viaggiare.
unimportant: senza importanza.
varying: variando, variare.

A short **dialogue** on the subject of the country **ensued**, on either side **calm** and concise--and soon put an end to by the entrance of Charlotte and her sister, just returned from her walk. The tete-a-tete surprised them. Mr. Darcy related the mistake which had occasioned his **intruding** on Miss Bennet, and after sitting a few minutes longer without saying much to anybody, went away.

"What can be the meaning of this?" said Charlotte, as soon as he was gone. "My dear, Eliza, he must be in love with you, or he would never have called us in this familiar way."

But when Elizabeth told of his silence; it did not seem very likely, even to Charlotte's wishes, to be the case; and after **various** conjectures, they could at last only suppose his visit to **proceed** from the difficulty of finding anything to do, which was the more **probable** from the time of year. All **field sports** were over. Within doors there was Lady Catherine, books, and a billiard-table, but gentlemen **cannot** always be within doors; and in the **nearness** of the Parsonage, or the **pleasantness** of the walk to it, or of the people who lived in it, the two cousins found a **temptation** from this period of walking **thither** almost every day. They called at various times of the morning, sometimes **separately**, sometimes together, and now and then accompanied by their aunt. It was **plain** to them all that Colonel Fitzwilliam came because he had pleasure in their society, a **persuasion** which of course recommended him still more; and Elizabeth was **reminded** by her own satisfaction in being with him, as well as by his evident **admiration** of her, of her former favourite George Wickham; and though, in **comparing** them, she saw there was less **captivating softness** in Colonel Fitzwilliam's **manners**, she believed he might have the best informed mind.

But why Mr. Darcy came so often to the Parsonage, it was more difficult to understand. It could not be for society, as he frequently sat there ten minutes together without opening his lips; and when he did speak, it seemed the effect of **necessity** rather than of choice--a **sacrifice** to **propriety**, not a pleasure to himself. He **seldom** appeared really **animated**. Mrs. Collins knew not what to make of him. Colonel Fitzwilliam's occasionally **laughing** at his **stupidity**, proved that he

Italian

admiration: ammirazione.
animated: animato.
calm: calmo, calmare, tranquillo, calma, placare.
cannot: non potere.
captivating: affascinando, accattivante, affascinare.
comparing: confrontando, paragonando.
dialogue: dialogo.
ensued: seguito.
field: campo, settore.

intruding: imponendo.
laughing: ridere, risata.
manners: educazione.
nearness: vicinanza.
necessity: necessità, bisogno.
persuasion: persuasione.
plain: piano, pianura, evidente, distinto, chiaro.
pleasantness: piacevolezza.
probable: probabile.
proceed: procedere, procedete, procedono, procedo, procediamo,

procedi.
propriety: convenienza.
reminded: ricordato.
sacrifice: sacrificio, sacrificare, offrire.
seldom: raramente.
separately: separatamente.
softness: morbidezza.
sports: sport, sportivo.
stupidity: stupidità.
temptation: tentazione.
thither: là.
various: vario, differente.

was generally different, which her own knowledge of him could not have told her; and as she would liked to have **believed** this change the effect of love, and the object of that love her friend Eliza, she set herself **seriously** to work to find it out. She **watched** him **whenever** they were at Rosings, and whenever he came to Hunsford; but without much success. He certainly looked at her friend a great deal, but the **expression** of that look was **disputable**. It was an **earnest, steadfast gaze**, but she often doubted whether there were much **admiration** in it, and sometimes it seemed nothing but **absence** of mind.

She had once or twice suggested to Elizabeth the possibility of his being **partial** to her, but Elizabeth always laughed at the idea; and Mrs. Collins did not think it right to press the subject, from the danger of **raising expectations** which might only end in **disappointment**; for in her opinion it **admitted** not of a doubt, that all her friend's **dislike** would **vanish**, if she could suppose him to be in her power.

In her kind schemes for Elizabeth, she sometimes **planned** her **marrying** Colonel Fitzwilliam. He was beyond **comparison** the most **pleasant** man; he certainly **admired** her, and his situation in life was most **eligible**; but, to **counterbalance** these **advantages**, Mr. Darcy had considerable **patronage** in the church, and his **cousin** could have none at all.

CHAPTER 33

More than once did Elizabeth, in her **ramble** within the park, **unexpectedly** meet Mr. Darcy. She felt all the perverseness of the **mischance** that should bring him where no one else was brought, and, to prevent its ever **happening** again, took care to **inform** him at first that it was a **favourite haunt** of **hers**. How it could occur a second time, therefore, was very odd! Yet it did, and even a third. It seemed like **wilful** ill-nature, or a voluntary **penance**, for on these occasions it was not merely a few formal inquiries and an **awkward pause** and then away, but he actually thought it necessary to turn back and walk with her. He never said a great deal, nor did she give herself the trouble of talking or of listening much; but it **struck** her in the course of their third rencontre that he was asking some odd unconnected questions--about her pleasure in being at Hunsford, her love of **solitary walks**, and her opinion of Mr. and Mrs. Collins's **happiness**; and that in speaking of Rosings and her not perfectly understanding the house, he seemed to expect that **whenever** she came into Kent again she would be **staying** *there* too. His words seemed to **imply** it. Could he have Colonel Fitzwilliam in his thoughts? She supposed, if he meant anything, he must mean and **allusion** to what might **arise** in that quarter. It **distressed** her a little, and she was quite glad to find herself at the gate in the pales opposite the Parsonage.

She was **engaged** one day as she walked, in **perusing** Jane's last letter, and **dwelling** on some passages which proved that Jane had not written in spirits,

Italian

allusion: allusione.
arise: nascere, nasciamo, nasco, nasci, nascete, nascono, salire, sorgere, sorgete, sorgono, sorgi.
awkward: goffo, sgraziato.
distressed: afflitto.
dwelling: dimorando, abitando, dimora, abitazione.
engaged: occupato, innestato, impegnato.
favourite: preferito.
happening: succedendo, avvenendo,
avvenimento.
happiness: felicità.
haunt: frequentare.
hers: suo.
imply: significare, significa, significhi, significhiamo, significate, significano, significo, implicare, implicano, implicate, implichi.
inform: informare, informano, informate, informi, informiamo, informo, informa, insegnare.
mischance: disgrazia, sfortuna.
pause: pausa, sosta.
penance: penitenza.
perusing: esaminando.
ramble: giro, passeggiata, vagare.
solitary: solo, solitario.
staying: stando, restando.
struck: colpito.
unexpectedly: inaspettatamente.
walks: cammina.
whenever: ogni volta che, quando.
wilful: intenzionale, testardo.

when, instead of being again **surprised** by Mr. Darcy, she saw on looking up that Colonel Fitzwilliam was meeting her. Putting away the letter immediately and **forcing** a smile, she said:

"I did not know before that you ever walked this way."

"I have been making the **tour** of the park," he replied, "as I generally do every year, and **intend** to close it with a call at the Parsonage. Are you going much farther?"

"No, I should have turned in a moment."

And **accordingly** she did turn, and they walked towards the Parsonage together.

"Do you certainly leave Kent on Saturday?" said she.

"Yes--if Darcy does not put it off **again**. But I am at his **disposal**. He **arranges** the business just as he pleases."

"And if not able to please himself in the **arrangement**, he has at **least** **pleasure** in the great power of choice. I do not know **anybody** who seems more to enjoy the power of doing what he likes than Mr. Darcy."

"He likes to have his own way very well," replied Colonel Fitzwilliam. "But so we all do. It is only that he has better means of having it than many others, because he is rich, and many others are poor. I speak feelingly. A **younger** son, you know, must be **inured** to self-denial and **dependence**."

"In my opinion, the younger son of an **earl** can know very little of either. Now **seriously**, what have you ever known of self-denial and dependence? When have you been **prevented** by want of money from going **wherever** you chose, or **procuring** anything you had a **fancy** for?"

"These are home questions--and perhaps I **cannot** say that I have **experienced** many hardships of that nature. But in matters of greater weight, I may **suffer** from want of money. Younger sons cannot **marry** where they like."

"Unless where they like women of **fortune**, which I think they very often do."

Italian

accordingly: di conseguenza, quindi.
anybody: qualcuno, nessuno.
arrangement: accomodamento, disposizione, sistemazione, ordinamento, arrangiamento, assestamento, adattamento.
arranges: sistema, predispone, ordina.
cannot: non potere.
dependence: dipendenza.
disposal: disposizione, eliminazione, smaltimento.
earl: conte.

experienced: esperto.
fancy: figurarsi, capriccio, immaginazione.
forcing: forzatura.
fortune: fortuna, sorte, patrimonio.
intend: intendere, intendono, intendo, intendete, intendiamo, intendi.
inured: abituato, assuefatto.
least: minimo, meno.
marry: sposare, sposati, sposatevi, si sposi, si sposate, si sposano, ci sposiamo, mi sposo, maritarsi,

ammogliarsi, maritare.
pleasure: piacere, gradimento.
prevented: impedito, prevenuto.
procuring: procurando.
seriously: seriamente, gravemente.
suffer: soffrire, soffri, soffro, soffrono, soffrite, soffriamo, patire, subire, patiamo, patite, patiscono.
surprised: sorpreso, sorpresa.
tour: giro.
wherever: dovunque, laddove.
younger: più giovane.

"Our habits of expense make us too dependent, and there are too many in my rank of life who can **afford** to marry without some attention to money."

"Is this," thought Elizabeth, "meant for me?" and she **coloured** at the idea; but, **recovering** herself, said in a **lively** tone, "And **pray**, what is the usual **price** of an earl's younger son? Unless the **elder** brother is very **sickly**, I suppose you would not ask above fifty thousand pounds."

He answered her in the same style, and the subject dropped. To **interrupt** a silence which might make him **fancy** her affected with what had passed, she soon afterwards said:

"I imagine your **cousin** brought you down with him **chiefly** for the sake of having **someone** at his disposal. I wonder he does not marry, to secure a **lasting convenience** of that kind. But, perhaps, his sister does as well for the present, and, as she is under his **sole** care, he may do what he likes with her."

"No," said Colonel Fitzwilliam, "that is an advantage which he must **divide** with me. I am joined with him in the **guardianship** of Miss Darcy."

"Are you indeed? And pray what sort of guardians do you make? Does your **charge** give you much trouble? Young ladies of her age are sometimes a little difficult to manage, and if she has the true Darcy spirit, she may like to have her own way."

As she spoke she observed him looking at her **earnestly**; and the manner in which he immediately asked her why she supposed Miss Darcy likely to give them any **uneasiness**, convinced her that she had somehow or other got pretty near the truth. She directly replied:

"You need not be frightened. I never heard any harm of her; and I dare say she is one of the most **tractable** creatures in the world. She is a very great favourite with some ladies of my **acquaintance**, Mrs. Hurst and Miss Bingley. I think I have heard you say that you know them."

"I know them a little. Their brother is a pleasant gentlemanlike man--he is a great friend of Darcy's."

Italian

acquaintance: conoscenza, conoscente.
afford: permettere, permettersi, permettono, permettiamo, permettete, permetto, permetti, produrre.
charge: carica, carico, addebito, spese, onere, tassa, caricare, imputazione, accusa.
chiefly: principalmente, soprattutto.
coloured: colorato.
convenience: convenienza.
cousin: cugino, cugina.

divide: dividere, dividete, dividiamo, divido, dividono, dividi, separare, separa, separi, separiamo, separate.
earnestly: seriamente.
elder: maggiore, sambuco.
fancy: figurarsi, capriccio, immaginazione.
guardianship: tutela.
interrupt: interrompere, interruzione.
lasting: durevole, duraturo, permanente, continuo.
lively: vivace, spiritoso, vivo, animato,

vispo.
pray: pregare, pregate, prego, preghi, prega, preghiamo, pregano.
price: prezzo, tariffa.
recovering: ricuperando.
sickly: cagionevole, malaticcio, malatamente.
sole: sogliola, solo, suola, pianta, unico.
someone: qualcuno.
tractable: docile, trattabile.
uneasiness: disagio.

"Oh! yes," said Elizabeth drily; "Mr. Darcy is **uncommonly** kind to Mr. Bingley, and takes a **prodigious** deal of care of him."

"Care of him! Yes, I really believe Darcy *does* take care of him in those points where he most wants care. From something that he told me in our journey **hither**, I have reason to think Bingley very much **indebted** to him. But I ought to **beg** his **pardon**, for I have no right to suppose that Bingley was the person meant. It was all conjecture."

"What is it you mean?"

"It is a **circumstance** which Darcy could not wish to be generally known, because if it were to get round to the lady's family, it would be an **unpleasant** thing."

"You may **depend** upon my not mentioning it."

"And remember that I have not much reason for **supposing** it to be Bingley. What he told me was merely this: that he **congratulated** himself on having **lately** **saved** a friend from the inconveniences of a most **imprudent** marriage, but without mentioning names or any other **particulars**, and I only suspected it to be Bingley from **believing** him the kind of young man to get into a **scrape** of that sort, and from knowing them to have been together the whole of last summer."

"Did Mr. Darcy give you reasons for this **interference**?"

"I **understood** that there were some very strong **objections** against the lady."

"And what arts did he use to **separate** them?"

"He did not talk to me of his own arts," said Fitzwilliam, **smiling**. "He only told me what I have now told you."

Elizabeth made no answer, and walked on, her heart **swelling** with **indignation**. After watching her a little, Fitzwilliam asked her why she was so **thoughtful**.

"I am thinking of what you have been telling me," said she. "Your cousin's **conduct** does not suit my feelings. Why was he to be the judge?"

"You are rather **disposed** to call his interference officious?"

Italian

beg: mendicare, mendicano, mendica, mendicate, mendico, mendichiamo, mendichi, chiedere, elemosinare, supplicare.
believing: credendo, credere.
circumstance: circostanza.
conduct: condotta, condurre, guidare, comportamento.
congratulated: felicitato.
depend: dipendere, dipendete, dipendiamo, dipendo, dipendono, dipendi.

disposed: disposto.
hither: qui, quà.
imprudent: imprudente.
indebted: obbligato, indebitato.
indignation: indignazione, sdegno.
interference: interferenza.
lately: ultimamente, recentemente.
objections: obiezioni.
pardon: grazia, perdono, perdonare, scusare, scusa.
particulars: particolari.
prodigious: prodigioso.

saved: salvato, risparmiato.
scrape: raschiare, scrostare.
separate: separato, separare, dividere.
smiling: sorridere.
supposing: supponendo.
swelling: rigonfiamento, gonfiore, tumefazione, gonfiezza.
thoughtful: pensieroso, premuroso.
uncommonly: insolitamente.
understood: capito, compreso.
unpleasant: rude, spiacevole, brusco, sgradevole, scostante.

"I do not see what right Mr. Darcy had to decide on the **propriety** of his friend's **inclination**, or why, upon his own judgement alone, he was to determine and direct in what manner his friend was to be happy. But," she continued, **recollecting** herself, "as we know none of the **particulars**, it is not fair to **condemn** him. It is not to be supposed that there was much affection in the case."

"That is not an **unnatural** surmise," said Fitzwilliam, "but it is a **lessening** of the honour of my cousin's triumph very sadly."

This was spoken jestingly; but it appeared to her so just a picture of Mr. Darcy, that she would not trust herself with an answer, and therefore, **abruptly** changing the conversation talked on **indifferent** matters until they reached the Parsonage. There, shut into her own room, as soon as their visitor left them, she could think without **interruption** of all that she had heard. It was not to be supposed that any other people could be meant than those with whom she was connected. There could not **exist** in the world *two* men over whom Mr. Darcy could have such **boundless** influence. That he had been **concerned** in the measures taken to separate Bingley and Jane she had never doubted; but she had always **attributed** to Miss Bingley the principal design and arrangement of them. If his own **vanity**, however, did not **mislead** him, *he* was the cause, his pride and **caprice** were the cause, of all that Jane had suffered, and still continued to suffer. He had **ruined** for a while every hope of happiness for the most **affectionate**, generous heart in the world; and no one could say how **lasting** an evil he might have **inflicted**.

"There were some very strong objections against the lady," were Colonel Fitzwilliam's words; and those strong objections probably were, her having one uncle who was a country **attorney**, and another who was in business in London.

"To Jane herself," she **exclaimed**, "there could be no possibility of objection; all **loveliness** and **goodness** as she is!--her understanding excellent, her mind **improved**, and her **manners captivating**. Neither could anything be urged against my father, who, though with some peculiarities, has abilities Mr. Darcy himself need not **disdain**, and **respectability** which he will probably never each."

Italian

abruptly: improvvisamente.	biasimo, biasimiamo, biasimi.	permanente, continuo.
affectionate: affettuoso.	**disdain**: sdegno, sdegnare.	**lessening**: diminuendo.
attorney: procuratore, avvocato.	**exclaimed**: esclamato.	**loveliness**: bellezza.
attributed: attribuito.	**exist**: esistere, esisto, esistono, esisti,	**manners**: educazione.
boundless: illimitato.	esistete, esistiamo.	**mislead**: traviare.
caprice: capriccio.	**goodness**: bontà.	**particulars**: particolari.
captivating: affascinando,	**improved**: migliorato, perfezionato.	**propriety**: convenienza.
accattivante, affascinare.	**inclination**: inclinazione, pendenza.	**recollecting**: rammentando.
concerned: interessato.	**indifferent**: indifferente.	**respectability**: rispettabilità.
condemn: condannare, condannate,	**inflicted**: inflitto.	**ruined**: rovinato.
condanno, condanni, condannano,	**interruption**: interruzione.	**unnatural**: innaturale.
condanniamo, condanna, biasimare,	**lasting**: durevole, duraturo,	**vanity**: vanità.

When she thought of her mother, her **confidence** gave way a little; but she would not allow that any **objections** *there* had material weight with Mr. Darcy, whose **pride**, she was **convinced**, would receive a deeper **wound** from the want of importance in his friend's **connections**, than from their want of sense; and she was quite decided, at last, that he had been **partly governed** by this **worst** kind of pride, and partly by the wish of **retaining** Mr. Bingley for his sister.

The **agitation** and **tears** which the subject occasioned, brought on a **headache**; and it grew so much **worse** towards the evening, that, added to her **unwillingness** to see Mr. Darcy, it **determined** her not to **attend** her cousins to Rosings, where they were **engaged** to **drink** tea. Mrs. Collins, **seeing** that she was really **unwell**, did not press her to go and as much as possible **prevented** her husband from **pressing** her; but Mr. Collins could not **conceal** his **apprehension** of Lady Catherine's being rather **displeased** by her **staying** at home.

Italian

agitation: agitazione.
apprehension: apprensione, arresto.
attend: visitare, curare, assistere, curiamo, curi, curo, curano, visitate, visitiamo, cura, visiti.
conceal: nascondere, nascondono, nascondete, nascondi, nascondiamo, nascondo, occultare.
confidence: fiducia, confidenza, affidamento.
connections: accesso.
convinced: convinto.

determined: definito, fissato, determinato.
displeased: scontentato, scontento.
drink: bere, bevanda, bibita.
engaged: occupato, innestato, impegnato.
governed: governato.
headache: mal di testa, cefalea.
objections: obiezioni.
partly: in parte, parzialmente.
pressing: pressatura, urgente.
prevented: impedito, prevenuto.

pride: orgoglio, fierezza.
retaining: ritenendo, trattenendo.
seeing: vedendo, segando.
staying: stando, restando.
tears: lacrime.
unwell: indisposto.
unwillingness: renitenza, malavoglia.
worse: peggiore, peggio.
worst: peggiore.
wound: ferita, ferire.

CHAPTER 34

When they were gone, **Elizabeth**, as if **intending** to **exasperate** herself as much as possible against Mr. Darcy, chose for her employment the **examination** of all the **letters** which Jane had written to her since her being in Kent. They **contained** no actual **complaint**, nor was there any **revival** of past occurrences, or any communication of present suffering. But in all, and in almost every line of each, there was a want of that **cheerfulness** which had been used to **characterise** her style, and which, **proceeding** from the **serenity** of a mind at **ease** with itself and **kindly disposed** towards everyone, had been **scarcely** ever **clouded**. Elizabeth noticed every sentence **conveying** the idea of **uneasiness**, with an attention which it had **hardly received** on the first perusal. Mr. Darcy's **shameful boast** of what **misery** he had been able to **inflict**, gave her a keener sense of her sister's sufferings. It was some **consolation** to think that his visit to Rosings was to end on the day after the next--and, a still greater, that in less than a **fortnight** she should herself be with Jane again, and **enabled** to contribute to the recovery of her spirits, by all that **affection** could do.

She could not think of Darcy's leaving Kent without **remembering** that his **cousin** was to go with him; but Colonel Fitzwilliam had made it clear that he had no intentions at all, and **agreeable** as he was, she did not mean to be **unhappy** about him.

Italian

affection: affetto, affezione, amore.
agreeable: gradevole, piacevole, amabile.
boast: vanteria, vantarsi.
characterise: caratterizzare.
cheerfulness: contentezza, allegria.
clouded: annuvolato.
complaint: reclamo, lamentela.
consolation: consolazione.
contained: contenuto.
conveying: trasportando, trasporto.
cousin: cugino, cugina.

disposed: disposto.
ease: agio, facilità.
elizabeth: Elisabetta.
enabled: abilitato.
examination: esame, verifica.
exasperate: esasperare.
fortnight: due settimane.
hardly: appena, a malapena, a stento.
inflict: infliggere, infliggete, infliggo, infliggiamo, infliggono, infliggi.
intending: intendendo.
kindly: gentilmente, gentile.

letters: lettere.
misery: miseria.
proceeding: procedendo, procedimento.
received: ricevuto, accolto.
remembering: ricordando.
revival: rinascita.
scarcely: appena, a stento.
serenity: serenità.
shameful: vergognoso.
uneasiness: disagio.
unhappy: infelice, triste.

While settling this point, she was suddenly **roused** by the **sound** of the doorbell, and her spirits were a little fluttered by the idea of its being Colonel Fitzwilliam himself, who had once before called late in the evening, and might now come to **inquire** particularly after her. But this idea was soon **banished**, and her spirits were very differently affected, when, to her utter **amazement**, she saw Mr. Darcy walk into the room. In an hurried manner he immediately began an inquiry after her health, **imputing** his visit to a wish of hearing that she were better. She answered him with cold **civility**. He sat down for a few moments, and then getting up, walked about the room. Elizabeth was surprised, but said not a word. After a silence of several minutes, he came towards her in an **agitated** manner, and thus began:

"In **vain** I have struggled. It will not do. My feelings will not be **repressed**. You must allow me to tell you how **ardently** I admire and love you."

Elizabeth's **astonishment** was beyond expression. She stared, coloured, doubted, and was silent. This he considered sufficient encouragement; and the **avowal** of all that he felt, and had long felt for her, immediately followed. He spoke well; but there were feelings besides those of the heart to be **detailed**; and he was not more **eloquent** on the subject of **tenderness** than of pride. His sense of her inferiority--of its being a degradation--of the family **obstacles** which had always opposed to **inclination**, were dwelt on with a warmth which seemed due to the consequence he was wounding, but was very unlikely to recommend his suit.

In **spite** of her deeply-rooted dislike, she could not be **insensible** to the **compliment** of such a man's affection, and though her intentions did not vary for an instant, she was at first sorry for the pain he was to receive; till, roused to resentment by his **subsequent** language, she lost all compassion in anger. She tried, however, to **compose** herself to answer him with patience, when he should have done. He concluded with **representing** to her the strength of that attachment which, in spite of all his endeavours, he had found impossible to **conquer**; and with expressing his hope that it would now be rewarded by her acceptance of his hand. As he said this, she could easily see that he had no doubt

Italian

agitated: agitato.
amazement: stupore, meraviglia.
ardently: ardentemente.
astonishment: stupore, meraviglia, sorpresa.
avowal: ammissione.
banished: bandito.
civility: civiltà, cortesia.
compliment: complimento.
compose: comporre, componi, componiamo, compongo, compongono, componete.

conquer: conquistare, conquistate, conquisto, conquisti, conquistano, conquistiamo, conquista.
detailed: dettagliato.
eloquent: eloquente.
imputing: attribuendo, imputando.
inclination: inclinazione, pendenza.
inquire: domandare, informarsi, domandano, domandate, domandi, domandiamo, domando, indagare, domanda.
insensible: insensibile.

obstacles: ostacoli.
representing: rappresentando, figurando.
repressed: represso.
roused: incitato, spronato, stimolato.
sound: suono, sonare, suonare, solido, sondare, sano, scandagliare, rumore, sonda.
spite: dispetto.
subsequent: successivo, seguente.
tenderness: tenerezza, affettuosità.
vain: vanitoso, vano.

of a favourable answer. He *spoke* of **apprehension** and anxiety, but his **countenance** expressed real security. Such a **circumstance** could only **exasperate farther**, and, when he ceased, the colour rose into her cheeks, and she said:

"In such cases as this, it is, I believe, the established mode to express a sense of **obligation** for the sentiments **avowed**, however **unequally** they may be returned. It is natural that obligation should be felt, and if I could *feel* gratitude, I would now thank you. But I cannot--I have never desired your good opinion, and you have certainly **bestowed** it most **unwillingly**. I am sorry to have occasioned pain to anyone. It has been most **unconsciously** done, however, and I hope will be of short **duration**. The feelings which, you tell me, have long prevented the **acknowledgment** of your regard, can have little difficulty in **overcoming** it after this explanation."

Mr. Darcy, who was **leaning** against the mantelpiece with his eyes fixed on her face, seemed to catch her words with no less resentment than surprise. His **complexion** became pale with anger, and the **disturbance** of his mind was **visible** in every **feature**. He was **struggling** for the appearance of **composure**, and would not open his lips till he believed himself to have **attained** it. The pause was to Elizabeth's feelings dreadful. At length, with a voice of forced **calmness**, he said:

"And this is all the reply which I am to have the honour of **expecting**! I might, perhaps, wish to be informed why, with so little *endeavour* at **civility**, I am thus rejected. But it is of small importance."

"I might as well inquire," replied she, "why with so evident a desire of **offending** and **insulting** me, you chose to tell me that you liked me against your will, against your reason, and even against your character? Was not this some excuse for incivility, if I *was* **uncivil**? But I have other provocations. You know I have. Had not my feelings decided against you--had they been indifferent, or had they even been favourable, do you think that any consideration would **tempt** me to accept the man who has been the means of **ruining**, perhaps for ever, the happiness of a most **beloved** sister?"

Italian

acknowledgment: riconoscimento.
apprehension: apprensione, arresto.
attained: arrivato.
avowed: dichiarato.
beloved: caro, adorato, amato.
bestowed: concesso, tributato.
calmness: calma.
circumstance: circostanza.
civility: civiltà, cortesia.
complexion: carnagione.
composure: calma, compostezza.
countenance: approvare, viso.

disturbance: perturbazione, disturbo.
duration: durata.
exasperate: esasperare.
expecting: aspettando.
farther: più lontano.
feature: caratteristica, carattere, funzione.
insulting: insultare, insultante.
leaning: sporgente, propensione, pendente.
obligation: obbligo, obbligazione, dovere, impegno.

offending: offendendo, insultando, oltraggiando.
overcoming: superando, superamento.
ruining: rovinare.
struggling: lottare.
tempt: tentare, tento, tentiamo, tenti, tentate, tenta, tentano.
uncivil: incivile.
unconsciously: inconsciamente.
unequally: inegualmente.
unwillingly: malvolentieri.
visible: visibile.

As she **pronounced** these words, Mr. Darcy changed colour; but the **emotion** was short, and he listened without attempting to **interrupt** her while she continued:

"I have every reason in the world to think ill of you. No **motive** can excuse the **unjust** and ungenerous part you acted *there*. You dare not, you **cannot** deny, that you have been the principal, if not the only means of **dividing** them from each other--of **exposing** one to the **censure** of the world for **caprice** and **instability**, and the other to its **derision** for disappointed hopes, and **involving** them both in **misery** of the acutest kind."

She paused, and saw with no slight **indignation** that he was listening with an air which proved him wholly **unmoved** by any feeling of **remorse**. He even looked at her with a smile of affected incredulity.

"Can you deny that you have done it?" she repeated.

With **assumed tranquillity** he then replied: "I have no wish of **denying** that I did everything in my power to separate my friend from your sister, or that I **rejoice** in my success. Towards *him* I have been kinder than towards myself."

Elizabeth disdained the appearance of **noticing** this civil reflection, but its meaning did not escape, nor was it likely to **conciliate** her.

"But it is not merely this affair," she continued, "on which my **dislike** is **founded**. Long before it had taken place my opinion of you was decided. Your character was **unfolded** in the **recital** which I received many months ago from Mr. Wickham. On this subject, what can you have to say? In what **imaginary** act of friendship can you here defend yourself? or under what **misrepresentation** can you here impose upon others?"

"You take an **eager** interest in that gentleman's concerns," said Darcy, in a less tranquil tone, and with a **heightened** colour.

"Who that knows what his misfortunes have been, can help feeling an interest in him?"

"His misfortunes!" repeated Darcy **contemptuously**; "yes, his misfortunes have been great indeed."

Italian

assumed: presunto, supposto.
cannot: non potere.
caprice: capriccio.
censure: disapprovazione, criticare, censura.
conciliate: conciliare.
contemptuously: sprezzantemente.
denying: negando.
derision: derisione.
dislike: avversione, ripugnanza, antipatia.
dividing: dividendo, separando.

eager: avido, desideroso, bramoso, impaziente.
emotion: emozione, commozione.
exposing: esponendo.
founded: fondato.
heightened: innalzato.
imaginary: immaginario.
indignation: indignazione, sdegno.
instability: instabilità.
interrupt: interrompere, interruzione.
involving: coinvolgendo.
misery: miseria.

misrepresentation: travisamento.
motive: motivo, movente, ragione.
noticing: notare.
pronounced: pronunciato.
recital: concerto, recital, dizione.
rejoice: allietare, rallegrare.
remorse: rimorso.
tranquil: tranquillo, calmo.
tranquillity: tranquillità.
unfolded: spiegato.
unjust: ingiusto.
unmoved: impassibile.

"And of your infliction," cried Elizabeth with energy. "You have **reduced** him to his present state of **poverty**--comparative poverty. You have **withheld** the advantages which you must know to have been **designed** for him. You have deprived the best years of his life of that independence which was no less his due than his **desert**. You have done all this! and yet you can treat the mention of his **misfortune** with contempt and ridicule."

"And this," cried Darcy, as he walked with quick steps across the room, "is your opinion of me! This is the **estimation** in which you hold me! I thank you for explaining it so fully. My faults, **according** to this **calculation**, are **heavy** indeed! But perhaps," added he, stopping in his walk, and turning towards her, "these **offenses** might have been overlooked, had not your pride been hurt by my **honest confession** of the scruples that had long prevented my forming any serious design. These bitter accusations might have been suppressed, had I, with greater policy, **concealed** my struggles, and **flattered** you into the belief of my being **impelled** by **unqualified**, **unalloyed** inclination; by reason, by reflection, by everything. But **disguise** of every sort is my **abhorrence**. Nor am I ashamed of the feelings I related. They were natural and just. Could you expect me to **rejoice** in the **inferiority** of your connections?--to **congratulate** myself on the hope of relations, whose **condition** in life is so decidedly beneath my own?"

Elizabeth felt herself growing more angry every moment; yet she tried to the utmost to speak with **composure** when she said:

"You are mistaken, Mr. Darcy, if you suppose that the mode of your declaration affected me in any other way, than as it spared the concern which I might have felt in refusing you, had you **behaved** in a more gentlemanlike manner."

She saw him start at this, but he said nothing, and she continued:

"You could not have made the offer of your hand in any possible way that would have tempted me to accept it."

Again his astonishment was **obvious**; and he looked at her with an expression of **mingled incredulity** and **mortification**. She went on:

Italian

abhorrence: orrore, avversione, ribrezzo, ripugnanza.
according: secondo.
behaved: agito, comportato.
calculation: calcolo, conto.
composure: calma, compostezza.
concealed: nascosto.
condition: condizione, condizionare.
confession: confessione.
congratulate: felicitare, felicitate, felicito, feliciti, felicitano, felicita, felicitiamo.
desert: deserto, abbandonare.
designed: progettato.
disguise: travestimento, travestire.
estimation: stima, valutazione.
flattered: lusingato.
heavy: pesante, grave.
honest: onesto.
impelled: costretto, incitato.
incredulity: incredulità.
inferiority: inferiorità.
mingled: mischiato, mescolato.
misfortune: sfortuna, traversia,
disgrazia.
mortification: mortificazione.
obvious: ovvio, evidente, chiaro, palese.
offenses: offese.
poverty: povertà.
reduced: ridotto.
rejoice: allietare, rallegrare.
unalloyed: puro.
unqualified: non qualificato.
withheld: trattenuto.

"From the very beginning--from the first moment, I may almost say--of my **acquaintance** with you, your manners, impressing me with the fullest belief of your **arrogance**, your **conceit**, and your **selfish disdain** of the feelings of others, were such as to form the groundwork of **disapprobation** on which **succeeding** events have built so **immovable** a dislike; and I had not known you a month before I felt that you were the last man in the world whom I could ever be **prevailed** on to marry."

"You have said quite enough, madam. I perfectly **comprehend** your feelings, and have now only to be ashamed of what my own have been. Forgive me for having taken up so much of your time, and accept my best wishes for your health and happiness."

And with these words he **hastily** left the room, and Elizabeth heard him the next moment open the front door and quit the house.

The **tumult** of her mind, was now **painfully** great. She knew not how to support herself, and from **actual** weakness sat down and cried for half-an-hour. Her **astonishment**, as she **reflected** on what had passed, was increased by every review of it. That she should receive an offer of marriage from Mr. Darcy! That he should have been in love with her for so many months! So much in love as to wish to marry her in **spite** of all the objections which had made him prevent his friend's **marrying** her sister, and which must appear at least with equal force in his own case--was almost incredible! It was **gratifying** to have **inspired unconsciously** so strong an affection. But his pride, his **abominable** pride--his **shameless avowal** of what he had done with respect to Jane--his **unpardonable** assurance in **acknowledging**, though he could not justify it, and the **unfeeling** manner in which he had mentioned Mr. Wickham, his cruelty towards whom he had not attempted to deny, soon overcame the pity which the consideration of his **attachment** had for a moment excited. She continued in very **agitated** reflections till the sound of Lady Catherine's carriage made her feel how **unequal** she was to encounter Charlotte's observation, and hurried her away to her room.

Italian

abominable: abominevole, orribile, orrendo.
acknowledging: riconoscendo.
acquaintance: conoscenza, conoscente.
actual: reale, effettivo, attuale.
agitated: agitato.
arrogance: arroganza, alterigia.
astonishment: stupore, meraviglia, sorpresa.
attachment: accessorio, allegato, attaccamento.
avowal: ammissione.

comprehend: comprendere, comprendo, comprendono, comprendiamo, comprendi, comprendete.
conceit: presunzione.
disapprobation: disapprovazione.
disdain: sdegno, sdegnare.
gratifying: gratificando, gratificante.
hastily: frettolosamente.
immovable: immobile.
inspired: ispirato.
marrying: sposandosi.

painfully: dolorosamente.
prevailed: prevalso.
reflected: riflesso.
selfish: egoistico, egoista.
shameless: svergognato, spudorato.
spite: dispetto.
succeeding: riuscendo, successivo.
tumult: tumulto.
unconsciously: inconsciamente.
unequal: ineguale, disuguale.
unfeeling: insensibile.
unpardonable: imperdonabile.

CHAPTER 35

Elizabeth awoke the next morning to the same thoughts and meditations which had at length closed her eyes. She could not yet **recover** from the surprise of what had happened; it was impossible to think of anything else; and, totally **indisposed** for employment, she **resolved**, soon after **breakfast**, to **indulge** herself in air and exercise. She was **proceeding** directly to her **favourite** walk, when the **recollection** of Mr. Darcy's sometimes coming there stopped her, and instead of **entering** the park, she turned up the **lane**, which led **farther** from the turnpike-road. The park **paling** was still the **boundary** on one side, and she soon passed one of the **gates** into the ground.

After walking two or three times along that part of the lane, she was **tempted**, by the **pleasantness** of the morning, to stop at the gates and look into the park. The five weeks which she had now passed in Kent had made a great difference in the country, and every day was **adding** to the **verdure** of the early trees. She was on the point of **continuing** her walk, when she caught a **glimpse** of a gentleman within the sort of **grove** which edged the park; he was moving that way; and, **fearful** of its being Mr. Darcy, she was directly retreating. But the person who **advanced** was now near enough to see her, and stepping forward with **eagerness**, **pronounced** her name. She had turned away; but on **hearing** herself called, though in a voice which **proved** it to be Mr. Darcy, she moved again towards the gate. He had by that time reached it also, and, holding out a letter,

Italian

adding: aggiungendo, addizionando.
advanced: avanzato, progredito.
boundary: confine, frontiera, limite, delimitazione, contorno.
breakfast: colazione, prima colazione.
continuing: continuando, durando.
eagerness: impazienza.
entering: entrando, entrare.
farther: più lontano.
favourite: preferito.
fearful: spaventoso, pauroso.
gate: cancello, porta, saracinesca,

paratoia, uscita.
glimpse: intravedere, occhiata, rapido sguardo.
grove: boschetto.
hearing: udendo, sentendo, udito, udienza, ascolto.
indisposed: indisposto.
indulge: indulgere.
lane: vicolo, corsia.
paling: palizzata.
pleasantness: piacevolezza.
proceeding: procedendo,

procedimento.
pronounced: pronunciato.
proved: provato.
recollection: memoria, ricordo.
recover: ricuperare, ricupera, ricuperi, ricuperiamo, ricuperano, ricuperate, ricupero, recuperare, guarire, riprendere.
resolved: risolto.
tempted: tentato.
verdure: verdura.

which she **instinctively** took, said, with a look of **haughty composure**, "I have been walking in the **grove** some time in the hope of meeting you. Will you do me the honour of reading that letter?" And then, with a slight bow, turned **again** into the **plantation**, and was soon out of sight.

With no expectation of pleasure, but with the strongest **curiosity**, Elizabeth opened the letter, and, to her still increasing wonder, perceived an envelope **containing** two **sheets** of letter-paper, written quite through, in a very close hand. The envelope itself was **likewise** full. Pursuing her way along the lane, she then began it. It was **dated** from Rosings, at **eight** o'clock in the morning, and was as follows:--

"Be not **alarmed**, madam, on receiving this letter, by the **apprehension** of its containing any **repetition** of those sentiments or **renewal** of those offers which were last night so **disgusting** to you. I write without any intention of paining you, or **humbling** myself, by **dwelling** on wishes which, for the happiness of both, **cannot** be too soon forgotten; and the effort which the **formation** and the perusal of this letter must occasion, should have been **spared**, had not my character required it to be written and read. You must, therefore, pardon the **freedom** with which I demand your attention; your feelings, I know, will **bestow** it **unwillingly**, but I demand it of your justice.

"Two **offenses** of a very different nature, and by no means of equal **magnitude**, you last night laid to my charge. The first mentioned was, that, regardless of the sentiments of either, I had **detached** Mr. Bingley from your sister, and the other, that I had, in **defiance** of various claims, in defiance of honour and **humanity**, **ruined** the immediate **prosperity** and **blasted** the prospects of Mr. Wickham. Wilfully and wantonly to have thrown off the companion of my youth, the acknowledged favourite of my father, a young man who had scarcely any other dependence than on our **patronage**, and who had been brought up to expect its **exertion**, would be a **depravity**, to which the separation of two

Italian

alarmed: allarmato.
apprehension: apprensione, arresto.
bestow: tributare, concedere.
blasted: maledetto.
cannot: non potere.
composure: calma, compostezza.
containing: contenendo.
curiosity: curiosità.
dated: datato.
defiance: sfida.
depravity: depravazione.
detached: isolato, staccato, distaccato.

disgusting: disgustoso.
dwelling: dimorando, abitando, dimora, abitazione.
eight: otto.
exertion: sforzo.
formation: formazione.
freedom: libertà.
grove: boschetto.
haughty: altezzoso.
humanity: umanità.
humbling: umiliante.
instinctively: istintivamente.

likewise: anche, altrettanto.
magnitude: grandezza, magnitudine.
offenses: offese.
patronage: patrocinio, patronato.
plantation: piantagione.
prosperity: prosperità.
renewal: rinnovo, rinnovamento.
repetition: ripetizione, replica.
ruined: rovinato.
sheets: fogli, le lenzuola.
spared: risparmiato.
unwillingly: malvolentieri.

young persons, whose affection could be the growth of only a few weeks, could bear no comparison. But from the **severity** of that blame which was last night so **liberally bestowed**, **respecting** each **circumstance**, I shall hope to be in the future **secured**, when the following account of my actions and their motives has been read. If, in the explanation of them, which is due to myself, I am under the necessity of relating feelings which may be offensive to yours, I can only say that I am sorry. The necessity must be **obeyed**, and further **apology** would be absurd.

"I had not been long in Hertfordshire, before I saw, in common with others, that Bingley preferred your elder sister to any other young woman in the country. But it was not till the evening of the dance at Netherfield that I had any **apprehension** of his feeling a serious **attachment**. I had often seen him in love before. At that ball, while I had the honour of dancing with you, I was first made **acquainted**, by Sir William Lucas's **accidental** information, that Bingley's attentions to your sister had given **rise** to a general expectation of their marriage. He spoke of it as a certain event, of which the time alone could be **undecided**. From that moment I observed my friend's behaviour **attentively**; and I could then perceive that his **partiality** for Miss Bennet was beyond what I had ever witnessed in him. Your sister I also watched. Her look and manners were open, cheerful, and **engaging** as ever, but without any **symptom** of peculiar regard, and I remained convinced from the evening's **scrutiny**, that though she received his attentions with pleasure, she did not invite them by any **participation** of **sentiment**. If *you* have not been mistaken here, *I* must have been in error. Your superior knowledge of your sister must make the latter probable. If it be so, if I have been **misled** by such error to **inflict** pain on her, your resentment has not been unreasonable. But I shall not **scruple** to **assert**, that the **serenity** of your sister's **countenance** and air was such as might have given the most **acute observer** a conviction that, however **amiable** her temper, her heart was not likely to be easily touched. That I was

Italian

accidental: accidentale, fortuito.
acquainted: informato.
acute: acuto, aguzzo, appuntito.
amiable: amabile.
apology: scusa, apologia.
apprehension: apprensione, arresto.
assert: asserire, asserite, asseriscono, asserisci, asserisco, asseriamo, sostenere, affermare.
attachment: accessorio, allegato, attaccamento.
attentively: attentamente.

bestowed: concesso, tributato.
circumstance: circostanza.
countenance: approvare, viso.
engaging: innestando, attraente.
inflict: infliggere, infliggete, infliggo, infliggiamo, infliggono, infliggi.
liberally: liberalmente.
misled: fuorviato, traviato.
obeyed: ubbidito, obbedito.
observer: osservatore.
partiality: parzialità, predilezione.
participation: partecipazione.

respecting: rispettare.
rise: alzarsi, aumento, salire, rialzo, levarsi, sorgere, incremento.
scruple: scrupolo.
scrutiny: esame minuzioso, scrutinio.
secured: fissato.
sentiment: sentimento.
serenity: serenità.
severity: rigore.
symptom: sintomo, segno.
undecided: incerto, indeciso.

desirous of believing her **indifferent** is certain--but I will venture to say that my **investigation** and decisions are not **usually influenced** by my hopes or fears. I did not believe her to be indifferent because I wished it; I believed it on **impartial** conviction, as truly as I wished it in reason. My objections to the marriage were not merely those which I last night acknowledged to have the **utmost** force of passion to put aside, in my own case; the want of connection could not be so great an evil to my friend as to me. But there were other **causes** of **repugnance**; causes which, though still **existing**, and existing to an equal degree in both instances, I had myself endeavoured to forget, because they were not immediately before me. These causes must be stated, though briefly. The situation of your mother's family, though **objectionable**, was nothing in comparison to that total want of **propriety** so frequently, so almost **uniformly betrayed** by herself, by your three younger sisters, and occasionally even by your father. Pardon me. It **pains** me to **offend** you. But **amidst** your concern for the defects of your nearest relations, and your **displeasure** at this representation of them, let it give you **consolation** to consider that, to have **conducted yourselves** so as to avoid any share of the like **censure**, is praise no less generally **bestowed** on you and your elder sister, than it is honourable to the sense and disposition of both. I will only say **farther** that from what passed that evening, my opinion of all parties was confirmed, and every **inducement heightened** which could have led me before, to **preserve** my friend from what I **esteemed** a most unhappy connection. He left Netherfield for London, on the day following, as you, I am certain, remember, with the design of soon returning.

"The part which I acted is now to be explained. His sisters' **uneasiness** had been equally excited with my own; our **coincidence** of feeling was soon discovered, and, alike sensible that no time was to be lost in **detaching** their brother, we shortly resolved on joining him directly in London. We accordingly went--and there I readily engaged in the office of pointing out to my friend the certain evils of such a choice. I

Italian

amidst: tra, fra.
bestowed: concesso, tributato.
betrayed: tradito.
causes: causa.
censure: disapprovazione, criticare, censura.
coincidence: coincidenza.
conducted: condotto.
consolation: consolazione.
detaching: staccando, distaccando, staccare.
displeasure: scontento, dispiacere.

esteemed: stimato.
existing: esistendo, esistente.
farther: più lontano.
heightened: innalzato.
impartial: imparziale.
indifferent: indifferente.
inducement: incitamento.
influenced: influenzato.
investigation: indagine, ricerca, investigazione, esame, inchiesta.
objectionable: biasimevole.
offend: offendere, offendiamo,

offendo, offendi, offendete, offendono, insultare, insulto, insulti, insultate, insultano.
pains: dolori.
preserve: conservare, conserva.
propriety: convenienza.
repugnance: avversione, ripugnanza.
uneasiness: disagio.
uniformly: uniformemente.
usually: di solito, solitamente.
utmost: massimo.
yourselves: voi stessi.

described, and **enforced** them **earnestly**. But, however this **remonstrance** might have **staggered** or delayed his determination, I do not suppose that it would **ultimately** have prevented the marriage, had it not been seconded by the assurance that I **hesitated** not in giving, of your sister's indifference. He had before believed her to return his affection with **sincere**, if not with equal regard. But Bingley has great natural **modesty**, with a stronger dependence on my judgement than on his own. To convince him, therefore, that he had **deceived** himself, was no very difficult point. To persuade him against returning into Hertfordshire, when that conviction had been given, was scarcely the work of a moment. I **cannot** blame myself for having done thus much. There is but one **part** of my conduct in the whole affair on which I do not reflect with satisfaction; it is that I **condescended** to adopt the measures of art so far as to conceal from him your sister's being in town. I knew it myself, as it was known to Miss Bingley; but her brother is even yet **ignorant** of it. That they might have met without ill consequence is perhaps probable; but his regard did not appear to me enough **extinguished** for him to see her without some danger. Perhaps this **concealment**, this disguise was beneath me; it is done, however, and it was done for the best. On this subject I have nothing more to say, no other apology to offer. If I have **wounded** your sister's feelings, it was **unknowingly** done and though the motives which governed me may to you very naturally appear insufficient, I have not yet learnt to **condemn** them.

"With respect to that other, more **weighty accusation**, of having injured Mr. Wickham, I can only **refute** it by laying before you the whole of his connection with my family. Of what he has *particularly* accused me I am ignorant; but of the truth of what I shall relate, I can **summon** more than one witness of **undoubted veracity**.

"Mr. Wickham is the son of a very respectable man, who had for many years the management of all the Pemberley estates, and whose good conduct in the **discharge** of his trust naturally inclined my father to

Italian

accusation: accusa, incriminazione, imputazione, denuncia.
accused: accusato, imputato, caricato.
art: arte, l'arte.
cannot: non potere.
concealment: occultamento, nascondiglio, reticenza.
condemn: condannare, condannate, condanno, condanni, condannano, condanniamo, condanna, biasimare, biasimo, biasimiamo, biasimi.
condescended: degnato.

deceived: ingannato, truffato.
described: descritto.
discharge: scarico, scarica, portata, scaricare.
earnestly: seriamente.
enforced: imposto.
extinguished: spento, estinto.
hesitated: esitato, titubato.
ignorant: ignorante.
modesty: modestia, verecondia.
refute: confutare, confutano, confuto, confutiamo, confutate, confuta,

confuti.
remonstrance: rimostranza.
sincere: sincero.
staggered: sfalsato.
summon: convocare, chiamare, intimare, citare.
ultimately: finalmente, alla fine.
undoubted: indubbio.
unknowingly: inconsapevolmente.
veracity: veracità.
weighty: pesante.
wounded: ferito.

be of service to him; and on George Wickham, who was his **godson**, his **kindness** was therefore **liberally bestowed**. My father **supported** him at school, and afterwards at Cambridge--most important assistance, as his own father, always poor from the **extravagance** of his wife, would have been unable to give him a gentleman's education. My father was not only **fond** of this young man's society, whose manner were always **engaging**; he had also the highest opinion of him, and hoping the church would be his profession, intended to provide for him in it. As for myself, it is many, many years since I first began to think of him in a very different manner. The **vicious** propensities--the want of principle, which he was careful to guard from the knowledge of his best friend, could not escape the observation of a young man of nearly the same age with himself, and who had opportunities of seeing him in **unguarded** moments, which Mr. Darcy could not have. Here again shall give you pain--to what degree you only can tell. But whatever may be the sentiments which Mr. Wickham has created, a suspicion of their nature shall not prevent me from **unfolding** his real character--it adds even another **motive**.

"My excellent father died about five years ago; and his **attachment** to Mr. Wickham was to the last so steady, that in his will he particularly recommended it to me, to promote his **advancement** in the best manner that his profession might allow--and if he took **orders**, **desired** that a valuable family living might be his as soon as it became **vacant**. There was also a **legacy** of one thousand pounds. His own father did not long **survive** mine, and within half a year from these events, Mr. Wickham wrote to **inform** me that, having finally resolved against taking orders, he hoped I should not think it **unreasonable** for him to expect some more immediate **pecuniary** advantage, in **lieu** of the preferment, by which he could not be benefited. He had some intention, he added, of studying law, and I must be aware that the interest of one thousand pounds would be a very **insufficient** support **therein**. I rather wished, than believed him to be **sincere**; but, at any rate, was perfectly ready to

---

Italian

advancement: progresso, avanzamento.
attachment: accessorio, allegato, attaccamento.
bestowed: concesso, tributato.
desired: desiderato.
engaging: innestando, attraente.
extravagance: stravaganza, prodigalità.
fond: tenero, affettuoso, affezionato.
godson: figlioccio.
inform: informare, informano,
informate, informi, informiamo, informo, informa, insegnare.
insufficient: insufficiente.
kindness: gentilezza, bontà, cortesia.
legacy: eredità, lascito, legato.
liberally: liberalmente.
lieu: luogo.
motive: motivo, movente, ragione.
orders: ordine, comande ai tavoli.
pecuniary: pecuniario.
sincere: sincero.
supported: sostenuto.
survive: sopravvivere, sopravvivete, sopravvivono, sopravvivo, sopravviviamo, sopravvivi.
therein: in ciò.
unfolding: spiegamento, spiegare, spiegando.
unguarded: incustodito.
unreasonable: irragionevole.
vacant: vacante, libero.
vicious: vizioso.

accede to his proposal. I knew that Mr. Wickham ought not to be a **clergyman**; the business was therefore soon settled--he resigned all claim to assistance in the church, were it possible that he could ever be in a situation to receive it, and accepted in return three thousand pounds. All connection between us seemed now **dissolved**. I thought too ill of him to invite him to Pemberley, or admit his society in town. In town I believe he **chiefly** lived, but his studying the law was a mere **pretence**, and being now free from all restraint, his life was a life of **idleness** and **dissipation**. For about three years I heard little of him; but on the **decease** of the **incumbent** of the living which had been designed for him, he applied to me again by letter for the presentation. His **circumstances**, he assured me, and I had no difficulty in believing it, were **exceedingly** bad. He had found the law a most **unprofitable** study, and was now absolutely resolved on being **ordained**, if I would present him to the living in question--of which he **trusted** there could be little doubt, as he was well assured that I had no other person to provide for, and I could not have forgotten my **revered** father's intentions. You will hardly blame me for refusing to comply with this **entreaty**, or for **resisting** every **repetition** to it. His resentment was in proportion to the distress of his circumstances--and he was **doubtless** as violent in his **abuse** of me to others as in his reproaches to myself. After this period every appearance of **acquaintance** was dropped. How he lived I know not. But last summer he was again most **painfully obtruded** on my notice.

"I must now mention a circumstance which I would wish to forget myself, and which no obligation less than the present should **induce** me to **unfold** to any human being. Having said thus much, I feel no doubt of your **secrecy**. My sister, who is more than ten years my **junior**, was left to the **guardianship** of my mother's **nephew**, Colonel Fitzwilliam, and myself. About a year ago, she was taken from school, and an establishment formed for her in London; and last summer she went with the lady who **presided** over it, to Ramsgate; and **thither** also went Mr. Wickham, undoubtedly by design; for there proved to have been a prior

Italian

abuse: abuso, insultare, abusare, offendere, insulto.
acquaintance: conoscenza, conoscente.
chiefly: principalmente, soprattutto.
circumstance: circostanza.
clergyman: ecclesiastico, prete, curato, sacerdote.
decease: decedere, decesso.
dissipation: dispersione, dissipazione.
dissolved: dissolto, sciolto.
doubtless: senza dubbio.
entreaty: preghiera, domanda,

supplica.
exceedingly: estremamente.
guardianship: tutela.
idleness: ozio.
incumbent: incombente.
induce: dedurre, concludere, indurre, induci, inducono, induciamo, inducete, deducono, deduco, deduciamo, deducete.
junior: minore.
nephew: nipote.
obtruded: imposto.

ordained: destinato.
painfully: dolorosamente.
presided: presieduto.
pretence: pretesa.
repetition: ripetizione, replica.
resisting: resistendo.
revered: riverito.
secrecy: segretezza.
thither: là.
trusted: fidato.
unfold: spiegare.
unprofitable: non redditizio.

acquaintance between him and Mrs. Younge, in whose character we were most **unhappily deceived**; and by her **connivance** and **aid**, he so far recommended himself to Georgiana, whose **affectionate** heart **retained** a strong **impression** of his **kindness** to her as a child, that she was persuaded to believe herself in love, and to consent to an elopement. She was then but fifteen, which must be her excuse; and after **stating** her **imprudence**, I am happy to add, that I owed the knowledge of it to herself. I joined them unexpectedly a day or two before the intended elopement, and then Georgiana, unable to support the idea of **grieving** and **offending** a brother whom she almost looked up to as a father, acknowledged the whole to me. You may imagine what I felt and how I acted. Regard for my sister's credit and feelings prevented any public **exposure**; but I wrote to Mr. Wickham, who left the place immediately, and Mrs. Younge was of course removed from her charge.   Mr. Wickham's chief object was **unquestionably** my sister's fortune, which is thirty thousand pounds; but I **cannot** help **supposing** that the hope of revenging himself on me was a strong **inducement**. His revenge would have been complete indeed.

"This, madam, is a faithful **narrative** of every event in which we have been concerned together; and if you do not absolutely reject it as false, you will, I hope, **acquit** me **henceforth** of cruelty towards Mr. Wickham. I know not in what manner, under what form of **falsehood** he had imposed on you; but his success is not perhaps to be wondered at. Ignorant as you **previously** were of everything concerning either, **detection** could not be in your power, and suspicion certainly not in your **inclination**.

"You may possibly wonder why all this was not told you last night; but I was not then master enough of myself to know what could or ought to be **revealed**. For the truth of everything here related, I can appeal more particularly to the **testimony** of Colonel Fitzwilliam, who, from our near relationship and constant **intimacy**, and, still more, as one of the executors of my father's will, has been **unavoidably acquainted** with

---

Italian

acquainted: informato.
acquit: assolvere, assolvete, assolviamo, assolvo, assolvono, assolvi.
affectionate: affettuoso.
aid: aiutare, aiuto, assistere, assistenza, soccorrere, assistente, soccorso.
cannot: non potere.
connivance: connivenza.
deceived: ingannato, truffato.
detection: rivelazione, scoperta.

exposure: esposizione.
falsehood: falso, falsità, bugia, menzogna.
grieving: addolorando, accorando.
henceforth: d'ora in poi, d'ora innanzi.
impression: impressione, impronta.
imprudence: imprudenza.
inclination: inclinazione, pendenza.
inducement: incitamento.
intimacy: intimità.
kindness: gentilezza, bontà, cortesia.
narrative: descrizione, narrativo.

offending: offendendo, insultando, oltraggiando.
previously: precedentemente, davanti.
retained: ritenuto, trattenuto.
revealed: pubblicato, rivelato.
stating: dichiarare.
supposing: supponendo.
testimony: certificato attestato, testimonianza.
unavoidably: inevitabilmente.
unhappily: infelicemente.
unquestionably: indiscutibilmente.

every particular of these transactions. If your **abhorrence** of *me* should make *my* assertions **valueless**, you **cannot** be **prevented** by the same **cause** from **confiding** in my **cousin**; and that there may be the **possibility** of **consulting** him, I shall **endeavour** to find some **opportunity** of **putting** this **letter** in your **hands** in the **course** of the morning. I will only **add**, God **bless** you.

"Fitzwilliam Darcy."

Italian

abhorrence: orrore, avversione, ribrezzo, ripugnanza.
add: aggiungere, aggiungiamo, aggiungete, aggiungi, aggiungo, aggiungono, addizionare, addizioniamo, addizioni, addizionate, addizionano.
bless: benedire, benedi', benedite, benedicono, benedico, benedici, benediciamo.
cannot: non potere.
cause: causa, causare, provocare.

confiding: confidando, confidare.
consulting: consultando, interpellando, consultare.
course: corso, percorso, piatto, andamento, decorso, direzione, rotta, portata.
cousin: cugino, cugina.
endeavour: tentare, tentativo, sforzarsi.
hands: mani.
letter: lettera, la lettera.
opportunity: opportunità, occasione.

possibility: possibilità, eventualità.
prevented: impedito, prevenuto.
putting: mettendo, ponendo.
valueless: senza valore.

CHAPTER 36

If Elizabeth, when Mr. Darcy gave her the letter, did not expect it to contain a **renewal** of his offers, she had formed no **expectation** at all of its contents. But such as they were, it may well be supposed how **eagerly** she went through them, and what a contrariety of **emotion** they **excited**. Her feelings as she read were **scarcely** to be defined. With **amazement** did she first understand that he believed any **apology** to be in his power; and steadfastly was she **persuaded**, that he could have no explanation to give, which a just sense of **shame** would not **conceal**. With a strong **prejudice** against everything he might say, she began his account of what had happened at Netherfield. She read with an **eagerness** which hardly left her power of **comprehension**, and from **impatience** of knowing what the next sentence might bring, was **incapable** of **attending** to the sense of the one before her eyes. His belief of her sister's **insensibility** she instantly **resolved** to be false; and his account of the real, the worst **objections** to the match, made her too angry to have any wish of doing him justice. He expressed no regret for what he had done which satisfied her; his style was not **penitent**, but **haughty**. It was all pride and **insolence**.

But when this subject was succeeded by his account of Mr. Wickham--when she read with somewhat clearer attention a relation of events which, if true, must **overthrow** every **cherished** opinion of his worth, and which bore so **alarming** an **affinity** to his own history of himself--her feelings were yet more **acutely** painful

---

Italian

acutely: acutamente.
affinity: affinità, parentela, parentado.
alarming: allarmante.
amazement: stupore, meraviglia.
apology: scusa, apologia.
attending: visitando, curando, assistendo.
cherished: adorato.
comprehension: comprensione.
conceal: nascondere, nascondono, nascondete, nascondi, nascondiamo, nascondo, occultare.

eagerly: ardentemente.
eagerness: impazienza.
emotion: emozione, commozione.
excited: eccitato, concitato, emozionato.
expectation: attesa, aspettativa.
haughty: altezzoso.
impatience: impazienza.
incapable: incapace.
insensibility: insensibilità, indifferenza.
insolence: insolenza.

objections: obiezioni.
overthrow: rovesciare, rovesciate, rovesciano, rovesci, rovesciamo, rovescia, rovescio.
penitent: pentito, penitente.
persuaded: convinto, persuaso.
prejudice: pregiudizio, preconcetto, prevenzione.
renewal: rinnovo, rinnovamento.
resolved: risolto.
scarcely: appena, a stento.
shame: vergogna, pudore.

and more difficult of **definition**. Astonishment, **apprehension**, and even **horror**, **oppressed** her. She wished to **discredit** it entirely, repeatedly **exclaiming**, "This must be false! This **cannot** be! This must be the **grossest** falsehood!"--and when she had gone through the whole letter, though scarcely knowing anything of the last **page** or two, put it hastily away, **protesting** that she would not regard it, that she would never look in it again.

In this **perturbed** state of mind, with thoughts that could rest on nothing, she walked on; but it would not do; in half a minute the letter was **unfolded** again, and **collecting** herself as well as she could, she again began the **mortifying** perusal of all that related to Wickham, and commanded herself so far as to examine the meaning of every sentence. The account of his connection with the Pemberley family was exactly what he had related himself; and the kindness of the late Mr. Darcy, though she had not before known its **extent**, agreed equally well with his own words. So far each **recital** confirmed the other; but when she came to the will, the difference was great. What Wickham had said of the living was fresh in her memory, and as she **recalled** his very words, it was impossible not to feel that there was gross **duplicity** on one side or the other; and, for a few moments, she **flattered** herself that her wishes did not **err**. But when she read and re-read with the closest attention, the particulars immediately following of Wickham's **resigning** all pretensions to the living, of his receiving in **lieu** so considerable a **sum** as three thousand pounds, again was she forced to **hesitate**. She put down the letter, **weighed** every circumstance with what she meant to be impartiality--deliberated on the probability of each statement--but with little success. On both sides it was only assertion. Again she read on; but every line proved more **clearly** that the affair, which she had believed it impossible that any **contrivance** could so represent as to render Mr. Darcy's conduct in it less than **infamous**, was capable of a turn which must make him entirely **blameless** throughout the whole.

The **extravagance** and general profligacy which he scrupled not to lay at Mr. Wickham's charge, **exceedingly** shocked her; the more so, as she could bring no proof of its injustice. She had never heard of him before his entrance into the ----

Italian

apprehension: apprensione, arresto.
blameless: irreprensibile.
cannot: non potere.
clearly: chiaramente.
collecting: raccogliendo.
contrivance: congegno.
definition: definizione.
discredit: screditare.
duplicity: duplicità.
err: errare, errano, errate, erri, erriamo, erro, erra, sbagliarsi.
exceedingly: estremamente.

exclaiming: esclamando.
extent: limite.
extravagance: stravaganza, prodigalità.
flattered: lusingato.
gross: lordo.
hesitate: esitare, esitiamo, esiti, esitate, esita, esitano, esito, titubare, tituba, titubiamo, titubi.
horror: orrore, ribrezzo.
infamous: infame.
lieu: luogo.

mortifying: mortificando, umiliante.
oppressed: premuto, oppresso, serrato, stretto.
page: pagina, valletto.
perturbed: perturbato.
protesting: protestare.
recalled: ricordato.
recital: concerto, recital, dizione.
resigning: rassegnando, dimettendo.
sum: somma, importo, addizionare.
unfolded: spiegato.
weighed: pesato.

shire Militia, in which he had engaged at the persuasion of the young man who, on meeting him accidentally in town, had there renewed a slight acquaintance. Of his former way of life nothing had been known in Hertfordshire but what he told himself. As to his real character, had information been in her power, she had never felt a wish of **inquiring**. His countenance, voice, and manner had established him at once in the possession of every virtue. She tried to **recollect** some instance of goodness, some distinguished **trait** of integrity or **benevolence**, that might **rescue** him from the attacks of Mr. Darcy; or at least, by the **predominance** of virtue, **atone** for those **casual errors** under which she would endeavour to **class** what Mr. Darcy had described as the **idleness** and **vice** of many years' continuance. But no such recollection **befriended** her. She could see him instantly before her, in every charm of air and address; but she could remember no more **substantial** good than the general **approbation** of the neighbourhood, and the regard which his social powers had gained him in the **mess**. After pausing on this point a considerable while, she once more continued to read. But, **alas**! the story which followed, of his designs on Miss Darcy, received some confirmation from what had passed between Colonel Fitzwilliam and herself only the morning before; and at last she was **referred** for the truth of every particular to Colonel Fitzwilliam himself--from whom she had previously received the information of his near concern in all his cousin's affairs, and whose character she had no reason to question. At one time she had almost resolved on applying to him, but the idea was checked by the **awkwardness** of the application, and at length wholly **banished** by the conviction that Mr. Darcy would never have **hazarded** such a proposal, if he had not been well assured of his cousin's **corroboration**.

She perfectly **remembered** everything that had passed in conversation between Wickham and herself, in their first evening at Mr. Phillips's. Many of his expressions were still fresh in her memory. She was *now* struck with the **impropriety** of such **communications** to a stranger, and wondered it had escaped her before. She saw the **indelicacy** of putting himself forward as he had done, and the **inconsistency** of his professions with his conduct. She remembered that he had **boasted** of having no fear of seeing Mr. Darcy--that Mr.

Italian

alas: ahimè.
approbation: approvazione.
atone: espiare, espio, espii, espiate, espiano, espia, espiamo.
awkwardness: goffaggine.
banished: bandito.
befriended: aiutato.
benevolence: benevolenza.
boasted: vantato.
casual: casuale, accidentale.
class: classe, classificare, categoria.
communications: comunicazioni.

corroboration: conferma, corroborazione.
errors: errori.
hazarded: rischiato.
idleness: ozio.
impropriety: scorrettezza, improprietà.
inconsistency: inconsistenza, incoerenza.
indelicacy: indelicatezza.
inquiring: domandando, domandare.
mess: confusione, disordine.

predominance: prevalenza, predominio, predominanza.
recollect: rammenta, rammentano, rammentate, rammenti, rammentiamo, rammento, rammentare, ricordarsi.
referred: riferito.
remembered: ricordato.
rescue: salvataggio, salvare, soccorso.
substantial: sostanziale, sostanzioso.
trait: caratteristica, tratto.
vice: morsa, vizio, virtù.

Darcy might leave the country, but that *he* should stand his **ground**; yet he had **avoided** the Netherfield ball the very next week. She remembered also that, till the Netherfield family had quitted the country, he had told his story to no one but herself; but that after their removal it had been **everywhere discussed**; that he had then no reserves, no scruples in sinking Mr. Darcy's character, though he had assured her that respect for the father would always prevent his **exposing** the son.

How differently did everything now appear in which he was concerned! His attentions to Miss King were now the consequence of views solely and **hatefully mercenary**; and the **mediocrity** of her fortune proved no longer the **moderation** of his wishes, but his **eagerness** to **grasp** at anything. His behaviour to herself could now have had no **tolerable** motive; he had either been **deceived** with regard to her fortune, or had been **gratifying** his **vanity** by encouraging the preference which she believed she had most incautiously **shown**. Every **lingering** struggle in his favour grew fainter and fainter; and in **farther justification** of Mr. Darcy, she could not but allow Mr. Bingley, when questioned by Jane, had long ago **asserted** his blamelessness in the affair; that proud and **repulsive** as were his manners, she had never, in the whole course of their acquaintance--an acquaintance which had **latterly** brought them much together, and given her a sort of **intimacy** with his ways--seen anything that betrayed him to be **unprincipled** or unjust--anything that spoke him of **irreligious** or **immoral** habits; that among his own connections he was **esteemed** and valued--that even Wickham had allowed him merit as a brother, and that she had often heard him speak so **affectionately** of his sister as to prove him capable of *some* **amiable** feeling; that had his actions been what Mr. Wickham represented them, so gross a **violation** of everything right could hardly have been concealed from the world; and that friendship between a person capable of it, and such an amiable man as Mr. Bingley, was **incomprehensible**.

She grew absolutely ashamed of herself. Of neither Darcy nor Wickham could she think without feeling she had been blind, partial, **prejudiced**, absurd.

Italian

affectionately: affettuosamente.
amiable: amabile.
asserted: asserito.
avoided: evitato.
deceived: ingannato, truffato.
discussed: discusso.
eagerness: impazienza.
esteemed: stimato.
everywhere: dappertutto, ovunque, dovunque, in ogni luogo.
exposing: esponendo.
farther: più lontano.

grasp: afferrare, stretta, comprendere.
gratifying: gratificando, gratificante.
ground: suolo, fondo, terra, massa, terreno.
hatefully: odiosamente.
immoral: immorale.
incomprehensible: incomprensibile.
intimacy: intimità.
irreligious: irreligioso.
justification: giustificazione, giustezza.
latterly: ultimamente.

lingering: indugiando, indugiare, prolungato.
mediocrity: mediocrità.
mercenary: mercenario.
moderation: moderazione.
prejudiced: prevenuto.
repulsive: ripulsivo, ripugnante.
shown: mostrato.
tolerable: tollerabile.
unprincipled: senza scrupoli.
vanity: vanità.
violation: violazione, infrazione.

"How despicably I have acted!" she cried; "I, who have prided myself on my **discernment**! I, who have **valued** myself on my abilities! who have often disdained the generous **candour** of my sister, and **gratified** my **vanity** in useless or blameable **mistrust**! How **humiliating** is this discovery! Yet, how just a **humiliation**! Had I been in love, I could not have been more **wretchedly** blind! But vanity, not love, has been my **folly**. Pleased with the preference of one, and **offended** by the **neglect** of the other, on the very beginning of our **acquaintance**, I have courted prepossession and ignorance, and driven reason away, where either were concerned. Till this moment I never knew myself."

From herself to Jane--from Jane to Bingley, her thoughts were in a line which soon brought to her **recollection** that Mr. Darcy's explanation *there* had appeared very insufficient, and she read it again. Widely different was the effect of a second perusal. How could she deny that credit to his assertions in one instance, which she had been obliged to give in the other? He declared himself to be totally unsuspicious of her sister's **attachment**; and she could not help remembering what Charlotte's opinion had always been. Neither could she deny the justice of his description of Jane. She felt that Jane's feelings, though **fervent**, were little displayed, and that there was a constant **complacency** in her air and manner not often united with great **sensibility**.

When she came to that part of the letter in which her family were mentioned in terms of such **mortifying**, yet **merited reproach**, her sense of shame was severe. The justice of the charge struck her too forcibly for **denial**, and the circumstances to which he particularly **alluded** as having passed at the Netherfield ball, and as **confirming** all his first **disapprobation**, could not have made a stronger impression on his mind than on hers.

The **compliment** to herself and her sister was not unfelt. It **soothed**, but it could not **console** her for the contempt which had thus been self-attracted by the rest of her family; and as she considered that Jane's disappointment had in fact been the work of her nearest relations, and reflected how **materially** the credit of both must be hurt by such **impropriety** of conduct, she felt **depressed** beyond anything she had ever known before.

Italian

acquaintance: conoscenza, conoscente.
alluded: alluso.
attachment: accessorio, allegato, attaccamento.
candour: franchezza.
complacency: compiacimento.
compliment: complimento.
confirming: confermando.
console: consolare, consolle, console.
denial: negazione, rifiuto, smentita.
depressed: depresso.
disapprobation: disapprovazione.

discernment: discernimento.
fervent: fervente.
folly: follia.
gratified: gratificato.
humiliating: umiliando, umiliante.
humiliation: umiliazione.
impropriety: scorrettezza, improprietà.
materially: materialmente.
merited: meritato.
mistrust: diffidenza, sfiducia.
mortifying: mortificando, umiliante.

neglect: trascurare, negligere, negligenza, trascuratezza.
offended: offeso, insultato, oltraggiato.
recollection: memoria, ricordo.
reproach: rimprovero, rimproverare, riprendere.
sensibility: sensibilità.
soothed: calmato.
valued: valutato, stimato.
vanity: vanità.
wretchedly: infelicemente.

After **wandering** along the **lane** for two hours, giving way to every **variety** of thought--re-considering events, **determining** probabilities, and **reconciling** herself, as well as she could, to a change so **sudden** and so important, **fatigue**, and a **recollection** of her long **absence**, made her at **length** return home; and she **entered** the house with the wish of **appearing cheerful** as **usual**, and the **resolution** of **repressing** such reflections as must make her **unfit** for conversation.

She was immediately told that the two gentlemen from Rosings had each called during her absence; Mr. Darcy, only for a few minutes, to take leave--but that Colonel Fitzwilliam had been **sitting** with them at **least** an hour, **hoping** for her return, and almost resolving to walk after her **till** she could be found. **Elizabeth** could but just *affect* concern in **missing** him; she really **rejoiced** at it. Colonel Fitzwilliam was no **longer an object**; she could think only of her letter.

Italian

absence: assenza, mancanza.
affect: riguardare, riguarda, riguardo, riguardano, riguardate, riguardi, riguardiamo, affettare.
appearing: apparendo.
cheerful: allegro.
determining: definendo, fissando, definito, fissato, determinato, determinando.
elizabeth: Elisabetta.
entered: entrato.
fatigue: fatica, affaticare, stancare, stanchezza, affaticamento.
hoping: sperando.
lane: vicolo, corsia.
least: minimo, meno.
length: lunghezza, durata.
longer: oltre, più lungo.
missing: disperso, mancante.
object: oggetto, cosa, scopo.
recollection: memoria, ricordo.
reconciling: riconciliando, conciliando.
rejoiced: allietato, gioito, rallegrato.
repressing: reprimendo.
resolution: risoluzione, definizione, deliberazione.
sitting: sedendo, covando, seduta.
sudden: subitaneo, improvviso.
till: finchè, coltivare, cassa, fino, arare.
unfit: inadatto.
usual: usuale, consueto, solito, generale, abituale.
variety: varietà, variazione.
wandering: vagando, peregrinazione.

CHAPTER 37

The two gentlemen left Rosings the next morning, and Mr. Collins having been in waiting near the lodges, to make them his **parting obeisance**, was able to bring home the **pleasing intelligence**, of their **appearing** in very good health, and in as **tolerable** spirits as could be expected, after the **melancholy** scene so **lately** gone through at Rosings. To Rosings he then **hastened**, to **console** Lady Catherine and her daughter; and on his return brought back, with great **satisfaction**, a message from her **ladyship**, **importing** that she felt herself so **dull** as to make her very **desirous** of having them all to **dine** with her.

Elizabeth could not see Lady Catherine without **recollecting** that, had she **chosen** it, she might by this time have been **presented** to her as her future **niece**; nor could she think, without a smile, of what her ladyship's **indignation** would have been. "What would she have said? how would she have behaved?" were questions with which she **amused** herself.

Their first subject was the **diminution** of the Rosings party. "I **assure** you, I feel it exceedingly," said Lady Catherine; "I believe no one **feels** the loss of friends so much as I do. But I am particularly **attached** to these young men, and know them to be so much attached to me! They were **excessively** sorry to go! But so they always are. The dear Colonel rallied his spirits **tolerably till** just at last; but Darcy seemed to feel it most **acutely**, more, I think, than last year. His **attachment** to Rosings certainly increases."

Italian

acutely: acutamente.	**diminution**: diminuzione.	**lately**: ultimamente, recentemente.
amused: divertito.	**dine**: cenare.	**melancholy**: malinconia, malinconico.
appearing: apparendo.	**dull**: opaco, smussato, spuntato.	**niece**: nipote.
assure: assicurare, assicura,	**elizabeth**: Elisabetta.	**obeisance**: riverenza, inchino.
assicuriamo, assicurate, assicuri,	**excessively**: eccessivamente.	**parting**: separazione, divisione.
assicurano, assicuro, garantire.	**feels**: sente, tasta, tocca, trova, prova.	**pleasing**: piacevole.
attached: fissato, attaccato, allegato.	**hastened**: affrettato, sollecitato.	**presented**: presentato.
attachment: accessorio, allegato,	**importing**: importazione, importatore,	**recollecting**: rammentando.
attaccamento.	importare.	**satisfaction**: soddisfazione.
chosen: scelto, eletto.	**indignation**: indignazione, sdegno.	**till**: finchè, coltivare, cassa, fino, arare.
console: consolare, consolle, console.	**intelligence**: intelligenza.	**tolerable**: tollerabile.
desirous: desideroso.	**ladyship**: signoria.	**tolerably**: tollerabilmente.

Mr. Collins had a **compliment**, and an **allusion** to throw in here, which were **kindly** smiled on by the mother and daughter.

Lady Catherine observed, after dinner, that Miss **Bennet** seemed out of spirits, and immediately **accounting** for it by herself, by **supposing** that she did not like to go home again so soon, she added:

"But if that is the case, you must write to your mother and **beg** that you may stay a little longer. Mrs. Collins will be very glad of your company, I am sure."

"I am much **obliged** to your **ladyship** for your kind invitation," replied Elizabeth, "but it is not in my power to accept it. I must be in town next Saturday."

"Why, at that **rate**, you will have been here only six weeks. I expected you to stay two months. I told Mrs. Collins so before you came. There can be no occasion for your going so soon. Mrs. Bennet could certainly spare you for another fortnight."

"But my father **cannot**. He wrote last week to **hurry** my return."

"Oh! your father of course may spare you, if your mother can. Daughters are never of so much consequence to a father. And if you will stay another *month* complete, it will be in my power to take one of you as far as London, for I am going there early in June, for a week; and as Dawson does not object to the barouche-box, there will be very good room for one of you--and indeed, if the weather should happen to be cool, I should not object to taking you both, as you are neither of you large."

"You are all **kindness**, madam; but I believe we must **abide** by our **original** plan."

Lady Catherine seemed **resigned**. "Mrs. Collins, you must send a **servant** with them. You know I always speak my mind, and I cannot bear the idea of two young women travelling **post** by themselves. It is highly **improper**. You must **contrive** to send somebody. I have the greatest **dislike** in the world to that sort of thing. Young women should always be properly **guarded** and attended, **according** to their situation in life. When my **niece** Georgiana went to Ramsgate

Italian

abide: aspettare, aspettiamo, aspetta, aspettano, aspetti, aspetto, aspettate, restare, sopportare.
according: secondo.
accounting: contabilità, ragioneria, contabile.
allusion: allusione.
beg: mendicare, mendicano, mendica, mendicate, mendico, mendichiamo, mendichi, chiedere, elemosinare, supplicare.
bennet: cariofillata, erba benedetta.

cannot: non potere.
compliment: complimento.
contrive: escogitano, escogito, escogitiamo, escogitate, escogita, escogiti, escogitare.
dislike: avversione, ripugnanza, antipatia.
guarded: guardingo, custodito.
hurry: affrettarsi, fretta.
improper: improprio.
kindly: gentilmente, gentile.
kindness: gentilezza, bontà, cortesia.

ladyship: signoria.
niece: nipote.
obliged: obbligato.
original: originale.
post: posta, palo, impiego, funzione, posto, montante, imbucare.
rate: tasso, stimare, valutare, aliquota, tariffa, apprezzare, ritmo, percentuale.
resigned: rassegnato.
servant: servire, servo, servitore.
supposing: supponendo.

last summer, I made a point of her having two men-servants go with her. Miss Darcy, the daughter of Mr. Darcy, of Pemberley, and Lady Anne, could not have appeared with **propriety** in a different manner. I am **excessively attentive** to all those things. You must send John with the young ladies, Mrs. Collins. I am glad it occurred to me to mention it; for it would really be **discreditable** to *you* to let them go alone."

"My uncle is to send a servant for us."

"Oh! Your uncle! He keeps a man-servant, does he? I am very glad you have somebody who thinks of these things. Where shall you change horses? Oh! Bromley, of course. If you mention my name at the Bell, you will be attended to."

Lady Catherine had many other questions to ask **respecting** their journey, and as she did not answer them all herself, attention was necessary, which Elizabeth believed to be lucky for her; or, with a mind so occupied, she might have forgotten where she was. Reflection must be reserved for **solitary** hours; whenever she was alone, she gave way to it as the greatest relief; and not a day went by without a solitary walk, in which she might **indulge** in all the delight of unpleasant recollections.

Mr. Darcy's letter she was in a fair way of soon knowing by heart. She **studied** every sentence; and her feelings towards its writer were at times **widely** different. When she remembered the style of his address, she was still full of **indignation**; but when she considered how **unjustly** she had condemned and **upbraided** him, her anger was turned against herself; and his disappointed feelings became the object of **compassion**. His **attachment** excited **gratitude**, his general character respect; but she could not approve him; nor could she for a moment **repent** her refusal, or feel the slightest **inclination** ever to see him again. In her own past behaviour, there was a constant **source** of **vexation** and regret; and in the unhappy defects of her family, a subject of yet **heavier chagrin**. They were **hopeless** of **remedy**. Her father, **contented** with laughing at them, would never **exert** himself to **restrain** the wild **giddiness** of his youngest daughters; and her mother, with manners so far from right herself, was entirely **insensible** of the

Italian

attachment: accessorio, allegato, attaccamento.
attentive: attento, premuroso.
chagrin: dispiacere, cruccio.
compassion: compassione.
contented: contento.
discreditable: vergognoso, disonorevole.
excessively: eccessivamente.
exert: praticare, esercitare, eserciti, pratico, pratichiamo, pratichi, praticate, praticano, pratica,

esercitiamo, esercitate.
giddiness: capogiro, vertigine.
gratitude: gratitudine, riconoscenza, grazie.
heavier: più pesante.
hopeless: disperato, senza speranza.
inclination: inclinazione, pendenza.
indignation: indignazione, sdegno.
indulge: indulgere.
insensible: insensibile.
propriety: convenienza.
remedy: rimedio, medicina, rimediare.

repent: pentirsi.
respecting: rispettare.
restrain: dominare, domina, domino, dominiamo, dominano, dominate, domini, reprimere, governare.
solitary: solo, solitario.
source: fonte, sorgente, origine.
studied: studiato.
unjustly: ingiustamente.
upbraided: rimproverato.
vexation: irritazione.
widely: largamente.

evil. Elizabeth had frequently united with Jane in an endeavour to check the **imprudence** of Catherine and Lydia; but while they were supported by their mother's **indulgence**, what chance could there be of improvement? Catherine, weak-spirited, **irritable**, and completely under Lydia's guidance, had been always affronted by their advice; and Lydia, self-willed and **careless**, would scarcely give them a hearing. They were **ignorant**, idle, and **vain**. While there was an officer in Meryton, they would **flirt** with him; and while Meryton was within a walk of Longbourn, they would be going there forever.

Anxiety on Jane's behalf was another **prevailing** concern; and Mr. Darcy's explanation, by **restoring** Bingley to all her former good opinion, **heightened** the sense of what Jane had lost. His affection was proved to have been **sincere**, and his conduct **cleared** of all blame, unless any could attach to the **implicitness** of his confidence in his friend. How **grievous** then was the thought that, of a situation so desirable in every respect, so **replete** with advantage, so promising for happiness, Jane had been deprived, by the folly and indecorum of her own family!

When to these recollections was added the development of Wickham's character, it may be easily believed that the happy spirits which had seldom been depressed before, were now so much affected as to make it almost impossible for her to appear **tolerably** cheerful.

Their engagements at Rosings were as frequent during the last week of her stay as they had been at first. The very last evening was spent there; and her **ladyship** again **inquired minutely** into the **particulars** of their journey, gave them directions as to the best method of **packing**, and was so **urgent** on the necessity of placing **gowns** in the only right way, that Maria thought herself obliged, on her return, to **undo** all the work of the morning, and pack her **trunk afresh**.

When they parted, Lady Catherine, with great **condescension**, wished them a good journey, and invited them to come to Hunsford again next year; and Miss de Bourgh **exerted** herself so far as to **curtsey** and **hold** out her hand to both.

Italian

afresh: di nuovo, ancora, da capo.
careless: sbadato, noncurante, negligente, trascurato.
cleared: chiaro.
condescension: condiscendenza.
curtsey: inchino.
exerted: esercitato, praticato.
flirt: flirtare, civettare.
gowns: vestiti.
grievous: doloroso.
heightened: innalzato.
hold: tenere, stiva, stretta, mantenere,

ritenere.
ignorant: ignorante.
implicitness: l'essere implicito.
imprudence: imprudenza.
indulgence: indulgenza.
inquired: domandato.
irritable: irritabile.
ladyship: signoria.
minutely: minutamente.
packing: imballaggio, impacchettamento.
particulars: particolari.

prevailing: prevalente, prevalendo.
replete: pieno.
restoring: ripristinando, restaurando.
sincere: sincero.
tolerably: tollerabilmente.
trunk: tronco, baule, proboscide, torso, bagagliaio.
undo: disfare, disfate, disfa', disfacciamo, disfaccio, disfai, disfanno.
urgent: urgente.
vain: vanitoso, vano.

CHAPTER 38

On Saturday morning Elizabeth and Mr. Collins met for breakfast a few minutes before the others appeared; and he took the opportunity of paying the **parting** civilities which he **deemed indispensably** necessary.

"I know not, Miss Elizabeth," said he, "whether Mrs. Collins has yet expressed her sense of your **kindness** in coming to us; but I am very certain you will not leave the house without **receiving** her thanks for it. The **favor** of your company has been much felt, I **assure** you. We know how little there is to **tempt** anyone to our **humble abode**. Our **plain** manner of living, our small rooms and few **domestics**, and the little we see of the world, must make Hunsford extremely **dull** to a young lady like yourself; but I hope you will believe us **grateful** for the **condescension**, and that we have done everything in our power to prevent your **spending** your time unpleasantly."

Elizabeth was **eager** with her thanks and assurances of **happiness**. She had spent six weeks with great **enjoyment**; and the pleasure of being with Charlotte, and the kind attentions she had received, must make *her* feel the **obliged**. Mr. Collins was **gratified**, and with a more **smiling solemnity** replied:

"It gives me great pleasure to hear that you have passed your time not disagreeably. We have certainly done our best; and most **fortunately** having it in our power to introduce you to very **superior** society, and, from our connection with Rosings, the **frequent** means of **varying** the humble home scene, I think we

Italian

abode: residenza, appartamento, alloggio, dimora.
assure: assicurare, assicura, assicuriamo, assicurate, assicuri, assicurano, assicuro, garantire.
condescension: condiscendenza.
deemed: creduto.
domestics: domestico.
dull: opaco, smussato, spuntato.
eager: avido, desideroso, bramoso, impaziente.
enjoyment: godimento.

favor: favore, favorire, cortesia.
fortunately: fortunatamente, per fortuna.
frequent: frequente, bazzicare.
grateful: riconoscente, grato.
gratified: gratificato.
happiness: felicità.
humble: umile, modesto.
indispensably: indispensabilmente.
kindness: gentilezza, bontà, cortesia.
obliged: obbligato.
parting: separazione, divisione.

plain: piano, pianura, evidente, distinto, chiaro.
receiving: ricevendo, accogliendo, ricezione, ricevere, ricevente.
smiling: sorridere.
solemnity: solennità.
spending: spendendo, passando.
superior: superiore.
tempt: tentare, tento, tentiamo, tenti, tentate, tenta, tentano.
varying: variando, variare.

may **flatter** ourselves that your Hunsford visit **cannot** have been entirely **irksome**. Our situation with regard to Lady Catherine's family is indeed the sort of extraordinary advantage and **blessing** which few can **boast**. You see on what a **footing** we are. You see how continually we are engaged there. In truth I must acknowledge that, with all the disadvantages of this humble **parsonage**, I should not think anyone **abiding** in it an object of **compassion**, while they are sharers of our **intimacy** at Rosings."

Words were insufficient for the **elevation** of his feelings; and he was obliged to walk about the room, while Elizabeth tried to **unite civility** and truth in a few short sentences.

"You may, in fact, carry a very favourable report of us into Hertfordshire, my dear cousin. I flatter myself at least that you will be able to do so. Lady Catherine's great attentions to Mrs. Collins you have been a daily witness of; and altogether I trust it does not appear that your friend has drawn an unfortunate-- but on this point it will be as well to be silent. Only let me assure you, my dear Miss Elizabeth, that I can from my heart most **cordially** wish you equal **felicity** in marriage. My dear Charlotte and I have but one mind and one way of thinking. There is in everything a most remarkable **resemblance** of character and ideas between us. We seem to have been designed for each other."

Elizabeth could safely say that it was a great happiness where that was the case, and with equal **sincerity** could add, that she firmly believed and **rejoiced** in his domestic comforts. She was not sorry, however, to have the **recital** of them interrupted by the lady from whom they sprang. Poor Charlotte! it was **melancholy** to leave her to such society! But she had chosen it with her eyes open; and though evidently regretting that her visitors were to go, she did not seem to ask for compassion. Her home and her **housekeeping**, her parish and her **poultry**, and all their dependent concerns, had not yet lost their charms.

At length the **chaise** arrived, the trunks were **fastened** on, the parcels placed within, and it was pronounced to be ready. After an **affectionate parting** between the friends, Elizabeth was attended to the carriage by Mr. Collins, and as they walked down the garden he was **commissioning** her with his best

Italian

abiding: durevole, permanente, continuo, aspettando.
affectionate: affettuoso.
blessing: benedicendo, benedizione.
boast: vanteria, vantarsi.
cannot: non potere.
chaise: calesse.
civility: civiltà, cortesia.
commissioning: messa in servizio.
compassion: compassione.
cordially: cordialmente.
elevation: elevazione, altezza,

prospetto.
fastened: fissato.
felicity: felicità.
flatter: lusingare, lusingate, lusingo, lusinghi, lusingano, lusinghiamo, lusinga, adulare.
footing: punto d'appoggio.
housekeeping: economia domestica, operazioni di gestione interna.
intimacy: intimità.
irksome: seccante.
melancholy: malinconia, malinconico.

parsonage: canonica.
parting: separazione, divisione.
poultry: pollame.
recital: concerto, recital, dizione.
rejoiced: allietato, gioito, rallegrato.
resemblance: somiglianza, rassomiglianza.
sincerity: sincerità.
unite: unire, congiungere, unirsi, unite, uniscono, unisco, uniamo, unisci.

respects to all her family, not **forgetting** his thanks for the **kindness** he had received at Longbourn in the winter, and his **compliments** to Mr. and Mrs. Gardiner, though unknown. He then handed her in, Maria followed, and the door was on the point of being closed, when he suddenly reminded them, with some **consternation**, that they had **hitherto** forgotten to leave any message for the ladies at Rosings.

"But," he added, "you will of course wish to have your **humble** respects delivered to them, with your grateful thanks for their kindness to you while you have been here."

Elizabeth made no **objection**; the door was then allowed to be shut, and the **carriage** drove off.

"Good gracious!" cried Maria, after a few minutes' silence, "it seems but a day or two since we first came! and yet how many things have happened!"

"A great many indeed," said her **companion** with a **sigh**.

"We have **dined** nine times at Rosings, besides **drinking** tea there twice! How much I shall have to tell!"

Elizabeth added **privately**, "And how much I shall have to conceal!"

Their journey was performed without much conversation, or any **alarm**; and within four hours of their leaving Hunsford they reached Mr. Gardiner's house, where they were to remain a few days.

Jane looked well, and Elizabeth had little opportunity of **studying** her spirits, **amidst** the various engagements which the kindness of her aunt had **reserved** for them. But Jane was to go home with her, and at Longbourn there would be leisure enough for observation.

It was not without an effort, meanwhile, that she could wait even for Longbourn, before she told her sister of Mr. Darcy's proposals. To know that she had the power of **revealing** what would so **exceedingly astonish** Jane, and must, at the same time, so highly **gratify** whatever of her own **vanity** she had not yet been able to reason away, was such a **temptation** to **openness** as nothing could have **conquered** but the state of **indecision** in which she remained as to the

Italian

alarm: allarme, sveglia, allarmare.
amidst: tra, fra.
astonish: stupire, stupisciti, si stupite, si stupiscono, si stupisci, mi stupisco, ci stupiamo, stupitevi, sorprendere, sbalordire.
carriage: vettura, carrello, vagone, carro, carrozza.
companion: compagno, accompagnatore.
compliments: complimenti.
conquered: conquistato.

consternation: sbigottimento, costernazione.
dined: pranzato, cenato.
drinking: bere.
exceedingly: estremamente.
forgetting: dimenticando.
gratify: gratificare, gratificano, gratifico, gratifichiamo, gratifichi, gratificate, gratifica.
hitherto: finora.
humble: umile, modesto.
indecision: indecisione.

kindness: gentilezza, bontà, cortesia.
objection: obiezione, opposizione.
openness: apertura, franchezza.
privately: privatamente.
reserved: riservato.
revealing: pubblicando, rivelando.
sigh: sospirare, sospiro.
studying: studio.
temptation: tentazione.
vanity: vanità.

extent of what she should **communicate**; and her **fear**, if she once **entered** on the **subject**, of being **hurried** into **repeating** something of Bingley which might only **grieve** her **sister** further.

Italian

communicate: comunicare, comunicano, comunico, comunichi, comunica, communicate, comunichiamo, annunciare, infettare.
entered: entrato.
extent: limite.
fear: paura, temere, angoscia, timore, aver timore.
grieve: affliggersi, addolorare, addolorarsi.
hurried: affrettato, frettoloso.
repeating: ripetendo.

sister: sorella, la sorella.
subject: soggetto, argomento, oggetto, sottoporre, tema, suddito, assoggettato.

CHAPTER 39

It was the second week in May, in which the three young ladies set out together from Gracechurch Street for the town of ----, in Hertfordshire; and, as they drew near the **appointed inn** where Mr. Bennet's carriage was to meet them, they **quickly** perceived, in **token** of the coachman's **punctuality**, both Kitty and Lydia looking out of a dining-room upstairs. These two girls had been above an hour in the place, happily employed in visiting an opposite **milliner**, watching the **sentinel** on guard, and dressing a **salad** and **cucumber**.

After **welcoming** their sisters, they **triumphantly** displayed a table set out with such cold meat as an inn **larder** usually **affords**, **exclaiming**, "Is not this nice? Is not this an agreeable surprise?"

"And we mean to treat you all," added Lydia, "but you must **lend** us the money, for we have just spent **ours** at the **shop** out there." Then, showing her purchases--"Look here, I have **bought** this **bonnet**. I do not think it is very pretty; but I thought I might as well **buy** it as not. I shall **pull** it to pieces as soon as I get home, and see if I can make it up any better."

And when her sisters **abused** it as **ugly**, she added, with perfect **unconcern**, "Oh! but there were two or three much uglier in the shop; and when I have bought some prettier-coloured **satin** to **trim** it with fresh, I think it will be very **tolerable**. Besides, it will not much **signify** what one wears this summer, after the ----shire have left Meryton, and they are going in a fortnight."

Italian

abused: abusato.
affords: permette.
appointed: nominato.
bonnet: cofano, cappotta, cuffia.
bought: comprato.
buy: comprare, comperare, acquisto, acquistare, compra.
cucumber: cetriolo, il cetriolo.
exclaiming: esclamando.
inn: locanda, osteria.
larder: dispensa.
lend: prestare, presta, prestiamo, presti, prestate, prestano, presto, imprestare.
milliner: modista.
ours: nostro.
pull: tirare, tirano, tiriamo, tirate, tira, tiri, tiro, trarre, tirata.
punctuality: puntualità.
quickly: presto, rapidamente, velocemente.
salad: insalata, l'insalata.
satin: raso, satin.
sentinel: sentinella.
shop: negozio, spaccio, bottega, officina.
signify: significare, significate, significo, significhi, significa, significhiamo, significano.
token: segno, gettone, prova.
tolerable: tollerabile.
trim: rifilare.
triumphantly: trionfalmente.
ugly: brutto.
unconcern: noncuranza.
welcoming: accogliendo.

"Are they indeed!" cried Elizabeth, with the greatest satisfaction.

"They are going to be **encamped** near Brighton; and I do so want **papa** to take us all there for the summer! It would be such a **delicious** scheme; and I **dare** say would hardly cost anything at all. Mamma would like to go too of all things! Only think what a **miserable** summer else we shall have!"

"Yes," thought Elizabeth, "*that* would be a **delightful** scheme indeed, and completely do for us at once. Good Heaven! Brighton, and a whole campful of soldiers, to us, who have been overset already by one poor **regiment** of **militia**, and the **monthly balls** of Meryton!"

"Now I have got some news for you," said Lydia, as they sat down at table. "What do you think? It is excellent news--capital news--and about a certain person we all like!"

Jane and Elizabeth looked at each other, and the **waiter** was told he need not stay. Lydia laughed, and said:

"Aye, that is just like your **formality** and **discretion**. You thought the waiter must not hear, as if he cared! I dare say he often **hears** worse things said than I am going to say. But he is an **ugly fellow**! I am **glad** he is gone. I never saw such a long **chin** in my life. Well, but now for my news; it is about dear Wickham; too good for the waiter, is it not? There is no **danger** of Wickham's **marrying** Mary King. There's for you! She is gone down to her **uncle** at Liverpool: gone to stay. Wickham is safe."

"And Mary King is safe!" added Elizabeth; "safe from a **connection imprudent** as to fortune."

"She is a great **fool** for going away, if she liked him."

"But I hope there is no strong **attachment** on either side," said Jane.

"I am sure there is not on *his*. I will answer for it, he never cared three straws about her--who could about such a **nasty** little **freckled** thing?"

Italian

attachment: accessorio, allegato, attaccamento.
balls: sfere, palla, balli.
chin: mento, il mento.
connection: coincidenza, accoppiamento, connessione, collegamento, relazione, banda.
danger: pericolo.
dare: osare, oso, osiamo, osi, osate, osano, osa, sfida.
delicious: squisito.
delightful: delizioso, piacevole.

discretion: discrezione.
encamped: accampato.
fellow: uomo.
fool: babbeo, sciocco, allocco, ingannare.
formality: formalità.
freckled: lentigginoso.
glad: contento, felice, lieto.
hears: ode, sente.
imprudent: imprudente.
marrying: sposandosi.
militia: milizia.

miserable: miserabile, misero, afflitto, cattivo, triste, povero, miserevole, miserando.
monthly: mensile, mensilmente, al mese.
nasty: schifoso, sgradevole, cattivo, mostruoso, disonesto, spiacevole.
papa: papà.
regiment: reggimento.
ugly: brutto.
uncle: zio, lo zio.
waiter: cameriere, il cameriere.

Elizabeth was shocked to think that, however **incapable** of such **coarseness** of *expression* herself, the coarseness of the *sentiment* was little other than her own **breast** had harboured and **fancied** liberal!

As soon as all had ate, and the **elder** ones paid, the **carriage** was ordered; and after some **contrivance**, the whole party, with all their **boxes**, work-bags, and parcels, and the **unwelcome addition** of Kitty's and Lydia's **purchases**, were **seated** in it.

"How **nicely** we are all crammed in," cried Lydia. "I am glad I bought my **bonnet**, if it is only for the **fun** of having another **bandbox**! Well, now let us be quite comfortable and **snug**, and talk and laugh all the way home. And in the first place, let us hear what has happened to you all since you went away. Have you seen any **pleasant** men? Have you had any flirting? I was in great hopes that one of you would have got a husband before you came back. Jane **will** be quite an old **maid** soon, I **declare**. She is almost three-and-twenty! Lord, how **ashamed** I should be of not being married before three-and-twenty! My **aunt** Phillips wants you so to get husbands, you can't think. She says Lizzy had better have taken Mr. Collins; but *I* do not think there would have been any fun in it. Lord! how I should like to be married before any of you; and then I would **chaperon** you about to all the **balls**. Dear me! we had such a good piece of fun the other day at Colonel Forster's. Kitty and me were to spend the day there, and Mrs. Forster promised to have a little dance in the evening; (by the **bye**, Mrs. Forster and me are *such* friends!) and so she asked the two Harringtons to come, but Harriet was ill, and so Pen was forced to come by herself; and then, what do you think we did? We **dressed** up Chamberlayne in woman's clothes on purpose to pass for a lady, only think what fun! Not a **soul** knew of it, but Colonel and Mrs. Forster, and Kitty and me, except my aunt, for we were forced to **borrow** one of her **gowns**; and you **cannot** imagine how well he looked! When Denny, and Wickham, and Pratt, and two or three more of the men came in, they did not know him in the least. Lord! how I laughed! and so did Mrs. Forster. I thought I should have died. And *that* made the men **suspect** something, and then they soon found out what was the matter."

Italian

addition: aggiunta, addizione.
ashamed: vergognoso.
aunt: zia, la zia.
balls: sfere, palla, balli.
bandbox: cappelliera.
bonnet: cofano, cappotta, cuffia.
borrow: prendere in prestito.
boxes: scatole.
breast: petto, seno, mammella.
bye: arrivederci, addio, ciao.
cannot: non potere.
carriage: vettura, carrello, vagone,

carro, carrozza.
chaperon: accompagnatrice.
coarseness: grossolanità, ruvidezza.
contrivance: congegno.
declare: dichiarare, dichiara, dichiaro,
dichiariamo, dichiari, dichiarano,
dichiarate.
dressed: vestito.
elder: maggiore, sambuco.
fancied: fantastico.
fun: divertimento, spasso, piacere.
gowns: vestiti.

ill: malato, ammalato.
incapable: incapace.
maid: cameriera, ragazza.
nicely: piacevolmente.
pleasant: piacevole, gradevole, ameno.
purchases: acquisti.
seated: seduto.
sentiment: sentimento.
snug: accogliente, comodo, raccolto.
soul: anima.
suspect: sospettare, sospetto.
unwelcome: sgradito.

With such kinds of histories of their parties and good jokes, did Lydia, **assisted** by Kitty's hints and **additions, endeavour** to **amuse** her companions all the way to Longbourn. Elizabeth listened as little as she could, but there was no escaping the frequent mention of Wickham's name.

Their reception at home was most kind. Mrs. **Bennet rejoiced** to see Jane in undiminished beauty; and more than once during dinner did Mr. Bennet say **voluntarily** to Elizabeth:

"I am glad you are come back, Lizzy."

Their party in the dining-room was large, for almost all the Lucases came to meet Maria and hear the news; and various were the subjects that occupied them: Lady Lucas was **inquiring** of Maria, after the **welfare** and **poultry** of her **eldest** daughter; Mrs. Bennet was **doubly** engaged, on one hand **collecting** an account of the present fashions from Jane, who sat some way below her, and, on the other, **retailing** them all to the younger Lucases; and Lydia, in a voice rather louder than any other person's, was **enumerating** the various pleasures of the morning to anybody who would hear her.

"Oh! Mary," said she, "I wish you had gone with us, for we had such fun! As we went along, Kitty and I drew up the **blinds**, and **pretended** there was nobody in the coach; and I should have gone so all the way, if Kitty had not been sick; and when we got to the George, I do think we **behaved** very **handsomely**, for we treated the other three with the nicest cold **luncheon** in the world, and if you would have gone, we would have treated you too. And then when we came away it was such fun! I thought we never should have got into the coach. I was ready to die of laughter. And then we were so **merry** all the way home! we talked and laughed so loud, that anybody might have heard us ten miles off!"

To this Mary very **gravely** replied, "Far be it from me, my dear sister, to **depreciate** such pleasures! They would **doubtless** be **congenial** with the **generality** of female minds. But I **confess** they would have no charms for *me*--I should **infinitely** prefer a book."

Italian

additions: addizioni.
amuse: divertire, divertiamo, divertono, diverto, diverto, diverti, divertite.
assisted: assistito, aiutato.
behaved: agito, comportato.
bennet: cariofillata, erba benedetta.
blinds: acceca.
collecting: raccogliendo.
confess: confessare, confessa, confessano, confessate, confessi, confessiamo, confesso.
congenial: congeniale.

depreciate: svalutiamo, svalutate, deprezziamo, deprezzi, deprezzate, deprezza, deprezzano, deprezzo, svalutano, svaluto, svaluti.
doubly: doppiamente.
doubtless: senza dubbio.
eldest: maggiore, il più vecchio.
endeavour: tentare, tentativo, sforzarsi.
enumerating: enumerando.
generality: generalità.
gravely: tomba, seriamente.

handsomely: bellamente.
infinitely: infinitamente.
inquiring: domandando, domandare.
luncheon: pranzo.
merry: allegro, festoso, gaio.
poultry: pollame.
pretended: finto.
rejoiced: allietato, gioito, rallegrato.
retailing: commercio al dettaglio, commercio al minuto.
voluntarily: volontariamente.
welfare: benessere.

But of this answer Lydia heard not a word. She **seldom listened** to **anybody** for more than half a **minute**, and never **attended** to Mary at all.

In the **afternoon** Lydia was **urgent** with the rest of the girls to walk to Meryton, and to see how **everybody** went on; but Elizabeth **steadily opposed** the scheme. It should not be said that the Miss Bennets could not be at home half a day before they were in **pursuit** of the officers. There was another reason too for her **opposition**. She dreaded **seeing** Mr. Wickham again, and was **resolved** to avoid it as long as possible. The **comfort** to *her* of the regiment's **approaching removal** was indeed beyond expression. In a **fortnight** they were to go--and once gone, she **hoped** there could be nothing more to **plague** her on his account.

She had not been many hours at home before she found that the Brighton scheme, of which Lydia had given them a **hint** at the **inn**, was under **frequent** discussion between her parents. Elizabeth saw directly that her father had not the smallest **intention** of **yielding**; but his **answers** were at the same time so **vague** and **equivocal**, that her mother, though often **disheartened**, had never yet despaired of **succeeding** at last.

Italian

afternoon: pomeriggio.
answers: risposta, risposte.
anybody: qualcuno, nessuno.
approaching: avvicinamento.
attended: visitato, curato, assistito.
comfort: consolare, comodità, confortare, comfort, benessere.
disheartened: sconfortato, avvilito, scoraggiato.
equivocal: ambiguo, equivoco.
everybody: ognuno, tutti, ogni, tutto.
fortnight: due settimane.

frequent: frequente, bazzicare.
hint: alludere, suggerimento, allusione, cenno.
hoped: sperato.
inn: locanda, osteria.
intention: intenzione, proposito.
listened: ascoltato.
minute: minuto, il minuto, minuscolo, momento.
opposed: opposto, contrapposto.
opposition: opposizione.
plague: peste.

pursuit: inseguimento, ricerca.
removal: rimozione, asportazione, eliminazione.
resolved: risolto.
seeing: vedendo, segando.
seldom: raramente.
steadily: costantemente, fermamente.
succeeding: riuscendo, successivo.
urgent: urgente.
vague: vago.
yielding: cedendo.

CHAPTER 40

Elizabeth's **impatience** to **acquaint** Jane with what had happened could no longer be **overcome**; and at length, resolving to **suppress** every particular in which her sister was concerned, and **preparing** her to be surprised, she related to her the next morning the chief of the scene between Mr. Darcy and herself.

Miss Bennet's **astonishment** was soon **lessened** by the strong **sisterly partiality** which made any **admiration** of Elizabeth appear perfectly natural; and all surprise was **shortly** lost in other feelings. She was sorry that Mr. Darcy should have **delivered** his sentiments in a manner so little suited to **recommend** them; but still more was she **grieved** for the **unhappiness** which her sister's **refusal** must have given him.

"His being so sure of **succeeding** was wrong," said she, "and certainly ought not to have appeared; but consider how much it must increase his disappointment!"

"Indeed," replied Elizabeth, "I am **heartily** sorry for him; but he has other feelings, which will probably soon drive away his **regard** for me. You do not **blame** me, however, for refusing him?"

"Blame you! Oh, no."

"But you blame me for having **spoken** so **warmly** of Wickham?"

"No--I do not know that you were wrong in saying what you did."

Italian

acquaint: informare, informi, informa, informate, informiamo, informo, informano, insegnare.
admiration: ammirazione.
astonishment: stupore, meraviglia, sorpresa.
blame: colpa, biasimare, riprendere, incolpare, biasimo.
delivered: consegnato.
grieved: accorato, addolorato.
heartily: cordialmente.
impatience: impazienza.

lessened: diminuito.
overcome: superare.
partiality: parzialità, predilezione.
preparing: preparando, allestendo, apprestando.
recommend: raccomandare, raccomanda, raccomandano, raccomandate, raccomandi, raccomandiamo, raccomando, consigliare, vantare.
refusal: rifiuto.
regard: riguardo, considerazione,

considerare, rispetto, considerano, consideriamo, considero, considera, consideri, considerate, stima.
shortly: prossimamente.
sisterly: sorella.
spoken: parlato.
succeeding: riuscendo, successivo.
suppress: soffocare, opprimere, soffoca, soffocano, soffocate, soffochi, soffochiamo, soffoco.
unhappiness: tristezza, infelicità.
warmly: caldamente, calorosamente.

"But you *will* know it, when I tell you what happened the very next day."

She then spoke of the letter, **repeating** the whole of its contents as far as they concerned George Wickham. What a **stroke** was this for poor Jane! who would **willingly** have gone through the world without **believing** that so much **wickedness existed** in the whole **race** of **mankind**, as was here **collected** in one individual. Nor was Darcy's **vindication**, though grateful to her feelings, capable of **consoling** her for such discovery. Most **earnestly** did she labour to prove the probability of error, and seek to clear the one without involving the other.

"This will not do," said Elizabeth; "you never will be able to make both of them good for anything. Take your choice, but you must be satisfied with only one. There is but such a **quantity** of **merit** between them; just enough to make one good sort of man; and of late it has been **shifting** about pretty much. For my part, I am **inclined** to believe it all Darcy's; but you shall do as you choose."

It was some time, however, before a smile could be **extorted** from Jane.

"I do not know when I have been more shocked," said she. "Wickham so very bad! It is almost past belief. And poor Mr. Darcy! Dear Lizzy, only consider what he must have suffered. Such a disappointment! and with the knowledge of your ill opinion, too! and having to relate such a thing of his sister! It is really too **distressing**. I am sure you must feel it so."

"Oh! no, my regret and **compassion** are all done away by seeing you so full of both. I know you will do him such **ample** justice, that I am growing every moment more **unconcerned** and **indifferent**. Your **profusion** makes me **saving;** and if you **lament** over him much longer, my heart will be as light as a feather."

"Poor Wickham! there is such an expression of goodness in his **countenance**! such an **openness** and **gentleness** in his manner!"

"There certainly was some great **mismanagement** in the education of those two young men. One has got all the goodness, and the other all the appearance of it."

"I never thought Mr. Darcy so **deficient** in the *appearance* of it as you used to do."

Italian

ample: ampio.
believing: credendo, credere.
collected: raccolto.
compassion: compassione.
consoling: consolare.
countenance: approvare, viso.
deficient: deficiente, carente, difettoso, insufficiente.
distressing: doloroso, penoso, angoscioso.
earnestly: seriamente.
existed: esistito.
extorted: estorto.
gentleness: delicatezza.
inclined: disposto, inclinato, propenso.
indifferent: indifferente.
lament: lamento, lamentare.
mankind: umanità.
merit: meritare, merito, benemerenza, pregio.
mismanagement: cattiva gestione.
openness: apertura, franchezza.
profusion: profusione.
quantity: quantità, grandezza.
race: razza, corsa, correre.
repeating: ripetendo.
saving: salvando, risparmio, risparmiando.
shifting: spostare, spostamento.
stroke: accarezzare, corsa, apoplessia, colpo, ictus, colpo apoplettico.
unconcerned: indifferente.
vindication: rivendicazione.
wickedness: cattiveria.
willingly: volentieri.

"And yet I meant to be **uncommonly** clever in taking so decided a **dislike** to him, **without** any reason. It is such a **spur** to one's **genius**, such an opening for wit, to have a dislike of that kind. One may be **continually abusive** without saying anything just; but one **cannot** always be laughing at a man without now and then **stumbling** on something witty."

"Lizzy, when you first read that letter, I am sure you could not treat the matter as you do now."

"Indeed, I could not. I was **uncomfortable** enough, I may say **unhappy**. And with no one to speak to about what I felt, no Jane to comfort me and say that I had not been so very weak and **vain** and **nonsensical** as I knew I had! Oh! how I wanted you!"

"How **unfortunate** that you should have used such very strong **expressions** in speaking of Wickham to Mr. Darcy, for now they *do* appear wholly undeserved."

"Certainly. But the **misfortune** of speaking with **bitterness** is a most natural consequence of the **prejudices** I had been encouraging. There is one point on which I want your advice. I want to be told whether I ought, or ought not, to make our **acquaintances** in general understand Wickham's character."

Miss Bennet paused a little, and then replied, "Surely there can be no occasion for **exposing** him so dreadfully. What is your opinion?"

"That it ought not to be attempted. Mr. Darcy has not authorised me to make his communication public. On the **contrary**, every particular relative to his sister was meant to be kept as much as possible to myself; and if I **endeavour** to **undeceive** people as to the rest of his conduct, who will believe me? The general prejudice against Mr. Darcy is so violent, that it would be the death of half the good people in Meryton to attempt to place him in an **amiable** light. I am not equal to it. Wickham will soon be gone; and therefore it will not **signify** to anyone here what he really is. Some time **hence** it will be all found out, and then we may laugh at their **stupidity** in not knowing it before. At present I will say nothing about it."

Italian

abusive: abusivo, offensivo.
acquaintances: conoscenze.
amiable: amabile.
bitterness: amarezza.
cannot: non potere.
continually: continuamente.
contrary: contrario.
dislike: avversione, ripugnanza, antipatia.
endeavour: tentare, tentativo, sforzarsi.
exposing: esponendo.

expressions: espressioni.
genius: genio.
hence: da qui, quindi.
misfortune: sfortuna, traversia, disgrazia.
nonsensical: assurdo, privo di senso.
prejudice: pregiudizio, preconcetto, prevenzione.
signify: significare, significate, significo, significhi, significa, significhiamo, significano.
spur: sperone, sprone, spronare.

stumbling: inciampare.
stupidity: stupidità.
uncomfortable: scomodo, disagiato.
uncommonly: insolitamente.
undeceive: disinganno, disingannare, disinganniamo, disinganna, disingannano, disingannate, disinganni.
unfortunate: sfortunato, sventurato.
unhappy: infelice, triste.
vain: vanitoso, vano.
wit: arguzia.

"You are quite right. To have his errors made public might **ruin** him for ever. He is now, perhaps, sorry for what he has done, and anxious to re-establish a character. We must not make him desperate."

The **tumult** of Elizabeth's mind was **allayed** by this conversation. She had got rid of two of the secrets which had **weighed** on her for a fortnight, and was certain of a willing **listener** in Jane, whenever she might wish to talk again of either. But there was still something lurking behind, of which **prudence** forbade the **disclosure**. She **dared** not relate the other half of Mr. Darcy's letter, nor explain to her sister how sincerely she had been **valued** by her friend. Here was knowledge in which no one could **partake**; and she was sensible that nothing less than a perfect understanding between the parties could justify her in throwing off this last **encumbrance** of **mystery**. "And then," said she, "if that very **improbable** event should ever take place, I shall merely be able to tell what Bingley may tell in a much more **agreeable** manner himself. The liberty of communication **cannot** be mine till it has lost all its value!"

She was now, on being settled at home, at leisure to observe the real state of her sister's spirits. Jane was not happy. She still **cherished** a very tender affection for Bingley. Having never even **fancied** herself in love before, her regard had all the warmth of first **attachment**, and, from her age and **disposition**, greater **steadiness** than most first attachments often **boast**; and so fervently did she value his **remembrance**, and prefer him to every other man, that all her good sense, and all her attention to the feelings of her friends, were **requisite** to check the **indulgence** of those regrets which must have been **injurious** to her own health and their **tranquillity**.

"Well, Lizzy," said Mrs. **Bennet** one day, "what is your opinion *now* of this **sad** business of Jane's? For my part, I am determined never to speak of it again to anybody. I told my sister Phillips so the other day. But I cannot find out that Jane saw anything of him in London. Well, he is a very **undeserving** young man--and I do not suppose there's the least chance in the world of her ever getting him now. There is no talk of his coming to Netherfield again in the summer; and I have **inquired** of everybody, too, who is likely to know."

Italian

agreeable: gradevole, piacevole, amabile.
allayed: alleviato, acquietato.
attachment: accessorio, allegato, attaccamento.
bennet: cariofillata, erba benedetta.
boast: vanteria, vantarsi.
cannot: non potere.
cherished: adorato.
dared: osato.
disclosure: rivelazione, scoperta.
disposition: disposizione,

predisposizione, ingegno, talento.
encumbrance: ingombro.
fancied: fantastico.
improbable: improbabile.
indulgence: indulgenza.
injurious: nocivo, dannoso.
inquired: domandato.
listener: ascoltatore.
mystery: mistero.
partake: partecipo, partecipa, partecipano, partecipate, partecipi, partecipiamo, partecipare.

prudence: prudenza.
remembrance: rimembranza, ricordo, memoria.
requisite: requisito.
ruin: rovinare, rovina.
sad: triste, afflitto.
steadiness: costanza, fermezza.
tranquillity: tranquillità.
tumult: tumulto.
undeserving: immeritevole.
valued: valutato, stimato.
weighed: pesato.

"I do not believe he **will** ever live at Netherfield any more."

"Oh well! it is just as he **chooses**. Nobody wants him to come. Though I shall always say he used my daughter extremely ill; and if I was her, I would not have put up with it. Well, my **comfort** is, I am sure Jane will **die** of a broken heart; and then he will be sorry for what he has done."

But as Elizabeth could not receive comfort from any such **expectation**, she made no answer.

"Well, Lizzy," continued her mother, soon **afterwards**, "and so the Collinses live very **comfortable**, do they? Well, well, I only hope it will last. And what sort of table do they keep? Charlotte is an excellent **manager**, I **dare** say. If she is half as **sharp** as her mother, she is **saving** enough. There is nothing **extravagant** in *their* **housekeeping**, I dare say."

"No, nothing at all."

"A great deal of good management, **depend** upon it. Yes, yes. *They* will take care not to **outrun** their income. *They* will never be **distressed** for money. Well, much good may it do them! And so, I suppose, they often talk of having Longbourn when your father is dead. They look upon it as quite their own, I dare say, **whenever** that happens."

"It was a subject which they could not **mention** before me."

"No; it would have been strange if they had; but I make no **doubt** they often talk of it between themselves. Well, if they can be easy with an **estate** that is not **lawfully** their own, so much the better. I should be **ashamed** of having one that was only entailed on me."

Italian

afterwards: dopo, dietro, in seguito, successivamente.
ashamed: vergognoso.
chooses: sceglie, elegge.
comfort: consolare, comodità, confortare, comfort, benessere.
comfortable: comodo, confortevole.
dare: osare, oso, osiamo, osi, osate, osano, osa, sfida.
depend: dipendere, dipendete, dipendiamo, dipendo, dipendono, dipendi.

die: morire, muoio, muori, muoiono, morite, moriamo, dado, cubo, matrice, stampo.
distressed: afflitto.
doubt: dubitare, dubbio.
estate: fattoria, patrimonio, tenuta.
expectation: attesa, aspettativa.
extravagant: stravagante.
housekeeping: economia domestica, operazioni di gestione interna.
ill: malato, ammalato.
lawfully: legalmente, legittimamente.

manager: direttore, amministratore, manager, gestore, gerente, dirigente, amministratore delegato.
mention: menzionare, menzione, cenno.
outrun: oltrepassare.
saving: salvando, risparmio, risparmiando.
sharp: affilato, aguzzo, acuto, tagliente, appuntito, piccante, giusto, giustamente, aspro, diesis, nitido.
whenever: ogni volta che, quando.

CHAPTER 41

The first week of their return was soon gone. The second began. It was the last of the **regiment's** stay in Meryton, and all the young **ladies** in the **neighbourhood** were drooping **apace**. The **dejection** was almost **universal**. The **elder** Miss **Bennets alone** were still able to eat, drink, and sleep, and **pursue** the usual course of their employments. Very frequently were they **reproached** for this **insensibility** by Kitty and Lydia, whose own **misery** was **extreme**, and who could not **comprehend** such hard-heartedness in any of the family.

"Good Heaven! what is to become of us? What are we to do?" would they often **exclaiming** the **bitterness** of **woe**. "How can you be **smiling** so, Lizzy?"

Their **affectionate** mother **shared** all their **grief**; she **remembered** what she had herself **endured** on a similar **occasion**, five-and-twenty years ago.

"I am sure," said she, "I cried for two days together when Colonel Miller's regiment went away. I thought I should have broken my heart."

"I am sure I shall break *mine*," said Lydia.

"If one could but go to Brighton!" **observed** Mrs. Bennet.

"Oh, yes!--if one could but go to Brighton! But **papa** is so disagreeable."

"A little sea-bathing would set me up forever."

Italian

affectionate: affettuoso.
alone: solo, da solo, solamente.
apace: di buon passo.
bennet: cariofillata, erba benedetta.
bitterness: amarezza.
comprehend: comprendere, comprendo, comprendono, comprendiamo, comprendi, comprendete.
dejection: deiezione, abbattimento, scoraggiamento, depressione.
elder: maggiore, sambuco.

endured: sopportato, durato.
exclaiming: esclamando.
extreme: estremo.
grief: dolore, pena.
insensibility: insensibilità, indifferenza.
ladies: signore.
misery: miseria.
neighbourhood: circondario, distretto, vicinato, quartiere.
observed: osservato.
occasion: occasione.

papa: papà.
pursue: perseguire, persegui, perseguite, perseguo, perseguiamo, perseguono, perseguitare, inseguire.
regiment: reggimento.
remembered: ricordato.
reproached: rimproverato.
shared: dividere, condiviso, diviso.
smiling: sorridere.
universal: universale.
woe: dolore, calamità, afflizione.

"And my aunt Phillips is sure it would do *me* a great deal of good," added Kitty.

Such were the kind of lamentations **resounding perpetually** through Longbourn House. Elizabeth tried to be **diverted** by them; but all sense of pleasure was lost in shame. She felt **anew** the justice of Mr. Darcy's objections; and never had she been so much **disposed** to pardon his interference in the views of his friend.

But the gloom of Lydia's prospect was shortly cleared away; for she received an invitation from Mrs. Forster, the wife of the colonel of the regiment, to accompany her to Brighton. This invaluable friend was a very young woman, and very lately married. A **resemblance** in good humour and good spirits had recommended her and Lydia to each other, and out of their *three* months' **acquaintance** they had been intimate *two*.

The **rapture** of Lydia on this occasion, her **adoration** of Mrs. Forster, the delight of Mrs. **Bennet**, and the **mortification** of Kitty, are scarcely to be described. Wholly **inattentive** to her sister's feelings, Lydia flew about the house in **restless ecstasy**, calling for everyone's **congratulations**, and laughing and talking with more violence than ever; whilst the **luckless** Kitty continued in the **parlour** repined at her **fate** in terms as unreasonable as her **accent** was **peevish**.

"I **cannot** see why Mrs. Forster should not ask *me* as well as Lydia," said she, "Though I am *not* her particular friend. I have just as much right to be asked as she has, and more too, for I am two years older."

In **vain** did Elizabeth attempt to make her reasonable, and Jane to make her resigned. As for Elizabeth herself, this invitation was so far from **exciting** in her the same feelings as in her mother and Lydia, that she considered it as the death **warrant** of all possibility of common sense for the latter; and **detestable** as such a step must make her were it known, she could not help **secretly advising** her father not to let her go. She represented to him all the improprieties of Lydia's general behaviour, the little advantage she could **derive** from the friendship of such a woman as Mrs. Forster, and the probability of her being yet more

Italian

accent: accento, accentare, accentano, accentate, accenti, accentiamo, accenta.
acquaintance: conoscenza, conoscente.
adoration: adorazione, venerazione.
advising: consigliando.
anew: di nuovo, ancora.
bennet: cariofillata, erba benedetta.
cannot: non potere.
congratulations: congratulazioni.
derive: derivare, derivo, deriviamo, derivi, derivano, derivate, deriva,

discendere, trarre.
detestable: detestabile.
disposed: disposto.
diverted: stornato, sviato, deviato.
ecstasy: estasi.
exciting: eccitando, eccitante, emozionante.
fate: destino, fato, sorte.
inattentive: disattento.
luckless: sfortunato.
mortification: mortificazione.
parlour: salotto.

peevish: permaloso, stizzoso.
perpetually: perennemente, perpetuamente.
rapture: rapimento, estasi.
resemblance: somiglianza, rassomiglianza.
resounding: risuonando, echeggiando, riecheggiando, risonante, clamoroso.
restless: inquieto, irrequieto.
secretly: segretamente.
vain: vanitoso, vano.
warrant: garanzia, mandato.

imprudent with such a companion at Brighton, where the temptations must be greater than at home. He heard her **attentively**, and then said:

"Lydia will never be easy until she has **exposed** herself in some public place or other, and we can never expect her to do it with so little expense or inconvenience to her family as under the present circumstances."

"If you were aware," said Elizabeth, "of the very great disadvantage to us all which must arise from the public notice of Lydia's **unguarded** and imprudent manner--nay, which has already **arisen** from it, I am sure you would judge differently in the affair."

"Already arisen?" repeated Mr. **Bennet**. "What, has she frightened away some of your lovers? Poor little Lizzy! But do not be cast down. Such **squeamish** youths as **cannot** bear to be connected with a little **absurdity** are not worth a regret. Come, let me see the list of **pitiful** fellows who have been kept **aloof** by Lydia's folly."

"Indeed you are mistaken. I have no such injuries to resent. It is not of particular, but of general evils, which I am now **complaining**. Our importance, our respectability in the world must be affected by the wild **volatility**, the assurance and **disdain** of all restraint which mark Lydia's character. Excuse me, for I must speak plainly. If you, my dear father, will not take the trouble of **checking** her **exuberant** spirits, and of teaching her that her present pursuits are not to be the business of her life, she will soon be beyond the reach of amendment. Her character will be fixed, and she will, at sixteen, be the most determined **flirt** that ever made herself or her family ridiculous; a flirt, too, in the worst and meanest degree of **flirtation**; without any **attraction** beyond youth and a **tolerable** person; and, from the ignorance and **emptiness** of her mind, wholly unable to **ward** off any portion of that universal contempt which her **rage** for admiration will **excite**. In this danger Kitty also is **comprehended**. She will follow wherever Lydia leads. Vain, ignorant, idle, and absolutely **uncontrolled**! Oh! my dear father, can you suppose it possible that they will not be **censured** and despised wherever they are known, and that their sisters will not be often involved in the disgrace?"

Italian

absurdity: assurdità.
aloof: appartato, in disparte, alla larga, a distanza, distante.
arisen: nato, sorto.
attentively: attentamente.
attraction: attrazione, forza attrattiva, attrattiva.
bennet: cariofillata, erba benedetta.
cannot: non potere.
censured: censurato.
checking: verifica, controllo.
complaining: lamentandosi, reclamando.
comprehended: compreso.
despised: disprezzato.
disdain: sdegno, sdegnare.
emptiness: vuoto.
excite: eccitare, ecciti, eccitiamo, eccitano, eccita, eccito, eccitate, spronare, incitare.
exposed: esposto.
exuberant: esuberante.
flirt: flirtare, civettare.
flirtation: flirt.
imprudent: imprudente.
pitiful: pietoso.
rage: furore, ira, furia, collera.
squeamish: schifiltoso, schizzinoso.
tolerable: tollerabile.
uncontrolled: sfrenato.
unguarded: incustodito.
volatility: volatilità.
ward: corsia, tutela, quartiere, proteggere, distretto, custodire, reparto, custodia.

Mr. **Bennet** saw that her whole heart was in the subject, and **affectionately** taking her hand said in reply:

"Do not make yourself uneasy, my love. Wherever you and Jane are known you must be respected and valued; and you will not appear to less advantage for having a **couple** of--or I may say, three--very silly sisters. We shall have no peace at Longbourn if Lydia does not go to Brighton. Let her go, then. Colonel Forster is a sensible man, and will keep her out of any real **mischief**; and she is luckily too poor to be an object of **prey** to anybody. At Brighton she will be of less importance even as a common **flirt** than she has been here. The officers will find women better worth their notice. Let us hope, therefore, that her being there may teach her her own **insignificance**. At any rate, she **cannot** grow many **degrees** worse, without authorising us to **lock** her up for the rest of her life."

With this answer Elizabeth was forced to be **content**; but her own opinion continued the same, and she left him disappointed and sorry. It was not in her nature, however, to increase her vexations by dwelling on them. She was confident of having performed her duty, and to **fret** over **unavoidable** evils, or **augment** them by anxiety, was no part of her disposition.

Had Lydia and her mother known the **substance** of her conference with her father, their **indignation** would hardly have found expression in their united **volubility**. In Lydia's imagination, a visit to Brighton comprised every possibility of **earthly** happiness. She saw, with the **creative** eye of fancy, the **streets** of that **gay** bathing-place covered with officers. She saw herself the object of attention, to **tens** and to scores of them at present unknown. She saw all the glories of the camp--its tents **stretched** forth in beauteous **uniformity** of lines, crowded with the young and the gay, and **dazzling** with scarlet; and, to complete the view, she saw herself seated beneath a tent, **tenderly** flirting with at least six officers at once.

Had she known her sister sought to tear her from such prospects and such realities as these, what would have been her sensations? They could have been understood only by her mother, who might have felt nearly the same. Lydia's

Italian

affectionately: affettuosamente.
augment: ingrandire, ingrandite, ingrandiscono, ingrandisco, ingrandisci, ingrandiamo, aumentare, aumenta, aumentano, aumentate, aumenti.
bennet: cariofillata, erba benedetta.
cannot: non potere.
content: contenuto, contento, soddisfatto, soddisfare.
couple: coppia, accoppiare, paio, consorti, coniugi, agganciare.

creative: creativo.
dazzling: abbagliare, abbagliante, accecante.
degrees: gradi.
earthly: terrestre, terreno, mondano.
flirt: flirtare, civettare.
fret: agitazione, consumare, greca.
gay: allegro, gaio.
indignation: indignazione, sdegno.
insignificance: banalità, futilità.
lock: serratura, serrare a chiave, chiusa, bloccaggio, bloccare, blocco,

fermo, ciocca.
mischief: birichinata.
prey: preda.
streets: strade.
stretched: teso, allungato.
substance: sostanza, materia.
tenderly: teneramente.
tens: dieci.
tent: tenda.
unavoidable: inevitabile.
uniformity: uniformità.
volubility: loquacità.

going to Brighton was all that **consoled** her for her **melancholy** conviction of her husband's never **intending** to go there himself.

But they were entirely **ignorant** of what had passed; and their raptures continued, with little **intermission**, to the very day of Lydia's leaving home.

Elizabeth was now to see Mr. Wickham for the last time. Having been frequently in company with him since her return, **agitation** was pretty well over; the agitations of formal **partiality** entirely so. She had even learnt to **detect**, in the very **gentleness** which had first delighted her, an **affectation** and a **sameness** to **disgust** and weary. In his present behaviour to herself, moreover, she had a fresh source of **displeasure**, for the **inclination** he soon **testified** of renewing those intentions which had marked the early part of their acquaintance could only **serve**, after what had since passed, to **provoke** her. She lost all concern for him in finding herself thus selected as the object of such idle and **frivolous gallantry**; and while she steadily **repressed** it, could not but feel the **reproof** contained in his believing, that however long, and for whatever cause, his attentions had been withdrawn, her **vanity** would be **gratified**, and her preference secured at any time by their renewal.

On the very last day of the regiment's remaining at Meryton, he **dined**, with other of the officers, at Longbourn; and so little was Elizabeth **disposed** to part from him in good humour, that on his making some inquiry as to the manner in which her time had passed at Hunsford, she mentioned Colonel Fitzwilliam's and Mr. Darcy's having both spent three weeks at Rosings, and asked him, if he was **acquainted** with the former.

He looked surprised, **displeased, alarmed**; but with a moment's **recollection** and a returning smile, replied, that he had formerly seen him often; and, after observing that he was a very gentlemanlike man, asked her how she had liked him. Her answer was **warmly** in his favour. With an air of indifference he soon afterwards added:

"How long did you say he was at Rosings?"

"Nearly three weeks."

Italian

acquainted: informato.
affectation: affettazione, posa.
agitation: agitazione.
alarmed: allarmato.
consoled: consolato.
detect: scoprire, scopri, scoprono, scopro, scoprite, scopriamo.
dined: pranzato, cenato.
disgust: ripugnanza, avversione, disgustare, disgusto, nauseare.
displeased: scontentato, scontento.
displeasure: scontento, dispiacere.

disposed: disposto.
frivolous: vanitoso, frivolo.
gallantry: galanteria, valore, prodezza.
gentleness: delicatezza.
gratified: gratificato.
ignorant: ignorante.
inclination: inclinazione, pendenza.
intending: intendendo.
intermission: interruzione, intervallo.
melancholy: malinconia, malinconico.
partiality: parzialità, predilezione.
provoke: spronare, provocare, incitare,

provochi, sproniamo, sprono, sproni, spronate, spronano, sprona, provoco.
recollection: memoria, ricordo.
renewing: rinnovando.
repressed: represso.
reproof: biasimo.
sameness: uniformità.
serve: servire, serviamo, servi, servono, servite, servo.
testified: testimoniato.
vanity: vanità.
warmly: caldamente, calorosamente.

"And you saw him frequently?"

"Yes, almost every day."

"His **manners** are very different from his cousin's."

"Yes, very different. But I think Mr. Darcy **improves** upon **acquaintance**."

"Indeed!" cried Mr. Wickham with a look which did not escape her. "And **pray**, may I ask?--" But **checking** himself, he added, in a gayer tone, "Is it in address that he improves? Has he **deigned** to add aught of **civility** to his **ordinary** style?--for I dare not hope," he continued in a lower and more serious tone, "that he is improved in **essentials**."

"Oh, no!" said Elizabeth. "In essentials, I believe, he is very much what he ever was."

While she spoke, Wickham looked as if **scarcely** knowing whether to **rejoice** over her words, or to **distrust** their meaning. There was a something in her **countenance** which made him listen with an **apprehensive** and anxious attention, while she added:

"When I said that he improved on acquaintance, I did not mean that his mind or his manners were in a state of improvement, but that, from knowing him better, his **disposition** was better understood."

Wickham's **alarm** now appeared in a **heightened complexion** and **agitated** look; for a few minuted he was silent, till, **shaking** off his **embarrassment**, he turned to her again, and said in the gentlest of **accents**:

"You, who so well know my feeling towards Mr. Darcy, will readily **comprehend** how **sincerely** I must rejoice that he is wise enough to assume even the *appearance* of what is right. His pride, in that direction, may be of service, if not to himself, to many others, for it must only **deter** him from such **foul misconduct** as I have suffered by. I only fear that the sort of cautiousness to which you, I imagine, have been **alluding**, is merely **adopted** on his visits to his aunt, of whose good opinion and judgement he stands much in **awe**. His fear of her has always **operated**, I know, when they were together; and a good deal is to

Italian

accents: accenta.	comprendo, comprendono,	**heightened**: innalzato.
acquaintance: conoscenza, conoscente.	comprendiamo, comprendi,	**improves**: migliora, perfeziona.
adopted: adottato, adottivo.	comprendete.	**manners**: educazione.
agitated: agitato.	**countenance**: approvare, viso.	**misconduct**: cattiva condotta.
alarm: allarme, sveglia, allarmare.	**deigned**: degnato.	**operated**: operato, azionato.
alluding: alludendo.	**deter**: impaurire, spaventare.	**ordinary**: ordinario, normale, comune.
apprehensive: apprensivo.	**disposition**: disposizione,	**pray**: pregare, pregate, prego, preghi,
awe: soggezione, timore.	predisposizione, ingegno, talento.	prega, preghiamo, pregano.
checking: verifica, controllo.	**distrust**: diffidenza.	**rejoice**: allietare, rallegrare.
civility: civiltà, cortesia.	**embarrassment**: imbarazzo.	**scarcely**: appena, a stento.
complexion: carnagione.	**essentials**: essenziale.	**shaking**: scuotendo.
comprehend: comprendere,	**foul**: fallo.	**sincerely**: sinceramente, francamente.

be **imputed** to his wish of **forwarding** the match with Miss de Bourgh, which I am certain he has very much at heart."

Elizabeth could not **repress** a smile at this, but she answered only by a slight **inclination** of the head. She saw that he wanted to **engage** her on the old subject of his grievances, and she was in no **humour** to **indulge** him. The rest of the evening passed with the *appearance*, on his side, of usual **cheerfulness**, but with no further attempt to distinguish Elizabeth; and they parted at last with mutual **civility**, and possibly a mutual desire of never meeting again.

When the party **broke** up, Lydia returned with Mrs. Forster to Meryton, from **whence** they were to set out early the next morning. The **separation** between her and her family was rather **noisy** than **pathetic**. Kitty was the only one who **shed** tears; but she did **weep** from **vexation** and **envy**. Mrs. **Bennet** was **diffuse** in her good wishes for the **felicity** of her daughter, and **impressive** in her injunctions that she should not miss the opportunity of enjoying herself as much as possible--advice which there was every reason to believe would be well attended to; and in the **clamorous happiness** of Lydia herself in **bidding farewell**, the more gentle adieus of her sisters were uttered without being heard.

Italian

bennet: cariofillata, erba benedetta.
bidding: offerta, licitazione, comando.
broke: al verde, rovinato, scarti di fabbricazione.
cheerfulness: contentezza, allegria.
civility: civiltà, cortesia.
clamorous: clamoroso.
diffuse: diffuso, diffondere.
engage: innestare, innestiamo, innesta, innestano, innestate, innesti, ingaggiare, ingranare, impegnare, assumere, innesto.

envy: invidia, invidiare, invidio, invidiate, invidiano, invidi, invidiamo.
farewell: addio, congedo.
felicity: felicità.
forwarding: invio, inoltro, spedizione.
happiness: felicità.
humour: umore, umorismo.
impressive: impressionante.
imputed: attribuito, imputato.
inclination: inclinazione, pendenza.
indulge: indulgere.

noisy: rumoroso, chiassoso.
pathetic: patetico.
repress: reprimere.
separation: separazione, distacco.
shed: baracca, versare, versate, verso, versiamo, versato, versano, versa, versi, capannone, tettoia.
vexation: irritazione.
weep: piangere, piangete, piangi, piangiamo, piangono, piango, lacrimare.
whence: da dove, donde.

CHAPTER 42

Had Elizabeth's opinion been all drawn from her own family, she could not have formed a very **pleasing** opinion of **conjugal felicity** or domestic comfort. Her father, **captivated** by youth and beauty, and that appearance of good humour which youth and beauty generally give, had married a woman whose weak understanding and **illiberal** mind had very early in their marriage put and end to all real affection for her. Respect, **esteem**, and confidence had **vanished** for ever; and all his views of domestic happiness were **overthrown**. But Mr. **Bennet** was not of a **disposition** to seek comfort for the disappointment which his own **imprudence** had brought on, in any of those pleasures which too often **console** the **unfortunate** for their **folly** of their **vice**. He was **fond** of the country and of books; and from these tastes had **arisen** his principal enjoyments. To his wife he was very little otherwise **indebted**, than as her **ignorance** and folly had contributed to his **amusement**. This is not the sort of happiness which a man would in general wish to owe to his wife; but where other powers of entertainment are wanting, the true **philosopher** will **derive** benefit from such as are given.

Elizabeth, however, had never been blind to the **impropriety** of her father's behaviour as a husband. She had always seen it with pain; but **respecting** his abilities, and grateful for his **affectionate** treatment of herself, she endeavoured to forget what she could not **overlook**, and to **banish** from her thoughts that

Italian

affectionate: affettuoso.
amusement: divertimento, spasso, svago.
arisen: nato, sorto.
banish: bandire, bandisci, bandisco, bandiscono, bandite, bandiamo, esiliare.
bennet: cariofillata, erba benedetta.
captivated: affascinato.
conjugal: coniugale.
console: consolare, consolle, console.
derive: derivare, derivo, deriviamo,

derivi, derivano, derivate, deriva, discendere, trarre.
disposition: disposizione, predisposizione, ingegno, talento.
esteem: stima, rispetto, stimare, considerazione, considerare, rispettare, riguardo.
felicity: felicità.
folly: follia.
fond: tenero, affettuoso, affezionato.
ignorance: ignoranza.
illiberal: illiberale.

impropriety: scorrettezza, improprietà.
imprudence: imprudenza.
indebted: obbligato, indebitato.
overlook: trascurare.
overthrown: rovesciato.
philosopher: filosofo.
pleasing: piacevole.
respecting: rispettare.
unfortunate: sfortunato, sventurato.
vanished: sparito.
vice: morsa, vizio, virtù.

continual breach of **conjugal** obligation and **decorum** which, in **exposing** his wife to the **contempt** of her own children, was so highly **reprehensible**. But she had never felt so strongly as now the disadvantages which must attend the children of so **unsuitable** a marriage, nor ever been so fully aware of the evils arising from so ill-judged a direction of talents; talents, which, **rightly** used, might at least have preserved the **respectability** of his daughters, even if **incapable** of **enlarging** the mind of his wife.

When Elizabeth had **rejoiced** over Wickham's departure she found little other cause for satisfaction in the loss of the **regiment**. Their parties **abroad** were less varied than before, and at home she had a mother and sister whose constant repinings at the **dullness** of everything around them threw a real **gloom** over their domestic circle; and, though Kitty might in time **regain** her natural degree of sense, since the disturbers of her **brain** were removed, her other sister, from whose **disposition** greater evil might be **apprehended**, was likely to be **hardened** in all her **folly** and assurance by a situation of such double danger as a watering-place and a **camp**. Upon the whole, therefore, she found, what has been sometimes been found before, that an event to which she had been looking with **impatient** desire did not, in taking place, bring all the satisfaction she had promised herself. It was consequently necessary to name some other period for the **commencement** of actual felicity--to have some other point on which her wishes and hopes might be fixed, and by again enjoying the pleasure of **anticipation**, **console** herself for the present, and prepare for another disappointment. Her tour to the Lakes was now the object of her happiest thoughts; it was her best **consolation** for all the uncomfortable hours which the discontentedness of her mother and Kitty made inevitable; and could she have included Jane in the scheme, every part of it would have been perfect.

"But it is fortunate," thought she, "that I have something to wish for. Were the whole arrangement complete, my disappointment would be certain. But here, by **carrying** with me one **ceaseless** source of regret in my sister's absence, I may reasonably hope to have all my expectations of pleasure realised. A scheme of which every part promises delight can never be successful; and general

Italian

abroad: all'estero, fuori.
anticipation: anticipazione, previsione.
apprehended: capito, compreso, afferrato, temuto.
brain: cervello.
camp: campo, campeggiare, campeggio, accampamento, accamparsi.
carrying: portando, trasportando.
ceaseless: incessante.
commencement: inizio, principio.

conjugal: coniugale.
consolation: consolazione.
console: consolare, consolle, console.
contempt: sprezzo, disprezzo.
continual: continuo, costante.
decorum: decoro.
disposition: disposizione, predisposizione, ingegno, talento.
dullness: ottusità.
enlarging: ingrandendo, ampliando.
exposing: esponendo.
folly: follia.

gloom: malinconia, tristezza.
hardened: indurito, temprato.
impatient: impaziente.
incapable: incapace.
regain: ricuperare, riprendere.
regiment: reggimento.
rejoiced: allietato, gioito, rallegrato.
reprehensible: riprovevole, biasimevole.
respectability: rispettabilità.
rightly: giustamente.
unsuitable: disadatto.

disappointment is only warded off by the **defence** of some little **peculiar** vexation."

When Lydia went away she promised to write very often and very **minutely** to her mother and Kitty; but her letters were always long expected, and always very short. Those to her mother contained little else than that they were just returned from the library, where such and such officers had attended them, and where she had seen such beautiful ornaments as made her quite wild; that she had a new **gown**, or a new **parasol**, which she would have described more fully, but was **obliged** to leave off in a violent **hurry**, as Mrs. Forster called her, and they were going off to the camp; and from her **correspondence** with her sister, there was still less to be learnt--for her letters to Kitty, though rather longer, were much too full of lines under the words to be made public.

After the first **fortnight** or three weeks of her absence, health, good humour, and **cheerfulness** began to **reappear** at Longbourn. Everything wore a happier aspect. The families who had been in town for the winter came back again, and summer finery and summer engagements arose. Mrs. **Bennet** was restored to her usual querulous **serenity**; and, by the middle of June, Kitty was so much recovered as to be able to enter Meryton without tears; an event of such happy promise as to make Elizabeth hope that by the following Christmas she might be so **tolerably** reasonable as not to mention an officer above once a day, unless, by some **cruel** and **malicious** arrangement at the War Office, another **regiment** should be quartered in Meryton.

The time fixed for the beginning of their **northern** tour was now fast **approaching**, and a fortnight only was wanting of it, when a letter arrived from Mrs. Gardiner, which at once **delayed** its **commencement** and **curtailed** its extent. Mr. Gardiner would be **prevented** by business from **setting** out till a fortnight later in July, and must be in London again within a month, and as that left too short a period for them to go so far, and see so much as they had proposed, or at least to see it with the leisure and comfort they had built on, they were obliged to give up the Lakes, and **substitute** a more **contracted** tour, and, **according** to the present plan, were to go no **farther northwards** than

Italian

according: secondo.
approaching: avvicinamento.
bennet: cariofillata, erba benedetta.
cheerfulness: contentezza, allegria.
commencement: inizio, principio.
contracted: contratto.
correspondence: corrispondenza, carteggio.
cruel: crudele.
curtailed: abbreviato.
defence: difesa, retroguardia.
delayed: ritardato.

disappointment: delusione, disappunto.
farther: più lontano.
fortnight: due settimane.
gown: abito, vestito, toga.
hurry: affrettarsi, fretta.
malicious: maligno, doloso, malizioso.
minutely: minutamente.
northern: settentrionale, nordico.
northwards: verso nord.
obliged: obbligato.
parasol: parasole, ombrellino.

peculiar: strano, peculiare, particolare.
prevented: impedito, prevenuto.
reappear: riapparire, riapparite, riappaio, riappaiono, riappari, riappariamo.
regiment: reggimento.
serenity: serenità.
setting: regolazione.
substitute: sostituto, sostituire, supplente, rimpiazzare, succedaneo, surrogato.
tolerably: tollerabilmente.

Derbyshire. In that county there was enough to be seen to **occupy** the chief of their three weeks; and to Mrs. Gardiner it had a **peculiarly** strong attraction. The town where she had formerly passed some years of her life, and where they were now to spend a few days, was **probably** as great an object of her **curiosity** as all the **celebrated** beauties of Matlock, Chatsworth, Dovedale, or the Peak.

Elizabeth was **excessively** disappointed; she had set her heart on seeing the Lakes, and still thought there might have been time enough. But it was her business to be satisfied--and certainly her **temper** to be happy; and all was soon right again.

With the mention of Derbyshire there were many ideas connected. It was impossible for her to see the word without thinking of Pemberley and its **owner**. "But surely," said she, "I may enter his county without **impunity**, and rob it of a few **petrified spars** without his **perceiving** me."

The period of expectation was now **doubled**. Four weeks were to pass away before her uncle and aunt's arrival. But they did pass away, and Mr. and Mrs. Gardiner, with their four children, did at length appear at Longbourn. The children, two girls of six and eight years old, and two younger boys, were to be left under the particular care of their cousin Jane, who was the general favourite, and whose steady sense and **sweetness** of temper exactly **adapted** her for attending to them in every way--teaching them, **playing** with them, and **loving** them.

The Gardiners stayed only one night at Longbourn, and set off the next morning with Elizabeth in **pursuit** of **novelty** and **amusement**. One **enjoyment** was certain--that of suitableness of companions; a suitableness which **comprehended** health and temper to bear inconveniences--cheerfulness to **enhance** every pleasure--and affection and intelligence, which might supply it among themselves if there were disappointments abroad.

It is not the object of this work to give a description of Derbyshire, nor of any of the remarkable places through which their **route thither** lay; Oxford, Blenheim, Warwick, Kenilworth, Birmingham, **etc**. are sufficiently known. A small part of Derbyshire is all the present concern. To the little town of Lambton,

Italian

adapted: adattato.
amusement: divertimento, spasso, svago.
celebrated: celebrato, festeggiato, famoso.
comprehended: compreso.
curiosity: curiosità.
doubled: raddoppiato.
enhance: accrescere, aumentare.
enjoyment: godimento.
etc: ecc.
excessively: eccessivamente.

impunity: impunità.
loving: affettuoso.
novelty: novità.
occupy: occupare, occupano, occupo, occupiamo, occupate, occupa, occupi.
owner: proprietario, titolare, possessore.
peculiarly: particolarmente.
perceiving: percependo, scorgendo, intravedendo.
petrified: terrorizzato, impietrito, pietrificato.

playing: giocando, suonando.
pursuit: inseguimento, ricerca.
rob: derubare, deruba, derubano, derubate, derubi, derubiamo, derubo, svaligiare, rubare.
route: strada, cammino, itinerario, via, pista, percorso, corsia, tracciato, rotta.
spars: litiga.
sweetness: dolcezza.
temper: umore, temperamento, tempra.
thither: là.

the scene of Mrs. Gardiner's former residence, and where she had **lately** learned some **acquaintance** still remained, they **bent** their steps, after having seen all the principal wonders of the country; and within five miles of Lambton, Elizabeth found from her aunt that Pemberley was **situated**. It was not in their direct road, nor more than a mile or two out of it. In talking over their route the evening before, Mrs. Gardiner expressed an **inclination** to see the place again. Mr. Gardiner declared his **willingness**, and Elizabeth was applied to for her approbation.

"My love, should not you like to see a place of which you have heard so much?" said her aunt; "a place, too, with which so many of your **acquaintances** are connected. Wickham passed all his youth there, you know."

Elizabeth was **distressed**. She felt that she had no business at Pemberley, and was **obliged** to assume a **disinclination** for seeing it. She must own that she was tired of seeing great houses; after going over so many, she really had no pleasure in fine carpets or **satin curtains**.

Mrs. Gardiner **abused** her **stupidity**. "If it were merely a fine house **richly** furnished," said she, "I should not care about it myself; but the grounds are **delightful**. They have some of the finest **woods** in the country."

Elizabeth said no more--but her mind could not **acquiesce**. The possibility of meeting Mr. Darcy, while **viewing** the place, **instantly** occurred. It would be **dreadful**! She **blushed** at the very idea, and thought it would be better to speak **openly** to her aunt than to run such a risk. But against this there were **objections**; and she finally resolved that it could be the last **resource**, if her private inquiries to the absence of the family were unfavourably answered.

Accordingly, when she retired at night, she asked the **chambermaid** whether Pemberley were not a very fine place? what was the name of its **proprietor**? and, with no little alarm, whether the family were down for the summer? A most welcome negative followed the last question--and her alarms now being removed, she was at leisure to feel a great deal of **curiosity** to see the house herself; and when the subject was **revived** the next morning, and she was again applied to, could readily answer, and with a proper air of **indifference**, that she

Italian

abused: abusato.	**delightful**: delizioso, piacevole.	**proprietor**: proprietario.
acquaintance: conoscenza, conoscente.	**disinclination**: avversione.	**resource**: risorsa.
acquaintances: conoscenze.	**distressed**: afflitto.	**revived**: rianimato.
acquiesce: acconsentire, acconsentite,	**dreadful**: terribile.	**richly**: riccamente.
acconsenti, acconsentiamo,	**inclination**: inclinazione, pendenza.	**satin**: raso, satin.
acconsento, acconsentono, essere	**indifference**: indifferenza.	**situated**: situato.
acquiescente.	**instantly**: direttamente,	**stupidity**: stupidità.
bent: curvo, piegato.	istantaneamente, immediatamente.	**viewing**: veduta, osservare,
blushed: arrossito.	**lately**: ultimamente, recentemente.	osservazione.
chambermaid: cameriera.	**objections**: obiezioni.	**willingness**: volontà.
curiosity: curiosità.	**obliged**: obbligato.	**woods**: bosco.
curtains: tendaggio, tenda.	**openly**: apertamente.	

had not really any **dislike** to the **scheme**. To Pemberley, therefore, they were to go.

Italian

dislike: avversione, ripugnanza, antipatia.
scheme: progetto, schema, piano.

CHAPTER 43

Elizabeth, as they drove along, watched for the first appearance of Pemberley Woods with some **perturbation**; and when at length they turned in at the **lodge**, her spirits were in a high flutter.

The park was very large, and contained great variety of ground. They entered it in one of its **lowest** points, and drove for some time through a beautiful **wood stretching** over a wide extent.

Elizabeth's mind was too full for conversation, but she saw and **admired** every remarkable spot and point of view. They gradually **ascended** for half-a-mile, and then found themselves at the **top** of a considerable **eminence**, where the wood **ceased**, and the eye was **instantly** caught by Pemberley House, **situated** on the opposite side of a **valley**, into which the road with some **abruptness wound**. It was a large, **handsome stone building,** standing well on rising ground, and **backed** by a **ridge** of high **woody** hills; and in front, a **stream** of some natural importance was **swelled** into greater, but without any **artificial** appearance. Its **banks** were neither formal nor **falsely adorned.** Elizabeth was delighted. She had never seen a place for which nature had done more, or where natural beauty had been so little **counteracted** by an **awkward** taste. They were all of them warm in their **admiration**; and at that moment she felt that to be **mistress** of Pemberley might be something!

Italian

abruptness: precipitazione.
admiration: ammirazione.
admired: ammirato.
adorned: decorato.
artificial: artificiale, artefatto.
ascended: salito, asceso.
awkward: goffo, sgraziato.
backed: sostenuto.
banks: banche.
building: edificio, costruzione, palazzo, stabile, manufatto edilizio, fabbricato, l'edificio.

ceased: cessato.
counteracted: neutralizzato.
eminence: eminenza.
falsely: falsamente.
handsome: bello, carino.
instantly: direttamente, istantaneamente, immediatamente.
lodge: casetta, alloggiare, ospitare.
lowest: infimo.
mistress: padrona.
perturbation: perturbazione.
ridge: cresta, crinale.

situated: situato.
stone: pietra, calcolo, sasso, la pietra, ciottolo.
stream: ruscello, corrente, flusso, corso d'acqua.
stretching: stiramento, allungamento.
swelled: gonfiato.
top: cima.
valley: valle, vallata.
wood: legno, bosco, selva, legna.
woody: legnoso.
wound: ferita, ferire.

They **descended** the **hill**, crossed the **bridge**, and drove to the door; and, while examining the nearer aspect of the house, all her **apprehension** of meeting its owner returned. She dreaded **lest** the **chambermaid** had been mistaken. On applying to see the place, they were admitted into the hall; and Elizabeth, as they waited for the **housekeeper**, had leisure to wonder at her being where she was.

The housekeeper came; a respectable-looking **elderly** woman, much less fine, and more civil, than she had any notion of finding her. They followed her into the dining-parlour. It was a large, well **proportioned** room, **handsomely** fitted up. Elizabeth, after slightly **surveying** it, went to a window to enjoy its prospect. The hill, crowned with wood, which they had descended, receiving increased **abruptness** from the distance, was a beautiful object. Every **disposition** of the ground was good; and she looked on the whole scene, the **river**, the trees **scattered** on its banks and the **winding** of the valley, as far as she could **trace** it, with delight. As they passed into other rooms these objects were taking different positions; but from every window there were beauties to be seen. The rooms were **lofty** and handsome, and their furniture **suitable** to the fortune of its **proprietor**; but Elizabeth saw, with admiration of his taste, that it was neither **gaudy** nor **uselessly** fine; with less of **splendour**, and more real **elegance**, than the furniture of Rosings.

"And of this place," thought she, "I might have been mistress! With these rooms I might now have been **familiarly acquainted**! Instead of viewing them as a stranger, I might have **rejoiced** in them as my own, and welcomed to them as visitors my uncle and aunt. But no,"--recollecting herself--"that could never be; my uncle and aunt would have been lost to me; I should not have been allowed to invite them."

This was a lucky recollection--it saved her from something very like regret.

She longed to **inquire** of the housekeeper whether her master was really absent, but had not the courage for it. At length however, the question was asked by her uncle; and she turned away with alarm, while Mrs. Reynolds replied that he was, adding, "But we expect him to-morrow, with a large party of

Italian

abruptness: precipitazione.
acquainted: informato.
apprehension: apprensione, arresto.
bridge: ponte, ponte di comando, ponticello, plancia.
chambermaid: cameriera.
descended: sceso, disceso.
disposition: disposizione, predisposizione, ingegno, talento.
elderly: anziano.
elegance: eleganza.
familiarly: familiarmente.

gaudy: fastoso.
handsomely: bellamente.
hill: collina, colle, altura.
housekeeper: governante.
inquire: domandare, informarsi, domandano, domandate, domandi, domandiamo, domando, indagare, domanda.
lest: affinchè non, per paura che.
lofty: alto, elevato.
proportioned: proporzionato, proporzione.

proprietor: proprietario.
rejoiced: allietato, gioito, rallegrato.
river: fiume.
scattered: versato, sparso.
splendour: splendore.
suitable: adatto, conveniente, idoneo, appropriato, utile, capace, decente, utilizzabile.
surveying: agrimensura.
trace: traccia, tracciare, delimitare.
uselessly: inutilmente.
winding: tortuoso, avvolgimento.

friends." How **rejoiced** was Elizabeth that their own **journey** had not by any **circumstance** been **delayed** a day!

Her **aunt** now called her to look at a **picture**. She approached and saw the **likeness** of Mr. Wickham, **suspended, amongst** several other miniatures, over the mantelpiece. Her aunt asked her, **smilingly**, how she liked it. The **housekeeper** came forward, and told them it was a picture of a young **gentleman**, the son of her late **master's steward**, who had been brought up by him at his own **expense**. "He is now gone into the army," she added; "but I am **afraid** he has turned out very wild."

Mrs. Gardiner looked at her **niece** with a **smile**, but Elizabeth could not return it.

"And that," said Mrs. Reynolds, **pointing** to another of the miniatures, "is my master--and very like him. It was **drawn** at the same time as the other--about eight years ago."

"I have heard much of your master's fine person," said Mrs. Gardiner, looking at the picture; "it is a **handsome** face. But, Lizzy, you can tell us whether it is like or not."

Mrs. Reynolds **respect** for Elizabeth seemed to increase on this **intimation** of her **knowing** her master.

"Does that young **lady** know Mr. Darcy?"

Elizabeth **coloured**, and said: "A little."

"And do not you think him a very handsome gentleman, ma'am?"

"Yes, very handsome."

"I am sure I know **none** so handsome; but in the **gallery upstairs** you will see a finer, **larger** picture of him than this. This room was my late master's **favourite** room, and these miniatures are just as they used to be then. He was very **fond** of them."

This accounted to Elizabeth for Mr. Wickham's being among them.

Italian

afraid: pauroso, inquieto, spaventato, angoscioso, impaurito.
amongst: fra, tra.
aunt: zia, la zia.
circumstance: circostanza.
coloured: colorato.
delayed: ritardato.
drawn: disegnato.
expense: spese, spesa.
favourite: preferito.
fond: tenero, affettuoso, affezionato.
gallery: galleria, ballatoio.

gentleman: signore, galantuomo, gentiluomo.
handsome: bello, carino.
housekeeper: governante.
intimation: accenno.
journey: viaggio, viaggiare.
knowing: conoscendo, sapendo.
lady: signora, dama.
larger: più grande.
likeness: somiglianza, rassomiglianza.
master: maestro, padrone, principale, master, dominare, anagrafica.

niece: nipote.
none: nessuno.
picture: immagine, illustrazione, pittura, figura, quadro.
pointing: indicare.
rejoiced: allietato, gioito, rallegrato.
respect: rispettare, rispetto, stima.
smile: sorriso, sorridere.
smilingly: sorridere.
steward: maggiordomo, dispensiere.
suspended: sospeso.
upstairs: di sopra.

Mrs. Reynolds then **directed** their attention to one of Miss Darcy, drawn when she was only eight years old.

"And is Miss Darcy as **handsome** as her brother?" said Mrs. Gardiner.

"Oh! yes--the handsomest young lady that ever was seen; and so accomplished!--She **plays** and **sings** all day long. In the next room is a new **instrument** just come down for her--a present from my master; she comes here to-morrow with him."

Mr. Gardiner, whose **manners** were very easy and **pleasant**, **encouraged** her communicativeness by his questions and **remarks**; Mrs. Reynolds, either by **pride** or **attachment**, had **evidently** great **pleasure** in talking of her master and his sister.

"Is your master much at Pemberley in the course of the year?"

"Not so much as I could wish, sir; but I **dare** say he may spend half his time here; and Miss Darcy is always down for the summer months."

"Except," thought Elizabeth, "when she **goes** to Ramsgate."

"If your master would **marry**, you might see more of him."

"Yes, sir; but I do not know when *that* will be. I do not know who is good enough for him."

Mr. and Mrs. Gardiner smiled. Elizabeth could not help saying, "It is very much to his credit, I am sure, that you should think so."

"I say no more than the truth, and everybody will say that knows him," replied the other. Elizabeth thought this was going **pretty** far; and she **listened** with increasing **astonishment** as the **housekeeper** added, "I have never known a cross word from him in my life, and I have known him ever since he was four years old."

This was **praise**, of all others most **extraordinary**, most **opposite** to her ideas. That he was not a good-tempered man had been her firmest opinion. Her keenest attention was **awakened**; she longed to hear more, and was **grateful** to her **uncle** for saying:

Italian

astonishment: stupore, meraviglia, sorpresa.
attachment: accessorio, allegato, attaccamento.
awakened: svegliato, risvegliato.
dare: osare, oso, osiamo, osi, osate, osano, osa, sfida.
directed: diretto.
encouraged: incoraggiato.
evidently: evidentemente.
extraordinary: straordinario, eccezionale.

goes: va.
grateful: riconoscente, grato.
handsome: bello, carino.
housekeeper: governante.
instrument: strumento, apparecchio.
listened: ascoltato.
manners: educazione.
marry: sposare, sposati, sposatevi, si sposi, si sposate, si sposano, ci sposiamo, mi sposo, maritarsi, ammogliarsi, maritare.
opposite: dirimpetto, opposto,

contrario, contro, di fronte a, di fronte.
plays: gioca, suona.
pleasant: piacevole, gradevole, ameno.
pleasure: piacere, gradimento.
praise: lodare, lode, elogiare, encomio, elogio.
pretty: grazioso, bellino, carino, bello.
pride: orgoglio, fierezza.
remarks: osservazioni.
sings: canta.
uncle: zio, lo zio.

"There are very few people of whom so much can be said. You are lucky in having such a master."

"Yes, sir, I know I am. If I were to go through the world, I could not meet with a better. But I have always observed, that they who are **good**-natured when children, are good-natured when they grow up; and he was always the sweetest-tempered, most generous-hearted **boy** in the world."

Elizabeth almost stared at her. "Can this be Mr. Darcy?" thought she.

"His father was an excellent man," said Mrs. Gardiner.

"Yes, ma'am, that he was indeed; and his son will be just like him--just as **affable** to the poor."

Elizabeth **listened**, wondered, doubted, and was **impatient** for more. Mrs. Reynolds could interest her on no other point. She related the subjects of the pictures, the **dimensions** of the rooms, and the price of the **furniture**, in **vain**, Mr. Gardiner, highly **amused** by the kind of family **prejudice** to which he **attributed** her **excessive commendation** of her master, soon led again to the subject; and she dwelt with **energy** on his many merits as they **proceeded** together up the great **staircase**.

"He is the best **landlord**, and the best master," said she, "that ever lived; not like the wild young men **nowadays**, who think of nothing but themselves. There is not one of his tenants or servants but will give him a good name. Some people call him **proud**; but I am sure I never saw anything of it. To my **fancy**, it is only because he does not **rattle** away like other young men."

"In what an **amiable** light does this place him!" thought Elizabeth.

"This fine account of him," **whispered** her **aunt** as they walked, "is not quite **consistent** with his behaviour to our poor friend."

"Perhaps we might be deceived."

"That is not very likely; our authority was too good."

On reaching the **spacious lobby** above they were shown into a very pretty sitting-room, **lately fitted** up with greater **elegance** and **lightness** than the

Italian

affable: affabile, cortese, gradevole, amichevole, grazioso, carino, benevole.
amiable: amabile.
amused: divertito.
attributed: attribuito.
aunt: zia, la zia.
boy: ragazzo, servire.
commendation: raccomandazione.
consistent: costante.
dimensions: dimensioni, ingombri.
elegance: eleganza.

energy: energia.
excessive: eccessivo.
fancy: figurarsi, capriccio, immaginazione.
fitted: aderente, adatto, attrezzato.
furniture: mobili, mobilia.
good-natured: gradevole, cortese.
impatient: impaziente.
landlord: proprietario, locatore, affittacamere.
lately: ultimamente, recentemente.
lightness: leggerezza.

listened: ascoltato.
lobby: lobby, atrio, vestibolo.
nowadays: oggigiorno.
prejudice: pregiudizio, preconcetto, prevenzione.
proceeded: proceduto.
proud: orgoglioso, fiero.
rattle: sonaglio, rantolo.
spacious: ampio, spazioso.
staircase: scala.
vain: vanitoso, vano.
whispered: bisbigliato.

apartments below; and were informed that it was but just done to give pleasure to Miss Darcy, who had taken a **liking** to the room when last at Pemberley.

"He is certainly a good brother," said Elizabeth, as she walked towards one of the windows.

Mrs. Reynolds **anticipated** Miss Darcy's **delight**, when she should enter the room. "And this is always the way with him," she added. "Whatever can give his sister any pleasure is sure to be done in a moment. There is nothing he would not do for her."

The picture-gallery, and two or three of the principal bedrooms, were all that remained to be shown. In the former were many good paintings; but Elizabeth knew nothing of the art; and from such as had been already visible below, she had **willingly** turned to look at some drawings of Miss Darcy's, in crayons, whose subjects were usually more interesting, and also more **intelligible**.

In the gallery there were many family portraits, but they could have little to **fix** the attention of a **stranger**. Elizabeth walked in **quest** of the only face whose features would be known to her. At last it arrested her--and she **beheld** a **striking resemblance** to Mr. Darcy, with such a smile over the face as she remembered to have sometimes seen when he looked at her. She stood several minutes before the picture, in **earnest contemplation**, and returned to it again before they quitted the gallery. Mrs. Reynolds informed them that it had been taken in his father's **lifetime**.

There was certainly at this moment, in Elizabeth's mind, a more gentle **sensation** towards the original than she had ever felt at the height of their **acquaintance**. The **commendation bestowed** on him by Mrs. Reynolds was of no **trifling** nature. What **praise** is more valuable than the praise of an **intelligent servant**? As a brother, a landlord, a master, she considered how many people's **happiness** were in his guardianship!--how much of pleasure or pain was it in his power to bestow!--how much of good or **evil** must be done by him! Every idea that had been brought forward by the **housekeeper** was **favourable** to his character, and as she stood before the **canvas** on which he was represented, and fixed his eyes upon herself, she thought of his regard with a deeper **sentiment** of

Italian

acquaintance: conoscenza, conoscente.
anticipated: anticipato.
beheld: guardato.
bestowed: concesso, tributato.
canvas: tela, canovaccio.
commendation: raccomandazione.
contemplation: contemplazione.
delight: delizia, deliziare, dilettare, diletto, godimento, rallegrare, gioia.
earnest: serio, caparra.
evil: male, cattivo, malvagio.
favourable: favorevole.

fix: fissare, fissa, fissano, fissate, fissi, fissiamo, fisso, riparare, aggiustare, ripara, ripariamo.
happiness: felicità.
housekeeper: governante.
intelligent: intelligente.
intelligible: intelligibile.
liking: predilezione, simpatia.
praise: lodare, lode, elogiare, encomio, elogio.
quest: ricerca.

resemblance: somiglianza, rassomiglianza.
sensation: sensazione.
sentiment: sentimento.
servant: servire, servo, servitore.
stranger: sconosciuto, estraneo, forestiero.
striking: impressionante.
trifling: insignificante.
willingly: volentieri.

gratitude than it had ever raised before; she remembered its warmth, and **softened** its **impropriety** of expression.

When all of the house that was open to general **inspection** had been seen, they returned downstairs, and, taking leave of the **housekeeper**, were **consigned** over to the **gardener**, who met them at the hall-door.

As they walked across the hall towards the river, Elizabeth turned back to look again; her uncle and aunt stopped also, and while the former was conjecturing as to the **date** of the building, the owner of it himself suddenly came forward from the road, which led behind it to the stables.

They were within twenty **yards** of each other, and so **abrupt** was his appearance, that it was impossible to avoid his sight. Their eyes instantly met, and the cheeks of both were **overspread** with the deepest **blush**. He absolutely **started**, and for a moment seemed **immovable** from surprise; but shortly recovering himself, advanced towards the party, and spoke to Elizabeth, if not in terms of perfect **composure**, at least of perfect **civility**.

She had **instinctively** turned away; but stopping on his approach, received his **compliments** with an embarrassment impossible to be overcome. Had his first appearance, or his **resemblance** to the picture they had just been examining, been insufficient to assure the other two that they now saw Mr. Darcy, the gardener's expression of surprise, on **beholding** his master, must immediately have told it. They stood a little **aloof** while he was talking to their **niece**, who, **astonished** and confused, scarcely dared **lift** her eyes to his face, and knew not what answer she returned to his civil inquiries after her family. **Amazed** at the **alteration** of his manner since they last parted, every sentence that he uttered was increasing her embarrassment; and every idea of the impropriety of her being found there **recurring** to her mind, the few minutes in which they continued were some of the most uncomfortable in her life. Nor did he seem much more at ease; when he spoke, his accent had none of its usual sedateness; and he repeated his inquiries as to the time of her having left Longbourn, and of her having stayed in Derbyshire, so often, and in so hurried a way, as plainly spoke the **distraction** of his thoughts.

Italian

abrupt: brusco, ripido, subitaneo, improvviso.
aloof: appartato, in disparte, alla larga, a distanza, distante.
alteration: alterazione, modifica, cambiamento, variazione.
amazed: sbalordito, stupito, si stupito.
astonished: stupito, si stupito.
beholding: guardando.
blush: rossore, arrossire.
civility: civiltà, cortesia.
compliments: complimenti.

composure: calma, compostezza.
consigned: consegnato.
date: data, dattero, datare, appuntamento.
distraction: distrazione.
gardener: giardiniere.
housekeeper: governante.
immovable: immobile.
impropriety: scorrettezza, improprietà.
inspection: ispezione, controllo, collaudo.

instinctively: istintivamente.
lift: ascensore, alzare, sollevare, salire, sollevamento, alzata, passaggio.
niece: nipote.
overspread: coprire, cospargere.
recurring: ricorrendo, ritornando, ricorrente.
resemblance: somiglianza, rassomiglianza.
softened: ammorbidito.
started: cominciato.
yards: iarde.

At length every idea seemed to fail him; and, after standing a few moments without saying a word, he suddenly **recollected** himself, and took leave.

The others then joined her, and expressed **admiration** of his figure; but Elizabeth heard not a word, and wholly **engrossed** by her own feelings, followed them in silence. She was **overpowered** by **shame** and **vexation**. Her coming there was the most **unfortunate**, the most ill-judged thing in the world! How strange it must appear to him! In what a **disgraceful** light might it not strike so **vain** a man! It might seem as if she had **purposely** thrown herself in his way again! Oh! why did she come? Or, why did he thus come a day before he was expected? Had they been only ten minutes **sooner**, they should have been beyond the reach of his **discrimination**; for it was **plain** that he was that moment arrived--that moment alighted from his horse or his **carriage**. She **blushed** again and again over the perverseness of the meeting. And his behaviour, so strikingly altered--what could it mean? That he should even speak to her was amazing!-- but to speak with such **civility**, to **inquire** after her family! Never in her life had she seen his **manners** so little **dignified**, never had he spoken with such **gentleness** as on this **unexpected** meeting. What a **contrast** did it offer to his last address in Rosings Park, when he put his letter into her hand! She knew not what to think, or how to account for it.

They had now entered a beautiful walk by the side of the water, and every step was bringing forward a nobler fall of ground, or a finer reach of the woods to which they were **approaching**; but it was some time before Elizabeth was sensible of any of it; and, though she answered **mechanically** to the repeated appeals of her uncle and aunt, and seemed to direct her eyes to such objects as they pointed out, she **distinguished** no part of the scene. Her thoughts were all fixed on that one spot of Pemberley House, **whichever** it might be, where Mr. Darcy then was. She longed to know what at the moment was passing in his mind--in what manner he thought of her, and whether, in **defiance** of everything, she was still dear to him. Perhaps he had been civil only because he felt himself at ease; yet there had been *that* in his voice which was not like ease.

Italian

admiration: ammirazione.
approaching: avvicinamento.
blushed: arrossito.
carriage: vettura, carrello, vagone, carro, carrozza.
civility: civiltà, cortesia.
contrast: contrasto.
defiance: sfida.
dignified: dignitoso.
discrimination: discriminazione, distinzione.
disgraceful: disgraziata, vergognoso,

disonorevole.
distinguished: distinto.
engrossed: assorbito.
gentleness: delicatezza.
inquire: domandare, informarsi, domandano, domandate, domandi, domandiamo, domando, indagare, domanda.
manners: educazione.
mechanically: meccanicamente.
overpowered: sopraffatto.
plain: piano, pianura, evidente,

distinto, chiaro.
purposely: intenzionalmente.
recollected: rammentato.
shame: vergogna, pudore.
sooner: prima.
unexpected: inatteso, imprevisto, inaspettato.
unfortunate: sfortunato, sventurato.
vain: vanitoso, vano.
vexation: irritazione.
whichever: qualunque, chiunque, qualsiasi.

Whether he had felt more of pain or of pleasure in seeing her she could not tell, but he certainly had not seen her with composure.

At length, however, the remarks of her companions on her absence of mind **aroused** her, and she felt the necessity of appearing more like herself.

They entered the woods, and **bidding adieu** to the river for a while, **ascended** some of the higher **grounds**; when, in spots where the opening of the trees gave the eye power to **wander**, were many charming views of the valley, the opposite hills, with the long range of woods overspreading many, and occasionally part of the stream. Mr. Gardiner expressed a wish of going round the whole park, but feared it might be beyond a walk. With a **triumphant** smile they were told that it was ten miles round. It settled the matter; and they pursued the **accustomed circuit**; which **brought** them again, after some time, in a descent among **hanging** woods, to the edge of the water, and one of its **narrowest** parts. They crossed it by a **simple** bridge, in character with the general air of the scene; it was a spot less **adorned** than any they had yet visited; and the valley, here contracted into a glen, allowed room only for the stream, and a narrow walk **amidst** the rough coppice-wood which bordered it. Elizabeth longed to **explore** its windings; but when they had crossed the bridge, and perceived their distance from the house, Mrs. Gardiner, who was not a great walker, could go no **farther**, and thought only of returning to the carriage as quickly as possible. Her **niece** was, therefore, obliged to **submit**, and they took their way towards the house on the opposite side of the river, in the nearest direction; but their progress was **slow**, for Mr. Gardiner, though seldom able to **indulge** the taste, was very fond of **fishing**, and was so much engaged in watching the occasional appearance of some **trout** in the water, and talking to the man about them, that he advanced but little. Whilst wandering on in this slow manner, they were again surprised, and Elizabeth's **astonishment** was quite equal to what it had been at first, by the sight of Mr. Darcy approaching them, and at no great distance. The walk here being here less sheltered than on the other side, allowed them to see him before they met. Elizabeth, however astonished, was at least more prepared for an **interview** than before, and

Italian

accustomed: consueto, abituato, usuale, solito, avvezzo.
adieu: addio.
adorned: decorato.
amidst: tra, fra.
aroused: suscitato, risvegliato, destato.
ascended: salito, asceso.
astonishment: stupore, meraviglia, sorpresa.
bidding: offerta, licitazione, comando.
circuit: circuito.
explore: esplorare, esplorano, esplorate, esplori, esploriamo, esploro, esplora.
farther: più lontano.
fishing: pesca, pescaggio.
grounds: fondamento, stessa connessione a terra.
hanging: impiccagione.
indulge: indulgere.
interview: intervista, colloquio.
narrow: stretto, ristretto, angusto.
niece: nipote.
rough: rude, brusco, ruvido, crudo, approssimativo, rozzo, grossolano, scabro, grezzo.
simple: semplice.
slow: lento.
submit: sottomettere, sottoporre.
triumphant: trionfante.
trout: trota.
wander: vagare, vago, errare, vaghiamo, vaga, vagano, vaghi, vagate, vagabondare.

resolved to appear and to speak with **calmness**, if he really intended to meet them. For a few moments, indeed, she felt that he would probably strike into some other path. The idea **lasted** while a turning in the walk **concealed** him from their view; the turning past, he was immediately before them. With a glance, she saw that he had lost none of his recent **civility**; and, to **imitate** his **politeness**, she began, as they met, to **admire** the beauty of the place; but she had not got beyond the words "delightful," and "charming," when some **unlucky** recollections **obtruded**, and she **fancied** that praise of Pemberley from her might be **mischievously construed**. Her colour changed, and she said no more.

Mrs. Gardiner was standing a little behind; and on her pausing, he asked her if she would do him the honour of introducing him to her friends. This was a stroke of civility for which she was quite **unprepared**; and she could hardly **suppress** a smile at his being now seeking the **acquaintance** of some of those very people against whom his pride had **revolted** in his offer to herself. "What will be his surprise," thought she, "when he knows who they are? He takes them now for people of fashion."

The introduction, however, was immediately made; and as she named their relationship to herself, she **stole** a sly look at him, to see how he bore it, and was not without the expectation of his decamping as fast as he could from such **disgraceful** companions. That he was *surprised* by the connection was evident; he **sustained** it, however, with **fortitude**, and so far from going away, turned his back with them, and entered into conversation with Mr. Gardiner. Elizabeth could not but be pleased, could not but triumph. It was **consoling** that he should know she had some relations for whom there was no need to **blush**. She listened most **attentively** to all that passed between them, and gloried in every expression, every sentence of her uncle, which marked his intelligence, his taste, or his good **manners**.

The conversation soon turned upon fishing; and she heard Mr. Darcy **invite** him, with the greatest civility, to fish there as often as he chose while he continued in the neighbourhood, offering at the same time to supply him with fishing **tackle**, and pointing out those parts of the stream where there was

Italian

acquaintance: conoscenza, conoscente.
admire: ammirare, ammiriamo, ammira, ammirano, ammiro, ammiri, ammirate.
attentively: attentamente.
blush: rossore, arrossire.
calmness: calma.
civility: civiltà, cortesia.
concealed: nascosto.
consoling: consolare.
construed: analizzato, interpretato.
disgraceful: disgraziata, vergognoso, disonorevole.

fancied: fantastico.
fortitude: forza d'animo.
imitate: imitare, imitano, imito, imitiamo, imitate, imita, imiti, contraffare.
invite: invitare, invita, invitano, invitate, inviti, invitiamo, invito.
lasted: durato.
manners: educazione.
obtruded: imposto.
politeness: cortesia, garbo.

revolted: rivoltato.
sly: furbo, astuto, scaltro.
stole: stola.
suppress: soffocare, opprimere, soffoca, soffocano, soffocate, soffochi, soffochiamo, soffoco.
sustained: sostenuto, costante, poggiato.
tackle: paranco, attrezzatura.
unlucky: sfortunato, disgraziato.
unprepared: impreparato.

usually most sport.   Mrs. Gardiner, who was walking arm-in-arm with Elizabeth, gave her a look **expressive** of wonder.   Elizabeth said nothing, but it **gratified** her **exceedingly**; the **compliment** must be all for herself.   Her **astonishment**, however, was extreme, and **continually** was she **repeating**, "Why is he so **altered**? From what can it proceed? It **cannot** be for *me*--it cannot be for *my* sake that his **manners** are thus **softened**. My reproofs at Hunsford could not work such a change as this. It is impossible that he should still love me."

After walking some time in this way, the two ladies in front, the two gentlemen behind, on **resuming** their places, after **descending** to the **brink** of the river for the better inspection of some curious water-plant, there **chanced** to be a little **alteration**. It **originated** in Mrs. Gardiner, who, **fatigued** by the exercise of the morning, found Elizabeth's arm **inadequate** to her support, and consequently preferred her husband's. Mr. Darcy took her place by her **niece**, and they walked on together. After a short silence, the lady first spoke. She wished him to know that she had been assured of his absence before she came to the place, and accordingly began by **observing**, that his arrival had been very unexpected--"for your housekeeper," she added, "informed us that you would certainly not be here till to-morrow; and indeed, before we left Bakewell, we understood that you were not immediately expected in the country." He acknowledged the truth of it all, and said that business with his **steward** had occasioned his coming forward a few hours before the rest of the party with whom he had been travelling. "They will join me early to-morrow," he continued, "and among them are some who will claim an **acquaintance** with you--Mr. Bingley and his sisters."

Elizabeth answered only by a slight **bow**. Her thoughts were **instantly** driven back to the time when Mr. Bingley's name had been the last mentioned between them; and, if she might judge by his **complexion**, *his* mind was not very **differently engaged**.

"There is also one other person in the party," he continued after a **pause**, "who more particularly wishes to be known to you. Will you allow me, or do I ask too much, to introduce my sister to your acquaintance during your stay at Lambton?"

Italian

acquaintance: conoscenza, conoscente.
alteration: alterazione, modifica, cambiamento, variazione.
altered: alterato.
astonishment: stupore, meraviglia, sorpresa.
bow: arco, prua, fiocco, inchino, inchinarsi, curva, archetto.
brink: orlo.
cannot: non potere.
chanced: successo.
complexion: carnagione.

compliment: complimento.
continually: continuamente.
descending: scendendo, discendendo.
differently: diversamente, in modo diverso.
engaged: occupato, innestato, impegnato.
exceedingly: estremamente.
expressive: espressivo.
fatigued: affaticato.
gratified: gratificato.
inadequate: inadeguato, insufficiente.

instantly: direttamente, istantaneamente, immediatamente.
manners: educazione.
niece: nipote.
observing: osservando.
originated: disceso.
pause: pausa, sosta.
repeating: ripetendo.
resuming: riprendendo.
softened: ammorbidito.
steward: maggiordomo, dispensiere.

The surprise of such an application was great indeed; it was too great for her to know in what manner she **acceded** to it. She immediately felt that whatever desire Miss Darcy might have of being **acquainted** with her must be the work of her brother, and, without looking **farther**, it was satisfactory; it was **gratifying** to know that his **resentment** had not made him think really ill of her.

They now walked on in silence, each of them deep in thought. Elizabeth was not comfortable; that was impossible; but she was **flattered** and pleased. His wish of **introducing** his sister to her was a **compliment** of the highest kind. They soon outstripped the others, and when they had reached the **carriage**, Mr. and Mrs. Gardiner were half a quarter of a mile behind.

He then asked her to walk into the house--but she declared herself not tired, and they stood together on the **lawn**. At such a time much might have been said, and silence was very **awkward**. She wanted to talk, but there seemed to be an **embargo** on every subject. At last she **recollected** that she had been **travelling**, and they talked of Matlock and Dove Dale with great **perseverance**. Yet time and her aunt moved slowly--and her **patience** and her ideas were nearly **worn** our before the tete-a-tete was over. On Mr. and Mrs. Gardiner's coming up they were all pressed to go into the house and take some **refreshment**; but this was declined, and they parted on each side with **utmost politeness**. Mr. Darcy handed the ladies into the carriage; and when it drove off, Elizabeth saw him walking slowly towards the house.

The observations of her uncle and aunt now began; and each of them **pronounced** him to be **infinitely superior** to anything they had expected. "He is perfectly well **behaved**, polite, and unassuming," said her uncle.

"There *is* something a little **stately** in him, to be sure," replied her aunt, "but it is **confined** to his air, and is not **unbecoming**. I can now say with the **housekeeper**, that though some people may call him proud, I have seen nothing of it."

"I was never more surprised than by his behaviour to us. It was more than civil; it was really **attentive**; and there was no **necessity** for such attention. His **acquaintance** with Elizabeth was very trifling."

Italian

acceded: concordato, accesso.
acquaintance: conoscenza, conoscente.
acquainted: informato.
attentive: attento, premuroso.
awkward: goffo, sgraziato.
behaved: agito, comportato.
carriage: vettura, carrello, vagone, carro, carrozza.
compliment: complimento.
confined: limitato.
embargo: embargo.
farther: più lontano.

flattered: lusingato.
gratifying: gratificando, gratificante.
housekeeper: governante.
infinitely: infinitamente.
introducing: presentando, introducendo.
lawn: prato, tappeto erboso, linone.
necessity: necessità, bisogno.
patience: pazienza.
perseverance: perseveranza.
polite: cortese, educato.
politeness: cortesia, garbo.

pronounced: pronunciato.
recollected: rammentato.
refreshment: rinfresco, ristoro.
resentment: risentimento, astio.
stately: imponente.
superior: superiore.
travelling: itinerante, viaggiante, viaggiare.
unbecoming: indecoroso.
utmost: massimo.
worn: consumato, usato, esausto, portato, logoro.

"To be sure, Lizzy," said her **aunt**, "he is not so **handsome** as Wickham; or, rather, he has not Wickham's **countenance**, for his features are perfectly good. But how came you to tell me that he was so disagreeable?"

Elizabeth excused herself as well as she could; said that she had liked him better when they had met in Kent than before, and that she had never seen him so **pleasant** as this morning.

"But perhaps he may be a little **whimsical** in his civilities," replied her **uncle**. "Your great men often are; and therefore I shall not take him at his word, as he might change his mind another day, and **warn** me off his grounds."

Elizabeth felt that they had entirely **misunderstood** his character, but said nothing.

"From what we have seen of him," continued Mrs. Gardiner, "I really should not have thought that he could have **behaved** in so **cruel** a way by anybody as he has done by poor Wickham. He has not an ill-natured look. On the **contrary**, there is something **pleasing** about his **mouth** when he **speaks**. And there is something of **dignity** in his countenance that would not give one an **unfavourable** idea of his heart. But, to be sure, the good lady who showed us his house did give him a most **flaming** character! I could hardly help **laughing aloud** sometimes. But he is a liberal master, I suppose, and *that* in the eye of a **servant comprehends** every virtue."

Elizabeth here felt herself called on to say something in **vindication** of his behaviour to Wickham; and therefore gave them to understand, in as **guarded** a manner as she could, that by what she had heard from his relations in Kent, his actions were capable of a very different **construction**; and that his character was by no means so **faulty**, nor Wickham's so **amiable**, as they had been considered in Hertfordshire. In **confirmation** of this, she related the **particulars** of all the **pecuniary** transactions in which they had been **connected**, without actually naming her authority, but **stating** it to be such as such as might be **relied** on.

Mrs. Gardiner was surprised and concerned; but as they were now **approaching** the scene of her former pleasures, every idea gave way to the charm

---

Italian

aloud: ad alta voce.
amiable: amabile.
approaching: avvicinamento.
aunt: zia, la zia.
behaved: agito, comportato.
comprehends: comprende.
confirmation: conferma.
connected: collegato, legato, connesso.
construction: costruzione.
contrary: contrario.
countenance: approvare, viso.
cruel: crudele.

dignity: dignità, decoro.
faulty: difettoso.
flaming: fiammeggiante.
guarded: guardingo, custodito.
handsome: bello, carino.
laughing: ridere, risata.
misunderstood: incompreso, frainteso.
mouth: bocca, imboccatura, foce, la bocca, apertura.
particulars: particolari.
pecuniary: pecuniario.
pleasant: piacevole, gradevole, ameno.

pleasing: piacevole.
relied: confidato.
servant: servire, servo, servitore.
speaks: parla.
stating: dichiarare.
uncle: zio, lo zio.
unfavourable: sfavorevole.
vindication: rivendicazione.
warn: avvertire, avvertiamo, avvertono, avverti, avverto, avvertite, ammonire, avvisare.
whimsical: capriccioso.

of **recollection**; and she was too much **engaged** in **pointing** out to her **husband** all the **interesting** spots in its **environs** to think of anything else. Fatigued as she had been by the morning's **walk** they had no **sooner dined** than she set off again in **quest** of her **former acquaintance**, and the **evening** was **spent** in the satisfactions of a **intercourse renewed** after many years' discontinuance.

The occurrences of the day were too full of interest to **leave** Elizabeth much **attention** for any of these new **friends**; and she could do nothing but think, and think with **wonder**, of Mr. Darcy's **civility**, and, above all, of his wishing her to be **acquainted** with his **sister**.

Italian

acquaintance: conoscenza, conoscente.
acquainted: informato.
attention: attenzione.
civility: civiltà, cortesia.
dined: pranzato, cenato.
engaged: occupato, innestato, impegnato.
environs: ambiente, dintorni.
evening: sera, la sera, serata.
former: precedente, passato.
friends: amici.
husband: marito, sposo.

intercourse: rapporti.
interesting: interessante.
leave: lasciare, abbandonare, partire, lasciano, partono, partite, partiamo, parti, lasciate, lasciamo, lascia.
pointing: indicare.
quest: ricerca.
recollection: memoria, ricordo.
renewed: rinnovato.
sister: sorella, la sorella.
sooner: prima.
spent: speso, passato.

walk: camminare, cammino, cammina, camminano, camminate, cammini, camminiamo, camminata, passeggiare, passeggiata.
wonder: stupirsi, stupore, meraviglia, domandarsi, meravigliarsi.

CHAPTER 44

Elizabeth had **settled** it that Mr. Darcy would bring his sister to visit her the very day after her reaching Pemberley; and was **consequently resolved** not to be out of sight of the **inn** the whole of that morning. But her conclusion was **false**; for on the very morning after their **arrival** at Lambton, these visitors came. They had been walking about the place with some of their new friends, and were just returning to the inn to dress themselves for **dining** with the same family, when the sound of a **carriage** drew them to a window, and they saw a gentleman and a lady in a curricle **driving** up the street. Elizabeth immediately **recognizing** the **livery, guessed** what it meant, and **imparted** no small degree of her surprise to her relations by **acquainting** them with the **honour** which she expected. Her **uncle** and **aunt** were all **amazement**; and the **embarrassment** of her manner as she spoke, joined to the **circumstance** itself, and many of the circumstances of the **preceding** day, opened to them a new idea on the business. Nothing had ever suggested it before, but they felt that there was no other way of **accounting** for such attentions from such a quarter than by **supposing** a **partiality** for their **niece**. While these newly-born notions were **passing** in their heads, the **perturbation** of Elizabeth's feelings was at every moment increasing. She was quite **amazed** at her own discomposure; but amongst other **causes** of **disquiet**, she dreaded **lest** the partiality of the brother should have said too much in her

Italian

accounting: contabilità, ragioneria, contabile.
acquainting: informando.
amazed: sbalordito, stupito, si stupito.
amazement: stupore, meraviglia.
arrival: arrivo, venuta.
aunt: zia, la zia.
carriage: vettura, carrello, vagone, carro, carrozza.
causes: causa.
circumstance: circostanza.
consequently: conseguentemente.

dining: pranzando, cenando.
disquiet: inquietudine.
driving: guida.
embarrassment: imbarazzo.
false: falso, finto.
guessed: indovinato.
honour: onore.
imparted: impartito.
inn: locanda, osteria.
lest: affinchè non, per paura che.
livery: livrea.
niece: nipote.

partiality: parzialità, predilezione.
passing: passeggero, passare, passaggio.
perturbation: perturbazione.
preceding: precedendo, precedente.
recognizing: riconoscendo.
resolved: risolto.
settled: regolato, stabilito, stabile, fermo, fisso, popolato, saldato, sistemato, deciso.
supposing: supponendo.
uncle: zio, lo zio.

favour; and, more than **commonly** anxious to please, she naturally suspected that every power of **pleasing** would fail her.

She **retreated** from the window, **fearful** of being seen; and as she walked up and down the room, endeavouring to **compose** herself, saw such looks of **inquiring** surprise in her uncle and aunt as made everything worse.

Miss Darcy and her brother appeared, and this **formidable** introduction took place. With **astonishment** did Elizabeth see that her new **acquaintance** was at least as much **embarrassed** as herself. Since her being at Lambton, she had heard that Miss Darcy was **exceedingly** proud; but the observation of a very few minutes convinced her that she was only exceedingly **shy**. She found it difficult to obtain even a word from her beyond a **monosyllable**.

Miss Darcy was tall, and on a larger scale than Elizabeth; and, though little more than sixteen, her figure was formed, and her appearance **womanly** and **graceful**. She was less handsome than her brother; but there was sense and good humour in her face, and her **manners** were perfectly **unassuming** and gentle. Elizabeth, who had expected to find in her as acute and unembarrassed an observer as ever Mr. Darcy had been, was much relieved by **discerning** such different feelings.

They had not long been together before Mr. Darcy told her that Bingley was also coming to wait on her; and she had **barely** time to express her satisfaction, and prepare for such a visitor, when Bingley's quick step was heard on the stairs, and in a moment he entered the room. All Elizabeth's anger against him had been long done away; but had she still felt any, it could hardly have stood its ground against the **unaffected cordiality** with which he expressed himself on seeing her again. He **inquired** in a friendly, though general way, after her family, and looked and spoke with the same good-humoured ease that he had ever done.

To Mr. and Mrs. Gardiner he was scarcely a less interesting **personage** than to herself. They had long wished to see him. The whole party before them, indeed, **excited** a lively attention. The suspicions which had just **arisen** of Mr. Darcy and their **niece** directed their observation towards each with an earnest

Italian

acquaintance: conoscenza, conoscente.
arisen: nato, sorto.
astonishment: stupore, meraviglia, sorpresa.
barely: appena, a mala pena.
commonly: comunemente.
compose: comporre, componi, componiamo, compongo, compongono, componete.
cordiality: cordialità.
discerning: discernendo, distinguendo, percependo, percepire,
perspicace, acuto.
embarrassed: imbarazzato.
exceedingly: estremamente.
excited: eccitato, concitato, emozionato.
fearful: spaventoso, pauroso.
formidable: formidabile, straordinario.
graceful: grazioso, aggraziato.
inquired: domandato.
inquiring: domandando, domandare.
manners: educazione.
monosyllable: monosillabo.
niece: nipote.
personage: personaggio.
pleasing: piacevole.
retreated: ritirato.
shy: timido, ritroso.
unaffected: spontaneo, non affettato, semplice.
unassuming: senza pretese.
womanly: femminile.

though **guarded** inquiry; and they soon drew from those inquiries the full conviction that one of them at least knew what it was to love. Of the lady's sensations they remained a little in doubt; but that the gentleman was **overflowing** with **admiration** was evident enough.

Elizabeth, on her side, had much to do. She wanted to **ascertain** the feelings of each of her visitors; she wanted to **compose** her own, and to make herself **agreeable** to all; and in the latter object, where she **feared** most to fail, she was most sure of success, for those to whom she endeavoured to give pleasure were prepossessed in her favour. Bingley was ready, Georgiana was **eager**, and Darcy determined, to be pleased.

In seeing Bingley, her thoughts naturally flew to her sister; and, oh! how **ardently** did she long to know whether any of his were directed in a like manner. Sometimes she could **fancy** that he talked less than on former occasions, and once or twice pleased herself with the notion that, as he looked at her, he was trying to trace a **resemblance**. But, though this might be **imaginary**, she could not be **deceived** as to his behaviour to Miss Darcy, who had been set up as a **rival** to Jane. No look appeared on either side that spoke particular regard. Nothing occurred between them that could justify the hopes of his sister. On this point she was soon satisfied; and two or three little circumstances occurred ere they parted, which, in her anxious **interpretation**, **denoted** a **recollection** of Jane not untinctured by **tenderness**, and a wish of saying more that might lead to the mention of her, had he **dared**. He observed to her, at a moment when the others were talking together, and in a tone which had something of real **regret**, that it "was a very long time since he had had the pleasure of seeing her;" and, before she could reply, he added, "It is above eight months. We have not met since the 26th of November, when we were all **dancing** together at Netherfield."

Elizabeth was pleased to find his memory so exact; and he afterwards took occasion to ask her, when **unattended** to by any of the rest, whether *all* her sisters were at Longbourn. There was not much in the question, nor in the **preceding** **remark**; but there was a look and a manner which gave them meaning.

Italian

admiration: ammirazione.
agreeable: gradevole, piacevole, amabile.
ardently: ardentemente.
ascertain: constatare, constatiamo, constati, constatate, constato, constatano, constata, accertare, accerto, accertiamo, accerti.
compose: comporre, componi, componiamo, compongo, compongono, componete.
dancing: ballando.

dared: osato.
deceived: ingannato, truffato.
denoted: denotato.
eager: avido, desideroso, bramoso, impaziente.
fancy: figurarsi, capriccio, immaginazione.
feared: temuto.
guarded: guardingo, custodito.
imaginary: immaginario.
interpretation: interpretazione.
overflowing: traboccante.

preceding: precedendo, precedente.
recollection: memoria, ricordo.
regret: rincrescere, rammarico, rimpiangere, rimpianto, rincrescimento.
remark: commento, osservazione, nota.
resemblance: somiglianza, rassomiglianza.
rival: rivale.
tenderness: tenerezza, affettuosità.
unattended: incustodito.

It was not often that she could turn her eyes on Mr. Darcy himself; but, whenever she did catch a **glimpse**, she saw an expression of general **complaisance**, and in all that he said she heard an accent so removed from hauteur or **disdain** of his companions, as convinced her that the improvement of **manners** which she had yesterday **witnessed** however temporary its existence might prove, had at least outlived one day. When she saw him thus seeking the **acquaintance** and **courting** the good opinion of people with whom any **intercourse** a few months ago would have been a disgrace--when she saw him thus civil, not only to herself, but to the very relations whom he had openly disdained, and **recollected** their last lively scene in Hunsford Parsonage--the difference, the change was so great, and struck so forcibly on her mind, that she could hardly **restrain** her **astonishment** from being visible. Never, even in the company of his dear friends at Netherfield, or his **dignified** relations at Rosings, had she seen him so **desirous** to please, so free from self-consequence or **unbending** reserve, as now, when no importance could result from the success of his endeavours, and when even the acquaintance of those to whom his attentions were addressed would draw down the **ridicule** and **censure** of the ladies both of Netherfield as Rosings.

Their visitors stayed with them above half-an-hour; and when they arose to **depart**, Mr. Darcy called on his sister to join him in expressing their wish of seeing Mr. and Mrs. Gardiner, and Miss Bennet, to dinner at Pemberley, before they left the country. Miss Darcy, though with a **diffidence** which marked her little in the habit of giving invitations, readily **obeyed**. Mrs. Gardiner looked at her **niece**, desirous of knowing how *she*, whom the invitation most concerned, felt **disposed** as to its acceptance, but Elizabeth had turned away her head. Presuming however, that this studied **avoidance** spoke rather a **momentary** embarrassment than any **dislike** of the proposal, and seeing in her husband, who was fond of society, a perfect willingness to accept it, she **ventured** to engage for her attendance, and the day after the next was fixed on.

Bingley expressed great pleasure in the certainty of seeing Elizabeth again, having still a great deal to say to her, and many inquiries to make after all their

Italian

acquaintance: conoscenza, conoscente.
astonishment: stupore, meraviglia, sorpresa.
avoidance: annullamento, evitare.
censure: disapprovazione, criticare, censura.
complaisance: compiacenza.
courting: corteggiare, corteggiamento.
depart: partire, partite, partiamo, parti, partono, parto, andarsene.
desirous: desideroso.
diffidence: timidezza.

dignified: dignitoso.
disdain: sdegno, sdegnare.
dislike: avversione, ripugnanza, antipatia.
disposed: disposto.
glimpse: intravedere, occhiata, rapido sguardo.
intercourse: rapporti.
manners: educazione.
momentary: momentaneo.
niece: nipote.
obeyed: ubbidito, obbedito.

recollected: rammentato.
restrain: dominare, domina, domino, dominiamo, dominano, dominate, domini, reprimere, governare.
ridicule: ridicolo, ridicolizzare.
unbending: inflessibile.
ventured: avventurato.
witnessed: testimoniato.

Hertfordshire friends. Elizabeth, **construing** all this into a wish of hearing her speak of her sister, was pleased, and on this account, as well as some others, found herself, when their visitors left them, capable of considering the last half-hour with some satisfaction, though while it was passing, the **enjoyment** of it had been little. Eager to be alone, and **fearful** of inquiries or hints from her uncle and aunt, she stayed with them only long enough to hear their **favourable** opinion of Bingley, and then **hurried** away to dress.

But she had no reason to fear Mr. and Mrs. Gardiner's **curiosity**; it was not their wish to force her communication. It was evident that she was much better **acquainted** with Mr. Darcy than they had before any idea of; it was evident that he was very much in love with her. They saw much to interest, but nothing to **justify** inquiry.

Of Mr. Darcy it was now a matter of anxiety to think well; and, as far as their **acquaintance** reached, there was no fault to find. They could not be **untouched** by his **politeness**; and had they drawn his character from their own feelings and his **servant's** report, without any reference to any other account, the circle in Hertfordshire to which he was known would not have recognized it for Mr. Darcy. There was now an interest, however, in **believing** the **housekeeper**; and they soon became sensible that the authority of a servant who had known him since he was four years old, and whose own **manners** indicated **respectability**, was not to be **hastily** rejected. Neither had anything occurred in the intelligence of their Lambton friends that could **materially lessen** its weight. They had nothing to **accuse** him of but pride; pride he probably had, and if not, it would certainly be **imputed** by the **inhabitants** of a small market-town where the family did not visit. It was **acknowledged**, however, that he was a liberal man, and did much good among the poor.

With respect to Wickham, the travellers soon found that he was not held there in much **estimation**; for though the chief of his concerns with the son of his **patron** were **imperfectly** understood, it was yet a well-known fact that, on his **quitting** Derbyshire, he had left many debts behind him, which Mr. Darcy afterwards **discharged**.

Italian

accuse: accusare, accusate, accusi, accusiamo, accuso, accusano, accusa, caricare, caricano, carico, carichiamo.
acknowledged: riconosciuto.
acquaintance: conoscenza, conoscente.
acquainted: informato.
believing: credendo, credere.
construing: analizzando, interpretando.
curiosity: curiosità.
discharged: scaricato.
enjoyment: godimento.

estimation: stima, valutazione.
favourable: favorevole.
fearful: spaventoso, pauroso.
hastily: frettolosamente.
housekeeper: governante.
hurried: affrettato, frettoloso.
imperfectly: imperfettamente.
imputed: attribuito, imputato.
inhabitants: fruitori della casa.
justify: giustificare, giustificate, giustifico, giustifichiamo, giustificano, giustifici, giustifica.

lessen: diminuire, diminuiamo, diminuisci, diminuisco, diminuiscono, diminuite.
manners: educazione.
materially: materialmente.
patron: patrono, mecenate.
politeness: cortesia, garbo.
quitting: abbandonando.
respectability: rispettabilità.
servant: servire, servo, servitore.
untouched: intatto.

As for Elizabeth, her thoughts were at Pemberley this evening more than the last; and the evening, though as it passed it seemed long, was not long enough to determine her feelings towards *one* in that **mansion**; and she lay awake two whole hours endeavouring to make them out. She certainly did not hate him. No; **hatred** had vanished long ago, and she had almost as long been ashamed of ever feeling a dislike against him, that could be so called. The respect created by the conviction of his valuable qualities, though at first **unwillingly** admitted, had for some time ceased to be **repugnant** to her feeling; and it was now **heightened** into somewhat of a friendlier nature, by the **testimony** so highly in his favour, and bringing forward his **disposition** in so **amiable** a light, which yesterday had produced. But above all, above respect and **esteem**, there was a motive within her of **goodwill** which could not be overlooked. It was **gratitude**; gratitude, not merely for having once loved her, but for loving her still well enough to forgive all the petulance and **acrimony** of her manner in rejecting him, and all the **unjust** accusations **accompanying** her rejection. He who, she had been persuaded, would avoid her as his greatest enemy, seemed, on this **accidental** meeting, most eager to preserve the **acquaintance**, and without any **indelicate** display of regard, or any **peculiarity** of manner, where their two selves only were concerned, was **soliciting** the good opinion of her friends, and bent on making her known to his sister. Such a change in a man of so much pride exciting not only **astonishment** but gratitude--for to love, **ardent** love, it must be attributed; and as such its impression on her was of a sort to be encouraged, as by no means unpleasing, though it could not be exactly defined. She respected, she **esteemed**, she was grateful to him, she felt a real interest in his welfare; and she only wanted to know how far she wished that welfare to depend upon herself, and how far it would be for the happiness of both that she should employ the power, which her fancy told her she still **possessed**, of bringing on her the renewal of his addresses.

It had been settled in the evening between the aunt and the **niece**, that such a striking **civility** as Miss Darcy's in coming to see them on the very day of her arrival at Pemberley, for she had reached it only to a late breakfast, ought to be **imitated**, though it could not be equalled, by some **exertion** of **politeness** on

Italian

accidental: accidentale, fortuito.
accompanying: accompagnando.
acquaintance: conoscenza, conoscente.
acrimony: acrimonia.
amiable: amabile.
ardent: ardente.
astonishment: stupore, meraviglia, sorpresa.
civility: civiltà, cortesia.
disposition: disposizione, predisposizione, ingegno, talento.
esteem: stima, rispetto, stimare, considerazione, considerare, rispettare, riguardo.
esteemed: stimato.
exertion: sforzo.
goodwill: avviamento, buona volontà, avviamento commerciale.
gratitude: gratitudine, riconoscenza, grazie.
hatred: odio.
heightened: innalzato.
imitated: imitato.
indelicate: indelicato.
mansion: palazzo.
niece: nipote.
peculiarity: caratteristica, peculiarità.
politeness: cortesia, garbo.
possessed: posseduto.
repugnant: ripugnante.
soliciting: adescamento, sollecitando.
testimony: certificato attestato, testimonianza.
unjust: ingiusto.
unwillingly: malvolentieri.

their side; and, **consequently**, that it would be **highly expedient** to **wait** on her at Pemberley the following morning. They were, therefore, to go. Elizabeth was **pleased**; though when she asked **herself** the **reason**, she had very little to say in reply.

Mr. Gardiner left them **soon** after **breakfast**. The **fishing scheme** had been **renewed** the day before, and a **positive engagement** made of his **meeting** some of the gentlemen at Pemberley before **noon**.

Italian

breakfast: colazione, prima colazione.
consequently: conseguentemente.
engagement: fidanzamento, assunzione.
expedient: espediente, conveniente.
fishing: pesca, pescaggio.
herself: stesso, sè.
highly: altamente, estremamente.
meeting: incontrando, convegno, riunione, incontro, adunanza, comizio, assemblea.
noon: mezzogiorno, mezzodì.

pleased: contento, soddisfatto.
positive: positivo.
reason: ragione, causa, intelletto, ragionare, argomentare, motivo.
renewed: rinnovato.
scheme: progetto, schema, piano.
soon: fra poco, presto.
wait: aspettare, aspetto, aspetta, aspettano, aspettate, aspetti, aspettiamo, attesa.

CHAPTER 45

Convinced as Elizabeth now was that Miss Bingley's **dislike** of her had **originated** in **jealousy**, she could not help feeling how **unwelcome** her appearance at Pemberley must be to her, and was **curious** to know with how much **civility** on that lady's side the **acquaintance** would now be renewed.

On reaching the house, they were shown through the hall into the **saloon**, whose northern aspect **rendered** it **delightful** for summer. Its windows opening to the ground, admitted a most **refreshing** view of the high **woody** hills behind the house, and of the beautiful **oaks** and Spanish **chestnuts** which were **scattered** over the **intermediate lawn**.

In this house they were received by Miss Darcy, who was sitting there with Mrs. Hurst and Miss Bingley, and the lady with whom she lived in London. Georgiana's **reception** of them was very civil, but attended with all the **embarrassment** which, though **proceeding** from **shyness** and the fear of doing wrong, would easily give to those who felt themselves **inferior** the belief of her being proud and **reserved**. Mrs. Gardiner and her **niece**, however, did her justice, and pitied her.

By Mrs. Hurst and Miss Bingley they were noticed only by a **curtsey**; and, on their being **seated**, a **pause**, **awkward** as such pauses must always be, **succeeded** for a few moments. It was first broken by Mrs. Annesley, a **genteel**, agreeable-looking woman, whose **endeavour** to introduce some kind of **discourse** proved

Italian

acquaintance: conoscenza, conoscente.
awkward: goffo, sgraziato.
chestnuts: castagna, castagne.
civility: civiltà, cortesia.
curious: curioso.
curtsey: inchino.
delightful: delizioso, piacevole.
discourse: discorso.
dislike: avversione, ripugnanza, antipatia.
embarrassment: imbarazzo.
endeavour: tentare, tentativo,

sforzarsi.
genteel: distinto.
inferior: inferiore.
intermediate: intermedio.
jealousy: gelosia.
lawn: prato, tappeto erboso, linone.
niece: nipote.
oaks: querce.
originated: disceso.
pause: pausa, sosta.
proceeding: procedendo, procedimento.

reception: ricezione, ricevimento, accettazione, reception, portineria.
refreshing: rinfrescante.
rendered: reso.
reserved: riservato.
saloon: salone, berlina.
scattered: versato, sparso.
seated: seduto.
shyness: timidezza.
succeeded: riuscito.
unwelcome: sgradito.
woody: legnoso.

her to be more truly well-bred than either of the others; and between her and Mrs. Gardiner, with occasional help from Elizabeth, the conversation was carried on. Miss Darcy looked as if she wished for **courage** enough to join in it; and sometimes did **venture** a short sentence when there was least danger of its being heard.

Elizabeth soon saw that she was herself **closely** watched by Miss Bingley, and that she could not speak a word, especially to Miss Darcy, without calling her attention. This observation would not have **prevented** her from trying to talk to the latter, had they not been **seated** at an **inconvenient** distance; but she was not sorry to be **spared** the **necessity** of saying much. Her own thoughts were employing her. She expected every moment that some of the gentlemen would enter the room. She wished, she **feared** that the master of the house might be amongst them; and whether she wished or feared it most, she could **scarcely** determine. After sitting in this manner a quarter of an hour without hearing Miss Bingley's voice, Elizabeth was **roused** by **receiving** from her a cold inquiry after the health of her family. She answered with equal **indifference** and **brevity**, and the others said no more.

The next **variation** which their visit **afforded** was produced by the entrance of servants with cold meat, **cake**, and a variety of all the finest fruits in season; but this did not take place till after many a significant look and smile from Mrs. Annesley to Miss Darcy had been given, to **remind** her of her post. There was now employment for the whole party--for though they could not all talk, they could all eat; and the beautiful pyramids of **grapes**, nectarines, and peaches soon collected them round the table.

While thus **engaged**, Elizabeth had a fair opportunity of **deciding** whether she most feared or wished for the appearance of Mr. Darcy, by the feelings which **prevailed** on his **entering** the room; and then, though but a moment before she had believed her wishes to **predominate**, she began to **regret** that he came.

He had been some time with Mr. Gardiner, who, with two or three other gentlemen from the house, was engaged by the river, and had left him only on **learning** that the ladies of the family intended a visit to Georgiana that morning.

Italian

afforded: permesso.
brevity: brevità.
cake: torta, focaccia, la torta.
closely: attentamente.
courage: coraggio.
deciding: decidendo.
engaged: occupato, innestato, impegnato.
entering: entrando, entrare.
feared: temuto.
grapes: uva.
inconvenient: difficile, pesante,

inconveniente, incomodo.
indifference: indifferenza.
learning: imparando, apprendimento.
necessity: necessità, bisogno.
predominate: predominare, predominiamo, predominano, predomino, predominate, predomina, predomini.
prevailed: prevalso.
prevented: impedito, prevenuto.
receiving: ricevendo, accogliendo, ricezione, ricevere, ricevente.

regret: rincrescere, rammarico, rimpiangere, rimpianto, rincrescimento.
remind: ricordare, ricorda, ricordo, ricordiamo, ricordi, ricordate, ricordano.
roused: incitato, spronato, stimolato.
scarcely: appena, a stento.
seated: seduto.
spared: risparmiato.
variation: variazione, variante.
venture: arrischiare, impresa.

No sooner did he appear than Elizabeth **wisely** resolved to be perfectly easy and unembarrassed; a resolution the more necessary to be made, but perhaps not the more easily kept, because she saw that the suspicions of the whole party were **awakened** against them, and that there was scarcely an eye which did not **watch** his behaviour when he first came into the room.   In no **countenance** was **attentive** curiosity so strongly marked as in Miss Bingley's, in **spite** of the smiles which **overspread** her face whenever she spoke to one of its objects; for jealousy had not yet made her **desperate**, and her attentions to Mr. Darcy were by no means over.   Miss Darcy, on her brother's entrance, **exerted** herself much more to talk, and Elizabeth saw that he was anxious for his sister and herself to get **acquainted**, and forwarded as much as possible, every attempt at conversation on either side.   Miss Bingley saw all this likewise; and, in the **imprudence** of anger, took the first opportunity of saying, with **sneering civility**:

"Pray, Miss Eliza, are not the ----shire Militia removed from Meryton?   They must be a great loss to *your* family."

In Darcy's presence she dared not mention Wickham's name; but Elizabeth instantly **comprehended** that he was uppermost in her thoughts; and the various recollections connected with him gave her a moment's distress; but **exerting** herself **vigorously** to **repel** the ill-natured attack, she presently answered the question in a **tolerably** detached tone.   While she spoke, an **involuntary** glance showed her Darcy, with a **heightened complexion**, **earnestly** looking at her, and his sister overcome with confusion, and unable to lift up her eyes.   Had Miss Bingley known what pain she was then giving her **beloved** friend, she undoubtedly would have refrained from the hint; but she had merely intended to **discompose** Elizabeth by bringing forward the idea of a man to whom she believed her partial, to make her **betray** a **sensibility** which might **injure** her in Darcy's opinion, and, perhaps, to remind the latter of all the follies and absurdities by which some part of her family were connected with that corps. Not a **syllable** had ever reached her of Miss Darcy's **meditated** elopement.   To no creature had it been revealed, where **secrecy** was possible, except to Elizabeth; and from all Bingley's connections her brother was particularly anxious to

Italian

acquainted: informato.
attentive: attento, premuroso.
awakened: svegliato, risvegliato.
beloved: caro, adorato, amato.
betray: tradire, tradisci, tradite,
  tradisco, tradiamo, tradiscono.
civility: civiltà, cortesia.
complexion: carnagione.
comprehended: compreso.
countenance: approvare, viso.
desperate: disperato.
discompose: scomporre, agitare.

earnestly: seriamente.
exerted: esercitato, praticato.
exerting: esercitando, praticando.
heightened: innalzato.
imprudence: imprudenza.
injure: danneggiare, danneggia,
  danneggiamo, danneggiano,
  danneggiate, danneggio, danneggi,
  ferire, ferisco, feriscono, feriamo.
involuntary: involontario.
meditated: meditato.
overspread: coprire, cospargere.

repel: respingere, respingete, respingi,
  respingiamo, respingo, respingono.
secrecy: segretezza.
sensibility: sensibilità.
sneering: sogghignare.
spite: dispetto.
syllable: sillaba.
tolerably: tollerabilmente.
vigorously: vigorosamente.
watch: orologio, guardare, sorvegliare,
  guardia, sentinella, osservare.
wisely: saggiamente.

conceal it, from the very wish which Elizabeth had long ago **attributed** to him, of their becoming **hereafter** her own. He had certainly formed such a plan, and without meaning that it should effect his **endeavour** to separate him from Miss Bennet, it is **probable** that it might add something to his lively concern for the welfare of his friend.

Elizabeth's collected behaviour, however, soon quieted his emotion; and as Miss Bingley, **vexed** and disappointed, **dared** not approach nearer to Wickham, Georgiana also recovered in time, though not enough to be able to speak any more. Her brother, whose eye she feared to meet, scarcely **recollected** her interest in the affair, and the very **circumstance** which had been designed to turn his thoughts from Elizabeth seemed to have fixed them on her more and more **cheerfully**.

Their visit did not continue long after the question and answer above mentioned; and while Mr. Darcy was attending them to their carriage Miss Bingley was venting her feelings in criticisms on Elizabeth's person, behaviour, and dress. But Georgiana would not join her. Her brother's recommendation was enough to ensure her favour; his judgement could not **err**. And he had spoken in such terms of Elizabeth as to leave Georgiana without the power of finding her otherwise than lovely and **amiable**. When Darcy returned to the **saloon**, Miss Bingley could not help **repeating** to him some part of what she had been saying to his sister.

"How very ill Miss Eliza Bennet looks this morning, Mr. Darcy," she cried; "I never in my life saw anyone so much altered as she is since the winter. She is grown so **brown** and **coarse**! Louisa and I were **agreeing** that we should not have known her again."

However little Mr. Darcy might have liked such an address, he **contented** himself with **coolly** replying that he perceived no other **alteration** than her being rather **tanned**, no **miraculous** consequence of travelling in the summer.

"For my own part," she **rejoined**, "I must **confess** that I never could see any beauty in her. Her face is too thin; her **complexion** has no **brilliancy**; and her features are not at all handsome. Her **nose** wants character--there is nothing

Italian

agreeing: concordando, pattuendo.
alteration: alterazione, modifica, cambiamento, variazione.
amiable: amabile.
attributed: attribuito.
brilliancy: splendore.
brown: marrone, bruno, rosolare, castano.
cheerfully: allegramente.
circumstance: circostanza.
coarse: rozzo, grossolano.
complexion: carnagione.

conceal: nascondere, nascondono, nascondete, nascondi, nascondiamo, nascondo, occultare.
confess: confessare, confessa, confessano, confessate, confessi, confessiamo, confesso.
contented: contento.
coolly: frescamente.
dared: osato.
endeavour: tentare, tentativo, sforzarsi.
err: errare, errano, errate, erri, erriamo,

erro, erra, sbagliarsi.
hereafter: in futuro.
miraculous: miracoloso.
nose: naso, il naso, fiuto.
probable: probabile.
recollected: rammentato.
rejoined: riunito.
repeating: ripetendo.
saloon: salone, berlina.
tanned: abbronzato.
vexed: irritato, indispettito, vessato, contrariato.

marked in its lines. Her teeth are **tolerable**, but not out of the common way; and as for her eyes, which have sometimes been called so fine, I could never see anything **extraordinary** in them. They have a **sharp**, **shrewish** look, which I do not like at all; and in her air **altogether** there is a self-sufficiency without fashion, which is intolerable."

Persuaded as Miss Bingley was that Darcy **admired** Elizabeth, this was not the best method of **recommending** herself; but **angry** people are not always **wise**; and in seeing him at last look somewhat **nettled**, she had all the success she expected. He was **resolutely silent**, however, and, from a **determination** of making him speak, she continued:

"I remember, when we first knew her in Hertfordshire, how **amazed** we all were to find that she was a **reputed beauty**; and I particularly **recollect** your saying one night, after they had been **dining** at Netherfield, '*she* a beauty!--I should as soon call her mother a wit.' But afterwards she seemed to improve on you, and I believe you thought her rather pretty at one time."

"Yes," replied Darcy, who could contain himself no longer, "but *that* was only when I first saw her, for it is many months since I have considered her as one of the handsomest women of my acquaintance."

He then went away, and Miss Bingley was left to all the **satisfaction** of having forced him to say what gave no one any pain but herself.

Mrs. Gardiner and Elizabeth **talked** of all that had **occurred** during their visit, as they returned, except what had particularly interested them both. The look and behaviour of everybody they had seen were discussed, except of the person who had **mostly engaged** their attention. They talked of his sister, his friends, his house, his fruit--of everything but himself; yet Elizabeth was **longing** to know what Mrs. Gardiner thought of him, and Mrs. Gardiner would have been highly **gratified** by her niece's beginning the subject.

Italian

admired: ammirato.
altogether: tutto, complessivamente.
amazed: sbalordito, stupito, si stupito.
angry: arrabbiato, irato, stizzito.
beauty: bellezza.
determination: determinazione.
dining: pranzando, cenando.
engaged: occupato, innestato, impegnato.
extraordinary: straordinario, eccezionale.
gratified: gratificato.

longing: bramoso.
mostly: maggiormente, soprattutto.
nettled: irritato.
occurred: successo, accaduto.
recollect: rammenta, rammentano, rammentate, rammenti, rammentiamo, rammento, rammentare, ricordarsi.
recommending: raccomandando.
reputed: reputato, stimato, supposto.
resolutely: risoluto, risolutamente, decisamente.

satisfaction: soddisfazione.
sharp: affilato, aguzzo, acuto, tagliente, appuntito, piccante, giusto, giustamente, aspro, diesis, nitido.
shrewish: bisbetico.
silent: silenzioso, zitto.
talked: parlato.
tolerable: tollerabile.
wise: saggio, assennato.

CHAPTER 46

Elizabeth had been a good deal **disappointed** in not **finding** a letter from Jane on their first **arrival** at Lambton; and this **disappointment** had been **renewed** on each of the mornings that had now been spent there; but on the third her repining was over, and her sister **justified**, by the **receipt** of two letters from her at once, on one of which was **marked** that it had been missent elsewhere. Elizabeth was not **surprised** at it, as Jane had written the direction **remarkably ill**.

They had just been **preparing** to walk as the letters came in; and her **uncle** and **aunt**, leaving her to enjoy them in quiet, set off by themselves. The one missent must first be **attended** to; it had been written five days ago. The beginning **contained** an account of all their little parties and engagements, with such news as the country **afforded**; but the latter half, which was **dated** a day later, and written in evident **agitation**, gave more important **intelligence**. It was to this effect:

"Since writing the above, dearest Lizzy, something has **occurred** of a most **unexpected** and serious nature; but I am **afraid** of **alarming** you--be **assured** that we are all well. What I have to say **relates** to poor Lydia. An express came at twelve last night, just as we were all gone to bed, from Colonel Forster, to **inform** us that she was gone off to Scotland with one of his officers; to own the truth, with Wickham! Imagine our surprise. To Kitty, however, it does not seem so

Italian

afforded: permesso.
afraid: pauroso, inquieto, spaventato, angoscioso, impaurito.
agitation: agitazione.
alarming: allarmante.
arrival: arrivo, venuta.
assured: assicurato, certo.
attended: visitato, curato, assistito.
aunt: zia, la zia.
contained: contenuto.
dated: datato.
disappointed: deluso.

disappointment: delusione, disappunto.
finding: fondendo, fondando.
ill: malato, ammalato.
inform: informare, informano, informate, informi, informiamo, informo, informa, insegnare.
intelligence: intelligenza.
justified: giustificato.
marked: marcato, contrassegnato.
occurred: successo, accaduto.
preparing: preparando, allestendo,

apprestando.
receipt: ricevuta, quietanza, quietanzare, ricezione, scontrino.
relates: racconta.
remarkably: notevolmente.
renewed: rinnovato.
surprise: sorprendere, sorpresa, meraviglia, stupore.
surprised: sorpreso, sorpresa.
uncle: zio, lo zio.
unexpected: inatteso, imprevisto, inaspettato.

wholly unexpected. I am very, very sorry. So **imprudent** a match on both sides! But I am willing to hope the best, and that his character has been **misunderstood**. Thoughtless and **indiscreet** I can easily believe him, but this step (and let us **rejoice** over it) marks nothing bad at heart. His choice is **disinterested** at least, for he must know my father can give her nothing. Our poor mother is **sadly grieved**. My father bears it better. How **thankful** am I that we never let them know what has been said against him; we must forget it ourselves. They were off Saturday night about **twelve**, as is conjectured, but were not **missed** till yesterday morning at eight. The express was sent off directly. My dear Lizzy, they must have passed within ten miles of us. Colonel **Forster** gives us reason to expect him here soon. Lydia left a few lines for his wife, **informing** her of their intention. I must **conclude**, for I **cannot** be long from my poor mother. I am afraid you will not be able to make it out, but I hardly know what I have written."

Without allowing herself time for consideration, and **scarcely** knowing what she felt, Elizabeth on **finishing** this letter **instantly seized** the other, and opening it with the **utmost impatience**, read as **follows**: it had been written a day later than the conclusion of the first.

"By this time, my dearest sister, you have received my **hurried** letter; I wish this may be more **intelligible**, but though not **confined** for time, my head is so **bewildered** that I cannot answer for being **coherent**. Dearest Lizzy, I hardly know what I would write, but I have bad news for you, and it cannot be **delayed**. Imprudent as the marriage between Mr. Wickham and our poor Lydia would be, we are now anxious to be **assured** it has taken place, for there is but too much reason to fear they are not gone to Scotland. Colonel Forster came yesterday, having left Brighton the day before, not many hours after the express. Though Lydia's short letter to Mrs. F. gave them to understand that they were going to Gretna Green, something was dropped by Denny **expressing** his belief that W. never intended to go there, or to marry Lydia at all, which was repeated to Colonel F., who, instantly taking the **alarm**, set off from B. **intending** to trace their route. He did trace them easily to Clapham, but no further; for on entering

Italian

alarm: allarme, sveglia, allarmare.
assured: assicurato, certo.
bewildered: sconcertato.
cannot: non potere.
coherent: coerente.
conclude: concludere, concludo, concludono, concludiamo, concludi, concludete.
confined: limitato.
delayed: ritardato.
disinterested: disinteressato, imparziale.

expressing: esprimendo.
f: effe.
finishing: finendo, finitura, finire, finissaggio, ultimando, rifinitura.
follows: segue.
grieved: accorato, addolorato.
hurried: affrettato, frettoloso.
impatience: impazienza.
imprudent: imprudente.
indiscreet: indiscreto.
informing: informando.
instantly: direttamente,

istantaneamente, immediatamente.
intelligible: intelligibile.
intending: intendendo.
missed: mancato.
misunderstood: incompreso, frainteso.
rejoice: allietare, rallegrare.
sadly: tristemente.
scarcely: appena, a stento.
seized: afferrato.
thankful: riconoscente, grato.
twelve: dodici.
utmost: massimo.

that place, they removed into a hackney coach, and dismissed the **chaise** that brought them from Epsom. All that is known after this is, that they were seen to continue the London road. I know not what to think. After making every possible inquiry on that side London, Colonel F. came on into Hertfordshire, **anxiously renewing** them at all the turnpikes, and at the inns in Barnet and Hatfield, but without any success--no such people had been seen to pass through. With the kindest concern he came on to Longbourn, and broke his apprehensions to us in a manner most **creditable** to his heart. I am **sincerely grieved** for him and Mrs. F., but no one can throw any blame on them. Our **distress**, my dear Lizzy, is very great. My father and mother believe the worst, but I **cannot** think so ill of him. Many circumstances might make it more **eligible** for them to be married **privately** in town than to pursue their first plan; and even if *he* could form such a design against a young woman of Lydia's connections, which is not likely, can I suppose her so lost to everything? Impossible! I grieve to find, however, that Colonel F. is not **disposed** to depend upon their marriage; he shook his head when I expressed my hopes, and said he fear W. was not a man to be **trusted**. My poor mother is really ill, and keeps her room. Could she **exert** herself, it would be better; but this is not to be expected. And as to my father, I never in my life saw him so affected. Poor Kitty has anger for having **concealed** their **attachment**; but as it was a matter of confidence, one cannot wonder. I am truly glad, dearest Lizzy, that you have been **spared** something of these **distressing** scenes; but now, as the first shock is over, shall I own that I long for your return? I am not so **selfish**, however, as to press for it, if **inconvenient**. Adieu! I take up my pen again to do what I have just told you I would not; but circumstances are such that I cannot help **earnestly begging** you all to come here as soon as possible. I know my dear uncle and aunt so well, that I am not afraid of requesting it, though I have still something more to ask of the former. My father is going to London with Colonel Forster **instantly**, to try to discover her. What he means to do I am sure I know not; but his **excessive** distress will not allow him to pursue any measure in the best and **safest** way, and Colonel Forster is **obliged** to be at Brighton again to-morrow evening. In such and exigence, my uncle's advice and assistance would be everything in the

Italian

anxiously: ansiosamente.
attachment: accessorio, allegato, attaccamento.
begging: mendicando.
cannot: non potere.
chaise: calesse.
concealed: nascosto.
creditable: lodevole.
disposed: disposto.
distress: pericolo.
distressing: doloroso, penoso, angoscioso.

earnestly: seriamente.
eligible: eleggibile.
excessive: eccessivo.
exert: praticare, esercitare, eserciti, pratico, pratichiamo, pratichi, praticate, praticano, pratica, esercitiamo, esercitate.
grieve: affliggersi, addolorare, addolorarsi.
grieved: accorato, addolorato.
inconvenient: difficile, pesante, inconveniente, incomodo.

instantly: direttamente, istantaneamente, immediatamente.
obliged: obbligato.
privately: privatamente.
renewing: rinnovando.
safest: il più sicuro.
selfish: egoistico, egoista.
sincerely: sinceramente, francamente.
spared: risparmiato.
trusted: fidato.

world; he will immediately **comprehend** what I must feel, and I **rely** upon his goodness."

"Oh! where, where is my uncle?" cried Elizabeth, darting from her seat as she finished the letter, in **eagerness** to follow him, without **losing** a moment of the time so **precious**; but as she reached the door it was opened by a servant, and Mr. Darcy appeared. Her pale face and **impetuous** manner made him start, and before he could recover himself to speak, she, in whose mind every idea was **superseded** by Lydia's situation, hastily exclaimed, "I beg your pardon, but I must leave you. I must find Mr. Gardiner this moment, on business that **cannot** be delayed; I have not an instant to lose."

"Good God! what is the matter?" cried he, with more feeling than **politeness**; then **recollecting** himself, "I will not **detain** you a minute; but let me, or let the servant go after Mr. and Mrs. Gardiner. You are not well enough; you cannot go yourself."

Elizabeth hesitated, but her knees **trembled** under her and she felt how little would be gained by her attempting to pursue them. Calling back the servant, therefore, she commissioned him, though in so **breathless** an accent as made her almost **unintelligible**, to fetch his master and mistress home instantly.

On his **quitting** the room she sat down, unable to support herself, and looking so **miserably** ill, that it was impossible for Darcy to leave her, or to **refrain** from saying, in a tone of **gentleness** and **commiseration**, "Let me call your maid. Is there nothing you could take to give you present relief? A **glass** of wine; shall I get you one? You are very ill."

"No, I thank you," she replied, endeavouring to recover herself. "There is nothing the matter with me. I am quite well; I am only **distressed** by some dreadful news which I have just received from Longbourn."

She burst into tears as she **alluded** to it, and for a few minutes could not speak another word. Darcy, in **wretched suspense**, could only say something **indistinctly** of his concern, and observe her in **compassionate** silence. At length she spoke again. "I have just had a letter from Jane, with such dreadful news. It

Italian

alluded: alluso.
breathless: ansante, senza fiato.
cannot: non potere.
commiseration: commiserazione.
compassionate: compassionevole.
comprehend: comprendere, comprendo, comprendono, comprendiamo, comprendi, comprendete.
detain: ritenere, riteniamo, ritieni, ritenete, ritengo, ritengono.
distressed: afflitto.

eagerness: impazienza.
gentleness: delicatezza.
glass: vetro, bicchiere, cristallo.
impetuous: impetuoso.
indistinctly: indistintamente.
losing: perdendo.
miserably: miserabilmente, miseramente.
politeness: cortesia, garbo.
precious: prezioso.
quitting: abbandonando.
recollecting: rammentando.

refrain: ritornello, astenersi.
rely: confida, confidano, confidate, confidi, confidiamo, confido, confidare, fare affidamento, fidarsi.
superseded: sostituito, soppiantato, rimpiazzato.
suspense: apprensione.
trembled: tremato.
unintelligible: inintelligibile, incomprensibile.
wretched: misero, miserabile, povero, infelice.

cannot be **concealed** from anyone. My younger sister has left all her friends--has **eloped**; has thrown herself into the power of--of Mr. Wickham. They are gone off together from Brighton. *You* know him too well to doubt the rest. She has no money, no connections, nothing that can **tempt** him to--she is lost for ever."

Darcy was fixed in **astonishment**. "When I consider," she added in a yet more **agitated** voice, "that I might have **prevented** it! I, who knew what he was. Had I but explained some part of it only--some part of what I learnt, to my own family! Had his character been known, this could not have happened. But it is all--all too late now."

"I am **grieved** indeed," cried Darcy; "grieved--shocked. But is it certain--absolutely certain?"

"Oh, yes! They left Brighton together on Sunday night, and were traced almost to London, but not beyond; they are certainly not gone to Scotland."

"And what has been done, what has been attempted, to recover her?"

"My father is gone to London, and Jane has written to **beg** my uncle's immediate assistance; and we shall be off, I hope, in half-an-hour. But nothing can be done--I know very well that nothing can be done. How is such a man to be worked on? How are they even to be discovered? I have not the smallest hope. It is every way horrible!"

Darcy shook his head in silent **acquiescence**.

"When *my* eyes were opened to his real character--Oh! had I known what I ought, what I **dared** to do! But I knew not--I was afraid of doing too much. Wretched, **wretched** mistake!"

Darcy made no answer. He seemed **scarcely** to hear her, and was walking up and down the room in **earnest meditation**, his **brow contracted**, his air **gloomy**. Elizabeth soon observed, and instantly understood it. Her power was **sinking**; everything *must* sink under such a proof of family weakness, such an **assurance** of the deepest **disgrace**. She could neither wonder nor **condemn**, but the belief of his self-conquest brought nothing to her **consolatory** to her **bosom**, afforded

Italian

acquiescence: acquiescenza.
agitated: agitato.
assurance: assicurazione, promessa.
astonishment: stupore, meraviglia, sorpresa.
beg: mendicare, mendicano, mendica, mendicate, mendico, mendichiamo, mendichi, chiedere, elemosinare, supplicare.
bosom: petto, seno.
brow: sopracciglio, fronte.
concealed: nascosto.

condemn: condannare, condannate, condanno, condanni, condannano, condanniamo, condanna, biasimare, biasimo, biasimiamo, biasimi.
consolatory: consolatorio.
contracted: contratto.
dared: osato.
disgrace: vergogna, disgrazia, disonorare, disonore.
earnest: serio, caparra.
eloped: scappato.
gloomy: tetro, tenebroso, oscuro.

grieved: accorato, addolorato.
meditation: meditazione.
prevented: impedito, prevenuto.
scarcely: appena, a stento.
sink: lavandino, lavello, affondare, acquaio.
sinking: affondamento, sprofondamento.
tempt: tentare, tento, tentiamo, tenti, tentate, tenta, tentano.
wretched: misero, miserabile, povero, infelice.

no palliation of her distress. It was, on the **contrary**, exactly calculated to make her understand her own wishes; and never had she so honestly felt that she could have loved him, as now, when all love must be **vain**.

But **self**, though it would **intrude**, could not **engross** her. Lydia--the humiliation, the misery she was bringing on them all, soon swallowed up every private care; and covering her face with her **handkerchief**, Elizabeth was soon lost to everything else; and, after a pause of several minutes, was only recalled to a sense of her situation by the voice of her companion, who, in a manner which, though it spoke compassion, spoke likewise restraint, said, "I am afraid you have been long desiring my absence, nor have I anything to **plead** in excuse of my stay, but real, though **unavailing** concern. Would to Heaven that anything could be either said or done on my part that might offer consolation to such distress! But I will not **torment** you with vain wishes, which may seem **purposely** to ask for your thanks. This unfortunate affair will, I fear, prevent my sister's having the pleasure of seeing you at Pemberley to-day."

"Oh, yes. Be so kind as to **apologise** for us to Miss Darcy. Say that urgent business **calls** us home immediately. Conceal the unhappy truth as long as it is possible, I know it **cannot** be long."

He readily assured her of his secrecy; again expressed his sorrow for her distress, wished it a happier conclusion than there was at present reason to hope, and leaving his **compliments** for her relations, with only one serious, **parting** look, went away.

As he quitted the room, Elizabeth felt how **improbable** it was that they should ever see each other again on such terms of **cordiality** as had marked their several meetings in Derbyshire; and as she threw a **retrospective** glance over the whole of their acquaintance, so full of contradictions and **varieties**, sighed at the perverseness of those feelings which would now have **promoted** its continuance, and would formerly have **rejoiced** in its **termination**.

If gratitude and **esteem** are good foundations of affection, Elizabeth's change of sentiment will be neither improbable nor **faulty**. But if otherwise--if regard **springing** from such sources is unreasonable or **unnatural**, in comparison of

Italian

apologise: scusarsi.
calls: chiama.
cannot: non potere.
compliments: complimenti.
contrary: contrario.
cordiality: cordialità.
engross: assorbo, assorbono, assorbiamo, assorbi, assorbite, assorbire.
esteem: stima, rispetto, stimare, considerazione, considerare, rispettare, riguardo.

faulty: difettoso.
handkerchief: fazzoletto.
improbable: improbabile.
intrude: impongo, imponiamo, imponete, imponi, impongono, imporre.
parting: separazione, divisione.
plead: peroro, supplico, supplichiamo, supplichi, supplicate, supplica, peroriamo, perori, perorano, perora, imploro.
promoted: promosso.

purposely: intenzionalmente.
rejoiced: allietato, gioito, rallegrato.
retrospective: retrospettiva, retrospettivo.
self: stesso.
springing: saltare, correzione.
termination: fine, terminazione.
torment: tormento.
unavailing: inutile.
unnatural: innaturale.
vain: vanitoso, vano.
varieties: varietà.

what is so often described as arising on a first interview with its object, and even before two words have been **exchanged**, nothing can be said in her defence, except that she had given somewhat of a trial to the latter method in her **partiality** for Wickham, and that its ill success might, perhaps, **authorise** her to seek the other less interesting mode of **attachment**. Be that as it may, she saw him go with regret; and in this early example of what Lydia's **infamy** must produce, found **additional anguish** as she reflected on that **wretched** business. Never, since reading Jane's second letter, had she **entertained** a hope of Wickham's meaning to marry her. No one but Jane, she thought, could **flatter** herself with such an expectation. Surprise was the least of her feelings on this development. While the contents of the first letter remained in her mind, she was all surprise--all **astonishment** that Wickham should marry a girl whom it was impossible he could marry for money; and how Lydia could ever have attached him had appeared **incomprehensible**. But now it was all too natural. For such an attachment as this she might have sufficient charms; and though she did not suppose Lydia to be **deliberately engaging** in an elopement without the intention of marriage, she had no difficulty in believing that neither her virtue nor her understanding would preserve her from falling an easy prey.

She had never perceived, while the regiment was in Hertfordshire, that Lydia had any partiality for him; but she was convinced that Lydia wanted only encouragement to attach herself to anybody. Sometimes one officer, sometimes another, had been her favourite, as their attentions raised them in her opinion. Her affections had continually been **fluctuating** but never without an object. The **mischief** of **neglect** and mistaken **indulgence** towards such a girl--oh! how **acutely** did she now feel it!

She was wild to be at home--to hear, to see, to be upon the spot to share with Jane in the cares that must now fall wholly upon her, in a family so **deranged**, a father absent, a mother **incapable** of **exertion**, and requiring constant **attendance**; and though almost persuaded that nothing could be done for Lydia, her uncle's interference seemed of the **utmost** importance, and till he entered the room her **impatience** was severe. Mr. and Mrs. Gardiner had hurried back in

Italian

acutely: acutamente.
additional: aggiuntivo, addizionale, supplementare.
anguish: angoscia.
astonishment: stupore, meraviglia, sorpresa.
attach: fissare, attaccare, fissi, attacca, fissate, fissano, fisso, attacchi, attacchiamo, attaccate, attaccano.
attachment: accessorio, allegato, attaccamento.
attendance: servizio, presenza.

authorise: autorizzare.
deliberately: apposta, deliberatamente.
deranged: squilibrato.
engaging: innestando, attraente.
entertained: intrattenuto.
exchanged: scambiato.
exertion: sforzo.
flatter: lusingare, lusingate, lusingo, lusinghi, lusingano, lusinghiamo, lusinga, adulare.
fluctuating: fluttuando.

impatience: impazienza.
incapable: incapace.
incomprehensible: incomprensibile.
indulgence: indulgenza.
infamy: infamia.
mischief: birichinata.
neglect: trascurare, negligere, negligenza, trascuratezza.
partiality: parzialità, predilezione.
utmost: massimo.
wretched: misero, miserabile, povero, infelice.

alarm, supposing by the servant's account that their **niece** was taken suddenly ill; but **satisfying** them instantly on that head, she **eagerly communicated** the cause of their **summons**, reading the two letters **aloud**, and **dwelling** on the **postscript** of the last with **trembling** energy, though Lydia had never been a favourite with them, Mr. and Mrs. Gardiner could not but be deeply **afflicted**. Not Lydia only, but all were concerned in it; and after the first exclamations of surprise and horror, Mr. Gardiner promised every assistance in his power. Elizabeth, though expecting no less, **thanked** him with tears of **gratitude**; and all three being **actuated** by one spirit, everything relating to their journey was **speedily** settled. They were to be off as soon as possible. "But what is to be done about Pemberley?" cried Mrs. Gardiner. "John told us Mr. Darcy was here when you sent for us; was it so?"

"Yes; and I told him we should not be able to keep our **engagement**. *that* is all settled."

"What is all settled?" repeated the other, as she ran into her room to prepare. "And are they upon such terms as for her to **disclose** the real truth? Oh, that I knew how it was!"

But wishes were **vain**, or at least could only serve to **amuse** her in the **hurry** and confusion of the following hour. Had Elizabeth been at leisure to be **idle**, she would have remained certain that all employment was impossible to one so **wretched** as herself; but she had her share of business as well as her aunt, and amongst the rest there were **notes** to be written to all their friends at Lambton, with false excuses for their sudden departure. An hour, however, saw the whole **completed**; and Mr. Gardiner meanwhile having settled his account at the **inn**, nothing remained to be done but to go; and Elizabeth, after all the **misery** of the morning, found herself, in a shorter **space** of time than she could have supposed, **seated** in the carriage, and on the road to Longbourn.

Italian

actuated: azionato.
afflicted: afflitto.
aloud: ad alta voce.
amuse: divertire, divertiamo, divertono, diverto, diverti, divertite.
communicated: comunicato.
completed: finito, completato, terminato.
disclose: svelare.
dwelling: dimorando, abitando, dimora, abitazione.
eagerly: ardentemente.
engagement: fidanzamento, assunzione.
gratitude: gratitudine, riconoscenza, grazie.
hurry: affrettarsi, fretta.
idle: ozioso, pigro, folle, inattivo.
inn: locanda, osteria.
misery: miseria.
niece: nipote.
notes: note.
postscript: poscritto.
satisfying: soddisfacendo,
accontentando, soddisfacente.
seated: seduto.
space: spazio, intervallo.
speedily: rapidamente.
summons: citazione, ingiunzione.
thanked: ringraziato.
trembling: tremolante, tremulo, tremolio, tremito, tremante, tremore, tremare.
vain: vanitoso, vano.
wretched: misero, miserabile, povero, infelice.

CHAPTER 47

"I have been thinking it over again, Elizabeth," said her **uncle**, as they **drove** from the town; "and really, upon serious consideration, I am much more **inclined** than I was to **judge** as your **eldest sister** does on the matter. It **appears** to me so very **unlikely** that any young man should form such a design against a girl who is by no means **unprotected** or **friendless**, and who was actually **staying** in his colonel's family, that I am **strongly** inclined to hope the best. Could he expect that her friends would not **step** forward? Could he expect to be noticed again by the **regiment**, after such an **affront** to Colonel Forster? His **temptation** is not **adequate** to the risk!"

"Do you really think so?" cried Elizabeth, **brightening** up for a moment.

"Upon my word," said Mrs. Gardiner, "I begin to be of your uncle's **opinion**. It is really too great a **violation** of **decency**, **honour**, and interest, for him to be **guilty** of. I **cannot** think so very **ill** of Wickham. Can you yourself, Lizzy, so **wholly** give him up, as to believe him **capable** of it?"

"Not, perhaps, of **neglecting** his own interest; but of every other neglect I can believe him capable. If, indeed, it should be so! But I **dare** not hope it. Why should they not go on to Scotland if that had been the case?"

"In the first place," replied Mr. Gardiner, "there is no **absolute proof** that they are not gone to Scotland."

Italian

absolute: assoluto, completo.
adequate: adeguato, sufficiente.
affront: affronto, insulto, insultare.
appears: appare.
brightening: schiarimento.
cannot: non potere.
capable: capace, abile, idoneo, adatto.
dare: osare, oso, osiamo, osi, osate, osano, osa, sfida.
decency: decenza.
drove: gregge.
eldest: maggiore, il più vecchio.

friendless: senza amici.
guilty: colpevole.
honour: onore.
ill: malato, ammalato.
inclined: disposto, inclinato, propenso.
judge: giudice, giudicare, critico.
neglect: trascurare, negligere, negligenza, trascuratezza.
opinion: parere, opinione, avviso.
proof: prova, bozza, dimostrazione, provino, impermeabilizzare,

resistente.
regiment: reggimento.
sister: sorella, la sorella.
staying: stando, restando.
step: passo, gradino, scalino.
strongly: fortemente.
temptation: tentazione.
uncle: zio, lo zio.
unlikely: improbabile.
unprotected: indifeso.
violation: violazione, infrazione.
wholly: interamente, completamente.

"Oh! but their **removing** from the **chaise** into a hackney coach is such a **presumption**! And, besides, no traces of them were to be found on the Barnet road."

"Well, then--supposing them to be in London. They may be there, though for the purpose of **concealment**, for no more exceptional purpose. It is not likely that money should be very **abundant** on either side; and it might strike them that they could be more **economically**, though less expeditiously, married in London than in Scotland."

"But why all this **secrecy**? Why any fear of **detection**? Why must their marriage be private? Oh, no, no--this is not likely. His most particular friend, you see by Jane's account, was persuaded of his never **intending** to marry her. Wickham will never marry a woman without some money. He **cannot** afford it. And what claims has Lydia--what **attraction** has she beyond youth, health, and good humour that could make him, for her sake, **forego** every chance of benefiting himself by **marrying** well? As to what **restraint** the apprehensions of **disgrace** in the **corps** might throw on a **dishonourable** elopement with her, I am not able to judge; for I know nothing of the effects that such a step might produce. But as to your other **objection**, I am afraid it will hardly hold good. Lydia has no brothers to step forward; and he might imagine, from my father's behaviour, from his **indolence** and the little attention he has ever seemed to give to what was going forward in his family, that *he* would do as little, and think as little about it, as any father could do, in such a matter."

"But can you think that Lydia is so lost to everything but love of him as to consent to live with him on any terms other than marriage?"

"It does seem, and it is most **shocking** indeed," replied Elizabeth, with tears in her eyes, "that a sister's sense of **decency** and virtue in such a point should admit of doubt. But, really, I know not what to say. Perhaps I am not doing her justice. But she is very young; she has never been taught to think on serious subjects; and for the last half-year, **nay**, for a twelvemonth--she has been given up to nothing but **amusement** and **vanity**. She has been allowed to **dispose** of her time in the most **idle** and **frivolous** manner, and to adopt any opinions that

Italian

abundant: abbondante.

amusement: divertimento, spasso, svago.

attraction: attrazione, forza attrattiva, attrattiva.

cannot: non potere.

chaise: calesse.

concealment: occultamento, nascondiglio, reticenza.

corps: corpo.

decency: decenza.

detection: rivelazione, scoperta.

disgrace: vergogna, disgrazia, disonorare, disonore.

dishonourable: disonorevole.

dispose: disporre, disponete, dispongo, dispongono, disponi, disponiamo.

economically: economicamente.

forego: precedere.

frivolous: vanitoso, frivolo.

idle: ozioso, pigro, folle, inattivo.

indolence: indolenza.

intending: intendendo.

marrying: sposandosi.

nay: anzi.

objection: obiezione, opposizione.

presumption: presunzione, supposizione.

removing: togliendo, asportando, rimuovendo.

restraint: restrizione.

secrecy: segretezza.

shocking: irritante, scandaloso.

vanity: vanità.

came in her way. Since the ----shire were first quartered in Meryton, nothing but love, **flirtation**, and officers have been in her head. She has been doing everything in her power by thinking and talking on the subject, to give greater-- what shall I call it? **susceptibility** to her feelings; which are naturally **lively** enough. And we all know that Wickham has every **charm** of person and address that can **captivate** a woman."

"But you see that Jane," said her **aunt**, "does not think so very **ill** of Wickham as to believe him capable of the attempt."

"Of whom does Jane ever think ill? And who is there, whatever might be their former **conduct**, that she would think capable of such an attempt, till it were proved against them? But Jane knows, as well as I do, what Wickham really is. We both know that he has been profligate in every sense of the word; that he has neither **integrity** nor **honour**; that he is as **false** and **deceitful** as he is insinuating."

"And do you really know all this?" cried Mrs. Gardiner, whose **curiosity** as to the **mode** of her **intelligence** was all alive.

"I do indeed," replied Elizabeth, **colouring**. "I told you, the other day, of his **infamous** behaviour to Mr. Darcy; and you yourself, when last at Longbourn, heard in what manner he spoke of the man who had **behaved** with such **forbearance** and **liberality** towards him. And there are other circumstances which I am not at liberty--which it is not worth while to **relate**; but his lies about the whole Pemberley family are **endless**. From what he said of Miss Darcy I was **thoroughly** prepared to see a **proud, reserved, disagreeable** girl. Yet he knew to the **contrary** himself. He must know that she was as **amiable** and **unpretending** as we have found her."

"But does Lydia know nothing of this? can she be **ignorant** of what you and Jane seem so well to understand?"

"Oh, yes!--that, that is the worst of all. Till I was in Kent, and saw so much both of Mr. Darcy and his **relation** Colonel Fitzwilliam, I was ignorant of the truth myself. And when I returned home, the ----shire was to leave Meryton in a

Italian

amiable: amabile.
aunt: zia, la zia.
behaved: agito, comportato.
captivate: affascinare.
charm: fascino, incanto.
colouring: coloritura.
conduct: condotta, condurre, guidare, comportamento.
contrary: contrario.
curiosity: curiosità.
deceitful: ingannevole, falso.
disagreeable: sgradevole.

endless: senza fine, infinito, interminabile.
false: falso, finto.
flirtation: flirt.
forbearance: pazienza.
honour: onore.
ignorant: ignorante.
ill: malato, ammalato.
infamous: infame.
integrity: integrità.
intelligence: intelligenza.
liberality: liberalità.

lively: vivace, spiritoso, vivo, animato, vispo.
mode: modo, moda, maniera.
proud: orgoglioso, fiero.
relate: raccontare, raccontiamo, racconta, raccontano, raccontate, racconti, racconto, narrare.
relation: relazione, rapporto.
reserved: riservato.
susceptibility: suscettibilità.
thoroughly: completamente.
unpretending: senza pretese.

week or fortnight's time. As that was the case, neither Jane, to whom I related the whole, nor I, thought it necessary to make our knowledge public; for of what use could it **apparently** be to any one, that the good opinion which all the **neighbourhood** had of him should then be **overthrown**? And even when it was settled that Lydia should go with Mrs. Forster, the **necessity** of opening her eyes to his character never occurred to me. That *she* could be in any danger from the **deception** never entered my head. That such a consequence as *this* could **ensue**, you may easily believe, was far enough from my thoughts."

"When they all removed to Brighton, therefore, you had no reason, I suppose, to believe them **fond** of each other?"

"Not the slightest. I can remember no **symptom** of **affection** on either side; and had anything of the kind been **perceptible**, you must be aware that **ours** is not a family on which it could be thrown away. When first he entered the **corps**, she was ready enough to **admire** him; but so we all were. Every girl in or near Meryton was out of her **senses** about him for the first two months; but he never **distinguished** *her* by any particular attention; and, consequently, after a **moderate** period of **extravagant** and wild **admiration**, her **fancy** for him gave way, and others of the **regiment**, who treated her with more distinction, again became her favourites."

It may be easily believed, that however little of **novelty** could be added to their fears, hopes, and conjectures, on this interesting subject, by its repeated discussion, no other could **detain** them from it long, during the whole of the journey. From Elizabeth's thoughts it was never **absent**. Fixed there by the keenest of all **anguish**, self-reproach, she could find no **interval** of ease or **forgetfulness**.

They travelled as expeditiously as possible, and, **sleeping** one night on the road, reached Longbourn by dinner time the next day. It was a comfort to Elizabeth to consider that Jane could not have been **wearied** by long expectations.

Italian

absent: assente.
admiration: ammirazione.
admire: ammirare, ammiriamo, ammira, ammirano, ammiro, ammiri, ammirate.
affection: affetto, affezione, amore.
anguish: angoscia.
apparently: evidentemente, apparentemente.
corps: corpo.
deception: inganno.
detain: ritenere, riteniamo, ritieni,

ritenete, ritengo, ritengono.
distinguished: distinto.
ensue: seguire, segui, seguono, seguo, seguiamo, seguite, conseguire, risultare.
extravagant: stravagante.
fancy: figurarsi, capriccio, immaginazione.
fond: tenero, affettuoso, affezionato.
forgetfulness: dimenticanza.
interval: intervallo.
moderate: moderato, moderare.

necessity: necessità, bisogno.
neighbourhood: circondario, distretto, vicinato, quartiere.
novelty: novità.
ours: nostro.
overthrown: rovesciato.
perceptible: percettibile.
regiment: reggimento.
senses: sensi.
sleeping: dormendo, addormentato.
symptom: sintomo, segno.
wearied: stanco.

The little Gardiners, **attracted** by the sight of a **chaise**, were standing on the steps of the house as they entered the **paddock**; and, when the **carriage** drove up to the door, the **joyful** surprise that **lighted** up their faces, and displayed itself over their whole bodies, in a variety of **capers** and frisks, was the first **pleasing earnest** of their welcome.

Elizabeth jumped out; and, after giving each of them a **hasty kiss, hurried** into the **vestibule**, where Jane, who came running down from her mother's **apartment**, immediately met her.

Elizabeth, as she **affectionately embraced** her, whilst tears **filled** the eyes of both, lost not a moment in asking whether anything had been heard of the fugitives.

"Not yet," replied Jane. "But now that my dear **uncle** is come, I hope everything will be well."

"Is my father in town?"

"Yes, he went on Tuesday, as I wrote you word."

"And have you heard from him often?"

"We have heard only twice. He wrote me a few lines on Wednesday to say that he had arrived in **safety**, and to give me his **directions**, which I particularly **begged** him to do. He merely added that he should not write again till he had something of importance to mention."

"And my mother--how is she? How are you all?"

"My mother is **tolerably** well, I trust; though her spirits are **greatly shaken**. She is **upstairs** and will have great **satisfaction** in seeing you all. She does not yet leave her dressing-room. **Mary** and Kitty are, thank Heaven, are quite well."

"But you--how are you?" cried Elizabeth. "You look **pale**. How much you must have gone through!"

Her sister, however, **assured** her of her being perfectly well; and their conversation, which had been **passing** while Mr. and Mrs. Gardiner were **engaged** with their children, was now put an end to by the approach of the

---

Italian

affectionately: affettuosamente.
apartment: appartamento.
assured: assicurato, certo.
attracted: attirato, attratto.
begged: mendicato.
capers: capperi.
carriage: vettura, carrello, vagone, carro, carrozza.
chaise: calesse.
directions: avvertenze.
earnest: serio, caparra.
elizabeth: Elisabetta.

embraced: abbracciato.
engaged: occupato, innestato, impegnato.
filled: pieno.
greatly: molto, grandemente.
hasty: affrettato, frettoloso.
hurried: affrettato, frettoloso.
joyful: gioioso.
jumped: saltato.
kiss: bacio, baciare, baciarsi.
lighted: illuminato.
mary: Maria.

paddock: paddock, recinto.
pale: pallido, smorto, impallidire.
passing: passeggero, passare, passaggio.
pleasing: piacevole.
safety: sicurezza.
satisfaction: soddisfazione.
shaken: scosso.
tolerably: tollerabilmente.
uncle: zio, lo zio.
upstairs: di sopra.
vestibule: vestibolo.

whole party. Jane ran to her uncle and aunt, and welcomed and **thanked** them both, with **alternate** smiles and tears.

When they were all in the drawing-room, the questions which Elizabeth had already asked were of course repeated by the others, and they soon found that Jane had no intelligence to give. The **sanguine** hope of good, however, which the **benevolence** of her heart suggested had not yet **deserted** her; she still expected that it would all end well, and that every morning would bring some letter, either from Lydia or her father, to explain their **proceedings**, and, perhaps, **announce** their marriage.

Mrs. **Bennet**, to whose **apartment** they all **repaired**, after a few minutes' conversation together, received them exactly as might be expected; with tears and lamentations of regret, invectives against the **villainous** conduct of Wickham, and complaints of her own sufferings and ill-usage; **blaming** everybody but the person to whose ill-judging **indulgence** the errors of her daughter must **principally** be **owing**.

"If I had been able," said she, "to carry my point in going to Brighton, with all my family, *this* would not have happened; but poor dear Lydia had nobody to take care of her. Why did the Forsters ever let her go out of their sight? I am sure there was some great **neglect** or other on their side, for she is not the kind of girl to do such a thing if she had been well looked after. I always thought they were very **unfit** to have the charge of her; but I was **overruled**, as I always am. Poor dear child! And now here's Mr. Bennet gone away, and I know he will **fight** Wickham, wherever he **meets** him and then he will be **killed**, and what is to become of us all? The Collinses will turn us out before he is cold in his **grave**, and if you are not kind to us, brother, I do not know what we shall do."

They all **exclaimed** against such **terrific** ideas; and Mr. Gardiner, after general assurances of his **affection** for her and all her family, told her that he meant to be in London the very next day, and would assist Mr. Bennet in every **endeavour** for **recovering** Lydia.

"Do not give way to **useless** alarm," added he; "though it is right to be prepared for the worst, there is no occasion to look on it as certain. It is not quite

Italian

affection: affetto, affezione, amore.
alternate: alternare, alterno, alternato.
announce: annunciare, annunciate, annunci, annuncia, annunciamo, annunciano, annunziare, annuncio, annunziate, annunzi, annunzia.
apartment: appartamento.
benevolence: benevolenza.
bennet: cariofillata, erba benedetta.
blaming: biasimare.
deserted: abbandonato, deserto.
endeavour: tentare, tentativo,

sforzarsi.
exclaimed: esclamato.
fight: combattere, duellare, lotta, lottare, battaglia, picchiarsi, combattimento.
grave: tomba, grave.
indulgence: indulgenza.
killed: ucciso.
meets: incontra.
neglect: trascurare, negligere, negligenza, trascuratezza.
overruled: annullato, revocato.

owing: dovere.
principally: principalmente, soprattutto.
proceedings: atti.
recovering: ricuperando.
repaired: riparato.
sanguine: rubicondo, sanguigno.
terrific: straordinario.
thanked: ringraziato.
unfit: inadatto.
useless: inutile, inservibile.
villainous: infame, malvagio.

a week since they left Brighton. In a few days more we may gain some news of them; and till we know that they are not married, and have no design of **marrying**, do not let us give the matter over as lost. As soon as I get to town I shall go to my brother, and make him come home with me to Gracechurch Street; and then we may **consult** together as to what is to be done."

"Oh! my dear brother," replied Mrs. **Bennet**, "that is exactly what I could most wish for. And now do, when you get to town, find them out, **wherever** they may be; and if they are not married already, *make* them marry. And as for wedding clothes, do not let them wait for that, but tell Lydia she shall have as much money as she **chooses** to buy them, after they are married. And, above all, keep Mr. Bennet from **fighting**. Tell him what a **dreadful** state I am in, that I am frighted out of my wits--and have such tremblings, such flutterings, all over me-- such spasms in my side and **pains** in my head, and such beatings at heart, that I can get no rest by night nor by day. And tell my dear Lydia not to give any **directions** about her clothes till she has seen me, for she does not know which are the best warehouses. Oh, brother, how kind you are! I know you will **contrive** it all."

But Mr. Gardiner, though he **assured** her again of his **earnest** endeavours in the cause, could not avoid **recommending moderation** to her, as well in her hopes as her fear; and after talking with her in this manner till dinner was on the table, they all left her to **vent** all her feelings on the **housekeeper**, who attended in the absence of her **daughters**.

Though her brother and sister were **persuaded** that there was no real occasion for such a **seclusion** from the family, they did not attempt to **oppose** it, for they knew that she had not **prudence** enough to hold her tongue before the servants, while they waited at table, and **judged** it better that *one* only of the **household**, and the one whom they could most trust should **comprehend** all her fears and **solicitude** on the subject.

In the dining-room they were soon joined by Mary and Kitty, who had been too **busily engaged** in their separate apartments to make their appearance before. One came from her books, and the other from her toilette. The faces of

---

Italian

assured: assicurato, certo.
bennet: cariofillata, erba benedetta.
busily: attivamente, indaffaratamente.
chooses: sceglie, elegge.
comprehend: comprendere, comprendo, comprendono, comprendiamo, comprendi, comprendete.
consult: consultare.
contrive: escogitano, escogito, escogitiamo, escogitate, escogita, escogiti, escogitare.

daughters: figlie.
directions: avvertenze.
dreadful: terribile.
earnest: serio, caparra.
engaged: occupato, innestato, impegnato.
fighting: lotta, combattente.
household: famiglia.
housekeeper: governante.
judged: giudicato.
marrying: sposandosi.
moderation: moderazione.

oppose: contrapporre, contrapponete, contrapponi, contrapponiamo, contrappongono, contrappongo, opporre.
pains: dolori.
persuaded: convinto, persuaso.
prudence: prudenza.
recommending: raccomandando.
seclusion: isolamento.
solicitude: sollecitudine.
vent: sfogo, apertura.
wherever: dovunque, laddove.

both, however, were **tolerably** calm; and no change was visible in either, except that the loss of her favourite sister, or the anger which she had herself **incurred** in this business, had given more of fretfulness than usual to the **accents** of Kitty. As for Mary, she was mistress enough of herself to whisper to Elizabeth, with a **countenance** of grave reflection, soon after they were seated at table:

"This is a most unfortunate affair, and will probably be much talked of. But we must **stem** the tide of **malice**, and **pour** into the wounded bosoms of each other the **balm** of **sisterly** consolation."

Then, **perceiving** in Elizabeth no **inclination** of replying, she added, "Unhappy as the event must be for Lydia, we may draw from it this useful **lesson**: that loss of virtue in a female is **irretrievable**; that one false step **involves** her in endless ruin; that her reputation is no less **brittle** than it is beautiful; and that she **cannot** be too much **guarded** in her behaviour towards the **undeserving** of the other sex."

Elizabeth lifted up her eyes in **amazement**, but was too much **oppressed** to make any reply. Mary, however, continued to **console** herself with such kind of **moral** extractions from the evil before them.

In the afternoon, the two elder Miss Bennets were able to be for half-an-hour by themselves; and Elizabeth instantly **availed** herself of the opportunity of making any inquiries, which Jane was equally eager to satisfy. After joining in general lamentations over the dreadful **sequel** of this event, which Elizabeth considered as all but certain, and Miss Bennet could not **assert** to be wholly impossible, the former continued the subject, by saying, "But tell me all and everything about it which I have not already heard. Give me further **particulars**. What did Colonel Forster say? Had they no **apprehension** of anything before the elopement took place? They must have seen them together for ever."

"Colonel Forster did own that he had often suspected some **partiality**, especially on Lydia's side, but nothing to give him any alarm. I am so **grieved** for him! His behaviour was **attentive** and kind to the **utmost**. He *was* coming to us, in order to assure us of his concern, before he had any idea of their not being

Italian

accents: accenta.
amazement: stupore, meraviglia.
apprehension: apprensione, arresto.
assert: asserire, asserite, asseriscono, asserisci, asserisco, asseriamo, sostenere, affermare.
attentive: attento, premuroso.
availed: servito.
balm: balsamo.
brittle: fragile, croccante, friabile.
cannot: non potere.
console: consolare, consolle, console.

countenance: approvare, viso.
grieved: accorato, addolorato.
guarded: guardingo, custodito.
inclination: inclinazione, pendenza.
incurred: incorso.
involves: coinvolge.
irretrievable: irrecuperabile.
lesson: lezione.
malice: malevolenza, livore, dolo, malizia, malignità.
moral: morale.
oppressed: premuto, oppresso,

serrato, stretto.
partiality: parzialità, predilezione.
particulars: particolari.
perceiving: percependo, scorgendo, intravedendo.
pour: versare.
sequel: seguito.
sisterly: sorella.
stem: gambo, tronco, stelo, fusto.
tolerably: tollerabilmente.
undeserving: immeritevole.
utmost: massimo.

gone to Scotland: when that **apprehension** first got **abroad**, it **hastened** his journey."

"And was Denny **convinced** that Wickham would not **marry**? Did he know of their **intending** to go off? Had Colonel Forster seen Denny himself?"

"Yes; but, when questioned by *him*, Denny **denied** knowing anything of their plans, and would not give his real opinion about it. He did not **repeat** his **persuasion** of their not marrying--and from *that*, I am **inclined** to hope, he might have been **misunderstood** before."

"And **till** Colonel Forster came himself, not one of you **entertained** a doubt, I suppose, of their being really married?"

"How was it possible that such an idea should enter our **brains**? I felt a little uneasy--a little **fearful** of my sister's **happiness** with him in marriage, because I knew that his **conduct** had not been always quite right. My father and mother knew nothing of that; they only felt how **imprudent** a match it must be. Kitty then **owned**, with a very natural **triumph** on knowing more than the rest of us, that in Lydia's last letter she had prepared her for such a step. She had known, it seems, of their being in love with each other, many weeks."

"But not before they went to Brighton?"

"No, I believe not."

"And did Colonel Forster appear to think well of Wickham himself? Does he know his real character?"

"I must **confess** that he did not speak so well of Wickham as he **formerly** did. He believed him to be imprudent and **extravagant**. And since this **sad affair** has taken place, it is said that he left Meryton **greatly** in debt; but I hope this may be false."

"Oh, Jane, had we been less **secret**, had we told what we knew of him, this could not have happened!"

Italian

abroad: all'estero, fuori.
affair: affare, faccenda, caso.
apprehension: apprensione, arresto.
brains: mente, cervello.
conduct: condotta, condurre, guidare, comportamento.
confess: confessare, confessa, confessano, confessate, confessi, confessiamo, confesso.
convinced: convinto.
denied: negato.
entertained: intrattenuto.

extravagant: stravagante.
fearful: spaventoso, pauroso.
formerly: precedentemente, davanti, in passato, un tempo.
greatly: molto, grandemente.
happiness: felicità.
hastened: affrettato, sollecitato.
imprudent: imprudente.
inclined: disposto, inclinato, propenso.
intending: intendendo.
marry: sposare, sposati, sposatevi, si

sposi, si sposate, si sposano, ci sposiamo, mi sposo, maritarsi, ammogliarsi, maritare.
misunderstood: incompreso, frainteso.
owned: posseduto.
persuasion: persuasione.
repeat: ripetere, ripetono, ripetete, ripetiamo, ripeto, ripeti, ripetizione.
sad: triste, afflitto.
secret: segreto.
till: finchè, coltivare, cassa, fino, arare.
triumph: vittoria, trionfo.

"Perhaps it would have been better," replied her sister. "But to **expose** the former faults of any person without **knowing** what their present feelings were, seemed **unjustifiable**. We acted with the best intentions."

"Could Colonel Forster **repeat** the **particulars** of Lydia's note to his wife?"

"He brought it with him for us to see."

Jane then took it from her pocket-book, and gave it to Elizabeth. These were the **contents**:

> My dear Harriet,
>   You will **laugh** when you know where I am gone, and I **cannot** help **laughing** myself at your **surprise** to-morrow morning, as soon as I am **missed**. I am going to Gretna Green, and if you cannot **guess** with who, I shall think you a **simpleton**, for there is but one man in the world I love, and he is an **angel**. I should never be happy without him, so think it no **harm** to be off. You need not send them word at Longbourn of my going, if you do not like it, for it will make the surprise the greater, when I write to them and sign my name 'Lydia Wickham.' What a good **joke** it will be! I can hardly write for laughing. Pray make my **excuses** to Pratt for not keeping my **engagement**, and **dancing** with him to-night. Tell him I hope he will excuse me when he knows all; and tell him I will **dance** with him at the next ball we meet, with great pleasure. I shall send for my clothes when I get to Longbourn; but I wish you would tell Sally to **mend** a great **slit** in my **worked muslin gown** before they are packed up. Good-bye. Give my love to Colonel Forster. I hope you will drink to our good **journey**.
>
>   Your **affectionate** friend,
>   "Lydia Bennet."

"Oh! **thoughtless**, thoughtless Lydia!" cried Elizabeth when she had finished it. "What a letter is this, to be written at such a moment! But at least it shows

Italian

affectionate: affettuoso.
angel: angelo.
cannot: non potere.
contents: contenuto.
dance: ballare, ballo, danza.
dancing: ballando.
engagement: fidanzamento, assunzione.
excuse: scusa, scusare, giustificazione, pretesto.
expose: esporre, esponete, espongo, espongono, esponi, esponiamo.

gown: abito, vestito, toga.
guess: supporre, indovinare, supposizione, congettura.
harm: danno, nuócere, danneggiare.
joke: scherzo, scherzare, barzelletta, celia, lazzo.
journey: viaggio, viaggiare.
knowing: conoscendo, sapendo.
laugh: ridere, riso, risata.
laughing: ridere, risata.
mend: riparare, rammendare, accomodare.

missed: mancato.
muslin: mussolina, mussola.
particulars: particolari.
repeat: ripetere, ripetono, ripetete, ripetiamo, ripeto, ripeti, ripetizione.
simpleton: sempliciotto.
slit: fessura, fenditura.
surprise: sorprendere, sorpresa, meraviglia, stupore.
thoughtless: sconsiderato.
unjustifiable: ingiustificabile.
worked: lavorato.

that *she* was serious on the subject of their journey. Whatever he might afterwards **persuade** her to, it was not on her side a *scheme* of **infamy**. My poor father! how he must have felt it!"

"I never saw anyone so shocked. He could not speak a word for full ten minutes. My mother was taken **ill** immediately, and the whole house in such confusion!"

"Oh! Jane," cried Elizabeth, "was there a **servant belonging** to it who did not know the whole story before the end of the day?"

"I do not know. I hope there was. But to be **guarded** at such a time is very difficult. My mother was in **hysterics**, and though I endeavoured to give her every assistance in my power, I am afraid I did not do so much as I might have done! But the **horror** of what might possibly happen almost took from me my faculties."

"Your **attendance** upon her has been too much for you. You do not look well. Oh that I had been with you! you have had every care and **anxiety** upon yourself alone."

"Mary and Kitty have been very kind, and would have shared in every **fatigue**, I am sure; but I did not think it right for either of them. Kitty is slight and **delicate**; and Mary studies so much, that her hours of **repose** should not be broken in on. My aunt Phillips came to Longbourn on Tuesday, after my father went away; and was so good as to stay till Thursday with me. She was of great use and **comfort** to us all. And Lady Lucas has been very kind; she walked here on Wednesday morning to condole with us, and offered her services, or any of her daughters', if they should be of use to us."

"She had better have stayed at home," cried Elizabeth; "perhaps she *meant* well, but, under such a **misfortune** as this, one **cannot** see too little of one's neighbours. Assistance is impossible; **condolence insufferable**. Let them **triumph** over us at a distance, and be satisfied."

She then **proceeded** to **inquire** into the measures which her father had intended to **pursue**, while in town, for the **recovery** of his daughter.

Italian

anxiety: ansia, ansietà, angoscia, inquietudine.
attendance: servizio, presenza.
belonging: appartenendo.
cannot: non potere.
comfort: consolare, comodità, confortare, comfort, benessere.
condolence: condoglianza.
delicate: delicato.
fatigue: fatica, affaticare, stancare, stanchezza, affaticamento.
guarded: guardingo, custodito.

horror: orrore, ribrezzo.
hysterics: isterico.
ill: malato, ammalato.
infamy: infamia.
inquire: domandare, informarsi, domandano, domandate, domandi, domandiamo, domando, indagare, domanda.
insufferable: insopportabile.
misfortune: sfortuna, traversia, disgrazia.
persuade: convincere, convincono,

convincete, convinci, convinciamo, convinco, persuadere, persuadono, persuado, persuadiamo, persuadi.
proceeded: proceduto.
pursue: perseguire, persegui, perseguite, perseguo, perseguiamo, perseguono, perseguitare, inseguire.
recovery: guarigione, ricupero, recupero, ripresa.
repose: riposo, riposarsi.
servant: servire, servo, servitore.
triumph: vittoria, trionfo.

"He **meant** I believe," replied Jane, "to go to Epsom, the place where they last changed horses, see the postilions and try if anything could be made out from them. His **principal object** must be to **discover** the number of the hackney **coach** which took them from Clapham. It had come with a **fare** from London; and as he thought that the **circumstance** of a **gentleman** and lady's **removing** from one **carriage** into another might be remarked he meant to make inquiries at Clapham. If he could **anyhow** discover at what house the **coachman** had before set down his fare, he **determined** to make inquiries there, and **hoped** it might not be **impossible** to find out the **stand** and number of the coach. I do not know of any other designs that he had **formed**; but he was in such a **hurry** to be **gone**, and his spirits so **greatly** discomposed, that I had **difficulty** in **finding** out even so much as this."

Italian

anyhow: comunque.
carriage: vettura, carrello, vagone, carro, carrozza.
circumstance: circostanza.
coach: vettura, vagone, carrozza, allenatore, allenare.
coachman: cocchiere, vetturino.
determined: definito, fissato, determinato.
difficulty: difficoltà.
discover: scoprire, scopri, scoprono, scopro, scoprite, scopriamo.

fare: tariffa.
finding: fondendo, fondando.
formed: formato.
gentleman: signore, galantuomo, gentiluomo.
gone: andato.
greatly: molto, grandemente.
hoped: sperato.
hurry: affrettarsi, fretta.
impossible: impossibile.
meant: significato.
object: oggetto, cosa, scopo.

principal: principale, committente, capitale, mandante.
removing: togliendo, asportando, rimuovendo.
stand: stare in piedi, granaio, alzarsi, bancarella.

CHAPTER 48

The whole party were in **hopes** of a letter from Mr. **Bennet** the next morning, but the post came in without bringing a single line from him. His family knew him to be, on all common **occasions**, a most **negligent** and **dilatory** **correspondent**; but at such a time they had hoped for **exertion**. They were forced to **conclude** that he had no **pleasing intelligence** to send; but even of *that* they would have been glad to be certain. Mr. Gardiner had **waited** only for the letters before he set off.

When he was gone, they were certain at least of receiving constant information of what was going on, and their **uncle promised**, at **parting**, to **prevail** on Mr. Bennet to return to Longbourn, as soon as he could, to the great **consolation** of his sister, who considered it as the only security for her husband's not being killed in a **duel**.

Mrs. Gardiner and the children were to remain in Hertfordshire a few days longer, as the former thought her presence might be **serviceable** to her nieces. She shared in their **attendance** on Mrs. Bennet, and was a great **comfort** to them in their hours of freedom. Their other **aunt** also **visited** them frequently, and always, as she said, with the design of **cheering** and **heartening** them up-- though, as she never came without **reporting** some fresh **instance** of Wickham's **extravagance** or **irregularity**, she **seldom** went away without leaving them more **dispirited** than she found them.

Italian

attendance: servizio, presenza.
aunt: zia, la zia.
bennet: cariofillata, erba benedetta.
cheering: applauso.
comfort: consolare, comodità, confortare, comfort, benessere.
conclude: concludere, concludo, concludono, concludiamo, concludi, concludete.
consolation: consolazione.
correspondent: corrispondente.
dilatory: dilatorio.

dispirited: abbattuto, scoraggiato.
duel: duello.
exertion: sforzo.
extravagance: stravaganza, prodigalità.
heartening: incoraggiante.
hopes: spera.
instance: istanza, esempio.
intelligence: intelligenza.
irregularity: irregolarità.
negligent: negligente, noncurante, sbadato.

occasions: occasioni.
parting: separazione, divisione.
pleasing: piacevole.
prevail: prevalere, prevalete, prevalgo, prevalgono, prevali, prevaliamo.
promised: promesso.
reporting: reporting.
seldom: raramente.
serviceable: utilizzabile.
uncle: zio, lo zio.
visited: visitato.
waited: aspettato.

All Meryton seemed **striving** to **blacken** the man who, but three months before, had been almost an **angel** of light. He was declared to be in debt to every **tradesman** in the place, and his intrigues, all honoured with the **title** of **seduction**, had been extended into every tradesman's family. Everybody declared that he was the wickedest young man in the world; and everybody began to find out that they had always **distrusted** the appearance of his **goodness**. Elizabeth, though she did not credit above half of what was said, believed enough to make her former **assurance** of her sister's **ruin** more certain; and even Jane, who believed still less of it, became almost **hopeless**, more especially as the time was now come when, if they had gone to Scotland, which she had never before entirely despaired of, they must in all **probability** have gained some news of them.

Mr. Gardiner left Longbourn on Sunday; on Tuesday his wife received a letter from him; it told them that, on his arrival, he had immediately found out his brother, and **persuaded** him to come to Gracechurch Street; that Mr. **Bennet** had been to Epsom and Clapham, before his arrival, but without gaining any satisfactory information; and that he was now determined to **inquire** at all the principal **hotels** in town, as Mr. Bennet thought it possible they might have gone to one of them, on their first coming to London, before they **procured** lodgings. Mr. Gardiner himself did not expect any success from this measure, but as his brother was **eager** in it, he meant to assist him in **pursuing** it. He added that Mr. Bennet seemed wholly disinclined at present to leave London and promised to write again very soon. There was also a **postscript** to this effect:

"I have written to Colonel Forster to desire him to find out, if possible, from some of the young man's intimates in the **regiment**, whether Wickham has any relations or **connections** who would be likely to know in what part of town he has now **concealed** himself. If there were anyone that one could apply to with a probability of gaining such a **clue** as that, it might be of **essential** consequence. At present we have nothing to guide us. Colonel Forster will, I **dare** say, do everything in his power to **satisfy** us on this head. But, on second thoughts,

Italian

angel: angelo.
assurance: assicurazione, promessa.
bennet: cariofillata, erba benedetta.
blacken: annerire, annerisci, annerite, annerisco, anneriamo, anneriscono.
clue: indizio.
concealed: nascosto.
connections: accesso.
dare: osare, oso, osiamo, osi, osate, osano, osa, sfida.
distrusted: diffidato.
eager: avido, desideroso, bramoso,

impaziente.
essential: essenziale.
goodness: bontà.
hopeless: disperato, senza speranza.
hotels: alberghi.
inquire: domandare, informarsi, domandano, domandate, domandi, domandiamo, domando, indagare, domanda.
persuaded: convinto, persuaso.
postscript: poscritto.
probability: probabilità.

procured: procurato.
pursuing: perseguendo.
regiment: reggimento.
ruin: rovinare, rovina.
satisfy: soddisfare, accontentare, soddisfano, soddisfiamo, soddisfa, soddisfate, soddisfo, accontentate, accontento, soddisfi, accontentano.
seduction: seduzione.
striving: sforzandosi.
title: titolo.
tradesman: commerciante.

perhaps, Lizzy could tell us what relations he has now living, better than any other person."

Elizabeth was at no loss to understand from **whence** this **deference** to her authority **proceeded**; but it was not in her power to give any information of so **satisfactory** a nature as the **compliment deserved**. She had never heard of his having had any relations, except a father and mother, both of whom had been dead many years. It was possible, however, that some of his companions in the ----shire might be able to give more information; and though she was not very **sanguine** in **expecting** it, the application was a something to look forward to.

Every day at Longbourn was now a day of **anxiety**; but the most anxious part of each was when the post was expected. The arrival of letters was the **grand** object of every morning's **impatience**. Through letters, whatever of good or bad was to be told would be **communicated**, and every **succeeding** day was expected to bring some news of importance.

But before they heard again from Mr. Gardiner, a letter arrived for their father, from a different quarter, from Mr. Collins; which, as Jane had received **directions** to open all that came for him in his absence, she **accordingly** read; and Elizabeth, who knew what **curiosities** his letters always were, looked over her, and read it **likewise**. It was as follows:

"My dear Sir,
"I feel myself called upon, by our relationship, and my situation in life, to condole with you on the **grievous affliction** you are now **suffering** under, of which we were yesterday **informed** by a letter from Hertfordshire. Be **assured**, my dear sir, that Mrs. Collins and myself **sincerely** sympathise with you and all your **respectable** family, in your present **distress**, which must be of the bitterest kind, because **proceeding** from a cause which no time can remove. No **arguments** shall be **wanting** on my part that can **alleviate** so severe a misfortune--or that may comfort you, under a **circumstance** that must be of all others the most **afflicting** to a parent's mind. The death of your daughter would have

Italian

accordingly: di conseguenza, quindi.
afflicting: affliggendo.
affliction: afflizione.
alleviate: alleviare, allevio, allevi, allevia, alleviamo, alleviano, alleviate.
anxiety: ansia, ansietà, angoscia, inquietudine.
arguments: argomenti.
assured: assicurato, certo.
circumstance: circostanza.
communicated: comunicato.

compliment: complimento.
curiosities: curiosità.
deference: deferenza.
deserved: meritato.
directions: avvertenze.
distress: pericolo.
expecting: aspettando.
grand: grande, grandioso.
grievous: doloroso.
impatience: impazienza.
informed: informato.
likewise: anche, altrettanto.

proceeded: proceduto.
proceeding: procedendo, procedimento.
respectable: rispettabile, onorevole.
sanguine: rubicondo, sanguigno.
satisfactory: soddisfacente.
sincerely: sinceramente, francamente.
succeeding: riuscendo, successivo.
suffering: soffrendo, sofferenza, soffrire, patendo.
wanting: volendo.
whence: da dove, donde.

been a **blessing** in comparison of this. And it is the more to be **lamented**, because there is reason to suppose as my dear Charlotte **informs** me, that this **licentiousness** of behaviour in your daughter has **proceeded** from a **faulty** degree of **indulgence**; though, at the same time, for the **consolation** of yourself and Mrs. **Bennet**, I am inclined to think that her own **disposition** must be naturally bad, or she could not be guilty of such an **enormity**, at so early an age. Howsoever that may be, you are grievously to be pitied; in which opinion I am not only joined by Mrs. Collins, but likewise by Lady Catherine and her daughter, to whom I have related the affair. They agree with me in **apprehending** that this false step in one daughter will be **injurious** to the fortunes of all the others; for who, as Lady Catherine herself condescendingly says, will **connect** themselves with such a family? And this consideration leads me moreover to reflect, with **augmented** satisfaction, on a certain event of last November; for had it been otherwise, I must have been involved in all your **sorrow** and **disgrace**. Let me then advise you, dear sir, to **console** yourself as much as possible, to throw off your **unworthy** child from your affection for ever, and leave her to **reap** the fruits of her own **heinous offense**.

"I am, dear Sir, etc., etc."

Mr. Gardiner did not write again till he had received an answer from Colonel Forster; and then he had nothing of a pleasant nature to send. It was not known that Wickham had a single relationship with whom he kept up any connection, and it was certain that he had no near one living. His former **acquaintances** had been numerous; but since he had been in the **militia**, it did not appear that he was on terms of particular friendship with any of them. There was no one, therefore, who could be pointed out as likely to give any news of him. And in the **wretched** state of his own **finances**, there was a very powerful motive for **secrecy**, in addition to his fear of discovery by Lydia's relations, for it had just **transpired** that he had left **gaming** debts behind him to a very considerable

Italian

acquaintances: conoscenze.
apprehending: temendo, comprendendo, capendo, afferrando.
augmented: ingrandito, aumentato.
bennet: cariofillata, erba benedetta.
blessing: benedicendo, benedizione.
connect: legare, lego, lega, legano, legate, leghi, leghiamo, collegare, colleghi, colleghiamo, collego.
consolation: consolazione.
console: consolare, consolle, console.
disgrace: vergogna, disgrazia,

disonorare, disonore.
disposition: disposizione, predisposizione, ingegno, talento.
enormity: enormità.
faulty: difettoso.
finances: finanze.
gaming: gioco.
heinous: atroce.
indulgence: indulgenza.
informs: informa.
injurious: nocivo, dannoso.
lamented: piangere, pianto, lamento.

licentiousness: licenziosità.
militia: milizia.
offense: offesa.
proceeded: proceduto.
reap: mietere, mietono, mieto, mieti, mietete, mietiamo.
secrecy: segretezza.
sorrow: tristezza, cordoglio.
transpired: traspirato.
unworthy: indegno.
wretched: misero, miserabile, povero, infelice.

amount. **Colonel** Forster believed that more than a thousand pounds would be necessary to clear his **expenses** at Brighton. He owed a good deal in town, but his debts of **honour** were still more **formidable**. Mr. Gardiner did not attempt to **conceal** these **particulars** from the Longbourn family. Jane heard them with **horror**. "A gamester!" she cried. "This is **wholly unexpected**. I had not an idea of it."

Mr. Gardiner added in his letter, that they might expect to see their father at home on the following day, which was Saturday. **Rendered spiritless** by the ill-success of all their endeavours, he had **yielded** to his brother-in-law's **entreaty** that he would return to his family, and leave it to him to do whatever occasion might suggest to be **advisable** for continuing their **pursuit**. When Mrs. **Bennet** was told of this, she did not express so much satisfaction as her children expected, considering what her **anxiety** for his life had been before.

"What, is he coming home, and without poor Lydia?" she cried. "Sure he will not leave London before he has found them. Who is to fight Wickham, and make him marry her, if he comes away?"

As Mrs. Gardiner began to wish to be at home, it was settled that she and the children should go to London, at the same time that Mr. Bennet came from it. The coach, therefore, took them the first **stage** of their journey, and brought its master back to Longbourn.

Mrs. Gardiner went away in all the **perplexity** about Elizabeth and her Derbyshire friend that had attended her from that part of the world. His name had never been **voluntarily** mentioned before them by her **niece**; and the kind of half-expectation which Mrs. Gardiner had formed, of their being followed by a letter from him, had ended in nothing. Elizabeth had received none since her return that could come from Pemberley.

The present **unhappy** state of the family rendered any other excuse for the **lowness** of her spirits **unnecessary**; nothing, therefore, could be **fairly** conjectured from *that*, though Elizabeth, who was by this time **tolerably** well **acquainted** with her own feelings, was perfectly aware that, had she known

Italian

acquainted: informato.
advisable: consigliabile.
amount: importo, somma, ammontare, numero.
anxiety: ansia, ansietà, angoscia, inquietudine.
bennet: cariofillata, erba benedetta.
colonel: colonnello.
conceal: nascondere, nascondono, nascondete, nascondi, nascondiamo, nascondo, occultare.
entreaty: preghiera, domanda,

supplica.
expenses: spese.
fairly: abbastanza, equamente.
formidable: formidabile, straordinario.
honour: onore.
horror: orrore, ribrezzo.
lowness: bassezza.
niece: nipote.
particulars: particolari.
perplexity: perplessità.
pursuit: inseguimento, ricerca.

rendered: reso.
spiritless: avvilito.
stage: palcoscenico, fase, stadio, scena, palco.
tolerably: tollerabilmente.
unexpected: inatteso, imprevisto, inaspettato.
unhappy: infelice, triste.
unnecessary: inutile, non necessario.
voluntarily: volontariamente.
wholly: interamente, completamente.
yielded: ceduto.

nothing of Darcy, she could have borne the **dread** of Lydia's **infamy** somewhat better. It would have **spared** her, she thought, one **sleepless** night out of two.

When Mr. **Bennet** arrived, he had all the appearance of his usual **philosophic composure**. He said as little as he had ever been in the habit of saying; made no mention of the business that had taken him away, and it was some time before his daughters had **courage** to speak of it.

It was not till the afternoon, when he had joined them at tea, that Elizabeth **ventured** to introduce the subject; and then, on her briefly **expressing** her **sorrow** for what he must have **endured**, he replied, "Say nothing of that. Who should suffer but myself? It has been my own doing, and I ought to feel it."

"You must not be too severe upon yourself," replied Elizabeth.

"You may well **warn** me against such an **evil**. Human nature is so **prone** to fall into it! No, Lizzy, let me once in my life feel how much I have been to blame. I am not afraid of being **overpowered** by the impression. It will pass away soon enough."

"Do you suppose them to be in London?"

"Yes; where else can they be so well concealed?"

"And Lydia used to want to go to London," added Kitty.

"She is happy then," said her father drily; "and her **residence** there will probably be of some duration."

Then after a short silence he continued:

"Lizzy, I bear you no ill-will for being **justified** in your advice to me last May, which, considering the event, shows some **greatness** of mind."

They were **interrupted** by Miss Bennet, who came to **fetch** her mother's tea.

"This is a parade," he cried, "which does one good; it gives such an **elegance** to **misfortune**! Another day I will do the same; I will sit in my library, in my **nightcap** and powdering **gown**, and give as much trouble as I can; or, perhaps, I may **defer** it till Kitty **runs** away."

Italian

bennet: cariofillata, erba benedetta.
composure: calma, compostezza.
courage: coraggio.
defer: rinviate, rinvio, dilaziono, differiamo, differisci, differisco, differiscono, differite, dilaziona, dilazionano, dilazionate.
dread: temere.
elegance: eleganza.
endured: sopportato, durato.
evil: male, cattivo, malvagio.
expressing: esprimendo.

fetch: portare, portiamo, porto, porti, portate, portano, porta, ottenere, andare a prendere.
gown: abito, vestito, toga.
greatness: grandezza.
infamy: infamia.
interrupted: interrotto, sospeso.
justified: giustificato.
misfortune: sfortuna, traversia, disgrazia.
nightcap: berretto da notte.
overpowered: sopraffatto.

philosophic: filosofico.
prone: prono, incline.
residence: residenza, alloggio, appartamento.
runs: corre, scorre.
sleepless: insonne.
sorrow: tristezza, cordoglio.
spared: risparmiato.
ventured: avventurato.
warn: avvertire, avvertiamo, avvertono, avverti, avverto, avvertite, ammonire, avvisare.

"I am not going to run away, papa," said Kitty fretfully. "If I should ever go to Brighton, I would **behave** better than Lydia."

"*You* go to Brighton. I would not **trust** you so near it as Eastbourne for **fifty** pounds! No, Kitty, I have at last learnt to be **cautious**, and you will feel the effects of it. No **officer** is ever to **enter** into my house again, **nor** even to **pass** through the **village**. Balls will be **absolutely prohibited**, **unless** you **stand** up with one of your sisters. And you are never to **stir** out of doors **till** you can **prove** that you have **spent** ten minutes of every day in a **rational** manner."

Kitty, who took all these **threats** in a **serious light**, began to cry.

"Well, well," said he, "do not make **yourself unhappy**. If you are a good **girl** for the next ten years, I will take you to a **review** at the end of them."

Italian

absolutely: assolutamente, infatti, davvero, completamente.
behave: comportarsi, condursi.
cautious: cauto, prudente.
enter: entrare, entra, entrano, entrate, entri, entriamo, entro, invio.
fifty: cinquanta.
girl: ragazza, piccola, la ragazza.
light: luce, leggero, accendere, chiaro, illuminare, fanale, lampada, luminoso, debole.
nor: ne.

officer: funzionario, ufficiale, impiegato.
pass: passare, passaggio, lasciapassare, passata, trascorrere, passo.
prohibited: vietato, proibito.
prove: provare, proviamo, provi, provate, provano, provo, prova, comprovare, dimostrare.
rational: razionale, ragionevole.
review: revisione, rassegna, rivista, recensione.
serious: serio, grave, importante.

spent: speso, passato.
stand: stare in piedi, granaio, alzarsi, bancarella.
stir: mescolare, agitare, muovere.
threats: minaccia.
till: finchè, coltivare, cassa, fino, arare.
trust: fiducia, trust, confidenza, affidamento.
unhappy: infelice, triste.
unless: a meno che, eccetto che.
village: villaggio, paese, borgo.
yourself: ti.

CHAPTER 49

Two days after Mr. Bennet's return, as Jane and Elizabeth were **walking** together in the **shrubbery** behind the house, they saw the **housekeeper** coming towards them, and, **concluding** that she came to call them to their mother, went forward to meet her; but, **instead** of the **expected summons**, when they approached her, she said to Miss Bennet, "I **beg** your **pardon**, madam, for interrupting you, but I was in **hopes** you might have got some good news from town, so I took the **liberty** of coming to ask."

"What do you mean, **Hill**? We have heard nothing from town."

"Dear madam," cried Mrs. Hill, in great **astonishment**, "don't you know there is an **express** come for **master** from Mr. Gardiner? He has been here this half-hour, and master has had a letter."

Away ran the **girls**, too **eager** to get in to have time for **speech**. They ran through the **vestibule** into the breakfast-room; from **thence** to the library; their father was in **neither**; and they were on the point of **seeking** him **upstairs** with their mother, when they were **met** by the **butler**, who said:

"If you are looking for my master, ma'am, he is walking towards the little copse."

Italian

astonishment: stupore, meraviglia, sorpresa.
beg: mendicare, mendicano, mendica, mendicate, mendico, mendichiamo, mendichi, chiedere, elemosinare, supplicare.
butler: maggiordomo.
concluding: concludendo, concludere.
eager: avido, desideroso, bramoso, impaziente.
expected: aspettato, atteso.
express: espresso, esprimere,
esprimete, esprimi, esprimiamo, esprimo, esprimono, direttissimo.
girls: ragazze.
hill: collina, colle, altura.
hopes: spera.
housekeeper: governante.
instead: invece.
liberty: libertà.
master: maestro, padrone, principale, master, dominare, anagrafica.
met: incontrato.
neither: ne, neanche, nemmeno,
neppure.
pardon: grazia, perdono, perdonare, scusare, scusa.
seeking: cercando.
shrubbery: boschetto.
speech: discorso, orazione, parola.
summons: citazione, ingiunzione.
thence: di là.
upstairs: di sopra.
vestibule: vestibolo.
walking: camminando, camminare.

Upon this information, they **instantly** passed through the hall once more, and ran across the **lawn** after their father, who was **deliberately pursuing** his way towards a small wood on one side of the paddock.

Jane, who was not so light nor so much in the **habit** of running as Elizabeth, soon lagged behind, while her sister, **panting** for breath, came up with him, and **eagerly** cried out:

"Oh, **papa**, what news--what news? Have you heard from my uncle?"

"Yes I have had a letter from him by express."

"Well, and what news does it bring--good or bad?"

"What is there of good to be expected?" said he, taking the letter from his **pocket**. "But perhaps you would like to read it."

Elizabeth **impatiently** caught it from his hand. Jane now came up.

"Read it aloud," said their father, "for I hardly know myself what it is about."

"Gracechurch Street, Monday, August 2.
"My dear brother,

"At last I am able to send you some tidings of my **niece**, and such as, upon the whole, I hope it will give you **satisfaction**. Soon after you left me on Saturday, I was **fortunate** enough to find out in what part of London they were. The **particulars** I **reserve** till we meet; it is enough to know they are discovered. I have seen them both--"

"Then it is as I always hoped," cried Jane; "they are married!" Elizabeth read on: "I have seen them both. They are not married, nor can I find there was any intention of being so; but if you are **willing** to **perform** the **engagements** which I have **ventured** to make on your side, I hope it will not be long before they are. All that is required of you is, to **assure** to your daughter, by **settlement**, her equal share of the five thousand pounds **secured** among your children after the **decease** of yourself and my sister; and, moreover, to enter into an engagement of

Italian

assure: assicurare, assicura, assicuriamo, assicurate, assicuri, assicurano, assicuro, garantire.
decease: decedere, decesso.
deliberately: apposta, deliberatamente.
eagerly: ardentemente.
engagement: fidanzamento, assunzione.
fortunate: fortunato, felice.
habit: abitudine, costume, vizio, consuetudine.

impatiently: impazientemente.
instantly: direttamente, istantaneamente, immediatamente.
lawn: prato, tappeto erboso, linone.
niece: nipote.
panting: ansimare.
papa: papà.
particulars: particolari.
perform: eseguire, eseguono, eseguo, eseguite, eseguiamo, esegui, compiere, fare, apparire, entrare, commettere.

pocket: tasca, intascare, la tasca, sacca.
pursuing: perseguendo.
reserve: riservare, riserva, prenotare, ordinare.
satisfaction: soddisfazione.
secured: fissato.
settlement: liquidazione, pareggiamento dei conti, accordo, assestamento, composizione, definizione transattiva.
ventured: avventurato.
willing: disposto, volenteroso.

allowing her, during your life, one **hundred** pounds per annum. These are conditions which, considering everything, I had no **hesitation** in **complying** with, as far as I thought myself **privileged**, for you. I shall send this by express, that no time may be lost in bringing me your answer. You will easily **comprehend**, from these **particulars**, that Mr. Wickham's circumstances are not so **hopeless** as they are generally believed to be. The world has been **deceived** in that respect; and I am happy to say there will be some little money, even when all his debts are **discharged**, to **settle** on my **niece**, in **addition** to her own **fortune**. If, as I **conclude** will be the case, you send me full powers to act in your name throughout the whole of this business, I will immediately give **directions** to Haggerston for **preparing** a proper settlement. There will not be the smallest occasion for your coming to town again; therefore stay quiet at Longbourn, and depend on my **diligence** and care. Send back your answer as fast as you can, and be careful to write **explicitly**. We have **judged** it best that my niece should be married from this house, of which I hope you will **approve**. She comes to us to-day. I shall write again as soon as anything more is determined on. Yours, etc.,

"Edw. Gardiner."

"Is it possible?" cried Elizabeth, when she had finished. "Can it be possible that he will marry her?"

"Wickham is not so **undeserving**, then, as we thought him," said her sister. "My dear father, I **congratulate** you."

"And have you answered the letter?" cried Elizabeth.

"No; but it must be done soon."

Most **earnestly** did she then **entreaty** him to lose no more time before he wrote.

"Oh! my dear father," she cried, "come back and write immediately. Consider how important every moment is in such a case."

Italian

addition: aggiunta, addizione.
approve: approvare, approvate, approvano, approvi, approvo, approva, approviamo.
complying: accondiscendendo, ottemperando.
comprehend: comprendere, comprendo, comprendono, comprendiamo, comprendi, comprendete.
conclude: concludere, concludo, concludono, concludiamo, concludi,
concludete.
congratulate: felicitare, felicitate, felicito, feliciti, felicitano, felicita, felicitiamo.
deceived: ingannato, truffato.
diligence: diligenza.
directions: avvertenze.
discharged: scaricato.
earnestly: seriamente.
entreaty: preghiera, domanda, supplica.
explicitly: esplicitamente.
fortune: fortuna, sorte, patrimonio.
hesitation: esitazione, tentennamento.
hopeless: disperato, senza speranza.
hundred: cento, centinaio.
judged: giudicato.
niece: nipote.
particulars: particolari.
preparing: preparando, allestendo, apprestando.
privileged: privilegiato.
settle: sistemare, regolare, saldare.
undeserving: immeritevole.

"Let me write for you," said Jane, "if you **dislike** the trouble yourself."

"I dislike it very much," he replied; "but it must be done."

And so saying, he turned back with them, and **walked** towards the house.

"And may I ask--" said Elizabeth; "but the terms, I suppose, must be **complied** with."

"Complied with! I am only **ashamed** of his **asking** so little."

"And they *must* **marry**! Yet he is *such* a man!"

"Yes, yes, they must marry. There is nothing else to be done. But there are two things that I want very much to know; one is, how much money your **uncle** has **laid** down to bring it about; and the other, how am I ever to pay him."

"Money! My uncle!" cried Jane, "what do you mean, sir?"

"I mean, that no man in his **senses** would marry Lydia on so **slight** a **temptation** as one hundred a year during my life, and fifty after I am gone."

"That is very true," said Elizabeth; "though it had not **occurred** to me before. His debts to be **discharged**, and something **still** to remain! Oh! it must be my uncle's doings! Generous, good man, I am **afraid** he has **distressed** himself. A small **sum** could not do all this."

"No," said her father; "Wickham's a **fool** if he takes her with a farthing less than ten thousand pounds. I should be sorry to think so ill of him, in the very beginning of our relationship."

"Ten thousand pounds! Heaven **forbid**! How is half such a sum to be repaid?"

Mr. **Bennet** made no answer, and each of them, deep in thought, continued **silent** till they reached the house. Their father then went on to the library to write, and the girls walked into the breakfast-room.

"And they are really to be married!" cried Elizabeth, as soon as they were by themselves. "How strange this is! And for *this* we are to be **thankful**. That they should marry, small as is their chance of **happiness**, and **wretched** as is his character, we are **forced** to **rejoice**. Oh, Lydia!"

Italian

afraid: pauroso, inquieto, spaventato, angoscioso, impaurito.
ashamed: vergognoso.
asking: chiedendo, domandando.
bennet: cariofillata, erba benedetta.
complied: accondisceso, ottemperato.
discharged: scaricato.
dislike: avversione, ripugnanza, antipatia.
distressed: afflitto.
fool: babbeo, sciocco, allocco, ingannare.

forbid: vietare, vieti, vietate, vietano, vietiamo, vieta, vieto, proibire, proibite, proibiamo, proibisci.
forced: forzato.
happiness: felicità.
ill: malato, ammalato.
laid: posato.
marry: sposare, sposati, sposatevi, si sposi, si sposate, si sposano, ci sposiamo, mi sposo, maritarsi, ammogliarsi, maritare.
occurred: successo, accaduto.

rejoice: allietare, rallegrare.
senses: sensi.
silent: silenzioso, zitto.
slight: leggero, lieve.
sum: somma, importo, addizionare.
temptation: tentazione.
thankful: riconoscente, grato.
till: finchè, coltivare, cassa, fino, arare.
uncle: zio, lo zio.
walked: camminato.
wretched: misero, miserabile, povero, infelice.

"I comfort myself with thinking," replied Jane, "that he certainly would not marry Lydia if he had not a real regard for her. Though our kind uncle has done something towards **clearing** him, I **cannot** believe that ten thousand pounds, or anything like it, has been advanced. He has children of his own, and may have more. How could he spare half ten thousand pounds?"

"If he were ever able to learn what Wickham's debts have been," said Elizabeth, "and how much is settled on his side on our sister, we shall exactly know what Mr. Gardiner has done for them, because Wickham has not sixpence of his own. The **kindness** of my uncle and aunt can never be requited. Their taking her home, and **affording** her their personal protection and **countenance**, is such a **sacrifice** to her advantage as years of **gratitude** cannot enough **acknowledge**. By this time she is actually with them! If such **goodness** does not make her **miserable** now, she will never **deserve** to be happy! What a meeting for her, when she first sees my aunt!"

"We must **endeavour** to forget all that has passed on either side," said Jane: "I hope and trust they will yet be happy. His **consenting** to marry her is a proof, I will believe, that he is come to a right way of thinking. Their **mutual affection** will steady them; and I **flatter** myself they will settle so quietly, and live in so rational a manner, as may in time make their past **imprudence** forgotten."

"Their conduct has been such," replied Elizabeth, "as neither you, nor I, nor anybody can ever forget. It is **useless** to talk of it."

It now occurred to the girls that their mother was in all **likelihood** perfectly **ignorant** of what had happened. They went to the library, therefore, and asked their father whether he would not wish them to make it known to her. He was writing and, without **raising** his head, **coolly** replied:

"Just as you please."

"May we take my uncle's letter to read to her?"

"Take whatever you like, and get away."

Elizabeth took the letter from his writing-table, and they went upstairs together. Mary and Kitty were both with Mrs. **Bennet**: one communication

---

Italian

acknowledge: riconoscere, riconoscono, riconosco, riconosciamo, riconosci, riconoscete, confessare, confermare, prendere atto.
affection: affetto, affezione, amore.
affording: permettendo.
bennet: cariofillata, erba benedetta.
cannot: non potere.
clearing: compensazione, radura.
consenting: acconsentire.
coolly: frescamente.
countenance: approvare, viso.

deserve: meritare, meritano, merita, meritate, meritiamo, meriti, merito.
endeavour: tentare, tentativo, sforzarsi.
flatter: lusingare, lusingate, lusingo, lusinghi, lusingano, lusinghiamo, lusinga, adulare.
goodness: bontà.
gratitude: gratitudine, riconoscenza, grazie.
ignorant: ignorante.
imprudence: imprudenza.

kindness: gentilezza, bontà, cortesia.
likelihood: verosimiglianza, probabilità.
miserable: miserabile, misero, afflitto, cattivo, triste, povero, miserevole, miserando.
mutual: reciproco.
raising: sollevamento, allevamento, sopraelevazione, aumento.
sacrifice: sacrificio, sacrificare, offrire.
useless: inutile, inservibile.

would, therefore, do for all. After a **slight** preparation for good news, the letter was read **aloud**. Mrs. **Bennet** could hardly contain herself. As soon as Jane had read Mr. Gardiner's hope of Lydia's being soon married, her **joy burst forth**, and every following sentence added to its **exuberance**. She was now in an **irritation** as **violent** from **delight**, as she had ever been **fidgety** from **alarm** and **vexation**. To know that her daughter would be married was enough. She was **disturbed** by no fear for her **felicity**, nor **humbled** by any **remembrance** of her misconduct.

"My dear, dear Lydia!" she cried. "This is **delightful** indeed! She will be married! I shall see her again! She will be married at **sixteen**! My good, kind brother! I knew how it would be. I knew he would manage everything! How I long to see her! and to see dear Wickham too! But the clothes, the wedding clothes! I will write to my sister Gardiner about them directly. Lizzy, my dear, run down to your father, and ask him how much he will give her. Stay, stay, I will go myself. Ring the **bell**, Kitty, for Hill. I will put on my things in a moment. My dear, dear Lydia! How **merry** we shall be together when we meet!"

Her **eldest** daughter endeavoured to give some relief to the violence of these transports, by leading her thoughts to the obligations which Mr. Gardiner's behaviour laid them all under.

"For we must **attribute** this happy conclusion," she added, "in a great measure to his **kindness**. We are **persuaded** that he has **pledged** himself to assist Mr. Wickham with money."

"Well," cried her mother, "it is all very right; who should do it but her own uncle? If he had not had a family of his own, I and my children must have had all his money, you know; and it is the first time we have ever had anything from him, except a few **presents**. Well! I am so happy! In a short time I shall have a daughter married. Mrs. Wickham! How well it sounds! And she was only sixteen last June. My dear Jane, I am in such a **flutter**, that I am sure I can't write; so I will **dictate**, and you write for me. We will **settle** with your father about the money afterwards; but the things should be ordered immediately."

Italian

alarm: allarme, sveglia, allarmare.
aloud: ad alta voce.
attribute: attributo, attribuire.
bell: campana, campanello.
bennet: cariofillata, erba benedetta.
burst: scoppiare, scoppio, crepa, screpolatura, fessura, esplosione, crepare, irrompere, burst.
delight: delizia, deliziare, dilettare, diletto, godimento, rallegrare, gioia.
delightful: delizioso, piacevole.
dictate: dettare, dettano, dettate, detti,

dettiamo, detta, detto.
disturbed: disturbato.
eldest: maggiore, il più vecchio.
exuberance: esuberanza.
felicity: felicità.
fidgety: agitato, irrequieto.
flutter: svolazzare.
forth: avanti.
humbled: umiliato.
irritation: irritazione.
joy: gioia.
kindness: gentilezza, bontà, cortesia.

merry: allegro, festoso, gaio.
persuaded: convinto, persuaso.
pledged: impegnato.
presents: presenta.
remembrance: rimembranza, ricordo, memoria.
settle: sistemare, regolare, saldare.
sixteen: sedici.
slight: leggero, lieve.
vexation: irritazione.
violent: violento.

She was then **proceeding** to all the **particulars** of **calico, muslin,** and **cambric,** and would shortly have **dictated** some very **plentiful** orders, had not Jane, though with some difficulty, **persuaded** her to wait till her father was at leisure to be **consulted.** One day's **delay,** she observed, would be of small importance; and her mother was too happy to be quite so **obstinate** as usual. Other schemes, too, came into her head.

"I will go to Meryton," said she, "as soon as I am dressed, and tell the good, good news to my sister Philips. And as I come back, I can call on Lady Lucas and Mrs. Long. Kitty, run down and order the **carriage.** An **airing** would do me a great deal of good, I am sure. Girls, can I do anything for you in Meryton? Oh! Here comes Hill! My dear Hill, have you heard the good news? Miss Lydia is going to be married; and you shall all have a **bowl** of **punch** to make **merry** at her wedding."

Mrs. Hill began **instantly** to express her **joy.** Elizabeth received her **congratulations** amongst the rest, and then, **sick** of this **folly,** took **refuge** in her own room, that she might think with freedom.

Poor Lydia's situation must, at best, be bad enough; but that it was no worse, she had need to be **thankful.** She felt it so; and though, in looking forward, neither **rational happiness** nor **worldly prosperity** could be **justly** expected for her sister, in looking back to what they had **feared,** only two hours ago, she felt all the advantages of what they had gained.

Italian

airing: aerazione, aria.
bowl: scodella, ciotola, bacino, coppa, vaschetta, boccia.
calico: calice.
cambric: cambrì, percalle.
carriage: vettura, carrello, vagone, carro, carrozza.
congratulations: congratulazioni.
consulted: consultato, interpellato.
delay: ritardo, tardare, ritardare, indugio, indugiare.
dictated: dettato.

feared: temuto.
folly: follia.
happiness: felicità.
instantly: direttamente, istantaneamente, immediatamente.
joy: gioia.
justly: giustamente.
merry: allegro, festoso, gaio.
muslin: mussolina, mussola.
obstinate: ostinato.
particulars: particolari.
persuaded: convinto, persuaso.

plentiful: abbondante, copioso.
proceeding: procedendo, procedimento.
prosperity: prosperità.
punch: punzone, ponce, perforatore, forare, punzonare, perforatrice, punch.
rational: razionale, ragionevole.
refuge: rifugio.
sick: malato, ammalato.
thankful: riconoscente, grato.
worldly: mondano.

CHAPTER 50

Mr. **Bennet** had very often **wished** before this period of his life that, instead of **spending** his whole income, he had **laid** by an annual **sum** for the better provision of his children, and of his wife, if she **survived** him. He now wished it more than ever. Had he done his duty in that respect, Lydia need not have been **indebted** to her **uncle** for whatever of **honour** or credit could now be **purchased** for her. The **satisfaction** of **prevailing** on one of the most **worthless** young men in Great Britain to be her husband might then have **rested** in its proper place.

He was seriously concerned that a cause of so little advantage to anyone should be forwarded at the **sole expense** of his brother-in-law, and he was determined, if possible, to find out the extent of his **assistance**, and to **discharge** the **obligation** as soon as he could.

When first Mr. Bennet had married, economy was held to be **perfectly useless**, for, of course, they were to have a son. The son was to join in cutting off the **entail**, as soon as he should be of age, and the **widow** and younger children would by that means be provided for. Five **daughters successively entered** the world, but yet the son was to come; and Mrs. Bennet, for many years after Lydia's birth, had been certain that he would. This event had at last been despaired of, but it was then too late to be **saving**. Mrs. Bennet had no turn for economy, and her husband's love of **independence** had **alone prevented** their **exceeding** their income.

Italian

alone: solo, da solo, solamente.
assistance: assistenza, aiuto.
bennet: cariofillata, erba benedetta.
daughters: figlie.
discharge: scarico, scarica, portata, scaricare.
entail: comportare.
entered: entrato.
exceeding: eccedendo.
expense: spese, spesa.
honour: onore.
indebted: obbligato, indebitato.

independence: indipendenza.
laid: posato.
obligation: obbligo, obbligazione, dovere, impegno.
perfectly: perfettamente.
prevailing: prevalente, prevalendo.
prevented: impedito, prevenuto.
purchased: comprato, acquistato.
rested: riposato.
satisfaction: soddisfazione.
saving: salvando, risparmio, risparmiando.

sole: sogliola, solo, suola, pianta, unico.
spending: spendendo, passando.
successively: successivamente.
sum: somma, importo, addizionare.
survived: sopravvissuto.
uncle: zio, lo zio.
useless: inutile, inservibile.
widow: vedova.
wished: desiderato.
worthless: immeritevole, dappoco, indegno.

Five thousand pounds was settled by marriage articles on Mrs. **Bennet** and the children. But in what proportions it should be divided amongst the latter depended on the will of the **parents**. This was one point, with regard to Lydia, at least, which was now to be settled, and Mr. Bennet could have no hesitation in **acceding** to the proposal before him. In terms of grateful **acknowledgment** for the kindness of his brother, though expressed most **concisely**, he then delivered on paper his perfect **approbation** of all that was done, and his willingness to **fulfil** the engagements that had been made for him. He had never before supposed that, could Wickham be **prevailed** on to marry his daughter, it would be done with so little **inconvenience** to himself as by the present arrangement. He would scarcely be ten pounds a year the **loser** by the hundred that was to be paid them; for, what with her **board** and pocket allowance, and the **continual** presents in money which passed to her through her mother's hands, Lydia's expenses had been very little within that sum.

That it would be done with such **trifling exertion** on his side, too, was another very welcome surprise; for his wish at present was to have as little trouble in the business as possible. When the first transports of rage which had produced his activity in seeking her were over, he naturally returned to all his former **indolence**. His letter was soon **dispatched**; for, though **dilatory** in **undertaking** business, he was quick in its execution. He **begged** to know further particulars of what he was **indebted** to his brother, but was too angry with Lydia to send any **message** to her.

The good news spread quickly through the house, and with **proportionate speed** through the neighbourhood. It was borne in the latter with **decent philosophy**. To be sure, it would have been more for the advantage of conversation had Miss Lydia Bennet come upon the town; or, as the happiest alternative, been **secluded** from the world, in some distant **farmhouse**. But there was much to be talked of in **marrying** her; and the **good**-natured wishes for her well-doing which had proceeded before from all the **spiteful** old ladies in Meryton lost but a little of their spirit in this change of circumstances, because with such an husband her misery was considered certain.

Italian

acceding: accedendo, concordando.
acknowledgment: riconoscimento.
approbation: approvazione.
begged: mendicato.
bennet: cariofillata, erba benedetta.
board: consiglio, asse, tavola, commissione, bordo, scheda, pannello.
concisely: concisamente.
continual: continuo, costante.
decent: decente.
dilatory: dilatorio.

dispatched: spedito.
exertion: sforzo.
farmhouse: cascina, fattoria.
fulfil: adempiere.
good-natured: gradevole, cortese.
inconvenience: inconvenienza, disagio, disturbo.
indebted: obbligato, indebitato.
indolence: indolenza.
loser: perdente.
marrying: sposandosi.
message: messaggio, comunicato,

annunzio, comunicazione.
parents: genitori, i genitori, padre e madre.
philosophy: filosofia.
prevailed: prevalso.
proportionate: proporzionato.
secluded: appartato.
speed: velocità, andatura, rapidità.
spiteful: dispettoso.
trifling: insignificante.
undertaking: intraprendendo, impresa.

It was a fortnight since Mrs. **Bennet** had been downstairs; but on this happy day she again took her seat at the head of her table, and in spirits **oppressively** high. No **sentiment** of shame gave a **damp** to her triumph. The marriage of a daughter, which had been the first object of her wishes since Jane was sixteen, was now on the point of **accomplishment**, and her thoughts and her words ran wholly on those attendants of elegant **nuptials**, fine muslins, new carriages, and servants. She was **busily searching** through the neighbourhood for a proper situation for her daughter, and, without knowing or considering what their income might be, rejected many as **deficient** in **size** and importance.

"Haye Park might do," said she, "if the Gouldings could **quit** it--or the great house at Stoke, if the drawing-room were larger; but Ashworth is too far off! I could not bear to have her ten miles from me; and as for Pulvis Lodge, the attics are dreadful."

Her husband allowed her to talk on without **interruption** while the servants remained. But when they had withdrawn, he said to her: "Mrs. Bennet, before you take any or all of these houses for your son and daughter, let us come to a right understanding. Into *one* house in this neighbourhood they shall never have **admittance**. I will not encourage the **impudence** of either, by receiving them at Longbourn."

A long dispute followed this declaration; but Mr. Bennet was firm. It soon led to another; and Mrs. Bennet found, with **amazement** and horror, that her husband would not advance a guinea to buy clothes for his daughter. He protested that she should receive from him no mark of affection whatever on the occasion. Mrs. Bennet could hardly **comprehend** it. That his anger could be carried to such a point of **inconceivable resentment** as to refuse his daughter a privilege without which her marriage would scarcely seem **valid**, **exceeded** all she could believe possible. She was more **alive** to the **disgrace** which her want of new clothes must reflect on her daughter's nuptials, than to any sense of shame at her **eloping** and living with Wickham a fortnight before they took place.

Elizabeth was now most **heartily** sorry that she had, from the **distress** of the moment, been led to make Mr. Darcy **acquainted** with their fears for her sister;

Italian

accomplishment: compimento, adempimento.
acquainted: informato.
admittance: ammettenza.
alive: vivo.
amazement: stupore, meraviglia.
bennet: cariofillata, erba benedetta.
busily: attivamente, indaffaratamente.
comprehend: comprendere, comprendo, comprendono, comprendiamo, comprendi, comprendete.

damp: umido.
deficient: deficiente, carente, difettoso, insufficiente.
disgrace: vergogna, disgrazia, disonorare, disonore.
distress: pericolo.
eloping: scappando.
exceeded: ecceduto.
heartily: cordialmente.
impudence: impudenza.
inconceivable: inconcepibile.
interruption: interruzione.

nuptials: nozze.
oppressively: oppressivamente.
quit: abbandonare, abbandonato, abbandono, abbandoni, abbandonate, abbandonano, abbandona, abbandoniamo, smettere.
resentment: risentimento, astio.
searching: ricerca.
sentiment: sentimento.
size: dimensione, grandezza, formato, taglia, grossezza, misura.
valid: valido, valevole.

for since her marriage would so shortly give the proper **termination** to the elopement, they might hope to conceal its **unfavourable** beginning from all those who were not immediately on the spot.

She had no fear of its **spreading farther** through his means. There were few people on whose **secrecy** she would have more confidently **depended**; but, at the same time, there was no one whose knowledge of a sister's **frailty** would have **mortified** her so much--not, however, from any fear of disadvantage from it **individually** to herself, for, at any rate, there seemed a **gulf impassable** between them. Had Lydia's marriage been concluded on the most honourable terms, it was not to be supposed that Mr. Darcy would connect himself with a family where, to every other objection, would now be added an **alliance** and relationship of the nearest kind with a man whom he so **justly** scorned.

From such a connection she could not wonder that he would **shrink**. The wish of **procuring** her regard, which she had assured herself of his feeling in Derbyshire, could not in rational expectation survive such a **blow** as this. She was **humbled**, she was **grieved**; she repented, though she hardly knew of what. She became jealous of his **esteem**, when she could no longer hope to be benefited by it. She wanted to hear of him, when there seemed the least chance of gaining intelligence. She was convinced that she could have been happy with him, when it was no longer likely they should meet.

What a triumph for him, as she often thought, could he know that the proposals which she had **proudly** spurned only four months ago, would now have been most **gladly** and **gratefully** received! He was as generous, she doubted not, as the most generous of his sex; but while he was **mortal**, there must be a triumph.

She began now to **comprehend** that he was exactly the man who, in **disposition** and talents, would most suit her. His understanding and temper, though **unlike** her own, would have answered all her wishes. It was an union that must have been to the advantage of both; by her ease and **liveliness**, his mind might have been **softened**, his manners improved; and from his

Italian

alliance: alleanza.
blow: soffiare, colpo, botta, botto.
comprehend: comprendere, comprendo, comprendono, comprendiamo, comprendi, comprendete.
depended: dipeso.
disposition: disposizione, predisposizione, ingegno, talento.
esteem: stima, rispetto, stimare, considerazione, considerare, rispettare, riguardo.

farther: più lontano.
frailty: fragilità.
gladly: volentieri, con piacere.
gratefully: con gratitudine.
grieved: accorato, addolorato.
gulf: golfo, abisso, burrone.
humbled: umiliato.
impassable: impraticabile.
individually: individualmente.
justly: giustamente.
liveliness: vivacità.
mortal: mortale.

mortified: mortificato.
procuring: procurando.
proudly: orgogliosamente.
secrecy: segretezza.
shrink: restringere, restringersi.
softened: ammorbidito.
spreading: spandimento, spalmatura, propagazione.
termination: fine, terminazione.
unfavourable: sfavorevole.
unlike: diversamente da, a differenza di.

judgement, **information**, and knowledge of the world, she must have received benefit of greater importance.

But no such happy marriage could now teach the **admiring multitude** what connubial **felicity** really was. An union of a different tendency, and **precluding** the possibility of the other, was soon to be formed in their family.

How Wickham and Lydia were to be supported in **tolerable** independence, she could not imagine. But how little of **permanent happiness** could **belong** to a couple who were only brought together because their passions were stronger than their virtue, she could easily **conjecture**.

Mr. Gardiner soon wrote again to his brother. To Mr. Bennet's acknowledgments he briefly replied, with **assurance** of his **eagerness** to promote the welfare of any of his family; and concluded with entreaties that the subject might never be mentioned to him again. The principal **purport** of his letter was to inform them that Mr. Wickham had resolved on **quitting** the **militia**.

"It was greatly my wish that he should do so," he added, "as soon as his marriage was fixed on. And I think you will agree with me, in considering the removal from that **corps** as highly **advisable**, both on his account and my niece's. It is Mr. Wickham's intention to go into the **regulars**; and among his former friends, there are still some who are able and willing to assist him in the **army**. He has the promise of an ensigncy in General ----'s **regiment**, now quartered in the North. It is an advantage to have it so far from this part of the **kingdom**. He **promises** fairly; and I hope among different people, where they may each have a character to **preserve**, they will both be more **prudent**. I have written to Colonel Forster, to inform him of our present arrangements, and to request that he will satisfy the various creditors of Mr. Wickham in and near Brighton, with assurances of **speedy payment**, for which I have **pledged** myself. And will you give yourself the trouble of carrying **similar** assurances to his creditors in Meryton, of whom I shall subjoin a **list according** to his information? He has given in all his debts; I hope at

Italian

according: secondo.
admiring: ammirando, ammirativo.
advisable: consigliabile.
army: esercito, armata.
assurance: assicurazione, promessa.
belong: appartenere, appartieni, apparteniamo, appartengono, appartenete, appartengo.
conjecture: congettura.
corps: corpo.
eagerness: impazienza.
felicity: felicità.

happiness: felicità.
inform: informare, informano, informate, informi, informiamo, informo, informa, insegnare.
kingdom: regno, reame.
list: lista, elenco, elencare, nota, distinta, catalogare, repertorio.
militia: milizia.
multitude: affluenza, folla, moltitudine.
payment: pagamento.
permanent: permanente, costante.

pledged: impegnato.
precluding: precludendo.
preserve: conservare, conserva.
promises: promette.
prudent: prudente, sensato.
purport: senso, significare, significato.
quitting: abbandonando.
regiment: reggimento.
regulars: regolare.
similar: simile.
speedy: rapido.
tolerable: tollerabile.

least he has not **deceived** us. Haggerston has our **directions**, and all will be completed in a week. They will then join his **regiment**, unless they are first invited to Longbourn; and I understand from Mrs. Gardiner, that my **niece** is very **desirous** of seeing you all before she leaves the South. She is well, and **begs** to be dutifully remembered to you and your mother.--Yours, etc.,

"E. Gardiner."

Mr. **Bennet** and his **daughters** saw all the **advantages** of Wickham's **removal** from the ----shire as clearly as Mr. Gardiner could do. But Mrs. Bennet was not so well pleased with it. Lydia's being **settled** in the North, just when she had expected most pleasure and **pride** in her company, for she had by no means given up her plan of their **residing** in Hertfordshire, was a severe **disappointment**; and, **besides**, it was such a **pity** that Lydia should be taken from a regiment where she was **acquainted** with everybody, and had so many favourites.

"She is so **fond** of Mrs. Forster," said she, "it will be quite **shocking** to send her away! And there are several of the young men, too, that she likes very much. The officers may not be so **pleasant** in General----'s regiment."

His daughter's request, for such it might be considered, of being admitted into her family again before she set off for the North, received at first an absolute negative. But Jane and Elizabeth, who agreed in wishing, for the sake of their sister's feelings and consequence, that she should be noticed on her marriage by her parents, urged him so **earnestly** yet so **rationally** and so **mildly**, to receive her and her husband at Longbourn, as soon as they were married, that he was **prevailed** on to think as they thought, and act as they wished. And their mother had the **satisfaction** of knowing that she would be able to show her married daughter in the **neighbourhood** before she was **banished** to the North. When Mr. Bennet wrote again to his brother, therefore, he sent his permission for them to come; and it was settled, that as soon as the **ceremony** was over, they should **proceed** to Longbourn. Elizabeth was surprised, however, that Wickham should

Italian

acquainted: informato.
advantages: vantaggi.
banished: bandito.
begs: mendica.
bennet: cariofillata, erba benedetta.
besides: inoltre, d'altronde.
ceremony: cerimonia.
daughters: figlie.
deceived: ingannato, truffato.
desirous: desideroso.
directions: avvertenze.
disappointment: delusione,

disappunto.
earnestly: seriamente.
fond: tenero, affettuoso, affezionato.
mildly: dolcemente, gentilmente.
neighbourhood: circondario, distretto, vicinato, quartiere.
niece: nipote.
pity: compassione, pietà.
pleasant: piacevole, gradevole, ameno.
prevailed: prevalso.
pride: orgoglio, fierezza.
proceed: procedere, procedete,

procedono, procedo, procediamo, procedi.
rationally: razionalmente.
regiment: reggimento.
removal: rimozione, asportazione, eliminazione.
residing: risiedendo.
satisfaction: soddisfazione.
settled: regolato, stabilito, stabile, fermo, fisso, popolato, saldato, sistemato, deciso.
shocking: irritante, scandaloso.

consent to such a **scheme,** and had she **consulted** only her own **inclination,** any **meeting** with him would have been the last **object** of her wishes.

Italian

consent: consenso, concordare, essere d'accordo, accordo, benestare, assenso, acconsentire.
consulted: consultato, interpellato.
inclination: inclinazione, pendenza.
meeting: incontrando, convegno, riunione, incontro, adunanza, comizio, assemblea.
object: oggetto, cosa, scopo.
scheme: progetto, schema, piano.

CHAPTER 51

Their sister's wedding day arrived; and Jane and Elizabeth felt for her probably more than she felt for herself. The carriage was sent to meet them at ---- , and they were to return in it by dinner-time. Their arrival was dreaded by the **elder** Miss **Bennets**, and Jane more especially, who gave Lydia the feelings which would have attended herself, had she been the **culprit**, and was **wretched** in the thought of what her sister must **endure**.

They came. The family were **assembled** in the breakfast room to receive them. Smiles **decked** the face of Mrs. Bennet as the carriage drove up to the door; her husband looked impenetrably **grave**; her **daughters, alarmed**, anxious, **uneasy**.

Lydia's voice was heard in the **vestibule**; the door was thrown open, and she ran into the room. Her mother stepped **forwards, embraced** her, and **welcomed** her with **rapture**; gave her hand, with an **affectionate** smile, to Wickham, who followed his lady; and wished them both joy with an **alacrity** which shewed no doubt of their **happiness**.

Their **reception** from Mr. Bennet, to whom they then turned, was not quite so **cordial**. His **countenance** rather gained in **austerity**; and he **scarcely** opened his lips. The easy **assurance** of the young couple, indeed, was enough to **provoke** him. Elizabeth was disgusted, and even Miss Bennet was shocked. Lydia was Lydia still; **untamed**, unabashed, wild, **noisy**, and **fearless**. She turned from

Italian

affectionate: affettuoso.
alacrity: entusiasmo, alacrità.
alarmed: allarmato.
assembled: montato, assemblato.
assurance: assicurazione, promessa.
austerity: austerità.
bennet: cariofillata, erba benedetta.
cordial: cordiale.
countenance: approvare, viso.
culprit: colpevole.
daughters: figlie.
decked: adornato.

elder: maggiore, sambuco.
embraced: abbracciato.
endure: sopportare, sopporta, sopporto, sopportiamo, sopporti, sopportano, sopportate, tollerare, durare, duriamo, dura.
fearless: intrepido, impavido.
forwards: in avanti, avanti.
grave: tomba, grave.
happiness: felicità.
noisy: rumoroso, chiassoso.
provoke: spronare, provocare, incitare,

provochi, sproniamo, sprono, sproni, spronate, spronano, sprona, provoco.
rapture: rapimento, estasi.
reception: ricezione, ricevimento, accettazione, reception, portineria.
scarcely: appena, a stento.
uneasy: inquieto.
untamed: indomito.
vestibule: vestibolo.
welcomed: accolto.
wretched: misero, miserabile, povero, infelice.

sister to sister, **demanding** their **congratulations**; and when at length they all sat down, looked **eagerly** round the room, took notice of some little **alteration** in it, and observed, with a laugh, that it was a great while since she had been there.

Wickham was not at all more **distressed** than herself, but his **manners** were always so **pleasing**, that had his character and his marriage been exactly what they ought, his smiles and his easy address, while he claimed their relationship, would have delighted them all. Elizabeth had not before believed him quite equal to such assurance; but she sat down, resolving within herself to draw no **limits** in future to the **impudence** of an **impudent** man. She **blushed**, and Jane blushed; but the cheeks of the two who caused their confusion suffered no variation of colour.

There was no want of discourse. The **bride** and her mother could neither of them talk fast enough; and Wickham, who happened to sit near Elizabeth, began **inquiring** after his **acquaintance** in that **neighbourhood**, with a good humoured ease which she felt very unable to equal in her replies. They seemed each of them to have the happiest memories in the world. Nothing of the past was **recollected** with pain; and Lydia led **voluntarily** to subjects which her sisters would not have **alluded** to for the world.

"Only think of its being three months," she cried, "since I went away; it seems but a **fortnight** I **declare**; and yet there have been things enough happened in the time. Good **gracious**! when I went away, I am sure I had no more idea of being married till I came back again! though I thought it would be very good fun if I was."

Her father lifted up his eyes. Jane was distressed. Elizabeth looked **expressively** at Lydia; but she, who never heard nor saw anything of which she chose to be **insensible**, **gaily** continued, "Oh! **mamma**, do the people **hereabouts** know I am married to-day? I was afraid they might not; and we overtook William Goulding in his curricle, so I was determined he should know it, and so I let down the side-glass next to him, and took off my **glove**, and let my hand just rest upon the window frame, so that he might see the ring, and then I **bowed** and smiled like anything."

Italian

acquaintance: conoscenza, conoscente.
alluded: alluso.
alteration: alterazione, modifica, cambiamento, variazione.
blushed: arrossito.
bowed: chino.
bride: sposa, fidanzata, novella sposa.
congratulations: congratulazioni.
declare: dichiarare, dichiara, dichiaro, dichiariamo, dichiari, dichiarano, dichiarate.
demanding: esigente.

distressed: afflitto.
eagerly: ardentemente.
expressively: espressivamente.
fortnight: due settimane.
gaily: gaiamente.
glove: guanto.
gracious: grazioso.
hereabouts: qui vicino.
impudence: impudenza.
impudent: impudente, sfacciato.
inquiring: domandando, domandare.
insensible: insensibile.

limits: limiti.
mamma: mamma.
manners: educazione.
neighbourhood: circondario, distretto, vicinato, quartiere.
pleasing: piacevole.
recollected: rammentato.
voluntarily: volontariamente.

Elizabeth could **bear** it no longer. She got up, and ran out of the room; and returned no more, **till** she heard them **passing** through the hall to the **dining parlour**. She then **joined** them soon enough to see Lydia, with **anxious parade**, walk up to her mother's right hand, and hear her say to her **eldest** sister, "Ah! Jane, I take your place now, and you must go lower, because I am a married woman."

It was not to be **supposed** that time would give Lydia that **embarrassment** from which she had been so **wholly** free at first. Her **ease** and good spirits increased. She longed to see Mrs. Phillips, the Lucases, and all their other neighbours, and to hear herself called "Mrs. Wickham" by each of them; and in the mean time, she went after **dinner** to show her **ring**, and **boast** of being married, to Mrs. **Hill** and the two housemaids.

"Well, **mamma**," said she, when they were all returned to the **breakfast** room, "and what do you think of my husband? Is not he a **charming** man? I am sure my sisters must all **envy** me. I only hope they may have half my good **luck**. They must all go to Brighton. That is the place to get husbands. What a **pity** it is, mamma, we did not all go."

"Very true; and if I had my will, we should. But my **dear** Lydia, I don't at all like your going such a way off. Must it be so?"

"Oh, **lord**! yes;--there is nothing in that. I shall like it of all things. You and **papa**, and my sisters, must come down and see us. We shall be at Newcastle all the winter, and I **dare** say there will be some **balls**, and I will take care to get good partners for them all."

"I should like it beyond anything!" said her mother.

"And then when you go away, you may leave one or two of my sisters behind you; and I dare say I shall get husbands for them before the winter is over."

"I thank you for my share of the favour," said Elizabeth; "but I do not particularly like your way of getting husbands."

Italian

anxious: ansioso.
balls: sfere, palla, balli.
bear: orso, produrre, ribassista, partorire, l'orso, portare.
boast: vanteria, vantarsi.
breakfast: colazione, prima colazione.
charming: affascinante, grazioso, amabile, incantevole.
dare: osare, oso, osiamo, osi, osate, osano, osa, sfida.
dear: caro, costoso, egregio.
dining: pranzando, cenando.

dinner: pranzo, colazione, cena, desinare.
ease: agio, facilità.
eldest: maggiore, il più vecchio.
embarrassment: imbarazzo.
envy: invidia, invidiare, invidio, invidiate, invidiano, invidi, invidiamo.
hill: collina, colle, altura.
joined: congiunto, legato, unito, collegato.
lord: signore.

luck: fortuna.
mamma: mamma.
papa: papà.
parade: parata, chiamata.
parlour: salotto.
passing: passeggero, passare, passaggio.
pity: compassione, pietà.
ring: anello, circolo.
supposed: supposto.
till: finchè, coltivare, cassa, fino, arare.
wholly: interamente, completamente.

Their visitors were not to remain above ten days with them. Mr. Wickham had received his commission before he left London, and he was to join his **regiment** at the end of a fortnight.

No one but Mrs. **Bennet regretted** that their stay would be so short; and she made the most of the time by **visiting** about with her daughter, and having very **frequent** parties at home. These parties were acceptable to all; to avoid a family circle was even more **desirable** to such as did think, than such as did not.

Wickham's **affection** for Lydia was just what Elizabeth had expected to find it; not equal to Lydia's for him. She had **scarcely** needed her present **observation** to be **satisfied**, from the reason of things, that their **elopement** had been brought on by the strength of her love, rather than by his; and she would have wondered why, without **violently caring** for her, he chose to elope with her at all, had she not felt certain that his **flight** was **rendered** necessary by **distress** of circumstances; and if that were the case, he was not the young man to **resist** an opportunity of having a **companion**.

Lydia was **exceedingly fond** of him. He was her dear Wickham on every occasion; no one was to be put in competition with him. He did every thing best in the world; and she was sure he would **kill** more birds on the first of September, than any body else in the country.

One morning, soon after their arrival, as she was sitting with her two **elder** sisters, she said to Elizabeth:

"Lizzy, I never gave *you* an account of my **wedding**, I believe. You were not by, when I told **mamma** and the others all about it. Are not you **curious** to hear how it was managed?"

"No really," replied Elizabeth; "I think there **cannot** be too little said on the subject."

"La! You are so strange! But I must tell you how it went off. We were married, you know, at St. Clement's, because Wickham's lodgings were in that parish. And it was **settled** that we should all be there by **eleven** o'clock. My uncle and **aunt** and I were to go together; and the others were to meet us at the

Italian

affection: affetto, affezione, amore.
aunt: zia, la zia.
bennet: cariofillata, erba benedetta.
cannot: non potere.
caring: premuroso.
companion: compagno, accompagnatore.
curious: curioso.
desirable: desiderabile.
distress: pericolo.
elder: maggiore, sambuco.
eleven: undici.

elope: scappa, scappano, scappate, scappi, scappiamo, scappo, scappare.
exceedingly: estremamente.
flight: volo, fuga.
fond: tenero, affettuoso, affezionato.
frequent: frequente, bazzicare.
kill: uccidere, ammazzare.
mamma: mamma.
observation: osservazione.
regiment: reggimento.
regretted: rammaricato.
rendered: reso.

resist: resistere, resistete, resistono, resisto, resistiamo, resisti.
satisfied: soddisfatto, contento, accontentato.
scarcely: appena, a stento.
settled: regolato, stabilito, stabile, fermo, fisso, popolato, saldato, sistemato, deciso.
violently: violentemente.
visiting: visitando.
wedding: nozze, matrimonio, sposalizio.

church.   Well, Monday morning came, and I was in such a **fuss**! I was so afraid, you know, that something would happen to put it off, and then I should have gone quite **distracted**.   And there was my **aunt**, all the time I was **dressing**, **preaching** and talking away just as if she was reading a **sermon**.   However, I did not hear above one word in ten, for I was thinking, you may suppose, of my dear Wickham.   I longed to know whether he would be married in his **blue** coat."

"Well, and so we breakfasted at ten as usual; I thought it would never be over; for, by the **bye**, you are to understand, that my **uncle** and aunt were **horrid unpleasant** all the time I was with them.   If you'll believe me, I did not once put my **foot** out of doors, though I was there a **fortnight**.   Not one party, or scheme, or anything.   To be sure London was rather thin, but, however, the Little Theatre was open.   Well, and so just as the **carriage** came to the door, my uncle was called away upon business to that horrid man Mr. Stone.   And then, you know, when once they get together, there is no end of it. Well, I was so **frightened** I did not know what to do, for my uncle was to give me away; and if we were beyond the hour, we could not be married all day.   But, **luckily**, he came back again in ten minutes' time, and then we all set out.   However, I **recollected** afterwards that if he had been **prevented** going, the **wedding** need not be put off, for Mr. Darcy might have done as well."

"Mr. Darcy!" **repeated** Elizabeth, in **utter amazement**.

"Oh, yes!--he was to come there with Wickham, you know.   But **gracious** me! I quite **forgot**!   I ought not to have said a word about it.   I **promised** them so **faithfully**!   What will Wickham say?   It was to be such a secret!"

"If it was to be secret," said Jane, "say not another word on the subject.   You may **depend** upon my **seeking** no further."

"Oh! certainly," said Elizabeth, though **burning** with **curiosity**; "we will ask you no questions."

"Thank you," said Lydia, "for if you did, I should certainly tell you all, and then Wickham would be angry."

Italian

amazement: stupore, meraviglia.
aunt: zia, la zia.
blue: blu, azzurro, turchino.
burning: bruciare, bruciatura.
bye: arrivederci, addio, ciao.
carriage: vettura, carrello, vagone, carro, carrozza.
curiosity: curiosità.
depend: dipendere, dipendete, dipendiamo, dipendo, dipendono, dipendi.
distracted: distratto.
dressing: fasciatura, condimento.
faithfully: fedelmente.
foot: piede, base, il piede, zampa.
forgot: dimenticato.
fortnight: due settimane.
frightened: spaventato.
fuss: armeggiare, agitarsi, confusione.
gracious: grazioso.
horrid: orrendo.
luckily: fortunatamente.
preaching: predicando.
prevented: impedito, prevenuto.
promised: promesso.
recollected: rammentato.
repeated: ripetuto.
seeking: cercando.
sermon: predica, sermone.
uncle: zio, lo zio.
unpleasant: rude, spiacevole, brusco, sgradevole, scostante.
utter: totale, completo, proferire, emettere.
wedding: nozze, matrimonio, sposalizio.

On such **encouragement** to ask, Elizabeth was forced to put it out of her power, by running away.

But to live in **ignorance** on such a point was impossible; or at least it was impossible not to try for information.   Mr. Darcy had been at her sister's **wedding**.   It was exactly a scene, and exactly among people, where he had apparently least to do, and least **temptation** to go.   Conjectures as to the meaning of it, **rapid** and wild, **hurried** into her brain; but she was **satisfied** with none. Those that best **pleased** her, as **placing** his **conduct** in the noblest light, seemed most **improbable**.   She could not bear such **suspense**; and **hastily seizing** a sheet of paper, wrote a short letter to her **aunt**, to request an explanation of what Lydia had dropt, if it were **compatible** with the **secrecy** which had been intended.

"You may **readily** comprehend," she added, "what my **curiosity** must be to know how a person unconnected with any of us, and (comparatively speaking) a **stranger** to our family, should have been amongst you at such a time.   Pray write **instantly**, and let me understand it--unless it is, for very **cogent** reasons, to remain in the secrecy which Lydia seems to think necessary; and then I must **endeavour** to be satisfied with ignorance."

"Not that I *shall*, though," she added to herself, as she finished the letter; "and my dear aunt, if you do not tell me in an **honourable** manner, I shall certainly be reduced to tricks and stratagems to find it out."

Jane's **delicate** sense of honour would not allow her to speak to Elizabeth **privately** of what Lydia had let fall; Elizabeth was **glad** of it;--till it appeared whether her inquiries would receive any **satisfaction**, she had rather be without a confidante.

Italian

aunt: zia, la zia.
cogent: convincente.
compatible: compatibile.
conduct: condotta, condurre, guidare, comportamento.
curiosity: curiosità.
delicate: delicato.
encouragement: incoraggiamento.
endeavour: tentare, tentativo, sforzarsi.
glad: contento, felice, lieto.
hastily: frettolosamente.

honour: onore.
honourable: onorevole.
hurried: affrettato, frettoloso.
ignorance: ignoranza.
improbable: improbabile.
instantly: direttamente, istantaneamente, immediatamente.
placing: collocamento.
pleased: contento, soddisfatto.
privately: privatamente.
rapid: rapido.
readily: prontamente.

satisfaction: soddisfazione.
satisfied: soddisfatto, contento, accontentato.
secrecy: segretezza.
seizing: afferrando, grippaggio.
stranger: sconosciuto, estraneo, forestiero.
suspense: apprensione.
temptation: tentazione.
wedding: nozze, matrimonio, sposalizio.

CHAPTER 52

Elizabeth had the **satisfaction** of **receiving** an answer to her letter as soon as she possibly could. She was no **sooner** in **possession** of it than, hurrying into the little copse, where she was least likely to be **interrupted**, she sat down on one of the **benches** and prepared to be happy; for the length of the letter **convinced** her that it did not contain a denial.

"Gracechurch Street, Sept. 6.

"My dear **niece**,

"I have just received your letter, and shall **devote** this whole morning to **answering** it, as I **foresee** that a *little* writing will not **comprise** what I have to tell you. I must **confess** myself **surprised** by your application; I did not expect it from *you*. Don't think me angry, however, for I only mean to let you know that I had not **imagined** such inquiries to be necessary on *your* side. If you do not choose to understand me, **forgive** my **impertinence**. Your **uncle** is as much surprised as I am--and nothing but the belief of your being a party concerned would have allowed him to act as he has done. But if you are really **innocent** and **ignorant**, I must be more **explicit**. On the very day of my coming home from Longbourn, your uncle had a most **unexpected** **visitor**. Mr. Darcy called, and was **shut** up with him several hours. It was all over before I arrived; so my

Italian

answering: risposta, rispondere.
benches: panchine.
comprise: comprendere, contenere, conteniamo, comprendo, contieni, contengono, contengo, comprendono, comprendiamo, comprendi, comprendete.
confess: confessare, confessa, confessano, confessate, confessi, confessiamo, confesso.
convinced: convinto.
devote: consacrare.

explicit: esplicito.
foresee: prevedere, prevedo, prevediamo, prevedi, prevedete, prevedono.
forgive: perdonare, perdonano, perdoniamo, perdona, perdonate, perdoni, perdono.
ignorant: ignorante.
imagined: immaginato.
impertinence: impertinenza.
innocent: innocente.
interrupted: interrotto, sospeso.

niece: nipote.
possession: possesso.
receiving: ricevendo, accogliendo, ricezione, ricevere, ricevente.
satisfaction: soddisfazione.
shut: chiudere, chiuso.
sooner: prima.
surprised: sorpreso, sorpresa.
uncle: zio, lo zio.
unexpected: inatteso, imprevisto, inaspettato.
visitor: visitatore, ospite.

curiosity was not so dreadfully racked as *your's* seems to have been. He came to tell Mr. Gardiner that he had found out where your sister and Mr. Wickham were, and that he had seen and talked with them both; Wickham **repeatedly**, Lydia once. From what I can collect, he left Derbyshire only one day after ourselves, and came to town with the resolution of **hunting** for them. The **motive professed** was his conviction of its being **owing** to himself that Wickham's worthlessness had not been so well known as to make it impossible for any young woman of character to love or **confide** in him. He **generously imputed** the whole to his **mistaken** pride, and **confessed** that he had before thought it beneath him to lay his private actions open to the world. His character was to speak for itself. He called it, therefore, his duty to step forward, and **endeavour** to remedy an **evil** which had been brought on by himself. If he *had another* motive, I am sure it would never **disgrace** him. He had been some days in town, before he was able to discover them; but he had something to direct his search, which was more than *we* had; and the consciousness of this was another reason for his resolving to follow us. There is a lady, it seems, a Mrs. Younge, who was some time ago **governess** to Miss Darcy, and was **dismissed** from her charge on some cause of **disapprobation**, though he did not say what. She then took a large house in Edward-street, and has since maintained herself by letting lodgings. This Mrs. Younge was, he knew, **intimately acquainted** with Wickham; and he went to her for intelligence of him as soon as he got to town. But it was two or three days before he could get from her what he wanted. She would not **betray** her trust, I suppose, without **bribery** and **corruption**, for she really did know where her friend was to be found. Wickham indeed had gone to her on their first arrival in London, and had she been able to receive them into her house, they would have taken up their **abode** with her. At length, however, our kind friend **procured** the wished-for direction. They were in ---- street. He saw Wickham, and afterwards **insisted** on seeing Lydia. His first object with her, he acknowledged, had been to persuade her to **quit** her present

Italian

abode: residenza, appartamento, alloggio, dimora.
acquainted: informato.
betray: tradire, tradisci, tradite, tradisco, tradiamo, tradiscono.
bribery: corruzione.
confessed: confessato.
confide: confidare, confidi, confidiamo, confidate, confidano, confida, confido.
corruption: corruzione.
curiosity: curiosità.

disapprobation: disapprovazione.
disgrace: vergogna, disgrazia, disonorare, disonore.
dismissed: licenziato.
endeavour: tentare, tentativo, sforzarsi.
evil: male, cattivo, malvagio.
generously: generosamente.
governess: istitutrice, governante.
hunting: cacciando, caccia.
imputed: attribuito, imputato.
insisted: insistito.

intimately: intimamente.
mistaken: sbagliato.
motive: motivo, movente, ragione.
owing: dovere.
procured: procurato.
professed: professato, dichiarare, dichiarato.
quit: abbandonare, abbandonato, abbandono, abbandoni, abbandonate, abbandonano, abbandona, abbandoniamo, smettere.
repeatedly: ripetutamente.

disgraceful situation, and return to her friends as soon as they could be **prevailed** on to receive her, **offering** his assistance, as far as it would go. But he found Lydia absolutely **resolved** on remaining where she was. She cared for none of her friends; she wanted no help of his; she would not hear of leaving Wickham. She was sure they should be married some time or other, and it did not much **signify** when. Since such were her feelings, it only remained, he thought, to secure and **expedite** a marriage, which, in his very first conversation with Wickham, he easily learnt had never been *his* design. He **confessed** himself **obliged** to leave the **regiment**, on account of some debts of **honour**, which were very **pressing**; and scrupled not to lay all the ill-consequences of Lydia's flight on her own **folly** alone. He meant to **resign** his commission immediately; and as to his future situation, he could **conjecture** very little about it. He must go somewhere, but he did not know where, and he knew he should have nothing to live on. Mr. Darcy asked him why he had not married your sister at once. Though Mr. **Bennet** was not **imagined** to be very rich, he would have been able to do something for him, and his situation must have been benefited by marriage. But he found, in reply to this question, that Wickham still **cherished** the hope of more effectually making his **fortune** by marriage in some other country. Under such circumstances, however, he was not likely to be **proof** against the **temptation** of immediate relief. They met several times, for there was much to be discussed. Wickham of course wanted more than he could get; but at length was reduced to be reasonable. Every thing being **settled** between *them*, Mr. Darcy's next step was to make your uncle **acquainted** with it, and he first called in Gracechurch street the evening before I came home. But Mr. Gardiner could not be seen, and Mr. Darcy found, on further inquiry, that your father was still with him, but would **quit** town the next morning. He did not judge your father to be a person whom he could so properly **consult** as your uncle, and therefore readily **postponed** seeing him till after the **departure** of the former. He did not leave his name, and till the next day it was only

Italian

acquainted: informato.
bennet: cariofillata, erba benedetta.
cherished: adorato.
confessed: confessato.
conjecture: congettura.
consult: consultare.
departure: partenza.
disgraceful: disgraziata, vergognoso, disonorevole.
expedite: accelerare, affrettare.
folly: follia.
fortune: fortuna, sorte, patrimonio.

honour: onore.
imagined: immaginato.
obliged: obbligato.
offering: offerta.
postponed: rimandato.
pressing: pressatura, urgente.
prevailed: prevalso.
proof: prova, bozza, dimostrazione, provino, impermeabilizzare, resistente.
quit: abbandonare, abbandonato, abbandono, abbandoni, abbandonate,

abbandonano, abbandona, abbandoniamo, smettere.
regiment: reggimento.
resign: dimettere, dimettersi.
resolved: risolto.
settled: regolato, stabilito, stabile, fermo, fisso, popolato, saldato, sistemato, deciso.
signify: significare, significate, significo, significhi, significa, significhiamo, significano.
temptation: tentazione.

known that a gentleman had called on business. On Saturday he came again. Your father was gone, your uncle at home, and, as I said before, they had a great deal of talk together. They met again on Sunday, and then *I* saw him too. It was not all settled before Monday: as soon as it was, the express was sent off to Longbourn. But our **visitor** was very **obstinate**. I **fancy**, Lizzy, that **obstinacy** is the real **defect** of his character, after all. He has been accused of many faults at different times, but *this* is the true one. Nothing was to be done that he did not do himself; though I am sure (and I do not speak it to be **thanked**, therefore say nothing about it), your uncle would most readily have settled the whole. They **battled** it together for a long time, which was more than either the gentleman or lady concerned in it **deserved**. But at last your uncle was forced to **yield**, and instead of being allowed to be of use to his **niece**, was forced to put up with only having the **probable** credit of it, which went **sorely** against the **grain**; and I really believe your letter this morning gave him great pleasure, because it required an explanation that would rob him of his borrowed feathers, and give the **praise** where it was due. But, Lizzy, this must go no **farther** than yourself, or Jane at most. You know pretty well, I suppose, what has been done for the young people. His debts are to be paid, amounting, I believe, to considerably more than a thousand pounds, another thousand in **addition** to her own settled upon *her*, and his commission **purchased**. The reason why all this was to be done by him alone, was such as I have given above. It was **owing** to him, to his **reserve** and want of proper consideration, that Wickham's character had been so **misunderstood**, and **consequently** that he had been received and noticed as he was. Perhaps there was some truth in *this*; though I doubt whether *his* reserve, or *anybody's* reserve, can be **answerable** for the event. But in **spite** of all this fine talking, my dear Lizzy, you may rest perfectly **assured** that your uncle would never have **yielded**, if we had not given him credit for *another interest* in the affair. When all this was **resolved** on, he returned again to his friends, who were still staying at Pemberley; but it was

Italian

addition: aggiunta, addizione.
answerable: responsabile.
assured: assicurato, certo.
battled: combattuto.
consequently: conseguentemente.
defect: difetto, imperfezione, mancanza.
deserved: meritato.
fancy: figurarsi, capriccio, immaginazione.
farther: più lontano.
grain: grana, grano, chicco, granello, venatura.
misunderstood: incompreso, frainteso.
niece: nipote.
obstinacy: ostinazione.
obstinate: ostinato.
owing: dovere.
praise: lodare, lode, elogiare, encomio, elogio.
probable: probabile.
purchased: comprato, acquistato.
reserve: riservare, riserva, prenotare, ordinare.
resolved: risolto.
rob: derubare, deruba, derubano, derubate, derubi, derubiamo, derubo, svaligiare, rubare.
sorely: dolorosamente.
spite: dispetto.
thanked: ringraziato.
visitor: visitatore, ospite.
yield: cedere, cedete, cedi, cediamo, cedo, cedono, resa, rendimento, prodotto, fruttare.
yielded: ceduto.

agreed that he should be in London once more when the wedding took place, and all money matters were then to receive the last finish. I believe I have now told you every thing. It is a relation which you tell me is to give you great surprise; I hope at least it will not afford you any **displeasure**. Lydia came to us; and Wickham had constant **admission** to the house. *He* was exactly what he had been, when I knew him in Hertfordshire; but I would not tell you how little I was **satisfied** with her behaviour while she **staid** with us, if I had not **perceived**, by Jane's letter last Wednesday, that her conduct on coming home was exactly of a piece with it, and therefore what I now tell you can give you no fresh pain. I talked to her **repeatedly** in the most serious manner, representing to her all the **wickedness** of what she had done, and all the **unhappiness** she had brought on her family. If she heard me, it was by good luck, for I am sure she did not listen. I was sometimes quite **provoked**, but then I **recollected** my dear Elizabeth and Jane, and for their sakes had **patience** with her. Mr. Darcy was **punctual** in his return, and as Lydia informed you, attended the wedding. He **dined** with us the next day, and was to leave town again on Wednesday or Thursday. Will you be very angry with me, my dear Lizzy, if I take this opportunity of saying (what I was never **bold** enough to say before) how much I like him. His behaviour to us has, in every respect, been as **pleasing** as when we were in Derbyshire. His understanding and opinions all please me; he wants nothing but a little more **liveliness**, and *that*, if he marry *prudently*, his wife may teach him. I thought him very sly;--he hardly ever mentioned your name. But **slyness** seems the fashion. Pray **forgive** me if I have been very **presuming**, or at least do not **punish** me so far as to **exclude** me from P. I shall never be quite happy till I have been all round the park. A low phaeton, with a nice little pair of ponies, would be the very thing. But I must write no more. The children have been wanting me this half hour.

Yours, very **sincerely**,
"M. Gardiner."

Italian

admission: ammissione, confessione, immissione, accoglimento, accoglienza, ingresso.
bold: grassetto, spesso, grosso, audace.
dined: pranzato, cenato.
displeasure: scontento, dispiacere.
exclude: escludere, escludete, escludi, escludiamo, escludo, escludono.
forgive: perdonare, perdonano, perdoniamo, perdona, perdonate, perdoni, perdono.

liveliness: vivacità.
patience: pazienza.
perceived: scorto, percepito, intravisto.
pleasing: piacevole.
presuming: supponendo, presumendo, presumere.
provoked: spronato, incitato, provocato.
prudently: prudentemente, giudiziosamente.
punctual: esatto, puntuale, preciso.

punish: punire, puniamo, punisci, punisco, puniscono, punite, castigare, castiga, castigano, castigate, castighi.
recollected: rammentato.
repeatedly: ripetutamente.
satisfied: soddisfatto, contento, accontentato.
sincerely: sinceramente, francamente.
slyness: astuzia.
staid: serio.
unhappiness: tristezza, infelicità.
wickedness: cattiveria.

The   contents of this letter threw Elizabeth into a **flutter** of spirits, in which it was difficult to determine whether pleasure or pain bore the greatest share. The vague and **unsettled** suspicions which uncertainty had produced of what Mr. Darcy might have been doing to forward her sister's match, which she had feared to encourage as an **exertion** of goodness too great to be probable, and at the same time dreaded to be just, from the pain of obligation, were proved beyond their greatest extent to be true! He had followed them **purposely** to town, he had taken on himself all the trouble and **mortification attendant** on such a research; in which **supplication** had been necessary to a woman whom he must **abominate** and **despise**, and where he was reduced to meet, frequently meet, reason with, persuade, and finally **bribe**, the man whom he always most wished to avoid, and whose very name it was punishment to him to **pronounce**. He had done all this for a girl whom he could neither regard nor **esteem**. Her heart did whisper that he had done it for her. But it was a hope shortly checked by other considerations, and she soon felt that even her **vanity** was insufficient, when required to depend on his affection for her --for a woman who had already refused him--as able to overcome a sentiment so natural as **abhorrence** against relationship with Wickham. Brother-in-law of Wickham! Every kind of pride must revolt from the connection. He had, to be sure, done much. She was ashamed to think how much. But he had given a reason for his interference, which asked no extraordinary stretch of belief. It was reasonable that he should feel he had been wrong; he had **liberality**, and he had the means of exercising it; and though she would not place herself as his principal **inducement**, she could, perhaps, believe that remaining **partiality** for her might assist his endeavours in a cause where her peace of mind must be **materially** concerned. It was painful, exceedingly painful, to know that they were under obligations to a person who could never receive a return. They owed the restoration of Lydia, her character, every thing, to him. Oh! how **heartily** did she **grieve** over every ungracious sensation she had ever encouraged, every **saucy** speech she had ever directed towards him. For herself she was **humbled**; but she was proud of him. Proud that in a cause of compassion and honour, he had been able to get the better of

Italian

abhorrence: orrore, avversione, ribrezzo, ripugnanza.
abominate: detestare, detestate, detesta, detestano, detestiamo, detesti, detesto, abominare, abomina, abomino, abominate.
attendant: custode, compagno, inserviente.
bribe: bustarella, corrompere, dono.
despise: disprezzare, disprezza, disprezzano, disprezzate, disprezzi, disprezziamo, disprezzo.

esteem: stima, rispetto, stimare, considerazione, considerare, rispettare, riguardo.
exertion: sforzo.
flutter: svolazzare.
grieve: affliggersi, addolorare, addolorarsi.
heartily: cordialmente.
humbled: umiliato.
inducement: incitamento.
liberality: liberalità.
materially: materialmente.

mortification: mortificazione.
partiality: parzialità, predilezione.
pronounce: pronunciare, pronunciano, pronunciate, pronunciamo, pronunci, pronuncio, pronuncia.
purposely: intenzionalmente.
saucy: impertinente, sfacciato.
supplication: preghiera, domanda, implorazione, supplica.
unsettled: sconvolto, disordinato.
vanity: vanità.

himself. She read over her **aunt's commendation** of him again and again. It was
hardly enough; but it **pleased** her. She was even **sensible** of some pleasure,
though **mixed** with **regret**, on finding how steadfastly both she and her **uncle**
had been **persuaded** that **affection** and confidence **subsisted** between Mr. Darcy
and herself.

She was **roused** from her seat, and her reflections, by some one's approach;
and before she could strike into another path, she was **overtaken** by Wickham.

"I am afraid I **interrupt** your **solitary ramble**, my dear sister?" said he, as he
joined her.

"You certainly do," she replied with a smile; "but it does not follow that the
interruption must be unwelcome."

"I should be sorry indeed, if it were. We were always good friends; and now
we are better."

"True. Are the others coming out?"

"I do not know. Mrs. **Bennet** and Lydia are going in the **carriage** to Meryton.
And so, my dear **sister**, I find, from our uncle and aunt, that you have actually
seen Pemberley."

She replied in the **affirmative**.

"I almost **envy** you the pleasure, and yet I believe it would be too much for
me, or else I could take it in my way to Newcastle. And you saw the old
housekeeper, I suppose? Poor Reynolds, she was always very **fond** of me. But
of course she did not **mention** my name to you."

"Yes, she did."

"And what did she say?"

"That you were gone into the army, and she was afraid had --not turned out
well. At such a distance as *that*, you know, things are **strangely** misrepresented."

"Certainly," he replied, **biting** his lips. Elizabeth **hoped** she had silenced
him; but he soon **afterwards** said:

Italian

affection: affetto, affezione, amore.
affirmative: affermativo.
afterwards: dopo, dietro, in seguito, successivamente.
aunt: zia, la zia.
bennet: cariofillata, erba benedetta.
biting: pungente, mordace.
carriage: vettura, carrello, vagone, carro, carrozza.
commendation: raccomandazione.
envy: invidia, invidiare, invidio, invidiate, invidiano, invidi,
invidiamo.
fond: tenero, affettuoso, affezionato.
hoped: sperato.
housekeeper: governante.
interrupt: interrompere, interruzione.
interruption: interruzione.
mention: menzionare, menzione, cenno.
mixed: misto, mescolato.
overtaken: sorpassato.
persuaded: convinto, persuaso.
pleased: contento, soddisfatto.
ramble: giro, passeggiata, vagare.
regret: rincrescere, rammarico, rimpiangere, rimpianto, rincrescimento.
roused: incitato, spronato, stimolato.
sensible: sensato, ragionevole, sensibile.
solitary: solo, solitario.
strangely: stranamente.
subsisted: esistito, sussistito.
uncle: zio, lo zio.

"I was **surprised** to see Darcy in town last month. We **passed** each other several times. I **wonder** what he can be doing there."

"Perhaps **preparing** for his **marriage** with Miss de Bourgh," said Elizabeth. "It must be something particular, to take him there at this time of year."

"Undoubtedly. Did you see him while you were at Lambton? I **thought** I **understood** from the Gardiners that you had."

"Yes; he **introduced** us to his sister."

"And do you like her?"

"Very much."

"I have heard, indeed, that she is **uncommonly improved** within this year or two. When I last saw her, she was not very **promising**. I am very **glad** you liked her. I hope she will turn out well."

"I **dare** say she will; she has got over the most trying age."

"Did you go by the village of Kympton?"

"I do not **recollect** that we did."

"I **mention** it, because it is the **living** which I ought to have had. A most **delightful** place!--Excellent Parsonage House! It would have suited me in every respect."

"How should you have liked making sermons?"

"Exceedingly well. I should have **considered** it as part of my **duty**, and the **exertion** would soon have been nothing. One ought not to repine;--but, to be sure, it would have been such a thing for me! The **quiet**, the **retirement** of such a life would have answered all my ideas of **happiness**! But it was not to be. Did you ever hear Darcy mention the **circumstance**, when you were in Kent?"

"I have heard from authority, which I thought *as good*, that it was left you **conditionally** only, and at the will of the present patron."

"You have. Yes, there was something in *that*; I told you so from the first, you may remember."

Italian

circumstance: circostanza.
conditionally: condizionalmente.
considered: considerato.
dare: osare, oso, osiamo, osi, osate, osano, osa, sfida.
delightful: delizioso, piacevole.
duty: dovere, dazio, imposta, mansione.
exertion: sforzo.
glad: contento, felice, lieto.
happiness: felicità.
improved: migliorato, perfezionato.

introduced: presentato, introdotto.
living: vivendo, abitando, vivo, vivente.
marriage: matrimonio.
mention: menzionare, menzione, cenno.
ought: dovere.
passed: passato.
preparing: preparando, allestendo, apprestando.
promising: promettendo, promettente.
quiet: calmare, tranquillo, placare,

quieto, calmo, zitto, silenzioso, quiete.
recollect: rammenta, rammentano, rammentate, rammenti, rammentiamo, rammento, rammentare, ricordarsi.
retirement: pensionamento, ritiro.
surprised: sorpreso, sorpresa.
uncommonly: insolitamente.
understood: capito, compreso.
wonder: stupirsi, stupore, meraviglia, domandarsi, meravigliarsi.

"I *did* hear, too, that there was a time, when sermon-making was not so palatable to you as it seems to be at present; that you actually declared your resolution of never taking orders, and that the business had been compromised accordingly."

"You did! and it was not wholly without foundation. You may remember what I told you on that point, when first we talked of it."

They were now almost at the door of the house, for she had walked fast to get rid of him; and unwilling, for her sister's sake, to provoke him, she only said in reply, with a good-humoured smile:

"Come, Mr. Wickham, we are brother and sister, you know. Do not let us quarrel about the past. In future, I hope we shall be always of one mind."

She held out her hand; he kissed it with affectionate gallantry, though he hardly knew how to look, and they entered the house.

Italian

affectionate: affettuoso.
brother: fratello, il fratello.
compromised: compromesso.
declared: dichiarato.
entered: entrato.
fast: veloce, digiuno, velocemente, presto, digiunare, rapido.
foundation: fondazione, fondamento, fondo, base, fondamenta.
future: futuro, avvenire.
gallantry: galanteria, valore, prodezza.
hardly: appena, a malapena, a stento.

hear: udire, odono, odi, odo, udite, udiamo, sentire, sentono, sento, sentite, senti.
kissed: baciato.
orders: ordine, comande ai tavoli.
palatable: gustoso, appetitoso.
provoke: spronare, provocare, incitare, provochi, sproniamo, sprono, sproni, spronate, spronano, sprona, provoco.
quarrel: lite, litigare, bisticciare, bisticcio, litigio.
reply: risposta, rispondere, replicare,

replica.
resolution: risoluzione, definizione, deliberazione.
rid: sbarazzare.
sake: causa.
sister: sorella, la sorella.
smile: sorriso, sorridere.
unwilling: riluttante, restio.
walked: camminato.
wholly: interamente, completamente.

CHAPTER 53

Mr. Wickham was so **perfectly satisfied** with this **conversation** that he never again **distressed** himself, or **provoked** his **dear sister** Elizabeth, by **introducing** the subject of it; and she was **pleased** to find that she had said enough to keep him quiet.

The day of his and Lydia's **departure** soon came, and Mrs. **Bennet** was **forced** to **submit** to a **separation**, which, as her husband by no means **entered** into her scheme of their all going to Newcastle, was likely to continue at **least** a twelvemonth.

"Oh! my dear Lydia," she cried, "when shall we meet again?"

"Oh, lord! I don't know. Not these two or three years, perhaps."

"Write to me very often, my dear."

"As often as I can. But you know **married** women have never much time for **writing**. My sisters may **write** to *me*. They will have nothing else to do."

Mr. Wickham's adieus were much more **affectionate** than his wife's. He **smiled**, looked **handsome**, and said many **pretty** things.

"He is as fine a fellow," said Mr. Bennet, as soon as they were out of the house, "as ever I saw. He simpers, and smirks, and makes love to us all. I am **prodigiously proud** of him. I **defy** even Sir William Lucas himself to **produce** a more **valuable** son-in-law."

Italian

affectionate: affettuoso.
bennet: cariofillata, erba benedetta.
conversation: conversazione, discorso.
dear: caro, costoso, egregio.
defy: sfidare, sfidano, sfidiamo, sfidate, sfidi, sfido, sfida.
departure: partenza.
distressed: afflitto.
entered: entrato.
forced: forzato.
handsome: bello, carino.
introducing: presentando,

introducendo.
least: minimo, meno.
married: sposato, si sposato.
perfectly: perfettamente.
pleased: contento, soddisfatto.
pretty: grazioso, bellino, carino, bello.
prodigiously: prodigiosamente.
produce: produrre, produciamo, produco, produci, producete, producono, produzione, prodotti, fabbricare, prodotto.
proud: orgoglioso, fiero.

provoked: spronato, incitato, provocato.
satisfied: soddisfatto, contento, accontentato.
separation: separazione, distacco.
sister: sorella, la sorella.
smiled: sorriso.
submit: sottomettere, sottoporre.
valuable: costoso, caro, prezioso.
write: scrivere, scrivi, scrivono, scriviamo, scrivete, scrivo.
writing: scrivendo, scrittura.

The loss of her daughter made Mrs. **Bennet** very **dull** for several days.

"I often think," said she, "that there is nothing so bad as **parting** with one's friends. One seems so **forlorn** without them."

"This is the **consequence**, you see, Madam, of **marrying** a daughter," said Elizabeth. "It must make you better **satisfied** that your other four are single."

"It is no such thing. Lydia does not leave me because she is married, but only because her husband's **regiment** happens to be so far off. If that had been nearer, she would not have gone so soon."

But the **spiritless** condition which this event threw her into was **shortly relieved**, and her mind opened again to the **agitation** of hope, by an article of news which then began to be in **circulation**. The **housekeeper** at Netherfield had received orders to **prepare** for the **arrival** of her master, who was coming down in a day or two, to **shoot** there for several weeks. Mrs. Bennet was quite in the fidgets. She looked at Jane, and smiled and shook her head by **turns**.

"Well, well, and so Mr. Bingley is coming down, sister," (for Mrs. Phillips first brought her the news). "Well, so much the better. Not that I care about it, though. He is nothing to us, you know, and I am sure _I_ never want to see him again. But, however, he is very welcome to come to Netherfield, if he likes it. And who knows what _may_ happen? But that is nothing to us. You know, sister, we agreed long ago never to **mention** a word about it. And so, is it quite certain he is coming?"

"You may **depend** on it," replied the other, "for Mrs. Nicholls was in Meryton last night; I saw her **passing** by, and went out myself on purpose to know the truth of it; and she told me that it was certain true. He comes down on Thursday at the **latest**, very likely on Wednesday. She was going to the butcher's, she told me, on purpose to order in some **meat** on Wednesday, and she has got three couple of ducks just fit to be killed."

Miss Bennet had not been able to hear of his coming without **changing** colour. It was many months since she had mentioned his name to Elizabeth; but now, as soon as they were alone together, she said:

Italian

agitation: agitazione.
arrival: arrivo, venuta.
bennet: cariofillata, erba benedetta.
changing: cambiare.
circulation: circolazione, diffusione.
consequence: conseguenza, risultato.
depend: dipendere, dipendete, dipendiamo, dipendo, dipendono, dipendi.
dull: opaco, smussato, spuntato.
forlorn: derelitto, abbandonato, misero.

housekeeper: governante.
latest: ultimo, recentissimo.
marrying: sposandosi.
meat: carne, la carne.
mention: menzionare, menzione, cenno.
parting: separazione, divisione.
passing: passeggero, passare, passaggio.
prepare: preparare, prepari, prepariamo, preparate, preparano, prepara, preparo, allestire,

allestiamo, allestisci, allestisco.
regiment: reggimento.
relieved: alleviato.
satisfied: soddisfatto, contento, accontentato.
shoot: sparare, spara, spariamo, spari, sparate, sparano, sparo, tirare, getto, germoglio, fucilare.
shortly: prossimamente.
spiritless: avvilito.
turns: gira, svolta, cambia.

"I saw you look at me to-day, Lizzy, when my aunt told us of the present report; and I know I appeared **distressed**. But don't imagine it was from any silly cause. I was only **confused** for the moment, because I felt that I *should* be looked at. I do **assure** you that the news does not affect me either with pleasure or pain. I am glad of one thing, that he comes alone; because we shall see the less of him. Not that I am afraid of *myself*, but I **dread** other people's remarks."

Elizabeth did not know what to make of it. Had she not seen him in Derbyshire, she might have supposed him capable of coming there with no other view than what was **acknowledged**; but she still thought him **partial** to Jane, and she **wavered** as to the greater **probability** of his coming there *with* his friend's permission, or being **bold** enough to come without it.

"Yet it is hard," she sometimes thought, "that this poor man **cannot** come to a house which he has **legally hired**, without **raising** all this **speculation**! I *will* leave him to himself."

In **spite** of what her sister declared, and really believed to be her feelings in the **expectation** of his arrival, Elizabeth could easily **perceive** that her spirits were affected by it. They were more **disturbed**, more **unequal**, than she had often seen them.

The subject which had been so **warmly** canvassed between their parents, about a twelvemonth ago, was now brought forward again.

"As soon as ever Mr. Bingley comes, my dear," said Mrs. **Bennet**, "you will wait on him of course."

"No, no. You forced me into **visiting** him last year, and promised, if I went to see him, he should marry one of my **daughters**. But it ended in nothing, and I will not be sent on a fool's **errand** again."

His wife represented to him how absolutely necessary such an attention would be from all the **neighbouring** gentlemen, on his returning to Netherfield.

"'Tis an **etiquette** I despise," said he. "If he wants our society, let him seek it. He knows where we live. I will not spend my hours in running after my neighbours every time they go away and come back again."

Italian

acknowledged: riconosciuto.
assure: assicurare, assicura, assicuriamo, assicurate, assicuri, assicurano, assicuro, garantire.
bennet: cariofillata, erba benedetta.
bold: grassetto, spesso, grosso, audace.
cannot: non potere.
confused: confuso.
daughters: figlie.
distressed: afflitto.
disturbed: disturbato.

dread: temere.
errand: messaggio, commissione.
etiquette: etichetta, galateo.
expectation: attesa, aspettativa.
hired: noleggiato.
legally: legalmente.
neighbouring: vicino.
partial: parziale.
perceive: percepire, accorgersi, scorgere, percepiamo, scorgo, scorgiamo, scorgi, scorgete, percepite, scorgono, percepiscono.

probability: probabilità.
raising: sollevamento, allevamento, sopraelevazione, aumento.
speculation: speculazione.
spite: dispetto.
unequal: ineguale, disuguale.
visiting: visitando.
warmly: caldamente, calorosamente.
wavered: esitato.

"Well, all I know is, that it will be **abominably rude** if you do not wait on him. But, however, that shan't prevent my asking him to **dine** here, I am determined. We must have Mrs. Long and the Gouldings soon. That will make **thirteen** with ourselves, so there will be just room at table for him."

Consoled by this resolution, she was the better able to bear her husband's incivility; though it was very **mortifying** to know that her neighbours might all see Mr. Bingley, in consequence of it, before *they* did. As the day of his arrival drew near:

"I begin to be sorry that he comes at all," said Jane to her sister. "It would be nothing; I could see him with perfect **indifference**, but I can hardly bear to hear it thus **perpetually** talked of. My mother means well; but she does not know, no one can know, how much I suffer from what she says. Happy shall I be, when his stay at Netherfield is over!"

"I wish I could say anything to **comfort** you," replied Elizabeth; "but it is **wholly** out of my power. You must feel it; and the usual satisfaction of **preaching patience** to a sufferer is denied me, because you have always so much."

Mr. Bingley arrived. Mrs. **Bennet**, through the assistance of servants, **contrived** to have the earliest tidings of it, that the period of **anxiety** and fretfulness on her side might be as long as it could. She **counted** the days that must **intervene** before their **invitation** could be sent; **hopeless** of seeing him before. But on the third morning after his arrival in Hertfordshire, she saw him, from her dressing-room window, enter the **paddock** and ride towards the house.

Her **daughters** were **eagerly** called to **partake** of her joy. Jane **resolutely** kept her place at the table; but Elizabeth, to **satisfy** her mother, went to the window-- she looked,--she saw Mr. Darcy with him, and sat down again by her sister.

"There is a gentleman with him, mamma," said Kitty; "who can it be?"

"Some **acquaintance** or other, my dear, I suppose; I am sure I do not know."

"La!" replied Kitty, "it looks just like that man that used to be with him before. Mr. what's-his-name. That tall, proud man."

Italian

abominably: abominevolmente.
acquaintance: conoscenza, conoscente.
anxiety: ansia, ansietà, angoscia, inquietudine.
bennet: cariofillata, erba benedetta.
comfort: consolare, comodità, confortare, comfort, benessere.
contrived: escogitato.
counted: contato.
daughters: figlie.
dine: cenare.
eagerly: ardentemente.

hopeless: disperato, senza speranza.
indifference: indifferenza.
intervene: intervenire, intervenite, intervieni, intervengo, intervengono, interveniamo.
invitation: invito.
mortifying: mortificando, umiliante.
paddock: paddock, recinto.
partake: partecipo, partecipa, partecipano, partecipate, partecipi, partecipiamo, partecipare.
patience: pazienza.

perpetually: perennemente, perpetuamente.
preaching: predicando.
resolutely: risoluto, risolutamente, decisamente.
rude: scortese, rozzo, maleducato.
satisfy: soddisfare, accontentare, soddisfano, soddisfiamo, soddisfa, soddisfate, soddisfo, accontentate, accontento, soddisfi, accontentano.
thirteen: tredici.
wholly: interamente, completamente.

"Good gracious! Mr. Darcy!--and so it does, I **vow**. Well, any friend of Mr. Bingley's will always be welcome here, to be sure; but else I must say that I **hate** the very sight of him."

Jane looked at Elizabeth with surprise and concern. She knew but little of their meeting in Derbyshire, and therefore felt for the **awkwardness** which must attend her sister, in seeing him almost for the first time after **receiving** his **explanatory** letter. Both sisters were **uncomfortable** enough. Each felt for the other, and of course for themselves; and their mother talked on, of her **dislike** of Mr. Darcy, and her resolution to be civil to him only as Mr. Bingley's friend, without being heard by either of them. But Elizabeth had sources of **uneasiness** which could not be suspected by Jane, to whom she had never yet had **courage** to shew Mrs. Gardiner's letter, or to relate her own change of **sentiment** towards him. To Jane, he could be only a man whose proposals she had refused, and whose **merit** she had **undervalued**; but to her own more extensive information, he was the person to whom the whole family were **indebted** for the first of benefits, and whom she regarded herself with an interest, if not quite so **tender**, at least as reasonable and just as what Jane felt for Bingley. Her **astonishment** at his coming--at his coming to Netherfield, to Longbourn, and **voluntarily** seeking her again, was almost equal to what she had known on first witnessing his **altered** behaviour in Derbyshire.

The colour which had been driven from her face, returned for half a minute with an additional **glow**, and a smile of **delight** added **lustre** to her eyes, as she thought for that space of time that his **affection** and wishes must still be unshaken. But she would not be secure.

"Let me first see how he behaves," said she; "it will then be early enough for expectation."

She sat **intently** at work, **striving** to be **composed**, and without **daring** to lift up her eyes, till anxious **curiosity** carried them to the face of her sister as the **servant** was **approaching** the door. Jane looked a little paler than usual, but more **sedate** than Elizabeth had expected. On the gentlemen's **appearing**, her colour increased; yet she received them with **tolerable** ease, and with a propriety

Italian

affection: affetto, affezione, amore.
altered: alterato.
appearing: apparendo.
approaching: avvicinamento.
astonishment: stupore, meraviglia, sorpresa.
awkwardness: goffaggine.
composed: composto.
courage: coraggio.
curiosity: curiosità.
daring: osando, audace.
delight: delizia, deliziare, dilettare, diletto, godimento, rallegrare, gioia.
dislike: avversione, ripugnanza, antipatia.
explanatory: esplicativo.
glow: ardore.
hate: odiare, odio, detestare.
indebted: obbligato, indebitato.
intently: intensamente.
lustre: lucentezza.
merit: meritare, merito, benemerenza, pregio.
receiving: ricevendo, accogliendo, ricezione, ricevere, ricevente.
sedate: calmo.
sentiment: sentimento.
servant: servire, servo, servitore.
striving: sforzandosi.
tender: tenero, dolce, offerta, tender.
tolerable: tollerabile.
uncomfortable: scomodo, disagiato.
undervalued: sottovalutato.
uneasiness: disagio.
voluntarily: volontariamente.
vow: voto.

of behaviour equally free from any **symptom** of **resentment** or any **unnecessary** complaisance.

Elizabeth said as little to either as **civility** would allow, and sat down again to her work, with an **eagerness** which it did not often command. She had **ventured** only one glance at Darcy. He looked serious, as usual; and, she thought, more as he had been used to look in Hertfordshire, than as she had seen him at Pemberley. But, perhaps he could not in her mother's presence be what he was before her uncle and aunt. It was a **painful**, but not an **improbable, conjecture**.

Bingley, she had **likewise** seen for an **instant**, and in that short period saw him looking both pleased and **embarrassed**. He was received by Mrs. **Bennet** with a degree of civility which made her two **daughters ashamed**, especially when contrasted with the cold and **ceremonious politeness** of her **curtsey** and address to his friend.

Elizabeth, particularly, who knew that her mother owed to the latter the **preservation** of her favourite daughter from **irremediable infamy**, was hurt and **distressed** to a most painful degree by a distinction so ill applied.

Darcy, after **inquiring** of her how Mr. and Mrs. Gardiner did, a question which she could not answer without confusion, said **scarcely** anything. He was not **seated** by her; perhaps that was the reason of his silence; but it had not been so in Derbyshire. There he had talked to her friends, when he could not to herself. But now several minutes **elapsed** without bringing the sound of his voice; and when occasionally, unable to **resist** the **impulse** of **curiosity**, she raised he eyes to his face, she as often found him looking at Jane as at herself, and frequently on no object but the ground. More **thoughtfulness** and less anxiety to please, than when they last met, were plainly expressed. She was **disappointed**, and angry with herself for being so.

"Could I expect it to be otherwise!" said she. "Yet why did he come?"

She was in no **humour** for conversation with anyone but himself; and to him she had hardly **courage** to speak.

She **inquired** after his sister, but could do no more.

Italian

ashamed: vergognoso.
bennet: cariofillata, erba benedetta.
ceremonious: cerimonioso.
civility: civiltà, cortesia.
conjecture: congettura.
courage: coraggio.
curiosity: curiosità.
curtsey: inchino.
daughters: figlie.
disappointed: deluso.
distressed: afflitto.
eagerness: impazienza.

elapsed: trascorso.
embarrassed: imbarazzato.
humour: umore, umorismo.
improbable: improbabile.
impulse: impulso.
infamy: infamia.
inquired: domandato.
inquiring: domandando, domandare.
instant: istante, momento, immediato.
irremediable: irrimediabile.
likewise: anche, altrettanto.
painful: doloroso, penoso.

politeness: cortesia, garbo.
preservation: conservazione, preservazione.
resentment: risentimento, astio.
resist: resistere, resistete, resistono, resisto, resistiamo, resisti.
scarcely: appena, a stento.
seated: seduto.
symptom: sintomo, segno.
thoughtfulness: pensosità.
unnecessary: inutile, non necessario.
ventured: avventurato.

"It is a long time, Mr. Bingley, since you went away," said Mrs. **Bennet**.

He **readily** agreed to it.

"I **began** to be afraid you would never come back again. People *did* say you meant to **quit** the place entirely at Michaelmas; but, however, I hope it is not true. A great many changes have happened in the **neighbourhood**, since you went away. Miss Lucas is married and settled. And one of my own **daughters**. I suppose you have heard of it; indeed, you must have seen it in the papers. It was in The Times and The Courier, I know; though it was not put in as it ought to be. It was only said, 'Lately, George Wickham, Esq. to Miss Lydia Bennet,' without there being a **syllable** said of her father, or the place where she lived, or anything. It was my brother Gardiner's drawing up too, and I wonder how he came to make such an **awkward** business of it. Did you see it?"

Bingley replied that he did, and made his **congratulations. Elizabeth dared** not **lift** up her eyes. How Mr. Darcy looked, therefore, she could not tell.

"It is a **delightful** thing, to be sure, to have a daughter well married," continued her mother, "but at the same time, Mr. Bingley, it is very hard to have her taken such a way from me. They are gone down to Newcastle, a place quite **northward**, it seems, and there they are to stay I do not know how long. His **regiment** is there; for I suppose you have heard of his leaving the ----shire, and of his being gone into the **regulars**. Thank Heaven! he has *some* friends, though perhaps not so many as he deserves."

Elizabeth, who knew this to be levelled at Mr. Darcy, was in such **misery** of **shame**, that she could hardly keep her seat. It drew from her, however, the **exertion** of speaking, which nothing else had so effectually done before; and she asked Bingley whether he meant to make any stay in the country at present. A few weeks, he believed.

"When you have killed all your own birds, Mr. Bingley," said her mother, "I beg you will come here, and **shoot** as many as you please on Mr. Bennet's **manor**. I am sure he will be **vastly** happy to **oblige** you, and will save all the best of the covies for you."

Italian

awkward: goffo, sgraziato.
beg: mendicare, mendicano, mendica, mendicate, mendico, mendichiamo, mendichi, chiedere, elemosinare, supplicare.
bennet: cariofillata, erba benedetta.
congratulations: congratulazioni.
dared: osato.
daughters: figlie.
delightful: delizioso, piacevole.
elizabeth: Elisabetta.
exertion: sforzo.

lift: ascensore, alzare, sollevare, salire, sollevamento, alzata, passaggio.
manor: feudo.
misery: miseria.
neighbourhood: circondario, distretto, vicinato, quartiere.
northward: verso nord.
oblige: obbligare, obblighiamo, obbliga, obbligano, obbligate, obblighi, obbligo.
quit: abbandonare, abbandonato, abbandono, abbandoni, abbandonate,

abbandonano, abbandona, abbandoniamo, smettere.
readily: prontamente.
regiment: reggimento.
regulars: regolare.
shame: vergogna, pudore.
shoot: sparare, spara, spariamo, spari, sparate, sparano, sparo, tirare, getto, germoglio, fucilare.
syllable: sillaba.
vastly: vastamente.

Elizabeth's **misery** increased, at such **unnecessary**, such **officious** attention! Were the same fair prospect to arise at present as had **flattered** them a year ago, every thing, she was persuaded, would be **hastening** to the same **vexatious** conclusion. At that **instant**, she felt that years of **happiness** could not make Jane or herself **amends** for moments of such painful confusion.

"The first wish of my heart," said she to herself, "is never more to be in company with either of them. Their society can afford no pleasure that will **atone** for such wretchedness as this! Let me never see either one or the other again!"

Yet the misery, for which years of happiness were to offer no **compensation**, received soon afterwards material relief, from **observing** how much the beauty of her sister re-kindled the **admiration** of her former **lover**. When first he came in, he had spoken to her but little; but every five minutes seemed to be giving her more of his attention. He found her as **handsome** as she had been last year; as good natured, and as **unaffected**, though not quite so **chatty**. Jane was anxious that no difference should be perceived in her at all, and was really persuaded that she talked as much as ever. But her mind was so **busily engaged**, that she did not always know when she was silent.

When the gentlemen rose to go away, Mrs. **Bennet** was **mindful** of her intended **civility**, and they were invited and engaged to **dine** at Longbourn in a few days time.

"You are quite a visit in my debt, Mr. Bingley," she added, "for when you went to town last winter, you promised to take a family dinner with us, as soon as you returned. I have not **forgot**, you see; and I **assure** you, I was very much **disappointed** that you did not come back and keep your engagement."

Bingley looked a little silly at this reflection, and said something of his concern at having been **prevented** by business. They then went away.

Mrs. Bennet had been strongly **inclined** to ask them to stay and dine there that day; but, though she always kept a very good table, she did not think anything less than two courses could be good enough for a man on whom she

Italian

admiration: ammirazione.
amends: emenda, ammenda.
assure: assicurare, assicura, assicuriamo, assicurate, assicuri, assicurano, assicuro, garantire.
atone: espiare, espio, espii, espiate, espiano, espia, espiamo.
bennet: cariofillata, erba benedetta.
busily: attivamente, indaffaratamente.
chatty: chiacchierino.
civility: civiltà, cortesia.
compensation: compensazione,

ricompensa, indennizzo, risarcimento, indennità.
dine: cenare.
disappointed: deluso.
engaged: occupato, innestato, impegnato.
flattered: lusingato.
forgot: dimenticato.
handsome: bello, carino.
happiness: felicità.
hastening: affrettando, sollecitando.
inclined: disposto, inclinato,

propenso.
instant: istante, momento, immediato.
lover: amante.
mindful: attento.
misery: miseria.
observing: osservando.
officious: ufficioso, invadente.
prevented: impedito, prevenuto.
unaffected: spontaneo, non affettato, semplice.
unnecessary: inutile, non necessario.
vexatious: irritante.

had such **anxious** designs, or **satisfy** the **appetite** and **pride** of one who had ten **thousand** a year.

Italian

anxious: ansioso.
appetite: appetito.
pride: orgoglio, fierezza.
satisfy: soddisfare, accontentare, soddisfano, soddisfiamo, soddisfa, soddisfate, soddisfo, accontentate, accontento, soddisfi, accontentano.
thousand: mille.

CHAPTER 54

As soon as they were gone, Elizabeth walked out to **recover** her spirits; or in other words, to **dwell** without **interruption** on those subjects that must **deaden** them more. Mr. Darcy's behaviour **astonished** and **vexed** her.

"Why, if he came only to be **silent**, **grave**, and **indifferent**," said she, "did he come at all?"

She could **settle** it in no way that gave her pleasure.

"He could be still **amiable**, still **pleasing**, to my **uncle** and **aunt**, when he was in town; and why not to me? If he fears me, why come **hither**? If he no longer cares for me, why silent? Teasing, teasing, man! I will think no more about him."

Her **resolution** was for a short time **involuntarily** kept by the approach of her sister, who joined her with a **cheerful** look, which showed her better **satisfied** with their visitors, than Elizabeth.

"Now," said she, "that this first meeting is over, I feel perfectly easy. I know my own strength, and I shall never be **embarrassed** again by his coming. I am glad he **dines** here on Tuesday. It will then be **publicly** seen that, on both sides, we meet only as common and indifferent acquaintance."

"Yes, very indifferent indeed," said Elizabeth, **laughingly**. "Oh, Jane, take care."

"My dear Lizzy, you **cannot** think me so **weak**, as to be in danger now?"

Italian

amiable: amabile.
astonished: stupito, si stupito.
aunt: zia, la zia.
cannot: non potere.
cheerful: allegro.
deaden: ammortizzare, ammortizza, ammortizzano, ammortizzate, ammortizzi, ammortizziamo, ammortizzo.
dines: pranza, cena.
dwell: abitare, dimorare, dimorate, dimoro, dimori, dimorano, dimora,

abitiamo, abiti, abitate, abitano.
embarrassed: imbarazzato.
grave: tomba, grave.
hither: qui, quà.
indifferent: indifferente.
interruption: interruzione.
involuntarily: involontariamente.
laughingly: ridere.
pleasing: piacevole.
publicly: pubblicamente.
recover: ricuperare, ricupera, ricuperi, ricuperiamo, ricuperano, ricuperate,

ricupero, recuperare, guarire, riprendere.
resolution: risoluzione, definizione, deliberazione.
satisfied: soddisfatto, contento, accontentato.
settle: sistemare, regolare, saldare.
silent: silenzioso, zitto.
uncle: zio, lo zio.
vexed: irritato, indispettito, vessato, contrariato.
weak: debole, fiacco.

"I think you are in very great danger of making him as much in love with you as ever."

They did not see the gentlemen again till Tuesday; and Mrs. **Bennet**, in the meanwhile, was giving way to all the happy schemes, which the good humour and common **politeness** of Bingley, in half an hour's visit, had revived.

On Tuesday there was a large party **assembled** at Longbourn; and the two who were most **anxiously** expected, to the credit of their **punctuality** as sportsmen, were in very good time. When they **repaired** to the dining-room, Elizabeth **eagerly** watched to see whether Bingley would take the place, which, in all their former parties, had **belonged** to him, by her sister. Her **prudent** mother, occupied by the same ideas, **forbore** to **invite** him to sit by herself. On entering the room, he seemed to **hesitate**; but Jane happened to look round, and happened to smile: it was decided. He placed himself by her.

Elizabeth, with a **triumphant sensation**, looked towards his friend. He bore it with **noble indifference**, and she would have **imagined** that Bingley had received his **sanction** to be happy, had she not seen his eyes **likewise** turned towards Mr. Darcy, with an expression of half-laughing alarm.

His behaviour to her sister was such, during dinner time, as showed an **admiration** of her, which, though more **guarded** than formerly, persuaded Elizabeth, that if left wholly to himself, Jane's **happiness**, and his own, would be **speedily secured**. Though she **dared** not depend upon the consequence, she yet received pleasure from **observing** his behaviour. It gave her all the **animation** that her spirits could **boast**; for she was in no **cheerful** humour. Mr. Darcy was almost as far from her as the table could divide them. He was on one side of her mother. She knew how little such a situation would give pleasure to either, or make either appear to advantage. She was not near enough to hear any of their discourse, but she could see how **seldom** they spoke to each other, and how formal and cold was their manner whenever they did. Her mother's ungraciousness, made the sense of what they owed him more painful to Elizabeth's mind; and she would, at times, have given anything to be privileged

Italian

admiration: ammirazione.
animation: animazione, vivacità.
anxiously: ansiosamente.
assembled: montato, assemblato.
belonged: appartenuto.
bennet: cariofillata, erba benedetta.
boast: vanteria, vantarsi.
bore: annoiare, alesaggio, foro, forare, succiello, seccare, alesare, perforare, trivellare.
cheerful: allegro.
dared: osato.

eagerly: ardentemente.
guarded: guardingo, custodito.
happiness: felicità.
hesitate: esitare, esitiamo, esiti, esitate, esita, esitano, esito, titubare, tituba, titubiamo, titubi.
imagined: immaginato.
indifference: indifferenza.
invite: invitare, invita, invitano, invitate, inviti, invitiamo, invito.
likewise: anche, altrettanto.
noble: nobile, gentilizio, nobiliare.

observing: osservando.
politeness: cortesia, garbo.
prudent: prudente, sensato.
punctuality: puntualità.
repaired: riparato.
sanction: sanzione.
secured: fissato.
seldom: raramente.
sensation: sensazione.
speedily: rapidamente.
triumphant: trionfante.

to tell him that his **kindness** was neither unknown nor unfelt by the whole of the family.

She was in hopes that the evening would afford some opportunity of bringing them together; that the whole of the visit would not pass away without **enabling** them to enter into something more of conversation than the **mere ceremonious salutation attending** his entrance. Anxious and **uneasy**, the period which passed in the drawing-room, before the gentlemen came, was **wearisome** and **dull** to a degree that almost made her **uncivil**. She looked forward to their entrance as the point on which all her chance of pleasure for the evening must depend.

"If he does not come to me, *then*," said she, "I shall give him up for ever."

The gentlemen came; and she thought he looked as if he would have answered her hopes; but, **alas**! the ladies had **crowded** round the table, where Miss Bennet was making tea, and Elizabeth **pouring** out the coffee, in so close a **confederacy** that there was not a single **vacancy** near her which would admit of a chair. And on the gentlemen's **approaching**, one of the girls moved closer to her than ever, and said, in a **whisper**:

"The men shan't come and part us, I am determined. We want none of them; do we?"

Darcy had walked away to another part of the room. She followed him with her eyes, **envied** everyone to whom he spoke, had **scarcely patience** enough to help anybody to coffee; and then was **enraged** against herself for being so **silly**!

"A man who has once been refused! How could I ever be **foolish** enough to expect a **renewal** of his love? Is there one among the sex, who would not **protest** against such a **weakness** as a second proposal to the same woman? There is no **indignity** so **abhorrent** to their feelings!"

She was a little **revived**, however, by his bringing back his coffee **cup** himself; and she **seized** the opportunity of saying:

"Is your sister at Pemberley still?"

"Yes, she will remain there till Christmas."

Italian

abhorrent: ripugnante, orrendo, orribile, avverso, detestabile.
alas: ahimè.
approaching: avvicinamento.
attending: visitando, curando, assistendo.
ceremonious: cerimonioso.
confederacy: confederazione.
crowded: affollato.
cup: tazza, coppa, la tazza, calice.
dull: opaco, smussato, spuntato.
enabling: abilitando.

enraged: irritato, arrabbiato, incollerito, adirato.
envied: invidiato.
foolish: sciocco, stupido, stolto, ignorante, fesso.
indignity: trattamento indegno.
kindness: gentilezza, bontà, cortesia.
mere: mero, laghetto, semplice.
patience: pazienza.
pouring: versare, torrenziale, colata.
protest: protesta, protestare.
renewal: rinnovo, rinnovamento.

revived: rianimato.
salutation: saluto.
scarcely: appena, a stento.
seized: afferrato.
silly: sciocco, stupido.
uncivil: incivile.
uneasy: inquieto.
vacancy: posto vacante.
weakness: debolezza.
wearisome: faticoso, tedioso.
whisper: sussurrare, bisbigliare, bisbiglio.

"And quite alone? Have all her friends left her?"

"Mrs. Annesley is with her. The others have been gone on to Scarborough, these three weeks."

She could think of nothing more to say; but if he **wished** to **converse** with her, he might have better success. He stood by her, however, for some minutes, in silence; and, at last, on the young lady's **whispering** to Elizabeth again, he walked away.

When the tea-things were removed, and the card-tables placed, the **ladies** all rose, and Elizabeth was then **hoping** to be soon joined by him, when all her views were **overthrown** by seeing him fall a **victim** to her mother's **rapacity** for whist players, and in a few moments after **seated** with the rest of the party. She now lost every **expectation** of pleasure. They were **confined** for the evening at different **tables**, and she had nothing to hope, but that his eyes were so often turned towards her side of the room, as to make him play as unsuccessfully as herself.

Mrs. **Bennet** had designed to keep the two Netherfield gentlemen to **supper**; but their **carriage** was **unluckily ordered** before any of the others, and she had no opportunity of **detaining** them.

"Well girls," said she, as soon as they were left to themselves, "What say you to the day? I think every thing has passed off **uncommonly** well, I **assure** you. The dinner was as well **dressed** as any I ever saw. The **venison** was **roasted** to a turn--and everybody said they never saw so **fat** a **haunch**. The **soup** was fifty times better than what we had at the Lucases' last week; and even Mr. Darcy **acknowledged**, that the partridges were **remarkably** well done; and I suppose he has two or three French cooks at least. And, my dear Jane, I never saw you look in greater beauty. Mrs. Long said so too, for I asked her whether you did not. And what do you think she said **besides**? 'Ah! Mrs. Bennet, we shall have her at Netherfield at last.' She did indeed. I do think Mrs. Long is as good a **creature** as ever lived--and her nieces are very pretty **behaved** girls, and not at all **handsome**: I like them prodigiously."

Italian

acknowledged: riconosciuto.
assure: assicurare, assicura, assicuriamo, assicurate, assicuri, assicurano, assicuro, garantire.
behaved: agito, comportato.
bennet: cariofillata, erba benedetta.
besides: inoltre, d'altronde.
carriage: vettura, carrello, vagone, carro, carrozza.
confined: limitato.
converse: contrario.
creature: creatura.

detaining: ritenendo.
dressed: vestito.
expectation: attesa, aspettativa.
fat: grasso, grosso, pingue, spesso.
handsome: bello, carino.
haunch: coscia, anca.
hoping: sperando.
ladies: signore.
ordered: ordinato, disposto.
overthrown: rovesciato.
rapacity: rapacità.
remarkably: notevolmente.

roasted: arrostito.
seated: seduto.
soup: minestra, brodo, zuppa, la minestra.
supper: cena.
tables: tavoli.
uncommonly: insolitamente.
unluckily: sfortunatamente.
venison: carne di cervo.
victim: vittima.
whispering: sussurrio.
wished: desiderato.

Mrs. **Bennet**, in short, was in very great spirits; she had seen enough of Bingley's behaviour to Jane, to be **convinced** that she would get him at last; and her expectations of advantage to her family, when in a happy **humour**, were so far beyond reason, that she was quite **disappointed** at not seeing him there again the next day, to make his proposals.

"It has been a very **agreeable** day," said Miss Bennet to Elizabeth. "The party seemed so well **selected**, so suitable one with the other. I hope we may often meet again."

Elizabeth smiled.

"Lizzy, you must not do so. You must not **suspect** me. It **mortifies** me. I **assure** you that I have now learnt to enjoy his conversation as an agreeable and **sensible** young man, without having a wish beyond it. I am perfectly **satisfied**, from what his **manners** now are, that he never had any design of **engaging** my **affection**. It is only that he is **blessed** with greater **sweetness** of address, and a stronger desire of generally **pleasing**, than any other man."

"You are very cruel," said her sister, "you will not let me smile, and are **provoking** me to it every moment."

"How hard it is in some cases to be believed!"

"And how impossible in others!"

"But why should you wish to **persuade** me that I feel more than I acknowledge?"

"That is a question which I hardly know how to answer. We all love to **instruct**, though we can **teach** only what is not worth knowing. Forgive me; and if you **persist** in **indifference**, do not make me your confidante."

Italian

affection: affetto, affezione, amore.
agreeable: gradevole, piacevole, amabile.
assure: assicurare, assicura, assicuriamo, assicurate, assicuri, assicurano, assicuro, garantire.
bennet: cariofillata, erba benedetta.
blessed: benedetto, beato.
convinced: convinto.
disappointed: deluso.
engaging: innestando, attraente.
humour: umore, umorismo.

indifference: indifferenza.
instruct: istruire, istruiamo, istruisci, istruisco, istruiscono, istruite.
manners: educazione.
mortifies: mortifica.
persist: persistere, persistono, persisto, persistiamo, persisti, persistete.
persuade: convincere, convincono, convincete, convinci, convinciamo, convinco, persuadere, persuadono, persuado, persuadiamo, persuadi.
pleasing: piacevole.

provoking: incitando, provocando, spronando.
satisfied: soddisfatto, contento, accontentato.
selected: selezionato, scelto.
sensible: sensato, ragionevole, sensibile.
suspect: sospettare, sospetto.
sweetness: dolcezza.
teach: insegnare, insegna, insegnano, insegniamo, insegni, insegnate, insegno, istruire.

CHAPTER 55

A few days after this visit, Mr. Bingley called again, and **alone**. His friend had left him that morning for London, but was to return home in ten days time. He sat with them above an hour, and was in **remarkably** good spirits. Mrs. **Bennet invited** him to **dine** with them; but, with many **expressions** of **concern**, he **confessed** himself **engaged** elsewhere.

"Next time you call," said she, "I hope we shall be more lucky."

He should be particularly happy at any time, **etc**. etc.; and if she would give him leave, would take an early opportunity of **waiting** on them.

"Can you come to-morrow?"

Yes, he had no **engagement** at all for to-morrow; and her **invitation** was **accepted** with **alacrity**.

He came, and in such very good time that the **ladies** were **none** of them **dressed**. In ran Mrs. Bennet to her daughter's room, in her **dressing gown**, and with her **hair** half **finished**, **crying** out:

"My **dear** Jane, make **haste** and **hurry** down. He is come--Mr. Bingley is come. He is, indeed. Make haste, make haste. Here, Sarah, come to Miss Bennet this moment, and help her on with her gown. Never mind Miss Lizzy's hair."

"We will be down as soon as we can," said Jane; "but I **dare** say Kitty is **forwarder** than either of us, for she went up **stairs** half an hour ago."

Italian

accepted: accettato.
alacrity: entusiasmo, alacrità.
alone: solo, da solo, solamente.
bennet: cariofillata, erba benedetta.
concern: riguardare, concernere, cura, azienda, importanza, preoccupazione.
confessed: confessato.
crying: pianto, piangente, piangere.
dare: osare, oso, osiamo, osi, osate, osano, osa, sfida.
dear: caro, costoso, egregio.

dine: cenare.
dressed: vestito.
dressing: fasciatura, condimento.
engaged: occupato, innestato, impegnato.
engagement: fidanzamento, assunzione.
etc: ecc.
expressions: espressioni.
finished: finito, pronto, ultimato, terminato, rifinito.
forwarder: spedizioniere.

gown: abito, vestito, toga.
hair: capelli, capello, pelo, capigliatura.
haste: fretta, furia.
hurry: affrettarsi, fretta.
invitation: invito.
invited: invitato.
ladies: signore.
none: nessuno.
remarkably: notevolmente.
stairs: scala, scale.
waiting: aspettando, attesa, servizio.

"Oh! **hang** Kitty! what has she to do with it? Come be quick, be quick! Where is your **sash**, my dear?"

But when her mother was gone, Jane would not be **prevailed** on to go down without one of her sisters.

The same anxiety to get them by themselves was visible again in the evening. After tea, Mr. **Bennet** retired to the library, as was his **custom**, and Mary went up stairs to her instrument. Two **obstacles** of the five being thus removed, Mrs. Bennet sat looking and **winking** at Elizabeth and Catherine for a considerable time, without making any impression on them. Elizabeth would not **observe** her; and when at last Kitty did, she very **innocently** said, "What is the matter mamma? What do you keep winking at me for? What am I to do?"

"Nothing child, nothing. I did not wink at you." She then sat still five minutes longer; but unable to waste such a precious occasion, she suddenly got up, and saying to Kitty, "Come here, my love, I want to speak to you," took her out of the room. Jane **instantly** gave a look at Elizabeth which spoke her **distress** at such **premeditation**, and her **entreaty** that *she* would not give in to it. In a few minutes, Mrs. Bennet half-opened the door and called out:

"Lizzy, my dear, I want to speak with you."

Elizabeth was forced to go.

"We may as well leave them by themselves you know;" said her mother, as soon as she was in the hall. "Kitty and I are going upstairs to sit in my dressing-room."

Elizabeth made no attempt to reason with her mother, but remained quietly in the hall, till she and Kitty were out of sight, then returned into the drawing-room.

Mrs. Bennet's schemes for this day were **ineffectual**. Bingley was every thing that was **charming**, except the **professed** lover of her daughter. His ease and **cheerfulness rendered** him a most **agreeable** addition to their evening party; and he **bore** with the ill-judged **officiousness** of the mother, and heard all her

---

Italian

agreeable: gradevole, piacevole, amabile.
bennet: cariofillata, erba benedetta.
bore: annoiare, alesaggio, foro, forare, succiello, seccare, alesare, perforare, trivellare.
charming: affascinante, grazioso, amabile, incantevole.
cheerfulness: contentezza, allegria.
custom: costume, usanza, uso, abitudine, consuetudine.
distress: pericolo.

entreaty: preghiera, domanda, supplica.
hang: pendere, appendere, sospendere, impiccare.
ineffectual: inefficace, vano.
innocently: innocentemente.
instantly: direttamente, istantaneamente, immediatamente.
mamma: mamma.
observe: osservare, osservano, osservo, osserviamo, osservate, osserva, osservi, eseguire, compiere.

obstacles: ostacoli.
officiousness: ufficiosità, ingerenza, invadenza.
premeditation: premeditazione.
prevailed: prevalso.
professed: professato, dichiarare, dichiarato.
rendered: reso.
sash: fusciacca.
wink: ammiccare.

silly remarks with a **forbearance** and command of **countenance** particularly grateful to the daughter.

He scarcely needed an invitation to stay supper; and before he went away, an engagement was formed, **chiefly** through his own and Mrs. **Bennet's** means, for his coming next morning to shoot with her husband.

After this day, Jane said no more of her **indifference**. Not a word passed between the sisters concerning Bingley; but Elizabeth went to bed in the happy belief that all must **speedily** be concluded, unless Mr. Darcy returned within the stated time. Seriously, however, she felt **tolerably** persuaded that all this must have taken place with that gentleman's **concurrence**.

Bingley was **punctual** to his **appointment**; and he and Mr. Bennet spent the morning together, as had been agreed on. The latter was much more **agreeable** than his companion expected. There was nothing of **presumption** or **folly** in Bingley that could **provoke** his **ridicule**, or **disgust** him into silence; and he was more **communicative**, and less **eccentric**, than the other had ever seen him. Bingley of course returned with him to dinner; and in the evening Mrs. Bennet's **invention** was again at work to get every body away from him and her daughter. Elizabeth, who had a letter to write, went into the breakfast room for that purpose soon after tea; for as the others were all going to sit down to cards, she could not be wanted to **counteract** her mother's schemes.

But on returning to the drawing-room, when her letter was finished, she saw, to her **infinite** surprise, there was reason to fear that her mother had been too **ingenious** for her. On opening the door, she perceived her sister and Bingley standing together over the **hearth**, as if engaged in **earnest** conversation; and had this led to no suspicion, the faces of both, as they **hastily** turned round and moved away from each other, would have told it all. Their situation was awkward enough; but *her's* she thought was still worse. Not a **syllable** was uttered by either; and Elizabeth was on the point of going away again, when Bingley, who as well as the other had sat down, suddenly rose, and **whispering** a few words to her sister, ran out of the room.

Italian

agreeable: gradevole, piacevole, amabile.
appointment: appuntamento, nomina, inserimento.
bennet: cariofillata, erba benedetta.
chiefly: principalmente, soprattutto.
communicative: comunicativo.
concurrence: accordo.
countenance: approvare, viso.
counteract: neutralizzare, neutralizziamo, neutralizzo, neutralizzi, neutralizzate,

neutralizzano, neutralizza.
disgust: ripugnanza, avversione, disgustare, disgusto, nauseare.
earnest: serio, caparra.
eccentric: eccentrico, stravagante.
folly: follia.
forbearance: pazienza.
hastily: frettolosamente.
hearth: focolare.
indifference: indifferenza.
infinite: infinito.
ingenious: ingegnoso.

invention: invenzione.
presumption: presunzione, supposizione.
provoke: spronare, provocare, incitare, provochi, sproniamo, sprono, sproni, spronate, spronano, sprona, provoco.
punctual: esatto, puntuale, preciso.
ridicule: ridicolo, ridicolizzare.
speedily: rapidamente.
syllable: sillaba.
tolerably: tollerabilmente.
whispering: sussurrio.

Jane could have no **reserves** from Elizabeth, where confidence would give pleasure; and **instantly** embracing her, **acknowledged**, with the liveliest **emotion**, that she was the happiest **creature** in the world.

"'Tis too much!" she added, "by far too much. I do not **deserve** it. Oh! why is not everybody as happy?"

Elizabeth's **congratulations** were given with a **sincerity**, a **warmth**, a **delight**, which words could but **poorly** express. Every sentence of **kindness** was a fresh source of **happiness** to Jane. But she would not allow herself to stay with her sister, or say half that remained to be said for the present.

"I must go instantly to my mother;" she cried. "I would not on any account **trifle** with her **affectionate solicitude**; or allow her to hear it from anyone but myself. He is gone to my father already. Oh! Lizzy, to know that what I have to **relate** will give such pleasure to all my dear family! how shall I bear so much happiness!"

She then **hastened** away to her mother, who had **purposely** broken up the card party, and was sitting up stairs with Kitty.

Elizabeth, who was left by herself, now smiled at the **rapidity** and ease with which an affair was finally settled, that had given them so many previous months of **suspense** and **vexation**.

"And this," said she, "is the end of all his friend's anxious **circumspection**! of all his sister's **falsehood** and **contrivance**! the happiest, wisest, most reasonable end!"

In a few minutes she was joined by Bingley, whose conference with her father had been short and to the purpose.

"Where is your sister?" said he **hastily**, as he opened the door.

"With my mother up stairs. She will be down in a moment, I dare say."

He then shut the door, and, coming up to her, claimed the good wishes and affection of a sister. Elizabeth **honestly** and **heartily** expressed her delight in the prospect of their relationship. They shook hands with great **cordiality**; and then,

Italian

acknowledged: riconosciuto.
affection: affetto, affezione, amore.
affectionate: affettuoso.
circumspection: circospezione.
congratulations: congratulazioni.
contrivance: congegno.
cordiality: cordialità.
creature: creatura.
delight: delizia, deliziare, dilettare, diletto, godimento, rallegrare, gioia.
deserve: meritare, meritano, merita, meritate, meritiamo, meriti, merito.

emotion: emozione, commozione.
falsehood: falso, falsità, bugia, menzogna.
happiness: felicità.
hastened: affrettato, sollecitato.
hastily: frettolosamente.
heartily: cordialmente.
honestly: onestamente.
instantly: direttamente, istantaneamente, immediatamente.
kindness: gentilezza, bontà, cortesia.
poorly: male, poveramente.

purposely: intenzionalmente.
rapidity: rapidità, velocità.
relate: raccontare, raccontiamo, racconta, raccontano, raccontate, racconti, racconto, narrare.
reserves: riserve.
sincerity: sincerità.
solicitude: sollecitudine.
suspense: apprensione.
trifle: inezia, sciocchezza.
vexation: irritazione.
warmth: calore, cordialità, tepore.

till her sister came down, she had to listen to all he had to say of his own **happiness**, and of Jane's perfections; and in **spite** of his being a **lover**, Elizabeth really believed all his expectations of **felicity** to be **rationally** founded, because they had for **basis** the excellent understanding, and super-excellent **disposition** of Jane, and a general **similarity** of feeling and taste between her and himself.

It was an evening of no common delight to them all; the satisfaction of Miss **Bennet's** mind gave a **glow** of such sweet **animation** to her face, as made her look handsomer than ever. **Kitty** simpered and smiled, and hoped her turn was coming soon. Mrs. Bennet could not give her consent or speak her **approbation** in terms warm enough to satisfy her feelings, though she talked to Bingley of nothing else for half an hour; and when Mr. Bennet joined them at **supper**, his voice and manner plainly showed how really happy he was.

Not a word, however, passed his lips in **allusion** to it, till their visitor took his leave for the night; but as soon as he was gone, he turned to his daughter, and said:

"Jane, I **congratulate** you. You will be a very happy woman."

Jane went to him **instantly**, **kissed** him, and **thanked** him for his **goodness**.

"You are a good girl;" he replied, "and I have great pleasure in thinking you will be so happily settled. I have not a doubt of your doing very well together. Your tempers are by no means unlike. You are each of you so **complying**, that nothing will ever be resolved on; so easy, that every **servant** will **cheat** you; and so generous, that you will always **exceed** your income."

"I hope not so. Imprudence or **thoughtlessness** in money matters would be **unpardonable** in me."

"Exceed their income! My dear Mr. Bennet," cried his wife, "what are you talking of? Why, he has four or five thousand a year, and very likely more." Then **addressing** her daughter, "Oh! my dear, dear Jane, I am so happy! I am sure I shan't get a **wink** of sleep all night. I knew how it would be. I always said it must be so, at last. I was sure you could not be so beautiful for nothing! I remember, as soon as ever I saw him, when he first came into Hertfordshire last

Italian

addressing: indirizzamento.
allusion: allusione.
animation: animazione, vivacità.
approbation: approvazione.
basis: base.
bennet: cariofillata, erba benedetta.
cheat: ingannare, truffare, imbroglione, imbrogliare, barare.
complying: accondiscendendo, ottemperando.
congratulate: felicitare, felicitate, felicito, feliciti, felicitano, felicita,

felicitiamo.
disposition: disposizione, predisposizione, ingegno, talento.
exceed: eccedere, eccedono, eccedo, eccedete, eccedi, eccediamo, oltrepassare.
felicity: felicità.
glow: ardore.
goodness: bontà.
happiness: felicità.
instantly: direttamente, istantaneamente, immediatamente.

kissed: baciato.
kitty: gattino.
lover: amante.
rationally: razionalmente.
servant: servire, servo, servitore.
similarity: somiglianza, similarità.
spite: dispetto.
supper: cena.
thanked: ringraziato.
thoughtlessness: sconsideratezza.
unpardonable: imperdonabile.
wink: ammiccare.

year, I thought how likely it was that you should come together. Oh! he is the handsomest young man that ever was seen!"

Wickham, Lydia, were all **forgotten**. Jane was beyond competition her **favourite** child. At that moment, she cared for no other. Her **younger** sisters soon began to make interest with her for **objects** of **happiness** which she might in future be able to dispense.

Mary petitioned for the use of the library at Netherfield; and Kitty **begged** very hard for a few **balls** there every winter.

Bingley, from this time, was of course a daily **visitor** at Longbourn; coming frequently before **breakfast**, and always **remaining till** after **supper**; unless when some **barbarous neighbour**, who could not be enough **detested**, had given him an **invitation** to dinner which he thought himself **obliged** to accept.

Elizabeth had now but little time for **conversation** with her sister; for while he was present, Jane had no attention to **bestow** on anyone else; but she found herself **considerably** useful to both of them in those hours of **separation** that must sometimes occur. In the absence of Jane, he always **attached** himself to Elizabeth, for the **pleasure** of talking of her; and when Bingley was gone, Jane **constantly sought** the same means of relief.

"He has made me so happy," said she, one evening, "by telling me that he was totally **ignorant** of my being in town last spring! I had not believed it possible."

"I suspected as much," replied Elizabeth. "But how did he account for it?"

"It must have been his sister's doing. They were certainly no friends to his **acquaintance** with me, which I **cannot wonder** at, since he might have chosen so much more **advantageously** in many respects. But when they see, as I trust they will, that their brother is happy with me, they will learn to be **contented**, and we shall be on good terms again; though we can never be what we once were to each other."

Italian

acquaintance: conoscenza, conoscente.
advantageously: vantaggiosamente.
attached: fissato, attaccato, allegato.
balls: sfere, palla, balli.
barbarous: barbaro.
begged: mendicato.
bestow: tributare, concedere.
breakfast: colazione, prima colazione.
cannot: non potere.
considerably: considerevolmente.
constantly: costantemente.
contented: contento.

conversation: conversazione, discorso.
detested: detestato.
elizabeth: Elisabetta.
favourite: preferito.
forgotten: dimenticato.
happiness: felicità.
ignorant: ignorante.
invitation: invito.
neighbour: vicino.
objects: oggetti.
obliged: obbligato.
pleasure: piacere, gradimento.

remaining: rimanendo, restando, rimanente, restante.
separation: separazione, distacco.
sought: cercato.
supper: cena.
till: finchè, coltivare, cassa, fino, arare.
visitor: visitatore, ospite.
wonder: stupirsi, stupore, meraviglia, domandarsi, meravigliarsi.
younger: più giovane.

"That is the most **unforgiving** speech," said Elizabeth, "that I ever heard you **utter**. Good girl! It would **vex** me, indeed, to see you again the **dupe** of Miss Bingley's **pretended** regard."

"Would you believe it, Lizzy, that when he went to town last November, he really loved me, and nothing but a **persuasion** of *my* being **indifferent** would have **prevented** his coming down again!"

"He made a little mistake to be sure; but it is to the credit of his modesty."

This naturally introduced a **panegyric** from Jane on his **diffidence**, and the little value he put on his own good qualities. Elizabeth was pleased to find that he had not **betrayed** the **interference** of his friend; for, though Jane had the most generous and forgiving heart in the world, she knew it was a **circumstance** which must **prejudice** her against him.

"I am certainly the most **fortunate** creature that ever existed!" cried Jane. "Oh! Lizzy, why am I thus singled from my family, and **blessed** above them all! If I could but see *you* as happy! If there *were* but such another man for you!"

"If you were to give me **forty** such men, I never could be so happy as you. Till I have your **disposition**, your **goodness**, I never can have your happiness. No, no, let me **shift** for myself; and, perhaps, if I have very good luck, I may meet with another Mr. Collins in time."

The situation of affairs in the Longbourn family could not be long a secret. Mrs. **Bennet** was **privileged** to **whisper** it to Mrs. Phillips, and she **ventured**, without any permission, to do the same by all her neighbours in Meryton.

The Bennets were **speedily pronounced** to be the luckiest family in the world, though only a few weeks before, when Lydia had first run away, they had been generally proved to be marked out for **misfortune**.

Italian

bennet: cariofillata, erba benedetta.
betrayed: tradito.
blessed: benedetto, beato.
circumstance: circostanza.
diffidence: timidezza.
disposition: disposizione, predisposizione, ingegno, talento.
dupe: duplicato, ingannare, credulone, gonzo, babbeo.
forgiving: perdonando.
fortunate: fortunato, felice.
forty: quaranta.

goodness: bontà.
indifferent: indifferente.
interference: interferenza.
misfortune: sfortuna, traversia, disgrazia.
panegyric: panegirico.
persuasion: persuasione.
prejudice: pregiudizio, preconcetto, prevenzione.
pretended: finto.
prevented: impedito, prevenuto.
privileged: privilegiato.

pronounced: pronunciato.
shift: turno, spostare, cambio, spostamento, scorrimento, trasferire.
speedily: rapidamente.
utter: totale, completo, proferire, emettere.
ventured: avventurato.
vex: irritare, contrariare, indispettire, vessare, irritano, vesso, vessiamo, vessi, vessate, vessano, vessa.
whisper: sussurrare, bisbigliare, bisbiglio.

CHAPTER 56

One morning, about a week after Bingley's **engagement** with Jane had been formed, as he and the females of the family were sitting together in the dining-room, their attention was suddenly drawn to the window, by the sound of a **carriage**; and they **perceived** a **chaise** and four **driving** up the **lawn**. It was too early in the morning for **visitors**, and **besides**, the **equipage** did not answer to that of any of their neighbours. The horses were post; and neither the carriage, nor the **livery** of the **servant** who **preceded** it, were familiar to them. As it was certain, however, that somebody was coming, Bingley **instantly prevailed** on Miss **Bennet** to avoid the **confinement** of such an **intrusion**, and walk away with him into the **shrubbery**. They both set off, and the conjectures of the remaining three continued, though with little **satisfaction**, **till** the door was **thrown** open and their visitor entered. It was Lady Catherine de Bourgh.

They were of course all **intending** to be **surprised**; but their **astonishment** was beyond their **expectation**; and on the part of Mrs. Bennet and Kitty, though she was perfectly unknown to them, even **inferior** to what **Elizabeth** felt.

She entered the room with an air more than usually ungracious, made no other reply to Elizabeth's **salutation** than a **slight inclination** of the head, and sat down without saying a word. Elizabeth had mentioned her name to her mother on her ladyship's entrance, though no request of introduction had been made.

Italian

astonishment: stupore, meraviglia, sorpresa.
bennet: cariofillata, erba benedetta.
besides: inoltre, d'altronde.
carriage: vettura, carrello, vagone, carro, carrozza.
chaise: calesse.
confinement: reclusione, prigionia, confinamento.
driving: guida.
elizabeth: Elisabetta.
engagement: fidanzamento,
assunzione.
equipage: equipaggio.
expectation: attesa, aspettativa.
inclination: inclinazione, pendenza.
inferior: inferiore.
instantly: direttamente, istantaneamente, immediatamente.
intending: intendendo.
intrusion: intrusione.
lawn: prato, tappeto erboso, linone.
livery: livrea.
perceived: scorto, percepito,
intravisto.
preceded: preceduto.
prevailed: prevalso.
salutation: saluto.
satisfaction: soddisfazione.
servant: servire, servo, servitore.
shrubbery: boschetto.
slight: leggero, lieve.
surprised: sorpreso, sorpresa.
thrown: gettato.
till: finchè, coltivare, cassa, fino, arare.
visitor: visitatore, ospite.

Mrs. **Bennet**, all **amazement**, though **flattered** by having a **guest** of such high importance, received her with the **utmost politeness**. After sitting for a moment in silence, she said very **stiffly** to Elizabeth,

"I hope you are well, Miss Bennet. That lady, I suppose, is your mother."

Elizabeth replied very **concisely** that she was.

"And *that* I suppose is one of your sisters."

"Yes, madam," said Mrs. Bennet, **delighted** to speak to a Lady Catherine. "She is my youngest girl but one. My youngest of all is **lately** married, and my **eldest** is somewhere about the grounds, walking with a young man who, I believe, will soon become a part of the family."

"You have a very small park here," returned Lady Catherine after a short silence.

"It is nothing in **comparison** of Rosings, my lady, I **dare** say; but I **assure** you it is much larger than Sir William Lucas's."

"This must be a most **inconvenient** sitting room for the evening, in summer; the windows are full west."

Mrs. Bennet **assured** her that they never sat there after dinner, and then added:

"May I take the **liberty** of asking your **ladyship** whether you left Mr. and Mrs. Collins well."

"Yes, very well. I saw them the night before last."

Elizabeth now expected that she would produce a letter for her from Charlotte, as it seemed the only **probable motive** for her **calling**. But no letter appeared, and she was completely puzzled.

Mrs. Bennet, with great **civility**, **begged** her ladyship to take some **refreshment**; but Lady Catherine very **resolutely**, and not very **politely**, declined **eating** anything; and then, **rising** up, said to Elizabeth,

---

Italian

amazement: stupore, meraviglia.
assure: assicurare, assicura, assicuriamo, assicurate, assicuri, assicurano, assicuro, garantire.
assured: assicurato, certo.
begged: mendicato.
bennet: cariofillata, erba benedetta.
calling: chiamando, chiamata.
civility: civiltà, cortesia.
comparison: confronto, riscontro, comparazione, paragone.
concisely: concisamente.

dare: osare, oso, osiamo, osi, osate, osano, osa, sfida.
delighted: lietissimo.
eating: mangiando.
eldest: maggiore, il più vecchio.
flattered: lusingato.
guest: ospite, invitato.
inconvenient: difficile, pesante, inconveniente, incomodo.
ladyship: signoria.
lately: ultimamente, recentemente.
liberty: libertà.

motive: motivo, movente, ragione.
politely: cortesemente.
politeness: cortesia, garbo.
probable: probabile.
refreshment: rinfresco, ristoro.
resolutely: risoluto, risolutamente, decisamente.
rising: aumento, salita, sorgere, sorgente, levata, ascendente, ascesa, nascente, sommossa, levante, crescita.
stiffly: rigidamente.
utmost: massimo.

"Miss Bennet, there seemed to be a prettyish kind of a little **wilderness** on one side of your **lawn**. I should be glad to take a turn in it, if you will favour me with your company."

"Go, my dear," cried her mother, "and show her **ladyship** about the different **walks**. I think she will be pleased with the hermitage."

Elizabeth **obeyed**, and running into her own room for her **parasol**, attended her **noble** guest **downstairs**. As they passed through the hall, Lady Catherine opened the doors into the dining-parlour and drawing-room, and **pronouncing** them, after a short survey, to be **decent** looking rooms, walked on.

Her **carriage** remained at the door, and Elizabeth saw that her waiting-woman was in it. They **proceeded** in silence along the **gravel** walk that led to the copse; Elizabeth was determined to make no effort for conversation with a woman who was now more than usually **insolent** and **disagreeable**.

"How could I ever think her like her **nephew**?" said she, as she looked in her face.

As soon as they entered the copse, Lady Catherine began in the following manner:--

"You can be at no loss, Miss Bennet, to understand the reason of my journey **hither**. Your own heart, your own **conscience**, must tell you why I come."

Elizabeth looked with **unaffected astonishment**.

"Indeed, you are **mistaken**, Madam. I have not been at all able to account for the honour of seeing you here."

"Miss Bennet," replied her ladyship, in an angry tone, "you ought to know, that I am not to be trifled with. But however **insincere** *you* may choose to be, you shall not find *me* so. My character has ever been **celebrated** for its **sincerity** and **frankness**, and in a cause of such moment as this, I shall certainly not **depart** from it. A report of a most **alarming** nature reached me two days ago. I was told that not only your sister was on the point of being most **advantageously** married, but that you, that Miss Elizabeth Bennet, would, in all **likelihood**, be soon afterwards united to my nephew, my own nephew, Mr. Darcy. Though I *know* it

Italian

advantageously: vantaggiosamente.
alarming: allarmante.
astonishment: stupore, meraviglia, sorpresa.
carriage: vettura, carrello, vagone, carro, carrozza.
celebrated: celebrato, festeggiato, famoso.
conscience: coscienza.
decent: decente.
depart: partire, partite, partiamo, parti, partono, parto, andarsene.

disagreeable: sgradevole.
downstairs: giù dalle scale.
frankness: franchezza.
gravel: ghiaia.
hither: qui, quà.
insincere: falso, insincero.
insolent: insolente.
ladyship: signoria.
lawn: prato, tappeto erboso, linone.
likelihood: verosimiglianza, probabilità.
mistaken: sbagliato.

nephew: nipote.
noble: nobile, gentilizio, nobiliare.
obeyed: ubbidito, obbedito.
parasol: parasole, ombrellino.
proceeded: proceduto.
pronouncing: pronunciando.
sincerity: sincerità.
unaffected: spontaneo, non affettato, semplice.
walks: cammina.
wilderness: regione selvaggia.

must be a **scandalous falsehood**, though I would not **injure** him so much as to suppose the truth of it possible, I instantly resolved on setting off for this place, that I might make my sentiments known to you."

"If you believed it impossible to be true," said Elizabeth, **colouring** with **astonishment** and **disdain**, "I wonder you took the trouble of coming so far. What could your **ladyship propose** by it?"

"At once to insist upon having such a report **universally** contradicted."

"Your coming to Longbourn, to see me and my family," said Elizabeth **coolly**, "will be rather a **confirmation** of it; if, indeed, such a report is in existence."

"If! Do you then pretend to be **ignorant** of it? Has it not been **industriously** circulated by **yourselves**? Do you not know that such a report is spread abroad?"

"I never heard that it was."

"And can you **likewise declare**, that there is no foundation for it?"

"I do not pretend to possess equal **frankness** with your ladyship. You may ask questions which I shall not choose to answer."

"This is not to be borne. Miss Bennet, I insist on being satisfied. Has he, has my **nephew**, made you an offer of marriage?"

"Your ladyship has declared it to be impossible."

"It ought to be so; it must be so, while he **retains** the use of his reason. But your arts and allurements may, in a moment of **infatuation**, have made him forget what he owes to himself and to all his family. You may have drawn him in."

"If I have, I shall be the last person to **confess** it."

"Miss Bennet, do you know who I am? I have not been **accustomed** to such language as this. I am almost the nearest relation he has in the world, and am entitled to know all his dearest concerns."

Italian

accustomed: consueto, abituato, usuale, solito, avvezzo.
astonishment: stupore, meraviglia, sorpresa.
colouring: coloritura.
confess: confessare, confessa, confessano, confessate, confessi, confessiamo, confesso.
confirmation: conferma.
coolly: frescamente.
declare: dichiarare, dichiara, dichiaro, dichiariamo, dichiari, dichiarano,
dichiarate.
disdain: sdegno, sdegnare.
falsehood: falso, falsità, bugia, menzogna.
frankness: franchezza.
ignorant: ignorante.
industriously: diligente.
infatuation: infatuazione.
injure: danneggiare, danneggia, danneggiamo, danneggiano, danneggiate, danneggio, danneggi, ferire, ferisco, feriscono, feriamo.
ladyship: signoria.
likewise: anche, altrettanto.
nephew: nipote.
propose: proporre, proponiamo, proponi, propongono, proponete, propongo.
retains: ritiene, trattiene.
scandalous: scandaloso.
universally: universalmente.
yourselves: voi stessi.

"But you are not entitled to know mine; nor will such behaviour as this, ever **induce** me to be explicit."

"Let me be **rightly** understood.   This match, to which you have the **presumption** to **aspire**, can never take place. No, never. Mr. Darcy is engaged to my daughter. Now what have you to say?"

"Only this; that if he is so, you can have no reason to suppose he will make an offer to me."

Lady Catherine hesitated for a moment, and then replied:

"The **engagement** between them is of a peculiar kind. From their **infancy**, they have been intended for each other. It was the favourite wish of *his* mother, as well as of her's. While in their cradles, we planned the union: and now, at the moment when the wishes of both sisters would be **accomplished** in their marriage, to be prevented by a young woman of **inferior** birth, of no importance in the world, and wholly unallied to the family! Do you pay no regard to the wishes of his friends? To his **tacit** engagement with Miss de Bourgh? Are you lost to every feeling of **propriety** and **delicacy**? Have you not heard me say that from his earliest hours he was **destined** for his cousin?"

"Yes, and I had heard it before. But what is that to me? If there is no other **objection** to my **marrying** your **nephew**, I shall certainly not be kept from it by knowing that his mother and aunt wished him to marry Miss de Bourgh. You both did as much as you could in **planning** the marriage.   Its **completion depended** on others. If Mr. Darcy is neither by honour nor **inclination** confined to his cousin, why is not he to make another choice? And if I am that choice, why may not I accept him?"

"Because honour, **decorum, prudence, nay**, interest, **forbid** it. Yes, Miss Bennet, interest; for do not expect to be noticed by his family or friends, if you wilfully act against the inclinations of all. You will be **censured**, slighted, and **despised**, by everyone connected with him. Your alliance will be a **disgrace**; your name will never even be mentioned by any of us."

Italian

accomplished: compiuto.
aspire: aspirare, aspiri, aspira, aspirate, aspiro, aspiriamo, aspirano.
censured: censurato.
completion: completamento.
decorum: decoro.
delicacy: delicatezza.
depended: dipeso.
despised: disprezzato.
destined: destinato.
disgrace: vergogna, disgrazia, disonorare, disonore.

engagement: fidanzamento, assunzione.
forbid: vietare, vieti, vietate, vietano, vietiamo, vieta, vieto, proibire, proibite, proibiamo, proibisci.
inclination: inclinazione, pendenza.
induce: dedurre, concludere, indurre, induci, inducono, induciamo, inducete, deducono, deduco, deduciamo, deducete.
infancy: infanzia.
inferior: inferiore.

marrying: sposandosi.
nay: anzi.
nephew: nipote.
objection: obiezione, opposizione.
planning: pianificazione, progettazione, programmazione.
presumption: presunzione, supposizione.
propriety: convenienza.
prudence: prudenza.
rightly: giustamente.
tacit: tacito.

"These are heavy misfortunes," replied Elizabeth. "But the wife of Mr. Darcy must have such extraordinary sources of **happiness** necessarily attached to her situation, that she could, upon the whole, have no cause to repine."

"Obstinate, **headstrong** girl! I am **ashamed** of you! Is this your **gratitude** for my attentions to you last spring? Is nothing due to me on that score? Let us sit down. You are to understand, Miss Bennet, that I came here with the determined resolution of carrying my purpose; nor will I be **dissuaded** from it. I have not been used to **submit** to any person's whims. I have not been in the habit of brooking disappointment."

"*That* will make your ladyship's situation at present more **pitiable**; but it will have no effect on me."

"I will not be **interrupted**. Hear me in silence. My daughter and my **nephew** are formed for each other. They are **descended**, on the **maternal** side, from the same **noble** line; and, on the father's, from **respectable, honourable**, and ancient--though untitled--families. Their fortune on both sides is **splendid**. They are **destined** for each other by the voice of every **member** of their **respective** houses; and what is to **divide** them? The **upstart** pretensions of a young woman without family, connections, or fortune. Is this to be **endured**! But it must not, shall not be. If you were sensible of your own good, you would not wish to **quit** the **sphere** in which you have been brought up."

"In **marrying** your nephew, I should not consider myself as **quitting** that sphere. He is a gentleman; I am a gentleman's daughter; so far we are equal."

"True. You *are* a gentleman's daughter. But who was your mother? Who are your uncles and aunts? Do not imagine me **ignorant** of their condition."

"Whatever my connections may be," said Elizabeth, "if your nephew does not object to them, they can be nothing to *you*."

"Tell me once for all, are you **engaged** to him?"

Though Elizabeth would not, for the mere purpose of **obliging** Lady Catherine, have answered this question, she could not but say, after a moment's **deliberation**:

Italian

ashamed: vergognoso.
deliberation: deliberazione.
descended: sceso, disceso.
destined: destinato.
dissuaded: dissuaso.
divide: dividere, dividete, dividiamo, divido, dividono, dividi, separare, separa, separi, separiamo, separate.
endured: sopportato, durato.
engaged: occupato, innestato, impegnato.
gratitude: gratitudine, riconoscenza,

grazie.
happiness: felicità.
headstrong: testardo.
honourable: onorevole.
ignorant: ignorante.
interrupted: interrotto, sospeso.
marrying: sposandosi.
maternal: materno.
member: membro.
nephew: nipote.
noble: nobile, gentilizio, nobiliare.
obliging: obbligando, accomodante.

pitiable: pietoso.
quit: abbandonare, abbandonato, abbandono, abbandoni, abbandonate, abbandonano, abbandona, abbandoniamo, smettere.
quitting: abbandonando.
respectable: rispettabile, onorevole.
respective: rispettivo.
sphere: sfera.
splendid: splendido, magnifico.
submit: sottomettere, sottoporre.
upstart: parvenu.

"I am not."

Lady Catherine seemed pleased.

"And will you promise me, never to enter into such an engagement?"

"I will make no promise of the kind."

"Miss Bennet I am shocked and **astonished**. I expected to find a more reasonable young woman. But do not **deceive** yourself into a belief that I will ever **recede**. I shall not go away till you have given me the assurance I require."

"And I certainly *never* shall give it. I am not to be **intimidated** into anything so wholly **unreasonable**. Your **ladyship** wants Mr. Darcy to marry your daughter; but would my giving you the wished-for promise make their marriage at all more **probable? Supposing** him to be attached to me, would my refusing to accept his hand make him wish to **bestow** it on his cousin? Allow me to say, Lady Catherine, that the arguments with which you have supported this extraordinary application have been as **frivolous** as the application was ill-judged. You have widely **mistaken** my character, if you think I can be worked on by such persuasions as these. How far your **nephew** might **approve** of your **interference** in his affairs, I **cannot** tell; but you have certainly no right to concern yourself in mine. I must **beg**, therefore, to be **importuned** no **farther** on the subject."

"Not so **hasty**, if you please. I have by no means done. To all the **objections** I have already urged, I have still another to add. I am no **stranger** to the **particulars** of your youngest sister's **infamous** elopement. I know it all; that the young man's **marrying** her was a patched-up business, at the expence of your father and uncles. And is such a girl to be my nephew's sister? Is her husband, is the son of his late father's **steward**, to be his brother? Heaven and earth!--of what are you thinking? Are the shades of Pemberley to be thus polluted?"

"You can now have nothing further to say," she resentfully answered. "You have **insulted** me in every possible method. I must beg to return to the house."

And she rose as she spoke. Lady Catherine rose also, and they turned back. Her ladyship was highly **incensed**.

Italian

approve: approvare, approvate, approvano, approvi, approvo, approva, approviamo.
astonished: stupito, si stupito.
beg: mendicare, mendicano, mendica, mendicate, mendico, mendichiamo, mendichi, chiedere, elemosinare, supplicare.
bestow: tributare, concedere.
cannot: non potere.
deceive: ingannare, ingannano, inganniamo, ingannate, inganna,
inganni, inganno, truffare, truffate, truffano, truffiamo.
farther: più lontano.
frivolous: vanitoso, frivolo.
hasty: affrettato, frettoloso.
importuned: importunato.
incensed: incenso.
infamous: infame.
insulted: insultato.
interference: interferenza.
intimidated: intimidito.
ladyship: signoria.
marrying: sposandosi.
mistaken: sbagliato.
nephew: nipote.
objections: obiezioni.
particulars: particolari.
probable: probabile.
recede: recedere.
steward: maggiordomo, dispensiere.
stranger: sconosciuto, estraneo, forestiero.
supposing: supponendo.
unreasonable: irragionevole.

"You have no regard, then, for the honour and credit of my **nephew**! Unfeeling, **selfish** girl! Do you not consider that a connection with you must **disgrace** him in the eyes of everybody?"

"Lady Catherine, I have nothing further to say. You know my sentiments."

"You are then resolved to have him?"

"I have said no such thing. I am only resolved to act in that manner, which will, in my own opinion, **constitute** my **happiness**, without **reference** to *you*, or to any person so wholly unconnected with me."

"It is well. You refuse, then, to **oblige** me. You refuse to **obey** the claims of duty, honour, and **gratitude**. You are determined to **ruin** him in the opinion of all his friends, and make him the **contempt** of the world."

"Neither duty, nor honour, nor gratitude," replied Elizabeth, "have any possible claim on me, in the present instance. No principle of either would be **violated** by my marriage with Mr. Darcy. And with regard to the **resentment** of his family, or the **indignation** of the world, if the former *were* **excited** by his **marrying** me, it would not give me one moment's concern--and the world in general would have too much sense to join in the scorn."

"And this is your real opinion! This is your **final** resolve! Very well. I shall now know how to act. Do not imagine, Miss Bennet, that your **ambition** will ever be **gratified**. I came to try you. I hoped to find you reasonable; but, depend upon it, I will carry my point."

In this manner Lady Catherine talked on, till they were at the door of the carriage, when, turning **hastily** round, she added, "I take no leave of you, Miss Bennet. I send no **compliments** to your mother. You **deserve** no such attention. I am most seriously displeased."

Elizabeth made no answer; and without attempting to persuade her **ladyship** to return into the house, walked quietly into it herself. She heard the carriage drive away as she **proceeded** up stairs. Her mother **impatiently** met her at the door of the dressing-room, to ask why Lady Catherine would not come in again and rest herself.

Italian

ambition: ambizione.
compliments: complimenti.
constitute: costituire, costituiamo, costituisci, costituisco, costituiscono, costituite.
contempt: sprezzo, disprezzo.
deserve: meritare, meritano, merita, meritate, meritiamo, meriti, merito.
disgrace: vergogna, disgrazia, disonorare, disonore.
excited: eccitato, concitato, emozionato.

final: finale.
gratified: gratificato.
gratitude: gratitudine, riconoscenza, grazie.
happiness: felicità.
hastily: frettolosamente.
impatiently: impazientemente.
indignation: indignazione, sdegno.
ladyship: signoria.
marrying: sposandosi.
nephew: nipote.
obey: ubbidire, ubbidiamo, ubbidite,

ubbidiscono, ubbidisci, ubbidisco, obbedire, obbediamo, obbediscono, obbedisco, obbedisci.
oblige: obbligare, obblighiamo, obbliga, obbligano, obbligate, obblighi, obbligo.
proceeded: proceduto.
reference: riferimento, referenza.
resentment: risentimento, astio.
ruin: rovinare, rovina.
selfish: egoistico, egoista.
violated: violato, aggredito, assalito.

"She did not **choose** it," said her **daughter**, "she would go."

"She is a very fine-looking woman! and her **calling** here was **prodigiously** civil! for she only came, I **suppose**, to tell us the Collinses were well. She is on her road **somewhere**, I **dare** say, and so, **passing** through Meryton, thought she might as well call on you. I suppose she had nothing particular to say to you, Lizzy?"

Elizabeth was **forced** to give into a little **falsehood** here; for to **acknowledge** the **substance** of their **conversation** was impossible.

Italian

acknowledge: riconoscere, riconoscono, riconosco, riconosciamo, riconosci, riconoscete, confessare, confermare, prendere atto.
call: chiamare, chiami, chiamiamo, chiamo, chiamano, chiama, chiamate, chiamata, appello.
calling: chiamando, chiamata.
choose: scegliere, scegli, scegliamo, scegliete, scelgo, scelgono, eleggere, eleggete, eleggi, eleggiamo, eleggo.
civil: civile.

conversation: conversazione, discorso.
dare: osare, oso, osiamo, osi, osate, osano, osa, sfida.
daughter: figlia, figliola, figliuola, la figlia.
falsehood: falso, falsità, bugia, menzogna.
forced: forzato.
passing: passeggero, passare, passaggio.
prodigiously: prodigiosamente.
somewhere: in qualche luogo, da

qualche parte.
substance: sostanza, materia.
suppose: supporre, supponiamo, supponete, suppongo, suppongono, supponi.

CHAPTER 57

The discomposure of spirits which this extraordinary visit threw Elizabeth into, could not be easily **overcome**; nor could she, for many hours, learn to think of it less than **incessantly**. Lady Catherine, it appeared, had actually taken the trouble of this journey from Rosings, for the **sole** purpose of **breaking** off her supposed **engagement** with Mr. Darcy. It was a **rational** scheme, to be sure! but from what the report of their engagement could **originate**, Elizabeth was at a loss to imagine; till she **recollected** that *his* being the **intimate** friend of Bingley, and *her* being the sister of Jane, was enough, at a time when the **expectation** of one wedding made everybody **eager** for another, to supply the idea. She had not herself forgotten to feel that the marriage of her sister must bring them more frequently together. And her neighbours at Lucas Lodge, therefore (for through their communication with the Collinses, the report, she **concluded**, had reached lady Catherine), had only set that down as almost certain and immediate, which she had looked forward to as possible at some future time.

In **revolving** Lady Catherine's **expressions**, however, she could not help feeling some **uneasiness** as to the possible **consequence** of her **persisting** in this **interference**. From what she had said of her resolution to prevent their marriage, it occurred to Elizabeth that she must **meditate** an application to her **nephew**; and how *he* might take a similar **representation** of the evils **attached** to a connection with her, she **dared** not **pronounce**. She knew not the **exact** degree

Italian

attached: fissato, attaccato, allegato.
breaking: rottura.
concluded: concluso.
consequence: conseguenza, risultato.
dared: osato.
eager: avido, desideroso, bramoso, impaziente.
engagement: fidanzamento, assunzione.
exact: esatto, preciso.
expectation: attesa, aspettativa.
expressions: espressioni.

incessantly: incessantemente.
interference: interferenza.
intimate: intimo.
meditate: meditare, mediti, meditiamo, meditate, meditano, medita, medito.
nephew: nipote.
originate: discendere, discendete, discendi, discendiamo, discendo, discendono, provenire.
overcome: superare.
persisting: persistendo.

pronounce: pronunciare, pronunciano, pronunciate, pronunciamo, pronunci, pronuncio, pronuncia.
rational: razionale, ragionevole.
recollected: rammentato.
representation: rappresentanza, rappresentazione, figura.
revolving: ruotando, girando, girevole.
sole: sogliola, solo, suola, pianta, unico.
uneasiness: disagio.

of his **affection** for his aunt, or his **dependence** on her **judgment**, but it was natural to suppose that he thought much higher of her **ladyship** than *she* could do; and it was certain that, in **enumerating** the miseries of a marriage with *one*, whose immediate connections were so **unequal** to his own, his aunt would address him on his weakest side. With his notions of **dignity**, he would probably feel that the arguments, which to Elizabeth had appeared weak and **ridiculous**, **contained** much good sense and **solid** reasoning.

If he had been **wavering** before as to what he should do, which had often seemed likely, the advice and **entreaty** of so near a relation might settle every doubt, and determine him at once to be as happy as dignity **unblemished** could make him. In that case he would return no more. Lady Catherine might see him in her way through town; and his **engagement** to Bingley of coming again to Netherfield must give way.

"If, therefore, an excuse for not keeping his promise should come to his friend within a few days," she added, "I shall know how to understand it. I shall then give over every **expectation**, every wish of his **constancy**. If he is **satisfied** with only **regretting** me, when he might have obtained my affections and hand, I shall soon **cease** to regret him at all."

The surprise of the rest of the family, on hearing who their visitor had been, was very great; but they **obligingly** satisfied it, with the same kind of **supposition** which had **appeased** Mrs. Bennet's **curiosity**; and Elizabeth was **spared** from much teasing on the subject.

The next morning, as she was going **downstairs**, she was met by her father, who came out of his library with a letter in his hand.

"Lizzy," said he, "I was going to look for you; come into my room."

She followed him **thither**; and her curiosity to know what he had to tell her was **heightened** by the supposition of its being in some manner **connected** with the letter he held. It suddenly struck her that it might be from Lady Catherine; and she **anticipated** with **dismay** all the **consequent** explanations.

Italian

affection: affetto, affezione, amore.
anticipated: anticipato.
appeased: placato.
cease: cessare.
connected: collegato, legato, connesso.
consequent: conseguente.
constancy: costanza.
contained: contenuto.
curiosity: curiosità.
dependence: dipendenza.
dignity: dignità, decoro.
dismay: costernazione, costernare.

downstairs: giù dalle scale.
engagement: fidanzamento, assunzione.
entreaty: preghiera, domanda, supplica.
enumerating: enumerando.
expectation: attesa, aspettativa.
heightened: innalzato.
judgment: giudizio, sentenza.
ladyship: signoria.
obligingly: servizievole, cortesemente.
regret: rincrescere, rammarico,

rimpiangere, rimpianto, rincrescimento.
ridiculous: ridicolo, assurdo.
satisfied: soddisfatto, contento, accontentato.
solid: solido, massiccio, compatto.
spared: risparmiato.
supposition: supposizione.
thither: là.
unblemished: senza macchia.
unequal: ineguale, disuguale.
wavering: esitando.

She followed her father to the fire place, and they both sat down. He then said,

"I have received a letter this morning that has **astonished** me **exceedingly**. As it **principally** concerns yourself, you ought to know its contents. I did not know before, that I had two daughters on the **brink** of **matrimony**. Let me **congratulate** you on a very important conquest."

The colour now rushed into Elizabeth's cheeks in the **instantaneous** conviction of its being a letter from the **nephew**, instead of the aunt; and she was **undetermined** whether most to be pleased that he explained himself at all, or **offended** that his letter was not rather addressed to herself; when her father continued:

"You look conscious. Young ladies have great **penetration** in such matters as these; but I think I may **defy** even *your* **sagacity**, to discover the name of your **admirer**. This letter is from Mr. Collins."

"From Mr. Collins! and what can *he* have to say?"

"Something very much to the purpose of course. He begins with **congratulations** on the approaching **nuptials** of my **eldest** daughter, of which, it seems, he has been told by some of the **good**-natured, gossiping Lucases. I shall not sport with your **impatience**, by reading what he says on that point. What **relates** to yourself, is as follows: 'Having thus offered you the **sincere** congratulations of Mrs. Collins and myself on this happy event, let me now add a short hint on the subject of another; of which we have been **advertised** by the same authority. Your daughter Elizabeth, it is **presumed**, will not long bear the name of Bennet, after her elder sister has resigned it, and the chosen partner of her fate may be reasonably looked up to as one of the most **illustrious** personages in this land.'

"Can you possibly guess, Lizzy, who is meant by this?" 'This young gentleman is **blessed**, in a peculiar way, with every thing the heart of **mortal** can most desire,--splendid property, noble **kindred**, and extensive **patronage**. Yet in **spite** of all these temptations, let me warn my cousin Elizabeth, and yourself, of

Italian

admirer: ammiratore.
advertised: annunziato.
astonished: stupito, si stupito.
blessed: benedetto, beato.
brink: orlo.
congratulate: felicitare, felicitate, felicito, feliciti, felicitano, felicita, felicitiamo.
congratulations: congratulazioni.
defy: sfidare, sfidano, sfidiamo, sfidate, sfidi, sfido, sfida.
eldest: maggiore, il più vecchio.

exceedingly: estremamente.
good-natured: gradevole, cortese.
illustrious: illustre.
impatience: impazienza.
instantaneous: istantaneo.
kindred: parentela, affine.
matrimony: matrimonio.
mortal: mortale.
nephew: nipote.
nuptials: nozze.
offended: offeso, insultato, oltraggiato.

patronage: patrocinio, patronato.
penetration: penetrazione.
presumed: supposto, presunto.
principally: principalmente, soprattutto.
relates: racconta.
sagacity: sagacia.
sincere: sincero.
spite: dispetto.
undetermined: indeterminato.

what evils you may **incur** by a **precipitate closure with** this gentleman's proposals, which, of course, you will be **inclined** to take immediate advantage of.'

"Have you any idea, Lizzy, who this gentleman is? But now it comes out:

"'My **motive** for cautioning you is as follows. We have reason to imagine that his **aunt**, Lady Catherine de Bourgh, does not look on the match with a friendly eye.'

"MR. DARCY, you see, is the man! Now, Lizzy, I think I *have* surprised you. Could he, or the Lucases, have pitched on any man within the circle of our **acquaintance**, whose name would have given the **lie** more effectually to what they related? Mr. Darcy, who never looks at any woman but to see a **blemish**, and who probably never looked at you in his life! It is admirable!"

Elizabeth tried to join in her father's pleasantry, but could only force one most **reluctant** smile. Never had his wit been **directed** in a manner so little **agreeable** to her.

"Are you not diverted?"

"Oh! yes. Pray read on."

"'After mentioning the **likelihood** of this marriage to her **ladyship** last night, she immediately, with her usual **condescension**, expressed what she felt on the occasion; when it become apparent, that on the score of some family **objections** on the part of my **cousin**, she would never give her consent to what she termed so **disgraceful** a match. I thought it my duty to give the speediest **intelligence** of this to my cousin, that she and her **noble admirer** may be aware of what they are about, and not run **hastily** into a marriage which has not been properly sanctioned.' Mr. Collins moreover **adds**, 'I am truly **rejoiced** that my cousin Lydia's sad business has been so well hushed up, and am only concerned that their living together before the marriage took place should be so generally known. I must not, however, **neglect** the duties of my station, or **refrain** from **declaring** my **amazement** at hearing that you received the young couple into your house as soon as they were married. It was an **encouragement** of **vice**; and

Italian

acquaintance: conoscenza, conoscente.
adds: aggiunge, addiziona.
admirer: ammiratore.
agreeable: gradevole, piacevole, amabile.
amazement: stupore, meraviglia.
aunt: zia, la zia.
blemish: difetto.
closure: chiusura.
condescension: condiscendenza.
cousin: cugino, cugina.
declaring: dichiarando.

directed: diretto.
disgraceful: disgraziata, vergognoso, disonorevole.
encouragement: incoraggiamento.
hastily: frettolosamente.
inclined: disposto, inclinato, propenso.
incur: incorrere in, incorrere.
intelligence: intelligenza.
ladyship: signoria.
lie: mentire, bugia, giacere, menzogna.
likelihood: verosimiglianza,

probabilità.
motive: motivo, movente, ragione.
neglect: trascurare, negligere, negligenza, trascuratezza.
noble: nobile, gentilizio, nobiliare.
objections: obiezioni.
precipitate: precipitare, precipitato.
refrain: ritornello, astenersi.
rejoiced: allietato, gioito, rallegrato.
reluctant: riluttante, ritroso, restio.
vice: morsa, vizio, virtù.
wit: arguzia.

had I been the **rector** of Longbourn, I should very **strenuously** have opposed it. You ought certainly to **forgive** them, as a Christian, but never to admit them in your sight, or allow their names to be mentioned in your hearing.' That is his notion of Christian **forgiveness**! The rest of his letter is only about his dear Charlotte's situation, and his **expectation** of a young olive-branch. But, Lizzy, you look as if you did not enjoy it. You are not going to be *missish*, I hope, and **pretend** to be affronted at an **idle** report. For what do we live, but to make sport for our neighbours, and laugh at them in our turn?"

"Oh!" cried Elizabeth, "I am **excessively diverted**. But it is so strange!"

"Yes--*that* is what makes it **amusing**. Had they fixed on any other man it would have been nothing; but *his* perfect **indifference**, and *your* pointed **dislike**, make it so delightfully **absurd**! Much as I **abominate** writing, I would not give up Mr. Collins's **correspondence** for any consideration. Nay, when I read a letter of his, I **cannot** help giving him the preference even over Wickham, much as I value the **impudence** and **hypocrisy** of my son-in-law. And **pray**, Lizzy, what said Lady Catherine about this report? Did she call to refuse her consent?"

To this question his daughter replied only with a laugh; and as it had been asked without the least suspicion, she was not **distressed** by his **repeating** it. Elizabeth had never been more at a loss to make her feelings appear what they were not. It was necessary to laugh, when she would rather have cried. Her father had most **cruelly mortified** her, by what he said of Mr. Darcy's indifference, and she could do nothing but wonder at such a want of **penetration**, or fear that perhaps, instead of his seeing too little, she might have **fancied** too much.

Italian

abominate: detestare, detestate, detesta, detestano, detestiamo, detesti, detesto, abominare, abomina, abomino, abominate.
absurd: assurdo.
amusing: divertente, divertendo, spassoso.
cannot: non potere.
correspondence: corrispondenza, carteggio.
cruelly: crudelmente.
dislike: avversione, ripugnanza, antipatia.
distressed: afflitto.
diverted: stornato, sviato, deviato.
excessively: eccessivamente.
expectation: attesa, aspettativa.
fancied: fantastico.
forgive: perdonare, perdonano, perdoniamo, perdona, perdonate, perdoni, perdono.
forgiveness: perdono.
hypocrisy: ipocrisia.
idle: ozioso, pigro, folle, inattivo.
impudence: impudenza.
indifference: indifferenza.
mortified: mortificato.
penetration: penetrazione.
pray: pregare, pregate, prego, preghi, prega, preghiamo, pregano.
pretend: fingere, fingete, fingi, fingiamo, fingo, fingono, pretendere, simulare.
rector: rettore, parroco.
repeating: ripetendo.
strenuously: strenuamente.

CHAPTER 58

Instead of **receiving** any such letter of **excuse** from his friend, as Elizabeth half expected Mr. Bingley to do, he was able to bring Darcy with him to Longbourn before many days had passed after Lady Catherine's visit. The gentlemen **arrived** early; and, before Mrs. **Bennet** had time to tell him of their having seen his **aunt**, of which her daughter sat in **momentary dread**, Bingley, who wanted to be **alone** with Jane, **proposed** their all **walking** out. It was agreed to. Mrs. Bennet was not in the **habit** of walking; Mary could never **spare** time; but the **remaining** five set off together. Bingley and Jane, however, soon allowed the others to outstrip them. They lagged behind, while Elizabeth, Kitty, and Darcy were to **entertain** each other. Very little was said by either; Kitty was too much afraid of him to talk; Elizabeth was **secretly forming** a **desperate** resolution; and perhaps he might be doing the same.

They **walked** towards the Lucases, because Kitty **wished** to call upon Maria; and as Elizabeth saw no **occasion** for making it a general concern, when Kitty left them she went **boldly** on with him alone. Now was the moment for her resolution to be **executed**, and, while her **courage** was high, she immediately said:

"Mr. Darcy, I am a very **selfish creature**; and, for the **sake** of giving **relief** to my own feelings, care not how much I may be wounding your's. I can no longer help **thanking** you for your **unexampled kindness** to my poor sister. Ever since

Italian

alone: solo, da solo, solamente.
arrived: arrivato.
aunt: zia, la zia.
bennet: cariofillata, erba benedetta.
boldly: audacemente, arditamente.
courage: coraggio.
creature: creatura.
desperate: disperato.
dread: temere.
entertain: intrattenere, intrattenete, intrattieni, intratteniamo, intrattengo, intrattengono, ricevere.

excuse: scusa, scusare, giustificazione, pretesto.
executed: eseguito.
forming: formazione.
habit: abitudine, costume, vizio, consuetudine.
kindness: gentilezza, bontà, cortesia.
momentary: momentaneo.
occasion: occasione.
proposed: proposto.
receiving: ricevendo, accogliendo, ricezione, ricevere, ricevente.

relief: rilievo, sollievo.
remaining: rimanendo, restando, rimanente, restante.
sake: causa.
secretly: segretamente.
selfish: egoistico, egoista.
spare: risparmiare, scorta.
thanking: ringraziando.
unexampled: singolare.
walked: camminato.
walking: camminando, camminare.
wished: desiderato.

I have known it, I have been most anxious to **acknowledge** to you how **gratefully** I feel it. Were it known to the rest of my family, I should not have merely my own **gratitude** to express."

"I am sorry, **exceedingly** sorry," replied Darcy, in a tone of surprise and **emotion**, "that you have ever been informed of what may, in a **mistaken** light, have given you **uneasiness**. I did not think Mrs. Gardiner was so little to be trusted."

"You must not blame my aunt. Lydia's **thoughtlessness** first **betrayed** to me that you had been concerned in the matter; and, of course, I could not rest till I knew the **particulars**. Let me thank you again and again, in the name of all my family, for that generous **compassion** which **induced** you to take so much trouble, and bear so many mortifications, for the sake of **discovering** them."

"If you *will* thank me," he replied, "let it be for yourself alone. That the wish of giving **happiness** to you might add force to the other **inducements** which led me on, I shall not attempt to deny. But your *family* **owe** me nothing. Much as I respect them, I believe I thought only of *you*."

Elizabeth was too much **embarrassed** to say a word. After a short **pause**, her companion added, "You are too generous to **trifle** with me. If your feelings are still what they were last April, tell me so at once. *my* affections and wishes are **unchanged**, but one word from you will silence me on this subject for ever."

Elizabeth, feeling all the more than common **awkwardness** and anxiety of his situation, now forced herself to speak; and immediately, though not very **fluently**, gave him to understand that her sentiments had **undergone** so material a change, since the period to which he **alluded**, as to make her receive with gratitude and pleasure his present assurances. The happiness which this reply produced, was such as he had probably never felt before; and he expressed himself on the occasion as **sensibly** and as **warmly** as a man **violently** in love can be supposed to do. Had Elizabeth been able to **encounter** his eye, she might have seen how well the expression of **heartfelt** delight, **diffused** over his face, became him; but, though she could not look, she could listen, and he told her of

Italian

acknowledge: riconoscere, riconoscono, riconosco, riconosciamo, riconosci, riconoscete, confessare, confermare, prendere atto.
alluded: alluso.
awkwardness: goffaggine.
betrayed: tradito.
compassion: compassione.
diffused: diffuso.
discovering: scoprendo.
embarrassed: imbarazzato.
emotion: emozione, commozione.

encounter: incontro, incontrare, incontra, incontriamo, incontri, incontrano, incontrate.
exceedingly: estremamente.
fluently: fluentemente.
gratefully: con gratitudine.
gratitude: gratitudine, riconoscenza, grazie.
happiness: felicità.
heartfelt: sincero.
induced: indotto, concluso, dedotto.
inducements: incitamenti.

mistaken: sbagliato.
owe: dovere.
particulars: particolari.
pause: pausa, sosta.
sensibly: assennatamente.
thoughtlessness: sconsideratezza.
trifle: inezia, sciocchezza.
unchanged: immutato.
undergone: subito.
uneasiness: disagio.
violently: violentemente.
warmly: caldamente, calorosamente.

feelings, which, in **proving** of what importance she was to him, made his affection every moment more valuable.

They walked on, without knowing in what direction. There was too much to be thought, and felt, and said, for attention to any other objects. She soon learnt that they were **indebted** for their present good understanding to the efforts of his aunt, who did call on him in her return through London, and there relate her journey to Longbourn, its motive, and the substance of her conversation with Elizabeth; **dwelling emphatically** on every expression of the latter which, in her **ladyship's apprehension, peculiarly denoted** her perverseness and assurance; in the belief that such a relation must assist her endeavours to **obtain** that promise from her **nephew** which she had refused to give. But, **unluckily** for her ladyship, its effect had been exactly contrariwise.

"It taught me to hope," said he, "as I had scarcely ever allowed myself to hope before. I knew enough of your **disposition** to be certain that, had you been absolutely, **irrevocably** decided against me, you would have acknowledged it to Lady Catherine, **frankly** and openly."

Elizabeth coloured and laughed as she replied, "Yes, you know enough of my **frankness** to believe me capable of *that*. After **abusing** you so **abominably** to your face, I could have no **scruple** in abusing you to all your relations."

"What did you say of me, that I did not deserve? For, though your accusations were ill-founded, formed on mistaken **premises**, my behaviour to you at the time had **merited** the severest **reproof**. It was **unpardonable**. I **cannot** think of it without abhorrence."

"We will not **quarrel** for the greater share of blame **annexed** to that evening," said Elizabeth. "The conduct of neither, if **strictly** examined, will be **irreproachable**; but since then, we have both, I hope, improved in civility."

"I cannot be so easily **reconciled** to myself. The **recollection** of what I then said, of my conduct, my manners, my expressions during the whole of it, is now, and has been many months, **inexpressibly** painful to me. Your reproof, so well applied, I shall never forget: 'had you **behaved** in a more gentlemanlike manner.'

Italian

abominably: abominevolmente.
abusing: abusando.
annexed: annesso.
apprehension: apprensione, arresto.
behaved: agito, comportato.
cannot: non potere.
denoted: denotato.
disposition: disposizione, predisposizione, ingegno, talento.
dwelling: dimorando, abitando, dimora, abitazione.
emphatically: enfatico, enfaticamente.

frankly: francamente.
frankness: franchezza.
indebted: obbligato, indebitato.
inexpressibly: indicibilmente.
irreproachable: irreprensibile.
irrevocably: irrevocabilmente.
ladyship: signoria.
merited: meritato.
nephew: nipote.
obtain: ottenere, ottieni, ottenete, ottengono, otteniamo, ottengo, procurare.

peculiarly: particolarmente.
premises: locali, locale, premesse.
proving: provando.
quarrel: lite, litigare, bisticciare, bisticcio, litigio.
recollection: memoria, ricordo.
reconciled: conciliato, riconciliato.
reproof: biasimo.
scruple: scrupolo.
strictly: rigorosamente, strettamente.
unluckily: sfortunatamente.
unpardonable: imperdonabile.

Those were your words. You know not, you can **scarcely conceive**, how they have **tortured** me;--though it was some time, I **confess**, before I was reasonable enough to allow their justice."

"I was certainly very far from expecting them to make so strong an impression. I had not the smallest idea of their being ever felt in such a way."

"I can easily believe it. You thought me then **devoid** of every proper feeling, I am sure you did. The turn of your **countenance** I shall never forget, as you said that I could not have addressed you in any possible way that would **induce** you to accept me."

"Oh! do not repeat what I then said. These recollections will not do at all. I **assure** you that I have long been most **heartily ashamed** of it."

Darcy mentioned his letter. "Did it," said he, "did it soon make you think better of me? Did you, on reading it, give any credit to its contents?"

She explained what its effect on her had been, and how gradually all her former prejudices had been removed.

"I knew," said he, "that what I wrote must give you pain, but it was necessary. I hope you have destroyed the letter. There was one part especially, the opening of it, which I should **dread** your having the power of reading again. I can remember some **expressions** which might **justly** make you hate me."

"The letter shall certainly be **burnt**, if you believe it essential to the **preservation** of my regard; but, though we have both reason to think my opinions not entirely **unalterable**, they are not, I hope, quite so easily changed as that implies."

"When I wrote that letter," replied Darcy, "I believed myself perfectly calm and cool, but I am since convinced that it was written in a **dreadful bitterness** of spirit."

"The letter, perhaps, began in bitterness, but it did not end so. The **adieu** is charity itself. But think no more of the letter. The feelings of the person who wrote, and the person who received it, are now so widely different from what they were then, that every **unpleasant circumstance attending** it ought to be

Italian

adieu: addio.
ashamed: vergognoso.
assure: assicurare, assicura, assicuriamo, assicurate, assicuri, assicurano, assicuro, garantire.
attending: visitando, curando, assistendo.
bitterness: amarezza.
burnt: bruciato.
circumstance: circostanza.
conceive: concepire, concepiamo, concepisci, concepisco, concepiscono,

concepite.
confess: confessare, confessa, confessano, confessate, confessi, confessiamo, confesso.
countenance: approvare, viso.
devoid: privo.
dread: temere.
dreadful: terribile.
expressions: espressioni.
heartily: cordialmente.
induce: dedurre, concludere, indurre, induci, inducono, induciamo,

inducete, deducono, deduco, deduciamo, deducete.
justly: giustamente.
preservation: conservazione, preservazione.
scarcely: appena, a stento.
tortured: torturato.
unalterable: inalterabile.
unpleasant: rude, spiacevole, brusco, sgradevole, scostante.

forgotten. You must learn some of my philosophy. Think only of the past as its **remembrance** gives you pleasure."

"I **cannot** give you credit for any philosophy of the kind. Your retrospections must be so totally **void** of **reproach**, that the **contentment** arising from them is not of philosophy, but, what is much better, of **innocence**. But with me, it is not so. Painful recollections will **intrude** which cannot, which ought not, to be **repelled**. I have been a **selfish** being all my life, in practice, though not in principle. As a child I was taught what was right, but I was not taught to correct my **temper**. I was given good principles, but left to follow them in pride and **conceit**. Unfortunately an only son (for many years an only child), I was spoilt by my parents, who, though good themselves (my father, particularly, all that was **benevolent** and amiable), **allowed**, encouraged, almost taught me to be selfish and **overbearing**; to care for none beyond my own family circle; to think **meanly** of all the rest of the world; to wish at least to think meanly of their sense and worth **compared** with my own. Such I was, from eight to eight and twenty; and such I might still have been but for you, dearest, loveliest Elizabeth! What do I not owe you! You taught me a lesson, hard indeed at first, but most **advantageous**. By you, I was properly **humbled**. I came to you without a doubt of my reception. You showed me how **insufficient** were all my pretensions to please a woman **worthy** of being pleased."

"Had you then persuaded yourself that I should?"

"Indeed I had. What will you think of my **vanity**? I believed you to be wishing, expecting my addresses."

"My **manners** must have been in fault, but not **intentionally**, I **assure** you. I never meant to **deceive** you, but my spirits might often lead me wrong. How you must have **hated** me after *that* evening?"

"Hate you! I was angry perhaps at first, but my anger soon began to take a proper direction."

"I am almost afraid of asking what you thought of me, when we met at Pemberley. You blamed me for coming?"

Italian

advantageous: vantaggioso, utile.
assure: assicurare, assicura, assicuriamo, assicurate, assicuri, assicurano, assicuro, garantire.
benevolent: benevolo.
cannot: non potere.
compared: confrontato, paragonato.
conceit: presunzione.
contentment: soddisfazione.
deceive: ingannare, ingannano, inganniamo, ingannate, inganna, inganni, inganno, truffare, truffate,
truffano, truffiamo.
hated: odiato.
humbled: umiliato.
innocence: innocenza.
insufficient: insufficiente.
intentionally: intenzionalmente.
intrude: impongo, imponiamo, imponete, imponi, impongono, imporre.
manners: educazione.
meanly: meschinamente.
overbearing: arrogante.
owe: dovere.
remembrance: rimembranza, ricordo, memoria.
repelled: respinto.
reproach: rimprovero, rimproverare, riprendere.
selfish: egoistico, egoista.
temper: umore, temperamento, tempra.
vanity: vanità.
void: vuoto, nullo.
worthy: degno, meritevole.

"No indeed; I felt nothing but surprise."

"Your surprise could not be greater than *mine* in being noticed by you. My **conscience** told me that I **deserved** no extraordinary **politeness**, and I **confess** that I did not expect to receive *more* than my due."

"My object then," replied Darcy, "was to show you, by every **civility** in my power, that I was not so mean as to resent the past; and I hoped to obtain your **forgiveness**, to **lessen** your ill opinion, by letting you see that your reproofs had been attended to. How soon any other wishes introduced themselves I can hardly tell, but I believe in about half an hour after I had seen you."

He then told her of Georgiana's **delight** in her **acquaintance**, and of her **disappointment** at its sudden **interruption**; which naturally **leading** to the cause of that interruption, she soon learnt that his resolution of following her from Derbyshire in **quest** of her sister had been formed before he quitted the **inn**, and that his **gravity** and **thoughtfulness** there had **arisen** from no other struggles than what such a purpose must comprehend.

She expressed her **gratitude** again, but it was too painful a subject to each, to be dwelt on **farther**.

After walking several miles in a **leisurely** manner, and too **busy** to know anything about it, they found at last, on **examining** their watches, that it was time to be at home.

"What could become of Mr. Bingley and Jane!" was a wonder which introduced the discussion of their affairs. Darcy was **delighted** with their **engagement**; his friend had given him the earliest information of it.

"I must ask whether you were surprised?" said Elizabeth.

"Not at all. When I went away, I felt that it would soon happen."

"That is to say, you had given your permission. I **guessed** as much." And though he **exclaimed** at the term, she found that it had been pretty much the case.

Italian

acquaintance: conoscenza, conoscente.
arisen: nato, sorto.
busy: occupato, affaccendato, indaffarato.
civility: civiltà, cortesia.
confess: confessare, confessa, confessano, confessate, confessi, confessiamo, confesso.
conscience: coscienza.
delight: delizia, deliziare, dilettare, diletto, godimento, rallegrare, gioia.
delighted: lietissimo.

deserved: meritato.
disappointment: delusione, disappunto.
engagement: fidanzamento, assunzione.
examining: esaminando, esaminare.
exclaimed: esclamato.
farther: più lontano.
forgiveness: perdono.
gratitude: gratitudine, riconoscenza, grazie.
gravity: gravità.

guessed: indovinato.
inn: locanda, osteria.
interruption: interruzione.
leading: conducendo, guidando.
leisurely: comodo.
lessen: diminuire, diminuiamo, diminuisci, diminuisco, diminuiscono, diminuite.
politeness: cortesia, garbo.
quest: ricerca.
thoughtfulness: pensosità.

"On the evening before my going to London," said he, "I made a **confession** to him, which I believe I ought to have made long ago. I told him of all that had occurred to make my former **interference** in his affairs **absurd** and **impertinent**. His surprise was great. He had never had the slightest suspicion. I told him, moreover, that I believed myself **mistaken** in **supposing**, as I had done, that your sister was **indifferent** to him; and as I could easily **perceive** that his **attachment** to her was unabated, I felt no doubt of their happiness together."

Elizabeth could not help smiling at his easy manner of directing his friend.

"Did you speak from your own observation," said she, "when you told him that my sister loved him, or merely from my information last spring?"

"From the former. I had narrowly observed her during the two visits which I had **lately** made here; and I was convinced of her affection."

"And your assurance of it, I suppose, carried immediate conviction to him."

"It did. Bingley is most unaffectedly modest. His **diffidence** had prevented his **depending** on his own judgment in so anxious a case, but his **reliance** on mine made every thing easy. I was **obliged** to confess one thing, which for a time, and not **unjustly**, **offended** him. I could not allow myself to **conceal** that your sister had been in town three months last winter, that I had known it, and **purposely** kept it from him. He was angry. But his anger, I am persuaded, **lasted** no longer than he remained in any doubt of your sister's sentiments. He has **heartily forgiven** me now."

Elizabeth longed to observe that Mr. Bingley had been a most **delightful** friend; so easily **guided** that his worth was **invaluable**; but she checked herself. She remembered that he had yet to learn to be laughed at, and it was rather too early to begin. In **anticipating** the happiness of Bingley, which of course was to be **inferior** only to his own, he continued the conversation till they reached the house. In the hall they parted.

Italian

absurd: assurdo.
anticipating: anticipando.
attachment: accessorio, allegato, attaccamento.
conceal: nascondere, nascondono, nascondete, nascondi, nascondiamo, nascondo, occultare.
confess: confessare, confessa, confessano, confessate, confessi, confessiamo, confesso.
confession: confessione.
delightful: delizioso, piacevole.

depending: dipendendo.
diffidence: timidezza.
forgiven: perdonato.
guided: guidato.
heartily: cordialmente.
impertinent: impertinente, insolente.
indifferent: indifferente.
inferior: inferiore.
interference: interferenza.
invaluable: inestimabile.
lasted: durato.
lately: ultimamente, recentemente.

mistaken: sbagliato.
obliged: obbligato.
offended: offeso, insultato, oltraggiato.
perceive: percepire, accorgersi, scorgere, percepiamo, scorgo, scorgiamo, scorgi, scorgete, percepite, scorgono, percepiscono.
purposely: intenzionalmente.
reliance: fiducia.
supposing: supponendo.
unjustly: ingiustamente.

CHAPTER 59

"My dear Lizzy, where can you have been walking to?" was a question which Elizabeth received from Jane as soon as she **entered** their room, and from all the others when they sat down to table. She had only to say in **reply**, that they had **wandered** about, **till** she was beyond her own knowledge. She **coloured** as she spoke; but neither that, nor anything else, **awakened** a **suspicion** of the truth.

The evening passed **quietly**, unmarked by anything **extraordinary**. The **acknowledged** lovers **talked** and laughed, the **unacknowledged** were **silent**. Darcy was not of a **disposition** in which **happiness** overflows in **mirth**; and Elizabeth, **agitated** and **confused**, rather *knew* that she was happy than *felt* herself to be so; for, **besides** the immediate **embarrassment**, there were other evils before her. She **anticipated** what would be felt in the family when her situation became known; she was aware that no one liked him but Jane; and even **feared** that with the others it was a **dislike** which not all his **fortune** and **consequence** might do away.

At night she opened her heart to Jane. Though suspicion was very far from Miss Bennet's general habits, she was absolutely **incredulous** here.

"You are **joking**, Lizzy. This **cannot** be!--engaged to Mr. Darcy! No, no, you shall not **deceive** me. I know it to be impossible."

Italian

acknowledged: riconosciuto.
agitated: agitato.
anticipated: anticipato.
awakened: svegliato, risvegliato.
besides: inoltre, d'altronde.
cannot: non potere.
coloured: colorato.
confused: confuso.
consequence: conseguenza, risultato.
deceive: ingannare, ingannano, inganniamo, ingannate, inganna, inganni, inganno, truffare, truffate,
truffano, truffiamo.
dislike: avversione, ripugnanza, antipatia.
disposition: disposizione, predisposizione, ingegno, talento.
embarrassment: imbarazzo.
entered: entrato.
extraordinary: straordinario, eccezionale.
feared: temuto.
fortune: fortuna, sorte, patrimonio.
happiness: felicità.
incredulous: incredulo.
joking: scherzare, scherzoso.
mirth: gaiezza, allegria, ilarità, gioia.
quietly: tranquillamente.
reply: risposta, rispondere, replicare, replica.
silent: silenzioso, zitto.
suspicion: sospetto.
talked: parlato.
till: finchè, coltivare, cassa, fino, arare.
unacknowledged: non riconosciuto.
wandered: vagato.

"This is a **wretched** beginning indeed! My **sole dependence** was on you; and I am sure nobody else will believe me, if you do not. Yet, indeed, I am in **earnest**. I speak nothing but the truth. He still **loves** me, and we are engaged."

Jane looked at her doubtingly. "Oh, Lizzy! it **cannot** be. I know how much you **dislike** him."

"You know nothing of the matter. *That* is all to be **forgot**. Perhaps I did not always love him so well as I do now. But in such cases as these, a good memory is **unpardonable**. This is the last time I shall ever remember it myself."

Miss Bennet still looked all **amazement**. Elizabeth again, and more seriously **assured** her of its truth.

"Good Heaven! can it be really so! Yet now I must believe you," cried Jane. "My dear, dear Lizzy, I would--I do **congratulate** you--but are you certain? **forgive** the question --are you quite certain that you can be happy with him?"

"There can be no doubt of that. It is **settled** between us already, that we are to be the happiest couple in the world. But are you **pleased**, Jane? Shall you like to have such a brother?"

"Very, very much. Nothing could give either Bingley or myself more **delight**. But we considered it, we talked of it as impossible. And do you really love him quite well enough? Oh, Lizzy! do anything rather than **marry** without **affection**. Are you quite sure that you feel what you ought to do?"

"Oh, yes! You will only think I feel *more* than I ought to do, when I tell you all."

"What do you mean?"

"Why, I must **confess** that I love him better than I do Bingley. I am afraid you will be angry."

"My dearest sister, now *be* serious. I want to talk very seriously. Let me know every thing that I am to know, without **delay**. Will you tell me how long you have loved him?"

Italian

affection: affetto, affezione, amore.
amazement: stupore, meraviglia.
assured: assicurato, certo.
cannot: non potere.
confess: confessare, confessa, confessano, confessate, confessi, confessiamo, confesso.
congratulate: felicitare, felicitate, felicito, feliciti, felicitano, felicita, felicitiamo.
delay: ritardo, tardare, ritardare, indugio, indugiare.

delight: delizia, deliziare, dilettare, diletto, godimento, rallegrare, gioia.
dependence: dipendenza.
dislike: avversione, ripugnanza, antipatia.
earnest: serio, caparra.
forgive: perdonare, perdonano, perdoniamo, perdona, perdonate, perdoni, perdono.
forgot: dimenticato.
loves: amore.
marry: sposare, sposati, sposatevi, si

sposi, si sposate, si sposano, ci sposiamo, mi sposo, maritarsi, ammogliarsi, maritare.
pleased: contento, soddisfatto.
settled: regolato, stabilito, stabile, fermo, fisso, popolato, saldato, sistemato, deciso.
sole: sogliola, solo, suola, pianta, unico.
unpardonable: imperdonabile.
wretched: misero, miserabile, povero, infelice.

"It has been coming on so gradually, that I hardly know when it began. But I believe I must date it from my first seeing his beautiful grounds at Pemberley."

Another **entreaty** that she would be serious, **however**, produced the **desired** effect; and she soon **satisfied** Jane by her **solemn** assurances of **attachment**. When convinced on that **article**, Miss **Bennet** had nothing further to wish.

"Now I am quite happy," said she, "for you will be as happy as myself. I always had a value for him. Were it for nothing but his love of you, I must always have **esteemed** him; but now, as Bingley's friend and your husband, there can be only Bingley and yourself more dear to me. But Lizzy, you have been very **sly**, very **reserved** with me. How little did you tell me of what passed at Pemberley and Lambton! I owe all that I know of it to another, not to you."

Elizabeth told her the motives of her **secrecy**. She had been **unwilling** to mention Bingley; and the **unsettled** state of her own feelings had made her equally avoid the name of his friend. But now she would no longer **conceal** from her his share in Lydia's marriage. All was **acknowledged**, and half the night spent in conversation.

"Good gracious!" cried Mrs. Bennet, as she stood at a window the next morning, "if that **disagreeable** Mr. Darcy is not coming here again with our dear Bingley! What can he mean by being so **tiresome** as to be always coming here? I had no notion but he would go a-shooting, or something or other, and not **disturb** us with his company. What shall we do with him? Lizzy, you must walk out with him again, that he may not be in Bingley's way."

Elizabeth could hardly help laughing at so convenient a proposal; yet was really **vexed** that her mother should be always giving him such an **epithet**.

As soon as they entered, Bingley looked at her so **expressively**, and shook hands with such **warmth**, as left no doubt of his good information; and he soon afterwards said **aloud**, "Mrs. Bennet, have you no more **lanes hereabouts** in which Lizzy may lose her way again to-day?"

Italian

acknowledged: riconosciuto.
aloud: ad alta voce.
article: articolo, prodotto, oggetto, cosa, merce.
attachment: accessorio, allegato, attaccamento.
bennet: cariofillata, erba benedetta.
conceal: nascondere, nascondono, nascondete, nascondi, nascondiamo, nascondo, occultare.
desired: desiderato.
disagreeable: sgradevole.

disturb: disturbare, disturbiamo, disturba, disturbano, disturbate, disturbi, disturbo.
entreaty: preghiera, domanda, supplica.
epithet: epiteto.
esteemed: stimato.
expressively: espressivamente.
hereabouts: qui vicino.
lanes: canali.
owe: dovere.
reserved: riservato.

satisfied: soddisfatto, contento, accontentato.
secrecy: segretezza.
sly: furbo, astuto, scaltro.
solemn: solenne.
tiresome: seccante, fastidioso, noioso, faticoso.
unsettled: sconvolto, disordinato.
unwilling: riluttante, restio.
vexed: irritato, indispettito, vessato, contrariato.
warmth: calore, cordialità, tepore.

"I advise Mr. Darcy, and Lizzy, and Kitty," said Mrs. **Bennet**, "to walk to Oakham Mount this morning. It is a nice long walk, and Mr. Darcy has never seen the view."

"It may do very well for the others," replied Mr. Bingley; "but I am sure it will be too much for Kitty. Won't it, Kitty?" Kitty owned that she had rather stay at home. Darcy **professed** a great **curiosity** to see the view from the Mount, and Elizabeth **silently consented**. As she went up stairs to get ready, Mrs. Bennet followed her, saying:

"I am quite sorry, Lizzy, that you should be forced to have that **disagreeable** man all to yourself. But I hope you will not mind it: it is all for Jane's sake, you know; and there is no occasion for talking to him, except just now and then. So, do not put yourself to inconvenience."

During their walk, it was **resolved** that Mr. Bennet's consent should be asked in the course of the evening. Elizabeth **reserved** to herself the application for her mother's. She could not determine how her mother would take it; sometimes **doubting** whether all his wealth and **grandeur** would be enough to overcome her **abhorrence** of the man. But whether she were **violently** set against the match, or violently **delighted** with it, it was certain that her manner would be equally ill **adapted** to do credit to her sense; and she could no more bear that Mr. Darcy should hear the first raptures of her joy, than the first **vehemence** of her **disapprobation**.

In the evening, soon after Mr. Bennet withdrew to the library, she saw Mr. Darcy rise also and follow him, and her **agitation** on seeing it was extreme. She did not fear her father's opposition, but he was going to be made **unhappy**; and that it should be through her means--that *she*, his favourite child, should be **distressing** him by her choice, should be **filling** him with fears and regrets in **disposing** of her--was a **wretched reflection**, and she sat in **misery** till Mr. Darcy appeared again, when, looking at him, she was a little **relieved** by his smile. In a few minutes he approached the table where she was sitting with Kitty; and, while **pretending** to **admire** her work said in a **whisper**, "Go to your father, he wants you in the library." She was gone directly.

Italian

abhorrence: orrore, avversione, ribrezzo, ripugnanza.
adapted: adattato.
admire: ammirare, ammiriamo, ammira, ammirano, ammiro, ammiri, ammirate.
agitation: agitazione.
bennet: cariofillata, erba benedetta.
consented: acconsentito.
curiosity: curiosità.
delighted: lietissimo.
disagreeable: sgradevole.

disapprobation: disapprovazione.
disposing: disponendo.
distressing: doloroso, penoso, angoscioso.
doubting: dubitare.
filling: otturazione, ripieno, riempimento.
grandeur: grandiosità.
misery: miseria.
pretending: fingendo.
professed: professato, dichiarare, dichiarato.

reflection: riflesso, riflessione.
relieved: alleviato.
reserved: riservato.
resolved: risolto.
silently: silenziosamente.
unhappy: infelice, triste.
vehemence: veemenza.
violently: violentemente.
whisper: sussurrare, bisbigliare, bisbiglio.
wretched: misero, miserabile, povero, infelice.

Her father was walking about the room, looking **grave** and anxious. "Lizzy," said he, "what are you doing? Are you out of your **senses**, to be **accepting** this man? Have not you always **hated** him?"

How **earnestly** did she then wish that her former opinions had been more reasonable, her **expressions** more **moderate**! It would have **spared** her from explanations and professions which it was **exceedingly awkward** to give; but they were now necessary, and she **assured** him, with some confusion, of her **attachment** to Mr. Darcy.

"Or, in other words, you are determined to have him. He is rich, to be sure, and you may have more fine clothes and fine carriages than Jane. But will they make you happy?"

"Have you any other objection," said Elizabeth, "than your belief of my indifference?"

"None at all. We all know him to be a proud, **unpleasant** sort of man; but this would be nothing if you really liked him."

"I do, I do like him," she replied, with tears in her eyes, "I love him. Indeed he has no **improper** pride. He is perfectly **amiable**. You do not know what he really is; then **pray** do not pain me by speaking of him in such terms."

"Lizzy," said her father, "I have given him my consent. He is the kind of man, indeed, to whom I should never dare refuse anything, which he **condescended** to ask. I now give it to *you*, if you are **resolved** on having him. But let me advise you to think better of it. I know your **disposition**, Lizzy. I know that you could be neither happy nor **respectable**, unless you truly **esteemed** your husband; unless you looked up to him as a **superior**. Your **lively** talents would place you in the greatest danger in an **unequal** marriage. You could **scarcely** escape **discredit** and **misery**. My child, let me not have the **grief** of seeing *you* unable to respect your partner in life. You know not what you are about."

Elizabeth, still more affected, was earnest and **solemn** in her reply; and at length, by repeated assurances that Mr. Darcy was really the object of her choice,

Italian

accepting: accettando.
amiable: amabile.
assured: assicurato, certo.
attachment: accessorio, allegato, attaccamento.
awkward: goffo, sgraziato.
condescended: degnato.
discredit: screditare.
disposition: disposizione, predisposizione, ingegno, talento.
earnest: serio, caparra.
earnestly: seriamente.

esteemed: stimato.
exceedingly: estremamente.
expressions: espressioni.
grave: tomba, grave.
grief: dolore, pena.
hated: odiato.
improper: improprio.
lively: vivace, spiritoso, vivo, animato, vispo.
misery: miseria.
moderate: moderato, moderare.
pray: pregare, pregate, prego, preghi,

prega, preghiamo, pregano.
resolved: risolto.
respectable: rispettabile, onorevole.
scarcely: appena, a stento.
senses: sensi.
solemn: solenne.
spared: risparmiato.
superior: superiore.
unequal: ineguale, disuguale.
unpleasant: rude, spiacevole, brusco, sgradevole, scostante.

by explaining the **gradual** change which her **estimation** of him had undergone, relating her absolute certainty that his affection was not the work of a day, but had stood the **test** of many months **suspense**, and **enumerating** with energy all his good qualities, she did **conquer** her father's **incredulity**, and **reconcile** him to the match.

"Well, my dear," said he, when she ceased speaking, "I have no more to say. If this be the case, he deserves you. I could not have parted with you, my Lizzy, to anyone less worthy."

To complete the favourable impression, she then told him what Mr. Darcy had **voluntarily** done for Lydia. He heard her with **astonishment**.

"This is an evening of wonders, indeed! And so, Darcy did every thing; made up the match, gave the money, paid the fellow's debts, and got him his commission! So much the better. It will **save** me a world of trouble and economy. Had it been your uncle's doing, I must and *would* have paid him; but these violent young lovers carry every thing their own way. I shall offer to pay him to-morrow; he will **rant** and **storm** about his love for you, and there will be an end of the matter."

He then **recollected** her embarrassment a few days before, on his reading Mr. Collins's letter; and after laughing at her some time, allowed her at last to go-- saying, as she quitted the room, "If any young men come for Mary or Kitty, send them in, for I am quite at leisure."

Elizabeth's mind was now relieved from a very heavy weight; and, after half an hour's quiet reflection in her own room, she was able to join the others with **tolerable composure**. Every thing was too recent for **gaiety**, but the evening passed tranquilly away; there was no longer anything material to be dreaded, and the comfort of ease and **familiarity** would come in time.

When her mother went up to her dressing-room at night, she followed her, and made the important communication. Its effect was most extraordinary; for on first hearing it, Mrs. **Bennet** sat quite still, and unable to utter a **syllable**. Nor was it under many, many minutes that she could **comprehend** what she heard;

Italian

astonishment: stupore, meraviglia, sorpresa.
bennet: cariofillata, erba benedetta.
composure: calma, compostezza.
comprehend: comprendere, comprendo, comprendono, comprendiamo, comprendi, comprendete.
conquer: conquistare, conquistate, conquisto, conquisti, conquistano, conquistiamo, conquista.
enumerating: enumerando.

estimation: stima, valutazione.
familiarity: dimestichezza.
gaiety: gaiezza.
gradual: graduale.
incredulity: incredulità.
rant: declamazione, declamare.
recollected: rammentato.
reconcile: conciliare, riconciliare, riconciliamo, riconcili, conciliate, conciliano, conciliamo, concilia, riconcilia, riconciliano, riconciliate.
save: salvare, salvi, salviamo, salvate,

salvano, salvo, salva, risparmiare, risparmiate, risparmiano, risparmiamo.
storm: tempesta, burrasca, temporale, bufera.
suspense: apprensione.
syllable: sillaba.
test: prova, provare, test, esame, collaudo, collaudare, esaminare, saggio, testare.
tolerable: tollerabile.
voluntarily: volontariamente.

though not in general **backward** to credit what was for the advantage of her family, or that came in the shape of a **lover** to any of them. She began at length to recover, to **fidget** about in her chair, get up, sit down again, wonder, and **bless** herself.

"Good **gracious**! Lord bless me! only think! dear me! Mr. Darcy! Who would have thought it! And is it really true? Oh! my sweetest Lizzy! how rich and how great you will be! What pin-money, what jewels, what carriages you will have! Jane's is nothing to it--nothing at all. I am so pleased--so happy. Such a **charming** man!--so **handsome**! so tall!--Oh, my dear Lizzy! **pray apologise** for my having disliked him so much before. I hope he will **overlook** it. Dear, dear Lizzy. A house in town! Every thing that is charming! Three daughters married! Ten thousand a year! Oh, Lord! What will become of me. I shall go distracted."

This was enough to prove that her **approbation** need not be doubted: and Elizabeth, **rejoicing** that such an **effusion** was heard only by herself, soon went away. But before she had been three minutes in her own room, her mother followed her.

"My dearest child," she cried, "I can think of nothing else! Ten thousand a year, and very likely more! 'Tis as good as a Lord! And a special **licence**. You must and shall be married by a special licence. But my dearest love, tell me what **dish** Mr. Darcy is particularly **fond** of, that I may have it to-morrow."

This was a sad **omen** of what her mother's behaviour to the gentleman himself might be; and Elizabeth found that, though in the certain possession of his warmest **affection**, and secure of her relations' consent, there was still something to be wished for. But the **morrow** passed off much better than she expected; for Mrs. **Bennet luckily** stood in such **awe** of her intended son-in-law that she **ventured** not to speak to him, unless it was in her power to offer him any attention, or mark her **deference** for his opinion.

Elizabeth had the satisfaction of seeing her father taking **pains** to get **acquainted** with him; and Mr. Bennet soon **assured** her that he was rising every hour in his **esteem**.

Italian

acquainted: informato.
affection: affetto, affezione, amore.
apologise: scusarsi.
approbation: approvazione.
assured: assicurato, certo.
awe: soggezione, timore.
backward: indietro, a rovescio, supino, deficiente.
bennet: cariofillata, erba benedetta.
bless: benedire, benedi', benedite, benedicono, benedico, benedici, benediciamo.
charming: affascinante, grazioso, amabile, incantevole.
deference: deferenza.
dish: piatto, pietanza.
effusion: versamento, effusione.
esteem: stima, rispetto, stimare, considerazione, considerare, rispettare, riguardo.
fidget: dimenarsi, irrequietezza, agitarsi.
fond: tenero, affettuoso, affezionato.
gracious: grazioso.
handsome: bello, carino.
licence: licenza, concessione, patente.
lover: amante.
luckily: fortunatamente.
morrow: domani.
omen: augurio, presagio.
overlook: trascurare.
pains: dolori.
pray: pregare, pregate, prego, preghi, prega, preghiamo, pregano.
rejoicing: gioia.
ventured: avventurato.

"I **admire** all my three sons-in-law highly," said he. "Wickham, perhaps, is my **favourite**; but I think I shall like *your* **husband** quite as well as Jane's."

Italian

admire: ammirare, ammiriamo,
  ammira, ammirano, ammiro, ammiri,
  ammirate.
favourite: preferito.
husband: marito, sposo.

CHAPTER 60

Elizabeth's spirits soon **rising** to playfulness again, she wanted Mr. Darcy to account for his having ever fallen in love with her. "How could you begin?" said she. "I can **comprehend** your going on **charmingly**, when you had once made a beginning; but what could set you off in the first place?"

"I **cannot fix** on the hour, or the spot, or the look, or the words, which laid the foundation. It is too long ago. I was in the middle before I knew that I *had* begun."

"My beauty you had early **withstood**, and as for my manners--my behaviour to *you* was at least always **bordering** on the **uncivil**, and I never spoke to you without rather wishing to give you pain than not. Now be **sincere**; did you **admire** me for my **impertinence**?"

"For the **liveliness** of your mind, I did."

"You may as well call it impertinence at once. It was very little less. The fact is, that you were **sick** of **civility**, of **deference**, of **officious** attention. You were disgusted with the women who were always speaking, and looking, and thinking for *your* **approbation** alone. I **roused**, and interested you, because I was so unlike *them*. Had you not been really **amiable**, you would have **hated** me for it; but in **spite** of the **pains** you took to **disguise** yourself, your feelings were always **noble** and just; and in your heart, you **thoroughly despised** the persons

Italian

admire: ammirare, ammiriamo, ammira, ammirano, ammiro, ammiri, ammirate.
amiable: amabile.
approbation: approvazione.
bordering: orlare, confinante, cingente.
cannot: non potere.
charmingly: affascinantemente.
civility: civiltà, cortesia.
comprehend: comprendere, comprendo, comprendono,

comprendiamo, comprendi, comprendete.
deference: deferenza.
despised: disprezzato.
disguise: travestimento, travestire.
fix: fissare, fissa, fissano, fissate, fissi, fissiamo, fisso, riparare, aggiustare, ripara, ripariamo.
hated: odiato.
impertinence: impertinenza.
liveliness: vivacità.
noble: nobile, gentilizio, nobiliare.

officious: ufficioso, invadente.
pains: dolori.
rising: aumento, salita, sorgere, sorgente, levata, ascendente, ascesa, nascente, sommossa, levante, crescita.
roused: incitato, spronato, stimolato.
sick: malato, ammalato.
sincere: sincero.
spite: dispetto.
thoroughly: completamente.
uncivil: incivile.
withstood: resistito.

who so **assiduously** courted you. There--I have **saved** you the trouble of **accounting** for it; and really, all things considered, I begin to think it perfectly reasonable. To be sure, you knew no actual good of me--but nobody thinks of *that* when they fall in love."

"Was there no good in your **affectionate** behaviour to Jane while she was **ill** at Netherfield?"

"Dearest Jane! who could have done less for her? But make a **virtue** of it by all means. My good qualities are under your protection, and you are to **exaggerate** them as much as possible; and, in return, it **belongs** to me to find occasions for teasing and quarrelling with you as often as may be; and I shall begin directly by asking you what made you so **unwilling** to come to the point at last. What made you so **shy** of me, when you first called, and afterwards **dined** here? Why, especially, when you called, did you look as if you did not care about me?"

"Because you were **grave** and silent, and gave me no encouragement."

"But I was embarrassed."

"And so was I."

"You might have talked to me more when you came to dinner."

"A man who had felt less, might."

"How **unlucky** that you should have a reasonable answer to give, and that I should be so reasonable as to admit it! But I wonder how long you *would* have gone on, if you had been left to yourself. I wonder when you *would* have spoken, if I had not asked you! My resolution of **thanking** you for your **kindness** to Lydia had certainly great effect. *Too much*, I am afraid; for what becomes of the moral, if our **comfort** springs from a **breach** of promise? for I ought not to have mentioned the subject. This will never do."

"You need not **distress** yourself. The moral will be perfectly fair. Lady Catherine's **unjustifiable** endeavours to separate us were the means of **removing** all my **doubts**. I am not **indebted** for my present **happiness** to your **eager** desire of **expressing** your **gratitude**. I was not in a **humour** to wait for any opening of

Italian

accounting: contabilità, ragioneria, contabile.
affectionate: affettuoso.
assiduously: assiduamente.
belongs: appartiene.
breach: violazione, breccia, rottura, infrazione, inadempimento.
comfort: consolare, comodità, confortare, comfort, benessere.
dined: pranzato, cenato.
distress: pericolo.
doubts: dubbio.

eager: avido, desideroso, bramoso, impaziente.
exaggerate: esagerare, esagero, esageriamo, esageri, esagerate, esagera, esagerano.
expressing: esprimendo.
gratitude: gratitudine, riconoscenza, grazie.
grave: tomba, grave.
happiness: felicità.
humour: umore, umorismo.
ill: malato, ammalato.

indebted: obbligato, indebitato.
kindness: gentilezza, bontà, cortesia.
removing: togliendo, asportando, rimuovendo.
saved: salvato, risparmiato.
shy: timido, ritroso.
thanking: ringraziando.
unjustifiable: ingiustificabile.
unlucky: sfortunato, disgraziato.
unwilling: riluttante, restio.
virtue: virtù.

your's. My aunt's intelligence had given me hope, and I was determined at once to know every thing."

"Lady Catherine has been of **infinite** use, which ought to make her happy, for she **loves** to be of use. But tell me, what did you come down to Netherfield for? Was it merely to ride to Longbourn and be **embarrassed**? or had you intended any more serious consequence?"

"My real purpose was to see *you*, and to judge, if I could, whether I might ever hope to make you love me. My **avowed** one, or what I avowed to myself, was to see whether your sister were still partial to Bingley, and if she were, to make the **confession** to him which I have since made."

"Shall you ever have courage to **announce** to Lady Catherine what is to **befall** her?"

"I am more likely to want more time than courage, Elizabeth. But it ought to done, and if you will give me a sheet of paper, it shall be done directly."

"And if I had not a letter to write myself, I might sit by you and **admire** the **evenness** of your writing, as another young lady once did. But I have an aunt, too, who must not be longer neglected."

From an **unwillingness** to confess how much her **intimacy** with Mr. Darcy had been over-rated, Elizabeth had never yet answered Mrs. Gardiner's long letter; but now, having *that* to **communicate** which she knew would be most welcome, she was almost **ashamed** to find that her uncle and aunt had already lost three days of happiness, and immediately wrote as follows:

"I would have **thanked** you before, my dear aunt, as I ought to have done, for your long, kind, satisfactory, detail of **particulars**; but to say the truth, I was too cross to write. You supposed more than really existed. But *now* suppose as much as you choose; give a loose **rein** to your fancy, **indulge** your imagination in every possible flight which the subject will afford, and unless you believe me actually married, you **cannot** greatly **err**. You must write again very soon, and **praise** him a great deal more than you did in your last. I thank you, again and again, for not going to the Lakes. How could I be so silly as to wish it! Your idea of the

Italian

admire: ammirare, ammiriamo, ammira, ammirano, ammiro, ammiri, ammirate.
announce: annunciare, annunciate, annunci, annuncia, annunciamo, annunciano, annunziare, annuncio, annunziate, annunzi, annunzia.
ashamed: vergognoso.
avowed: dichiarato.
befall: succedete, succedi, succediamo, succedo, succedono, succedere.
cannot: non potere.

communicate: comunicare, comunicano, comunico, comunichi, comunica, communicate, comunichiamo, annunciare, infettare.
confess: confessare, confessa, confessano, confessate, confessi, confessiamo, confesso.
confession: confessione.
embarrassed: imbarazzato.
err: errare, errano, errate, erri, erriamo, erro, erra, sbagliarsi.
evenness: uniformità.

indulge: indulgere.
infinite: infinito.
intimacy: intimità.
loves: amore.
particulars: particolari.
praise: lodare, lode, elogiare, encomio, elogio.
rein: redine, briglia.
thanked: ringraziato.
unwillingness: renitenza, malavoglia.

ponies is **delightful**. We will go round the Park every day. I am the happiest **creature** in the world. Perhaps other people have said so before, but not one with such justice. I am happier even than Jane; she only smiles, I laugh. Mr. Darcy **sends** you all the love in the world that he can **spare** from me. You are all to come to Pemberley at Christmas. Yours, etc."

Mr. Darcy's letter to Lady Catherine was in a different style; and still different from either was what Mr. **Bennet** sent to Mr. Collins, in reply to his last.

"Dear Sir,

"I must trouble you once more for **congratulations**. Elizabeth will soon be the wife of Mr. Darcy. Console Lady Catherine as well as you can. But, if I were you, I would stand by the **nephew**. He has more to give.

"Yours **sincerely**, etc."

Miss Bingley's congratulations to her brother, on his **approaching** marriage, were all that was **affectionate** and **insincere**. She wrote even to Jane on the occasion, to express her delight, and repeat all her former professions of regard. Jane was not **deceived**, but she was affected; and though feeling no **reliance** on her, could not help writing her a much kinder answer than she knew was **deserved**.

The **joy** which Miss Darcy expressed on **receiving** similar information, was as sincere as her brother's in **sending** it. Four sides of paper were **insufficient** to contain all her delight, and all her **earnest** desire of being loved by her sister.

Before any answer could arrive from Mr. Collins, or any congratulations to Elizabeth from his wife, the Longbourn family heard that the Collinses were come themselves to Lucas Lodge. The reason of this sudden **removal** was soon **evident**. Lady Catherine had been **rendered** so **exceedingly** angry by the **contents** of her nephew's letter, that Charlotte, really **rejoicing** in the match, was anxious to get away till the **storm** was **blown** over. At such a moment, the arrival of her friend was a sincere pleasure to Elizabeth, though in the course of their meetings she must sometimes think the pleasure **dearly** bought, when she

Italian

affectionate: affettuoso.
approaching: avvicinamento.
bennet: cariofillata, erba benedetta.
blown: dischiuso.
congratulations: congratulazioni.
contents: contenuto.
creature: creatura.
dearly: caramente.
deceived: ingannato, truffato.
delight: delizia, deliziare, dilettare, diletto, godimento, rallegrare, gioia.
delightful: delizioso, piacevole.

deserved: meritato.
earnest: serio, caparra.
evident: evidente, chiaro, palese, lampante.
exceedingly: estremamente.
insincere: falso, insincero.
insufficient: insufficiente.
joy: gioia.
nephew: nipote.
receiving: ricevendo, accogliendo, ricezione, ricevere, ricevente.
rejoicing: gioia.

reliance: fiducia.
removal: rimozione, asportazione, eliminazione.
rendered: reso.
sending: mandando, spedendo.
sends: manda, spedisce.
sincere: sincero.
sincerely: sinceramente, francamente.
spare: risparmiare, scorta.
storm: tempesta, burrasca, temporale, bufera.

saw Mr. Darcy **exposed** to all the **parading** and **obsequious civility** of her husband. He **bore** it, however, with **admirable calmness**. He could even listen to Sir William Lucas, when he complimented him on carrying away the brightest **jewel** of the country, and expressed his hopes of their all meeting **frequently** at St. James's, with very **decent composure**. If he did **shrug** his shoulders, it was not till Sir William was out of sight.

Mrs. Phillips's **vulgarity** was another, and perhaps a greater, tax on his **forbearance**; and though Mrs. Phillips, as well as her sister, stood in too much **awe** of him to speak with the **familiarity** which Bingley's good **humour** encouraged, yet, whenever she *did* speak, she must be vulgar. Nor was her respect for him, though it made her more quiet, at all likely to make her more **elegant**. Elizabeth did all she could to **shield** him from the frequent notice of either, and was ever anxious to keep him to herself, and to those of her family with whom he might **converse** without **mortification**; and though the **uncomfortable** feelings **arising** from all this took from the season of **courtship** much of its pleasure, it added to the hope of the future; and she looked forward with **delight** to the time when they should be removed from society so little **pleasing** to either, to all the comfort and **elegance** of their family party at Pemberley.

Italian

admirable: ammirabile, ammirevole, mirabile.
arising: nascendo, sorgendo.
awe: soggezione, timore.
bore: annoiare, alesaggio, foro, forare, succiello, seccare, alesare, perforare, trivellare.
calmness: calma.
civility: civiltà, cortesia.
comfort: consolare, comodità, confortare, comfort, benessere.
composure: calma, compostezza.

converse: contrario.
courtship: corteggiamento.
decent: decente.
delight: delizia, deliziare, dilettare, diletto, godimento, rallegrare, gioia.
elegance: eleganza.
elegant: elegante.
exposed: esposto.
familiarity: dimestichezza.
forbearance: pazienza.
frequent: frequente, bazzicare.
humour: umore, umorismo.

jewel: gioiello, gemma, gioia.
mortification: mortificazione.
obsequious: ossequioso, servile.
parading: sfilare.
pleasing: piacevole.
shield: scudo, riparo, proteggere, schermo, schermare.
shrug: alzata di spalle.
uncomfortable: scomodo, disagiato.
vulgar: volgare, triviale.
vulgarity: volgarità.

CHAPTER 61

Happy for all her **maternal** feelings was the day on which Mrs. **Bennet** got **rid** of her two most **deserving daughters**. With what **delighted pride** she afterwards **visited** Mrs. Bingley, and **talked** of Mrs. Darcy, may be **guessed**. I wish I could say, for the **sake** of her family, that the **accomplishment** of her **earnest** desire in the establishment of so many of her children produced so happy an effect as to make her a sensible, **amiable**, well-informed woman for the rest of her life; though perhaps it was **lucky** for her husband, who might not have relished domestic **felicity** in so unusual a form, that she still was **occasionally nervous** and **invariably silly**.

Mr. Bennet **missed** his second daughter **exceedingly**; his **affection** for her drew him oftener from home than anything else could do. He delighted in going to Pemberley, especially when he was least expected.

Mr. Bingley and Jane remained at Netherfield only a twelvemonth. So near a vicinity to her mother and Meryton relations was not **desirable** even to *his* easy **temper**, or *her* **affectionate** heart. The **darling** wish of his sisters was then **gratified**; he bought an estate in a **neighbouring** county to Derbyshire, and Jane and Elizabeth, in **addition** to every other source of **happiness**, were within thirty miles of each other.

Kitty, to her very material advantage, spent the chief of her time with her two **elder** sisters. In society so **superior** to what she had generally known, her

Italian

accomplishment: compimento, adempimento.
addition: aggiunta, addizione.
affection: affetto, affezione, amore.
affectionate: affettuoso.
amiable: amabile.
bennet: cariofillata, erba benedetta.
darling: prediletto, tesoro, caro.
daughters: figlie.
delighted: lietissimo.
deserving: meritando, meritevole.
desirable: desiderabile.

earnest: serio, caparra.
elder: maggiore, sambuco.
exceedingly: estremamente.
felicity: felicità.
gratified: gratificato.
guessed: indovinato.
happiness: felicità.
invariably: invariabilmente.
kitty: gattino.
lucky: fortunato.
maternal: materno.
missed: mancato.

neighbouring: vicino.
nervous: nervoso.
occasionally: occasionalmente.
pride: orgoglio, fierezza.
rid: sbarazzare.
sake: causa.
silly: sciocco, stupido.
superior: superiore.
talked: parlato.
temper: umore, temperamento, tempra.
visited: visitato.

improvement was great. She was not of so **ungovernable** a **temper** as Lydia; and, removed from the influence of Lydia's example, she became, by proper attention and management, less **irritable**, less **ignorant**, and less **insipid**. From the further **disadvantage** of Lydia's society she was of course carefully kept, and though Mrs. Wickham frequently invited her to come and stay with her, with the promise of **balls** and young men, her father would never consent to her going.

Mary was the only daughter who remained at home; and she was necessarily drawn from the **pursuit** of **accomplishments** by Mrs. Bennet's being quite unable to sit alone. Mary was **obliged** to **mix** more with the world, but she could still **moralize** over every morning visit; and as she was no longer **mortified** by comparisons between her sisters' beauty and her own, it was suspected by her father that she **submitted** to the change without much **reluctance**.

As for Wickham and Lydia, their characters suffered no **revolution** from the marriage of her sisters. He **bore** with **philosophy** the **conviction** that Elizabeth must now become **acquainted** with whatever of his **ingratitude** and **falsehood** had before been unknown to her; and in **spite** of every thing, was not **wholly** without hope that Darcy might yet be **prevailed** on to make his **fortune**. The congratulatory letter which Elizabeth received from Lydia on her marriage, explained to her that, by his wife at least, if not by himself, such a hope was **cherished**. The letter was to this effect:

"My dear Lizzy,

"I wish you **joy**. If you love Mr. Darcy half as well as I do my dear Wickham, you must be very happy. It is a great **comfort** to have you so rich, and when you have nothing else to do, I hope you will think of us. I am sure Wickham would like a place at court very much, and I do not think we shall have quite money enough to live upon without some help. Any place would do, of about three or four hundred a year; but however, do not speak to Mr. Darcy about it, if you had rather not.

"Yours, etc."

Italian

accomplishments: compimenti.
acquainted: informato.
balls: sfere, palla, balli.
bore: annoiare, alesaggio, foro, forare, succiello, seccare, alesare, perforare, trivellare.
cherished: adorato.
comfort: consolare, comodità, confortare, comfort, benessere.
conviction: convinzione, condanna.
disadvantage: svantaggio.
falsehood: falso, falsità, bugia, menzogna.
fortune: fortuna, sorte, patrimonio.
ignorant: ignorante.
ingratitude: ingratitudine.
insipid: insipido, insulso, scipito.
irritable: irritabile.
joy: gioia.
mix: mescolare, mischiare, impastare, mescolanza, miscela.
moralize: moraleggiare, moralizzare.
mortified: mortificato.
obliged: obbligato.
philosophy: filosofia.
prevailed: prevalso.
pursuit: inseguimento, ricerca.
reluctance: riluttanza.
revolution: rivoluzione, giro, rotazione.
spite: dispetto.
submitted: sottomesso, sottoposto.
temper: umore, temperamento, tempra.
ungovernable: indisciplinato.
wholly: interamente, completamente.

As it happened that Elizabeth had *much* rather not, she endeavoured in her answer to put an end to every **entreaty** and **expectation** of the kind. Such relief, however, as it was in her power to afford, by the practice of what might be called economy in her own private expences, she frequently sent them. It had always been evident to her that such an income as **theirs**, under the direction of two persons so **extravagant** in their wants, and **heedless** of the future, must be very insufficient to their support; and whenever they changed their quarters, either Jane or herself were sure of being applied to for some little assistance towards discharging their **bills**. Their manner of living, even when the restoration of peace dismissed them to a home, was **unsettled** in the extreme. They were always moving from place to place in **quest** of a **cheap** situation, and always spending more than they ought. His affection for her soon sunk into **indifference**; her's **lasted** a little longer; and in **spite** of her youth and her **manners**, she **retained** all the claims to reputation which her marriage had given her.

Though Darcy could never receive *him* at Pemberley, yet, for Elizabeth's sake, he **assisted** him further in his profession. Lydia was occasionally a visitor there, when her husband was gone to enjoy himself in London or Bath; and with the Bingleys they both of them frequently **staid** so long, that even Bingley's good humour was overcome, and he **proceeded** so far as to talk of giving them a hint to be gone.

Miss Bingley was very deeply **mortified** by Darcy's marriage; but as she thought it **advisable** to retain the right of visiting at Pemberley, she dropt all her **resentment**; was **fonder** than ever of Georgiana, almost as **attentive** to Darcy as heretofore, and paid off every **arrear** of **civility** to Elizabeth.

Pemberley was now Georgiana's home; and the **attachment** of the sisters was exactly what Darcy had hoped to see. They were able to love each other even as well as they intended. Georgiana had the highest opinion in the world of Elizabeth; though at first she often listened with an **astonishment bordering** on alarm at her lively, **sportive**, manner of talking to her brother. He, who had always inspired in herself a respect which almost overcame her affection, she

Italian

advisable: consigliabile.

arrear: arretrato.

assisted: assistito, aiutato.

astonishment: stupore, meraviglia, sorpresa.

attachment: accessorio, allegato, attaccamento.

attentive: attento, premuroso.

bills: effetti, banconote.

bordering: orlare, confinante, cingente.

cheap: a buon mercato, economico,

conveniente.

civility: civiltà, cortesia.

entreaty: preghiera, domanda, supplica.

expectation: attesa, aspettativa.

extravagant: stravagante.

fonder: più affettuoso.

heedless: sbadato, disattento.

indifference: indifferenza.

lasted: durato.

manners: educazione.

mortified: mortificato.

proceeded: proceduto.

quest: ricerca.

resentment: risentimento, astio.

retain: ritenere, ritengo, ritieni, ritenete, riteniamo, ritengono, trattenere, trattenete, trattengo, trattengono, tratteniamo.

spite: dispetto.

sportive: allegro.

staid: serio.

theirs: loro.

unsettled: sconvolto, disordinato.

now saw the object of open pleasantry. Her mind received knowledge which had never before fallen in her way. By Elizabeth's instructions, she began to **comprehend** that a woman may take liberties with her husband which a brother will not always allow in a sister more than ten years younger than himself.

Lady Catherine was extremely **indignant** on the marriage of her **nephew**; and as she gave way to all the **genuine frankness** of her character in her reply to the letter which announced its **arrangement**, she sent him language so very **abusive**, especially of Elizabeth, that for some time all **intercourse** was at an end. But at length, by Elizabeth's **persuasion**, he was **prevailed** on to **overlook** the offence, and seek a **reconciliation**; and, after a little further resistance on the part of his **aunt**, her **resentment** gave way, either to her **affection** for him, or her **curiosity** to see how his wife **conducted** herself; and she **condescended** to wait on them at Pemberley, in **spite** of that pollution which its **woods** had received, not merely from the presence of such a **mistress**, but the **visits** of her uncle and aunt from the city.

With the Gardiners, they were always on the most **intimate** terms. Darcy, as well as Elizabeth, really loved them; and they were both ever **sensible** of the warmest **gratitude** towards the persons who, by bringing her into Derbyshire, had been the means of **uniting** them.

Italian

abusive: abusivo, offensivo.
affection: affetto, affezione, amore.
arrangement: accomodamento, disposizione, sistemazione, ordinamento, arrangiamento, assestamento, adattamento.
aunt: zia, la zia.
comprehend: comprendere, comprendo, comprendono, comprendiamo, comprendi, comprendete.
condescended: degnato.

conducted: condotto.
curiosity: curiosità.
frankness: franchezza.
genuine: genuino, autentico.
gratitude: gratitudine, riconoscenza, grazie.
indignant: indignato.
intercourse: rapporti.
intimate: intimo.
mistress: padrona.
nephew: nipote.
overlook: trascurare.

persuasion: persuasione.
prevailed: prevalso.
reconciliation: riconciliazione, conciliazione.
resentment: risentimento, astio.
sensible: sensato, ragionevole, sensibile.
spite: dispetto.
uniting: unendo.
visits: visita.
woods: bosco.

GLOSSARY

abatement: riduzione, detrazione, diminuzione, abbattimento, abolizione

abhorrence: orrore, avversione, ribrezzo, ripugnanza

abhorrent: ripugnante, orrendo, orribile, avverso, detestabile

abide: aspettare, aspettiamo, aspetta, aspettano, aspetti, aspetto, aspettate, restare, sopportare

abiding: durevole, permanente, continuo, aspettando

abilities: abilità

ablution: abluzione

abode: residenza, appartamento, alloggio, dimora

abominable: abominevole, orribile, orrendo

abominably: abominevolmente

abominate: detestare, detestate, detesta, detestano, detestiamo, detesti, detesto, abominare, abomina, abomino, abominate

abound: abbondare, abbondano, abbondate, abbondi, abbondiamo, abbondo, abbonda

abrupt: brusco, ripido, subitaneo, improvviso

abruptly: improvvisamente

abruptness: precipitazione

absent: assente

absolute: assoluto, completo

absurd: assurdo

absurdity: assurdità

abundant: abbondante

abundantly: abbondantemente

abuse: abuso, insultare, abusare, offendere, insulto

abused: abusato

abusing: abusando

abusive: abusivo, offensivo

accede: concordare, accedere, concordo, concordate, concordiamo, concordi, concordano, accedono, accedo, accedi, accediamo

acceded: concordato, accesso

acceding: accedendo, concordando

accent: accento, accentare, accentano, accentate, accenti, accentiamo, accenta

accents: accenta

acceptable: accettabile

acceptance: accettazione, accoglienza, accoglimento

accepting: accettando

accidental: accidentale, fortuito

accidentally: accidentalmente

accompanied: accompagnato

accompany: accompagnare, accompagna, accompagniamo, accompagno, accompagni, accompagnate, accompagnano

accompanying: accompagnando

accomplished: compiuto

accomplishment: compimento, adempimento

accomplishments: compimenti

according: secondo

accordingly: di conseguenza, quindi

accosted: abbordato, accostato, avvicinato

accounting: contabilità, ragioneria, contabile

accuracy: accuratezza, esattezza, precisione

accurate: esatto, preciso, accurato

accusation: accusa, incriminazione, imputazione, denuncia

accuse: accusare, accusate, accusi, accusiamo, accuso, accusano, accusa, caricare, caricano, carico, carichiamo

accusing: accusando, caricando

accustomed: consueto, abituato, usuale, solito, avvezzo

achieving: compiendo, conseguendo

acknowledge: riconoscere, riconoscono, riconosco, riconosciamo, riconosci, riconoscete, confessare, confermare, prendere atto

acknowledged: riconosciuto

acknowledging: riconoscendo

acknowledgment: riconoscimento

acquaint: informare, informi, informa, informate, informiamo, informo, informano, insegnare

acquaintance: conoscenza, conoscente

acquaintances: conoscenze

acquainted: informato

acquainting: informando

acquiesce: acconsentire, acconsentite, acconsenti, acconsentiamo, acconsento, acconsentono, essere acquiescente

acquiescence: acquiescenza

acquire: acquisire, acquisiamo, acquisisco, acquisiscono, acquisite, acquisisci, acquistare

acquired: acquisito

acquisition: acquisizione, acquisto, guadagno, compra

acquit: assolvere, assolvete, assolviamo, assolvo, assolvono, assolvi

acrimony: acrimonia

actuated: azionato

acute: acuto, aguzzo, appuntito

acutely: acutamente

adapted: adattato

adding: aggiungendo, addizionando

addition: aggiunta, addizione

additions: addizioni

addressed: rivolto

addresses: indirizzi

addressing: indirizzamento

adds: aggiunge, addiziona

adept: esperto, abile

adequate: adeguato, sufficiente

adhered: aderito

adhering: aderendo

adieu: addio

adjusting: aggiustando, regolando

admirable: ammirabile, ammirevole, mirabile

admiration: ammirazione

admire: ammirare, ammiriamo, ammira, ammirano, ammiro, ammiri, ammirate

admired: ammirato

admirer: ammiratore
admires: ammira
admiring: ammirando, ammirativo
admission: ammissione, confessione, immissione, accoglimento, accoglienza, ingresso
admit: confessare, confessa, confessiamo, confessi, confessate, confessano, confesso, ammettere, permettere, ammetto, ammettiamo
admittance: ammettenza
admitting: confessando, ammettendo
adopt: adottare, adotta, adotto, adottiamo, adotti, adottano, adottate
adoration: adorazione, venerazione
adorned: decorato
advancement: progresso, avanzamento
advances: avanzamenti
advantageous: vantaggioso, utile
advantageously: vantaggiosamente
advantages: vantaggi
adventure: avventura
advertised: annunziato
advisable: consigliabile
advise: consigliare, consigliano, consigli, consiglia, consigliamo, consigliate, consiglio, raccomandare
advised: consigliato
advising: consigliando
affability: affabilità
affable: affabile, cortese, gradevole, amichevole, grazioso, carino, benevole
affair: affare, faccenda, caso
affectation: affettazione, posa
affection: affetto, affezione, amore
affectionate: affettuoso
affectionately: affettuosamente
affinity: affinità, parentela, parentado
affirmative: affermativo
afflicted: afflitto
afflicting: affliggendo
affliction: afflizione
afforded: permesso
affording: permettendo
affords: permette
affront: affronto, insulto, insultare
afresh: di nuovo, ancora, da capo
agitated: agitato
agitation: agitazione
agony: agonia, angoscia
agreeable: gradevole, piacevole, amabile
agreeably: piacevolmente
agreeing: concordando, pattuendo
aimed: puntato, intenzionato, mirato
airing: aerazione, aria
alacrity: entusiasmo, alacrità
alarm: allarme, sveglia, allarmare
alarmed: allarmato
alarming: allarmante

alas: ahimè
alienated: alienato
alike: simile, similmente
allayed: alleviato, acquietato
alleviate: alleviare, allevio, allevi, allevia, alleviamo, alleviano, alleviate
alleviated: alleviato
alliance: alleanza
allowable: ammissibile
allowance: indennità, assegno, tolleranza, abbuono, detrazione, sconto, permesso
allowing: permettendo
allude: alludere, alludi, alludiamo, alludo, alludono, alludete
alluded: alluso
alluding: alludendo
allusion: allusione
aloof: appartato, in disparte, alla larga, a distanza, distante
aloud: ad alta voce
altar: altare
alter: cambiarsi, alterare, altera, alteriamo, alterano, alteri, alterate, altero, modificare, mutare, cambiare
alteration: alterazione, modifica, cambiamento, variazione
altered: alterato
alternate: alternare, alterno, alternato
altogether: tutto, complessivamente
amaze: sbalordire, sbalordiamo, sbalordisci, sbalordisco, sbalordiscono, sbalordite, stupire, si stupiscono, ci stupiamo, si stupisci, si stupite
amazed: sbalordito, stupito, si stupito
amazement: stupore, meraviglia
amazes: sbalordisce, si stupisce
amazing: sbalordendo, stupefacente, stupendosi, sorprendente, strabiliante
ambition: ambizione
amendment: emendamento, modifica, correzione
amends: emenda, ammenda
amiable: amabile
amid: tra, fra
amidst: tra, fra
amiss: male, inopportuno
ample: ampio
amply: ampiamente
amuse: divertire, divertiamo, divertono, diverto, diverti, divertite
amused: divertito
amusement: divertimento, spasso, svago
amusing: divertente, divertendo, spassoso
anecdote: aneddoto
anew: di nuovo, ancora
angel: angelo

angelic: angelico
anger: collera, rabbia, ira
angrily: irosamente
anguish: angoscia
animated: animato
animation: animazione, vivacità
ankle: caviglia
annexed: annesso
announce: annunciare, annunciate, annunci, annuncia, annunciamo, annunciano, annunziare, annuncio, annunziate, annunzi, annunzia
annoyed: infastidito, irritato, seccato
answerable: responsabile
answering: risposta, rispondere
answers: risposta, risposte
antagonist: antagonista
anticipate: anticipare, anticipiamo, anticipi, anticipate, anticipa, anticipano, anticipo, prevedere, prevenire
anticipated: anticipato
anticipating: anticipando
anticipation: anticipazione, previsione
anxiety: ansia, ansietà, angoscia, inquietudine
anxious: ansioso
anxiously: ansiosamente
anyhow: comunque
apace: di buon passo
apartment: appartamento
apologies: scuse
apologise: scusarsi
apology: scusa, apologia
apothecary: farmacista
apparel: vestimento, abito
appearing: apparendo
appease: placare, placo, plachiamo, plachi, placate, placano, placa, calmare
appeased: placato
appertain: appartieni, apparteniamo, appartengono, appartenete, appartengo, appartenere
appetite: appetito
applies: applica
applying: applicando
apprehended: capito, compreso, afferrato, temuto
apprehending: temendo, comprendendo, capendo, afferrando
apprehension: apprensione, arresto
apprehensive: apprensivo
approaching: avvicinamento
approbation: approvazione
approve: approvare, approvate, approvano, approvi, approvo, approva, approviamo
apt: adatto
arch: arco, volta
archbishop: arcivescovo

archly: arco
archness: malizia
ardent: ardente
ardently: ardentemente
arguing: argomentando, discutendo, disputando
arise: nascere, nasciamo, nasco, nasci, nascete, nascono, salire, sorgere, sorgete, sorgono, sorgi
arisen: nato, sorto
arising: nascendo, sorgendo
aroused: suscitato, risvegliato, destato
arrange: sistemare, sistemiamo, sistemate, sistemano, sistemo, sistemi, sistema, predisporre, predisponete, predispongo, predisponi
arranged: sistemato, predisposto, ordinato
arrangement: accomodamento, disposizione, sistemazione, ordinamento, arrangiamento, assestamento, adattamento
arranges: sistema, predispone, ordina
arranging: sistemando, predisponendo, ordinando
arrear: arretrato
arrested: arrestato
arrival: arrivo, venuta
arrive: arrivare, arrivano, arriva, arrivi, arriviamo, arrivate, arrivo, giungere
arriving: arrivando
arrogance: arroganza, alterigia
arrogant: arrogante, altezzoso
artful: astuto
artfully: astutamente
artificial: artificiale, artefatto
ascended: salito, asceso
ascertain: constatare, constatiamo, constati, constatate, constato, constatano, constata, accertare, accerto, accertiamo, accerti
ascertaining: constatando, accertando
ashamed: vergognoso
aside: da parte, a parte
asperity: asperità
aspire: aspirare, aspiri, aspira, aspirate, aspiro, aspiriamo, aspirano
assembled: montato, assemblato
assemblies: complessivi
assent: affermare, assentire, approvazione, assenso, acconsentire
assert: asserire, asserite, asseriscono, asserisci, asserisco, asseriamo, sostenere, affermare
asserted: asserito
asserting: asserendo
assertion: asserzione, affermazione
assiduous: assiduo, diligente
assiduously: assiduamente

assist: assistere, assistono, assistiamo, assistete, assisti, assisto, aiutare, aiuti, aiuta, aiutano, aiutate
assistant: assistente, aggiunto, aiutante, aiuto, coadiutore
assisted: assistito, aiutato
assisting: assistendo, aiutando
associating: associare
assumed: presunto, supposto
assurance: assicurazione, promessa
assure: assicurare, assicura, assicuriamo, assicurate, assicuri, assicurano, assicuro, garantire
assured: assicurato, certo
assuring: assicurando
astonish: stupire, stupisciti, si stupite, si stupiscono, si stupisci, mi stupisco, ci stupiamo, stupitevi, sorprendere, sbalordire
astonished: stupito, si stupito
astonishment: stupore, meraviglia, sorpresa
atone: espiare, espio, espii, espiate, espiano, espia, espiamo
atoned: espiato
atonement: espiazione, riparazione
attach: fissare, attaccare, fissi, attacca, fissate, fissano, fisso, attacchi, attacchiamo, attaccate, attaccano
attached: fissato, attaccato, allegato
attachment: accessorio, allegato, attaccamento
attained: arrivato
attempted: provato
attempting: provando
attend: visitare, curare, assistere, curiamo, curi, curo, curano, visitate, visitiamo, cura, visiti
attendance: servizio, presenza
attendant: custode, compagno, inserviente
attended: visitato, curato, assistito
attending: visitando, curando, assistendo
attentive: attento, premuroso
attentively: attentamente
attorney: procuratore, avvocato
attracted: attirato, attratto
attraction: attrazione, forza attrattiva, attrattiva
attribute: attributo, attribuire
attributed: attribuito
attributing: attribuire
audible: udibile
augment: ingrandire, ingrandite, ingrandiscono, ingrandisco, ingrandisci, ingrandiamo, aumentare, aumenta, aumentano, aumentate, aumenti
augmented: ingrandito, aumentato
aunt: zia, la zia
austerity: austerità

authorise: autorizzare
authoritative: autoritario, autorevole
authorized: autorizzato
avail: giovare, essere utile, servire, utilizzare
availed: servito
avarice: avarizia
avenue: viale
avoidance: annullamento, evitare
avoided: evitato
avoiding: evitando
avowal: ammissione
avowed: dichiarato
awaited: aspettato, atteso
awake: sveglio, svegliarsi
awakened: svegliato, risvegliato
awe: soggezione, timore
awful: orribile, orrendo, tremendo, terribile
awkward: goffo, sgraziato
awkwardness: goffaggine
backed: sostenuto
backgammon: backgammon
backward: indietro, a rovescio, supino, deficiente
backwards: indietro, a rovescio, all'indietro, supino
balls: sfere, palla, balli
balm: balsamo
bandbox: cappelliera
banish: bandire, bandisci, bandisco, bandiscono, bandite, bandiamo, esiliare
banished: bandito
barbarous: barbaro
barbarously: barbaramente
bare: nudo, denudare
barefaced: impudente
barely: appena, a mala pena
bashful: timido
bath: bagno, vasca da bagno, il bagno
battled: combattuto
bearing: cuscinetto, rapporto
beaux: fidanzati
befall: succedete, succedi, succediamo, succedo, succedono, succedere
beforehand: in anticipo
befriended: aiutato
beg: mendicare, mendicano, mendica, mendicate, mendico, mendichiamo, mendichi, chiedere, elemosinare, supplicare
begged: mendicato
begging: mendicando
begins: comincia, inizia
begs: mendica
behave: comportarsi, condursi
behaved: agito, comportato
behaves: agisce
behavior: condotta, comportamento
beheld: guardato

beholding: guardando
believing: credendo, credere
bell: campana, campanello
belong: appartenere, appartieni, apparteniamo, appartengono, appartenete, appartengo
belonged: appartenuto
belonging: appartenendo
belongs: appartiene
beloved: caro, adorato, amato
benches: panchine
beneficence: beneficenza
beneficial: giovevole, che reca giovamento, che fa bene, benefico, vantaggioso
benevolence: benevolenza
benevolent: benevolo
bennet: cariofillata, erba benedetta
bent: curvo, piegato
bequest: lascito
besides: inoltre, d'altronde
bestow: tributare, concedere
bestowed: concesso, tributato
bestowing: concedendo, tributando
betray: tradire, tradisci, tradite, tradisco, tradiamo, tradiscono
betrayed: tradito
bewailed: si lamentato
bewildered: sconcertato
bewitched: incantato
bewitching: incantando, affascinante
bid: offerta, offrire, chiedere
bidding: offerta, licitazione, comando
bills: effetti, banconote
biting: pungente, mordace
bitter: amaro
bitterly: amaramente
bitterness: amarezza
blacken: annerire, annerisci, annerite, annerisco, anneriamo, anneriscono
blame: colpa, biasimare, riprendere, incolpare, biasimo
blameless: irreprensibile
blaming: biasimare
blasted: maledetto
blemish: difetto
bless: benedire, benedi', benedite, benedicono, benedico, benedici, benediciamo
blessed: benedetto, beato
blessing: benedicendo, benedizione
blind: cieco, accecare, acceca, accechi, accechiamo, accecate, accecano, acceco
blinded: accecato
blinds: acceca
blow: soffiare, colpo, botta, botto
blown: dischiuso
blush: rossore, arrossire
blushed: arrossito
blushing: rosso, arrossire, rossore
boast: vanteria, vantarsi

boasted: vantato
boasting: vanteria
bold: grassetto, spesso, grosso, audace
boldly: audacemente, arditamente
bonnet: cofano, cappotta, cuffia
bordering: orlare, confinante, cingente
bore: annoiare, alesaggio, foro, forare, succiello, seccare, alesare, perforare, trivellare
borrow: prendere in prestito
bosom: petto, seno
bound: limite, confine
boundary: confine, frontiera, limite, delimitazione, contorno
boundless: illimitato
bounty: generosità
bow: arco, prua, fiocco, inchino, inchinarsi, curva, archetto
bowed: chino
bowing: archeggio
bowl: scodella, ciotola, bacino, coppa, vaschetta, boccia
bows: archetti
boxes: scatole
brains: mente, cervello
breach: violazione, breccia, rottura, infrazione, inadempimento
breaking: rottura
breast: petto, seno, mammella
breathed: respirato
breathing: respirando, respirazione, respiro
breathless: ansante, senza fiato
breeding: allevamento, riproduzione
brevity: brevità
bribe: bustarella, corrompere, dono
bribery: corruzione
bride: sposa, fidanzata, novella sposa
bridegroom: sposo
briefly: brevemente
brightening: schiarimento
brilliancy: splendore
brings: porta
brink: orlo
brittle: fragile, croccante, friabile
brotherly: fraterno
brothers: fratelli
brow: sopracciglio, fronte
burning: bruciare, bruciatura
burnt: bruciato
burst: scoppiare, scoppio, crepa, screpolatura, fessura, esplosione, crepare, irrompere, burst
burying: seppellendo
busily: attivamente, indaffaratamente
bustle: trambusto
butler: maggiordomo
buying: acquisto
bye: arrivederci, addio, ciao
cake: torta, focaccia, la torta

calculate: calcolare, calcoliamo, calcola, calcolano, calcolate, calcoli, calcolo
calculated: calcolato
calculation: calcolo, conto
calico: calice
calling: chiamando, chiamata
calm: calmo, calmare, tranquillo, calma, placare
calmly: con calma
calmness: calma
cambric: cambrì, percalle
camp: campo, campeggiare, campeggio, accampamento, accamparsi
candid: franco
candour: franchezza
cannot: non potere
canvas: tela, canovaccio
capers: capperi
caprice: capriccio
captivate: affascinare
captivated: affascinato
captivating: affascinando, accattivante, affascinare
captivation: attrazione
careless: sbadato, noncurante, negligente, trascurato
carelessness: negligenza
caring: premuroso
carriage: vettura, carrello, vagone, carro, carrozza
carter: carrettiere
carved: intagliato, tagliato, scolpito
casual: casuale, accidentale
catching: contagioso, prendendo, infettivo, colpendo, prendere
caution: avvertire, prudenza, avvertenza, cautela
cautious: cauto, prudente
cease: cessare
ceased: cessato
ceaseless: incessante
celebrated: celebrato, festeggiato, famoso
celerity: celerità
censure: disapprovazione, criticare, censura
censured: censurato
ceremonious: cerimonioso
ceremony: cerimonia
certainty: certezza
cessation: cessazione
chagrin: dispiacere, cruccio
chaise: calesse
chamber: camera
chambermaid: cameriera
chanced: successo
chaperon: accompagnatrice
characterise: caratterizzare
characteristic: caratteristico, caratteristica

charged: caricato
charity: elemosina
charm: fascino, incanto
charming: affascinante, grazioso, amabile, incantevole
charmingly: affascinantemente
chatty: chiacchierino
cheap: a buon mercato, economico, conveniente
cheat: ingannare, truffare, imbroglione, imbrogliare, barare
cheating: ingannare, frode, imbrogliare
checked: quadrettato
checking: verifica, controllo
cheerful: allegro
cheerfully: allegramente
cheerfulness: contentezza, allegria
cheering: applauso
cherish: adoriamo, adori, adorate, adorano, adora, adoro, adorare, curare teneramente
cherished: adorato
chestnuts: castagna, castagne
chicken: pollo, gallina, il pollo, pollastro
chiefly: principalmente, soprattutto
childhood: infanzia, fanciullezza
chin: mento, il mento
chooses: sceglie, elegge
choosing: scegliendo, eleggendo
christening: battesimo, battezzando
circle: circolo, cerchio, compagnia
circuit: circuito
circulating: circolante, circolare
circulation: circolazione, diffusione
circumspect: circospetto
circumspection: circospezione
circumstance: circostanza
civility: civiltà, cortesia
civilly: civile, civilmente
clamorous: clamoroso
cleanse: pulire, puliamo, pulisci, pulisco, puliscono, pulite
cleared: chiaro
clearing: compensazione, radura
clergy: clero
clergyman: ecclesiastico, prete, curato, sacerdote
clerical: clericale
clerk: commesso, cancelliere, impiegato
clever: intelligente, destro, abile, lesto, sveglio
clock: orologio
closet: armadio
closure: chiusura
clouded: annuvolato
clue: indizio
clump: gruppo
cluster: gruppo, grappolo, cluster
coach: vettura, vagone, carrozza,

allenatore, allenare
coachman: cocchiere, vetturino
coarse: rozzo, grossolano
coarseness: grossolanità, ruvidezza
coat: cappotto, rivestire
coaxed: persuaso, blandito
cogent: convincente
coherent: coerente
coincide: coincidere, coincidete, coincidi, coincidiamo, coincido, coincidono
coincided: coinciso
coincidence: coincidenza
coldly: freddamente
collect: raccogliere, raccolgono, raccolgo, raccogliete, raccogliamo, raccogli
collected: raccolto
collecting: raccogliendo
colonel: colonnello
coloured: colorato
colouring: coloritura
comfort: consolare, comodità, confortare, comfort, benessere
comfortably: piacevolmente
comforted: confortato
commanded: comandato
commencement: inizio, principio
commendable: lodevole
commendation: raccomandazione
commended: lodato
commerce: commercio
commiseration: commiserazione
commissioning: messa in servizio
commonly: comunemente
communicate: comunicare, comunicano, comunico, comunichi, comunica, communicate, comunichiamo, annunciare, infettare
communicated: comunicato
communications: comunicazioni
communicative: comunicativo
companion: compagno, accompagnatore
comparative: comparativo
comparatively: comparativamente
compare: confrontare, confronta, confrontiamo, confronti, confrontano, confrontate, confronto, paragonare, paragono, paragona, paragonate
comparing: confrontando, paragonando
comparison: confronto, riscontro, comparazione, paragone
compass: bussola, la bussola, compasso
compassion: compassione
compassionate: compassionevole
compatible: compatibile
compensation: compensazione, ricompensa, indennizzo,

risarcimento, indennità
complacency: compiacimento
complain: lagnarsi, lamentarsi, lamentare
complained: reclamato, si lamentò
complaining: lamentandosi, reclamando
complaint: reclamo, lamentela
complaints: reclami
complaisance: compiacenza
complaisant: compiacente
completion: completamento
complexion: carnagione
compliance: conformità, compliance, cedevolezza
complied: accondisceso, ottemperato
compliment: complimento
compliments: complimenti
comply: ottemperi, accondiscendiamo, ottemperiamo, ottempero, ottemperate, ottemperano, ottempera, accondiscendo, accondiscendi, accondiscendete, accondiscendono
complying: accondiscendendo, ottemperando
compose: comporre, componi, componiamo, compongo, compongono, componete
composed: composto
composure: calma, compostezza
comprehend: comprendere, comprendo, comprendono, comprendiamo, comprendi, comprendete
comprehended: compreso
comprehends: comprende
comprehension: comprensione
comprise: comprendere, contenere, conteniamo, comprendo, contieni, contengono, contengo, comprendono, comprendiamo, comprendi, comprendete
comprised: compreso, contenuto
compromised: compromesso
conceal: nascondere, nascondono, nascondete, nascondi, nascondiamo, nascondo, occultare
concealed: nascosto
concealing: nascondendo
concealment: occultamento, nascondiglio, reticenza
conceals: nasconde
conceit: presunzione
conceited: vanitoso, presuntuoso
conceive: concepire, concepiamo, concepisci, concepisco, concepiscono, concepite
conception: concepimento, concezione
concerning: concernere
conciliate: conciliare

conciliating: conciliando, conciliare
conciliatory: conciliativo
concisely: concisamente
conclude: concludere, concludo, concludono, concludiamo, concludi, concludete
concluded: concluso
concluding: concludendo, concludere
concurrence: accordo
condemn: condannare, condannate, condanno, condanni, condannano, condanniamo, condanna, biasimare, biasimo, biasimiamo, biasimi
condemned: condannato, biasimato
condescend: degna, degnano, degnate, degni, degniamo, degno, degnare
condescended: degnato
condescends: degna
condescension: condiscendenza
conditional: condizionale
conditionally: condizionalmente
condolence: condoglianza
conducted: condotto
confederacy: confederazione
confess: confessare, confessa, confessano, confessate, confessi, confessiamo, confesso
confessed: confessato
confession: confessione
confide: confidare, confidi, confidiamo, confidate, confidano, confida, confido
confident: fiducioso
confidential: confidenziale
confiding: confidando, confidare
confined: limitato
confinement: reclusione, prigionia, confinamento
confirm: confermare, confermiamo, confermo, confermano, confermate, confermi, conferma
confirmation: conferma
confirming: confermando
confirms: conferma
confused: confuso
confusion: confusione
congenial: congeniale
congratulate: felicitare, felicitate, felicito, feliciti, felicitano, felicita, felicitiamo
congratulated: felicitato
congratulation: felicitazione, rallegramento, congratulazione
congratulations: congratulazioni
conjecture: congettura
conjugal: coniugale
conjunction: congiunzione
connect: legare, lego, lega, legano, legate, leghi, leghiamo, collegare, colleghi, colleghiamo, collego
connected: collegato, legato, connesso

connection: coincidenza, accoppiamento, connessione, collegamento, relazione, banda
connections: accesso
connivance: connivenza
conquer: conquistare, conquistate, conquisto, conquisti, conquistano, conquistiamo, conquista
conquered: conquistato
conquest: conquista
conscience: coscienza
conscientious: coscienzioso
conscientiously: coscienziosamente
conscious: cosciente
consciousness: consapevolezza, coscienza
consent: consenso, concordare, essere d'accordo, accordo, benestare, assenso, acconsentire
consented: acconsentito
consenting: acconsentire
consequence: conseguenza, risultato
consequent: conseguente
consequential: conseguente
consequently: conseguentemente
considerably: considerevolmente
considering: considerando
consign: consegnare
consigned: consegnato
consisted: consistito, constato
consistency: consistenza, coerenza
consistent: costante
consists: consiste, consta
consolation: consolazione
consolatory: consolatorio
console: consolare, consolle, console
consoled: consolato
consoling: consolare
constancy: costanza
constantly: costantemente
consternation: sbigottimento, costernazione
constitute: costituire, costituiamo, costituisci, costituisco, costituiscono, costituite
constitution: costituzione
constrained: costretto
construed: analizzato, interpretato
construing: analizzando, interpretando
consult: consultare
consulted: consultato, interpellato
consulting: consultando, interpellando, consultare
contained: contenuto
contemplation: contemplazione
contempt: sprezzo, disprezzo
contemptuously: sprezzantemente
contented: contento
contentment: soddisfazione
contents: contenuto

continual: continuo, costante
continually: continuamente
continuing: continuando, durando
contracted: contratto
contradict: contraddire, contraddiciamo, contraddite, contraddico, contraddici, contraddi', contraddicono
contradicted: contraddetto
contrary: contrario
contribute: contribuire, contribuiamo, contribuisci, contribuisco, contribuiscono, contribuite
contributed: contribuito
contrivance: congegno
contrive: escogitano, escogito, escogitiamo, escogitate, escogita, escogiti, escogitare
contrived: escogitato
convenience: convenienza
convenient: conveniente
converse: contrario
conversed: conversato
convert: convertito, convertire
convey: trasportare
conveyed: trasportato
conveying: trasportando, trasporto
conviction: convinzione, condanna
convince: convincere, convincete, convinci, convinciamo, convinco, convincono, persuadere
convinced: convinto
cook: cuoco, cuoca, cucinare, cuocere
cooking: cucina
cool: fresco, raffreddare, freddo
coolly: frescamente
copied: copiato
coquetry: civetteria
cordial: cordiale
cordiality: cordialità
cordially: cordialmente
corps: corpo
correspond: corrispondere, corrispondete, corrispondi, corrispondiamo, corrispondo, corrispondono, avere la coincidenza
correspondence: corrispondenza, carteggio
correspondent: corrispondente
corroborated: confermato, corroborato
corroboration: conferma, corroborazione
corruption: corruzione
costing: valutazione dei costi, determinazione dei costi, costo, costare
cough: tossire, tosse
coughing: tosse, tossire
counted: contato
countenance: approvare, viso

counteract: neutralizzare, neutralizziamo, neutralizzo, neutralizzi, neutralizzate, neutralizzano, neutralizza
counteracted: neutralizzato
counterbalance: contrappeso
counterpart: controparte
counting: contare, conteggio
couples: coppia
courage: coraggio
courier: corriere
courteous: cortese
courtesy: cortesia
courtier: cortigiano
courting: corteggiare, corteggiamento
courtship: corteggiamento
cousin: cugino, cugina
covering: copertura, rivestimento, coprire, monta
cows: vacche
creative: creativo
creature: creatura
creditable: lodevole
criticise: criticare
crossed: attraversato
crossing: attraversamento, incrocio, traversata, passaggio
crowded: affollato
cruel: crudele
cruelly: crudelmente
cruelty: crudeltà
crushing: schiacciamento
cry: piangere, grido, gridare, urlare
crying: pianto, piangente, piangere
cucumber: cetriolo, il cetriolo
culprit: colpevole
cultivation: coltivazione
cunning: astuzia, astuto, furbo
curiosities: curiosità
curiosity: curiosità
curious: curioso
curtailed: abbreviato
curtains: tendaggio, tenda
curtsey: inchino
custody: custodia
custom: costume, usanza, uso, abitudine, consuetudine
cutting: taglio, tagliente, talea, affilato
dale: valle
damp: umido
dance: ballare, ballo, danza
danced: ballato, ballavo ballava
dancing: ballando
dare: osare, oso, osiamo, osi, osate, osano, osa, sfida
dared: osato
daring: osando, audace
darling: prediletto, tesoro, caro
dated: datato
daughters: figlie
dawdled: bighellonato, gingillato
dazzling: abbagliare, abbagliante,

accecante
deaden: ammortizzare, ammortizza, ammortizzano, ammortizzate, ammortizzi, ammortizziamo, ammortizzo
dearly: caramente
decease: decedere, decesso
deceitful: ingannevole, falso
deceive: ingannare, ingannano, inganniamo, ingannate, inganna, inganni, inganno, truffare, truffate, truffano, truffiamo
deceived: ingannato, truffato
deceives: inganna, truffa
deceiving: ingannando, truffando, ingannare
decency: decenza
decent: decente
deception: inganno
decidedly: decisamente
deciding: decidendo
decisive: decisivo
decked: adornato
declaration: dichiarazione
declare: dichiarare, dichiara, dichiaro, dichiariamo, dichiari, dichiarano, dichiarate
declared: dichiarato
declares: dichiara
declaring: dichiarando
decorum: decoro
deduced: dedotto
deemed: creduto
default: predefinito, inadempienza, contumacia, difetto, mancanza
defect: difetto, imperfezione, mancanza
defection: defezione, diserzione
defective: difettoso, difettivo
defend: difendere, difendi, difendiamo, difendo, difendono, difendete
defended: difeso
defense: difesa
defer: rinviate, rinvio, dilaziono, differiamo, differisci, differisco, differiscono, differite, dilaziona, dilazionano, dilazionate
deference: deferenza
deferred: differito
defiance: sfida
deficiency: deficienza, mancanza, carenza, difetto, disavanzo
deficient: deficiente, carente, difettoso, insufficiente
defied: sfidato
defy: sfidare, sfidano, sfidiamo, sfidate, sfidi, sfido, sfida
degenerate: degenerare, degenerato
degrees: gradi
deigned: degnato
dejection: deiezione, abbattimento,

scoraggiamento, depressione
delay: ritardo, tardare, ritardare, indugio, indugiare
delayed: ritardato
deliberately: apposta, deliberatamente
deliberation: deliberazione
delicacy: delicatezza
delicate: delicato
delicious: squisito
delight: delizia, deliziare, dilettare, diletto, godimento, rallegrare, gioia
delighted: lietissimo
delightful: delizioso, piacevole
delivered: consegnato
delivering: consegnando
demanding: esigente
denial: negazione, rifiuto, smentita
denied: negato
denominated: denominato
denoted: denotato
deny: negare, negate, negano, neghi, neghiamo, nego, nega
denying: negando
depart: partire, partite, partiamo, parti, partono, parto, andarsene
departed: partito
departure: partenza
depend: dipendere, dipendete, dipendiamo, dipendo, dipendono, dipendi
depended: dipeso
dependence: dipendenza
dependent: dipendente, persona a carico
depending: dipendendo
deportment: condotta, comportamento
depravity: depravazione
depreciate: svalutiamo, svalutate, deprezziamo, deprezzi, deprezzate, deprezza, deprezzano, deprezzo, svalutano, svaluto, svaluti
depressed: depresso
deprive: privare
deprived: privato, deprivato
deranged: squilibrato
derision: derisione
derive: derivare, derivo, deriviamo, derivi, derivano, derivate, deriva, discendere, trarre
derived: derivato
derives: deriva
descended: sceso, disceso
descending: scendendo, discendendo
descent: discesa, discendenza
describing: descrivendo
desert: deserto, abbandonare
deserted: abbandonato, deserto
desertion: diserzione
deserve: meritare, meritano, merita, meritate, meritiamo, meriti, merito

deserved: meritato
deserves: merita
deserving: meritando, meritevole
designing: progettazione, disegnare
desirable: desiderabile
desired: desiderato
desirous: desideroso
despair: disperazione, disperare
desperate: disperato
desperation: disperazione
despicable: disprezzabile, spregevole
despise: disprezzare, disprezza,
disprezzano, disprezzate, disprezzi,
disprezziamo, disprezzo
despised: disprezzato
despises: disprezza
despising: disprezzando
destined: destinato
destitute: indigente
destroyed: distrutto
destructive: distruttivo
detached: isolato, staccato, distaccato
detaching: staccando, distaccando,
staccare
detain: ritenere, riteniamo, ritieni,
ritenete, ritengo, ritengono
detained: ritenuto
detaining: ritenendo
detect: scoprire, scopri, scoprono,
scopro, scoprite, scopriamo
detected: scoperto
detection: rivelazione, scoperta
deter: impaurire, spaventare
determination: determinazione
determining: definendo, fissando,
definito, fissato, determinato,
determinando
detest: detestare, detestate, detesto,
detesti, detestano, detesta,
detestiamo
detestable: detestabile
detested: detestato
device: dispositivo, apparecchio,
congegno
devoid: privo
devote: consacrare
devoted: devoto
devoting: dedicando, consacrando
dialogue: dialogo
dictate: dettare, dettano, dettate,
detti, dettiamo, detta, detto
dictated: dettato
dictates: detta
dictating: dettando
dictatorial: dittatoriale
differ: differire
differently: diversamente, in modo
diverso
diffidence: timidezza
diffident: timido
diffuse: diffuso, diffondere
diffused: diffuso

dignified: dignitoso
dignity: dignità, decoro
dilatory: dilatorio
diligence: diligenza
dimensions: dimensioni, ingombri
diminution: diminuzione
dine: cenare
dined: pranzato, cenato
dines: pranza, cena
dining: pranzando, cenando
directed: diretto
directions: avvertenze
dirt: sporcizia, fango, sudiciume
dirty: sporco, sporcare, imbrattare,
insudiciare
disadvantage: svantaggio
disagreeable: sgradevole
disagreement: disaccordo
disappoint: deludere, deludo,
deludete, deludi, deludiamo,
deludono
disappointed: deluso
disappointing: deludendo
disappointment: delusione,
disappunto
disapprobation: disapprovazione
disapprove: disapprovare,
disapprova, disapprovo,
disapproviamo, disapprovi,
disapprovate, disapprovano,
biasimare, biasima, biasimano,
biasimate
disarm: disarmare, disarmiamo,
disarma, disarmano, disarmi,
disarmate, disarmo
discern: distinguo, distingui,
percepiamo, percepiscono,
percepisco, percepisci,
distinguiamo, percepite, distinguete,
discernono, discerno
discernible: distinguibile,
discernibile
discerning: discernendo,
distinguendo, percependo,
percepire, perspicace, acuto
discernment: discernimento
discharge: scarico, scarica, portata,
scaricare
discharged: scaricato
disclaim: negare, nego, neghiamo,
neghi, negate, negano, nega
disclaimed: negato
disclose: svelare
disclosed: dischiuso, svelato
disclosure: rivelazione, scoperta
discompose: scomporre, agitare
disconcerted: sconcertato, turbato
discontented: scontento
discontinuance: cessazione
discourage: impaurire, scoraggiare,
spaventare, impaurite, spavento,
spaventiamo, spaventi, spaventate,

spaventano, spaventa, scoraggio
discouraged: impaurito, spaventato,
scoraggiato
discourse: discorso
discover: scoprire, scopri, scoprono,
scopro, scoprite, scopriamo
discovering: scoprendo
discovery: scoperta
discredit: screditare
discreditable: vergognoso,
disonorevole
discretion: discrezione
discrimination: discriminazione,
distinzione
disdain: sdegno, sdegnare
disengaged: disimpegnato,
disinnestato
disgrace: vergogna, disgrazia,
disonorare, disonore
disgraceful: disgraziata, vergognoso,
disonorevole
disgracing: disonorare
disguise: travestimento, travestire
disgust: ripugnanza, avversione,
disgustare, disgusto, nauseare
disgusting: disgustoso
dish: piatto, pietanza
disheartened: sconfortato, avvilito,
scoraggiato
dishes: stoviglie
dishonesty: disonestà
dishonorable: disonorevole
dishonourable: disonorevole
disinclination: avversione
disinterested: disinteressato,
imparziale
disinterestedness: disinteresse
dislike: avversione, ripugnanza,
antipatia
dismay: costernazione, costernare
dismissed: licenziato
disobliging: scortese
dispatched: spedito
dispelling: dissipando, scacciando
dispense: distribuire, distribuiamo,
distribuiscono, distribuite,
distribuisci, distribuisco, dispensare
dispirited: abbattuto, scoraggiato
displease: dispiacere
displeased: scontentato, scontento
displeasure: scontento, dispiacere
disposal: disposizione, eliminazione,
smaltimento
dispose: disporre, disponete,
dispongo, dispongono, disponi,
disponiamo
disposed: disposto
disposing: disponendo
disposition: disposizione,
predisposizione, ingegno, talento
disputable: disputabile, discutibile,
opinabile

dispute: controversia
disquiet: inquietudine
disregarded: ignorato
disrespect: mancanza di rispetto
disrespectful: irriverente
dissatisfied: insoddisfatto
dissemble: dissimuli, dissimulo, dissimuliamo, dissimulano, dissimula, dissimulate, dissimulare
disservice: danno, disservizio
dissipation: dispersione, dissipazione
dissolved: dissolto, sciolto
dissuade: dissuadere, dissuadi, dissuadono, dissuadiamo, dissuadete, dissuado
dissuaded: dissuaso
distant: distante, lontano
distinguish: distinguere, distingui, distinguono, distinguiamo, distinguete, distinguo
distinguished: distinto
distinguishing: distinguendo
distracted: distratto
distraction: distrazione
distress: pericolo
distressed: afflitto
distressing: doloroso, penoso, angoscioso
distribute: distribuire, distribuite, distribuiscono, distribuiamo, distribuisco, distribuisci
distrust: diffidenza
distrusted: diffidato
disturb: disturbare, disturbiamo, disturba, disturbano, disturbate, disturbi, disturbo
disturbance: perturbazione, disturbo
disturbed: disturbato
diversified: diversificato, differenziato
diversion: diversione, deviazione, dirottamento
divert: deviare
diverted: stornato, sviato, deviato
divide: dividere, dividete, dividiamo, divido, dividono, dividi, separare, separa, separi, separiamo, separate
divided: diviso, separato
dividing: dividendo, separando
domestics: domestico
doorway: entrata, vano della porta
dose: dose
doubled: raddoppiato
doubly: doppiamente
doubtful: dubbioso
doubting: dubitare
doubtless: senza dubbio
doubts: dubbio
dove: colomba, piccione
downstairs: giù dalle scale
dozen: dozzina
draughts: dama

dread: temere
dreadful: terribile
dressed: vestito
dressing: fasciatura, condimento
drinking: bere
driven: guidato
driving: guida
duchess: duchessa
ductility: duttilità
duel: duello
dull: opaco, smussato, spuntato
dullness: ottusità
dupe: duplicato, ingannare, credulone, gonzo, babbeo
duplicity: duplicità
duration: durata
dwell: abitare, dimorare, dimorate, dimoro, dimori, dimorano, dimora, abitiamo, abiti, abitate, abitano
dwelling: dimorando, abitando, dimora, abitazione
dying: morendo, morente
eager: avido, desideroso, bramoso, impaziente
eagerly: ardentemente
eagerness: impazienza
ear: orecchio, spiga, l'orecchio, pannocchia
earl: conte
earnest: serio, caparra
earnestly: seriamente
earnestness: serietà
earthly: terrestre, terreno, mondano
ease: agio, facilità
easiness: facilità, agevolezza, comodità, con facilita
easter: Pasqua
eating: mangiando
eccentric: eccentrico, stravagante
echo: eco, echeggiare
economically: economicamente
ecstasy: estasi
educated: istruito, educato
effectual: efficace
efficacy: efficacia
effusion: versamento, effusione
elapsed: trascorso
elated: esaltato, esultante
elder: maggiore, sambuco
eldest: maggiore, il più vecchio
elegance: eleganza
elegant: elegante
elevate: elevare, elevate, elevo, elevi, eleva, eleviamo, elevano
elevated: elevato
elevating: elevando
elevation: elevazione, altezza, prospetto
eligibility: eleggibilità
eligible: eleggibile
elizabeth: Elisabetta
elope: scappa, scappano, scappate,

scappi, scappiamo, scappo, scappare
eloped: scappato
eloping: scappando
eloquence: eloquenza
eloquent: eloquente
eluded: eluso, schivato
embargo: embargo
embarrassed: imbarazzato
embarrassment: imbarazzo
embraced: abbracciato
emergence: emersione
eminence: eminenza
eminent: eminente
emotion: emozione, commozione
emphatic: enfatico
emphatically: enfatico, enfaticamente
employ: usare, impiegare, assumere, occupare
employed: impiegato
emptiness: vuoto
enabled: abilitato
enabling: abilitando
encamped: accampato
encounter: incontro, incontrare, incontra, incontriamo, incontri, incontrano, incontrate
encouragement: incoraggiamento
encouraging: incoraggiando, incoraggiante
encumbrance: ingombro
endeavour: tentare, tentativo, sforzarsi
endless: senza fine, infinito, interminabile
endurable: sopportabile, tollerabile
endure: sopportare, sopporta, sopporto, sopportiamo, sopporti, sopportano, sopportate, tollerare, durare, duriamo, dura
endured: sopportato, durato
enduring: sopportando, durando, durevole
enemy: nemico
energetic: energico, energetico
enforced: imposto
engage: innestare, innestiamo, innesta, innestano, innestate, innesti, ingaggiare, ingranare, impegnare, assumere, innesto
engaged: occupato, innestato, impegnato
engagement: fidanzamento, assunzione
engaging: innestando, attraente
engross: assorbo, assorbono, assorbiamo, assorbi, assorbite, assorbire
engrossed: assorbito
engrossing: assorbendo, assorbire
enhance: accrescere, aumentare
enjoying: piacendo, fruendo, godendo

enjoyment: godimento
enlarging: ingrandendo, ampliando
enormity: enormità
enraged: irritato, arrabbiato, incollerito, adirato
ensign: insegna, alfiere
ensue: seguire, segui, seguono, seguo, seguiamo, seguite, conseguire, risultare
ensued: seguito
ensuing: seguendo
entail: comportare
entailing: comportare
entering: entrando, entrare
entertain: intrattenere, intrattenete, intrattieni, intratteniamo, intrattengo, intrattengono, ricevere
entertained: intrattenuto
entertainment: divertimento, spettacolo
entitled: intitolato
entrance: entrata, ingresso, accesso, l'entrata, adito
entreat: supplicare
entreated: supplicato
entreating: supplicando, supplicare
entreaty: preghiera, domanda, supplica
enumerating: enumerando
enumeration: enumerazione
envelope: busta, la busta, involucro
envied: invidiato
environs: ambiente, dintorni
envy: invidia, invidiare, invidio, invidiate, invidiano, invidi, invidiamo
envying: invidiando
epithet: epiteto
equipage: equipaggio
equivalent: equivalente
equivocal: ambiguo, equivoco
err: errare, errano, errate, erri, erriamo, erro, erra, sbagliarsi
errand: messaggio, commissione
errors: errori
essence: essenza
essentials: essenziale
esteem: stima, rispetto, stimare, considerazione, considerare, rispettare, riguardo
esteemed: stimato
estimable: stimabile
estimation: stima, valutazione
etiquette: etichetta, galateo
evade: evitare, evitano, evita, evitate, eviti, evito, evitiamo, eludere, eludiamo, eludo, eludi
evenness: uniformità
everywhere: dappertutto, ovunque, dovunque, in ogni luogo
evident: evidente, chiaro, palese, lampante

evidently: evidentemente
evil: male, cattivo, malvagio
exact: esatto, preciso
exaggerate: esagerare, esagero, esageriamo, esageri, esagerate, esagera, esagerano
exaggeration: esagerazione
examine: esaminare, esaminate, esamino, esamini, esaminano, esamina, esaminiamo
examined: esaminato
examining: esaminando, esaminare
exasperate: esasperare
exceed: eccedere, eccedono, eccedo, eccedete, eccedi, eccediamo, oltrepassare
exceeded: ecceduto
exceeding: eccedendo
exceedingly: estremamente
excel: eccellere, eccelli, eccellono, eccello, eccellete, eccelliamo
excellence: eccellenza
excellency: eccellenza
excepting: salvo
exception: eccezione
exceptional: eccezionale
excess: eccesso, eccedenza, franchigia
excessive: eccessivo
excessively: eccessivamente
exchanged: scambiato
excite: eccitare, ecciti, eccitiamo, eccitano, eccita, eccito, eccitate, spronare, incitare
excited: eccitato, concitato, emozionato
exciting: eccitando, eccitante, emozionante
exclaimed: esclamato
exclaiming: esclamando
exclamation: esclamazione
exclude: escludere, escludete, escludi, escludiamo, escludo, escludono
exclusion: esclusione
excuse: scusa, scusare, giustificazione, pretesto
executed: eseguito
execution: esecuzione
exert: praticare, esercitare, eserciti, pratico, pratichiamo, pratichi, praticate, praticano, pratica, esercitiamo, esercitate
exerted: esercitato, praticato
exerting: esercitando, praticando
exertion: sforzo
exhausted: esausto, sfinito, esaurito
exhibit: esibire, allegato, documento, esposizione, esporre
existed: esistito
expectation: attesa, aspettativa
expectations: aspettativa, aspettative
expecting: aspettando
expects: aspetta

expedient: espediente, conveniente
expedite: accelerare, affrettare
expense: spese, spesa
expenses: spese
explaining: spiegando
explanatory: esplicativo
explicit: esplicito
explicitly: esplicitamente
explore: esplorare, esplorano, esplorate, esplori, esploriamo, esploro, esplora
expose: esporre, esponete, espongo, espongono, esponi, esponiamo
exposed: esposto
exposing: esponendo
exposure: esposizione
expressing: esprimendo
expressions: espressioni
expressive: espressivo
expressively: espressivamente
expressly: espressamente
exquisite: squisito
extenuating: attenuante
extinguished: spento, estinto
extort: estorcere, estorci, estorcono, estorcete, estorco, estorciamo
extorted: estorto
extraordinary: straordinario, eccezionale
extravagance: stravaganza, prodigalità
extravagant: stravagante
extreme: estremo
exuberance: esuberanza
exuberant: esuberante
exultation: esultanza
eyelashes: ciglio
fail: fallire, morire, mancare
failing: in mancanza di
faint: debole, svenire, svengo, svengono, sveniamo, svenite, svieni, svenimento, vago
faintly: debolmente
faithful: fedele, leale
faithfully: fedelmente
falls: cade
false: falso, finto
falsehood: falso, falsità, bugia, menzogna
falsely: falsamente
fame: fama
familiarity: dimestichezza
familiarly: familiarmente
fancied: fantastico
fancy: figurarsi, capriccio, immaginazione
fare: tariffa
farewell: addio, congedo
farmhouse: cascina, fattoria
farther: più lontano
fashionable: alla moda
fastened: fissato

fastidious: fastidioso
fat: grasso, grosso, pingue, spesso
fate: destino, fato, sorte
fatigue: fatica, affaticare, stancare, stanchezza, affaticamento
fatigued: affaticato
fault: difetto, faglia, guasto, fallo
faultless: irreprensibile, perfetto
faulty: difettoso
favor: favore, favorire, cortesia
favour: favorire, favore
favourable: favorevole
favourably: favorevolmente
favoured: favorito
favourite: preferito
feared: temuto
fearful: spaventoso, pauroso
fearless: intrepido, impavido
feather: penna, piuma
feels: sente, tasta, tocca, trova, prova
felicity: felicità
fellow: uomo
fender: parafango, parabordo
fervent: fervente
fetch: portare, portiamo, porto, porti, portate, portano, porta, ottenere, andare a prendere
fetched: portato
feverish: febbrile, febbricitante
fewer: meno
fidget: dimenarsi, irrequietezza, agitarsi
fidgety: agitato, irrequieto
fifth: quinto, quinta
filial: filiale
filled: pieno
filling: otturazione, ripieno, riempimento
finances: finanze
finds: fonde, fonda
fingering: diteggiatura
finishing: finendo, finitura, finire, finissaggio, ultimando, rifinitura
fireplace: camino, caminetto
firmness: fermezza
fishing: pesca, pescaggio
fitted: aderente, adatto, attrezzato
fix: fissare, fissa, fissano, fissate, fissi, fissiamo, fisso, riparare, aggiustare, ripara, ripariamo
fixing: fissando, riparando, fissazione, fissaggio, quotazione
flaming: fiammeggiante
flatter: lusingare, lusingate, lusingo, lusinghi, lusingano, lusinghiamo, lusinga, adulare
flattered: lusingato
flattering: lusingando, adulatorio
flirt: flirtare, civettare
flirtation: flirt
flogged: frustato, fustigato
flowing: fluente

fluctuating: fluttuando
fluently: fluentemente
flutter: svolazzare
flying: volando, volare, volante
folded: piegato
folly: follia
fond: tenero, affettuoso, affezionato
fonder: più affettuoso
fool: babbeo, sciocco, allocco, ingannare
foolish: sciocco, stupido, stolto, ignorante, fesso
footing: punto d'appoggio
footman: lacchè
footstool: sgabello
forbearance: pazienza
forbearing: indulgente, paziente
forbid: vietare, vieti, vietate, vietano, vietiamo, vieta, vieto, proibire, proibite, proibiamo, proibisci
forbidding: vietando, proibendo, ostile, spaventevole
forcing: forzatura
forego: precedere
foresee: prevedere, prevedo, prevediamo, prevedi, prevedete, prevedono
foreseen: previsto
foretold: predetto
forever: per sempre
forfeit: penalità, penale
forgetfulness: dimenticanza
forgets: dimentica
forgetting: dimenticando
forgive: perdonare, perdonano, perdoniamo, perdona, perdonate, perdoni, perdono
forgiven: perdonato
forgiveness: perdono
forgiving: perdonando
forgot: dimenticato
forlorn: derelitto, abbandonato, misero
formality: formalità
formerly: precedentemente, davanti, in passato, un tempo
formidable: formidabile, straordinario
forming: formazione
forth: avanti
fortitude: forza d'animo
fortnight: due settimane
fortunate: fortunato, felice
fortunately: fortunatamente, per fortuna
fortune: fortuna, sorte, patrimonio
forwarder: spedizioniere
forwarding: invio, inoltro, spedizione
forwards: in avanti, avanti
foul: fallo
founded: fondato
fourthly: in quarto luogo

frailty: fragilità
frame: telaio, intelaiatura, cornice, fotogramma, incorniciare, struttura, inquadrare, immagine, incastellatura, ordinata
frankly: francamente
frankness: franchezza
freckled: lentigginoso
freely: liberamente
frequent: frequente, bazzicare
fresher: matricola
fret: agitazione, consumare, greca
friendless: senza amici
friendship: amicizia
frighten: spaventare, spaventiamo, spaventi, spaventate, spaventano, spaventa, spavento, impaurire, intimorire
frightened: spaventato
frivolous: vanitoso, frivolo
frost: gelo, brina, gelata
fulfil: adempiere
fun: divertimento, spasso, piacere
furnish: fornire, fornite, forniscono, fornisco, fornisci, forniamo, arredare
furniture: mobili, mobilia
fuss: armeggiare, agitarsi, confusione
gaiety: gaiezza
gaily: gaiamente
gained: guadagnato
gallant: galante, coraggioso, valoroso
gallantry: galanteria, valore, prodezza
gaming: gioco
gardener: giardiniere
gate: cancello, porta, saracinesca, paratoia, uscita
gathered: raccolto
gathering: convegno, raccolta
gaudy: fastoso
gay: allegro, gaio
gaze: fissare, sguardo fisso
generality: generalità
generations: generazioni
generous: generoso, liberale, munifico
generously: generosamente
genius: genio
genteel: distinto
gentle: mite, gentile, dolce, delicato
gentleness: delicatezza
gentlewoman: signora, gentildonna
genuine: genuino, autentico
giddiness: capogiro, vertigine
gift: regalo, dono, presente, donazione, omaggio
gig: calesse
gladly: volentieri, con piacere
glance: occhiata, sguardo
glazing: vetrata
glimpse: intravedere, occhiata, rapido sguardo

gloom: malinconia, tristezza
gloomy: tetro, tenebroso, oscuro
glory: gloria
glove: guanto
glow: ardore
glowing: raggiante, ardente
godfather: padrino, compare
godson: figlioccio
good-natured: gradevole, cortese
goodness: bontà
goodwill: avviamento, buona
  volontà, avviamento commerciale
governed: governato
governess: istitutrice, governante
gown: abito, vestito, toga
gowns: vestiti
grace: grazia
graceful: grazioso, aggraziato
gracefully: con garbo
gracious: grazioso
graciously: graziosamente
gradual: graduale
gradually: gradualmente, poco a
  poco
grain: grana, grano, chicco, granello,
  venatura
grandeur: grandiosità
grapes: uva
grasp: afferrare, stretta, comprendere
grateful: riconoscente, grato
gratefully: con gratitudine
gratification: gratificazione,
  soddisfazione
gratified: gratificato
gratify: gratificare, gratificano,
  gratifico, gratifichiamo, gratifichi,
  gratificate, gratifica
gratifying: gratificando, gratificante
gratitude: gratitudine, riconoscenza,
  grazie
grave: tomba, grave
gravel: ghiaia
gravely: tomba, seriamente
gravity: gravità
greatly: molto, grandemente
greatness: grandezza
grief: dolore, pena
grieve: affliggersi, addolorare,
  addolorarsi
grieved: accorato, addolorato
grieving: addolorando, accorando
grievous: doloroso
gross: lordo
grouped: raggruppato
grove: boschetto
guard: capotreno, protezione,
  proteggere, guardia, carter, riparo,
  custodire, sorvegliare
guarded: guardingo, custodito
guardian: guardiano, tutore
guardianship: tutela
guess: supporre, indovinare,

supposizione, congettura
guessed: indovinato
guest: ospite, invitato
guidance: guida
guided: guidato
guiding: guidare
guilt: colpa
gulf: golfo, abisso, burrone
habit: abitudine, costume, vizio,
  consuetudine
habitual: abituale
hack: fare a pezzi
hackneyed: trito, trito e ritrito
ham: prosciutto, il prosciutto
handkerchief: fazzoletto
handsome: bello, carino
handsomely: bellamente
handwriting: calligrafia
hang: pendere, appendere,
  sospendere, impiccare
hanging: impiccagione
happening: succedendo, avvenendo,
  avvenimento
happily: felicemente
happiness: felicità
hardened: indurito, temprato
hardship: avversità
harm: danno, nuocere, danneggiare
harmony: armonia, accordo
harp: arpa
harshly: duramente
haste: fretta, furia
hasten: affrettarsi, affrettare
hastened: affrettato, sollecitato
hastening: affrettando, sollecitando
hastily: frettolosamente
hasty: affrettato, frettoloso
hat: cappello
hate: odiare, odio, detestare
hated: odiato
hatefully: odiosamente
hating: odiare
hatred: odio
haughty: altezzoso
haunch: coscia, anca
haunt: frequentare
hazarded: rischiato
headache: mal di testa, cefalea
headquarters: sede centrale
headstrong: testardo
heal: guarire, guarisco, guariscono,
  guariamo, guarite, guarisci, sanare
healthful: sano, salubre
healthy: sano
hears: ode, sente
heartening: incoraggiante
heartfelt: sincero
hearth: focolare
heartily: cordialmente
hearty: cordiale, caloroso
heaven: cielo, paradiso
heavier: più pesante

hedge: siepe, copertura, barriera
heedless: sbadato, disattento
heighten: innalzare
heightened: innalzato
heinous: atroce
heiress: erede
henceforth: d'ora in poi, d'ora
  innanzi
hereabouts: qui vicino
hereafter: in futuro
hermitage: eremitaggio, eremo
hers: suo
hesitate: esitare, esitiamo, esiti,
  esitate, esita, esitano, esito, titubare,
  tituba, titubiamo, titubi
hesitated: esitato, titubato
hesitating: esitando, titubando,
  esitare
hesitation: esitazione, tentennamento
hide: nascondere, nascondo,
  nascondiamo, nascondono,
  nascondete, nascondi, pelle,
  nascondersi, pellame, celare,
  occultare
hint: alludere, suggerimento,
  allusione, cenno
hinted: suggerito
hire: prendere in affitto, noleggio,
  noleggiare, noleggiate, noleggiano,
  noleggiamo, noleggia, noleggi,
  affitto, assumere
hired: noleggiato
hither: qui, quà
hitherto: finora
honest: onesto
honestly: onestamente
honour: onore
honourable: onorevole
hopeless: disperato, senza speranza
hopes: spera
hoping: sperando
horrid: orrendo
horror: orrore, ribrezzo
horseback: groppa, dorso del cavallo
horsewoman: amazzone, cavallerizza
hospitality: ospitalità
hotels: alberghi
housekeeper: governante
housekeeping: economia domestica,
  operazioni di gestione interna
housemaid: domestica
howsoever: comunque
hug: abbracciare, abbraccio
humanity: umanità
humble: umile, modesto
humbled: umiliato
humbling: umiliante
humiliating: umiliando, umiliante
humiliation: umiliazione
humility: umiltà
humour: umore, umorismo
hunting: cacciando, caccia

hurried: affrettato, frettoloso
hurry: affrettarsi, fretta
hurt: ferire, far male, ferita, dolere
hypocrisy: ipocrisia
hypocritical: ipocrita
hysterics: isterico
idle: ozioso, pigro, folle, inattivo
idleness: ozio
ignorance: ignoranza
ignorant: ignorante
ill: malato, ammalato
illiberal: illiberale
illiterate: analfabeta, illetterato
illness: malattia
illustration: illustrazione
illustrious: illustre
imaginable: immaginabile
imaginary: immaginario
imagination: immagine,
  immaginazione, fantasia
imagined: immaginato
imitate: imitare, imitano, imito,
  imitiamo, imitate, imita, imiti,
  contraffare
imitated: imitato
imitation: imitazione
immoral: immorale
immovable: immobile
imparted: impartito
impartial: imparziale
impassable: impraticabile
impatience: impazienza
impatient: impaziente
impatiently: impazientemente
impelled: costretto, incitato
imperfection: imperfezione
imperfectly: imperfettamente
impertinence: impertinenza
impertinent: impertinente, insolente
impetuous: impetuoso
implacability: implacabilità
implacable: implacabile
implicit: implicito
implicitness: l'essere implicito
implied: significato, implicito,
  implicato
implies: significa, implica
imply: significare, significa,
  signifchi, significhiamo, significate,
  significano, significo, implicare,
  implicano, implicate, implichi
impolitic: impolitico
importing: importazione,
  importatore, importare
importune: importunare
importuned: importunato
impose: imporre, imponete,
  imponiamo, imponi, impongo,
  impongono
imposed: imposto
imposing: imponente, imponendo
impressed: impressionato

impressive: impressionante
improbable: improbabile
improper: improprio
impropriety: scorrettezza,
  improprietà
improves: migliora, perfeziona
imprudence: imprudenza
imprudent: imprudente
impudence: impudenza
impudent: impudente, sfacciato
impulse: impulso
impulses: impulsi
impunity: impunità
impurities: impurità
impute: attribuire
imputed: attribuito, imputato
imputing: attribuendo, imputando
inadequate: inadeguato, insufficiente
inattention: disattenzione
inattentive: disattento
incapable: incapace
incensed: incenso
incessant: incessante
incessantly: incessantemente
inclination: inclinazione, pendenza
inclined: disposto, inclinato,
  propenso
incomprehensible: incomprensibile
inconceivable: inconcepibile
inconsistency: inconsistenza,
  incoerenza
inconvenience: inconvenienza,
  disagio, disturbo
inconvenient: difficile, pesante,
  inconveniente, incomodo
incredible: incredibile
incredulity: incredulità
incredulous: incredulo
incumbent: incombente
incur: incorrere in, incorrere
incurred: incorso
indebted: obbligato, indebitato
indecision: indecisione
indefinite: indefinito
indelicacy: indelicatezza
indelicate: indelicato
indicated: indicato
indifference: indifferenza
indifferent: indifferente
indignant: indignato
indignation: indignazione, sdegno
indignity: trattamento indegno
indirect: indiretto
indiscreet: indiscreto
indispensably: indispensabilmente
indisposed: indisposto
indistinctly: indistintamente
individually: individualmente
indolence: indolenza
indolent: indolente
induce: dedurre, concludere, indurre,
  induci, inducono, induciamo,

inducete, deducono, deduco,
  deduciamo, deducete
induced: indotto, concluso, dedotto
inducement: incitamento
inducements: incitamenti
indulge: indulgere
indulged: compiaciuto, indulto
indulgence: indulgenza
indulgent: indulgente
indulging: indulgendo, compiacendo
industriously: diligente
ineffectual: inefficace, vano
inevitable: inevitabile
inevitably: inevitabilmente
inexhaustible: inesauribile
inexpressible: inesprimibile
inexpressibly: indicibilmente
infamous: infame
infamy: infamia
infancy: infanzia
infatuation: infatuazione
inferior: inferiore
inferiority: inferiorità
infinite: infinito
infinitely: infinitamente
inflexibly: inflessibilmente
inflict: infliggere, infliggete, infliggo,
  infliggiamo, infliggono, infliggi
inflicted: inflitto
influenced: influenzato
inform: informare, informano,
  informate, informi, informiamo,
  informo, informa, insegnare
informality: tono familiare,
  familiarità, irregolarità
informed: informato
informing: informando
informs: informa
ingenious: ingegnoso
ingenuity: ingegnosità
ingratitude: ingratitudine
inhabitants: fruitori della casa
inherit: ereditare, erediti, ereditiamo,
  ereditano, ereditate, eredito, eredita
inherited: ereditato
inheriting: ereditando
inhumanity: inumanità
iniquitous: iniquo
injure: danneggiare, danneggia,
  danneggiamo, danneggiano,
  danneggiate, danneggio, danneggi,
  ferire, ferisco, feriscono, feriamo
injured: danneggiato, ferito
injuring: danneggiando, ferendo
injurious: nocivo, dannoso
injustice: ingiustizia
inn: locanda, osteria
innocence: innocenza
innocent: innocente
innocently: innocentemente
inoffensive: inoffensivo
inquire: domandare, informarsi,

domandano, domandate, domandi,
domandiamo, domando, indagare,
domanda
inquired: domandato
inquiring: domandando, domandare
inquiry: inchiesta
insensibility: insensibilità,
indifferenza
insensible: insensibile
insignificance: banalità, futilità
insignificant: insignificante
insincere: falso, insincero
insinuating: insinuando
insipid: insipido, insulso, scipito
insipidity: insipidezza
insist: insistere, insistiamo, insisto,
insistete, insistono, insisti
insisted: insistito
insists: insiste
insolence: insolenza
insolent: insolente
inspection: ispezione, controllo,
collaudo
inspire: ispirare, ispira, ispirate,
ispiri, ispiro, ispirano, ispiriamo
inspired: ispirato
inspires: ispira
inspiring: ispirando
instability: instabilità
instance: istanza, esempio
instant: istante, momento, immediato
instantaneous: istantaneo
instantly: direttamente,
istantaneamente, immediatamente
instinctively: istintivamente
instituted: istituito
instruct: istruire, istruiamo, istruisci,
istruisco, istruiscono, istruite
instructed: istruito
instructing: istruendo
instruction: istruzione
instructions: istruzioni
instrument: strumento, apparecchio
insufferable: insopportabile
insufficient: insufficiente
insulted: insultato
insulting: insultare, insultante
integrity: integrità
intelligence: intelligenza
intelligent: intelligente
intelligible: intelligibile
intend: intendere, intendono,
intendo, intendete, intendiamo,
intendi
intending: intendendo
intentionally: intenzionalmente
intently: intensamente
intercourse: rapporti
interfere: interferire, interferiamo,
interferite, interferiscono,
interferisco, interferisci
interference: interferenza

interfering: interferendo, interferire
intermarriage: matrimonio tra
consanguinei
intermediate: intermedio
intermission: interruzione, intervallo
interpose: interporre, interponete,
interponiamo, interponi,
interpongono, interpongo
interrupt: interrompere, interruzione
interrupted: interrotto, sospeso
interruption: interruzione
interval: intervallo
intervene: intervenire, intervenite,
intervieni, intervengo, intervengono,
interveniamo
intimacy: intimità
intimate: intimo
intimately: intimamente
intimation: accenno
intimidate: intimidire, intimidiamo,
intimidisci, intimidisco,
intimidiscono, intimidite, intimorire
intimidated: intimidito
intolerable: intollerabile
intricate: complicato, intricato
introduce: presentare, presenta,
presenti, presentiamo, presentate,
presentano, presento, introdurre,
introduci, introduciamo, introduco
introducing: presentando,
introducendo
intrude: impongo, imponiamo,
imponete, imponi, impongono,
imporre
intruder: intruso
intruding: imponendo
intrusion: intrusione
inured: abituato, assuefatto
invalid: non valido, invalido
invaluable: inestimabile
invariable: invariabile
invariably: invariabilmente
invent: inventare, inventano,
inventate, inventi, inventiamo,
invento, inventa
inventing: inventando
invention: invenzione
invitation: invito
invite: invitare, invita, invitano,
invitate, inviti, invitiamo, invito
inviting: invitando, invitare,
invitante
involuntarily: involontariamente
involuntary: involontario
involves: coinvolge
irksome: seccante
irregularity: irregolarità
irreligious: irreligioso
irremediable: irrimediabile
irreproachable: irreprensibile
irretrievable: irrecuperabile
irrevocably: irrevocabilmente

irritable: irritabile
irritated: irritato
irritation: irritazione
jealous: geloso
jealousy: gelosia
jewel: gioiello, gemma, gioia
jilt: pianta, piantano, piantate, pianti,
piantiamo, pianto, piantare, civetta
joining: congiungendo, legando,
unendo, collegando
joints: giunti
joke: scherzo, scherzare, barzelletta,
celia, lazzo
joking: scherzare, scherzoso
jot: annotare in fretta
joy: gioia
joyful: gioioso
joyfully: gioiosamente
judged: giudicato
judgement: giudizio, decreto,
deliberazione, sentenza
judging: giudicare
judgment: giudizio, sentenza
jumped: saltato
jumping: saltare
junior: minore
justification: giustificazione,
giustezza
justified: giustificato
justify: giustificare, giustificate,
giustifico, giustificiamo,
giustificano, giustifici, giustifica
justifying: giustificando
justly: giustamente
keeps: osserva, conserva, trattiene
kindly: gentilmente, gentile
kindness: gentilezza, bontà, cortesia
kindred: parentela, affine
kiss: bacio, baciare, baciarsi
kissed: baciato
kitty: gattino
knighthood: cavalierato
lace: pizzo, laccio, merletto,
allacciare, stringa
laconic: laconico
lad: ragazzo
ladies: signore
ladyship: signoria
laid: posato
laity: laicato
lament: lamento, lamentare
lamented: piangere, pianto, lamento
landing: pianerottolo, sbarco,
approdo, atterraggio
landlord: proprietario, locatore,
affittacamere
lanes: canali
languor: languore
larder: dispensa
lasted: durato
lasting: durevole, duraturo,
permanente, continuo

lastly: infine, ultimamente, per finire
lately: ultimamente, recentemente
latterly: ultimamente
laudable: lodevole
laugh: ridere, riso, risata
laughing: ridere, risata
laughingly: ridere
laughter: risa, risata, riso
laurel: alloro, lauro
lawfully: legalmente, legittimamente
lawn: prato, tappeto erboso, linone
laying: posando, posa
leads: conduce, guida
leaning: sporgente, propensione, pendente
lease: locazione, affitto, affittare, contratto d'affitto, noleggiare
legacy: eredità, lascito, legato
legally: legalmente
leisure: tempo libero, ozio, svago
leisurely: comodo
lend: prestare, presta, prestiamo, presti, prestate, prestano, presto, imprestare
lessen: diminuire, diminuiamo, diminuisci, diminuisco, diminuiscono, diminuite
lessened: diminuito
lessening: diminuendo
lesson: lezione
lest: affinchè non, per paura che
letting: affittando
liable: responsabile
liberality: liberalità
liberally: liberalmente
liberty: libertà
licence: licenza, concessione, patente
licentiousness: licenziosità
lieu: luogo
lifetime: vita
lighted: illuminato
lightness: leggerezza
likelihood: verosimiglianza, probabilità
likeness: somiglianza, rassomiglianza
likewise: anche, altrettanto
liking: predilezione, simpatia
limits: limiti
lingering: indugiando, indugiare, prolungato
listened: ascoltato
listener: ascoltatore
liveliness: vivacità
lively: vivace, spiritoso, vivo, animato, vispo
livery: livrea
lobby: lobby, atrio, vestibolo
lock: serratura, serrare a chiave, chiusa, bloccaggio, bloccare, blocco, fermo, ciocca
lodge: casetta, alloggiare, ospitare

lofty: alto, elevato
longing: bramoso
loo: gabinetto
loose: sciolto, lasco, slegare, slacciare, sciogliere
loser: perdente
losing: perdendo
lottery: lotteria
loud: forte, alto, rumoroso
loudly: forte, ad alta voce
loveliness: bellezza
lover: amante
loves: amore
loving: affettuoso
lowest: infimo
lowness: bassezza
luck: fortuna
luckily: fortunatamente
luckless: sfortunato
luncheon: pranzo
lustre: lucentezza
magistrate: magistrato
magnitude: grandezza, magnitudine
maid: cameriera, ragazza
maiden: nubile, fanciulla
maintained: mantenuto, conservato
maintaining: mantenendo, conservando
malice: malevolenza, livore, dolo, malizia, malignità
malicious: maligno, doloso, malizioso
mamma: mamma
manifold: collettore, molteplice
mankind: umanità
manners: educazione
manoeuvre: manovra, manovrare
manor: feudo
mansion: palazzo
marry: sposare, sposati, sposatevi, si sposi, si sposate, si sposano, ci sposiamo, mi sposo, maritarsi, ammogliarsi, maritare
marrying: sposandosi
masterly: magistrale
materially: materialmente
maternal: materno
matrimonial: matrimoniale
matrimony: matrimonio
mature: maturo, maturare, maturano, maturate, maturi, maturiamo, matura
meanly: meschinamente
meantime: frattanto, nel frattempo, intanto
meat: carne, la carne
mechanically: meccanicamente
mediocrity: mediocrità
meditate: meditare, mediti, meditiamo, meditate, meditano, medita, medito
meditated: meditato

meditating: meditando
meditation: meditazione
meets: incontra
melancholy: malinconia, malinconico
mend: riparare, rammendare, accomodare
mercenary: mercenario
mere: mero, laghetto, semplice
merit: meritare, merito, benemerenza, pregio
merited: meritato
merry: allegro, festoso, gaio
mess: confusione, disordine
messages: messaggio
mien: aspetto
mild: mite, dolce
mildly: dolcemente, gentilmente
mildness: mitezza
mile: miglio
militia: milizia
milliner: modista
mindful: attento
mingled: mischiato, mescolato
mingling: mescolando, mischiando
minutely: minutamente
minuteness: minuziosità, minutezza
miraculous: miracoloso
mirth: gaiezza, allegria, ilarità, gioia
mischance: disgrazia, sfortuna
mischief: birichinata
misconduct: cattiva condotta
miserable: miserabile, misero, afflitto, cattivo, triste, povero, miserevole, miserando
miserably: miserabilmente, miseramente
miserly: avaro
misery: miseria
misfortune: sfortuna, traversia, disgrazia
mislead: traviare
misleading: fuorviante
misleads: travia, fuorvia
misled: fuorviato, traviato
mismanagement: cattiva gestione
misrepresentation: travisamento
misrepresented: falsato, travisato
missing: disperso, mancante
mistake: errore, sbaglio, sbagliare, confondere, fallo
mistaken: sbagliato
mistress: padrona
mistrust: diffidenza, sfiducia
misunderstand: fraintendere, fraintendi, fraintendono, fraintendiamo, fraintendete, fraintendo
misunderstood: incompreso, frainteso
mix: mescolare, mischiare, impastare, mescolanza, miscela
mixed: misto, mescolato

mixing: mescolamento, miscelazione
mixture: mistura, miscela, commistione, impasto, mescolanza, miscuglio
mode: modo, moda, maniera
moderate: moderato, moderare
moderation: moderazione
modest: modesto, pudico
modesty: modestia, verecondia
momentary: momentaneo
monosyllable: monosillabo
monotonous: monotono, uniforme
monthly: mensile, mensilmente, al mese
moral: morale
morality: virtù, moralità, morale
moralize: moraleggiare, moralizzare
morrow: domani
mortal: mortale
mortification: mortificazione
mortified: mortificato
mortifies: mortifica
mortifying: mortificando, umiliante
mother-in-law: suocera
motive: motivo, movente, ragione
mount: montare, montatura, supporto, monte, cavalcatura, affusto
mountains: montagne
mounting: montaggio, salita
mud: fango, melma
muffin: focaccia
multitude: affluenza, folla, moltitudine
musical: musicale, musical
muslin: mussolina, mussola
mutual: reciproco
mutually: reciprocamente
mystery: mistero
named: nome
narrative: descrizione, narrativo
nasty: schifoso, sgradevole, cattivo, mostruoso, disonesto, spiacevole
nay: anzi
nearness: vicinanza
neat: pulito, puro, ordinato
neatness: pulizia, accuratezza
necessity: necessità, bisogno
needless: inutile
needlessly: inutilmente
needlework: cucito, lavoro ad ago, ricamo
neglect: trascurare, negligere, negligenza, trascuratezza
neglected: trascurato
negligence: negligenza, trascuratezza, condotta negligente
negligent: negligente, noncurante, sbadato
neighbour: vicino
neighbourhood: circondario, distretto, vicinato, quartiere

neighbouring: vicino
nephew: nipote
nerves: nervi, nervo
nervous: nervoso
netting: reticolato
nettled: irritato
nicely: piacevolmente
niece: nipote
nightcap: berretto da notte
noble: nobile, gentilizio, nobiliare
noisy: rumoroso, chiassoso
nominally: nominalmente
nonsense: nonsenso
nonsensical: assurdo, privo di senso
noon: mezzogiorno, mezzodì
northward: verso nord
northwards: verso nord
nothingness: inutilità, nullità
noticing: notare
notion: nozione, idea
nourishes: alimenta, nutrisce
novelty: novità
nowadays: oggigiorno
nowhere: in nessun luogo, da nessuna parte
numerous: numeroso
nuptials: nozze
nursing: allattamento
oaks: querce
obeisance: riverenza, inchino
obey: ubbidire, ubbidiamo, ubbidite, ubbidiscono, ubbidisci, ubbidisco, obbedire, obbediamo, obbediscono, obbedisco, obbedisci
obeyed: ubbidito, obbedito
objection: obiezione, opposizione
objectionable: biasimevole
objections: obiezioni
obligation: obbligo, obbligazione, dovere, impegno
oblige: obbligare, obblighiamo, obbliga, obbligano, obbligate, obblighi, obbligo
obliged: obbligato
obliging: obbligando, accomodante
obligingly: servizievole, cortesemente
obsequious: ossequioso, servile
obsequiousness: ossequiosità
observances: osservanze
observation: osservazione
observations: osservazioni
observe: osservare, osservano, osservo, osserviamo, osservate, osserva, osservi, eseguire, compiere
observer: osservatore
observing: osservando
obstacles: ostacoli
obstinacy: ostinazione
obstinate: ostinato
obtruded: imposto
occasional: occasionale

occupation: occupazione, mestiere, professione, impiego, lavoro
occupied: occupato
occupies: occupa
occupy: occupare, occupano, occupo, occupiamo, occupate, occupa, occupi
occurring: accadendo, succedendo
occurs: accade, succede
oddities: stranezze
oddity: stranezza
oddly: stranamente
odious: odioso
offend: offendere, offendiamo, offendo, offendi, offendete, offendono, insultare, insulto, insulti, insultate, insultano
offended: offeso, insultato, oltraggiato
offending: offendendo, insultando, oltraggiando
offense: offesa
offenses: offese
offensive: offensivo, offensiva
officious: ufficioso, invadente
officiousness: ufficiosità, ingerenza, invadenza
omen: augurio, presagio
omit: omettere, omettete, ometti, omettiamo, omettono, trascurare, ometto
omitted: omesso
openly: apertamente
openness: apertura, franchezza
operated: operato, azionato
oppose: contrapporre, contrapponete, contrapponi, contrapponiamo, contrappongono, contrappongo, opporre
opposed: opposto, contrapposto
oppressed: premuto, oppresso, serrato, stretto
oppressively: oppressivamente
ordained: destinato
ordered: ordinato, disposto
orderly: attendente
ordination: ordinazione
originate: discendere, discendete, discendi, discendiamo, discendo, discendono, provenire
originated: disceso
ostentation: ostentazione
ostentatious: ostentato
ours: nostro
outdone: superato, sorpassato
outrun: oltrepassare
overbearing: arrogante
overcome: superare
overcoming: superando, superamento
overflowing: traboccante
overhear: origlia, origliate, origlio,

origli, origliano, origliamo, origliare, udire per caso
overheard: origliato
overjoyed: felicissimo
overlook: trascurare
overpower: sopraffa', sopraffacciamo, sopraffaccio, sopraffai, sopraffanno, sopraffate, sopraffare
overpowered: sopraffatto
overpowering: sopraffacendo, opprimente, prepotente, schiacciante
overruled: annullato, revocato
overspread: coprire, cospargere
overtaken: sorpassato
overthrow: rovesciare, rovesciate, rovesciano, rovesci, rovesciamo, rovescia, rovescio
overthrowing: rovesciando
overthrown: rovesciato
owe: dovere
owing: dovere
owned: posseduto
pace: passo, andatura, velocità
pack: pacco, avvolgere, imballare, impaccare, muta
packing: imballaggio, impacchettamento
paddock: paddock, recinto
painful: doloroso, penoso
painfully: dolorosamente
pains: dolori
paint: dipingere, pittura, vernice, verniciare, tinta, tingere, pitturare
painter: pittore
paintings: dipinti
palatable: gustoso, appetitoso
pale: pallido, smorto, impallidire
paling: palizzata
palings: steccato, palizzata
paltry: meschino
panegyric: panegirico
pang: dolore acuto, spasimo
panting: ansimare
papa: papà
parade: parata, chiamata
parading: sfilare
parasol: parasole, ombrellino
pardon: grazia, perdono, perdonare, scusare, scusa
parental: parentale
parish: parrocchia
parlour: salotto
parsonage: canonica
partake: partecipo, partecipa, partecipano, partecipate, partecipi, partecipiamo, partecipare
partial: parziale
partiality: parzialità, predilezione
participation: partecipazione
particulars: particolari
parting: separazione, divisione

passing: passeggero, passare, passaggio
passion: ardore, passione
pathetic: patetico
patience: pazienza
patron: patrono, mecenate
patronage: patrocinio, patronato
patroness: patrona, patronessa
pause: pausa, sosta
pavement: marciapiede, selciato
peak: punta, picco, culmine, acme, visiera, cima, vetta
peculiar: strano, peculiare, particolare
peculiarity: caratteristica, peculiarità
peculiarly: particolarmente
pecuniary: pecuniario
pedantic: pedante
peep: occhieggiare, pigolio, pigolare, sbirciare
peevish: permaloso, stizzoso
pen: penna
penance: penitenza
penetration: penetrazione
penitent: pentito, penitente
perceive: percepire, accorgersi, scorgere, percepiamo, scorgo, scorgiamo, scorgi, scorgete, percepite, scorgono, percepiscono
perceived: scorto, percepito, intravisto
perceiving: percependo, scorgendo, intravedendo
perceptible: percettibile
perforce: necessariamente
perform: eseguire, eseguono, eseguo, eseguite, eseguiamo, esegui, compiere, fare, apparire, entrare, commettere
performed: eseguito
performer: esecutore
performs: esegue
permission: permesso, accordo, autorizzazione, nullaosta, licenza
permit: permettere, permesso, autorizzazione
permitted: permesso
perpetual: perpetuo
perpetually: perennemente, perpetuamente
perplexity: perplessità
perseverance: perseveranza
persevered: perseverato
persevering: perseverando
persist: persistere, persistono, persisto, persistiamo, persisti, persistete
persisted: persistito
persisting: persistendo
persists: persiste
personage: personaggio
persuade: convincere, convincono,

convincete, convinci, convinciamo, convinco, persuadere, persuadono, persuado, persuadiamo, persuadi
persuaded: convinto, persuaso
persuasion: persuasione
perturbation: perturbazione
perturbed: perturbato
perusing: esaminando
perverse: perverso
petition: petizione, istanza, supplica
petrified: terrorizzato, impietrito, pietrificato
petticoat: sottana, sottogonna, sottoveste
philosopher: filosofo
philosophic: filosofico
philosophy: filosofia
picturesque: pittoresco
piling: accatastamento
pitiable: pietoso
pitiful: pietoso
pity: compassione, pietà
placing: collocamento
plague: peste
plain: piano, pianura, evidente, distinto, chiaro
plantation: piantagione
plate: piatto, lastra, piastra, placca, lamiera, targa
playful: giocoso
plays: gioca, suona
plead: peroro, supplico, supplichiamo, supplichi, supplicate, supplica, peroriamo, perori, perorano, perora, imploro
pleasant: piacevole, gradevole, ameno
pleasantly: piacevolmente
pleasantness: piacevolezza
pleased: contento, soddisfatto
pleases: soddisfa
pleasing: piacevole
pledged: impegnato
plentiful: abbondante, copioso
pocket: tasca, intascare, la tasca, sacca
poetry: poesia
pointing: indicare
polished: lucidato
polite: cortese, educato
politely: cortesemente
politeness: cortesia, garbo
pollution: inquinamento, contaminazione
pompous: ampolloso, pomposo
pools: piscina, totocalcio
poorly: male, poveramente
pope: papa
popularity: popolarità
portion: parte, porzione
portrait: ritratto, verticale
positively: positivamente
possess: possedere, possedete,

possediamo, possiedi, possiedo,
possiedono
possessed: posseduto
possesses: possiede
possessing: possedendo
possession: possesso
possessor: possessore
possibilities: possibilità
posterity: posterità
postponed: rimandato
postscript: poscritto
poultry: pollame
pour: versare
poured: versato
pouring: versare, torrenziale, colata
poverty: povertà
practising: praticante
praise: lodare, lode, elogiare,
encomio, elogio
pray: pregare, pregate, prego, preghi,
prega, preghiamo, pregano
preaching: predicando
preceded: preceduto
preceding: precedendo, precedente
precious: prezioso
precipitate: precipitare, precipitato
precisely: precisamente
precision: precisione, accuratezza
precluding: precludendo
predict: predire, predici, prediciamo,
predico, predicono, predite, predi'
predominance: prevalenza,
predominio, predominanza
predominate: predominare,
predominiamo, predominano,
predomino, predominate,
predomina, predomini
preference: preferenza
preferred: preferito
prejudice: pregiudizio, preconcetto,
prevenzione
prejudiced: prevenuto
premeditated: premeditato
premeditation: premeditazione
premises: locali, locale, premesse
preparation: preparazione,
allestimento, preparativo
preparations: preparativi
prepare: preparare, prepari,
prepariamo, preparate, preparano,
prepara, preparo, allestire,
allestiamo, allestisci, allestisco
preparing: preparando, allestendo,
apprestando
presentation: presentazione,
rappresentazione
presently: attualmente
presents: presenta
preservation: conservazione,
preservazione
preservative: conservante,
preservativo, conservativo

preserve: conservare, conserva
preserved: conservato
preside: presiedere
presided: presieduto
pressed: premuto
pressing: pressatura, urgente
presume: supporre, supponiamo,
supponi, suppongono, suppongo,
supponete, presumere, presumiamo,
presumo, presumi, presumete
presumed: supposto, presunto
presuming: supponendo,
presumendo, presumere
presumption: presunzione,
supposizione
pretence: pretesa
pretend: fingere, fingete, fingi,
fingiamo, fingo, fingono,
pretendere, simulare
pretended: finto
pretending: fingendo
pretense: pretesa, finta, finzione
pretension: pretesa
prevail: prevalere, prevalete,
prevalgo, prevalgono, prevali,
prevaliamo
prevailed: prevalso
prevailing: prevalente, prevalendo
prevented: impedito, prevenuto
prevents: impedisce, previene
prey: preda
pride: orgoglio, fierezza
principal: principale, committente,
capitale, mandante
principally: principalmente,
soprattutto
prior: anteriore, precedente
privately: privatamente
privilege: privilegio, privilegiare
privileged: privilegiato
probability: probabilità
probable: probabile
probity: probità
proceed: procedere, procedete,
procedono, procedo, procediamo,
procedi
proceeded: proceduto
proceeding: procedendo,
procedimento
proclaim: proclamare, proclami,
proclamiamo, proclamate,
proclamano, proclamo, proclama,
pubblicare
procure: procurare, procurate,
procuro, procuri, procurano,
procuriamo, procacciare, procura
procured: procurato
procuring: procurando
prodigious: prodigioso
prodigiously: prodigiosamente
productive: produttivo
profess: dichiarare, professare

professed: professato, dichiarare,
dichiarato
professing: dichiarando, professando
profession: professione, mestiere
proficiency: competenza
proficient: competente
profuse: abbondante, profuso
profusion: profusione
prohibited: vietato, proibito
projected: proiettato, progettato
promise: promessa, promettere,
promettono, promettete, prometti,
promettiamo, prometto
promises: promette
promising: promettendo,
promettente
promote: promuovere, promuovi,
promuovono, promuoviamo,
promuovete, promuovo, favorire
promoted: promosso
prompt: preciso, esatto, sollecito,
pronto
prone: prono, incline
pronounce: pronunciare,
pronunciano, pronunciate,
pronunciamo, pronunci, pronuncio,
pronuncia
pronounced: pronunciato
pronouncing: pronunciando
proof: prova, bozza, dimostrazione,
provino, impermeabilizzare,
resistente
propitious: propizio
proportionate: proporzionato
proportioned: proporzionato,
proporzione
propose: proporre, proponiamo,
proponi, propongono, proponete,
propongo
proprietor: proprietario
propriety: convenienza
prospect: prospettiva, esplorare
prosperity: prosperità
prosperous: prospero, fiorente
protest: protesta, protestare
protesting: protestare
proud: orgoglioso, fiero
proudly: orgogliosamente
proverb: proverbio
proving: provando
provoke: spronare, provocare,
incitare, provochi, sproniamo,
sprono, sproni, spronate, spronano,
sprona, provoco
provoked: spronato, incitato,
provocato
provoking: incitando, provocando,
spronando
proxy: procura, procuratore,
mandatario
prudence: prudenza
prudent: prudente, sensato

prudential: prudenziale
prudently: prudentemente,
  giudiziosamente
publicly: pubblicamente
publish: pubblicare, pubblicate,
  pubblichi, pubblichiamo, pubblica,
  pubblicano, pubblico
punch: punzone, ponce, perforatore,
  forare, punzonare, perforatrice,
  punch
punctual: esatto, puntuale, preciso
punctuality: puntualità
punctually: puntualmente
punish: punire, puniamo, punisci,
  punisco, puniscono, punite,
  castigare, castiga, castigano,
  castigate, castighi
punishment: punizione, castigo, pena
purchased: comprato, acquistato
purchases: acquisti
pure: puro
purport: senso, significare, significato
purposely: intenzionalmente
purse: borsa, borsellino, portamonete
pursue: perseguire, persegui,
  perseguite, perseguo, perseguiamo,
  perseguono, perseguitare, inseguire
pursued: perseguito
pursuing: perseguendo
pursuit: inseguimento, ricerca
puzzle: puzzle, enigma, confondere,
  rendere perplesso, rompicapo
quadrille: quadriglia
qualification: qualificazione,
  qualifica
qualified: qualificato, abilitato
quantity: quantità, grandezza
quarrel: lite, litigare, bisticciare,
  bisticcio, litigio
quarrelsome: litigioso
quest: ricerca
quickness: prontezza, rapidità,
  lestezza
quit: abbandonare, abbandonato,
  abbandono, abbandoni,
  abbandonate, abbandonano,
  abbandona, abbandoniamo,
  smettere
quitting: abbandonando
rage: furore, ira, furia, collera
ragout: cibreo
raising: sollevamento, allevamento,
  sopraelevazione, aumento
ramble: giro, passeggiata, vagare
rank: rango, ordine, classificare
rant: declamazione, declamare
rapacity: rapacità
rapid: rapido
rapidity: rapidità, velocità
rapture: rapimento, estasi
rapturous: estatico
rashness: avventatezza

rated: nominale
rational: razionale, ragionevole
rationally: razionalmente
rattle: sonaglio, rantolo
readily: prontamente
readiness: prontezza
reanimated: rianimato
reap: mietere, mietono, mieto, mieti,
  mietete, mietiamo
reappear: riapparire, riapparite,
  riappaio, riappaiono, riappari,
  riappariamo
reasonableness: ragionevolezza
reasonably: ragionevolmente
reasoning: ragionamento,
  argomentazione
rebuke: biasimare, disapprovare,
  riprendere, sgridare, rimproverare
recall: richiamo, ricordare, richiamare
recalled: ricordato
recede: recedere
receipt: ricevuta, quietanza,
  quietanzare, ricezione, scontrino
receiving: ricevendo, accogliendo,
  ricezione, ricevere, ricevente
reception: ricezione, ricevimento,
  accettazione, reception, portineria
recital: concerto, recital, dizione
reckon: contare, computare, calcolare
reckoned: contato, calcolato,
  computato
recognized: riconosciuto
recognizing: riconoscendo
recollect: rammenta, rammentano,
  rammentate, rammenti,
  rammentiamo, rammento,
  rammentare, ricordarsi
recollected: rammentato
recollecting: rammentando
recollection: memoria, ricordo
recommend: raccomandare,
  raccomanda, raccomandano,
  raccomandate, raccomandi,
  raccomandiamo, raccomando,
  consigliare, vantare
recommendation: raccomandazione,
  consiglio
recommendations: raccomandazioni
recommended: raccomandato
recommending: raccomandando
reconcile: conciliare, riconciliare,
  riconciliamo, riconcili, conciliate,
  conciliano, conciliamo, concilia,
  riconcilia, riconciliano, riconciliate
reconciled: conciliato, riconciliato
reconciliation: riconciliazione,
  conciliazione
reconciling: riconciliando,
  conciliando
recover: ricuperare, ricupera,
  ricuperi, ricuperiamo, ricuperano,
  ricuperate, ricupero, recuperare,

guarire, riprendere
recovered: ricuperato
recovering: ricuperando
recreation: ricreazione
rectitude: rettitudine
rector: rettore, parroco
rectory: canonica
recurring: ricorrendo, ritornando,
  ricorrente
reel: bobina, aspo, mulinello,
  rocchetto
referred: riferito
reflect: riflettere, rifletti, riflettiamo,
  rifletto, riflettono, riflettete
reflected: riflesso
reflecting: riflettendo
reflection: riflesso, riflessione
refrain: ritornello, astenersi
refreshing: rinfrescante
refreshment: rinfresco, ristoro
refuge: rifugio
refusal: rifiuto
refuse: rifiutare, rifiutarsi, rifiuti
refute: confutare, confutano, confuto,
  confutiamo, confutate, confuta,
  confuti
regain: ricuperare, riprendere
regained: riacquistato, riconquistato,
  ricuperato, riguadagnato, ripreso
regarding: considerando
regardless: incurante
regiment: reggimento
regret: rincrescere, rammarico,
  rimpiangere, rimpianto,
  rincrescimento
regretted: rammaricato
regulars: regolare
regulate: regolare, regolano, regolate,
  regoli, regoliamo, regolo, regola
regulated: regolato
regulation: regolazione, regola,
  regolamento, regolamentazione,
  normativa
rein: redine, briglia
reject: rifiutare, respingere, scarto,
  rigettare, rifiutarsi, bocciare, scartare
rejected: respinto
rejection: rifiuto, rigetto
rejoice: allietare, rallegrare
rejoiced: allietato, gioito, rallegrato
rejoicing: gioia
rejoined: riunito
relate: raccontare, raccontiamo,
  racconta, raccontano, raccontate,
  racconti, racconto, narrare
relates: racconta
relating: raccontando
relation: relazione, rapporto
reliance: fiducia
relied: confidato
relieve: alleviare, allevio, allevi,
  allevia, alleviamo, alleviano,

alleviate, rilevare
relieved: alleviato
relinquish: cedere, cedete, cedono, cedo, cedi, cediamo, abbandonare
reluctance: riluttanza
reluctant: riluttante, ritroso, restio
rely: confida, confidano, confidate, confidi, confidiamo, confido, confidare, fare affidamento, fidarsi
remainder: resto, rimanenza
remark: commento, osservazione, nota
remarkable: notevole, eccezionale
remarkably: notevolmente
remarks: osservazioni
remedy: rimedio, medicina, rimediare
remembering: ricordando
remembrance: rimembranza, ricordo, memoria
remind: ricordare, ricorda, ricordo, ricordiamo, ricordi, ricordate, ricordano
reminded: ricordato
reminding: ricordando
remonstrance: rimostranza
remorse: rimorso
removal: rimozione, asportazione, eliminazione
removing: togliendo, asportando, rimuovendo
render: rendere, rendono, rendete, rendi, rendiamo, rendo
rendered: reso
rendering: rendering, rendendo, traduzione
renewal: rinnovo, rinnovamento
renewed: rinnovato
renewing: rinnovando
repaid: rimborsato, ripagato
repaired: riparato
repeat: ripetere, ripetono, ripetete, ripetiamo, ripeto, ripeti, ripetizione
repeated: ripetuto
repeatedly: ripetutamente
repeating: ripetendo
repel: respingere, respingete, respingi, respingiamo, respingo, respingono
repelled: respinto
repent: pentirsi
repentance: pentimento, rimpianto
repetition: ripetizione, replica
replete: pieno
reporting: reporting
repose: riposo, riposarsi
reprehensible: riprovevole, biasimevole
representation: rappresentanza, rappresentazione, figura
represented: rappresentato, figurato
representing: rappresentando,

figurando
repress: reprimere
repressed: represso
repressing: reprimendo
reproach: rimprovero, rimproverare, riprendere
reproached: rimproverato
reproof: biasimo
repugnance: avversione, ripugnanza
repugnant: ripugnante
repulsive: ripulsivo, ripugnante
reputed: reputato, stimato, supposto
requiring: richiedendo
requisite: requisito
rescue: salvataggio, salvare, soccorso
resemblance: somiglianza, rassomiglianza
resentful: risentito, astioso
resentment: risentimento, astio
reserve: riservare, riserva, prenotare, ordinare
reserved: riservato
reserves: riserve
residence: residenza, alloggio, appartamento
resides: risiede
residing: risiedendo
resign: dimettere, dimettersi
resignation: rassegnazione, dimissioni
resigned: rassegnato
resigning: rassegnando, dimettendo
resist: resistere, resistete, resistono, resisto, resistiamo, resisti
resisted: resistito
resisting: resistendo
resolute: risoluto, deciso
resolutely: risoluto, risolutamente, decisamente
resolution: risoluzione, definizione, deliberazione
resolve: risolvere
resolved: risolto
resounding: risuonando, echeggiando, riecheggiando, risonante, clamoroso
resource: risorsa
respectability: rispettabilità
respectable: rispettabile, onorevole
respected: rispettato
respectful: rispettoso
respecting: rispettare
respective: rispettivo
rested: riposato
restless: inquieto, irrequieto
restoration: restauro, ripristino, ristabilimento, restituzione, restaurazione
restored: ripristinato, restaurato
restoring: ripristinando, restaurando
restrain: dominare, domina, domino, dominiamo, dominano, dominate,

domini, reprimere, governare
restrained: dominato
restraint: restrizione
resume: riprendere, riprendete, riprendiamo, riprendo, riprendono, riprendi
resuming: riprendendo
retail: al dettaglio
retailing: commercio al dettaglio, commercio al minuto
retain: ritenere, ritengo, ritieni, ritenete, riteniamo, ritengono, trattenere, trattenete, trattengo, trattengono, tratteniamo
retained: ritenuto, trattenuto
retaining: ritenendo, trattenendo
retains: ritiene, trattiene
retaliate: rivalersi
retired: pensionato, ritirato, a riposo
retirement: pensionamento, ritiro
retort: replica, storta
retreated: ritirato
retrospective: retrospettiva, retrospettivo
revealed: pubblicato, rivelato
revealing: pubblicando, rivelando
revenge: vendetta
revered: riverito
reverie: fantasticheria
reverse: retromarcia, inverso, contrario, invertire, rovescio
reverting: ritornando
revival: rinascita
revive: rianimare, rianima, rianimano, rianimate, rianimi, rianimiamo, rianimo, rinascere
revived: rianimato
revolt: rivolta, ribellarsi
revolted: rivoltato
revolving: ruotando, girando, girevole
richly: riccamente
rid: sbarazzare
ride: camminare, giro, corsa, cavalcare, cavalcata
ridge: cresta, crinale
ridicule: ridicolo, ridicolizzare
ridiculing: ridicolizzare
ridiculous: ridicolo, assurdo
riding: equitazione, cavalcata
rightful: legittimo
rightly: giustamente
rings: anelli
risen: sorto
rising: aumento, salita, sorgere, sorgente, levata, ascendente, ascesa, nascente, sommossa, levante, crescita
rival: rivale
roasted: arrostito
rob: derubare, deruba, derubano, derubate, derubi, derubiamo,

derubo, svaligiare, rubare
romantic: romantico
rough: rude, brusco, ruvido, crudo,
   approssimativo, rozzo, grossolano,
   scabro, grezzo
roused: incitato, spronato, stimolato
rude: scortese, rozzo, maleducato
rudeness: villania, maleducazione
ruin: rovinare, rovina
ruined: rovinato
ruining: rovinare
runs: corre, scorre
sacrifice: sacrificio, sacrificare, offrire
sacrificed: sacrificato
sad: triste, afflitto
sadly: tristemente
safely: al sicuro, sicuramente
safest: il più sicuro
sagacity: sagacia
sake: causa
salad: insalata, l'insalata
saloon: salone, berlina
salutation: saluto
sameness: uniformità
sanction: sanzione
sanguine: rubicondo, sanguigno
sarah: Sara
sarcastic: sarcastico
sash: fusciacca
satin: raso, satin
satirical: satirico
satisfaction: soddisfazione
satisfactory: soddisfacente
satisfied: soddisfatto, contento,
   accontentato
satisfy: soddisfare, accontentare,
   soddisfano, soddisfiamo, soddisfa,
   soddisfate, soddisfo, accontentare,
   accontento, soddisfi, accontentano
satisfying: soddisfacendo,
   accontentando, soddisfacente
saucy: impertinente, sfacciato
savage: selvaggio, crudele
saved: salvato, risparmiato
saving: salvando, risparmio,
   risparmiando
scampering: sgambettando
scandalous: scandaloso
scarce: scarso, raro
scarcely: appena, a stento
scarcity: scarsità
scarlet: scarlatto
scattered: versato, sparso
scheming: intrigante
scold: sgridare, rimproverare,
   riprendere
scolding: rimprovero, sgridata
scope: portata, scopo, ambito, campo
scorn: disprezzo, disprezzare
scrape: raschiare, scrostare
scruple: scrupolo
scrutiny: esame minuzioso, scrutinio

searching: ricerca
seasonable: stagionale, di stagione
seated: seduto
secluded: appartato
seclusion: isolamento
secondly: in secondo luogo,
   secondariamente
secrecy: segretezza
secret: segreto
secretly: segretamente
secured: fissato
sedate: calmo
seduction: seduzione
seeking: cercando
seeming: parendo, sembrando,
   sembrare
sees: vede, sega
seize: afferrare, afferro, afferra,
   afferrano, afferrate, afferri,
   afferriamo, acciuffare, acchiappare,
   confiscare, prendere
seized: afferrato
seizing: afferrando, grippaggio
seldom: raramente
selected: selezionato, scelto
selecting: selezionando
self: stesso
selfish: egoistico, egoista
selfishness: egoismo
sending: mandando, spedendo
sends: manda, spedisce
seniority: anzianità
sensation: sensazione
senses: sensi
sensibility: sensibilità
sensible: sensato, ragionevole,
   sensibile
sensibly: assennatamente
sentiment: sentimento
sentinel: sentinella
separated: separato
separately: separatamente
separates: separa
separating: separare
separation: separazione, distacco
sequel: seguito
serenity: serenità
sermon: predica, sermone
servant: servire, servo, servitore
serviceable: utilizzabile
servility: servilismo
serving: servendo
settle: sistemare, regolare, saldare
settled: regolato, stabilito, stabile,
   fermo, fisso, popolato, saldato,
   sistemato, deciso
settling: regolando, saldando,
   sistemando, assestamento, regolare,
   sedimentazione
severity: rigore
shade: ombra, adombrare, tinta,
   ombreggiare, oscurità, sfumatura,

sfumare
shake: scuotere, scuotono, scuoto,
   scuotiamo, scuoti, scuotete, scossa
shaken: scosso
shaking: scuotendo
shame: vergogna, pudore
shameful: vergognoso
shameless: svergognato, spudorato
sharing: condivisione
sharpened: affilato, acuito
shed: baracca, versare, versate, verso,
   versiamo, versato, versano, versa,
   versi, capannone, tettoia
sheets: fogli, le lenzuola
sheltered: riparato
shelves: ripiani, scaffali
shield: scudo, riparo, proteggere,
   schermo, schermare
shift: turno, spostare, cambio,
   spostamento, scorrimento, trasferire
shifting: spostare, spostamento
shine: risplendere, brillare, lustro,
   splendere
shocking: irritante, scandaloso
shoes: scarpe
shoot: sparare, spara, spariamo,
   spari, sparate, sparano, sparo, tirare,
   getto, germoglio, fucilare
shopping: shopping
shorten: abbreviare, accorciare,
   accorciate, accorciano, accorciamo,
   accorcia, accorci, abbreviate,
   abbreviano, abbreviamo, abbrevia
shortness: bassa statura, brevità
shrewish: bisbetico
shrink: restringere, restringersi
shrubbery: boschetto
shrug: alzata di spalle
shy: timido, ritroso
shyness: timidezza
sick: malato, ammalato
sickly: cagionevole, malaticcio,
   malatamente
sideboard: armadio, credenza
sigh: sospirare, sospiro
signal: segnale, segno
signify: significare, significate,
   significo, significhi, significa,
   significhiamo, significano
silently: silenziosamente
silly: sciocco, stupido
similarity: somiglianza, similarità
simpleton: sempliciotto
sincere: sincero
sincerely: sinceramente, francamente
sincerity: sincerità
sing: cantare, canta, cantano, cantate,
   canti, cantiamo, canto
singing: cantando, canto
sings: canta
singular: singolare, strano
sink: lavandino, lavello, affondare,

acquaio

sinking: affondamento, sprofondamento

sister-in-law: cognata

sisterly: sorella

situated: situato

sixteen: sedici

sixth: sesto, sesta

sketch: schizzo, abbozzare, bozzetto, disegno, abbozzo, progetto, progettare, schema

skill: abilità, destrezza, maestria

slacken: allentare

slave: schiavo, sgobbare

sleeping: dormendo, addormentato

sleepless: insonne

sleeves: manicotti

slept: dormito

slight: leggero, lieve

slit: fessura, fenditura

sloping: inclinato

sly: furbo, astuto, scaltro

slyness: astuzia

smart: intelligente

smiling: sorridere

smilingly: sorridere

smoothly: facilmente, agevolmente

sneer: sogghigno, sogghignare, scherno

sneering: sogghignare

snug: accogliente, comodo, raccolto

softened: ammorbidito

softness: morbidezza

solace: conforto, consolare

sole: sogliola, solo, suola, pianta, unico

solely: solamente, soltanto, unicamente

solemn: solenne

solemnity: solennità

solicit: sollecito, sollecitare, sollecitate, solleciti, sollecitano, sollecita, sollecitiamo

solicitation: sollecitazione

soliciting: adescamento, sollecitando

solicitude: sollecitudine

solid: solido, massiccio, compatto

solidity: solidità

solitary: solo, solitario

solitude: solitudine

sonnet: sonetto

sooner: prima

soothe: calmare, calmano, calmiamo, calmi, calmate, calmo, calma, placare, lenire

soothed: calmato

sore: piaga, dolente

sorely: dolorosamente

sorrow: tristezza, cordoglio

sought: cercato

soul: anima

soup: minestra, brodo, zuppa, la

minestra

sour: acido, agro, brusco, rude, acerbo, aspro

spacious: ampio, spazioso

spanish: spagnolo

spare: risparmiare, scorta

spared: risparmiato

spars: litiga

speaks: parla

speculation: speculazione

speedily: rapidamente

speedy: rapido

spending: spendendo, passando

sphere: sfera

spiritless: avvilito

spite: dispetto

spiteful: dispettoso

spleen: milza, malumore

splendid: splendido, magnifico

splendour: splendore

spoken: parlato

sportive: allegro

spreading: spandimento, spalmatura, propagazione

springing: saltare, correzione

spur: sperone, sprone, spronare

squeamish: schifiltoso, schizzinoso

stability: stabilità

staggered: sfalsato

staid: serio

staircase: scala

stairs: scala, scale

stamp: francobollo, bollo, bollare, timbro, affrancare, timbrare

startled: spaventato

starve: affamare

stateliness: grandiosità

stately: imponente

stating: dichiarare

staying: stando, restando

stays: sta, resta

steadfast: risoluto, costante

steadily: costantemente, fermamente

steadiness: costanza, fermezza

steady: fisso

stem: gambo, tronco, stelo, fusto

steward: maggiordomo, dispensiere

stiffly: rigidamente

stiffness: rigidezza, rigidità

stir: mescolare, agitare, muovere

stirring: mescolare, eccitante, agitazione

stoke: riscaldare

stole: stola

stopping: fermando, cessando, interrompendo, smettendo, arrestando

storing: immagazzinamento, memorizzazione

storm: tempesta, burrasca, temporale, bufera

stout: forte, corpulento, robusto, birra

scura

strangely: stranamente

strangeness: stravaganza, stranezza

stranger: sconosciuto, estraneo, forestiero

stream: ruscello, corrente, flusso, corso d'acqua

strenuously: strenuamente

stretch: stendere, tendere, allungamento

stretched: teso, allungato

stretching: stiramento, allungamento

strictly: rigorosamente, strettamente

striking: impressionante

striving: sforzandosi

stroke: accarezzare, corsa, apoplessia, colpo, ictus, colpo apoplettico

stroll: passeggiata, passeggiare

struck: colpito

struggled: lottato

struggling: lottare

stubbornness: testardaggine, cocciutaggine

studied: studiato

studious: studioso

studying: studio

stumbling: inciampare

stupid: stupido, sciocco, ignorante, balordo

stupidity: stupidità

subjection: sottomissione, soggezione

submit: sottomettere, sottoporre

submitted: sottomesso, sottoposto

subsided: abbassato, calato, cessato, sprofondato

subsist: esistere, sussistere, sussisti, sussistono, sussistiamo, sussistete, esisto, esistiamo, esisti, esistete, sussisto

subsisted: esistito, sussistito

subsisting: sussistendo, esistendo

substance: sostanza, materia

substitute: sostituto, sostituire, supplente, rimpiazzare, succedaneo, surrogato

succeed: riuscire, riusciamo, riuscite, riescono, riesco, riesci, succedere

succeeded: riuscito

succeeding: riuscendo, successivo

succeeds: riesce

successfully: con successo

succession: successione

successively: successivamente

successor: successore, discendente

suddenness: subitaneità

suffer: soffrire, soffri, soffro, soffrono, soffrite, soffriamo, patire, subire, patiamo, patite, patiscono

suffering: soffrendo, sofferenza, soffrire, patendo

suffers: soffre, patisce

sufficiently: abbastanza, sufficientemente
suggesting: proponendo, suggerendo
suggestion: suggerimento, proposta, suggestione
summon: convocare, chiamare, intimare, citare
summoned: convocato
summons: citazione, ingiunzione
supercilious: altezzoso
superintended: soprinteso
superintendence: soprintendenza
superintends: soprintende
superior: superiore
superiority: superiorità
superseded: sostituito, soppiantato, rimpiazzato
supper: cena
supplication: preghiera, domanda, implorazione, supplica
supplied: fornito
supplying: approvvigionamento, fornitura
supposing: supponendo
supposition: supposizione
suppress: soffocare, opprimere, soffoca, soffocano, soffocate, soffochi, soffochiamo, soffoco
suppressed: soffocato, soppresso
surmise: supporre, congetturare
surmount: sormontare
surpass: sorpassare, superare
surpassing: senza pari, superare, sorpassando, sovrastando, superando
surrounded: circondato
surrounding: circondando, circostante
surveying: agrimensura
survive: sopravvivere, sopravvivete, sopravvivono, sopravvivo, sopravviviamo, sopravvivi
survived: sopravvissuto
survivor: superstite, sopravvissuto
susceptibility: suscettibilità
suspect: sospettare, sospetto
suspend: sospendere, sospendi, sospendono, sospendiamo, sospendete, sospendo
suspended: sospeso
suspense: apprensione
suspicion: sospetto
suspicious: sospettoso, sospetto
sustained: sostenuto, costante, poggiato
sweet: dolce, soave, caramella
sweetness: dolcezza
swell: gonfiare, dilatare, rigonfiamento, mare lungo, crescendo
swelled: gonfiato
swelling: rigonfiamento, gonfiore,

tumefazione, gonfiezza
syllable: sillaba
symmetry: simmetria
symptom: sintomo, segno
symptoms: sintomi
synonymously: sinonimo
tables: tavoli
tacit: tacito
taciturn: taciturno
tackle: paranco, attrezzatura
talent: talento, ingegno
talked: parlato
tanned: abbronzato
taught: insegnato
teach: insegnare, insegna, insegnano, insegniamo, insegni, insegnate, insegno, istruire
tear: strappo, lagrima, strappare, lacerare, lacrima
tease: irritare, stuzzicare
tedious: noioso, tedioso
tells: dice, racconta, narra
temper: umore, temperamento, tempra
tempered: temperato
tempt: tentare, tento, tentiamo, tenti, tentate, tenta, tentano
temptation: tentazione
tempted: tentato
tenant: affittuario, inquilino, locatario
tendency: tendenza
tender: tenero, dolce, offerta, tender
tenderly: teneramente
tenderness: tenerezza, affettuosità
tenor: tenore
tens: dieci
tent: tenda
termination: fine, terminazione
terrific: straordinario
testified: testimoniato
testifying: testimoniando
testimony: certificato attestato, testimonianza
thanked: ringraziato
thankful: riconoscente, grato
thankfully: riconoscentemente
thankfulness: gratitudine, riconoscenza
thanking: ringraziando
theirs: loro
thence: di là
thereby: con ciò
therein: in ciò
thereupon: in merito
thirdly: in terzo luogo
thirteen: tredici
thither: là
thorough: completo, accurato
thoroughly: completamente
thoughtful: pensieroso, premuroso
thoughtfulness: pensosità
thoughtless: sconsiderato

thoughtlessness: sconsideratezza
threadbare: liso
threatened: minacciato
threats: minaccia
throat: gola, la gola
throw: gettare, lanciare, lancio, tiro, alzata
throwing: lancio
thrown: gettato
thwarted: contrastato, ostacolato
tickets: biglietti
tide: marea
tired: stanco
tiresome: seccante, fastidioso, noioso, faticoso
token: segno, gettone, prova
tolerable: tollerabile
tolerably: tollerabilmente
tongue: lingua, linguetta, la lingua
topic: argomento, tema
torment: tormento
tormenting: tormentoso, tormento
tortured: torturato
touched: toccato
toward: verso, a
trace: traccia, tracciare, delimitare
tractable: docile, trattabile
tradesman: commerciante
trait: caratteristica, tratto
tranquil: tranquillo, calmo
tranquillity: tranquillità
transferred: trasferito, attraversato
transient: transitorio
transition: transizione, passaggio
transpired: traspirato
travelling: itinerante, viaggiante, viaggiare
treasure: tesoro
treat: trattare, guarire
treating: trattare
tremble: tremare
trembled: tremato
trembling: tremolante, tremulo, tremolio, tremito, tremante, tremore, tremare
trepidation: trepidazione
trespass: trasgredire, trasgressione, infrazione, sconfinare
tribute: tributo
trifle: inezia, sciocchezza
trifling: insignificante
trim: rifilare
trimming: guarnizione
triumph: vittoria, trionfo
triumphant: trionfante
triumphantly: trionfalmente
troop: truppa
troublesome: fastidioso, noioso
trout: trota
truly: davvero, infatti, veramente
trunk: tronco, baule, proboscide, torso, bagagliaio

trusted: fidato
trusting: fiducioso
tuesday: martedì
tumult: tumulto
turns: gira, svolta, cambia
ugly: brutto
ultimately: finalmente, alla fine
unaccountable: inesplicabile, irresponsabile
unacknowledged: non riconosciuto
unacquainted: non abituato
unaffected: spontaneo, non affettato, semplice
unalloyed: puro
unalterable: inalterabile
unanswerable: incontestabile, irrefutabile
unassuming: senza pretese
unattended: incustodito
unavailing: inutile
unavoidable: inevitabile
unavoidably: inevitabilmente
unaware: inconsapevole, ignaro, inconscio
unbecoming: indecoroso
unbending: inflessibile
unblemished: senza macchia
uncertain: incerto, malsicuro
uncertainty: incertezza
unchanged: immutato
uncivil: incivile
uncle: zio, lo zio
uncomfortable: scomodo, disagiato
uncommon: insolito, raro
uncommonly: insolitamente
unconcern: noncuranza
unconcerned: indifferente
unconsciously: inconsciamente
uncontrolled: sfrenato
undeceive: disinganno, disingannare, disinganniamo, disinganna, disingannano, disingannate, disinganni
undecided: incerto, indeciso
undergone: subito
undertaken: intrapreso
undertaking: intraprendendo, impresa
undervalued: sottovalutato
undervaluing: sottovalutando
undeserved: immeritato
undeserving: immeritevole
undetermined: indeterminato
undo: disfare, disfate, disfa', disfacciamo, disfaccio, disfai, disfanno
undone: disfatto
undoubted: indubbio
undoubtedly: indubbiamente, si capisce
uneasiness: disagio
uneasy: inquieto

unequal: ineguale, disuguale
unequally: inegualmente
unexampled: singolare
unexpected: inatteso, imprevisto, inaspettato
unexpectedly: inaspettatamente
unfavourable: sfavorevole
unfeeling: insensibile
unfit: inadatto
unfold: spiegare
unfolded: spiegato
unfolding: spiegamento, spiegare, spiegando
unfortunate: sfortunato, sventurato
ungovernable: indisciplinato
unguarded: incustodito
unhappily: infelicemente
unhappiness: tristezza, infelicità
unhappy: infelice, triste
unheard: non sentito
uniform: uniforme, divisa
uniformity: uniformità
uniformly: uniformemente
unimportant: senza importanza
unintelligible: inintelligibile, incomprensibile
unite: unire, congiungere, unirsi, unite, uniscono, unisco, uniamo, unisci
uniting: unendo
universal: universale
universally: universalmente
unjust: ingiusto
unjustifiable: ingiustificabile
unjustly: ingiustamente
unkindness: cattiveria, scortesia
unknowingly: inconsapevolmente
unluckily: sfortunatamente
unlucky: sfortunato, disgraziato
unmoved: impassibile
unnatural: innaturale
unnaturally: innaturalmente
unnecessarily: inutilmente
unnecessary: inutile, non necessario
unpardonable: imperdonabile
unpleasant: rude, spiacevole, brusco, sgradevole, scostante
unpleasantly: antipaticamente, spiacevolmente
unprepared: impreparato
unpretending: senza pretese
unprincipled: senza scrupoli
unprofitable: non redditizio
unprotected: indifeso
unqualified: non qualificato
unquestionably: indiscutibilmente
unreasonable: irragionevole
unrestrained: non represso
unsettled: sconvolto, disordinato
unstudied: spontaneo
unsuitable: disadatto
untamed: indomito

untidy: trasandato
untouched: intatto
unwelcome: sgradito
unwell: indisposto
unwilling: riluttante, restio
unwillingly: malvolentieri
unwillingness: renitenza, malavoglia
unworthily: indegnamente
unworthy: indegno
upbraided: rimproverato
upbraiding: rimproverando
uproar: baccano
upstairs: di sopra
upstart: parvenu
urgent: urgente
useless: inutile, inservibile
uselessly: inutilmente
utmost: massimo
utter: totale, completo, proferire, emettere
utterly: totalmente
vacancy: posto vacante
vacant: vacante, libero
vague: vago
vain: vanitoso, vano
valid: valido, valevole
valued: valutato, stimato
valueless: senza valore
vanish: sparire, spariscono, sparisco, sparisci, spariamo, sparite, svanire
vanished: sparito
vanity: vanità
variation: variazione, variante
varied: variato, vario
varieties: varietà
vary: variare, vario, variate, vari, varia, variamo, variano
varying: variando, variare
vastly: vastamente
vehemence: veemenza
veneration: venerazione
venison: carne di cervo
vent: sfogo, apertura
venture: arrischiare, impresa
ventured: avventurato
veracity: veracità
verdure: verdura
verily: molto
vestibule: vestibolo
vex: irritare, contrariare, indispettire, vessare, irritano, vesso, vessiamo, vessi, vessate, vessano, vessa
vexation: irritazione
vexatious: irritante
vexed: irritato, indispettito, vessato, contrariato
vexing: irritando, vessando, contrariando, indispettendo
vice: morsa, vizio, virtù
vicious: vizioso
victim: vittima
viewing: veduta, osservare,

osservazione
vigorously: vigorosamente
vigour: forza, vigore
villainous: infame, malvagio
vindication: rivendicazione
violated: violato, aggredito, assalito
violation: violazione, infrazione
violent: violento
violently: violentemente
virtue: virtù
visible: visibile
visiting: visitando
visitor: visitatore, ospite
visits: visita
vivacity: vivacità
vogue: moda
void: vuoto, nullo
volatility: volatilità
volubility: loquacità
voluntarily: volontariamente
vouch: attestare, attestano, attestate, attesti, attestiamo, attesto, attesta
vow: voto
vulgar: volgare, triviale
vulgarity: volgarità
waited: aspettato
waiter: cameriere, il cameriere
waived: rinunciato
waking: svegliare
walker: deambulatore, camminatore
walks: cammina
wander: vagare, vago, errare, vaghiamo, vaga, vagano, vaghi, vagate, vagabondare
wandered: vagato
wandering: vagando, peregrinazione
wanting: volendo
ward: corsia, tutela, quartiere, proteggere, distretto, custodire, reparto, custodia
warmly: caldamente, calorosamente
warmth: calore, cordialità, tepore
warn: avvertire, avvertiamo, avvertono, avverti, avverto, avvertite, ammonire, avvisare
warned: avvertito
warrant: garanzia, mandato
wasting: sprecare, sprecando
watchful: vigile, vigilante
watchfulness: vigilanza
wave: onda, ondata, sventolare, l'onda, ondeggiare
wavered: esitato
wavering: esitando
weak: debole, fiacco
weakened: indebolito, debilitato
weakness: debolezza
wearied: stanco
wearisome: faticoso, tedioso
weary: stanco, stancare, fiacco
wedding: nozze, matrimonio, sposalizio

weep: piangere, piangete, piangi, piangiamo, piangono, piango, lacrimare
weighed: pesato
weighty: pesante
welcomed: accolto
welcoming: accogliendo
wet: bagnato, bagnare, umido, inumidire
whence: da dove, donde
whenever: ogni volta che, quando
wherever: dovunque, laddove
whichever: qualunque, chiunque, qualsiasi
whimsical: capriccioso
whisper: sussurrare, bisbigliare, bisbiglio
whispered: bisbigliato
whispering: sussurrio
whither: dove
wholly: interamente, completamente
wickedness: cattiveria
widow: vedova
wilderness: regione selvaggia
wilful: intenzionale, testardo
willingly: volentieri
willingness: volontà
winding: tortuoso, avvolgimento
wink: ammiccare
wisdom: saggezza, freccia, sapienza
wise: saggio, assennato
wisely: saggiamente
wished: desiderato
wit: arguzia
withdrawing: ritirando, prelevando
withdrawn: ritirato, prelevato
withheld: trattenuto
withstood: resistito
witness: testimone, testimoniare
witnessed: testimoniato
woe: dolore, calamità, afflizione
womanly: femminile
wonderfully: meravigliosamente
woods: bosco
woody: legnoso
worldly: mondano
worn: consumato, usato, esausto, portato, logoro
worthless: immeritevole, dappoco, indegno
worthy: degno, meritevole
wound: ferita, ferire
wounded: ferito
wretched: misero, miserabile, povero, infelice
wretchedly: infelicemente
writes: scrive
yards: iarde
yawn: sbadigliare, sbadiglio
yawning: sbadiglio, sbadigliando
yield: cedere, cedete, cedi, cediamo, cedo, cedono, resa, rendimento,

prodotto, fruttare
yielded: ceduto
yielding: cedendo
yourselves: voi stessi

Printed in the United States
59638LVS00003B/59

9 780497 899707